Lecture Notes in Computer Science   14598

Founding Editors

Gerhard Goos
Juris Hartmanis

The series Lecture Notes in Computer Science (LNCS), including its subseries Lecture Notes in Artificial Intelligence (LNAI) and Lecture Notes in Bioinformatics (LNBI), has established itself as a medium for the publication of new developments in computer science and information technology research, teaching, and education.

LNCS enjoys close cooperation with the computer science R & D community, the series counts many renowned academics among its volume editors and paper authors, and collaborates with prestigious societies. Its mission is to serve this international community by providing an invaluable service, mainly focused on the publication of conference and workshop proceedings and postproceedings. LNCS commenced publication in 1973.

Isaac Sserwanga · Hideo Joho · Jie Ma ·
Preben Hansen · Dan Wu · Masanori Koizumi ·
Anne J. Gilliland

Editors

Wisdom, Well-Being, Win-Win

19th International Conference, iConference 2024
Changchun, China, April 15–26, 2024
Proceedings, Part III

 Springer

Editors
Isaac Sserwanga
iSchool organization
Berlin, Germany

Hideo Joho
University of Tsukuba
Tsukuba, Japan

Jie Ma
Jilin University
Changchun, China

Preben Hansen
Stockholm University
Stockholm, Sweden

Dan Wu
Wuhan University
Wuhan, China

Masanori Koizumi
University of Tsukuba
Tsukuba, Japan

Anne J. Gilliland
University of California
Los Angeles, CA, USA

ISSN 0302-9743   ISSN 1611-3349 (electronic)
Lecture Notes in Computer Science
ISBN 978-3-031-57866-3   ISBN 978-3-031-57867-0 (eBook)
https://doi.org/10.1007/978-3-031-57867-0

Preface

As we embark on the proceedings of iConference 2024, we reflect upon the changes since the iConference of 2023. This annual gathering represents a symbol of the resilience, adaptability, and innovation of the information community. Emerging from the challenges posed by the global COVID-19 pandemic, the iSchools community navigated the remote conference landscape, laying the foundation for a new normal where technology became the bridge connecting minds, ideas, and aspirations.

The success of the iSchools conference of 2023 reaffirmed the pivotal role of information technologies in fostering engagement and collaboration. It set the stage for the overarching theme of the 19th iConference: "Wisdom, Well-being, and Win-win." This theme encapsulates our commitment to exploring synergies, nurturing shared goals, and leveraging the power of information to enhance the well-being of individuals and communities. As we delve into the proceedings, we invite readers to witness the culmination of efforts aimed at not only advancing scholarly discourse but also contributing to the broader landscape of wisdom-driven innovation.

The virtual iConference 2024 took place from April 15–18, 2024 before the physical conference on April 22–26, 2024 at Changchun, China. Its hosts included Jilin University, China, and University of Tsukuba, Japan.

The conference theme attracted a total of 218 submissions with 109 Full Research Papers and 109 Short Research Papers.

In a double-blind review process by 319 internationally renowned experts, 91 entries were approved, including 36 Full Research Papers and 55 Short Research Papers. The approval rate was 33% for the Full Research Papers and 50.46% for the Short Research Papers. Additional submissions were selected for the Workshops and Panels, the Doctoral Colloquium, the Early Career Colloquium, the Student Symposium, Posters, and the Spanish-Portuguese and Chinese language paper sessions.

The Full and Short Research papers are published for the ninth time in Springer's *Lecture Notes in Computer Science* (LNCS). These proceedings are sorted into the following eighteen categories, reflecting the diversity of the information research areas: "Archives and Information Sustainability", "Behavioral Research", "AI and Machine Learning", "Information Science and Data Science", "Information and Digital Literacy", "Digital Humanities", "Intellectual Property Issues", "Social Media and Digital Networks", "Disinformation and Misinformation", "Libraries, Bibliometrics and Metadata", "Knowledge Management", "Information Science Education", "Information Governance and Ethics", "Health Informatics", "Human-AI Collaboration", "Information Retrieval", "Community Informatics" and "Scholarly, Communication and Open Access".

We greatly appreciate the reviewers for their expertise and valuable review work and the track chairs for their relentless effort and vast expert knowledge. We wish to extend our gratitude to the chairs and volume editors; Full Research Papers chairs, Hideo Joho from University of Tsukuba, Jie Ma from Jilin University, and Preben Hansen from

Stockholm University; Short Research Papers chairs, Dan Wu from Wuhan University, Masanori Koizumi from University of Tsukuba, and Anne J. Gilliland from University of California, Los Angeles.

    The iConference lived up to its global representation of iSchools to harness the synergy of research and teaching in the field of information and complementary areas of sustainability.

February 2024

Isaac Sserwanga
Hideo Joho
Jie Ma
Preben Hansen
Dan Wu
Masanori Koizumi
Anne J. Gilliland

Organization

Organizer

Jilin University, People's Republic of China
University of Tsukuba, Japan

Conference Chairs

Yingtong Guo	Jilin University, People's Republic of China
Atsushi Toshimori	University of Tsukuba, Japan
Atsuyuki Morishima	University of Tsukuba, Japan
Jun Deng	Jilin University, People's Republic of China

Program Chairs

Local Arrangement Chairs

Yingtong Guo	Jilin University, People's Republic of China
Jun Deng	Jilin University, People's Republic of China

Proceedings Chair

Isaac Sserwanga	Humboldt-Universität zu Berlin (iSchools Organisation), Germany

Full Research Paper Chairs

Hideo Joho	University of Tsukuba, Japan
Jie Ma	Jilin University, People's Republic of China
Preben Hansen	Stockholm University, Sweden

Short Research Paper Chairs

Dan Wu	Wuhan University, People's Republic of China
Masanori Koizumi	University of Tsukuba, Japan
Anne J. Gilliland	University of California, Los Angeles, USA

Poster Chairs

Alex Poole	Drexel University, USA
Lei Pei	Nanjing University, People's Republic of China
Ellie Sayyad Abdi	Curtin University, Australia

Spanish - Portuguese Papers Chairs

Sara Martínez Cardama	Universidad Carlos III de Madrid, Spain
Josep Cobarsí Morales	Universidad Carlos III de Madrid, Spain
Alan César Belo Angeluci	Universidade de São Paulo, Brazil
Diana Lucio Arias	Pontificia Universidad Javeriana, Colombia

Chinese Paper Chairs

Xiwei Wang	Jilin University, People's Republic of China
Yang Zhang	Sun Yat-sen University, People's Republic of China
Gaohui Cao	Central China Normal University, People's Republic of China

Workshops and Panel Chairs

Ina Fourie	University of Pretoria, South Africa
Chengzhi Zhang	Nanjing University, People's Republic of China
Wonsik Jeff Shim	Sungkyunkwan University, South Korea

Student Symposium Chairs

Hui Yan	Renmin University of China, People's Republic of China
Elizabeth Eikey	University of California, USA
Romain Herault	Linnaeus University, Sweden

Early Career Colloquium Chairs

Charles Senteio	Rutgers University, USA
Jiangping Chen	University of North Texas, USA
Debbie Meharg	Edinburgh Napier University, UK
YuXiang Zhao	Nanjing University, People's Republic of China

Doctoral Colloquium Chairs

Widad Mustafa El Hadi   University of Lille, France
Howard Rosenbaum   Indiana University Bloomington, USA
Tina Du   Charles Sturt University, Australia

Doctoral Dissertation Award Chair

Pengyi Zhang   Peking University, People's Republic of China

Conference Coordinators

Michael Seadle   iSchools Organization
Slava Sterzer   iSchools Organization
Katharina Gudat   iSchools Organization
Ulrike Liebner   iSchools Organization
Isaac Sserwanga   iSchools Organization
Wei Feng   iSchools Organization

Reviewers Full and Short Papers iConference 2024 (319)

Jacob Abbott
Naresh Kumar Agarwal
Daniel Agbaji
Aharony Noa Aharony
Farhan Ahmad Ahmad
Isola Ajiferuke
Mahir Akgun
Nicole D. Alemanne
Daniel Gelaw Alemneh
Lilach Alon
Misita Anwar
Tatjana Aparac-Jelusic
Rhea Rowena Ubana Apolinario
Lateef Ayinde
Dmitriy Babichenko
Ananth Balashankar
Sarah Barriage
Ofer Bergman
Arpita Bhattacharya
Jianxin Bi
Toine Bogers

Isak De Villiers {Diffie} Bosman
Theo J. D. Bothma
Guillaume Boutard
Sarah Elaine Bratt
Paulina Bressel
Jenny Bronstein
Leonard D. Brown
Yi Bu
Sarah A. Buchanan
Charles Bugre
Julia Bullard
Frada Burstein
Yu-Wei Chang
Haihua Chen
Hsin-liang Chen
Jiangping Chen
Xiaoyu Chen
Yi-Yun Cheng
Wonchan Choi
Yujin Choi
Yunseon Choi

Miyoung Chong
Josep Cobarsí-Morales
Isabella L. Corieri
Julian D. Cortes
Andrew Cox
Amber L. Cushing
Mats Dahlstrom
Gabriel David
Nilou Davoudi
Jun Deng
Sanhong Deng
Shengli Deng
Leyla Dewitz
Junhua Ding
Karsten Donnay
Philip Doty
Liz Dowthwaite
Yunfei Du
Zhenjia Fan
Bruce Ferwerda
Rachel Fleming-May
Ina Fourie
Rebecca D. Frank
Viviane Frings-Hessami
Hengyi Fu
Yaming Fu
Jonathan Furner
Henry Alexis Gabb
Maria Gäde
Abdullah Gadi
Chunmei Gan
Yubao Gao
Zheng Gao
Stanislava Gardasevic
Emmanouel Garoufallou
Diane Gill
Fausto Giunchiglia
Dion Goh
Patrick Thomas Golden
Liliana Gonzalez Perez
Anne Goulding
Christopher Graziul
Elke Greifeneder
Jenifer Daiane Grieger
Melissa Gross

Ece Gumusel
Qiuyan Guo
Vibhor Gupta
Ayse Gursoy
Hazel Hall
Ruohua Han
Yue Hao
Noriko Hara
Jenna Hartel
Bruce Hartpence
Stefanie Havelka
Alison Hicks
Liang Hong
Lingzi Hong
Md Khalid Hossain
Jingrui Hou
Amanda Hovious
Xinhui Hu
Yuerong Hu
Zhan Hu
Ying Huang
Shezin Waziha Hussain
Isto Huvila
Aylin Imeri (Ilhan)
Sharon Ince
Jonathan Isip
Hiroyoshi Ito
Corey Jackson
Eunmi Jeong
Jie Jiang
Michael Jones
Heidi Julien
Nicolas Jullien
Jaap Kamps
Ijay Kaz-Onyeakazi
Mat Kelly
Rebecca Kelly
Heikki Keskustalo
Mahmood Khosrowjerdi
Jiro Kikkawa
Heejun Kim
Jeonghyun Kim
Kyungwon Koh
Masanori Koizumi
Kushwanth Koya

Adam Kriesberg
Maja Krtalic
Bill Kules
Mucahid Kutlu
Sucheta Lahiri
Glen Layne-Worthey
Chengyi Le
Gregory Leazer
Deborah Lee
Kijung Lee
Lo Lee
Tae Hee Lee
Wan-Chen Lee
Kai Li
Lei Li
Muyan Li
Ying Li
Yingya Li
Yuan Li
Shaobo Liang
Chern Li Liew
Louise Limberg
Zack Lischer-Katz
Chang Liu
Jieli Liu
Annemaree Lloyd
Kun Lu
Ana Lucic
Zhuoran Luo
Lai Ma
Linqing Ma
Shutian Ma
Xiaoyue Ma
Emily Maemura
Sara Martínez-Cardama
Matthew Mayernik
Diane McAdie
Kate McDowell
Claire McGuinness
Pamela Ann McKinney
David McMenemy
Debbie Meharg
Jonas Ferrigolo Melo
Shuyuan Metcalfe
Anika Meyer

Eric Meyer
A. J. Million
J. Elizabeth Mills
Yue Ming
Lorri Mon
Atsuyuki Morishima
Heather Moulaison-Sandy
Widad Mustafa El Hadi/Prunier
Hyeong Suk Na
Maayan Nakash
Ha Quang Thinh Ngo
Huyen Nguyen
Sarah Nguyễn
David M. Nichols
Kathleen Obille
Lydia Oladapo
Gillian Oliver
Felipe Ortega
Giulia Osti
Kathleen Padova
Nayana Pampapura Madali
Hyoungjoo Park
Jinkyung Park
Min Sook Park
William Christopher Payne
Lei Pei
Olivia Pestana
Alina Petrushka
Leonor Gaspar Pinto
Alex H. Poole
Widiatmoko Adi Putranto
Xin Qian
Rahmi Rahmi
Priya Rajasagi
Arcot Rajasekar
Alexandria Rayburn
Gabby Resch
Jorge Revez
Fernanda Ribeiro
Cristian Roman Palacios
Milly Romeijn-Stout
Vassilis Routsis
Carsten Rudolph
Sarah Elizabeth Ryan
Özhan Sağlık

Songlak Sakulwichitsintu
Liliana Salas
Rachel Salzano
Madelyn Rose Sanfilippo
Vitor Santos
Ellie Sayyad Abdi
Kirsten Schlebbe
Michael Seadle
Subhasree Sengupta
Charles Senteio
Qingong Shi
Kristina Shiroma
Yan Shvartzshnaider
Luanne Sinnamon
Stephen C. Slota
Annique Smith
Vitaliy Snytyuk
António Lucas Soares
Amanda H. Sorensen
Clay Spinuzzi
Beth St. Jean
Rebecca Stallworth
Hrvoje Stancic
Ian Stockwell
Besiki Stvilia
Honglei Lia Sun
SeoYoon Sung
Jennifer Yoon Sunoo
Tokinori Suzuki
Tanja Svarre
Sue Yeon Syn
Masao Takaku
Anna Maria Tammaro
Rong Tang
Yi Tang
Zehra Taşkın
Paula Telo
Tien-I Tsai
Denise Tsunoda
Zhifang Tu
Rachel Tunis
Michael Twidale

Berthilde Uwamwezi
Neville Vakharia
Diego Vallejo-Huanga
Martie van Deventer
Brenda Van Wyk
Merce Væzquez
Travis L. Wagner
Yi Wan
Di Wang
June Wang
Ke-Rou Wang
Lin Wang
Linxu Wang
Peiling Wang
Shengang Wang
Yi-yu Wang
Zhongyi Wang
Xiaofei Wei
Brian Wentz
Namtip Wipawin
Christa Womser-Hacker
Jian Wu
Peng Wu
Peng Xiao
Iris Xie
Sherry Xie
Huimin Xu
Jian Xu
Xiao Xue
Erjia Yan
Hui Yan
Pu Yan
Feng Yang
Yuyu Yang
Ziruo Yi
Ayoung Yoon
JungWon Yoon
Sarah Young
Fei Yu
Vyacheslav I. Zavalin
Xianjin Zha
Yujia Zhai

Bin Zhang
Chengzhi Zhang
Chenwei Zhang
Jinchao Zhang
Mei Zhang
Xiaoqian Zhang
Yan Zhang

Yang Zhang
Yishan Zhang
Han Zheng
Kyrie Zhixuan Zhou
Lihong Zhou
Qinghua Zhu

Contents – Part III

Health Informatics

Human-AI Collaboration

Information Retrieval

Community Informatics

Scholarly, Communication and Open Access

Knowledge Management

A Network Portrait Divergence Approach to Measure Science-Technology Linkages

Kai Meng[1,2] ⓘ, Zhichao Ba[1,2(✉)] ⓘ, and Leilei Liu[1,2] ⓘ

[1] Laboratory of Data Intelligence and Interdisciplinary Innovation, Nanjing University,
Suzhou 215163, China
bazhichaoty@nju.edu.cn

[2] School of Information Management, Nanjing University, Nanjing 210023, China

Abstract. Science and technology (S&T) association has become an important pattern of promoting technological innovation. Detecting S&T linkages is a crucial way to discover their knowledge connections. Prior research mostly identifies S&T linkages by counting statistical distribution or calculating the semantic similarity of terms or topics between S&T, while is unequipped to reveal structural linkages between S&T systems. In this study, we proposed a novel knowledge network coupling approach to gauge network linkages between S&T based on a network portrait divergence algorithm. First, we extracted core knowledge elements in S&T and applied a word alignment approach to uniformly descript those elements. Then, by transforming the S&T knowledge system into knowledge networks, we constructed S&T knowledge networks based on word co-occurrence relations. Finally, a network portrait divergence algorithm is applied to generate network portraits and calculate portrait distance between S&T knowledge networks to gauge their dynamic structural coupling. The results demonstrated that the knowledge network-based coupling approach could detect the linkages and interaction patterns of S&T at a fine-grained level. This study can provide methodological tools and reference basis for the development and policymaking of S&T innovation.

Keywords: Science-technology Linkages · Knowledge network · Structural coupling · Interaction pattern · Network portrait divergence

1 Introduction

The contemporary relationship between S&T is progressively evolving into a closer linkage, characterized by a growing trend of mutual interdependence, transformation, and cross-fertilization. Nevertheless, there exists a significant challenge where certain scientific advancements are not promptly translated and applied in practical technological contexts[18, 23]. The translation of new drug development, the commercialization of biofuels, and the practical application of quantum communication are some of the practical examples. The establishment of a robust linkage between S&T through a knowledge organization system can serve as a means to fortify the bond between foundational scientific research and applied technological research [27]. Consequently, the exploration

I. Sserwanga et al. (Eds.): iConference 2024, LNCS 14598, pp. 3–22, 2024.
https://doi.org/10.1007/978-3-031-57867-0_1

of the intricate interactions between S&T, particularly concerning knowledge interconnections, interactions, and synergistic mechanisms, assumes paramount significance in the contemporary landscape of knowledge management and S&T innovation research.

The essence of the interaction between S&T linkage in the process of transformation is the nature, structure, and functionality brought about by the interactions between elements within S&T knowledge systems [7]. Consequently, the primary goal of S&T linkage detection is to uncover the intricate process of knowledge exchange between these two systems, while also discerning the direction, structure, and intensity of their interaction [20] Scientific literature stands as a significant manifestation of research outcomes in the realm of science, while technology patents serve as crucial carriers of technological innovation [27]. Through the correlation analysis of scientific literature and technology patent data, it has emerged as the most direct and effective method for comprehensively exploring the nexus between S&T.

Scholars have proposed various methodologies to analyze the connection between S&T, notably including thesis-patent mixed citation analysis [24], author-inventor correlation analysis [4], subject category mapping correlation analysis [6, 10], and topic-based correlation analysis [27]. Nevertheless, the prevailing approach to detecting the S&T relationship currently involves dissecting the linkages between scientific literature and technology patent data. However, contemporary research on the S&T linkages predominantly revolves around quantifying the relationship between S&T by tallying the distribution of specific features in papers and patents.

This paper is dedicated to the investigation of objective linkages among S&T resources. It aims to convert the knowledge structure system within the realm of S&T into an expressive knowledge network model. Additionally, it seeks to examine the interconnected interactions and synergistic pathways between different facets of S&T through the lens of network coupling. To achieve these objectives, this paper introduces a novel method that leverages physics knowledge networks for unveiling S&T interactions. This method facilitates a quantitative analysis of the interconnected knowledge structures in S&T at a micro level, thus enhancing the existing theories and methodologies in the field of S&T interconnection research.

2   Related Research Work

2.1   Science-Technology Linkage Detection

Drawing upon the framework of system dynamics, Bassecoulard & Zitt delved into the evolutionary processes within S&T systems [3]. Their investigation revealed a nonlinear interplay between S&T, characterized by the emergence of novel synergistic effects arising from reciprocal constraints and coupling, rather than a mere superposition of individual relationships. To effectively probe this intricate interaction, scholars in the realms of technical economics and bibliometrics have advanced several methodologies for discerning the nexus between S&T.

The analysis of citations in the realm of S&T unveils discernible characteristics and patterns that facilitate the tracking of knowledge flow and diffusion between these domains [24]. Consequently, patent citation analysis emerges as a widely acknowledged and superior method for detecting linkages between S&T. Notably, this analysis encompasses the exploration of patent citation papers, papers citing patents, and the innovative utilization of paper-patent hybrid co-citation analysis as the primary mechanism for mining citation features. Addressing the prevailing issue of limited integration between scientific literature and technological patents, the establishment of an effective knowledge organization system can be achieved through classification lists or subject word lists [7]. Scholars have endeavored to establish a mapping between subject classification systems and patent International Patent Classification (IPC) systems, thus reflecting the interconnectedness of knowledge and the structural correspondence between S&T [10]. Furthermore, an analysis of indicators such as the quantitative distribution of author-inventor associations, evolutionary characteristics, roles and functions, and S&T output can unveil the impact of engagement in scientific activities or technological research and development on the resulting S&T output [6].

To gain insights into the linkages between S&T from the perspective of research topics and the content of S&T literature, scholars have proposed the discovery of topic terms or topic associations within the body of knowledge in S&T [19]. This is achieved through the application of machine learning and data mining techniques to reveal the semantic connections between S&T.

The research methods described above investigate the correlation between S&T by examining various objective connections that exist between scientific literature and technology patent data. However, these methods exhibit certain limitations. Bibliometric-based approaches are influenced by factors such as sparse citations, author relationships, and a broad alignment between scientific literature and technology patent data [20]. While methods based on topic-specific or topic-related word associations can unveil semantic linkages between S&T on a granular level, they face challenges in elucidating the interplay between the organizational structure of S&T knowledge.

2.2 Network Coupling Measurements

Network coupling refers to the dynamic linkage characterized by interdependence, mutual coordination, and mutual promotion that arises from the positive interactions among internal modules or components within networks [1]. The coupling relationship within network structures is not solely manifested in the correlation of node attributes across networks but also the interconnectedness of nodes. Measurement of network structure coupling can draw upon established system coupling calculation methods. Prior research on system coupling measurement has predominantly employed techniques such as gray correlation analysis, combinatorial mathematical models, and other methodologies to construct the structural elements within the system and develop a system for evaluating coupling [15]. Alternatively, researchers have created coupling correlation models, coupling coordination models, and capacity coupling coefficient models within the realm of physics to calculate the correlations among system elements, thus characterizing the extent of coupling between systems [14].

The emergence of complex scientific disciplines and the growing field of complex network research have fostered the application of complex network analysis to investigate coupling mechanisms within the realm of flow space [17]. In the context of the ongoing trends in informatization, networking, and globalization, knowledge space has emerged as a virtual spatial construct. It represents a reconfiguration of knowledge resources and elements, imbued with distinctive attributes from temporal and spatial perspectives [1, 8]. These attributes encompass intangibility, sharing, fluid interactivity, heightened efficiency, and synergistic capabilities. Consequently, there exists a compelling need to investigate the coupling of knowledge systems or networks within the knowledge flow space.

3   Research Framework and Methodology

The establishment of an S&T knowledge network aims to investigate the S&T knowledge system association. We explore the method for detecting linkages within the S&T knowledge network from the perspective of knowledge network coupling. The comprehensive research framework is depicted in Fig. 1. To be specific, our methodology involves several steps: Initially, keywords are extracted from the titles and abstracts of papers and patent data, with the pre-processed keywords serving as the foundational elements of S&T knowledge. Subsequently, a S&T domain corpus is constructed and trained using Bidirectional Encoder Representations from Transformers (BERT). Leveraging this pre-trained semantic model, we align the core S&T knowledge elements to identify the distinctive and shared elements within the area of S&T. Following this, we proceed to construct S&T knowledge networks spanning different periods, utilizing co-occurrence associations among the knowledge elements. We employ Network Portrait Divergence (NPD) to quantify the temporal coupling strength between these S&T knowledge networks. Finally, we employ Multiscale Backbone Analysis to discern the flow and evolutionary trajectory of knowledge within the domain of S&T. This approach allows us to detect dynamic linkages within the S&T knowledge network by amalgamating the dynamic coupling of S&T time series with the lead-lag relationships.

3.1   Core Knowledge Meta-extraction and Knowledge Network Construction

In the realm of systematic knowledge, knowledge elements serve as fundamental units and foundational components that define the structure of domain-specific knowledge. This paper employs keywords extracted from both research papers and patents as alternative representations of these knowledge elements. Nevertheless, there exists a certain degree of granularity mismatch and expression disparities between scientific concepts and technical terminology. Consequently, rather than relying directly on the self-referenced keywords provided by the original authors, this paper employs an unsupervised methodology to extract keywords from the titles and abstracts of research papers and patents. Furthermore, to mitigate the potential adverse effects of synonymous phrases on subsequent experiments, this study adopts the BERT-ITPT-FiT (BERT + with In-Task Pre-Training + Fine-Tuning) strategy to achieve semantic alignment among the extracted keywords. Specific details of this process are illustrated in Fig. 1, Step 2.

To begin, the domain-specific corpus data is fed into the BERT model for In-Task Pre-Training, with a predefined limit on the number of iterations for fine-tuning the BERT model. Subsequently, we construct word vectors for the extracted keywords,

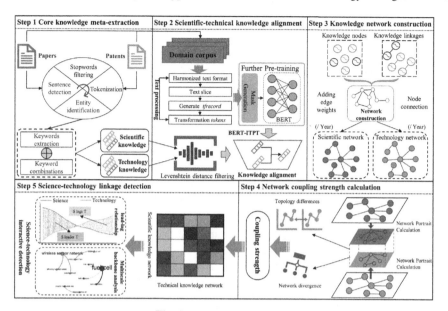

Fig. 1. Research framework.

which have been filtered using the Levenshtein Distance, employing the BERT-ITPT-FiT strategy generation model. These keywords are aligned using three distinct schemes: self-alignment within scientific papers, self-alignment within patents, and alignment between scientific papers and patents. Finally, the results of word alignment serve as the foundation for establishing an S&T knowledge network based on word co-occurrence relationships. For any given keyword, denoted as $k_i \in S_1$, we calculate the vector similarity with each of the other keywords, represented as $k_j \in S_2$, where S_1 and S_2 are distinct sets of keywords. The preservation of expected aligned keyword pairs is achieved through the creation of triads in the form of $< k_i, r_{<k_i,k_j>}, k_j >$. Simultaneously, we employ a similarity threshold, denoted as β, to filter out keyword pairs that exhibit substantial dissimilarity and are thus unsuitable for alignment.

3.2 Network Coupling Measure Based on Network Portrait Divergence

Examining and quantifying the linkage within the knowledge structure encompassing S&T, through the lens of knowledge network coupling, serves as the foundational framework for delving deeper into the mutually beneficial evolutionary processes between these two domains. Furthermore, it serves as a vital cornerstone for uncovering the driving forces behind this evolutionary coupling. These networks rely on interdependence, coordination, and mutual promotion throughout their generation and evolution. Importantly, this concept takes into account not only the relevance of the attributes associated with knowledge elements (nodes), but also the significance of the connections (edges) that link these corresponding knowledge elements. In this study, we employ a network portrait divergence algorithm to quantify the strength of coupling within S&T knowledge networks [2]. This algorithm's computational process can be primarily delineated into two distinct steps. The first step encompasses the generation of network portraits, while the second involves the calculation of portrait distances.

Network portraits serve as a valuable means for visualizing and encoding the structural attributes inherent in a given network. They prove particularly apt for facilitating the comparative analysis of networks based on mathematical principles. A network portrait, denoted as B, is an array comprising (δ, k) elements. The computation of the shortest path lengths within the portrait array is accomplished through a breadth-first search algorithm. Notably, a salient attribute of the network portrait is its robustness. It remains invariant regardless of the ordering or labeling of network nodes. The network portrait effectively encapsulates a comprehensive set of structural characteristics of the network, as delineated in Table 1 below. Furthermore, Fig. 2 provides an illustrative depiction of a pair of science-technology network alongside its corresponding portrait projection.

Table 1. Network portrait structural characteristics.

Portrait representation B of network G	$B_{\delta,k} \equiv$ Number of nodes with k linked nodes at distance δ $(0 \leq \delta \leq d, 0 \leq k \leq N - 1)$
Number of nodes in storage network G at row zero: N	$B_{0,k} = N\varphi_{k,1}$
The first row captures the node degree distribution $P_{(k)}$:	$B_{1,k} = NP_{(k)}$
The α row holds the distribution of nearest neighbor nodes $P_{(\alpha,k)}$	$B_{\alpha,k} = NP_{(\alpha,k)}$
Number of G-edges of the network: E	$\frac{\sum_{k=0}^{N} kB_{1,k}}{2}$
Diameter of network G: d	$max\{\delta | B_{\delta,k} > 0, for k > 0\}$

The probability combination of row representations in network portrait B is $P(k|\delta)$:

$$P(k|\delta) = \frac{k}{N^2} B_{\delta,k} \tag{1}$$

$KL(H||I)$ is the Kullback-Leibler (KL) scatter value between two probability distributions H and I, where H and I are defined according to Eq. (1). The joint KL dispersion distribution for all rows of portraits B_1, B_2 of networks G_1 and G_2 is as follows:

$$KL(P_1(k|\delta)||P_2(k|\delta)) = \sum_{\delta=0}^{max(d_1,d_2)} \sum_{k=0}^{N} P_1(k|\delta) * log_2 \frac{P_1(k|\delta)}{P_2(k|\delta)} \tag{2}$$

The coupling strength of networks G_1 and G_2 is defined as $1-d$ (G_1, G_2), and the portrait distance d (G_1, G_2) is calculated as shown in Eq. (3):

$$d(G_1, G_2) \equiv \frac{1}{2} * KL(P_1||M) + \frac{1}{2} * KL(P_2||M) \tag{3}$$

where $M = \frac{1}{2} * (P_1, P_2)$ is the mixture distribution of P_1 and P_2. P_1, P_2 are defined by Eq. (1), and the $KL(H||I)$ divergence is calculated by Eq. (2).

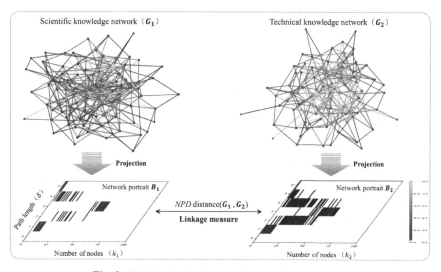

Fig. 2. Calculating S&T network portrait divergences.

3.3 Science-Technology Interactive Pattern Recognition

Through a comparative examination of the sequential progression of S&T topics along their evolutionary trajectory, we can effectively discern distinct interaction patterns within specific domains, shedding light on the pivotal role played by the lead-lag relationship in detecting S&T interactions. The S&T lead-lag relationship typically falls into categorized interaction modes encompassing science leading technology, technology leading science, and synchronized development of both S&T. In the context of this study, we leverage network portrait projection techniques to quantify the strength of S&T coupling, thereby enabling a comprehensive exploration of the dynamic interplay between S&T across time, specifically in terms of leading and lagging periods, with the aim of identifying the cyclical patterns characterizing S&T interactions. Building upon the complex weighted network features have constructed, we employ Multiscale Backbone analysis to decipher the knowledge flow and evolutionary dynamics inherent in the realm of S&T. The ensuing elucidation of our methodology is outlined as follows:

Step 1: Construct a portfolio of technology + science same-year and science n-year lag knowledge networks. Identify the technical knowledge elements, scientific knowledge elements, and S&T shared knowledge elements in the combined network.

Step 2: Filtering of an undirected weighted network based on the probability density function of a node taking a specific value of x.

Step 3: The continued filtering process, achieved by imposing a significance level denoted as 'α,' results in the identification of links with statistically significant weights. These significant weights play a pivotal role as the multiscale backbone within the composite network, which is constructed through the Step1 procedure.

4 Experimental Results

4.1 Data Sources

Energy conservation has risen to prominence as a pivotal domain, wielding a substantial influence in the advancement of energy conversion processes, all the while ameliorating environmental pollution. It stands as a highly efficacious solution for grappling with the enduring conundrum posed by the interplay between economic development and energy consumption in the pursuit of sustainability [25]. However, extensive research has illuminated a pronounced disparity in S&T advancements within the energy conservation sector [9, 22]. By conducting a comprehensive analysis of the dynamic interplay and interaction patterns between S&T in this field, we can offer enhanced support for innovations in environmentally friendly materials and technological enhancements in energy conservation.

The energy conservation domain, a quintessential domain of S&T innovation, boasts a substantial body of literature and patent data. Therefore, for reasons pertaining to data accessibility and future development prospects, this study opts to concentrate on the energy conservation sector for empirical analysis. Scientific literature and patent data primarily derive from the Web of Science (WoS) database and the United States Patent and Trademark Office (USPTO) database, as specified in Table 2 and Table 3. To ensure data integrity, the collected papers and patents underwent a rigorous process of deduplication and cleansing, ultimately yielding a dataset comprising 166,643 papers and 91,593 patents.

Table 2. Search regulations for scientific papers.

Database selection	Web of Science
Retrieval formula	TI = ((power-efficient) OR (energy efficiency) OR (low-power) OR (low-energy) OR (energy-saving) OR (fuel-efficient) OR (energy-conscious) OR (high-efficiency) OR (Low Power-Consumption) OR (energy efficient) OR (power allocation) OR (energy consumption) OR (smart grid) OR (smart metering) OR (enhancement of efficiency) OR (Energy Management) OR (Energy Performance) OR (Rational Use) OR (Electricity Consumption) OR (System Efficiency) OR (Energy Efficient Prosperity) OR (Eco-Power) OR (Energy-Efficient Window) OR (energy analysis) OR (efficiency factor) OR (Energy-saving awareness) OR (energy efficiency measures) OR (energy utilization) OR (energy conservation) OR (intelligent control) OR (energy demand) OR (sustainable energy) OR (energy policy) OR (energy efficient systems) OR (energy usage) OR (maximum efficiency) OR (energy efficiency ratio) OR (energy efficiency strategies) OR (energy simulation) OR (energy use) OR (energy storage) OR (energy forecasting) OR (consumption of energy) OR (Conscious use))
Type of Literature	DT = Article
Time window	PY = (1979–2021)

Table 3. Search regulations for patents.

Energy conservation	USPC	IPC
Energy storage or distribution	307;700/295+	H01M; H02J
Thermal	702/130+	F24H 7/00
Insulating	52/404.1+	E04B 1/74; E04B 2/00
Static structures	52/404.1	E04B 1/62; E04D; E06B 7/098; E06B
Transportation	244/172.7	B64G 1/44
Land vehicle	105; 180; 280	B60L 8/00; B60K 16/00
Alternative-power vehicle (e.g., hydrogen)	180/2.1–2.2, 54.1	B60L 8/00
Electric vehicle	180/65.1; 180/65.21; 701/22+	B60L 9/00
Fuel-cell-powered vehicles	180/65.21, 180/65.31	B60L 11/18
Drag reduction	105/1.1; 296/180.1+; 296/181.5	B62D 35/00
Human-powered vehicle	180/205; 280/200+	B62M
Hybrid-powered vehicle	180/65.21–65.29	B60K 6/20,6/00
Rail vehicle	105/49	B61C 1/00
Roadways (e.g., recycled surface, all-weather bikeways)	404	E01C 1/00
Wave-powered boat motors	440/9	B63H 19/02
Wind-powered boat motors	440/8	B63H 13/00
Wind-powered ships	114/102.1+	B63H 9/00

4.2 Core Knowledge Meta-extraction

To acquire a robust foundational knowledge base for constructing the science-technology knowledge network, this study employs five distinct algorithms for keyword extraction: word frequency analysis (TF-IDF), graph-based search (TextRank), node degree analysis (RAKE), word relationship assessment (Yake!), and semantic analysis (KeyBert). An evaluation of these various algorithms' performance in keyword extraction is conducted through a comprehensive blend of quantitative and qualitative methodologies. Ultimately, the most effective algorithm for generating keywords is identified as the output for S&T knowledge extraction.

The identified keywords are classified into three tiers based on their significance and pertinence to the primary focus of the source document [16]. Level 1 (score 1) comprises meaningful keywords that directly mirror the core theme of the document, while Level 2 (score 0.5) encompasses keywords that are tangentially related to the central theme. Level 3 (score 0) encompasses irrelevant and nonsensical keywords that do not bear any relevance to the document. The BM25F algorithm, widely employed in the domain of information retrieval for computing query-document matching scores, was selected to evaluate the matching scores between keywords and titles as well as abstracts.

In this study, a random selection process was employed to choose five documents annually from the total dataset, designating them as scientific papers and patents coding documents. Two independent coders were tasked with coding 1,100 keywords to each of the scientific papers and patents. The final Cohen's kappa coefficient for coding agreement was calculated to be 0.819, indicating a substantial level of agreement. The results presented in Table 4 demonstrate that KeyBert outperforms the other selected algorithms in scientific papers, while the traditional TF-IDF algorithm performs the least effectively.

Furthermore, the best match score calculation also utilized the aforementioned randomly sampled data. The distribution of average BM scores serves to validate the coding assessment. Notably, the KeyBert algorithm within the purple group exhibits the highest level of effectiveness, as depicted in Fig. 3. Consequently, the keywords generated by this algorithm have been chosen as the foundation for constructing the S&T knowledge network in this research.

Table 4. Performance comparison of keyword extraction algorithms in papers and patents.

Keyword extraction algorithms	Scientific papers				Technology patents			
	Max	Min	Mean	Avg standard error	Max	Min	Mean	Avg standard error
TF-IDF	0.75	0.1	0.413	0.102	0.45	0.1	0.311	0.092
TextRank	0.85	0.4	0.65	0.101	0.8	0.3	0.511	0.110
RAKE	0.9	0.4	0.65	0.100	0.8	0.4	0.634	0.110
Yake!	1	0.4	0.696	0.093	**0.9**	**0.55**	0.737	0.087
KeyBert	**0.9**	**0.5**	**0.784**	**0.091**	**0.9**	0.5	**0.780**	**0.086**

4.3 Scientific-Technical Knowledge Network Construction

Core knowledge elements are extracted utilizing the KeyBert algorithm, and an S&T knowledge network is subsequently formed through the co-occurrence relationships among these knowledge elements. During the network construction process, a noteworthy observation is made concerning the presence of numerous isolated knowledge nodes, with a particularly pronounced occurrence within the scientific network. To address this issue, this study computes the overall structure of the S&T network, as depicted in Fig. 4. In the 2000 S&T knowledge network, the row structure of the generative portrait is not characterized as clearly, and the scientific knowledge network is worse than the technical knowledge network. Building upon established methodologies for network construction, such as those relying on high-frequency words or node filtration [26], this paper opts for the inclusion of the TOP 10% of nodes within the S&T knowledge network, rather

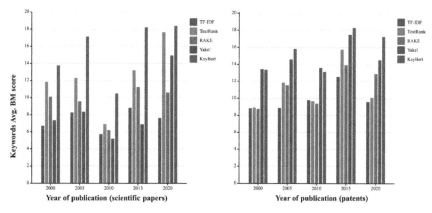

Fig. 3. Comparison of BM performance of keyword extraction algorithms in S&T.

than the entire network, when computing measures of S&T network coupling. This choice is made to mitigate potential errors stemming from isolated nodes lacking valid information that could impact the results.

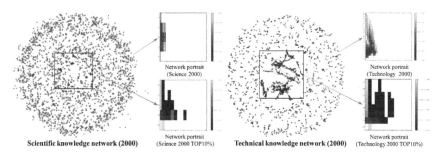

Fig. 4. S&T full network with TOP 10% strategy portrait generation (2000).

In this study, we have extracted a total of 66,052 and 30,409 keywords from the S&T knowledge network to construct a time-series network dedicated to S&T. These keywords were selected using the TOP 10% keyword strategy, resulting in 52,958 keywords that are common to the entire dataset. This observation underscores the presence of lexical variations in the representation of S&T. Consequently, in this paper, we have chosen to employ the BERT-ITPT-FiT scheme to align keywords within the framework of the TOP 10% strategy. Figure 5 presents a visual representation of the impact of S&T keyword alignment.

Throughout the keyword alignment process, it is evident that the self-alignment of scientific keywords exhibits a consistent and gradual growth pattern, with an average alignment ratio of 6.08%. Conversely, during the self-alignment of patent keywords, we observe a notable phenomenon: significant self-alignment of patent-related knowledge predating 2010, especially within a relatively limited body of knowledge. This observation suggests that in the early stages of patent development, innovators tend to focus on small-scale innovations and exhibit a preference for emulating similar technologies. The average alignment ratio for patent keyword self-alignment is 9.47%.

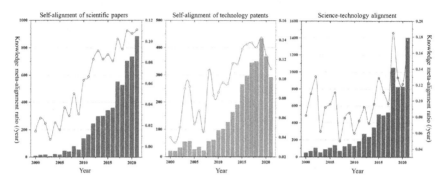

Fig. 5. Results of S&T knowledge meta-alignment based on BERT-ITPT-FiT.

Properties such as edges, nodes, and density show significant enhancement in S&T knowledge networks aligned by keywords. A comprehensive overview of the descriptive statistics for these knowledge networks before and after alignment can be found in Table 5. Over the period from 2000 to 2021, the time-series analysis generated a total of 22 pairs of S&T knowledge networks. Notably, the average network density showed a significant increase (Science: 1.76E−03 to 2.08E−03; Technology: 2.32E−03 to 2.39E−03), as did the average clustering coefficients (Science: 0.371 to 0.373; Technology: 0.254 to 0.255) following the enhancement of the S&T knowledge networks. Moreover, the number of network components experienced a notable reduction (Science: 739.5 to 641; Technology: 395.458 to 387.833). These findings suggest that the knowledge-aligned network exhibits fewer independent components, higher network density, increased clustering coefficients, and enhanced stability when compared to the initial network.

This paper aims to provide additional validation for the impact of the features embedded within the projection of the S&T knowledge network portrait using the TOP10% strategy, as illustrated in Fig. 6. As time progresses, the scope of the S&T knowledge network expands, consequently enriching the node pathways stored within the network portrait. Furthermore, the portrait projection encompasses a greater array of node probability combinations across varying scales.

4.4 Measurement of Coupled Scientific-Technical Knowledge Networks

This paper leverages the S&T knowledge network established in Sect. 4.3, alongside its portrait projection, to perform an analysis of the coupling between S&T along the temporal axis. This analysis is conducted from both overall and TOP10% perspective to determine the strength of coupling between these years. The results are depicted in Fig. 7 as a heatmap, illustrating the pairwise coupling of S&T knowledge networks over the period spanning from 2000 to 2021. Each cell's color in the heatmap signifies its respective coupling strength.

Table 5. Descriptive statistics for S&T knowledge network attributes (TOP 10% strategy).

Network attributes	Scientific knowledge networks (N = 22)			Technical knowledge networks (N = 22)		
	Min	Max	Mean	Min	Max	Mean
Initial networks						
Nodes	534	3383	1669.409	510	1571	938.375
Edges	687	3194	1482.5	384	1898	956.5
Avg. Clustering coefficient	0.196889	0.664932	0.371256	0.206705	0.310167	0.253773
Density	5.30E−04	4.83E−03	1.76E−03	1.45E−03	3.43E−03	2.32E−03
Components	216	1388	739.5	233	631	395.4583
Knowledge alignment networks						
Nodes	502	2913	1508.792	496	1535	912.875
Edges	676	3024	1467.083	376	1757	914.5
Avg. Clustering coefficient	0.201954	0.65009	0.372726	0.206978	0.305252	0.254519
Density	6.78E−04	5.38E−03	2.08E−03	1.45E−03	3.58E−03	2.39E−03
Components	189	1167	641	226	624	387.8333

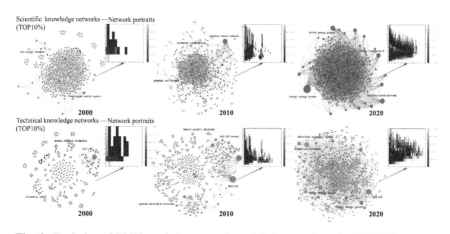

Fig. 6. Evolution of S&T knowledge networks and their portraits under TOP10% strategy.

In the context of the overall knowledge meta-constructed network coupling measurement, discerning differences in coupling strength proves challenging. The discrepancies primarily manifest near the diagonal, which corresponds to the coupling between the same years, while other regions exhibit similar coupling strengths. However, within the S&T knowledge network extracted using the TOP10% strategy, distinctive patterns of coupling strength emerge. Notably, there are varying degrees of coupling strength observed in the three cells preceding and succeeding the diagonal, alongside robust coupling precisely at the diagonal. These findings suggest the presence of a knowledge relationship characterized by either an advancement or a lag within the S&T interface. This dynamic has the potential to either facilitate or impede the flow of knowledge.

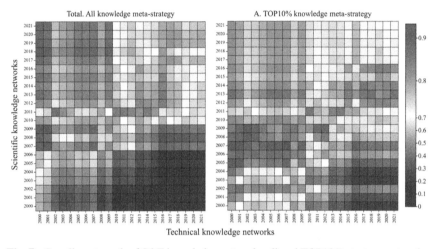

Fig. 7. Coupling strength of S&T knowledge networks all and TOP10% strategy networks.

This paper aims to investigate the influence of the lead-lag relationship on interactions between S&T. Specifically, we analyze the coupling interaction characteristics within the contemporaneous lead-lag phase of the S&T knowledge network under the TOP10% strategy, as depicted in Fig. 8. In this figure, the black line illustrates the coupling strength within the same year, and the red line represents the mean coupling strength for the three years following the year when technology led science. In contrast, the blue line displays the mean coupling strength for the three years during which science lagged behind technology. By examining changes in the lead-lag coupling strength relationship, we identify two primary cycles of differences. The subplot on the right provides a detailed examination of variations in the strength of the S&T network coupling for a given year within each cycle and for the one to three years both preceding and following that year.

Cycle 1: Technology takes the lead in science, primarily observed in the early stages of development within the energy efficiency field (2003–2005). This period coincides with increased global attention to energy security and climate change, alongside a surge in technological advancements in renewable energy [9, 11].

Cycle 2: Science assumes the leadership role in technology, occurring in the recent years from 2011 to 2021. Successive international reports have advocated significant investments in the promotion of electricity and alternative energy sources, which have stimulated scientific output and facilitated technological advances. This, in turn, has made technology development less challenging and has fostered advancements in related fields [5].

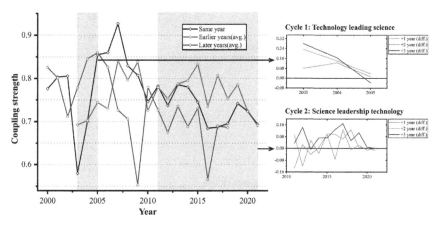

Fig. 8. Contemporaneous-lead-lag relationships in S&T knowledge networks.

This paper investigates the interaction patterns of knowledge backbones within the contexts of science-leading technology and technology-leading science, taking into consideration temporal disparities in S&T (see Fig. 9). In the context of technology leading the way, our analysis reveals that during the same year and three years subsequent to technological advancements, "Fuel Cell" and its subfields, namely "Fuel Cell Power" and "Fuel Cell Stack," served as pivotal components of knowledge sharing within the S&T landscape throughout this cycle. The dissemination of core knowledge in this period is predominantly driven by interactions within the existing body of S&T knowledge. Furthermore, the "Wireless Sensor Network" emerges as a focal point within the scientific domain during this cycle, with increasing research activities over the subsequent three years.

Turning our attention to the science leadership cycle, we base our observations on the most recent three years of combined networks. In this period, the core knowledge shared between S&T within the realm of energy efficiency evolved from earlier research on "Fuel Cell" to the more contemporary focus on "Energy Storage System." Notably, research in the domain of energy storage systems has experienced substantial growth; however, the emergence of alternative energy sources necessitates further scientific exploration to reduce the associated costs [21]. Within this context, science emphasizes cutting-edge topics like "Electrode Active" and "Electrolyte Secondary Battery," while technology continues to explore established areas such as "Wireless Sensor Network" and "Battery Pack Cooling."

4.5   Verifying Network Coupling Calculation Algorithms

In the context of the interconnected S&T knowledge network calculation, the primary focus of the network projection portrait calculation method is to assess both the dispersion patterns of knowledge network nodes and their structural characteristics. To bolster the robustness of our derived conclusions, this study employs various coupling calculation methods for comparative analysis. Figure 10 presents the outcomes derived from the

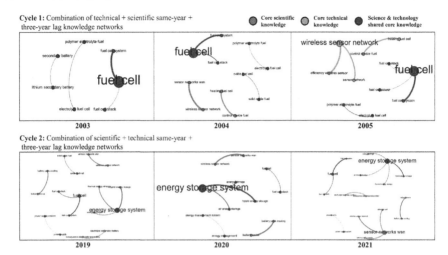

Fig. 9. Multi-scale knowledge backbone for S&T combinatorial networks.

application of these diverse network coupling calculation methods. Specifically, we reevaluate three algorithms within this paper:

(i) The Degree Divergence algorithm, which relies on degree distribution, quantifies the dissimilarity between two networks by computing the Jensen-Shannon scatter distribution of node degrees in both networks.
(ii) The Jaccard Distance algorithm, which is content based, evaluates network dispar-ities primarily by considering the proportion of shared nodes in relation to the total nodes in the original network.
(iii) The DMeasure algorithm, founded on structural disparities, gauges distinctions between networks through the computation of weighted metrics encompassing three distinct components. These components are as follows: firstly, the square root of the Jensen-Shannon scatter between the probabilities of average node distance; secondly, the absolute disparity between the square roots of network node disper-sion; and thirdly, the square root of the Jensen-Shannon scatter between network centrality and the probability distribution of its complementary graph.

The measures of network coupling strength are all represented as *1-distance* trans-formed initial distances. The three selected algorithms exhibit minimal distinctions in the transformed coupling matrix. Consequently, we proceed to compute the L2 norm (Euclidean distance) between the network portrait distance and the results obtained from the other three algorithms. The experimental findings reveal that the algorithm rooted in structural disparities (DMeasure) exhibits a higher degree of similarity to the structure of the portrait distance measure compared to the algorithms grounded in content and degree distribution.

Moreover, within this research, we opt for the Erdős-Rényi random network to gener-ate pairwise networks with an edge probability of 0.1, allowing us to discern variances in performance among the network portrait coupling measure and several alternative algo-rithms, as illustrated in Fig. 11. Notably, the portrait projection coupling method entails

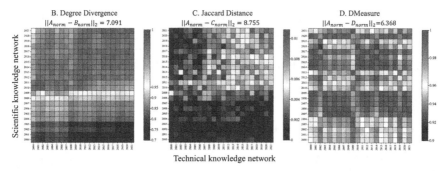

Fig. 10. Comparison of coupled S&T calculation algorithms.

a higher computational complexity and relatively longer execution times compared to its counterparts; however, it excels particularly in larger networks. Conversely, when dealing with smaller network sizes, the coupling computations of multiple algorithms yield more distinctive results, making it challenging to discern network similarities and disparities. As network size progressively expands, accompanied by an increase in node edges, we observe a greater alignment in trends between the network portrait measurement algorithm and the degree distribution algorithm's coupling estimates, though subtle differences persist. In stark contrast, the content-based (Jaccard Distance) and structure-based (DMeasure) algorithms encounter difficulties in accurately estimating differences in larger networks, with the Jaccard Distance measure exhibiting notable instability.

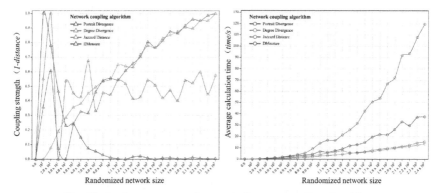

Fig. 11. Performance test of network distance coupling algorithms.

5   Discussion and Conclusion

S&T collaborative innovation stands as the principal driving force underpinning the advancement of innovation and the development of strategic emerging industries. This force operates through the real-time adaptation of knowledge and factors, facilitating mutual interaction and synergy within the realm of S&T. Consequently, it results in the overflow diffusion and dynamic coupling necessary to foster the continuous emergence of S&T innovation. Addressing the persistent issue of insufficiently potent and seamless transformation of S&T achievements into tangible productivity, an in-depth examination of the mechanisms underpinning science-technology-related interaction and collaborative innovation becomes imperative. Such an investigation can unearth win-win scenarios and optimize the effectiveness of science-technology collaborative innovation.

In this context, this paper adopts a vantage point centered on the coupling of science-technology knowledge networks. It introduces the calculation of network portrait projection distance as a means of identifying linkages among S&T knowledge. Furthermore, the paper leverages the BERT model to train and align shared knowledge elements within the S&T domain. Subsequently, it constructs a time-series knowledge network for measuring portrait distance, allowing for an analysis of knowledge mobility within the network backbone. This analysis is complemented by an exploration of instances of S&T overshooting and lagging linkages in the time-series network. To validate the efficacy and robustness of the network portrait divergence calculation method, extensive data from the field of energy conservation are employed as the empirical basis.

5.1 Theoretical and Practical Implications

This paper offers four primary theoretical and practical contributions.

(i) We introduce the portrait projection distance, for the detection of S&T linkages. This approach represents a breakthrough compared to existing coarse-grained detection schemes involving citation analysis, category mapping, and topic associations. It provides insights into the interplay between S&T by examining their core knowledge elements, thus advancing the theoretical and methodological aspects of "S&T linkage" research.

(ii) To address vocabulary disparities between the realms of S&T, we employ the BERT fine-tuning model. This step not only aligns the lexicons but also enhances the attributes of the S&T knowledge network, leading to improved accuracy in association distance detection based on knowledge elements.

(iii) We assess the effectiveness of the portrait projection distance method in detecting S&T linkages, utilizing large-scale samples from the field of energy conservation in S&T literature. Additionally, we conduct randomized network comparison experiments to validate its performance.

(iv) Using the portrait projection distance metric, we identify instances of overextension and lagging within S&T linkages. Furthermore, we analyze the knowledge flow evolution process in two distinct phases: science leading technology and technology leading science.

5.2 Limitations and Future Research

However, this paper exhibits certain limitations that warrant discussion. Firstly, during the process of constructing the core keyword network using literature in the field of S&T, we have identified instances of low connectivity among keyword nodes. These nodes, characterized by their minimal feature values, fail to contribute effectively to network projection construction. We are advisable to incorporate these low-degree nodes into the features of S&T linkages as sources of weak signal information [12, 13].

Secondly, it is essential to acknowledge the substantial complexity inherent in the calculation of network portrait projections. Additionally, the computation of coupling strength between extensive networks demands considerable time investment. In future investigations, researchers should endeavor to strike a balance between ensuring the validity of feature representations and expediting computational processes by implementing filtering mechanisms for portrait features.

References

1. Ba, Z., Liang, Z.: A novel approach to measuring science-technology linkage: from the perspective of knowledge network coupling. J. Informet. **15**(3), 101167 (2021). https://doi.org/10.1016/j.joi.2021.101167
2. Bagrow, J.P., Bollt, E.M.: An information-theoretic, all-scales approach to comparing networks. Appl. Netw. Sci. **4**(1), 1–15 (2019). https://doi.org/10.1007/s41109-019-0156-x
3. Bassecoulard, E., Zitt, M.: Patents and Publications. World Patent Inf. **27**(1), 335–347 (2005). https://doi.org/10.1007/1-4020-2755-9_31
4. Breschi, S., Catalini, C.: Tracing the links between science and technology: an exploratory analysis of scientists' and inventors' networks. Res. Policy **39**(1), 14–26 (2010). https://doi.org/10.1016/j.respol.2009.11.004
5. Canton, H.: The Europa Directory of International Organisation. United Nations Conference on Trade and Development—UNCTAD. Geneva (2021). https://doi.org/10.4324/9781003179900-26
6. Catalán, P., Navarrete, C., Figueroa, F.: The scientific and technological cross-space: Is technological diversification driven by scientific endogenous capacity? Res. Policy **51**(8), 104016 (2022). https://doi.org/10.1016/j.respol.2020.104016
7. Chen, X., et al.: Exploring science-technology linkages: a deep learning-empowered solution. Inf. Process. Manage. **60**, 103255 (2023). https://doi.org/10.1016/j.ipm.2022.103255
8. Colavizza, G.: A diachronic study of historiography. Scientometrics **117**(3), 2117–2131 (2018). https://doi.org/10.1007/s11192-018-2934-0
9. Dixon, R.K., McGowan, E., Onysko, G., Scheer, R.M.: US energy conservation and efficiency policies: challenges and opportunities. Energy Policy **38**, 6398–6408 (2010). https://doi.org/10.1016/j.enpol.2010.01.038
10. Han, F., Magee, C.L.: Testing the science/technology relationship by analysis of patent citations of scientific papers after decomposition of both science and technology. Scientometrics **116**(2), 767–796 (2018). https://doi.org/10.1007/s11192-018-2774-y
11. Hvelplund, F.: Renewable energy and the need for local energy markets. Energy **31**, 2293–2302 (2006). https://doi.org/10.1016/j.energy.2006.01.016
12. Joanny, G., Perani, S., Eulaerts, O.: Detection of disruptive technologies by automated identification of weak signals in technology development. In: Proceedings of the ISSI. International Society for Scientometrics and Informetrics, pp. 2644–2645 (2019)
13. Kim, J., Lee, C.: Novelty-focused weak signal detection in futuristic data: assessing the rarity and paradigm unrelatedness of signals. Technol. Forecast. Soc. Chang. **120**, 59–76 (2017). https://doi.org/10.1016/j.techfore.2017.04.006
14. Li, W., Yi, P.: Assessment of city sustainability-coupling coordinated development among economy, society, and environment. J. Clean. Prod. **256**(20), 120453 (2020). https://doi.org/10.1016/j.jclepro.2020.120453

15. Li, X., Tao, J.: The dynamic coupling analysis for coordinated development of the environment and economy based on cloud model: Case study of Henan. In: 2014 International Conference on Management Science and Engineering (ICMSE). IEEE, 726–735 (2014). https://doi.org/10.1109/ICMSE.2014.6930301

16. Li, K., Yan, E.: Are NIH-funded publications fulfilling the proposed research? An examination of concept-matchedness between NIH research grants and their supported publications. J. Informet. **13**(1), 226–237 (2019). https://doi.org/10.1016/j.joi.2019.01.001

17. Li, M., Wang, W., Zhou, K.: Exploring the technology emergence related to artificial intelligence: a perspective of coupling analyses. Technol. Forecast. Soc. Chang. **172**, 121064 (2021). https://doi.org/10.1016/j.techfore.2021.121064

18. Li, X., Xie, Q., Daim, T., Huang, L.: Forecasting technology trends using text mining of the gaps between science and technology: the case of perovskite solar cell technology. Technol. Forecast. Soc. Chang. **146**(3), 432–449 (2019). https://doi.org/10.1016/j.techfore.2019.01.012

19. Magerman, T., Looy, B., Debackere, K.: Does involvement in patenting jeopardize one's academic footprint? an analysis of patent-paper pairs in biotechnology. Res. Policy **44**(9), 1702–1713 (2015). https://doi.org/10.1016/j.respol.2015.06.005

20. Meyer, M.: Does science push technology? Patents citing scientific literature. Res. Policy **29**(3), 409–434 (2000). https://doi.org/10.1016/S0048-7333(99)00040-2

21. Olabi, A.G., Onumaegbu, C., Wilberforce, T., Ramadan, M.R., Abdelkareem, M.A., Alami, A.H.: Critical review of energy storage systems. Energy **214**, 118987 (2021). https://doi.org/10.1016/j.energy.2020.118987

22. Shahbaz, M., Zakaria, M., Shahzad, S.J.H., Mahalik, M.K.: The energy consumption and economic growth nexus in top ten energy-consuming countries: Fresh evidence from using the quantile-on-quantile approach. Energy Econ. **71**, 282–301 (2018). https://doi.org/10.1016/j.eneco.2018.02.023

23. Shibata, N., Kajikawa, Y., Sakata, I.: Extracting the commercialization gap between science and technology - case study of a solar cell. Technol. Forecast. Soc. Chang. **77**, 1147–1155 (2010). https://doi.org/10.1016/j.techfore.2010.03.008

24. Wang, L., Li, Z.: Knowledge flows from public science to industrial technologies. J. Technol. Transf. **46**(4), 1232–1255 (2021). https://doi.org/10.1007/s10961-019-09738-9

25. Wang, Y., Yin, S., Fang, X., Chen, W.: Interaction of economic agglomeration, energy conservation and emission reduction: evidence from three major urban agglomerations in China. Energy, **2**, 122519 (2021). https://doi.org/10.1016/j.energy.2021.122519

26. Xu, H., Yue, Z., Pang, H., Elahi, E., Li, J.Y., Wang, L.: Integrative model for discovering linked topics in science and technology. J. Informet. **16**, 101265 (2022). https://doi.org/10.1016/j.joi.2022.101265

27. Xu, S., Zhai, D., Wang, F., An, X., Pang, H., Sun, Y.: A novel method for topic linkages between scientific publications and patents. J. Am. Soc. Inf. Sci. **70**(9), 1–17 (2019). https://doi.org/10.1002/asi.24175

Data Augmentation on Problem and Method Sentence Classification Task in Scientific Paper: A Mechanism Analysis Study

Yingyi Zhang[1] and Chengzhi Zhang[2(✉)]

[1] Soochow University, Suzhou 215127, China
yyzhang9@suda.edu.cn
[2] Nanjing University of Science and Technology, Nanjing 210094, China
zhangcz@njust.edu.cn

Abstract. Billions of scientific papers lead to the need to identify essential parts of the massive text. Scientific research is an activity from putting forward problems to using methods. To learn the main idea from scientific papers, we focus on extracting problem and method sentences. Annotating sentences in scientific papers is labor-intensive, resulting in the creation of small-scale datasets that limit model learning. To tackle this challenge, data augmentation has been adopted due to its ability to generate synthetic data with minor variations, thereby expanding the scale of the original training dataset. Nowadays, there are various data augmentation methods, such as those based on random word replacement or back translation. Nevertheless, their suitability for sentence classification tasks in scientific papers remains unexplored. Thus, this paper constructs two manually annotation datasets and evaluates their performance. Furthermore, this paper delves into the mechanisms underlying their effects. Previous studies have suggested that data augmentation can diminish reliance on high-frequency patterns in models. Therefore, this paper employs attention values to represent the model's dependence on words and analyzes how data augmentation methods alter the attention values of individual words within sentences. The experimental results indicate that data augmentation methods can improve the macro F_1 score in sentence classification tasks. Furthermore, data augmentation methods effectively reduce the attention values assigned to stop words, commonly used words in scientific papers, and commonly used words in method and problem sentences.

Keywords: Data augmentation · Problem and Method Sentence Classification · Scientific Paper mining

1 Introduction

The number of scientific papers in the world has reached a billion [1]. Massive scientific papers exceed human processing capability. Scientific research is an activity from putting forward problems to using methods to solve them [18]. "Problem" and "method" are two essential parts of scientific papers [11]. Among them, the problem is the subject of the scientific paper and the technical problem, while the method is the process researchers used to achieve the goal. These "problem" and "method" elements find expression in sentences. Extracting these problems and method sentences is the objective of this paper. It has downstream applications, including academic information retrieval [3] and the summarization of scientific papers [2].

In recent years, several studies have focused on this task. Two noteworthy ones are by Sakai and Hirokawa [12] and Wang et al. [15]. Sakai and Hirokawa [12] extracted problem sentences and manually curated a 300 abstracts dataset. Wang et al. [15], on the other hand, concentrated on extracting method sentences and manually assembled a 100 abstracts dataset. As seen above, the process of manual annotation is labor-intensive, resulting in the creation of small-scale datasets. Consequently, neural networks tend to memorize specific patterns that do not generalize well [14]. Overreliance on these patterns can lead to a reduction in models' generalization ability.

To mitigate the issues of limited training data and pattern overreliance, this paper introduces data augmentation methods (data augmenters). Data augmenters construct synthetic data with minor changes [14]. Adding these synthetic sentences increases the scale of the original training dataset and reduces the models' dependency on high-frequency patterns [13]. Data augmenters have been used in various text classification tasks, but their effectiveness has not yet been demonstrated in the task of problem and method sentence classification.

Therefore, this paper constructs two datasets, and then analyzes whether data augmenters can improve the performance on these two datasets. Furthermore, it is important to analyze the underlying principles of how data augmenters work in this task. Following the viewpoint of Shakeel et al. [13], this paper analyzes whether data augmenters alter the pattern relied upon by the baseline model. To obtain these features, this paper uses attention value to represent the model's reliance on words.

The experimental results indicate that data augmenters can improve the macro F_1 score of problem and method sentence classification tasks. Additionally, data augmenters can reduce the attention values assigned to stop words, commonly used words in scientific papers and problem and method sentences.

2   Data Augmenters for Text Classification

Data augmenters for text classification tasks include word-level and sentence-level methods. Among the word-level augmenters, random methods are used [17], in which the words that need to be replaced and the newly inserted words are randomly selected. Different with random methods, TFIDF augmenters replace words with small TFIDF values [20], the embedding augmenters replace the randomly selected words with their synonyms [16], and the BERT augmenter first masks the words randomly, then uses a pretrained language model to predict the masked word [19].

Sentence-level augmenters generally use back translation methods [5, 7]. Taking an English sentence as an example, it first translates the sentence into other languages and then back translate it into English. Another line is use generation model like GPT. For example, a few studies first design prompt information for GPT-3 to generate entities, and then use GPT-3 to generate sentence with these generated entities [4].

3   Experimental Details

3.1   Sentence Definition

Table 1. The definition of three categories of sentences in scientific papers.

Proposed categories	Definition	Source literature	Status of application
Problem sentence	Describe the gap between the methods and the ideal solution	Sakai & Hirokawa, [12]	Exact adoption
	Describe the subject of the paper	Fisas, Saggion & Ronzano, [6]	Exact adoption
	Describe the subject in past work	-	New category
Method sentence	Describe the process researchers did that used to achieve a goal	Liu et al., [9]	Exact adoption
	Describe the details of the experimental setup	Fisas, Saggion & Ronzano, [6]	Exact adoption
	Describe the method used or mentioned in past work	Iwatsuki & Aizawa, [8]	Exact adoption
cooccurrence sentence	Describe the subject and the method used in the paper	-	New category
	Describe the subject and method of past work	-	New category
	Describe the method and the gap between this method and the ideal solution	-	New category

In Table 1, we give the definition of the problem and method sentence. We also define another category of sentences: the problem and method cooccurrence sentence (cooccurrence sentence). The definition is also shown in Table 1. Except for sentences of the above three categories, other sentences are defined as normal sentences, which contain neither the problem nor the method-related information.

3.2 Dataset Preparation

This paper constructs two datasets, i.e., an Abstract dataset and a Full-text dataset. The statistics information is shown in Table 2.

Abstract Dataset. The abstract dataset is a subset of the SCIERC dataset [10]. We selected 305 abstracts related to NLP from this dataset. There are 1,440 sentences in this dataset.

Full-Text Dataset. The full-text dataset consists of 74 Annual Meeting of the Association for Computational Linguistics conference (ACL) papers. The ACL anthology released the XML format of papers published from 1979 to 2015. We randomly sample two papers each year from the released dataset. There are 12,594 sentences in the dataset.

Table 2. Statistical information of two datasets.

Sentence Category	Abstract	Full-Text
Problem sentence	271	1,160
Method sentence	395	2,428
Cooccurrence sentence	562	2,061
Normal sentence	212	6,945

3.3 Baseline and Data Augmenters Selection

Baseline Model. This paper selects three baselines. The first is PLM-BiLSTM-ATT [22], consists of an attention module. The second is Prompt learning model based on sentence (Prompt-sen). The third is Prompt learning model based on paragraph (Prompt-para). These two models use "gpt-3.5-turbo". In Prompt-sen, the model predicts the category of each sentence. In Prompt-para, the model selects sentences with specific category from paragraphs.

Data Augmenters. This paper selects four word-level augmenters, i.e., Random augmenter (Random) [17], TFIDF augmenter (TFIDF) [20], Embedding augmenter (Embed) [16], Contextual embedding BERT augmenter (PLM) [19], and two sentence-level augmenters, i.e., Back translation augmenter (BackTrans) [5] and ChatGPT augmenter (ChatGPT) [4].

Augmented Sentence Discrimination Method. This paper uses the discrimination method proposed by Zeng et al. [21]. As shown in Fig. 1, we add the augmented sentence that can be correctly predicted to the original training dataset. It is called the "True-discrimination" strategy. In this paper, we also consider another situation that the label of added sentence is incorrectly predicted, which is called "Wrong-discrimination" strategy.

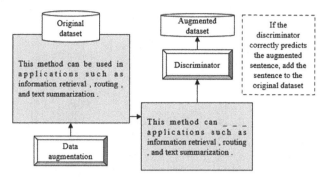

Fig. 1. The sentence quality discriminator of the data augmenters.

3.4 Parameter Setting

Parameter Setting on Data Augmenters. In data augmenters, the number of replaced words should not exceed 20% of the number of words in the original sentence. We use the PLM-BiLSTM-ATT to train the quality discriminator.

Parameter Setting on Sentence Extraction Models. The Adam optimizer is applied. The epochs of the Abstract and Full-text datasets are 20 and 10, respectively. The learning rate is 3e-5. The maximum sentence length is limited to 512. The number of neural in BiLSTM is 150.

3.5 Evaluation Metrics

The accuracy, precision (P), recall (R), F_1, *Macro P*, *Macro R*, and *Macro F_1* are used. We use the F_1@T, F_1@M, F_1@MT, and F_1@N to denote the F_1 in the problem sentence, method sentence, cooccurrence sentence, and normal sentence extraction, respectively.

4 Experimental Results

4.1 Experimental Results on Two Datasets

This section analyzes the performance of data augmenters on two datasets. Tables 3 and 4 present the experimental results for the Abstract and the Full-text datasets, respectively.

From Table 3, first, *on the abstract dataset, data augmenters can improve the macro F_1*. Among them, the BackTrans achieves the highest macro F_1, which is 72.88%. Second, *the performance of augmenters with "True-discrimination" strategy are better than augmenters with "Wrong-discrimination" strategy.*

From *Table 4, first, on the full-text dataset, the macro F1 of the four data augmenters, i.e., Random, Embed, BackTrans, ChatGPT, are higher than baseline models,* with ChatGPT being the best at 72.80%. Second, *the performance of augmenters with "Wrong-discrimination" strategy are better than augmenters with "True-discrimination" strategy.*

Table 3. Experiment results on Abstract dataset. In the table, "+ Random-True" indicates the PLM-BiLSTM-ATT combined with the random method and using "True-discrimination" strategy. "Wrong" denotes "Wrong-discrimination" strategy. And so on.

Model	Acc	Macro P	Macro R	Macro F_1	F_1@ T	F_1@ M	F_1@ MT	F_1@ N
PLM-BiLSTM-ATT	73.18	72.42	70.50	70.62	63.46	73.50	77.57	67.96
Prompt-Sen	32.02	24.14	26.20	21.97	3.18	36.21	38.65	9.83
Prompt-Para	25.85	25.96	26.57	23.07	13.13	37.88	21.20	20.08
+ Random-True	73.80	74.17	72.53	72.25	67.66	72.65	77.77	70.92
+ Random-Wrong	72.74	74.07	70.59	70.63	64.37	72.17	76.20	69.77
+ TFIDF-True	73.72	73.40	71.05	71.26	65.35	73.96	78.17	67.55
+ TFIDF- Wrong	71.52	73.11	68.42	68.95	63.67	71.28	76.35	64.49
+ Embed-True	73.47	73.50	72.73	72.07	66.03	74.22	75.75	72.27
+ Embed- Wrong	71.78	72.94	69.24	69.76	63.18	71.72	75.86	68.29
+ PLM-True	74.52	75.37	72.21	72.84	66.01	74.12	78.29	**72.95**
+ PLM- Wrong	70.42	70.90	69.81	69.22	61.72	71.22	73.31	70.61
+ BackTrans-True	**75.18**	**75.60**	**72.08**	**72.88**	67.32	**74.28**	**78.95**	70.95
+ BackTrans- Wrong	72.71	73.80	70.48	70.87	64.45	72.64	76.69	69.69
+ ChatGPT-True	74.03	74.91	71.84	71.96	**68.36**	72.92	78.65	67.93
+ ChatGPT- Wrong	69.74	70.00	68.07	67.80	64.73	68.03	73.85	64.61

Table 4. Experiment results on Full text Dataset

Model	Acc	Macro P	Macro R	Macro F_1	F_1@ T	F_1@ M	F_1@ MT	F_1@ N
PLM-BiLSTM-ATT	78.77	72.39	71.05	71.46	60.14	66.17	71.56	87.95
Prompt-Sen	37.80	23.17	26.65	22.77	2.24	16.05	23.36	49.41
Prompt-Para	32.39	26.99	27.25	21.70	16.77	13.32	5.08	51.65
+ Random-True	76.11	66.31	65.57	65.48	47.15	60.03	67.99	86.73
+ Random-Wrong	78.61	72.16	72.76	72.14	61.36	66.84	73.06	87.30
+ TFIDF-True	78.81	72.93	70.12	71.12	58.65	66.31	71.55	87.96
+ TFIDF- Wrong	78.26	71.83	71.27	71.25	60.38	65.73	71.43	87.40
+ Embed-True	76.48	68.39	67.70	66.98	53.11	58.33	69.44	87.04
+ Embed- Wrong	79.34	72.92	72.84	72.71	62.09	66.81	74.15	87.79
+ PLM-True	77.82	71.61	69.41	70.03	56.94	65.07	70.62	87.49
+ PLM- Wrong	77.84	71.64	70.58	70.56	59.41	65.04	70.60	87.17
+ BackTrans-True	78.84	72.13	72.44	71.96	60.15	67.31	72.44	87.95
+ BackTrans- Wrong	78.75	72.05	72.61	71.99	60.70	67.86	71.77	87.62
+ ChatGPT-True	**79.59**	**73.74**	72.13	**72.80**	**62.14**	67.52	72.20	**89.32**
+ ChatGPT- Wrong	79.51	73.00	**73.46**	72.77	61.63	**67.92**	**73.25**	88.26

Based on the aforementioned results, the performance across the two datasets exhibits variations when employing different discrimination strategies. In Sect. 4.2, we delve deeper into the factors contributing to this phenomenon.

4.2   Experimental Result on Datasets with Different Samples

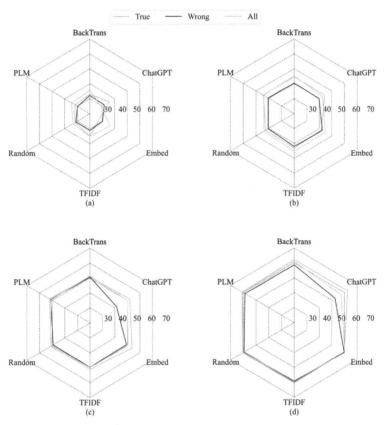

Fig. 2. The result of 50, 100, 200, and 500 samples of the Abstract Dataset. (a), (b), (c), (d) represent 50, 100, 200, and 500 samples. "True" indicates "True-discrimination" strategy, "wrong" indicates "Wrong-discrimination" strategy, and "all" indicates using all sentences. The same applies to the following figures.

This section analyzes the macro F_1 for different discrimination strategies on 50, 100, 200, and 500 samples. Figures 2 and 3 represent the results for the Abstract and Full-text dataset, respectively.

According to Fig. 2, for the Abstract dataset, when the dataset is small, using all augmented sentences yields high macro F_1 scores. *As the sample size increases, using "True discrimination" strategy results in high macro F_1 scores.*

As shown in Fig. 3, for the Full-text dataset, when the dataset is small, the macro F_1 of "True-discrimination" and "Wrong-discrimination" strategy are quite comparable. However, *as the dataset size grows, except for the ChatGPT method, using "Wrong discrimination" strategy achieves the optimal macro F_1 scores.*

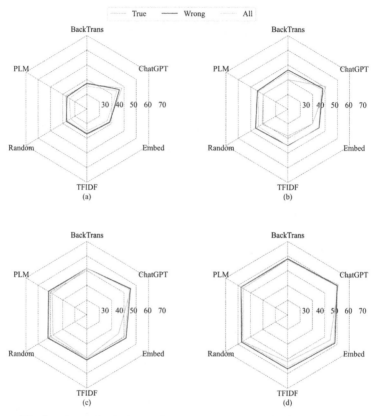

Fig. 3. The result of 50, 100, 200, and 500 samples of Full-text Dataset.

To analyze the reasons behind this phenomenon, the paper examined the label distribution of "True-discrimination" strategy selected sentences and "Wrong-discrimination" strategy selected sentences. It was found that there is a higher proportion of problem sentences in "Wrong-discrimination" strategy selected sentences. This can explain the phenomenon. First, *in the Abstract dataset, the number of sentences for each category is balanced. Adding a significant number of problem sentences would disrupt the distribution of sentence category in the dataset.* Second, in the Full-text dataset, there are significant differences in the number of sentences for different categories, with normal sentences being the most abundant and problem sentences being the least. *Adding problem sentences in the training dataset enhances the model's ability to recognize problem sentences, thus improving the model's performance.*

4.3 Attention Value Analysis of Data Augmenters

Table 5. The intersection results between the high-attention word set of baseline model and the low-attention word set of data augmenters in Abstract dataset. The bold word denoted the unique words in all results. The same applies to the following table.

Augmenter	50	100	200	500
Random	of	a; is; paper	of; model; ambiguity	of; for; system
TFIDF	is; the; this	a; paper	a; **by**; **task**; model	**on**; **that**; paper; **topic**; information
Embed	of; the	of	is; for; this; model	is; paper
PLM	this	is; model	have; **based**; **principle**	is; **and**; paper; **over**
BackTrans	of	a; is; paper	model; ambiguity	paper; **which**; **different**
ChatGPT	of; the; **achieve**; **language**	of; the	is; **both**; model; **using**	as; **MRR**; paper; system; information

Table 6. The intersection results between the high-attention word set of baseline model and the low-attention word set of data augmenters in Full-text dataset.

Augmenter	50	100	200	500
Random	a; as; or; and; the	a; **we**; in; the; this	a; of; for; the; system	is; the; user; from; system
TFIDF	in; of; and; for; the	a; to; of; for; the	of; the; from; **action**; system;	in; the; system; problem; **language**
Embed	of; in; the; and; for	a; is; of; and; the	of; to; and; the; **tag**	by; in; to; the; **dialogue**
PLM	is; of; and; for; **based**	is; in; of; the; this	of; or; is; the; for	is; the; user; **notion**; system
BackTrans	a; to; **on**; the; for	a; in; of; to; the	the; **example**	of; is; to; the; from
ChatGPT	of; to; the; and; **method**	is; in; of; and; the	is; the; this; **first**; system	is; of; the; system; problem

This section analyzes whether data augmenters can alleviate the model's reliance on high-frequency features.

To find features that are important in baseline models but not in models with data augmenters, this paper calculates the intersection between high-attention words set of PLM-BiLSTM-ATT and low-attention words set of data augmenters. Among them, high-attention words set consist of 4 words with biggest attention values, while low-attention words set consist of 4 words with lowest attention values. Tables 5 and 6 display the intersection results for the Abstract dataset and the Full-text dataset, respectively.

In Tables 5 and 6, the following conclusions can be drawn: first, *attention values for stop words in sentences decrease*, including "of" and "the". Second, *attention values for commonly used words in scientific paper decrease*, including "paper" and "information." Third, *attention values for commonly used words in problem and method sentences decrease*. These words include two categories: one is those related to problems and methods, such as "model" and "task," and another is those connecting problem and method entities, such as "by" and "for." Sentences containing these words may not necessarily be problem or method sentences. Forth, *the attention values for some nouns also decrease*, including nouns like "language" and "MRR." This phenomenon can be seen in large sample sizes.

5   Conclusion

This paper analyzes the performance and mechanisms of six data augmenters on both Abstract and Full-text datasets. Experimental results show that data augmenters can enhance the F_1 score. Sentence-level augmenters perform the best in both Abstract and Full-text datasets. Additionally, this paper examines the impact of different discrimination strategies on augmenters. Finally, the paper delves into the mechanisms of data augmenters. Through attention value analysis, it is found that data augmenters effectively reduce the attention values of stop words, commonly used words in scientific papers and problem and method sentences, thus alleviating the model's overreliance on these words. In future work, we plan to expand the domains and quantity of annotated datasets, use more data augmenters for mechanism analysis, and design suitable data augmenters for problem and method sentence classification.

Acknowledgments. This work is supported by National Natural Science Foundation of China (Grant No. 72074113).

References

1. Bornmann, L., Mutz, R.: Growth rates of modern science: a bibliometric analysis based on the number of publications and cited references. J. Am. Soc. Inf. Sci. **66**(11), 2215–2222 (2015)
2. Dernoncourt, F., Lee, J.Y.: Pubmed 200k rct: a dataset for sequential sentence classification in medical abstracts. In: Proceedings of the Eighth International Joint Conference on Natural Language Processing, IJCNLP, pp. 308–313. Asian Federation of Natural Language Processing, Taipei, Taiwan (2017)
3. Dernoncourt, F., Lee, J.Y., Szolovits, P.: Neural networks for joint sentence classification in medical paper abstracts. In: Proceedings of the 15th Conference of the European Chapter of the Association for Computational Linguistics, EACL, pp. 694–700. Association for Computational Linguistics, Valencia, Spain (2016)
4. Ding, B., Qin, C., Liu, L., Bing, L., Joty, S., Li, B.: Is gpt-3 a good data annotator?. arXiv preprint arXiv:2212.10450 (2022)
5. Ferreira, T.M., Costa, A.H.R.: DeepBT and NLP Data Augmentation Techniques: A New Proposal and a Comprehensive Study. In: Cerri, R., Prati, R.C. (eds.) BRACIS 2020. LNCS (LNAI), vol. 12319, pp. 435–449. Springer, Cham (2020). https://doi.org/10.1007/978-3-030-61377-8_30
6. Fisas, B., Saggion, H., Ronzano, F.: On the Discursive Structure of computer graphics research papers. In: Proceedings of the 2019 Conference of the North American Chapter of the Association for Computational Linguistics: Human Language Technologies, NAACL, pp. 42–51. Association for Computational Linguistics: Colorado, USA (2015)

7. Graa, M., Kim, Y., Schamper, J., Khadivi, S., Ney, H.: Generalizing back-translation in neural machine translation. In: Proceedings of the Fourth Conference on Machine Translation, WMT, pp. 45–52. Association for Computational Linguistics, Florence, Italy (2019)

8. Iwatsuki, K., Aizawa, A.: Communicative-function-based sentence classification for construction of an academic formulaic expression database. In Proceedings of the 16th Conference of the European Chapter of the Association for Computational Linguistics, EACL, pp. 3476–3497. Association for Computational Linguistics, Online (2021)

9. Liu, Y., et al.: Roberta: a robustly optimized bert pretraining approach. arXiv preprint arXiv: 1907.11692 (2019)

10. Luan, Y., He, L., Ostendorf, M., Hajishirzi, H.: Multi-task identification of entities, relations, and coreference for scientific knowledge graph construction. In: Proceedings of the 2018 Conference on Empirical Methods in Natural Language Processing, EMNLP, pp. 3219–3232. Association for Computational Linguistics, Brussels, Belgium (2018)

11. Luo, Z., Lu, W., He, J., Wang, Y.: Combination of research questions and methods: A new measurement of scientific novelty. J. Informet. **16**(2), 101282 (2022)

12. Sakai, T., Hirokawa, S.: Feature words that classify problem sentence in scientific article. In: Proceedings of the 14th International Conference on Information Integration and Web-based Applications & Services, IIWAS, pp. 360–367. Association for Computing Machinery, New York, USA (2012)

13. Shakeel, M.H., Karim, A., Khan, I.: A multi-cascaded model with data augmentation for enhanced paraphrase detection in short texts. Inf. Process. Manage. **57**(3), 102204 (2020)

14. Shorten, C., Khoshgoftaar, T.M., Furht, B.: Text data augmentation for deep learning. Journal of Big Data **8**(1), 101 (2021)

15. Wang, R., Zhang, C., Zhang, Y., Zhang, J.: Extracting Methodological Sentences from Unstructured Abstracts of Academic Articles. In: Sundqvist, A., Berget, G., Nolin, J., Skjerdingstad, K.I. (eds.) iConference 2020. LNCS, vol. 12051, pp. 790–798. Springer, Cham (2020). https://doi.org/10.1007/978-3-030-43687-2_66

16. Wang, W. Y., Yang, D.: That's so annoying!!!: a lexical and frame-semantic embedding based data augmentation approach to automatic categorization of annoying behaviors using# petpeeve tweets. In: Proceedings of the 2015 Conference on Empirical Methods in Natural Language Processing, EMNLP, pp. 2557–2563. Association for Computational Linguistics, Lisbon, Portugal (2015)

17. Wei, J., Zou, K.: EDA: Easy data augmentation techniques for boosting performance on text classification tasks. In: Proceedings of the 2019 Conference on Empirical Methods in Natural Language Processing and the 9th International Joint Conference on Natural Language Processing, EMNLP-IJCNLP, pp. 6382–6388. Association for Computational Linguistics, Hong Kong, China (2019)

18. Wilson, E.B.: An Introduction to Scientific Research. Dover Publications (1991)

19. Wu, X., Lv, S., Zang, L., Han, J., Hu, S.: Conditional BERT contextual augmentation. In: Proceedings of the International Conference on Computational Science, ICCS, pp. 84–95. Springer, Faro, Portugal (2018)

20. Xie, Q., Dai, Z., Hovy, E., Luong, M.T., Le, Q.V.: Unsupervised data augmentation for consistency training. In: Proceedings of the Advances in Neural Information Processing Systems, NIPS, pp. 6256–6268. Curran Associates Inc, Vancouver, Canada (2020)

21. Zeng, X., Li, Y., Zhai, Y., Zhang, Y.: Counterfactual generator: a weakly-supervised method for named entity recognition. In: Proceedings of the 2020 Conference on Empirical Methods in Natural Language Processing, EMNLP, pp. 7270–7280. Association for Computational Linguistics, Online: Association for Computational Linguistics (2020)
22. Zhang, H., Ren, F.: Bertatde at semeval-2020 task 6: extracting term-definition pairs in free text using pre-trained model. In: Proceedings of the Fourteenth Workshop on Semantic Evaluation, SemEval, pp. 690–696. International Committee for Computational Linguistics, Online (2020)

Key Factors of Government Knowledge Base Adoption in First-, Second- and Third-Tier Cities in China

Jing Zhou[1]([⊠]) [iD] and Li Si[1,2] [iD]

[1] Wuhan University, Wuhan, Hubei, People's Republic of China
zhoujingwinky@whu.edu.cn
[2] Center for Studies of Information Resources, Wuhan, Hubei, People's Republic of China

Abstract. The government knowledge base (GKB) has increasing significance nowadays as a means of achieving enhanced connectivity, productivity, availability, and efficiency. The facilitators and barriers to adopting a government knowledge base are unknown from the perspective of civil servants. This research seeks to identify and compare critical factors that impact government knowledge base adoption in first-, second- and third-tier cities in China. According to the literature review, factors from the UTAUT and TOE framework were integrated, and trust to knowledge base and intention to knowledge reuse were introduced to the research model. A questionnaire was designed based on the model and distributed to civil servants. The proposed model was validated, and the collected data was analyzed by PLS-SEM. The results show the factors (effort expectancy, social influence, competitive pressure, trust to knowledge base, intention to knowledge reuse) have a positive impact on the adoption of knowledge base in local governments in all cities while performance expectancy and compatibility have a positive impact on the adoption only in first- and second-tier cities. Facilitating conditions do not positively impact the adoption of a knowledge base in any city. The development of a new GKB adoption model has contributed to a new theoretical finding in the area of digital government. The outcomes will provide insights to local governments seeking to make investment decisions on knowledge base adoption.

Keywords: Government Knowledge Base · Knowledge Reuse · The Unified Theory of Acceptance and Use of Technology (UTAUT) · Technology-Organization-Environment (TOE) Framework · Local Government

1 Introduction

With the advent of digital governments, a wealth of valuable expertise and knowledge regarding public service and social governance has been amassed. Some of this knowledge is stored in electronic files and digital archives, while other aspects remain tacit in

Supplementary Information The online version contains supplementary material available at
https://doi.org/10.1007/978-3-031-57867-0_3.

the minds of civil servants, administrators, or experts, making them non-shareable and non-reusable. In this context, knowledge bases are introduced into local governments. A GKB is the product of collecting and organizing government information about a particular subject into a useful form, with strong knowledge integration, classification, storage, distribution, and decision support. A knowledge base is essential to civil servants because they need to access the expertise of a broad array of subject matters when responding to the plethora of citizens' requests [14]. Though knowledge bases are vital applications proceeding digital transformation, there has been no research focusing on how knowledge bases influence the digital transformation process in the context of government. This study aims to conduct in-depth research on facilitators and barriers to adopting emerging Information and Communications Technology (ICT) infrastructure, i.e., GKB, and how a GKB affects different levels of digital transformation and further improves digital innovation.

Previous research centered mainly on knowledge bases in firms [60]. In many countries, both developed countries and developing countries are utilizing industrial knowledge bases, to drive open innovation, and improve efficiency and user satisfaction [6, 30, 52]. In addition, knowledge bases have been utilized to enable transformational changes in private sector organizations, by improving the process of capturing, developing, sharing, and using organizational knowledge [16].

From the organizational perspective, knowledge bases serve as a critical construct to measure innovation capabilities in an industry. Organizations with different scales and sizes have different levels of innovation capabilities, thus behaving differently in knowledge base adoption [39, 60]. For instance, small and medium-sized enterprises (SMEs) face resource constraints in terms of human resources and scale limitations when adopting ICT [54]. Nevertheless, SMEs have larger organizational flexibility, less bureaucracy, and greater responsiveness to technology. As for large enterprises, they are endowed with monopoly power, which enables them to benefit more from innovations than small firms. This, in turn, is a driver to invest in product/service innovation [50]. Accordingly, it's easy to deduce that local governments in cities with different scales and levels of economic development and open innovation operate within different regulatory, policy, and organizational contexts and individual capabilities. Thus, local governments of these cities face diverse constraints that limit their ability to invest in knowledge bases. While in different levels of cities in developing countries, GKB is an emerging trend and they have not been subject to significant scholarly investigation.

From the individual perspective, prior research has found that knowledge bases accelerate the speed with which knowledge is acquired and disseminated to organizational members, and thus serve as a particularly effective intraorganizational learning mechanism [26]. Furthermore, usage behaviors have a significant impact on individual performance. When individuals exhibit greater levels of usage intensity, a higher level of professional experience may serve to reduce the effort to process information and garner greater cognitive benefits from knowledge bases usage [23]. As data contributors and users, civil servants relate all the daily businesses to GKB, so the opinions of civil servants are worth investigating. This study contributes to the knowledge base adoption literature by being among the first to listen to its civil servants and gain a perspective on what they think about the knowledge base.

Hence, this study aims to explore the influential role of organizational and individual factors on knowledge base adoption in first-, second- and third-tier cities in China from the perspective of civil servants. Since knowledge bases in first-, and second-tier cities have been developed well but are still being developed in third-tier cities, this study treats the data from first and second-tier cities as a single dataset and compares it with the data from third-tier cities during model measurement. Based on this, this study aims to fill the gap by addressing two questions:

RQ1. What are the facilitators and barriers for local governments to adopt and use knowledge base from the perspective of civil servants?
RQ2. How different are these facilitators and barriers in first-, second-, and third-tier cities of China?

2 Literature Review

2.1 Government Knowledge Base

By developing and introducing novel ICT, many local governments established integrated knowledge bases and online services, providing constituents with information at a variety of levels [58]. Government knowledge base could be adopted in diverse fields of public services, such as crime prevention [57], urban emergency management [35], jurisdictional domains [32], administrative process digitalization [11], e-participation [1], crisis management [10], et al.

2.2 Technology Adoption and Diffusion Models

Since the 1980s, the research on technology adoption, diffusion, and use behavior has received extensive attention. Previous pieces of research can be separated into two levels: individual and organizational levels.

As for the individual level, the UTAUT was proposed and is currently one of the most authoritative and basic models to explain and predict user technology acceptance and use behavior [12, 29]. It has shown that four core structures (Performance Expectancy, Effort Expectancy, Social Influence, Facilitating Conditions) are determinants of Behavioral Intention and Use Behavior, and these structures are in turn mediated by Gender, Age, Experience, and Voluntariness of Use [59]. According to the organizational level, the TOE framework can be invoked which comprises three dimensions: technological context, organizational context, and external environment context. Barriers to enhancing smarter governments have been demarcated as technological and operational barriers, managerial and organizational barriers, and political and institutional barriers [47]. Hence, the TOE framework has been extensively used for appreciating the adoption of technological innovations in government such as AI [40], and e-participation [28].

To extend the theoretical prowess of frameworks that suggest both individual and organizational contexts, some studies have called for a combined model of the UTAUT and TOE framework to examine the adoption of innovative new technology [25, 33, 41].

3 Research Context

In China, GKB was developed due to digital transformation in governments. *Guiding Opinions of the General Office of the State Council on Further Optimizing Local Government Service Hotlines* [55] pointed out that all cities are required to establish and maintain a GKB with "authoritative accuracy, unified standards, real-time updates, and joint construction and sharing". After that, some governments in first-tier cities started to construct knowledge bases. During the COVID-19 epidemic, more governments adopted knowledge bases to handle complicated business because of limited staffing in related departments. Therefore, a wider range of cities began to construct knowledge bases during the outbreak, and systematically record, organize, and manage the experience, lessons, and knowledge, to provide reference for future decision-making. With the intelligent development of knowledge bases, *Guiding Opinions of the State Council on Strengthening the Construction of Digital Government* [56] included GKB in more government affairs, such as social management and public services.

Hundreds of cities at different stages of development are divided into 3 tiers according to political status, economic development, city scale, and population in China. First-tier cities are Beijing, Shanghai, Guangzhou, and some other capital cities. Second-tier cities develop lagging behind the first-tier cities, but they prepare relatively well in innovation for GKB adoption. Third-tier cities are developing fast, but their comprehensive strength is much less than the other two tiers so the ICT infrastructures to build GKB are in the pipeline. According to the web survey conducted, all first-tier cities (19 overall) have constructed GKB and nearly all of them have rich functional modules and intelligent knowledge reasoning. Meanwhile, about 86.7% of second-tier cities (30 overall) and 72.9% of third-tier cities (70 overall) have constructed GKB. As for second-tier cities, 69.2% of GKBs have FAQs and AI-guided chatbots. As for third-tier cities, 20% of GKB have FAQs and 32.9% have AI-guided chatbots.

As is shown in Fig. 1, GKB has various data resources collected from citizens, civil servants, and governments. They are processed into knowledge through the Intelligent Conversation Platform and Intelligent Knowledge Reasoning Platform and provide service for enterprises, citizens, and civil servants, who have access to these applications through multiple entries, like web portals, Apps, hotline, etc. As for first- and second-tier cities in China, the functions of GKB and the level of its intelligence have developed well. In third-tier cities, though the framework and application have been promoted, the actual utilization rates and their influential factors are to be studied. Thus, this research focuses on GKB use in first-, second-, and third-tier cities to figure out and compare their facilitators and barriers.

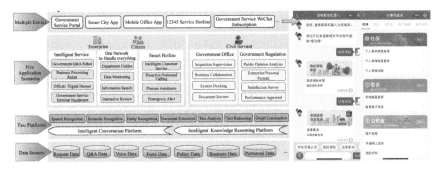

Fig. 1. The framework and application of GKB

4 Research Model and Hypotheses

Knowledge base adoption is both organizational and individual behavior. On the one hand, knowledge base adoption is an organization's behavior since some departments will adopt it for the benefit of the organization. On the other hand, this behavior depends extensively on distinct individuals, such as directors, deputy directors, civil servants, IT developers, and analysts. In this respect, the variables that are important from both an individual and an organizational perspective need to be examined for technology adoption. In this study, the UTAUT framework was used to explore the individual perspective, whereas the TOE was used to understand organizational perspectives. However, organizational context is excluded in this research for individual factors are used to target the members of organizations. Besides, "intention to knowledge reuse" and "trust to knowledge base" were introduced, as is shown in Fig. 2. Drawing on the conceptual model and insights from previous research, we presented the following eleven hypotheses to test the validity of each of the constructs contained within the research conceptual model:

As for individual factors, *Performance expectancy (PE)* indicates the degree to which an individual believes that using the system will help him or her to attain gains in job performance. *Effort Expectancy (EE)* represents the degree of ease associated with the use of the system. *Social Influence (SI)* refers to the degree to which an individual perceives that important others believe they should use the new system. *Facilitating Conditions (FC)* describes the degree to which an individual believes that an organizational and technical infrastructure exists to support the use of the system [59]. Previous studies have pointed out that these individual factors would affect behavior intention to use technology in local governments [22, 38, 60].

H1: Performance expectancy has a positive effect on behavior intention to use GKB.
H2: Effort expectancy has a positive effect on behavior intention to use GKB.
H3: Social influence has a positive effect on behavior intention to use GKB.
H4: Facilitating Conditions has a positive effect on behavior intention to use GKB.

Intention to knowledge reuse (IR) was introduced into the framework. So and Bolloju [49] tested that the intention to knowledge reuse positively affected IT service operations. Hence, we hypothesized intention to knowledge reuse affects behavioral intention to use. Chhim, Somers, and Chinnam [8] suggested technical and expectation factors interdependently affect knowledge reuse. So, we would test if compatibility would affect the intention to knowledge reuse. Kankanhalli, Lee, and Lim [24] found that perceived knowledge base capability positively affects knowledge reuse, which in turn impacts the benefits derived from using the system. Since the reuser does not have to reinvent solutions already present in the knowledge base, which makes it easier to use it, we included effort expectancy as a driving factor of intention to knowledge reuse.

H5: Effort expectancy has a positive effect on the intention to knowledge reuse.
H6: Intention to knowledge reuse has a positive effect on behavior intention to use GKB.
H7: Compatibility has a positive effect on the intention to knowledge reuse.

Competitive pressure (CP) refers to the extent of opposition that an organization feels from its competitive alliance [21]. The study of Oni, Musa, and Oni [42] supported the postulation that intense competition stimulates the rapid spread of innovation in public sectors. They are challenged with constant demands to increase efficiency and effectiveness while reducing non-compliance and maintaining a high level of service delivery [21].

H8: Competitive pressure has a positive effect on behavior intention to use GKB.

Compatibility (CB) describes the degree to which innovation is perceived as being consistent with the organization's existing technology [46]. A high level of compatibility can enhance the impact of newly adopted technology in an organization. Extant literature provided evidence of the link between compatibility and technology adoption (e.g., cloud computing [2], social media [48]) in local governments, and digital transformation in SMEs [53].

H9: Compatibility has a positive effect on behavior intention to use GKB.

Trust factors have a strong affection on knowledge base adoption and knowledge reuse. The trust of Internet factor was introduced, which is adopted by Carter and Bélanger [7]. Besides, trust in data and trust in the system were tested in open government data adoption [51]. In this study, we included *trust to knowledge base (TB)* as a moderating effect affecting behavioral intention to use and intention to knowledge reuse.

H10: Trust to knowledge base has a positive effect on behavior intention to use GKB.
H11: Trust to knowledge base has a positive effect on intention to knowledge reuse.

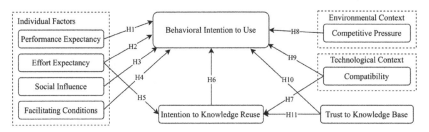

Fig. 2. Integration of UTAUT and TOE Framework

5 Model Validation and Data Analysis

5.1 Questionnaire and Sampling Procedure

A questionnaire with two main sections was developed to collect the data. The first section contained demographic information about the respondents. The second section consisted of the items measuring the constructs. In Table 1, this UTAUT and TOE combined model with each having several factors provided more comprehensive and insightful information in explaining the knowledge base adoption of government. The Likert five-point scale ranging from "strongly agree" to "strongly disagree" was used.

The initial questionnaire was designed based on the previous research mentioned in part 4 and distributed twice experimentally among 10 experts to ensure content validity and the questions were discussed in terms of simplicity and comprehensibility.

The non-probability sampling technique was adopted. Through purposive and snow-ball, we used experiential knowledge and judgment to choose the first few civil servants whose opinions best represented that of the government and then relied on their referrals for other likely participants.

Table 1. Measurement items in the UTAUT and TOE combined mode

Construct	ID	Measurement items
Performance Expectancy	PE1	I would find GKB helpful in my job
	PE2	Using GKB improves my job performance
	PE3	Using GKB improves my job efficiency
Effort Expectancy	EE1	I could use GKB through various channels
	EE2	It would be easy for me to become skillful at using GKB
	EE3	I would find GKB easy to learn and use
Social Influence	SI1	People who influence my behavior think that I should use GKB
	SI2	People who are important to me think that I should use GKB
	SI3	Many people around me use GKB
	SI4	The use frequency of GKB would increase if others recommend
Facilitating Conditions	FC1	I have the equipment necessary to use GKB
	FC2	I have the knowledge necessary to use GKB
	FC3	The organization provides training and instruction
Trust to Knowledge Base	TB1	I trust GKB and its services
	TB2	I think that GKB protects personal information and sensitive data
	TB3	In general, GKB is trusted tool that I can use to interact with the local government
Intention to Knowledge Reuse	IR1	I intend to reuse others' knowledge
	IR2	I am willing to share knowledge so others can reuse it
	IR3	I think GKB can satisfy my demand of knowledge reuse
Compatibility	CB1	GKB fits well with business processes
	CB2	GKB is compatible with hardware and software
	CB3	GKB fits well with other government service systems
Competitive Pressure	CP1	Some of local governments have already started using GKB
	CP2	Some of government departments have already started using GKB
	CP3	A competitive pressure is emerging from competitors to adopt GKB
Behavioral Intention to Use	BI1	I am willing to use GKB
	BI2	My organization plan to use GKB
	BI3	I would strongly recommend others to use GKB

5.2 Data Collection and Descriptive Analysis

By distributing online and offline questionnaires among civil servants, 252 completed questionnaires (84.1% response rate) were collected from 7 local governments in first- and second-tier cities, and 346 completed questionnaires (90.2% response rate) were collected from 12 local governments in third-tier cities. According to the screening criteria of invalid questionnaires defined by incomplete questionnaire filling, 207 valid questionnaires from first- and second-tier cities and 319 valid questionnaires from third-tier cities were finally determined after careful review and cleaning.

The descriptive analysis examined the respondents' demographic characteristics by calculating the frequency and percentage for each category of the characteristic, seen Appendix A. Characteristics involved in the analysis were age, gender, designation group, GKB adoption, and work experience in local government and GKB.

Descriptive analysis showed most respondents are under 45 years old and are more interested in and familiar with IT and knowledge base systems. More than half of the respondents are executives who may have an urgent need for GKB in their businesses. More than 70% of respondents have been working in local government for more than 1 year and are familiar with business and less than 30% of respondents have been employed for no more than one year. Compared to respondents in third-tier cities, more respondents have adopted or know GKB in first- and second-tier cities thanks to well-developed GKB in these cities. All in all, these respondents are enough to represent most civil servants who have a good command of their business and attempt to learn and apply the knowledge base to previous work.

5.3 Model Analysis

Structural Equation Modeling (SEM) analysis is good for this study given that the sample benchmark for SEM is 100 or 150 to 200 and above. Partial Least Square (PLS) is developed as a second generation of SEM [61] to handle situations where the latent variables and a series of cause-and-effect relationships exist [18]. A two-phase data analysis was employed based on PLS-SEM [19] i.e., a measurement model and structural model analysis. A measurement model analysis validates the reliability and validity of the relationships between the measurement items and the constructs, while a structural model analysis validates the relationship between the constructs, i.e., hypothesis testing.

Measurement Model

Construct Reliability and Validity. The reliability and validity are tested by calculating constructs' Cronbach's alpha, Composite reliability (rho_a), and Average variance extracted (AVE). Based on Appendix B, all Cronbach's alpha values are greater than 0.7. The composite reliability (rho_a) of FC is between 0.6 and 0.7. The values of Compo-site reliability (rho_a) for the rest of the constructs are greater than 0.7 which is ac-ceptable for this coefficient [20]. The AVE for all constructs is more than 0.5 and the value of CR is higher than AVE for each construct. Therefore, the reliability and valid-ity of the measurement model based on this index are confirmed [45].

Discriminant Validity. The discriminant validity was examined by two assessment outcomes: Fornell-Larcker and HTMT (Heterotrait-monotrait). First, the correlations between the items of potentially overlapping constructs were assessed according to For-nell and Larcker's [13] method. Appendix C shows the square root of AVEs is larger in all cases than the off-diagonal elements in their corresponding row and column, sug-gesting that the required discriminant validity has been achieved [9]. Second, Appendix D shows all HTMT ratios were less than the threshold limits of 0.85 and 0.90 suggested by Kline [27] and Gold, Malhotra, and Segars [17] for all constructs. Overall, the meas-urement model demonstrated adequate discriminant validity.

Structural Model. The main assessment criterion for the goodness of fit of the structural model is that the R2 measures the coefficient of determination and the level of significance of the path coefficients (β values) [19]. The results of this study showed that the R2 values for BI are 0.642 and 0.624 respectively, suggesting that as for first- and second-tier cities, 64.2% of the variance in BI can be explained by the proposed model, and as for third-tier cities, The proportion is 62.4%. The path coefficients of the structural model have been measured and bootstrap analysis (resampling $= 5000$) was performed to assess the statistical significance of the path coefficients. Figure 3 and Fig. 4 illustrate the PLS-SEM structural model testing results, indicating the path coefficient and path significances.

Regarding first- and second-tier cities, the results reveal that among the individual factors, PE, EE, and SI have significant relationships with BI: $\beta = 0.098, P < 0.05, \beta = 0.256, P < 0.001$ and $\beta = 0.284, P < 0.001$ respectively. Nevertheless, the relationship between FC and BI is non-significant: $\beta = -0.035$ p > 0.05. Regarding environmental context, CP has a significant relationship with BI: $\beta = 0.115, P < 0.001$. For the technological context, CB has a significant relationship with BI: $\beta = -0.113, P < 0.05$. As for TB, it also has a significant relationship with BI: $\beta = 0.231, P < 0.001$. Furthermore, EE, TB, and CB have significant relationships with IR: $\beta = 0.315, P < 0.001, \beta = 0.259, P < 0.01$, and $\beta = 0.268, P < 0.01$ respectively. And IR has a significant relationship with BI: $\beta = 0.162, P < 0.01$. Thus, according to the data of first- and second-tier cities, all hypotheses were supported except for H4.

Considering third-tier cities, the results indicate that among the individual factors, EE and SI have significant relationships with BI: $\beta = 0.220, P < 0.01$ and $\beta = 0.287, P < 0.001$ respectively. Nevertheless, the relationship between PE, FC, and BI is non-significant: $\beta = -0.055$ p > 0.05 and $\beta = -0.030$ p > 0.05 respectively. Regarding environmental context, CP has a significant relationship with BI: $\beta = 0.091, P < 0.05$.

But as for technological context, the relationship between CB and BI is non-significant: $\beta = -0.080$, $P > 0.05$. As for TB, it also has a significant relationship with BI: $\beta = 0.201$, $P < 0.001$. Furthermore, EE, TB, and CB have significant relationships with IR: $\beta = 0.302$, $P < 0.001$, $\beta = 0.257$, $P < 0.01$ and $\beta = 0.278$, $P < 0.01$ respectively. And IR has a significant relationship with BI: $\beta = 0.242$, $P < 0.01$. Thus, H2–3, H5–8, H10–11 are supported but H1, H4 and H9 are not supported.

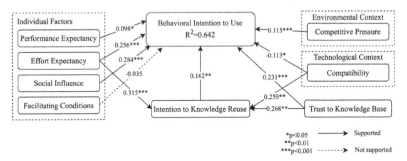

Fig. 3. Results of hypotheses testing (first- and second-tier cities)

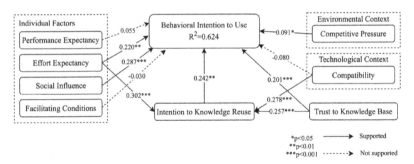

Fig. 4. Results of hypotheses testing (third-tier cities)

6   Discussion

This study empirically analyzed the factors that affect the behavioral intention to use GKB in local governments in first-, second-, and third-tier cities using the integration of the UTAUT and TOE framework.

Performance expectancy. The result differs in first-, second-, and third-tier cities. As for first- and second-tier cities, the positive result shows the degree of a civil servant's belief in GKB to help him to be successful in his job. The result is consistent with the findings from similar studies in developed nations such as Spain [5]; and developing nations such as The United Arab Emirates [36]. This could be a result of the fact that GKB provides a wide range of options and benefits to civil servants because of its usefulness, speed, and accessibility, which in turn can significantly reduce the cost and time that they must spend concerning carrying out those businesses in the traditional manner. However, as for third-tier cities, the result shows performance expectancy does not have an association with behavioral intention to use GKB. The result aligns with Kwateng, Atiemo, and Appiah's [31] findings. It shows that the perception of benefits is not enough as a driving factor to adopt GKB. It can happen when businesses are simpler and fewer in third-tier cities. It may also happen because users feel that if the app is not relatively easy to use, they can still exchange knowledge and get services through live visits. Then, the benefits of GKB affect its users slightly.

Effort expectancy. It has a positive association with behavioral intention to use GKB in all cities. As such, the study's finding is supported by the studies undertaken by Ammar and Ahmed [3]. The result shows that when they make less effort to learn and use the new system, they will probably use it. The EE hypothesis is covered in the questionnaire with three questions about the extent to which the civil servants perceived the ease of access and use of the GKB. It reveals most of the civil servants have gained expertise and become acquainted with the right way to access GKB without asking for help. As for grassroots staff, they care more about whether GKB is easy to use. Since the horizontal departmental and vertical hierarchical barriers of the government have set up many obstacles to data sharing, the staffs must learn and use multiple applications and duplicate the same datasets in these systems for business collaboration. Some of them think the usage of GKB will also increase the workload, which hinders its usage.

Social influence. It has a positive association with behavioral intention to use GKB. In this study, it is one of the strongest predictors of intention in all cities. The result echoes the study about blockchain adoption [43] and e-government [38, 44]. So, if others recommend or use GKB, there is more possibility for them to use it. For civil servants, they choose to use GKB mainly because of their leaders' or colleagues' beliefs, influence, or urges. Besides, they are more easily to adopt GKB when others whose business is related to theirs are using it.

Facilitating conditions. Opposed to other variables, it does not have a statistically significant relationship with behavioral intention to use GKB in all cities. The results are in line with the results reported in the study of Zuiderwijk, Janssen, and Dwivedi [63], especially given the involvement of more significant factors such as EE and SI, FC cannot be regarded as a good predictor for the behavioral intention to use. The FC hypothesis is tested through three questions, which focused on whether respondents feel that they had access to the equipment, knowledge, and other support to enable them to use GKB. Some users in this study believed that taking some effective measures such as increasing the technical and organizational support, holding educational courses, providing access to the system operation manual, and increasing the internet speed will increase the willingness to use the system. Despite such belief, most of the participants in the study regarded the other factors incorporated into the model as more important in increasing their willingness to use GKB.

Competitive pressure. It is found to have a positive effect on behavioral intention to use GKB in these cities. Through CP, some departments will replicate the GKB adoption behavior of other successful departments. They are competing to deliver their services in a perfect manner to increase service quality and efficiency. Also, local governments are not willing to be outdone in terms of invisible performance competition among different cities. For example, in China, some far-sighted leaders in local governments in developed cities like Guangzhou and Hangzhou began to realize the great importance and urgency of the adoption of a knowledge base. So, they carried out digital transformation to adopt GKB and achieved good performance, which stimulated more cities to imitate.

Compatibility. As for first- and second-tier cities, the result supports the proposed hypothesis and confirms that CB is an influential factor in the intention to use GKB. This finding is consistent with past studies on the adoption of cloud computing [2] and city management applications [4]. According to respondents, they may be reluctant to use GKB if the functionality offered is not compatible with organizational infrastructure, platforms, and other systems. Indeed, it is difficult to promote GKB in local governments because the traditional governance thinking and sunk costs in previous platforms may lead to the refusal of the knowledge base. And if GKB is developed externally, most of the functions it offers may not necessarily be customizable to meet specific local government needs and requirements. Moreover, GKB may not have any impact on local government operations if their users feel that GKB is incompatible with their existing routines. On the contrary, CB does not have an association with behavioral intention to use GKB in third-tier cities. In this study, local government organizations are tempted to use GKB even if it is not compatible with other systems. One possible reason is that it is related to the other finding of this study: effort expectancy has a significant effect on GKB use. That's to say, when the staff find it easy to handle business with GKB, even if they must learn how to use it, they will still choose to adopt it.

Intention to knowledge reuse. The research also shows that it plays an important supportive role in GKB adoption. EE and CB both have a significant effect on IR. Knowledge reuse is beneficial to the high efficiency of training and working considering the low effort and cost devoted to learning and adapting to the GKB system. On the one hand, due to the physical isolation between government departments, data could not be synchronized, which may cause conflicts and contradictions in the knowledge of various departments. At the same time, the knowledge collection often adopts a "starting from scratch" mode, which involves a lot of repetitive labor and low knowledge utilization efficiency. Through GKB, knowledge reuse can be operated in an open, convenient, and sharing platform so those who urgently need knowledge reuse tend to adopt GKB. On the other hand, knowledge reuse can also reduce the operating costs of training new staff when experienced staff depart. For a long time, urban management staff who undertake specific tasks in local communities referred to several work guidebooks, their own experience, seniors', and superiors' instructions. With their transferring to another position, it would take much time to train new staff and knowledge loss happened frequently. If the knowledge in their minds could be stored in GKB, it's easier to reuse it.

Trust to knowledge base. The study also identifies positive relationships between trust to knowledge base and behavioral intention to use GKB, intention to knowledge reuse. As for some respondents, they do not trust data privacy and security in GKB. Firstly, the leaders are concerned that entrenched departmental interests will be infringed because of data transparency in GKB. Secondly, data insecurity is a hidden danger if citizens' data is disclosed and may cause public panic, leading to mistrust in wider groups. On the contrary, trust to knowledge base can also promote behavioral intention to use GKB and intention to knowledge reuse because the trust shows those civil servants believe that the knowledge base can protect data security and personal privacy, and the system is robust enough to cope with an emergent IT crisis like system breakdown. The positive relationship between trust and e-government is consistent with the viewpoints of previous research [15, 34].

7 Conclusion

GKB is an important innovation that can reduce data duplication, enable broader data integration, increase knowledge reuse, and eliminate redundant integration activities among government organizations. However, despite the outward advantages of GKB, its adoption among local governments remains unknown with limited studies. This study has achieved its aim by constructing and validating a theoretical model that examined the effects of integration of the UTAUT and TOE framework on local governments' adoption of GKB in first-, second-, and third-tier cities. The findings of this study might be useful for government organizations implementing GKB initiatives that have not been successful in doing so. This study confirmed that individual determinants (effort expectancy and social influence), environmental determinants (competitive pressure), trust to knowledge base, and intention to knowledge reuse have significant effects on GKB adoption in all cities. Individual determinants (performance expectancy) and technological determinants (compatibility) have significant effects on GKB adoption in first- and second-tier cities but not in third-tier cities. Unexpectedly, the individual determinant (facilitating conditions) does not have significant relationships to the adoption of GKB in all cities.

The implications of this study are two-fold: theoretical and practical. First, the development of a new GKB adoption model has contributed to a new theoretical finding in the area of digital government. This study is the first to investigate individual, technological, and environmental determinants that affect GKB adoption by local government. In addition, the study reveals the relationship between knowledge base adoption and knowledge reuse which was first introduced. Moreover, the findings of this study have addressed distinctions of facilitators and barriers in different tiers of cities. Second, the results of this study make valuable practical contributions. In developing new GKB initiatives, the findings of this study would be beneficial for the GKB initiators in public sectors of first-, second- and third-tier cities respectively in China as well as other developing countries. In addition, policymakers can use the research findings as inputs in developing the GKB guidelines and procedures to allow horizontal knowledge sharing and reuse across multiple organizations within the public sectors.

Despite its contributions, this study faces limitations. The early-stage adoption of GKBs might hinder respondents' comprehension of its functionalities, potentially limiting the generalizability of the survey results. Future studies addressing respondents' knowledge and awareness levels regarding GKBs could yield more comprehensive and generalized conclusions. Additionally, certain variables might act as mediators, influencing the observed effects. Further exploration and discussion of these mediating variables can enhance the depth and scope of future research.

APPENDIX A. Descriptive Analysis of the Respondents

Demographics	Category	Respondents in second-tier cities		Respondents in third-tier cities	
		Frequency	Percentage (%)	Frequency	Percentage (%)
Age	18–25	53	25.6%	56	17.6%
	26–35	63	30.4%	166	52.0%
	36–45	56	27.1%	63	19.7%
	46–55	26	12.6%	19	6.0%
	>55	9	4.3%	15	4.7%
Gender	Male	92	44.4%	148	46.4%
	Female	115	55.6%	171	53.6%
Designation group	Top management	19	9.2%	24	7.5%
	Executive	112	54.1%	205	64.3%
	Support group	76	36.7%	90	28.2%
GKB adoption	Yes	156	75.7%	203	63.6%
	No, but know it	36	17.4%	49	15.4%
	No, never know it	15	7.2%	67	21.0%
Work experience in local government	<1 year	59	28.5%	83	26.0%
	1–5 years	114	55.1%	132	41.4%
	6–10 years	25	12.1%	28	8.8%
	>10 years	9	4.3%	76	23.8%

APPENDIX B. Results of Construct Reliability and Validity

Construct	Data of first- and second-tier cities			Data of third-tier cities		
	Cronbach's alpha	Composite reliability (rho_a)	Average variance extracted (AVE)	Cronbach's alpha	Composite reliability (rho_a)	Average variance extracted (AVE)
BI	0.859	0.859	0.780	0.883	0.883	0.81
CB	0.880	0.900	0.805	0.887	0.89	0.816
CP	0.905	0.915	0.842	0.911	0.919	0.85
EE	0.864	0.865	0.787	0.872	0.872	0.796
FC	0.711	0.687	0.606	0.713	0.717	0.617
IR	0.907	0.909	0.843	0.901	0.903	0.834
PE	0.903	0.906	0.838	0.906	0.908	0.842
SI	0.887	0.898	0.817	0.887	0.914	0.817
TB	0.798	0.858	0.718	0.826	0.842	0.746

APPENDIX C. Results of Fornell-Larcker Criterion

(First- and Second-tier Cities)

	BI	CB	CP	EE	FC	IR	PE	SI	TB
BI	0.883								
CB	0.442	0.897							
CP	0.51	0.532	0.918						
EE	0.66	0.452	0.382	0.887					
FC	0.237	0.277	0.317	0.187	0.778				
IR	0.555	0.544	0.49	0.581	0.225	0.918			
PE	0.463	0.397	0.255	0.479	0.129	0.207	0.915		
SI	0.653	0.488	0.547	0.524	0.327	0.361	0.468	0.904	
TB	0.655	0.528	0.472	0.555	0.332	0.58	0.416	0.58	0.847

(Third-tier Cities)

	BI	CB	CP	EE	FC	IR	PE	SI	TB
BI	0.9								
CB	0.467	0.903							
CP	0.495	0.575	0.922						
EE	0.638	0.418	0.358	0.892					
FC	0.136	0.198	0.197	0.09	0.785				
IR	0.592	0.542	0.446	0.56	0.159	0.914			
PE	0.428	0.395	0.27	0.459	0.084	0.228	0.918		
SI	0.642	0.508	0.552	0.524	0.172	0.37	0.486	0.904	
TB	0.645	0.548	0.481	0.546	0.253	0.575	0.431	0.592	0.863

APPENDIX D. Results of Heterotrait-Monotrait Ratio (HTMT)

(First- and Second-tier Cities)

	BI	CB	CP	EE	FC	IR	PE	SI	TB
BI									
CB	0.499								
CP	0.577	0.592							
EE	0.765	0.511	0.432						
FC	0.251	0.344	0.375	0.21					
IR	0.624	0.603	0.54	0.654	0.268				
PE	0.525	0.438	0.284	0.542	0.157	0.227			
SI	0.746	0.541	0.612	0.596	0.381	0.397	0.524		
TB	0.768	0.634	0.553	0.656	0.424	0.677	0.472	0.683	

(Third-tier Cities)

	BI	CB	CP	EE	FC	IR	PE	SI	TB
BI									
CB	0.523								
CP	0.552	0.637							
EE	0.726	0.474	0.403						
FC	0.151	0.251	0.244	0.111					
IR	0.659	0.604	0.492	0.629	0.2				
PE	0.478	0.437	0.299	0.517	0.104	0.251			
SI	0.716	0.567	0.618	0.595	0.21	0.401	0.544		
TB	0.747	0.644	0.558	0.638	0.318	0.664	0.492	0.689	

References

1. Abdulraheem, M.H., Affendi, S., bin Mohd Yusof.: Employing a knowledge base in the decision making in e-government. Adv. Sci. Lett. **23**(6), 5338–5341 (2017)
2. Ali, O., Shrestha, A., Osmanaj, V., Muhammed, S.: Cloud computing technology adoption: an evaluation of key factors in local governments. Inf. Technol. People **34**(2), 666–703 (2021)
3. Ammar, A., Ahmed, E.M.: Factors Influencing sudanese microfinance intention to adopt mobile banking. Cogent Bus. Manag. **3**(1), 1154257 (2016)
4. Annis, C., Hou, J., Tang, T.: Perceptions, motivators and barriers of using city management applications among citizens: a focus group approach. Inf. Technol. People **34**(4), 1338–1356 (2021)
5. Gaitán, A., Jorge, B.P., Peral, and Ma Ramón Jerónimo.: Elderly and Internet banking: an application of UTAUT2. J. Internet Bank. Commer. **20**(1), 1–23 (2015)
6. Aslesen, H.W., Freel, M.: Industrial knowledge bases as drivers of open innovation? Ind. Innov. **19**(7), 563–584 (2012)
7. Carter, L., Bélanger, F.: The utilization of e-government services: citizen trust, innovation and acceptance factors. Inf. Syst. J. **15**(1), 5–25 (2005)
8. Chhim, P.P., Somers, T.M., Chinnam, R.B.: Knowledge reuse through electronic knowledge repositories: a multi theoretical study. J. Knowl. Manag. **21**(4), 741–764 (2017)
9. Chin, W.W.: Commentary: Issues and Opinion on Structural Equation Modeling. MIS Q. **22**(1), 7–16 JSTOR (1998)
10. Cinque, M., et al.: Sector: secure common information space for the interoperability of first responders. Procedia Comput. Sci. **64**, 750–757 (2015)
11. Deutsch, C., Gottlieb, M., Pongratz, H.: Adoption of e-government requirements to higher education institutions regarding the digital transformation. Electronic Participation. In: 13th IFIP WG 8.5 International Conference, EPart 2021, Granada, Spain, September 7–9, 2021, Proceedings 13, 90–104 (2021)
12. Dwivedi, Y.K., Shareef, M.A., Simintiras, A.C., Lal, B., Weerakkody, V.: A generalised adoption model for services: a cross-country comparison of mobile health (m-Health). Gov. Inf. Q. **33**(1), 174–187 (2016)
13. Fornell, C., Larcker, D.F.: Evaluating structural equation models with unobservable variables and measurement error. J. Mark. Res. **18**(1), 39–50 (1981)
14. Giesbrecht, T., Scholl, H.J., Schwabe, G.: Smart advisors in the front office: designing employee-empowering and citizen-centric services. Gov. Inf. Q. **33**(4), 669–684 (2016)

15. Gil-Garcia, J.R., Flores-Zúñiga, M.Á.: Towards a comprehensive understanding of digital government success: integrating implementation and adoption factors. Gov. Inf. Q. **37**(4), 101518 (2020)

16. Girodon, J., Monticolo, D., Bonjour, E., Perrier, M.: An organizational approach to designing an intelligent knowledge-based system: application to the decision-making process in design projects. Adv. Eng. Inform. **29**(3), 696–713 (2015)

17. Gold, A.H., Malhotra, A., Segars, A.H.: Knowledge management: an organizational capabilities perspective. J. Manag. Inf. Syst. **18**(1), 185–214 (2001)

18. Gustafsson, A., Johnson, M.D.: Determining attribute importance in a service satisfaction model. J. Serv. Res. **7**(2), 124–141 (2004)

19. Hair, J.F., Tomas, G., Hult, M., Ringle, C.M., Sarstedt, M., Danks, N.P., Ray, S.: Partial Least Squares Structural Equation Modeling (PLS-SEM) using R: A workbook. Springer International Publishing, Cham (2021)

20. Jörg, H.: Partial Least Squares Path Modeling. Adv. Methods Model. Markets, 361–81 (2017)

21. Hiran, K.K., Henten, A.: An integrated TOE–DoI framework for cloud computing adoption in the higher education sector: case study of sub-saharan Africa, Ethiopia. Int. J. Syst. Assur. Eng. Manag. **11**, 441–449 (2020)

22. Hooda, A., Gupta, P., Jeyaraj, A., Giannakis, M., Dwivedi, Y.K.: The effects of trust on behavioral intention and use behavior within e-government contexts. Int. J. Inf. Manage. **67**, 102553 (2022)

23. Iyengar, K., Sweeney, J., Montealegre, R.: Pathways to individual performance: examining the interplay between knowledge bases and repository kms use. Inf. Manag. **58**(7), 103498 (2021)

24. Kankanhalli, A., Lee, O.-K., Lim, K.H.: Knowledge reuse through electronic repositories: a study in the context of customer service support. Inf. Manag. **48**(2–3), 106–113 (2011)

25. Khayer, A., Nusrat Jahan, M., Hossain, N., Yahin Hossain, M.: The adoption of cloud computing in small and medium enterprises: a developing country perspective. Vine J. Inf. Knowl. Manag. Syst. **51**(1), 64–91 (2021). https://doi.org/10.1108/VJIKMS-05-2019-0064

26. Kim, S.H., Mukhopadhyay, T., Kraut, R.E.: When does repository kms use lift performance? the role of alternative knowledge sources and task environments. MIS Q. **40**(1), 133–156 (2016)

27. Kline, R.B.: Principles and Practice of Structural Equation Modeling. Guilford publications (2023)

28. Krishnan, S., Teo, T.S.H., Lymm, J.: Determinants of electronic participation and electronic government maturity: insights from cross-country data. Int. J. Inf. Manage. **37**(4), 297–312 (2017)

29. Kurfalı, M., Arifoğlu, A., Tokdemir, G., Paçin, Y.: Adoption of e-government services in Turkey. Comput. Hum. Behav. **66**, 168–178 (2017)

30. Květoň, V., Kadlec, V.: Evolution of knowledge bases in European regions: searching for spatial regularities and links with innovation performance. Eur. Plan. Stud. **26**(7), 1366–1388 (2018)

31. Kwateng, K.O., Atiemo, K.A.O., Appiah, C.: Acceptance and use of mobile banking: an application of UTAUT2. J. Enterp. Inf. Manag. **32**(1), 118–151 (2018)

32. Lacasta, J., Lopez-Pellicer, F.J., Florczyk, A., Zarazaga-Soria, F.J., Nogueras-Iso, J.: Population of a spatio-temporal knowledge base for jurisdictional domains. Int. J. Geogr. Inf. Sci. **28**(9), 1964–1987 (2014)

33. Le, A.T.P., Puvaneswaran Kunasekaran, S., Rasoolimanesh, M., AriRagavan, N., Thomas, T.K.: Investigating the determinants and process of destination management system (DMS) implementation. J. Organ. Chang. Manag. **35**(2), 308–329 (2022). https://doi.org/10.1108/JOCM-11-2020-0352

34. Wenjuan, L.: The role of trust and risk in citizens' e-government services adoption: a perspective of the extended UTAUT model. Sustainability **13**(14), 7671 (2021)
35. Li, Z., Xiang T., Wang, J.: Decision support system on government emergency management for urban emergency. In: International Conference on Education, Management and Computing Technology (icemct-16), 1178–83, Atlantis Press (2016)
36. Mansoori, K.A., Al, J.S., Tchantchane, A.L.: Investigating emirati citizens' adoption of e-government services in Abu Dhabi using modified UTAUT model. Inf. Technol. People **31**(2), 455–481 (2018)
37. Mensah, I.K., Adams, S.: A comparative analysis of the impact of political trust on the adoption of e-government services. Int. J. Public Adm. **43**(8), 682–696 (2020)
38. Mensah, I.K., Zeng, G., Luo, C.: The effect of gender, age, and education on the adoption of mobile government services. Int. J. Semant. Web Inf. Syst. (IJSWIS) **16**(3), 35–52 (2020)
39. de Miguel Molina, B., Hervás-Oliver, J.L., Rafael, B.D.: Understanding innovation in creative industries: knowledge bases and innovation performance in art restoration organisations. Innovation **21**(3), 421–42 (2019)
40. Mikalef, P., et al.: Enabling AI capabilities in government agencies: a study of determinants for European municipalities. Gov. Inf. Q. 101596 (2021)
41. Nur Firas, N.A.Z.I.M., Nabiha Mohd, R.A.Z.I.S., Mohammad Firdaus Mohammad, H.A.T.T.A.: Behavioural intention to adopt blockchain technology among bankers in Islamic financial system: perspectives in Malaysia. Romanian J. Inf. Technol. Autom. **31**(1), 11–28 (2021). https://doi.org/10.33436/v31i1y202101
42. Oni, A.A., Musa, U., Oni, S.: E-Revenue adoption in state internal revenue service: interrogating the institutional factors. J. Organ. End User Comput. (JOEUC) **32**(1), 41–61 (2020)
43. Park, K.O.: A study on sustainable usage intention of blockchain in the big data era: logistics and supply chain management companies. Sustainability **12**(24), 10670 (2020)
44. Rey-Moreno, M., Felício, J.A., Medina-Molina, C., Rufín, R.: Facilitator and inhibitor factors: adopting e-government in a dual model. J. Bus. Res. **88**, 542–549 (2018)
45. Ringle, C.M., Sarstedt, M., Straub, D.W.: Editor's comments: a critical look at the use of PLS-SEM in 'MIS Quarterly.' MIS Q. **36**(1), iii–xiv (2012)
46. Rogers, Everett M, Arvind Singhal, and Margaret M Quinlan.: Diffusion of Innovations. In An Integrated Approach to Communication Theory and Research, 432–48, Routledge (2014)
47. Savoldelli, A., Codagnone, C., Misuraca, G.: Understanding the e-government paradox: learning from literature and practice on barriers to adoption. Gov. Inf. Q. **31**, S63-71 (2014)
48. Sharif, M.H., Mohd, I.T., Davidson, R.: Determinants of Social Media Impact in Local Government. J. Organ. End User Comput. **28**(3), 82–103 (2016)
49. So, J.C.F., Bolloju, N.: Explaining the intentions to share and reuse knowledge in the context of it service operations. J. Knowl. Manag. **9**(6), 30–41 (2005)
50. Spithoven, A., Vanhaverbeke, W., Roijakkers, N.: Open innovation practices in SMEs and large enterprises. Small Bus. Econ. **41**, 537–562 (2013)
51. Subedi, R., Nyamasvisva, T.E., Pokharel, M.: An integrated-based framework for open government data adoption in kathmandu. Webology **19**(2), 7936–7961 (2022)
52. Szakálné Kanó, I., Vas, Z., Klasová, S.: Emerging synergies in innovation systems: creative industries in central Europe. J. Knowl. Econ. **14**(1), 450–71 (2023)
53. Ta, V.A., Lin, C.-Y.: Exploring the determinants of digital transformation adoption for SMEs in an emerging economy. Sustainability **15**(9), 7093 (2023)
54. Teirlinck, P., Spithoven, A.: The R&D knowledge base in city-agglomerations and knowledge searching in product innovative SMEs. Entrep. Reg. Dev. **31**(5–6), 516–533 (2019)

55. The General Office of the State Council of the People's Republic of China. 2020. Guiding Opinions of the General Office of the State Council on Further Optimizing Local Government Service Convenience Hotlines (2020). http://www.gov.cn/zhengce/zhengceku/2021-01/06/content_5577419.htm

56. The State Council of the People's Republic of China. 2022. Guiding Opinions of the State Council on Strengthening the Construction of Digital Government. (2022). http://www.gov.cn/zhengce/content/2022-06/23/content_5697299.htm

57. Tilley, N., Laycock, G.: Developing a knowledge base for crime prevention: lessons learned from the British experience. Crime Prev. Commun. Safety **20**(4), 228–242 (2018)

58. Todevski, M., Janeska-Sarkanjac, S., Trajanov, D.: Analysis of introducing one stop shop administrative services: a case study of the republic of Macedonia. Transylvanian Rev. Adm. Sci. **9**(38), 180–201 (2013)

59. Venkatesh, V., Morris, M.G., Davis, G.B., Davis, F.D.: User acceptance of information technology: toward a unified view. MIS Q. **27**(3), 425–478 (2003)

60. Wei, S., Xu, D., Liu, H.: The effects of information technology capability and knowledge base on digital innovation: the moderating role of institutional environments. 2022 European J Innov. Manag. **25**(3), 720–740 (2021)

61. Wold, H.: Factors influencing the outcome of economic sanctions. Trabajos de Estadística e Investigación Operativa **36**, 325–337 (1985)

62. Zeebaree, M., Agoyi, M., Aqel, M.: Sustainable adoption of e-government from the UTAUT perspective. Sustainability **14**(9), 5370 (2022)

63. Zuiderwijk, A., Janssen, M., Dwivedi, Y.K.: Acceptance and use predictors of open data technologies: drawing upon the unified theory of acceptance and use of technology. Gov. Inf. Q. **32**(4), 429–440 (2015)

Beliefs, Values and Emotions in Education Practitioners' Engagements with Learning Analytics in Higher Education

Itzelle Medina-Perea[1]([✉]), Jo Bates[1], Monika Fratczak[1], and Erinma Ochu[2]

[1] Information School, University of Sheffield, Sheffield, UK
{i.medinaperea,jo.bates,m.fratczak}@sheffield.ac.uk
[2] College of Art, Technology and Environment at UWE, Bristol, UK
Erinma.Ochu@uwe.ac.uk

Abstract. The use of learning analytics (LA), defined as personalized learning environments through the continuous measurement, collection, analysis, and reporting of data about learners and their context, is rapidly expanding. A growing body of literature has questioned the benefits attributed to LA solutions and raised a number of concerns about the current developments in the education sector. However, we know little about how the beliefs, values, and emotions of different groups of educational practitioners shape how they engage with learning analytics technologies and influence the evolution of the cultures of practice shaping the adoption of learning analytics. Here we report on research that asks: how do culturally situated beliefs, values, and emotions shape UK-based higher education practitioners' engagements with learning analytics? We conducted 34 semi-structured interviews and four focus groups with staff from a provider of digital services for UK higher education and staff from UK universities. With insights from this research, we aim to contribute to empower practitioners in higher education and relevant stakeholders to foster the development of critical and reflective data cultures that are able to exploit the possibilities of learning analytics while being critically responsive to their societal implications and limitations.

Keywords: Beliefs · Values and Emotions · Data cultures · Learning Analytics · Higher Education

1 Introduction and Literature Review

Data mining and data analytics packages embedded in educational platforms are increasingly being used to track what students do in digital environments, evaluate their performances, and even predict their future outcomes [25]. The use of AI in education is not new, it has existed as a research field since the 1980s. After periods of intermittent interest, AI regained attention around 2010 [25]. The collection of educational data is not new either; however, a key shift is that today larger volumes of data of a wider variety and detail can be accessed almost in real-time [21]. In this context, the use of learning analytics (LA), which are defined as personalized learning environments through the continuous measurement, collection, analysis, and reporting of data about learners and their context, is rapidly growing [8].

I. Sserwanga et al. (Eds.): iConference 2024, LNCS 14598, pp. 54–61, 2024.
https://doi.org/10.1007/978-3-031-57867-0_4

Philanthropists, EdTech companies, and policymakers around the world have promoted the idea that big data and learning analytics (LA) have the potential to revolutionize education [23]. The drive to support the adoption of AI-based solutions in education is in sync with the uncritical belief that technology has the power to drive social progress. Some seem to embrace the belief that the adoption of LA solutions has the potential to 'fix' what they believe to be old-fashioned education systems that they assert limit students' potential [17].

A number of benefits have been attributed to the adoption of AI-based solutions in the education sector. It has been argued, for example, that they help increase student achievement as these tools can help students to develop mastery in different knowledge areas [20], enhance student success [13, 16, 20] and minimize inequalities by providing additional support to students from disadvantaged backgrounds [17]. It has also been claimed that by identifying patterns in student data, educators can promptly identify students' needs or weaknesses and act based on these data to improve their learning experience [16, 17].

However, a growing body of literature has questioned the benefits attributed to AI-based solutions, reflecting on the potential negative implications of adopting AI-based solutions and raising concerns about developments in the field [12, 21, 25, 26]. Studies have explored, for example, issues such as surveillance and loss of privacy, bias, and discrimination, and the marketisation of education [5, 11, 23, 26].

Despite this growing interest among researchers, we know little about how the beliefs, values, and emotions of different groups of higher education practitioners shape how they engage with AI-driven learning analytics technologies, and how these beliefs, values and feelings influence the evolution of the cultures of practice shaping the adoption of learning analytics.

In this paper, we report on research that asks: how do culturally situated beliefs, values, and emotions shape UK-based higher education practitioners' engagements with learning analytics? Through our research we aim to develop a foundation for engaging people that work with data mining and predictive machine learning - or the results of such computational processing - in critical and reflective dialogue. Our working assumption is that if we want to contribute to the development of more responsible cultures of AI practice, we first need to understand them.

2   Theoretical Framework: Values, Beliefs and Emotions

The theoretical approach underlying the study recognizes the interconnected nature of values, beliefs, and emotions in the constitution of social phenomena [1, 3, 24], in contrast to approaches that theorize reason and emotion as binary entities. Drawing on works by e.g., Bates [2] and Kitchin and Lauriault [15], we understand the values and beliefs within a given context of practice to be shaped by external social forces, such as economic and political factors. In this way, our theoretical lens reflects a social constructionist, rather than a cognitive approach, to understanding values, beliefs, and emotions.

We understand beliefs, values, and emotions as follows:

- Beliefs are ideas that people assert to be true, we understand widely accepted beliefs as "loose ideologies" [10] or fragmented common sense [9].

- Values are specific types of beliefs that people hold and care about regarding, for example, what is right or wrong, what is important and not important [18].
- Emotions are understood by us as "social feelings…conditioned by the culture of society…its norms, values, ideas, beliefs" [3] rather than "mere biological responses".

Previous research has identified a range of beliefs people have about data and AI, such as "dataism" [6] and "data-centric relationality [22], values around emergent tech practices e.g. 'human' values such as liberal values, human-centric values [19], or emotional responses to data and machine learning systems [7, 14]. However, values, feelings and beliefs have not been considered in interaction with one another. We are applying this theoretical understanding of beliefs, values, and emotion as a lens through which to guide our data collection and analysis.

3 Methodology

Through exploring the perspectives of practitioners in different roles, we aim to build a rich understanding about what they believe and how they feel about the application of predictive machine learning in higher education. Our data collection includes interviews and focus groups. We carried out semi-structured interviews of an average duration of 1 h with staff from Jisc, a provider of digital services for UK higher education (n~5) and staff from two different UK universities, including academic staff from different disciplines (n~16), learning technologists and others responsible for LA system implementation (n~5), and student advisors (n~4). We also conducted four focus groups with some of these participants, each with 3–5 people in different roles. In addition to this, we carried out semi-structured interviews (n~4) of an average duration of 1 h with staff from two further universities who were engaged in the Jisc learning analytics network or in piloting of Jisc's learning analytics systems. All participants from universities have engaged either with descriptive analytics, which can provide insights into a student's learning activities, or predictive analytics, which aims to predict their future academic performance. We recruited a total of 34 participants.

The interview questions and focus groups explored topics including:

- Their experience of working in higher education, including their engagement with learning analytics in their work.
- Their beliefs and feelings about recent developments and priorities around learning analytics adoption in their organization and sector.
- Aspects of their work that they feel positively and negatively about, and what they feel to be important about their work (i.e., what they value).
- Their engagement with colleagues about the adoption of learning analytics in the sector.
- Their expectations about the future use of learning analytics in higher education.

Data are being analyzed using a combination of thematic analysis [4], and close critical reading around key findings. We are currently in the early stages of data analysis, and here report key themes forming one of the thematic narratives identified through our analysis. We use pseudonyms to refer to participants as a means of preserving anonymity. Ethical approval for the study was gained from The University of Sheffield.

4 Findings and Discussion

The following outlines three themes forming one of the thematic narratives emerging from our early findings about how higher education practitioners' culturally situated beliefs, values and emotions shape their engagements with learning analytics in their work.

4.1 Recognizing the Potential and Staying Away from the Hype

It is clear that the beliefs, values, and emotions of practitioners about the use of LA in higher education, and consequently in their own work, are strongly influenced by participants' perceptions of what is happening externally to their organization.

While educational practitioners recognize the potential benefits of LA, their belief systems do not seem to embrace the overhyped discourse promoted by some EdTech providers and other stakeholders in which tools are promised to improve retention, increase efficiency, and 'fix' education. For the educational practitioners we engaged with, learning analytics is a tool that, if used carefully and responsibly, has the potential to enhance educators' work, but they are averse to the belief that it is "magic or [an] easy solution" (Interviewee, learning technologist, Oct-2022). For example, a lecturer that engages on a regular basis with a learning analytics dashboard provided by their university commented:

> The tool is an add on to your work...there's something wrong if we only use an online tool to get all your information... in my opinion, these are our tools to support our work and do it better...So we have to take care with artificial intelligence or in particular, analytics as a tool to help us and support our work, not as a solution for all our problems. (Felipe, lecturer, Oct-2022)

Practitioners in all roles also expressed a sense of frustration about the proliferation of the overhyped discourse that tends to over-claim the benefits of these tools. Some expressed a sense of disappointment about the lack of critical perspectives in the field and believed that more voices willing to challenge the values and beliefs being promoted by EdTech providers and other powerful stakeholders are needed:

> There's a view of like, this is brilliant, it's absolutely fantastic and it's done all of this. And then there's a view of a – there's other set of publications which go, well, it is helpful, it can be quite good in – when used in the right way but [this] view is not quite as upbeat and gung-ho as the [other] crowd. So, it's not a case of I think data analytics is a waste of time and we shouldn't be doing it. I think we should be doing it, but I think we've just got to be careful about not over-claiming benefits unless we're absolutely, you know, unless the information we've got is absolutely robust. And I think there's been an element of over-claiming if I'm being brutally honest. (Cameron, Lecturer, Nov-2022)

> ...the amount of critical voices are very few and far between... Because the overwhelming – you only need to pick up the latest issue of the Journal of Learning Analytics for example, and there'll be a dozen papers in there extolling the virtues of learning analytics, right? (Ted, Learning Technologist, Oct-2022)

These findings suggest that education practitioners believe that the utilization of learning analytics has the potential to enhance their practice, however, claims that assert that learning analytics can serve as a remedy for the various pedagogical issues they face has generated feelings of skepticism and frustration. Some believed that a more balanced and critical approach regarding the role of learning analytics in higher education is needed.

4.2   The Importance of Looking Beyond the Data and Prioritizing Meaningful Teacher-Student Relationships.

Practitioners' beliefs and values regarding the use or adoption of LA reflect the human-centric values [19] they hold in relation to their work in education. Participants reflect on the importance of keeping students at the forefront of their practice and seeing beyond the data. They refuse to make decisions based primarily on outputs provided by learning analytics dashboards, which are based on e.g., data about attendance and engagement with the virtual learning environment (VLE) because this goes against their values. Rather they believe it is crucial to use their experience and skills in conjunction with the outputs of LA systems. For example, a lecturer explained:

> The data might make you think there's nothing I can do about this student, it's terrible. But if you're using that in conjunction with your skills as a tutor, you may have other information about that student that tells you that actually it's not as bad as it looks, you know, I know something about it. I still need to have that sort of human contact with the student. I still need to know who that student is. I still need to say to them if you've got any issues you need to let me know. (Alice, Lecturer, Nov-2022)

One of the big promises of LA dashboards is that their outputs provide new insights about learners. However, educators believe that in most cases, these tools tend to confirm what they already know about students and only on rare occasions, indicate something new.

For some practitioners, getting confirmation from the system about their existing beliefs about students is helpful because it makes them feel reassured that their "thinking is right" or gives them more confidence:

> I look at data and I think well yeah that tells me what I already knew and that in itself is a positive because it reaffirms for me that my thinking is right. I kind of quite like that it tells me what I knew because it means that what I knew was probably accurate. Yes, so that for me is fine. And also, sometimes it tells me something that I didn't know but where it's really useful so for me, for example, I may not have known that somebody wasn't active and was unlikely to submit their work. (Alice, Lecturer, Nov 2022)

As discussed above, education practitioners hold the belief that learning analytics outputs do not provide the complete picture and therefore should thus be used in conjunction with skills and experience. But beyond this, they also believe that systems should not replace meaningful conversations or undermine the possibility of developing meaningful and positive student-teacher relationships, which are not only an important aspect of their practice, but also an enjoyable task.

Systems can only show you one side of things. They can only show you what the student's interacting with. You don't get to see their behavioral side of engagement, psychological types of things, you're only seeing one side of something... You need to get every – you need a human aspect of things. You can't just rely on systems and computer things. They're just there to help you but you always need that human interaction as well. (Amy, Student Advisor, Oct-2022)

These insights show that education practitioners believe it is crucial to place students at the heart of their practice and seeing beyond the data provided by learning analytics systems. Therefore, for them it is important to use outputs provided by such systems in conjunction with their own experience and skills. Student-teacher relations are valued and enjoyed by educators, who believe they are essential for understanding students' needs, motivations, and experiences.

4.3 Responsible Use of Technology and Resources

A number of participants believed that some developers in the LA sector were developing technology solutions for problems that did not always exist in practice and expressed frustration at this situation. They believed that the development of including learning analytics solutions should be driven by identification of areas where this technology can make a meaningful impact within the education context.

I think sometimes these new dashboards or algorithms or whatever exist because they can exist, rather than because they're actually targeted at a problem that exists... a solution looking for a problem. So I would like to see some of these new predictive learning analytics interventions really targeted towards problems that – identified problems that do exist. Instead of retrofitting them to problems that are perceived to exist...I find it very frustrating if I'm honest.

(Ted, Learning Technologist, Nov 2022)

Some participants highlighted the importance of reflecting and carefully evaluating when considering the adoption of learning analytics within the higher education sector. Some believed that if LA dashboards provide outcomes that are not convincing or good enough, raise ethical concerns, or threaten human-centric values [19] they hold regarding education practice it may be a good idea for institutions to stop using them, or not implement them in the first place. For example, a learning technologist who led on a project aimed at exploring the potential of the use of predictive learning analytics in a UK university explained:

And maybe the technology is not right, maybe the data collection isn't right, maybe the proxies are not right, maybe whole lots of things. So that's what we did as an institution. We tested it robustly I think with a research student who focused their area. It was relevant, I think our practice was the right one, our instincts were right to keep it away and not use it. Yeah, I still think we felt a little bit nervous about the ethics of taking action based on a predictive algorithm which may or may not be accurate. So we found that there are probably more human centered ways of achieving the same thing, or similar things (Max, Learning Technologist, Nov, 2022)

For some others, even if a learning analytics solution brings positive outcomes, it is crucial to evaluate if investing in it is the best choice, particularly in a context where resources are limited.

5 Conclusion

In conclusion, the emerging findings of this research highlight that education practitioners believe there are potential benefits of using learning analytics, however, they do not embrace the idea that the mere implementation of these tools will improve education. This challenges the overhyped discourse promoted by EdTech companies, internet entrepreneurs, AI enthusiasts, and other powerful stakeholders. This work also shows that the proliferation of this overhyped discourse that tends to overclaim the benefits of LA systems has provoked frustration among some education practitioners. Further, it shows that while these practitioners are open to the use of LA systems in higher education, they resist engaging with such systems in ways that could threaten important values for them, such as keeping students at the forefront of their practice and fostering the development of meaningful and positive student-teacher relationships. Through enhancing our understanding of the beliefs, values and emotional engagements of education practitioners with data and learning analytics systems, we aim to contribute to empower practitioners in higher education and relevant stakeholders to foster the development of critical and reflective data cultures that are able to exploit the possibilities of learning analytics, while being critically responsive to their societal implications and limitations.

References

1. Ahmed, S.: Cultural Politics of Emotion. Edinburgh University Press, Edinburgh (2014)
2. Bates, J.: Data cultures, power and the city. In: Data and the City, pp. 189–200 Routledge (2017)
3. Bericat, E.: The sociology of emotions: four decades of progress. Curr. Sociol. 64(3), 491–513 (2016). https://doi.org/10.1177/0011392115588355
4. Braun, V., Clarke, V.: Using thematic analysis in psychology. Qual. Res. Psychol. 3(2), 77–101 (2006)
5. Castañeda, L., Selwyn, N.: More than tools? Making sense of the ongoing digitizations of higher education. Int. J. Educ. Technol. High. Educ. 15(1), 22 (2018). https://doi.org/10.1186/s41239-018-0109-y
6. van Dijck, J.: Datafication, dataism and dataveillance: big data between scientific paradigm and ideology. Surveill. Soc. 12(2), 197–208 (2014)
7. Eubanks, V.: Automating Inequality: How High-Tech Tools Profile, Police, and Punish the Poor. St. Martin's Press, New York (2018)
8. Gašević, D., et al.: Let's not forget: learning analytics are about learning. Techtrends Tech. Trends 59(1), 64–71 (2015). https://doi.org/10.1007/s11528-014-0822-x

9. Hall, S.: Gramsci and Us. Marxism Today, 16–21 June 1987 (1987)
10. Harrison, K., Boyd, T.: The Role of Ideology in Politics and Society. Manchester University Press, Manchester (2018)
11. Hartong, S., Förschler, A.: Opening the black box of data-based school monitoring: data infrastructures, flows and practices in state education agencies. Big Data Soc. **6**(1), 2053951719853311 (2019). https://doi.org/10.1177/2053951719853311
12. Jarke, J., Macgilchrist, F.: Dashboard stories: how narratives told by predictive analytics reconfigure roles, risk and sociality in education. Big Data Soc. **8**(1), 20539517211025560 (2021). https://doi.org/10.1177/20539517211025561
13. Jisc: Can artificial intelligence transform the teaching and learning experience? https://www.timeshighereducation.com/hub/jisc/p/can-artificial-intelligence-transform-teaching-and-learning-experience. Accessed 10 Nov 2021
14. Kennedy, H., Hill, R.: The feeling of numbers: emotions in everyday engagements with data and their visualisation. Sociology **52**(4), 830–848 (2018)
15. Kitchin, R., Lauriault, T.: Towards Critical Data Studies: Charting and Unpacking Data Assemblages and Their Work. Social Science Research Network, Rochester (2014)
16. Luckin, R., et al.: Intelligence Unleashed: An Argument for AI in Education. Pearson, London (2016)
17. Microsoft: Understanding the new learning landscape: Accelerating learning analytics and AI in education (2021). https://edudownloads.azureedge.net/msdownloads/Microsoft-Accelerating-Learning-Analytics-and-AI-in-Education.pdf
18. Open University: Week 2: Values and beliefs: View as single page. https://www.open.edu/openlearn/ocw/mod/oucontent/view.php?id=21013&printable=1. Accessed 28 June 2021
19. Pasquale, F.: New Laws of Robotics — Frank Pasquale (2020)
20. Posner, Z.: Artificial Intelligence Comes to Learning. https://www.mheducation.com/ideas/artificial-intelligence-comes-to-learning.html. Accessed 10 Nov 2021
21. Prinsloo, P.: Of 'black boxes' and algorithmic decision-making in (higher) education – a commentary. Big Data Soc. **7**(1), 2053951720933994 (2020). https://doi.org/10.1177/2053951720933994
22. Ricaurte, P.: Data epistemologies, the coloniality of power, and resistance. Television New Media **20**(4), 350–365 (2019). https://doi.org/10.1177/1527476419831640
23. Roberts-Mahoney, H., et al.: Netflixing human capital development: personalized learning technology and the corporatization of K-12 education. J. Educ. Policy **31**(4), 405–420 (2016). https://doi.org/10.1080/02680939.2015.1132774
24. Ustek-Spilda, F., et al.: Engaging with ethics in internet of things: imaginaries in the social milieu of technology developers. Big Data Soc. **6**(2), 205395171987946 (2019). https://doi.org/10.1177/2053951719879468
25. Williamson, B.: Big Data in Education: The Digital Future of Learning, Policy and Practice. SAGE, Los Angeles (2017)
26. Yu, J., Couldry, N.: Education as a domain of natural data extraction: analysing corporate discourse about educational tracking. Inf. Commun. Soc. 1–18 (2020). https://doi.org/10.1080/1369118X.2020.1764604

Information Science Education

Promoting Academic Integrity Through Gamification: Testing the Effectiveness of a 3D Immersive Video Game

Xin Zhao[ID], Haoyu Xie(✉)[ID], Alec Roberts, and Laura Sbaffi[ID]

The University of Sheffield, Sheffield S10 2TN, UK
Xin.Zhao@Sheffield.ac.uk, hxie5@sheffield.ac.uk

Abstract. Academic integrity is the foundation of quality higher education. However, the resources explaining the concept tend to be definition-driven, have complex language and sometimes even a severe tone to discourage students from breaking rules. This project deployed a gamified approach, designing and evaluating a 3D immersive video game for university students to facilitate their understanding and adoption of academic integrity principles. The game allowed students to be immersed in a virtual campus through an avatar and navigate a campus (e.g., garden, library, cafe, student accommodation) with scenario-based, academic integrity related dialogues with in-game characters. The paper aims to showcase the game design and student feedback of the game. Observation and interviews were conducted with 15 participants. Thematic analysis of the data shows that the game greatly enhanced student understanding of academic integrity concepts by providing contextualized memorability whilst relieving anxiety. Students' engagement with the game was linked to game features such as appealing aesthetics, customization, and contextualization. The paper concludes by offering recommendations concerning the employment of gamification as an educational approach for instructing students in higher education on complex concepts, such as academic integrity.

Keywords: Academic Integrity · Gamification · 3D immersive video game · game design · game evaluation

1 Introduction

The escalating issues related to breaches in student academic integrity, whether inadvertent or deliberate, are increasingly challenging academic departments [1]. This necessitates a critical reflection on the mechanisms used to inform students about academic integrity and the prevention of academic misconduct. The most frequent incidents leading to such breaches are poor paraphrasing methods and inaccurate referencing formats, which often lead to instances of plagiarism [2].

Academic integrity as a concept is not universally comprehended. The myriad interpretations of academic integrity can sometimes result in misunderstandings among students and staff alike, thereby inadvertently fostering unethical academic practices

I. Sserwanga et al. (Eds.): iConference 2024, LNCS 14598, pp. 65–76, 2024.
https://doi.org/10.1007/978-3-031-57867-0_5

[3]. In recent years, universities have shown an increased commitment to addressing issues related to academic integrity [4]. However, the integration of these principles into teaching practices still leaves much to be desired [5, 6].

The challenges have been amplified by the emergence of contract cheating and the use of ghost-writing services [7], compounded by a poor understanding of academic integrity practices due to cultural variances in highly internationalized student cohorts. This has necessitated the exploration of innovative approaches in the higher education sector to support and guide students [8].

Several researchers have underscored the importance of proactive strategies in fostering academic integrity among students as they transition into new academic environments [5, 9]. One emerging approach is the use of gamification, although its application in promoting academic integrity is still in its infancy [7]. Gamification incorporates elements of gameplay, such as points and rewards, into the learning environment [10]. There is growing evidence that gamification can effectively facilitate learning by making it a more engaging and enjoyable process [7, 11].

The aim of this study was to design and evaluate a 3D interactive video game in English for university students to facilitate their understanding and adoption of academic integrity principles. The design of the video game was based on a previous study which surveyed 400+ students to explore their learning needs in terms of academic integrity concepts [12]. The pedagogical basis for creating this resource stems from the concept of 'edutainment,' an approach that combines learning with entertainment, particularly through a gamification approach [13]. Edutainment focuses on transforming educational content into a game-like environment to facilitate enjoyable learning [14, 15], while maintaining a harmonious balance between fun and educational value [16].

In this short paper, the design process of the 3D immersive video game is showcased. In addition, students' evaluations of the effectiveness of the game are presented through in-depth interviews.

2 Methodology

The process of designing, implementing, and evaluating the 3D immersive video game consists of three distinct stages. In the first stage, we developed a 3D video game based on the insights gathered from our previously published study, which involved conducting focus groups and surveys to understand students' learning needs regarding Academic Integrity (n = 177). Moving on to the second stage, we conducted a pilot of the game and gathered valuable feedback from participants through interviews and observations (n = 15). Subsequently, we refined the game based on the valuable insights obtained from the interview feedback. Finally, in the third stage, we officially launched the game and collected in-game data from a larger group of students (n = 317), alongside an evaluation survey (n = 257).

This paper primarily focuses on documenting the game design and refinement process, encompassing stages 1 and 2 (Fig. 1). Participants for this study were recruited through snowball sampling, initiated via university email announcements. We achieved sample saturation by the 15th interview, as the emergence of recurring themes indicated no further insights [25]. The interview design was semi-structured, encompassing questions about demographics, game-related aspects (e.g., 'What feature of the game did you like most/least?'), academic content (e.g., 'Were the questions worded clearly?'), and observations (e.g., 'I noticed frequent clicks in a specific game area, could you elaborate?'). The project received ethics approval from the University of Sheffield.

Fig. 1. Stages of the study

2.1 Game Design

The game creates a virtual campus that closely resembles a real educational institution. Players assume the role of a new student who has just arrived on campus and navigate the virtual environment using an avatar. They interact with other in-game characters, representing fellow students and help them with Academic Integrity related questions, through engaging dialogues. Players encounter four distinct scenes: the university garden, the academic library, the university cafe, and the student accommodations. Throughout these scenes, players are presented with 20 scenario-based academic integrity related quizzes.

The game was developed using the Unity game engine and programmed in C#. The Unity Game Framework is a modular framework that includes various modules, such as data syncing, special effects, player control, dialogue, and artificial intelligence (AI) for in-game characters. To enhance the player's experience, the game incorporated several elements for smoother gameplay. These included message panels, cursor animations, and in-game graphic tips that guided the player through conversations, navigating to destinations, transitioning between scenes, and more (Fig. 2).

In the game design phase, eye tracking technology was employed for usability tests of UI prototypes, as widely utilized in the field [17]. The attentional trajectory of participants was used to inform the development of the final UI design, ensuring that important information such as task prompts, scores, and dialogues were effectively presented to players (Fig. 3).

Players actively participate in quiz answering by engaging in dialogues with in-game characters (Fig. 4). The dialogue dynamically adjusts based on the player's responses, providing personalized feedback. Furthermore, to sustain motivation, the game incorporates a point-based system and a leaderboard (Fig. 5), encouraging players to strive for higher scores and fostering a sense of competition and achievement.

This game acts as a socio-technical structure, incorporating both technical elements and social interactions. Specifically, its technical aspects, such as programming and interaction mechanisms, create an interactive and immersive environment for the player.

Fig. 2. An example of in-game tips.

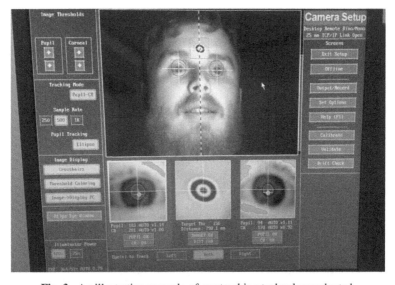

Fig. 3. An illustrative example of eye tracking technology adopted.

Players acquire social experience by engaging in conversations with other characters and exchanging body language, thus realizing the game's educational purpose. To enhance the game's realism and facilitate players' understanding and immersion in the textual storyline [18], rich character animations were employed to portray the emotions of in-game characters. These animations were implemented using humanoid animations controlled by a finite state machine (FSM) [18, 19]. During conversations, players can perform various body gestures such as waving, nodding, and clapping, aligning their

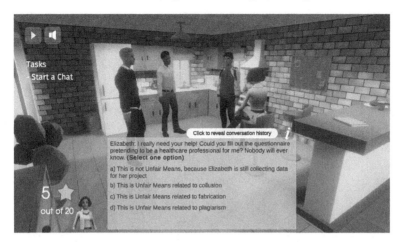

Fig. 4. Illustration of quiz UI.

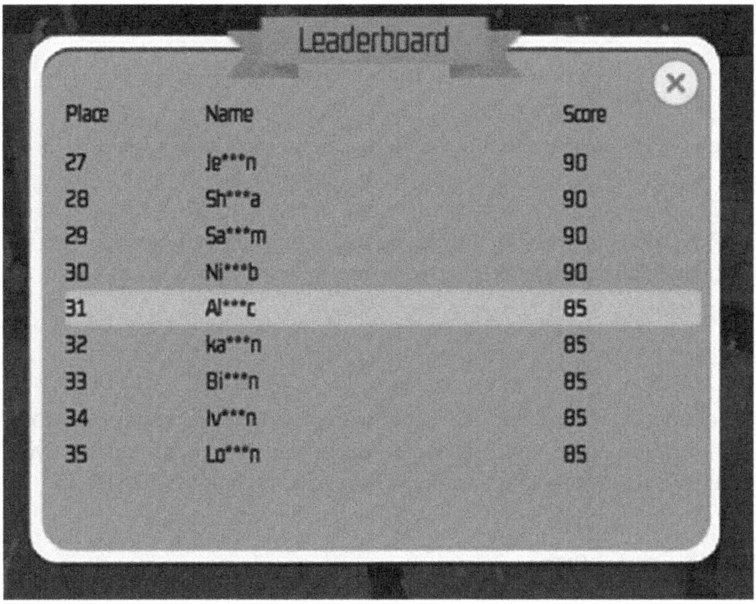

Place	Name	Score
27	Je***n	90
28	Sh***a	90
29	Sa***m	90
30	Ni***b	90
31	Al***c	85
32	ka***n	85
33	Bi***n	85
34	Iv***n	85
35	Lo***n	85

Fig. 5. Illustration of the leaderboard.

responses with the dialogue. Notably, when players provide correct answers, they are rewarded with congratulatory animations (Fig. 6), providing them with a more socially oriented incentive [19, 20].

Fig. 6. In-game animations.

2.2 Interview Process

The interviews were conducted either face-to-face or via Google Meets. During these interviews, students were asked to assess the gameplay and content of the game and provide suggestions for improvements in these areas. A total of 15 participants were recruited. The group consisted of 11 female and four male participants. The interview data were thematically analysed.

3 Results

The interview data revealed that the gamification of academic integrity provided an accessible, enjoyable, and engaging format from the three main perspectives: game design, academic knowledge (i.e., academic integrity contents) and usability.

3.1 Game Design Features

Four main topics were raised in relation to the design of the game. Students indicated that customization and the game aesthetics (music, art, and backgrounds) made the subject of academic integrity enjoyable, engaging and less anxiety-inducing [23]. Furthermore, the simplicity of the game and scoring system supported learning.

Customization. Many participants were initially intrigued by the game due to the ability to customize their avatars as personalisation provided enjoyment and direct choices for players:

> "I think it's very personalized because they allow me to choose the gender and clothes I like." [P13, Female, China]

Aesthetics. Aesthetic aspects continued to engage participants as the game progressed with the art and music engrossing participants into the subject matter [25]:

"I really liked the aesthetics. I liked going into the park and then automatically I was like 'Oh, this is fun. Oh, there's a duck!'... It just brought some life to the game." [P10, Female, UK]

Simplicity. Students found that the simplicity of the gameplay, where players interacted with characters through text options, suited academic integrity and assisted their learning:

"It was really helpful with a little list of what to do next... you literally just click where you wanna go and then the game does it for you so that was really helpful because it might have been quite frustrating." [P12, Female, UK]

Scoring System. With these features establishing a comfortable and accessible environment, participants noted that the high score system kept them hooked and motivated [21]. Participants especially appreciated the feedback they received on answers.

"You give feedback for every question, it helps you more. I submit a lot of questions for [other] quizzes and they give me maybe the third [question], this one, this one. I'm like, what did I answer? I already forgot! But for the game, there's more immediate feedback." [P4, Female, China]

3.2 Academic Knowledge

During the interviews, students reported increased engagement in academic integrity concepts.

Gamification Inspires Learning. Most students professed that the game taught or clarified key concepts of academic integrity that they found ambiguous, vague or were unaware of.

"I got to know all about academic integrity. Now I'll be more cautious regarding writing my assignments... I learnt something from it... I think the information after answering each question, for me, I think that was very informative." [P1, Female, China]

Contextualization Improves Knowledge Recall. Vital to learning new information is memorizing [22], as several participants discussed that gamifying the information assisted in recalling academic practices. Specifically, situating questions within a setting supported recollection of information which led to students comparing common resources and ranking their preference with the game being favoured:

"The game is best and the quiz is second and the presentation is last... I can learn more, I can remember more things because the story happens and I can remember which area like a cafe and garden so I can totally remember it." [P15, Female, China]

Gamification Relieves Anxiety. As a result of gamifying academic integrity, the game reduced apprehension or uneasiness:

> "Throughout my degree, I found it quite anxiety-inducing thinking about Academic Integrity. I think having it in the form of a game for someone else to instruct you is quite helpful." [P12, Female, UK]

Students contrasted other academic integrity resources, such as presentations and quizzes, with the greater engagement, fun, and motivation they experienced with the game:

> "If someone is talking to you like the presentation, you can't remember anything important... if you are involved, you really read the question and make some answers. That is good. But for the quiz... I can imagine how boring it is. So a game will definitely be better." [P13, Female, China]

Through gamification, students exhibited an increased understanding of academic integrity as the game clarified concepts and made information memorable through setting and relatability. The game also reduced a barrier of uneasiness in initially contemplating academic integrity. Therefore, participants expressed that teaching academic integrity is more effective and accessible through a gamified format, especially when compared to formats frequently used within universities of presentations and quizzes.

3.3 Usability

The participants highlighted several features that presented functional usability whilst also recommending improvements to the game that assisted in evaluating its impact on student learning. These aspects involved phrasing, contextual clarification, and emphasizing the gamification feel.

Phrasing. Whilst participants have cited how the customization, setting, and choices provide immersion and recollection of academic integrity, students also suggested that some phrasing of questions and responses disrupted the narrative and enjoyment of the game:

> "The least part of it was probably the questions. They are very stilted. They're like 'Oh, can you help me?.' They're not realistic. How they talk isn't real." [P3, Female, New Zealand]

Students recommended shortening, simplifying, or bullet-pointing key information to reduce the dependence on reading which would emphasize the gamified aspects over testing academic integrity knowledge.

Contextual Clarification. Throughout the game, a narrative was developed by introducing contextual information before each question to assist in understanding academic integrity. However, participants indicated that they often forgot the prior discussions and would struggle to interpret the questions. Students recommended including a back button or information icon to repeat or summarize the information from these conversations between characters:

"Sometimes when I select the answer and I forgot what the question is. So I want to turn back and look around but there is no function." [P15, Female, China].

Students also recommended functions to increase understanding of keywords. This often took the form of highlighting, underlining, or boldening these words. Participants whose first language was not English suggested keywords to have a pop-up definition which would quickly clarify terms.

Whilst participants expressed positive feedback on the game assisting memorizing key concepts, they also suggested this could be developed further with a summary page at the end of the game which would act as an overview for the questions with an indication of what academic integrity topics to revise and the information they may have missed:

"I think maybe a PDF copy of the questions to summarize and to get the results of which question you did wrong... Otherwise, when I close the game, I can't remember anything." [P13, Female, China].

Emphasizing Gamification. As previously highlighted, the gamification of academic integrity was described as a more engaging and accessible format by participants. However, the extent to which gamification occurred was often perceived as short of the expectations or potential for the game. Participants wanted further gamification with some students perceiving the game as being more of a quiz than a game:

"It did feel kind of like a dressed-up quiz in a way. I'm sure there's some kind of gameplay mechanics that would have made it more gamey." [P2, Male, UK]

Participants suggested expanding the interactive aspects of the game to move it beyond the questions that served as one of the minimal player inputs. Therefore, participants expressed further interactions to make the gameplay more enticing, enjoyable, and engaging. These ranged from simple inputs of clicking on animals for noises to utilizing the map with additional, more varied questions to increase high scores.

4   Discussion and Implications

This paper presents the design and evaluation of an educational game aimed at supporting student learning on the topic of academic integrity. The findings highlight the effectiveness of gamification approach in enhancing student engagement in learning academic integrity related concepts. The incorporation of appealing aesthetics, customization options, and simplicity in the game design were positively received by participants, making the learning experience enjoyable and less anxiety-inducing. Participants reported increased comprehension of academic integrity concepts through engaging dialogues with in-game characters, as the narrative nature provided relevant and relatable experiences that supported memorization and recollection. The game's affordance to simulate social scenarios related to unfair means plays a pivotal role in bridging the gap between theoretical knowledge and real-life application. By immersing students in these simulated environments, the game enhances their understanding of academic integrity principles and fosters the transferability of acquired knowledge to practical situations.

This aspect greatly contributes to the overall comprehensibility and applicability of students' learning experiences. This finding is consistent with the research by Birk et al. [23], who suggest that when players identify with an avatar in a game, it can contribute to an enhanced immersive experience and increase intrinsic motivation for learning.

Our study provides compelling evidence that gamification is highly effective in promoting learning through entertainment [13], especially for topics that tend to induce anxiety, such as academic integrity. This accords with existing literature that suggests gamification can enhance students' engagement, promote skills development, and optimize their learning [24]. The inclusion of gamification elements, such as a point system and leaderboard, contributes to enhancing intrinsic motivation among students. These elements provide students with clear goals and a sense of achievement, encouraging them to actively engage in the learning process. Additionally, the integration of achievement badges and congratulatory animations from other in-game characters serve as a rewarding mechanism, further incentivizing students to strive for excellence and perform their best [29, 30].

Despite the overall positive feedback, some areas for improvements were identified during the evaluation. Participants expressed concerns about the phrasing of questions and responses, highlighting the need for more realistic and concise expressions. They also recommended an inclusion of a back button or information icon to review prior conversations and a summary page to consolidate learning outcomes. Additionally, participants desired further gamification elements to enhance interaction and engagement, suggesting the inclusion of more interactive features, varied questions, and optional landmarks for exploration.

Our research demonstrates the effectiveness of combining observational methods, such as eye-tracking, with follow-up interviews for data collection. This integrated approach has proven particularly valuable in enriching our data. It has informed the development of the game's UI design and enhanced the relevance of observation-related questions during the interviews.

One limitation of our work is the small sample size for the interviews, and the fact that all participants were postgraduates from the Faculty of Social Science. This restricted sample may limit the generalizability of our findings to a broader population. Furthermore, this study focused exclusively on students' engagement and perceived learning gains, rather than evaluating their actual understanding of academic integrity before and after playing the game. Therefore, our follow-up research (Phase 3) will concentrate on this particular aspect.

References

1. Gallant, T.B.: Academic integrity as a teaching & learning issue: from theory to practice. Theory Into Practice. **56**, 88–94 (2017)
2. Greenberger, S., Holbeck, R., Steele, J., Dyer, T.: Plagiarism due to misunderstanding: online instructor perceptions. J. Sch. Teach. Learn. **16**, 72–84 (2016)
3. Palmer, A., Pegrum, M., Oakley, G.: A wake-up call? Issues with plagiarism in transnational higher education. Ethics Behav. **29**, 23–50 (2019)
4. Burbidge, T., Hamer, R.: Academic honesty in the international baccalaureate diploma programme: student, teacher, and school perspectives. J. Int. Stud. **10**, 265–285 (2020)

5. Bretag, T., et al.: 'Teach us how to do it properly!' An Australian academic integrity student survey. Stud. High. Educ. **39**, 1150–1169 (2014)
6. Gottardello, D., Karabag, S.F.: Ideal and actual roles of university professors in academic integrity management: a comparative study. Stud. High. Educ. **47**, 526–544 (2022)
7. Khan, Z.R., et al.: Initiating count down-gamification of academic integrity. Int. J. Educ. Integr. **17**, 1–15 (2021)
8. White, A.: Interactive approaches to learning about academic integrity: the role of fun and games. In: Bretag, T. (ed.) A Research Agenda for Academic Integrity. Edward Elgar Publishing (2020). https://doi.org/10.4337/9781789903775.00013
9. Newton, P.: Academic integrity: a quantitative study of confidence and understanding in students at the start of their higher education. Assess. Eval. High. Educ. **41**, 482–497 (2016)
10. Becker, K.: What's the difference between gamification, serious games, educational games, and game-based learning. Acad. Lett. **209**, 1–4 (2021)
11. Furdu, I., Tomozei, C., Kose, U.: Pros and cons gamification and gaming in classroom. arXiv preprint arXiv:1708.09337 (2017)
12. Sbaffi, L., Zhao, X.: Evaluating a pedagogical approach to promoting academic integrity in higher education: an online induction program. Front. Psychol. **13**, 1009305 (2022)
13. Aksakal, N.: Theoretical view to the approach of the edutainment. Procedia Soc. Behav. Sci. **186**, 1232–1239 (2015)
14. Shulman, J.L., Bowen, W.G.: The Game of Life: College Sports and Educational Values. Princeton University Press (2011). https://doi.org/10.1515/9781400840694
15. Moreno-Ger, P., Burgos, D., Martínez-Ortiz, I., Sierra, J.L., Fernández-Manjón, B.: Educational game design for online education. Comput. Hum. Behav. **24**, 2530–2540 (2008)
16. Prensky, M.: Digital game-based learning. Comput. Entertainment (CIE). **1**, 21–21 (2003)
17. Sunhem, W., Pasupa, K.: A scenario-based analysis of front-facing camera eye tracker for UX-UI survey on mobile banking app. In: 2020 12th International Conference on Knowledge and Smart Technology (KST), pp. 80–85 (2020). https://doi.org/10.1109/KST48564.2020.9059376
18. Taylor, M.J., Pountney, D.C., Baskett, M.: Using animation to support the teaching of computer game development techniques. Comput. Educ. **50**, 1258–1268 (2008)
19. Ho, E.S.L., Komura, T.: A finite state machine based on topology coordinates for wrestling games. Comput. Animation Virtual Worlds **22**, 435–443 (2011). https://doi.org/10.1002/cav.376
20. Thorn, A.: Unity Animation Essentials. Packt Publishing Ltd (2015)
21. Nielsen, R.K.L., Grabarczyk, P.: Are loot boxes gambling? Random reward mechanisms in video games. Trans. Digit. Games Res. Assoc. **4**, 171–207 (2019)
22. Vanduhe, V.Z., Nat, M., Hasan, H.F.: Continuance intentions to use gamification for training in higher education: integrating the technology acceptance model (TAM), social motivation, and task technology fit (TTF). IEEE Access. **8**, 21473–21484 (2020). https://doi.org/10.1109/ACCESS.2020.2966179
23. Davis, M.: Examining and improving inclusive practice in institutional academic integrity policies, procedures, teaching, and support. Int. J. Educ. Integr. **18**, 1–20 (2022)
24. Khaleel, F.L., Ashaari, N.S., Wook, T.: The impact of gamification on students learning engagement. Int. J. Electr. Comput. Eng. **10**, 4965 (2020)
25. Schwarz, A.F., Huertas-Delgado, F.J., Cardon, G., DeSmet, A.: Design features associated with user engagement in digital games for healthy lifestyle promotion in youth: a systematic review of qualitative and quantitative studies. Games Health J. **9**, 150–163 (2020)
26. Hernik, J., Jaworska, E.: The effect of enjoyment on learning. In: INTED2018 Proceedings, pp. 508–514. IATED (2018)

27. Birk, M.V., Atkins, C., Bowey, J.T., Mandryk, R.L.: Fostering intrinsic motivation through avatar identification in digital games. In: Proceedings of the 2016 CHI Conference on Human Factors in Computing Systems, pp. 2982–2995 (2016)
28. Smiderle, R., Rigo, S.J., Marques, L.B., Peçanha de Miranda Coelho, J.A., Jaques, P.A.: The impact of gamification on students' learning, engagement and behavior based on their personality traits. Smart Learn. Environ. **7**, 1–11 (2020). https://doi.org/10.1186/s40561-019-0098-x
29. Metzger, E.C., Lubin, L., Patten, R.T., Whyte, J.: Applied gamification: Creating reward systems for organizational professional development. In: Ifenthaler, D., Bellin-Mularski, N., Mah, D.K. (eds.) Foundation of Digital Badges and Micro-Credentials, pp. 457–466. Springer, Cham (2016). https://doi.org/10.1007/978-3-319-15425-1_25
30. Saleem, A.N., Noori, N.M., Ozdamli, F.: Gamification applications in e-learning: a literature review. Technol. Knowl. Learn. **27**, 139–159 (2022)
31. Boddy, C.R.: Sample size for qualitative research. Qual. Market Res. **19**, 426–432 (2016)

Information Governance and Ethics

Are We Practicing What We Preach? Towards Greater Transborder Inclusivity in Information Science Systematic Reviews

Stephanie Krueger[1,2,3,4](✉) 🆔 and Rebecca D. Frank[5,6] 🆔

[1] Berliner Hochschule für Technik, 13353 Berlin, Germany
stephanie.krueger@gmail.com
[2] Czech National Library of Technology (NTK), 16080 Prague, Czech Republic
[3] Czech Technical University in Prague, 16636 Prague, Czech Republic
[4] University of Chemistry and Technology, 16000 Prague, Czech Republic
[5] University of Tennessee Knoxville, Knoxville, TN 37006, USA
[6] Einstein Center Digital Future, 10117 Berlin, Germany

Abstract. Inclusiveness has been investigated in different ways by Information Science (InfoSci) researchers, often as a line of social justice inquiry. Systematic reviews (SRs), which bridge the gap between research and practice, are a key example of research impacted by inclusiveness. "Transborder" inclusiveness—the ability of researchers from different institutions, regions, and countries to access information, and the inclusion of information from researchers in regions and countries where English is not an official language in major collections of InfoSci research—influences how researchers perform SRs. Although this topic has been identified in other disciplines involved in Evidence Based Practice (EBP) such as nursing, it has received less attention in InfoSci. We address this need through a reflective case study of an SR in InfoSci which brings this transborder issue of inclusiveness into focus, demonstrating problems of access and the value of international collaboration and asking an overarching question: how can we make writing SRs in InfoSci research more inclusive?

Keywords: Transborder Inclusion · Academic Libraries · Evidence Based practice (EBP) · Information Science (InfoSci) Research · Systematic Reviews · PRISMA · Open Access · Reflective Single-site Case Study · Information Inequality

1 Introduction

1.1 Overview

Inclusiveness has been investigated in different ways by Information Science (InfoSci) researchers, often as a line of social justice inquiry (e.g., [1–7]). Systematic reviews (SRs), which bridge the gap between research and practice, are a key example of research impacted by inclusiveness. "Transborder" inclusiveness—the ability of researchers from

I. Sserwanga et al. (Eds.): iConference 2024, LNCS 14598, pp. 79–89, 2024.
https://doi.org/10.1007/978-3-031-57867-0_6

different institutions, regions, and countries to access information, and the inclusion of information from researchers in different regions and countries where English is not an official language in major collections of InfoSci research ([8–10])—influences how researchers perform SRs. Although this topic has been identified in other disciplines involved in Evidence Based Practice (EBP) such as nursing [11], it has received less attention in InfoSci. We address this need through a reflective case study of an SR, the first of its kind to the best of our knowledge in InfoSci, which brings this issue of transborder inclusiveness into focus, demonstrating problems of access and the value of international collaboration.

1.2 Issues in Transborder Research Inclusiveness

Issues of inclusiveness have been identified by notable InfoSci organizations such as the International Federation of Library Associations and Institution (IFLA) [12, p. 36] and the Association of College & Research Libraries (ACRL) in the United States (US) [13], as well as scholars from around the world [12–16]. One transborder issue is a dependence on English or "white-IST [white elitist] discourse" as the de facto language of international scholarly communications [12, 17–19], a topic specifically raised by Xu et al. [20] in relation to possible SR bias in InfoSci. Another transborder inclusiveness issue is "helicopter" or "parachute" research [12, p. 370], in which scholars from privileged regions conduct research in areas and/or places that are removed from their own lived experience [21]. A third is the disconnect between the promotion of Open Access (OA) initiatives and policies and the practices of scholars and publishers [22–26].

The current state of affairs has led to a mixture of open and subscription-based research in InfoSci [27]. Such a mixture of open/subscription-based content is common across the broader scholarly communications environment, recently characterized by Brembs et al. as reflecting three publishing crises: affordability, functionality, and replicability [28, p. 230206/2]. The resulting lack of access to the full range of InfoSci scholarship disadvantages scholars and practitioners at institutions that do not, or cannot, purchase costly subscriptions, as shown in the case study below.

While OA tools are available to everyone with the ability to access them, subscription-based abstracting, and indexing (A&I) tools in InfoSci such as Clarivate's Web of Science (WOS), Elsevier's Scopus, ProQuest's Library and Information Science Abstracts (LISA); and EBSCO's Library and Information Science Source (LISS) remain closed and inaccessible to many. At time of writing, only Library, Information Science and Technology Abstracts (LISTA) was openly accessible—while still being hosted on the commercial EBSCO platform [29].

1.3 Aim

Using a recent SR effort on the topic of satellite/remote sensing data in InfoSci, we conducted a reflective single-site case study [30–32]. In reflective case studies, researchers examine their own experiences in order to identify issues, problem solve, and/or enhance one's own practice [31, pp. 5–6]. This method is particularly useful when the researchers are working in a space that is relevant to their own professional practice, which is the case here.

Through this case study we examine our experience as researchers conducting an SR in order to explore how issues of access and availability of research publications in InfoSci reflect privilege and impede inclusiveness. We also highlight the disconnect between professed values and actions of the InfoSci research community with regard to perceptions of OA practices, attitudes, and policies that Scott et al. [24] identified.

In this paper, we ask the following research questions:

1. What issues or challenges regarding access to research publications arose for the research team during the process of conducting an SR?
   a. What adaptations were necessary to address those challenges?
   b. What impact did those adaptations have on the research team and/or their research project?
2. What are the implications of unequal access to research publications in InfoSci?

We briefly describe our research process using a modified Preferred Reporting Items for Systematic Reviews and Meta-Analyses (PRISMA) approach for an SR. We describe challenges accessing A&I databases and full-text publications, and the adaptations that addressed those challenges. We conclude with a discussion of the impacts these adaptations had on our work, and the implications of the unequal access we describe for InfoSci scholarship, using a levels of access framework based on Zhang et al. [11, pp. 105737/5–6]. This paper is part of a grant-funded research project whose aim is to understand data practices among people engaged in citizen-based monitoring for nuclear disarmament and nonproliferation. The project involves a transborder team of researchers whose institutional affiliations afford them different levels of access to scholarly resources and publications.

2 Case Study

In this study, we focus on two specific team members: Researcher A (RA, Rebecca D. Frank, co-author), is a faculty member at a very large US public research university (R1) with access to a second large US public research university library (R1). Researcher B (RB, Stephanie Krueger, corresponding author) is a contract consultant for the German institution managing the satellite data grant with no access to that institution's library resources. She had library access at a well-funded library in the Czech Republic. However, because of the library's focus on science and technology, it has few subscriptions to InfoSci content.

2.1 A Modified PRISMA Approach: Identifying, Obtaining, and Screening Titles for Analysis

We conducted a pilot scan of SR methods literature in InfoSci as well as broader SR guidelines [33–37]. We selected a modified PRISMA approach, as recommended by Xu, et al. [20, p. 297]. While we followed many of the processes outlined in the PRISMA checklist, we characterize our work as a modified PRISMA approach because our review addresses research across a variety of InfoSci sub-domains and research methods. As

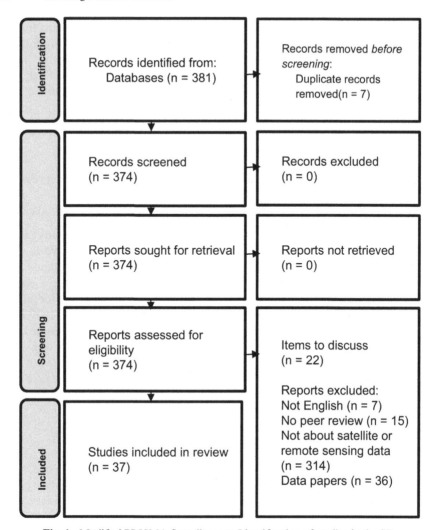

Fig. 1. Modified PRISMA flow diagram: Identification of studies in the SR.

such, it will not include statistical synthesis, one component of the PRISMA checklist intended for reviews of strictly quantitative research (Fig. 1).

For data collection, we used slight variations of the following full text keyword query:

((satellite* OR "remote sensing") AND (data OR image*)) AND ("data sharing" OR "data reuse" OR "open data").

Full-text searching enabled us to keep our search broad, necessary because of the narrow results found in searches limited to abstracts/titles or relying on index or subject terms during our initial scans. Further search parameters included limiting our searches to InfoSci peer-reviewed research (journal articles, conference papers, data papers), 1990-present.

After running queries in WOS, Scopus, LISA, and LISS/LISTA, we exported our results (citations and abstracts) in RIS format to Zotero, then ran "Find PDF" in Zotero to find full-text versions of open and/or available titles. Full-text versions of the remaining titles were located and downloaded individually by RA. She used interlibrary loan (ILL) services to locate full-text items not immediately available. Of the 381 titles identified for initial screening, there were seven duplicates.

For screening, we used two yes/no criteria (i.e., *Is this title written in English? Is this title a peer reviewed journal article, conference paper, and/or data paper?*) and one inclusion question (i.e., *Was the article primarily about satellite/remote sensing data?*). Both researchers conducted independent inclusion/exclusion scans, taking notes, and adding notes to a spreadsheet. A comparison of scanning efforts showed good agreement in decision-making, with less than 5.9% of articles needing to be discussed before a final inclusion/exclusion decision was made. 37 titles were included in the SR. Information about further analysis of this content is outside the scope of this paper.

2.2 Unequal Access

As described at the start of this section, RA and RB had differing levels of access to scholarly resources based on a number of factors. As a tenure-track faculty member at a large US research university, RA had extensive and relatively convenient access to the InfoSci resources needed for this SR. As noted in Sect. 2, RB did not have access to key resources.

We were able to overcome RB's limited access to key InfoSci resources by relying on RA to query three of the four databases used in this SR, and to locate full-text versions of all subscription-based titles. The final SR will include all relevant sources of information that the research team set out to use, but the distribution of work was unequal. While it can be argued that this alone was a challenge for the team, the greater issue was that RB did not have the same opportunity as RA to develop a deep familiarity with the data early in the research process.

2.3 Scopus and the InfoSci Subject Limiter

An access issue that arose while searching Scopus was the inability to limit one's search to InfoSci as a subject. Rather, InfoSci was included alongside several other topics under the umbrella of Social Science (SUBJAREA(SOCI)), without a clear way to query the individual subjects in this category. RA recruited the assistance of the InfoSci subject specialist librarian at her university, who suggested two solutions. First, a lengthy advanced query for limiting search to InfoSci content by journal title. Second, she was able to reach out to a representative at the publisher who provided the subject code ("SUBJTERMS (3309)) that RA used for the Scopus query—information that was not available in the search interface.

2.4   Uniqueness of A&I Results

Of the 379 titles identified through our searches, there were only seven duplicates. Of those, one was a title that appeared in WoS and EBSCO, and nine were titles that appeared in Scopus and ProQuest. The uniqueness of content across the four sources included in this study suggests that research teams with institutional access like RA seeking to conduct comprehensive SRs will have a comparative advantage over research teams whose access more closely resembles RB.

In this section, we provided a single-site narrative case study analysis, describing challenges encountered during a recent SR and discussing the ways that these challenges were addressed. In Sect. 3, we discuss broader implications for the transnational SR research process.

3   Discussion

3.1   Discussion Overview

This reflective case study examined the process of data collection for an SR of InfoSci scholarship on the topic of satellite data, focusing on issues of data availability, data sharing, and open data. We found that our research team encountered two major obstacles: (1) unequal access to scholarly resources, and (2) the need for transborder library support in using those scholarly resources. The results of our SR data collection also highlighted the uniqueness of content across A&I databases in InfoSci, an issue that has the potential to magnify those obstacles.

We were able to address both obstacles by relying on RA's institutional access. She was able to access the A&I databases necessary to identify titles for inclusion in this SR and was able to find full-text versions of nearly every title identified via institutional subscriptions and ILL services. She also received help from her library's InfoSci subject specialist librarian, who resolved the Scopus subject term issue by consulting with other librarians and reaching out directly to the publisher. The timely resolution of this issue depended on institutional access to a research library with staffing and resources available for consultation. InfoSci researchers without access to skilled librarians who have expertise in our research area(s) would likely have a difficult time resolving this type of problem.

The work required to address these obstacles resulted in an unequal distribution of work across team members, which led to negative consequences for both members of the research team. For RA, it meant taking on a far greater share of the work for data collection. As a result, RA and RB went into data analysis with differing levels of familiarity and knowledge about the data set. This created an imbalance of power, with RA having the privilege of being part of a more robust academic knowledge system than RB [38, p. 968]. As a result, while RA would have been able to collect the data for this SR on her own, RB was dependent on RA to carry out the necessary data collection for a comprehensive SR of English-language InfoSci scholarship.

3.2   Barriers to Transborder Inclusivity for SRs

These findings have several implications for InfoSci researchers at institutions that are not part of robust academic knowledge systems. These implications align with the access issue levels identified by Zhang et al. [11]: (1) institutional/infrastructure, (2) individual, and (3) lack of locally appropriate evidence levels (i.e., language barriers) (pp. 105737/5–6). We discuss our findings below using this framework.

Institutional/Infrastructure ("Transborder" Access) Barriers. The privilege that researchers with top-tier access to scholarly resources have is difficult to overstate. In this study, RA was able to access all the resources necessary for an SR of InfoSci literature. Access to highly skilled specialist librarians provided another advantage. Additionally, a substantial portion of InfoSci scholarship is behind a paywall, with Green OA versions of closed access publications often challenging to locate (e.g., [39, 40]). Researchers without access to scholarly literature, such as RB, must work much harder than those at privileged academic institutions to gain access to the tools they need for a comprehensive English-language SR in InfoSci.

Individual Barriers. Without access to subscription-based A&I tools, researchers conducting SRs need to reach out to more privileged colleagues, as was the case here with RB relying on RA. This indicates a possible incentive for "less privileged" researchers to participate in transborder collaborations. However, it also creates a power imbalance that disadvantages those same researchers (as with RB here), who must rely on the participation of a collaborator in order to carry out their research. On the other hand, lack of access may have a chilling effect on literature-based research. The difficulty in finding suitable and willing collaborators, coupled with conditions that create imbalanced relationships between members of research teams and unequal workloads for those team members, as was the case here with RA and RB, may make this type of transborder project an unattractive prospect for those with and without access.

Lack of Locally Appropriate Evidence/Language Barriers. Third, our English search terms yielded overwhelmingly English results, reflecting a limitation of our case study: potential bias against the InfoSci literature written in other languages. InfoSci research is dominated by English-language publications, with most highly ranked journals requiring English language submissions [27]. Tenure requirements for researchers (e.g., RA) often require publishing in those highly-ranked, English-language, journals. Therefore, SRs written in languages other than English are unlikely to find a wide audience or be published in those highly-ranked journals. Scholarship in languages other than English is also likely to be omitted from SRs.

3.3   Open Access

These findings illustrate a set of obstacles that exist in part due to the dominance of closed access publishing in InfoSci. The institutional/infrastructure (transborder) and individual level obstacles would be less significant if the majority of InfoSci publications were available OA, leveling the playing field in terms of access to scholarly outputs. Scholars such as Mercer [24] have noted the disconnect between values and practice in

InfoSci publishing. In this paper, we provide a concrete example of the consequences of this disconnect on scholars with and without the institutional affiliation and/or resources required to access closed publications. A scholarly communications ecosystem in which InfoSci scholars practices align with our professed values would be one in which transborder collaborations (such as the one described in this case study) are carried out by colleagues who have the opportunity to contribute equally to the process of producing and publishing high quality literature-based research such as SRs.

While proposing a solution to the thorny problem of scholarly publishing is outside the scope of this short paper, our findings have led us to pose the following question as a prompt or call for future research: *What can researchers and leaders in the iSchool community do to promote inclusiveness in literature-based research such as SRs?*

3.4 Limitations

This paper reports on the results of a reflexive single-site case study describing our SR process. While this case study demonstrates internal validity, [31, p. 9], it presents only a brief examination of one case. These findings would be strengthened by an extended investigation against a broader theoretical backdrop and in additional settings. Finally, the SR described in the case study scanned English literature only, and thus is biased to that corpus.

4   Conclusion

In this paper, we used a reflective single site case study to describe a recent SR conducted by our transnational research team on the topic of satellite data. This case study highlighted inclusiveness issues faced by InfoSci researchers with differing levels of access to the tools needed to conduct a comprehensive English-language SR. There are steps we as a community might take to extend access to A&I tools and help the iSchool community to better "practice what we preach" in terms of bridging the digital divides that persist in our scholarly knowledge systems, which reinforce both privilege and disadvantage for scholars in our own community. In our future research, including the aforementioned satellite data project, we hope to continue probing the impact of the inclusion issues that we have identified here on InfoSci research more broadly.

Acknowledgements. We would like to thank Calantha Tillotson, the Subject Expert Librarian for Information Science at Hodges Library at the University of Tennessee-Knoxville, whose support was essential to the research described in this article. We also greatly appreciated the manuscript review by Dr. Ann Medaille, University of Nevada Reno Libraries. This research was funded by a grant from the Deutsche Stiftung Friedensforschung for the Citizen-based Monitoring for Peace & Security in the Era of Synthetic Media and Deepfakes project (2023–2025).

References

1. Connaway, L.S., Chu, C.M., Kawooya, D., Mfengu, A.: Research frameworks for multiple ways of knowing: social justice, methodology, and policy. In: Zavalina, O., Poole, A. H. (eds.), Proceedings of the ALISE Annual Conference, (n.p.). Illinois Library IOPN, Urbana-Champaign (2022). https://doi.org/10.21900/j.alise.2022.1107
2. Cooke, N.A., Kitzie, V.L.: Outsiders-within-library and information science: reprioritizing the marginalized in critical sociocultural work. J. Am. Soc. Inf. Sci. **72**(10), 1285–1294 (2021). https://doi.org/10.1002/asi.24449
3. Inskip, C.: What are the options for library and information studies education reform in addressing racial inequity in the library profession in the UK? J. Libr. Inf. Sci. **55**(4), 972–998 (2022). https://doi.org/10.1177/09610006221114483
4. Jaeger, P.T., Taylor, N.G., Gorham, U.: Libraries, human rights, and social justice: Enabling access and promoting inclusion. Rowman & Littlefield, Lanham/London (2015). https://digitalcommons.usf.edu/si_facpub/418/
5. Jaeger, P.T., Shilton, K., Koepfler, J.: The rise of social justice as a guiding principle in library and information science research. Libr. Q. Inf. Community Policy **86**(1), 1–9 (2016). https://doi.org/10.1086/684142
6. Mehra, B.: Toward an impact-driven framework to operationalize social justice and implement ICT4D in the field of information. J. Assoc. Inf. Sci. Technol. **74**(12), 1419–1436 (2022). https://doi.org/10.1002/asi.24693
7. Winberry, J., Bishop, B.W.: Documenting social justice in library and information science research: a literature review. J. Documentation **77**(4), 743–753 (2020). https://doi.org/10.1108/JD-08-2020-0136
8. Heeks, R.: Digital inequality beyond the digital divide: conceptualizing adverse digital incorporation in the global south. Inf. Technol. Dev. **28**(4), 688–704 (2022). https://doi.org/10.1080/02681102.2022.2068492
9. Heyward-Rotimi, K.: Critiquing neocolonial digital barriers' impact on eLibraries and African scholarship. Ann. Anthropol. Pract. **47**(1), 5–19 (2023). https://doi.org/10.1111/napa.12193
10. Soto, S.: Transnational knowledge projects and failing racial etiquette. In: 2008 National Association for Chicana and Chicano Studies (NACCS) Conference Proceedings, pp. 69–72. SJSU ScholarWorks (2008). https://scholarworks.sjsu.edu/naccs/2008/Proceedings/8?utm_source=scholarworks.sjsu.edu%2Fnaccs%2F2008%2FProceedings%2F8&utm_medium=PDF&utm_campaign=PDFCoverPages
11. Zhang, M., Doi, L., Awua, J., Asare, H., Stenhouse, R.: Challenges and possible solutions for accessing scholarly literature among medical and nursing professionals and students in low-and-middle income countries: a systematic review. Nurse Educ. Today **123**, 105737 (2023). https://doi.org/10.1016/j.nedt.2023.105737
12. Matusiak, K., Bright, K., Schachter, D.: Conducting international research in the library and information science field: challenges and approaches. AIB Stud. **62**(2), 367–378 (2022). https://doi.org/10.2426/aibstudi-13396
13. Association of College & Research Libraries (ACRL). Equity, diversity, and inclusion. https://www.ala.org/acrl/issues/edi
14. Alabi, J.: From hostile to inclusive: strategies for improving the racial climate of academic libraries. Libr. Trends **67**(1), 131–146 (2018). https://doi.org/10.1353/lib.2018.0029
15. Hosoi, M., Lim, A., Pan, D., Seo, H.: Promotion and tenure in academic libraries: impact on librarians of color. https://scholarsphere.psu.edu/resources/62f62553-2a62-4d83-8a88-877e149a5531
16. Lor, P.J.: International and Comparative Librarianship: Concepts and Methods for Global Studies. Walter de Gruyter GmBH, Berlin/Boston (2019). https://doi.org/10.1515/9783110267990

17. Gray, L., Mehra, B.: Going against the current of hegemonic "white-IST" discourse: a doctoral program journey from critical student+ guide perspectives. J. Educ. Libr. Inf. Sci. **62**(2), 182–200 (2021). https://doi.org/10.3138/jelis.2020-0056

18. Chaka, C., Ndlangamandla, S.: Relocating English studies and SoTL in the global south: towards decolonizing English and critiquing the coloniality of language. J. Contemp. Issues Educ. **17**(2), 39–56 (2022). https://doi.org/10.20355/jcie29495

19. R'boul, H.: English and the dissemination of local knowledges. In: The Routledge Handbook of Language and the Global South/s, pp. 147–157. Routledge, Oxon/New York (2023). https://doi.org/10.4324/9781003007074-14

20. Xu, J., Kang, Q., Song, Z.: The current state of systematic reviews in library and information studies. Libr. Inf. Sci. Res. **37**(4), 296–310 (2015). https://doi.org/10.1016/j.lisr.2015.11.003

21. Gerwin, V.: Pack up the parachute: why global north-south collaborations need to change. Nature **619**(7971), 885–887 (2023). https://doi.org/10.1038/d41586-023-02313-1

22. ACRL policy statement on open access to scholarship by academic librarians. https://www.ala.org/acrl/standards/openaccess#:~:text=In%20support%20of%20transparency%20and,make%20openly%20accessible%20all%20products. Accessed 06 Jan 2024

23. IFLA statement on open access to scholarly literature and research documentation [2003]. https://www.ifla.org/publications/ifla-statement-on-open-access-to-scholarly-literature-and-research-documentation-2003/. Accessed 06 Jan 2024

24. Mercer, H.: Almost halfway there: an analysis of the open access behaviors of academic librarians. Coll. Res. Libr. **72**(5), 443–453 (2011). https://doi.org/10.5860/crl-167

25. Scott, R.E., Harrington, C., Dubnjakovic, A.: Exploring open access practices, attitudes, and policies in academic libraries. Portal Libr. Acad. **21**(2), 365–388 (2021). https://doi.org/10.1353/pla.2021.0020

26. Scott, R.E.: A selected comparison of music librarians' and musicologists' self-archiving practices. Portal Libr. Acad. **19**(4), 635–651 (2019). https://doi.org/10.1353/pla.2019.0039

27. Clarivate Journal Citation Reports, Information Science & Library Science filter applied, [NOTE: link varies according to institutional proxy server]. https://jcr-clarivate-com.ezproxy.[institutional domain]/jcr/browse-journals. Accessed 03 Aug 2023

28. Brembs, B., et al.: Replacing academic journals. Roy. Soc. Open Sci. **10**(7), 230206 (2023). https://doi.org/10.1098/rsos.230206

29. EBSCO Library, Information science and technology abstracts homepage. https://www.ebsco.com/products/research-databases/library-information-science-and-technology-abstracts. Accessed 06 Jan 2024

30. Panke, D.: Research design & method selection: making good choices in the social sciences. Research Design & Method Selection. Sage, Los Angeles (2018). https://uk.sagepub.com/en-gb/eur/research-design-method-selection/book260462

31. Tardi, S.: Case study: defining and differentiating among types of case studies. In: Baron, A., McNeal, K. Case study methodology in higher education, pp. 1–19. IGI Global, Brussels/London/Hong Kong/Washington DC (2019). https://doi.org/10.4018/978-1-5225-9429-1

32. Yin, R.K.: Case Study Research and Applications: Design and Methods. 6th edn. Sage, Los Angeles (2018). https://us.sagepub.com/en-us/nam/case-study-research-and-applications/book250150

33. Grant, M.J., Booth, A.: A typology of reviews: an analysis of 14 review types and associated methodologies. Health Info. Libr. J. **26**(2), 91–108 (2009). https://doi.org/10.1111/j.1471-1842.2009.00848.x

34. Donner, E.K.: Research data management systems and the organization of universities and research institutes: a systematic literature review. J. Librariansh. Inf. Sci. **55**(2), 261–281 (2023). https://doi.org/10.1177/09610006211070282

35. Page, M.J., et al.: The PRISMA 2020 statement: an updated guideline for reporting systematic reviews. Int. J. Surg. **88**, 105906 (2021). https://doi.org/10.1136/bmj.n71

36. Maemura, E., Moles, N., Becker, C.: Organizational assessment frameworks for digital preservation: a literature review and mapping. J. Assoc. Inf. Sci. Technol. **68**(7), 1619–37 (2017). https://hdl.handle.net/1807/73869

37. Vassilakaki, E., Moniarou-Papaconstaninou, V.: Librarians' support in improving health literacy: a systematic literature review. J. Librariansh. Inf. Sci. **255**(2), 500–514 (2023). https://doi.org/10.1177/09610006221093794

38. Reed, M.S., Rudman, H.: Re-thinking research impact: voice, context and power at the interface of science, policy and practice. Sustain. Sci. **18**(2), 967–981 (2023). https://doi.org/10.1007/s11625-022-01216-w

39. Khuntia, P., Munshi, S.A.: An overview of open access scholarly article discovery tools. Libr. Waves **8**(2), 106–16 (2022). http://www.librarywaves.com/index.php/lw/article/view/132

40. Baich, T.: Open access: help or hindrance to resource sharing? Interlending Document Supply **43**(2), 68–75 (2015). https://doi.org/10.1108/ILDS-01-2015-0003

Who Gets Left Behind in the Push for Smart Cities? Insights from Marginalized Communities

Sunyup Park[✉] [ID] and Jessica Vitak [ID]

University of Maryland, College Park, MD 20742, USA
{Sypark,jvitak}@umd.edu

Abstract. Smart cities take advantage of advances in ubiquitous computing and big data analytics to build and deploy technologies that increase efficiency and sustainability. However, benefits derived from smart cities are not equally distributed. In this paper, we consider how smart city initiatives can better serve and engage marginalized communities through a focus on the city of Baltimore, MD. Through focus groups with 43 Black Baltimore residents living in low-income neighborhoods, we identify key barriers they perceive to being more engaged in and trusting of smart city initiatives, as well as important disconnects between residents' needs and the city's solutions. Based on these findings, we make the case for cities to more deeply engage these communities in smart city initiatives, as many technologies are not designed with their unique needs in mind, and they are the most likely to experience harms from surveillance technologies that collect large quantities of data and build predictive models used by cities.

Keywords: Smart Cities · Privacy · Marginalized Communities · Digital Divide · Digital Literacy

1 Introduction

Over the last decade, cities around the world have implemented policies and technologies to make themselves "smarter." This has led to the coining of the term "smart cities," in-depth analyses by scholars, and corporate campaigns designed to profit from this increasing reliance on data-driven decision-making based on data collected from residents and their environment. Smart city technologies span nearly all aspects of cities, from energy and transportation to public safety and infrastructure.

Rob Kitchin [26] notes that definitions of smart cities tend to focus on two things: the technology itself and the development of a "knowledge economy." First, smart cities are only possible thanks to the tremendous rise in ubiquitous computing, leading to what Greenfield [16] refers to as "everyware"—an environment where computing is no longer limited to a small set of devices but instead can be found nearly everywhere and in everything, and is "used to monitor, manage and regulate city flows and processes, often in real-time" (p. 2). More broadly, smart cities reflect an increased focus on the knowledge economy being essential to growth. In other words, by collecting more data from cities and people moving through them, officials will be better positioned to innovate. Kitchin

I. Sserwanga et al. (Eds.): iConference 2024, LNCS 14598, pp. 90–104, 2024.
https://doi.org/10.1007/978-3-031-57867-0_7

[26] further notes that what makes a city "smart" is how technology is used in decision- and policy-making to leverage growth.

Given the vast amount of data collection occurring in smart cities, we must consider disparate impacts of data collection and surveillance on marginalized populations. Most US cities have higher concentrations of impoverished and of minority populations [15]. These groups face disproportionate amounts of government surveillance. Madden and colleagues [30] describe this as a "matrix of vulnerabilities that low-income people face as a result of the collection and aggregation of big data and the application of predictive analytics" (p. 53). They note that the increasing reliance on mobile and internet tech- nologies will likely increase privacy harms, especially given that many new technologies exhibit biases against these populations [36, 42].

In this paper, we consider one aspect of smart city initiatives: public transportation. Buses, light rails, and subways provide critical infrastructure to city residents, and they are often the only form of transportation available to low-income residents. Given the shift toward decentralization of employment in cities [14], many of the poorest residents live in central parts of the city but travel to outer parts for work. Research shows that lower-income residents endure more complex and longer trips on public transit, requiring multiple modes and/or transfers, when compared to higher-income residents [37]. This is especially important given the link between geographic and economic mobility: those who can move around more easily are more likely to improve their economic standing [23].

We focus on the city of Baltimore, Maryland, the state's largest city (population: 570,000). More than 60% of the population is Black, and more than 20% of the city's residents fall below the poverty line [43]. Baltimore has also been an early adopter in data analytics at scale; in 1999, the city launched CitiStat, a program that required government agencies to regularly generate and share performance data with the mayor's office [20]. By 2018, Baltimore was investing in various smart city initiatives, from more energy-efficient lighting to smart trash bins and ShotSpotter devices. However, public transportation has faced continuing challenges that have not been helped by the city's increasing reliance on technology, and the city's transit system is one of the most class- and race-segregated in the US [3].

We build on prior work considering how technology can support the needs of low- income residents of Baltimore City [28, 29]. They found that Black residents were frustrated with the quality of public transit and felt it limited access to work and educa- tional opportunities. Some of the most equity-disadvantaged neighborhoods in Baltimore have the highest percentage of people using public transit and longest commute times in the country [22]. That said, it's unclear whether these residents' voices and experi- ences are considered as part of decision-making about public transit, nor whether privacy considerations play any role in their thoughts on smart technology.

Lung-Amam and colleagues [28] noted that Baltimore should work closely with residents in addressing these challenges, so we set out to gain a deeper understanding of residents' needs, as well as barriers that may prevent them from being more engaged in smart city initiatives. We ask two key research questions:

RQ1: What barriers do Baltimore residents perceive to their engagement in the development and expansion of smart city initiatives?

RQ2: What do Baltimore residents want or need to promote the development and expansion of smart city initiatives?

Findings from focus groups with 43 Black, low-income Baltimore residents highlight two key barriers to feeling more engaged in smart city initiatives: low digital literacy and a lack of trust. In terms of needs, residents want solutions that are less about the technology and focus more on addressing challenges they face in their day-to-day lives. Beyond that, residents want greater transparency about data collection practices and more direct engagement with residents to identify and respond to their most pressing needs. Based on these findings, we argue that cities need to do more to involve residents and particularly residents like those we spoke to in the development and deployment of smart city initiatives. By including residents more deeply in the process and providing them with greater transparency about the data collected through smart technologies, cities may be able to build trust with their residents and ensure new initiatives do not create additional challenges for marginalized communities.

2 Background

Technology is at the core of most definitions of smart cities [17, 21, 41]. For example, Townsend [41] defines smart cities as "places where information technology is combined with infrastructure, architecture, everyday objects, and even our bodies to address social, economic, and environmental problems" (p. 15). These technologies make a city "smart" by collecting real-time data from sensors around the city. That data is then analyzed and visualized for city officials to aid decision-making.

Smart city technologies span government services, urban infrastructure, energy, and the environment. Of particular interest for this paper is how smart cities are reflected in public transportation. New technologies enable real-time data processing to make transportation smarter (e.g., real-time location information for tracking and monitoring public transportation services [34]). For example, Baltimore introduced a smartphone application[1] in 2023 to expand their assisted mobility services for smartphone users.

2.1 Privacy Concerns in Smart Cities

Most smart city technologies are integrated into city infrastructures to improve efficiency and quality of services [7]. These technologies collect, analyze, and distribute citizens' data [25, 26], and their use has privacy implications. Helbing et al. [19] argue that mass surveillance is why privacy is so often violated in smart cities. Data used for services can also be used for surveillance purposes [45], with potential harms arising when using data to draw inferences about residents as well as issues with anonymization, reidentification, and ineffective/absent notice and consent [24].

For residents to fully accept smart cities, 'respect of privacy' is a crucial value [32], as reflected in the need for transparency between public and private sectors involved in smart city development. In fact, when people's privacy concerns are not addressed, smart city projects fail, as seen in the case of Sidewalk Toronto, a project that faced backlash

---

[1] https://www.mta.maryland.gov/mobility-all-access.

from privacy advocates because of its lack of transparency and accountability around the collection and use of data [12, 31].

However, limited research has investigated residents' privacy concerns regarding smart cities. When people participate in smart city projects, information security is a concern, especially regarding data anonymity and access [8]. On the other hand, Belanche-Gracia et al. [1] found that smartcard users in Spain perceived smartcard data to be limited and trusted local authorities in managing the information. Calculation of tradeoffs also impacts acceptance of surveillance technologies; van Heek et al. [18] found that people are more likely to trade their privacy for safety in places they think are unsafe. To improve residents' confidence in using smart cities, Chatterjee et al. [6] emphasized the role of IT authorities to address privacy and security issues.

2.2 Increased Risk of Harms for Marginalized Communities

Smart city technologies can negatively impact marginalized communities' privacy. Research has highlighted that lower-income/education individuals have less awareness of privacy risks and are more vulnerable to data breaches and security-related harms [30]. Vitak et al. [44] found that economically disadvantaged internet users face barriers to understanding privacy risks, practicing privacy-protective behaviors, and trusting information intermediaries due to lower digital literacy. Likewise, marginalized communities rely on mobile phones over computers, which exacerbates vulnerabilities and risk exposure [29].

Given that smart cities frequently utilize crowdsourced data from citizens' smartphones to reduce infrastructure costs [8], the privacy and security implications—especially for marginalized communities—are concerning. Emami-Naeini et al. [11] argue that marginalized populations' perceptions of benefits and harms of smart cities might be more pronounced than—and not easily generalizable to—the general population because concerns are linked to socioeconomic status; lower-income respondents were more concerned about the ethical implications of certain scenarios (e.g., deploying gunshot spotters) because scenarios like gun violence were more relevant to them. Older adults also face increased privacy risks due to their lack of access to physical, social, and digital resources; Sourbati and Behrendt [40] argue this hinders inclusiveness in smart cities and may increase social inequality.

Lung-Amam et al. [29] note that few studies have considered the privacy implications for marginalized populations in smart cities. They investigated how smart city technology impacted low-income neighborhoods and found public transportation as one of residents' main interests. Building on their work, Frias-Martinez et al. [13] investigated how privacy might prevent low-income residents from participating in a city's mobile-based data collection efforts. They note that current metrics measuring mobility experience leave out transit-dependent, equity-challenged communities' experiences because they ignore the multi-modal/legged trips that lower-income residents must face.

3   Method

This study directly builds on Lung-Amam et al.'s [29] work and complements previous studies regarding marginalized populations in smart cities [11, 40] by investigating the lived experiences of low-income residents of color. This paper is part of a larger NSF-funded project developing privacy-preserving public transit tools to serve low-income residents in Baltimore, MD, a medium-sized city on the US' east coast. Baltimore launched a major smart city initiative in 2018 [9]. Among its goals was addressing chronic problems with public transportation [10]. Baltimore has one of the worst public transportation systems in the US, with some of the longest commute times for residents using public transportation [22].

3.1   Procedure

The project team includes several Baltimore-based partner organizations, and we worked closely with the Housing Authority of Baltimore City (HABC)[2] to identify low-income, majority Black neighborhoods where residents relied heavily on public transit and to help coordinate focus group sessions in these neighborhoods. Data collection was initially planned for late 2020; however, pandemic restrictions delayed data collection until summer 2021. We also planned to use a mix of interviews and focus groups; however, after conducting two pilot phone interviews, we determined that in-person, group-based discussions would better suit our research goals.

Coordinating with HABC staff working in these neighborhoods, we began recruiting residents in June 2021 for 90-min focus group sessions to be held in one of three HABC community spaces. Over the next 10 months, we held eight sessions with 43 residents (63% female; age range: 20s–70s) in the three locations through the city (see Table 1). While we purposefully did not collect detailed demographic information from participants, we did confirm there (1) were a resident of the neighborhood; (2) used public transportation (bus, light rail, subway, and/or mobility services) at least monthly; and (3) owned a smartphone. Each session included 4–8 participants as well as 1–3 team members. All sessions were audio recorded. Participants received a US$50 gift card to Amazon or Wal-Mart.

Focus groups were organized into four sections. First, we asked about participants' general experiences with public transportation. This was meant to build rapport with and between participants, and to get participants comfortable with the focus group format. Second, we discussed perceptions of smart city technology. To facilitate this, participants reviewed and discussed a handout with descriptions of common smart city technologies (e.g., trash cans, gunshot detectors) and mobile apps (e.g., contact tracing, public transit). Third, we asked participants to discuss their experiences with and perceptions toward public transit apps, as well as any data privacy concerns, they had used these apps or smartphones more generally. We concluded by asking them to share their needs and wants for public transit apps. The full protocol (including handouts) is in the supplemental materials.

---

[2] HABC provides numerous services to low-income residents, including management of public housing programs. As of 2023, they managed 7000 public housing units at 21 sites across Baltimore.

Table 1. Focus group locations and participants.

Location / Session ID	Date	# Participants	Participant IDs1	Community Description
A1	July 2021	6	P21-P26	Location A is in West Baltimore and has 200 + units for older adults. There is one bus stop nearby; to get to the closest grocery store takes 50 min by bus
B1	Aug 2021	4	P3-P6	Location B is in West Baltimore and has 200 + units. It primarily serves older adults and people with disabilities. Like Location A, it has a bus stop nearby but is not close to major grocery stores; there are accessible "corner stores" but prices are much higher. Many residents use Mobility or cab services
B2	Aug 2021	5	P7-P11	
B3	Aug 2021	5	P12-P16	
C1	Nov 2021	4	P17-P20	Location C is in Central Baltimore and has 1200 + units, primarily serving families. The community includes a daycare and aquatic center. There is one shopping center close by with a limited number of stores. Residents have no access to grocery stores in the area. Multiple forms of public transportation (bus stops and light rail) are within walking distance
C2	April 2022	5	P27-P31	
C3	April 2022	8	P32-P39	
C4	April 2022	6	P40-P45	

1 P1 and P2 were part of the pilot data collection; their data is not included in this analysis

3.2 Data Analysis

When recording sessions, we used multiple recorders to capture everyone's comments. However, the audio quality was relatively poor for several reasons. First, while we purposefully chose to collect data in the building/neighborhood where participants lived, these spaces were not optimal for data collection. At Location C, for example, sessions took place in a large space with high ceilings, causing some sound distortion. At Location B, sessions were conducted in a room adjacent to building construction, which added noise. In most sessions, participants were spread out and/or masked because of pandemic restrictions or concerns. We carefully reviewed each transcript, audio files, and researcher notes to fill in places where professional transcribers were unsure, noting places where audio quality was too poor to transcribe.

Transcripts were uploaded to Atlas.ti for qualitative analysis. Following Miles et al. [33], we developed an initial codebook based on the project's overarching research questions, the focus group protocol, and notes from the first four sessions. We continued collecting data for several months, determining saturation had been reached [39] after the April 2022 sessions. We revisited the codebook and discussed additional updates and clarifications to each code, then each transcript was read and coded by both authors. Following this, we exported excerpts and completed a thematic analysis [2, 38] of three codes: public transportation dislikes; data privacy concerns and management; and digital/tech literacy. For this step, the first author read through all excerpts for a given code multiple times to identify patterns across participants and sessions, then wrote detailed memos summarizing themes and providing examples from the data.

4 Findings

4.1 RQ1: Barriers to Engagement in Smart City Initiatives

RQ1 explored residents' attitudes toward smart city initiatives and barriers to being more engaged with the city's smart city initiatives. Below, we highlight two interconnected themes that emerged: low digital literacy and trust.

Barrier
#1: Low Digital Literacy and Limited Knowledge of Smart Technologies. Most participants reported having limited knowledge of smart technologies and low digital literacy. Many described challenges using their phone effectively to accomplish tasks. For example, P5 described constant frustration with her phone, saying, "I struggle with the different apps. I don't do nothing but make phone calls." Similarly, P4 described feeling uncomfortable using her smartphone: "I just had the feeling that I'm going to mess something up. If I get to pressing buttons and stuff like that, it's not going to register correctly."

While a few younger participants self-described themselves as more tech-savvy, many turned to family and neighbors for help using their smartphones. P3, who affectionately referred to her nine grandchildren as "computer geeks," regularly got technical help from them: "When it comes down to something I really don't understand, one of them will take time to explain it to me. And they know it's going to take a while, but they set it up, and they show me what to do after."

Struggles and successes with smartphone apps were often discussed as they related to transit apps, including Google Maps, ride-share apps, and public transportation apps like Transit, which provide real-time information about bus schedules. P31 and P41 relied heavily on grandchildren to help map out trips or find when the next bus was coming. When asked about reasons for *not* using public transportation apps, P41 replied, "I ask my children or grandchildren. I'll get frustrated by the time I look at it and find it and go through it, and I'm like, 'I do not understand. Will y'all tell me?'".

Given this low technical proficiency, it is unsurprising that participants' knowledge of smart city technology was limited. Most had never heard the term, and while some recognized examples because they encountered them in their everyday life, they frequently misunderstood how technologies worked. P14 thought that the Array of Things would expose him to radiation: "All that radiation, it's contaminating the neighborhood and yourself and the environment." P17 "found it upsetting" that the contact tracing application "made" the health department call her to get vaccinated, and eventually "took it off [her smartphone]."

Barrier #2: Low Trust in Technology and City Officials. As described above, many residents misunderstood aspects of how smart cities and smartphone applications worked, and sometimes that misunderstanding led them to distrust the effectiveness or utility of these technologies—or city officials. P19 strongly believed gunshot detectors were "a decoy to deter criminals," noting that "the city once admitted…that certain cameras in a certain community wasn't working." This made him skeptical of "how many times [workers] go around maintaining these cameras." P19 also expressed concerns about the city monitoring residents, saying "I want to feel free…. I don't want to be monitored all the time, where I go and what I do." P17 replied, "Big Brother is always watching. Ain't nothing we can do."

A similar skepticism was expressed regarding smart trash bins deployed throughout the city. Participants were surprised that the trash bins were "smart," with several noting that the technology didn't work properly. For example, P27 mentioned, "Trust me, I don't know if the sensor works, but it's full to capacity. I don't care what day you go past there, trash is hanging all over." Likewise, P17 mentioned seeing gunshot detectors attached to cameras but wasn't sure they were working because "I know they come periodically and change the cameras, but I never see them do anything with the ShotSpotter." P19 chimed in, asking: "How many of them [ShotSpotter] are fake? Because I'm sure some of them are fake."

Given data collection occurred during 2021–2022, we asked about contact tracing apps, which typically use Bluetooth and self-reports to alert people when they have been near someone who recently tested COVID-19 positive. There was definitely confusion about how they worked—we noted above that P17 thought she was getting calls from the city's health department because she downloaded the app. In fact, several participants expressed skepticism or unease with contact tracing apps because they erroneously believed they allowed government or health officials to track them. Research suggests trust in government decreased during the pandemic [40]; comments by our participants suggested there was either a lack of communication or miscommunication about contact tracing apps, leading to distrust or skepticism.

Participants also lacked trust in technology companies. During a conversation about how long apps should retain user data, P14 mentioned he wanted data deleted from his phone after "30–60 days, it should be gone. Because then I don't feel as though you may be infringing on my privacy." P13 replied, "But after whatever it goes on, and then they said it never goes away, it's always on there," adding, "None of us are probably technically equipped even fully on our own phones. Much less trying to dig into the people that can go and hack your stuff."

A heated discussion during Session C3 highlighted participants' low regarding data collection. When asked if they had any concerns about transit data being collected and shared with the local transit authority, P33 said, "If they want something off your phone, they can get anything off your phone." P38 replied, "All they need to know is trips I take with them. They don't need anything else…. They don't know me personally, why they need my history?" Others in this session strongly agreed with this sentiment. P36 then joined the conversation, suggesting that apps could access all phone data: "All the data is just there. They say, we'll get all the data from Transit, but you still got the rest of the data on your phone, got all the calls that she had within that day, that she caught the bus or something like that."

4.2   RQ2: Residents Highlight Key Needs for Smart City Engagement

In addressing RQ2, we found a mismatch between what residents needed and what the city offered them. We focus on two core themes: smart city initiatives that don't address core problems faced by residents, and a lack of community engagement in developing and communicating about changes to existing programs and services.

Need #1: Solutions That Address Residents' Issues Simply. In our discussions of smart city initiatives broadly—and transit apps specifically—residents were skeptical that technical solutions would solve city problems. Several participants primarily used MobilityLink, a specialized transit service for those with mobility limitations. To use this service, residents could use a website or, more recently, a smartphone app. However, given that many participants previously mentioned they either don't use transit apps or use them in limited ways, it was unsurprising that they said they preferred making reservations over the phone. P29 expressed his frustration with calling MobilityLink as "donuts," meaning that you would go around in circles on the phone: "[MobilityLink] sticks you to somebody else. Then they stick you to somebody else. It works like that." P41 also described difficulties making reservations over the phone, saying that "whoever's doing the scheduling does not know what they're doing." Participants complained there was no way to communicate with drivers or get information when a driver was running late, and this lack of information could make the process of getting transportation very tedious.

It was also clear to participants that some of the city's "smart" solutions were not all that smart. As noted above, discussions related to the smart trash bins highlighted that adding chips to them didn't seem to reduce the amount of trash on the ground, and participants were skeptical that devices like ShotSpotter were real. If such straightforward forms of smart technology (e.g., adding sensors to alert the city when the bin is full) don't work, why should residents trust that more complex technological solutions will? From our participants' perspective, their needs were much more basic and weren't being addressed through more complicated, technology-driven solutions.

Need #2: More Transparency from the City, More Direct Engagement with Residents. Participants repeatedly shared examples of recent changes to the city's bus system that made it more confusing and inconvenient. This included changes to routes, changes in the scheduling—including reducing the frequency of weekend buses—changes that required more transfers, and changes to how bus routes were labeled. Furthermore, participants said it was unclear *why* these changes were made, and they suspected that whoever made the changes did not use public transportation themselves. P17 said, "Whoever changed the MTA schedule and changed the buses from numbers to colors, he don't catch the bus. That's my whole problem. ...when you going to implement something, if you don't use it, I don't need your help." Similarly, P38 mentioned hearing the administrator brought in to update the bus system wasn't from Baltimore and P33 replied, "It's probably somebody that never even caught a bus. They probably don't even touch buses." So, when we asked participants what they wanted to make their public transportation experience better, all they wanted was for the city to undo these changes. P31 explained, "If [city officials are] going to consider things, why don't they consider restoring the skipped stops they moved for no just cause."

If there were clear reasons for these changes, residents were unaware. Such discrepancies between city services and what residents actually need are due, in part, to a lack of community engagement in planning and implementing changes to core city services. Prior comments from participants about their misunderstandings or lack of knowledge of smart city initiatives suggest that current strategies for communicating about changes are lacking. One example of this was seen during Session C1, where participants discussed a groundbreaking at a local park. P19 was frustrated he hadn't gotten any information about the event, saying, "I want to know what's going on in my community. They should have put fliers in everybody's door saying, 'This is going to happen this day.' No one on my block got a flier or anything."

Participants also wanted more transparency regarding data collected by the city to ensure it benefited their community. P43 asked, "Can we go to the library to find out who's collecting data and what the data is being used for, and whether they are able to use it for the community that they collected the data from?" Our participants demanded direct benefits to their community because they felt their communities have been neglected; for example, P43 said, "Sometimes they take your data and sell it, and other communities more affluent than ours benefit from our data." P43 also noted problematic ways data could be used: "They use that data to say, 'well this is why we don't want to build a supermarket in this community,' 'this is why we need a gated community.'" Finally, they wanted data collection to have clear benefits like improved safety, but they didn't see that happening, with P27 noting that "the data is not keeping the city safe."

While frustrated, participants also acknowledged the importance of participating in community meetings to help shape policy. For example, P21 said that for people "that don't have a car, they rely on public transportation. But you can't expect a bus to come on time, or … for them to put more buses on a line on Sunday if you don't go to a meeting and speak about it." Despite knowing and wanting to attend meetings, participants complained about the timing, saying meetings were held at unfavorable times and places. P17 noted that a lot of the community meetings were held far from their neighborhood. Instead, she suggested, "For every area where you have a bus situation, in all those areas they [could] have meetings."

5   Discussion

When we began collecting data for this study, we were most interested in residents' privacy concerns arising from smart city initiatives and the data collected from residents. However, it quickly became clear that data privacy was just not a priority for most residents. Instead, they were more concerned with changes that negatively impacted their daily life, such as changes to public buses that added time and inconvenience to their day. This disconnect is concerning and highlights how the needs and wants of the most vulnerable can be overlooked in the push to advance the city economically and technologically.

The findings from this study provide a direct extension to Lung-Amam et al.'s [28, 29] work, which engaged West Baltimore residents to explore smart city technologies and considered ways to better engage the community in planning and policymaking. Lung-Amam et al. [29] found that because many residents lacked reliable computer access and relied on mobile devices to complete tasks, the city should leverage this by creating more app-based services. However, our study, which included a significant number of adults ages 50+, found that many struggled to effectively use their smartphones. This was especially clear for participants who used MobilityLink services and preferred calling to using the website or mobile app. Given the shift to virtual scheduling, it's likely there are limited resources for residents who want to reserve via phone. It's also unclear if the city conducted any research with residents who use MobilityLink before building an app to see if that solution matched the needs and skills of its primary users.

The role of trust in building out smart cities cannot be understated. One of the largest smart city initiatives globally—featuring a collaboration between Google's Sidewalk Labs and the City of Toronto—collapsed in large part because the needs and goals of key stakeholders conflicted [12]. This was highlighted when privacy expert Ann Cavoukian resigned from the project in 2018 due to data privacy concerns [5]. Lung-Aman et al. [29] trace a long history of distrust by marginalized Baltimore residents toward city officials. In our conversations, we found this lack of trust extended to both smart city technologies—especially when they didn't work in expected ways or when there was high uncertainty regarding their purpose—as well as city officials collecting data from residents.

This mistrust is especially concerning when considering the wider landscape in which smart city data collection occurs. Poor and minoritized communities have histori- cally faced both greater surveillance and worse outcomes from surveillance [4, 30]. Prior work evaluating privacy risks faced by this population [44] found that low digital literacy and a lack of reliable computer access led many low-income families to distrust online content, companies, and the government; this distrust can lead to rejecting technologies outright or developing misconceptions about the uses of a given technology. Of course, when it comes to smart city initiatives, it is often difficult—if not impossible—to reject a technology. Those who rely on public transportation cannot opt-out of camera surveil- lance; those who use Google Maps or the Transit app may need to share their location to use the service. A few of our participants expressed unease with the growing use of everyware throughout the city, sometimes expressing resignation to being watched by "big brother."

Many of the barriers residents described that prevent them from greater engagement in smart city initiatives can be addressed by involving them in development and decision- making processes. This is certainly not a novel idea, but it's clear that cities are still largely ignoring the needs of their most marginalized residents. Lung-Amam and colleagues [29] make a compelling argument for institutionalizing engagement mechanisms to involve local communities in smart city initiatives, noting, "For smart city investments to work *for* communities, rather than just *in* them, smart city planning must help to build and repair community trust, leverage existing neighborhood assets, facilitate residents' access and choice, and recognize the diversity within and between disadvantaged neighborhoods" (p. 107, emphasis in original). Our research strongly supports this assertion and highlights places where current policies do not align with residents' needs.

Beyond seeking direct input from residents and involving them in the development process, our findings support the call for cities to be more open and transparent regarding smart city data collection and use. Data access initiatives can take many forms, but it's clear both from our data and previous studies [8, 29] that residents want access to their data and want to have a greater say in how that data is used. Such access could also reduce the likelihood of data being used in problematic ways, as residents and local organizations could review city policies, conduct data audits, and ensure data is not being used to engage in biased predictions—something that has a long history of causing harms to marginalized communities [36, 42].

6   Conclusion

The push toward smart cities may feel inevitable, but it's clear there are better and worse ways to implement technologies that collect massive amounts of data about residents. Techno-solutionism—the frequently heard refrain by those who think technology can fix any problem [35]—is especially problematic for those on the margins, whose experiences and needs differ from those with the money and knowledge to fully benefit from new technologies [11].

In this study, we extended prior work [28, 29] evaluating smart city initiatives in Baltimore, Maryland. Through focus groups with 43 low-income, Black residents, with a special focus on public transit, we explored barriers they perceive to greater engagement with smart city initiatives and the mismatch between their needs and city solutions. These findings reiterate the urgent need for greater citizen engagement—especially with those who most likely to be negatively affected by these initiatives—in needs assessment, development, and evaluation of data-driven projects. It is important to note that even though these residents had limited technical knowledge, they understood the importance of transparency regarding and access to their data.

Some of the challenges and concerns we identified may be addressed soon. In December 2023, the Baltimore City Office of Information and Technology released a five-year Digital Inclusion Strategy to reduce the digital divide and promote digital equity in the city [47]. Specific action goals (e.g., digital skills training) will help alleviate fundamental barriers our participants faced that prevented full engagement in the smart city. The strategy's plan to involve low-income and older residents of color in policy development [46] can further amplify marginalized populations' voice and highlight needs that are often neglected by current metrics for measuring quality of services.

While this study is limited to a small number of residents in one city in the US, we hope the experiences of Baltimore's residents reaffirm calls from prior researchers [27, 29] to pursue smart cities that create truly connected communities and create better futures for *all* residents.

Acknowledgments. This study was funded by the National Science Foundation, #1951924, SCC-IRG Track 1: Inclusive Public Transit Toolkit to Assess Quality of Service Across Socioeconomic Status in Baltimore City. We thank our partners at HABC and CMTA for helping coordinate data collection, as well as the residents who joined a focus group session.

References

1. Belanche-Gracia, D., et al.: Determinants of multi-service smartcard success for smart cities development: a study based on citizens' privacy and security perceptions. Gov. Inf. Q. **32**(2), 154–163 (2015). https://doi.org/10.1016/j.giq.2014.12.004
2. Braun, V., Clarke, V.: Using thematic analysis in psychology. Qual. Res. Psychol. **3**(2), 77–101 (2006). https://doi.org/10.1191/1478088706qp063oa
3. Brown, L.T.: The Black Butterfly: The Harmful Politics of Race and Space in America. JHU Press (2021)
4. Browne, S.: Dark Matters: On the Surveillance of Blackness. Duke University Press (2015)
5. Canon, G.: "City of surveillance": privacy expert quits Toronto's smart-city project (2018). https://www.theguardian.com/world/2018/oct/23/toronto-smart-city-surveillance-ann-cav oukian-resigns-privacy
6. Chatterjee, S., et al.: Alignment of IT authority and citizens of proposed smart cities in India: system security and privacy perspective. Glob. J. Flex. Syst. Manag. **19**(1), 95–107 (2018). https://doi.org/10.1007/s40171-017-0173-5
7. Chourabi, H., et al.: Understanding smart cities: an integrative framework. In: 2012 45th Hawaii International Conference on System Sciences, pp. 2289–2297 (2012). https://doi.org/10.1109/HICSS.2012.615
8. Cilliers, L., Flowerday, S.: Information security in a public safety, participatory crowdsourcing smart city project. In: World Congress on Internet Security (WorldCIS-2014), pp. 36–41 IEEE, London, United Kingdom (2014). https://doi.org/10.1109/WorldCIS.2014.7028163
9. City of Baltimore: 2018 Annual Report Baltimore City Office of Information and Technology (2019)
10. City of Baltimore, Maryland: B'Smart: Connecting Communities to Opportunities in Baltimore for a Safe, Efficient, Sustainable, Equitable and Economically Competitive Smart City (2016)
11. Emami-Naeini, P., et al.: Understanding people's concerns and attitudes toward smart cities. In: Proceedings of the 2023 CHI Conference on Human Factors in Computing Systems, pp. 1–24. ACM, Hamburg Germany (2023). https://doi.org/10.1145/3544548.3581558
12. Filion, P., et al.: Urban neoliberalism, smart city, and big tech: the aborted sidewalk labs Toronto experiment. J. Urban Aff. **45**(9), 1625–1643 (2023). https://doi.org/10.1080/073 52166.2022.2081171
13. Frias-Martinez, V., et al.: The BALTO toolkit - a new approach to ethical and sustainable data collection for equitable public transit. In: Proceedings of the 6th ACM SIGCAS/SIGCHI Conference on Computing and Sustainable Societies, pp. 129–133. ACM, Cape Town South Africa (2023). https://doi.org/10.1145/3588001.3609374
14. Glaeser, E.L., et al.: Decentralized Employment and the Transformation of the American City [with Comments]. Brookings-Wharton Papers on Urban Affairs, pp. 1–63 (2001)
15. Goldsmith, W., Blakely, E.: Separate Societies: Poverty and Inequality in U.S. Cities. Temple University Press (2010)
16. Greenfield, A.: Everyware: The Dawning Age of Ubiquitous Computing. New Riders (2010)
17. Harrison, C., et al.: Foundations for smarter cities. IBM J. Res. Dev. **54**(4), 1–16 (2010). https://doi.org/10.1147/JRD.2010.2048257
18. van Heek, J., et al.: "How fear of crime affects needs for privacy & safety": acceptance of surveillance technologies in smart cities. In: 2016 5th International Conference on Smart Cities and Green ICT Systems (SMARTGREENS), pp. 1–12. IEEE (2016)
19. Helbing, D., et al.: Ethics of smart cities: towards value-sensitive design and co-evolving city life. Sustainability **13**(20), 11162 (2021). https://doi.org/10.3390/su132011162

20. Henderson, L.J.: The Baltimore CitiStat Program. IBM Endowment for The Business of Government (2003)
21. Höjer, M., Wangel, J.: Smart sustainable cities: definition and challenges. In: Hilty, L.M., Aebischer, B. (eds.) ICT Innovations for Sustainability, pp. 333–349. Springer International Publishing, Cham (2015). https://doi.org/10.1007/978-3-319-09228-7_20
22. Iyer, S.: Lack of accessibility leads to high-commute time neighborhoods. https://medium.com/central-maryland-transportation-alliance/lack-of-accessibility-leads-to-high-commute-time-neighborhoods-28028c0f1197. Accessed 16 Sep 2023
23. Kaufman, S., et al.: Mobility, economic opportunity, and New York city neighborhoods (2014). https://papers.ssrn.com/abstract=2598566. https://doi.org/10.2139/ssrn.2598566
24. Kitchin, R.: Getting Smarter about Smart Cities: Improving Data Privacy and Data Security. Department of the Taoiseach on behalf of the Government Data Forum (2016)
25. Kitchin, R.: Reframing, reimagining, and remaking smart cities. In: Creating Smart Cities. Routledge (2018)
26. Kitchin, R.: The real-time city? Big data and smart urbanism. GeoJournal **79**(1), 1–14 (2014). https://doi.org/10.1007/s10708-013-9516-8
27. König, P.D.: Citizen-centered data governance in the smart city: from ethics to accountability. Sustain. Cities Soc. **75**, 103308 (2021). https://doi.org/10.1016/j.scs.2021.103308
28. Lung-Amam, W., et al.: Smart cities, connected communities: Using Technology to Meet the Needs of West Baltimore Residents. (2018)
29. Lung-Amam, W., et al.: Toward Engaged, Equitable, and Smart Communities: Lessons From West Baltimore. Housing Policy Debate, pp. 1–19 (2021). https://doi.org/10.1080/10511482.2019.1672082
30. Madden, M., et al.: Privacy, poverty, and big data: matrix of vulnerabilities for poor Americans. Washington Univ. Law Rev. **95**(1), 53–126 (2017)
31. Mann, M., et al.: #BlockSidewalk to Barcelona: technological sovereignty and the social license to operate smart cities. J. Am. Soc. Inf. Sci. **71**(9), 1103–1115 (2020). https://doi.org/10.1002/asi.24387
32. Mark, R., Anya, G.: Ethics of using smart city AI and big data: the case of four large European cities. ORBIT J. **2**(2), 1–36 (2019). https://doi.org/10.29297/orbit.v2i2.110
33. Miles, M.B., et al.: Qualitative Data Analysis: A Methods Sourcebook. SAGE Publications Inc, Los Angeles London New Delhi Singapore Washington DC Melbourne (2019)
34. Mohanty, S.P., et al.: Everything you wanted to know about smart cities: the Internet of things is the backbone. IEEE Consum. Electron. Mag. **5**(3), 60–70 (2016). https://doi.org/10.1109/MCE.2016.2556879
35. Morozov, E.: To Save Everything, Click Here: The Folly of Technological Solutionism. PublicAffairs (2013)
36. Noble, S.U.: Algorithms of Oppression: How Search Engines Reinforce Racism. In: Algorithms of Oppression. New York University Press (2018). https://doi.org/10.18574/nyu/9781479833641.001.0001
37. Nuworsoo, C., et al.: Analyzing equity impacts of transit fare changes: case study of alameda-contra costa Transit, California. Eval. Program Plann. **32**(4), 360–368 (2009). https://doi.org/10.1016/j.evalprogplan.2009.06.009
38. Saldaña, J.: The Coding Manual for Qualitative Researchers. Sage Publications Ltd, Los Angeles, London (2015)
39. Saunders, B., et al.: Saturation in qualitative research: exploring its conceptualization and operationalization. Qual. Quant. **52**(4), 1893–1907 (2018). https://doi.org/10.1007/s11135-017-0574-8
40. Sourbati, M., Behrendt, F.: Smart mobility, age, and data justice. New Media Soc. **23**(6), 1398–1414 (2021). https://doi.org/10.1177/1461444820902682

41. Townsend, A.M.: Smart Cities: Big Data, Civic Hackers, and the Quest for a New Utopia. W. W. Norton & Company (2013)

42. Turner Lee, N.: Detecting racial bias in algorithms and machine learning. J. Inf. Commun. Ethics Soc. **16**(3), 252–260 (2018). https://doi.org/10.1108/JICES-06-2018-0056

43. U.S. Census Bureau: QuickFacts: Baltimore city, Maryland. https://www.census.gov/quickfacts/fact/table/baltimorecitymaryland/PST045222. Accessed 16 Sep 2023

44. Vitak, J., et al.: 'I Knew It Was Too Good to Be True": the challenges economically disadvantaged internet users face in assessing trustworthiness, avoiding scams, and developing self-efficacy online. In: Proceedings of the ACM on Human-Computer Interaction 2(CSCW), pp. 1–25 (2018). https://doi.org/10.1145/3274445

45. van Zoonen, L.: Privacy concerns in smart cities. Gov. Inf. Q. **33**(3), 472–480 (2016). https://doi.org/10.1016/j.giq.2016.06.004

46. Baltimore City's Digital Inclusion Stragtegy 2024–2029. Baltimore City Office of Information and Technology (2023)

47. Mayor Scott, BCIT Release Five-Year Plan to Address the City's Digital Divide. Office of Broadband and Digital Equity (2023)

Enhancing Ethical Governance of Artificial Intelligence Through Dynamic Feedback Mechanism

Yaqi Liu$^{(\boxtimes)}$, Wenjie Zheng , and Yueli Su

Zhongnan University of Economics and Law, Wuhan, China
liuyaqi@zuel.edu.cn, {202211200036,202211200039}@stu.zuel.edu.cn

Abstract. The rapid advancement of Artificial Intelligence (AI) has ushered in significant opportunities while also giving rise to profound ethical concerns. Governments, non-governmental organizations, research institutions, and industries worldwide have fervently engaged in the exploration and implementation of AI ethics. This work reviews the research and practice of AI ethical governance issues worldwide, with a particular emphasis on AI ethics legislation and the practical application of ethical principles. Within the current landscape of AI ethics governance research, several pressing challenges emerge, including the establishment of a robust ethical decision-making framework, the integration of ethical principles into AI systems, and the formulation of guiding legal policies. Based on an extensive analysis of existing AI ethics governance theories and technological research, this study presents an innovative conceptual framework rooted in dynamic feedback reinforcement learning theory. This pioneering framework, cultivated through the collaboration of multiple stakeholders, encompasses various dimensions encompassing law, technology, and market dynamics. Additionally, it establishes an AI ethics governance committee tasked with supervising the behavior of AI systems, guiding their acquisition of ethical principles, and adapting to the ever-evolving environment. The overarching objective of this collaborative, multi-faceted AI ethics governance framework is to serve as a reference point for global AI ethics governance mechanisms and to promote the sustainable development of the AI industry. By taking into account legal, technological, and market factors, our aim is to facilitate a harmonious interaction between technology, humanity, and society, ultimately paving the way for a healthy and inclusive intelligent society.

Keywords: Artificial Intelligence Ethics · Ethical Governance ·
Artificial Intelligence Governance Framework · Feedback Reinforcement Learning

1 Introduction

In recent years, Artificial Intelligence (AI) has rapidly developed under the joint driving forces of algorithms, computing power, and data, becoming an impor-

I. Sserwanga et al. (Eds.): iConference 2024, LNCS 14598, pp. 105–121, 2024.
https://doi.org/10.1007/978-3-031-57867-0_8

tant driving force for the economy and society. Although AI is widely applied in finance, education, healthcare, and other fields, it has also raised ethical risks and challenges from different dimensions, such as biases and discrimination, lack of transparency in algorithms, privacy issues of training data, and safety and responsibility concerns in the clinical environment of AI application. Therefore, establishing governance mechanisms to ensure the reliable and secure development of AI has become an urgent issue.

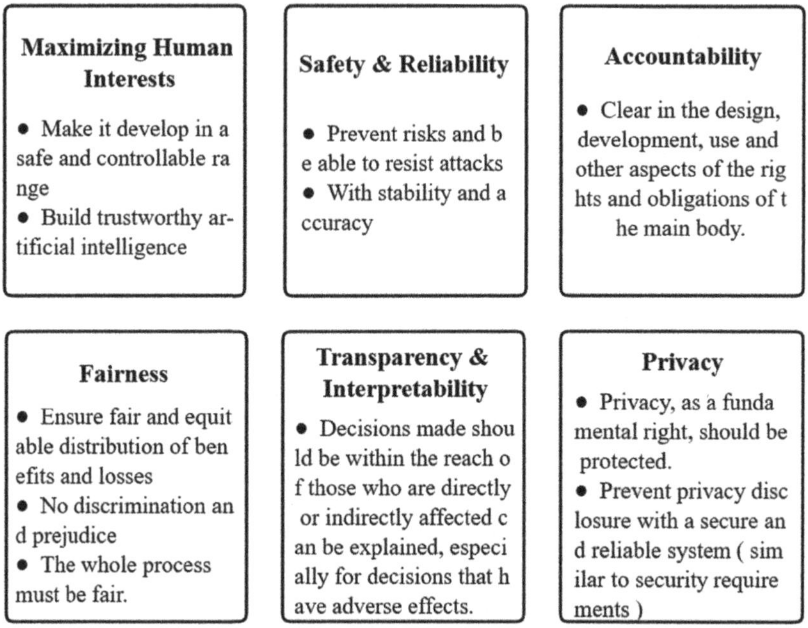

Maximizing Human Interests

- Make it develop in a safe and controllable range
- Build trustworthy artificial intelligence

Safety & Reliability

- Prevent risks and be able to resist attacks
- With stability and accuracy

Accountability

- Clear in the design, development, use and other aspects of the rights and obligations of the main body.

Fairness

- Ensure fair and equitable distribution of benefits and losses
- No discrimination and prejudice
- The whole process must be fair.

Transparency & Interpretability

- Decisions made should be within the reach of those who are directly or indirectly affected can be explained, especially for decisions that have adverse effects.

Privacy

- Privacy, as a fundamental right, should be protected.
- Prevent privacy disclosure with a secure and reliable system (similar to security requirements)

Fig. 1. Common goals of principles related to ethical governance of AI

Global stakeholders are increasingly concerned about ethical issues related to AI, and governments, non-governmental organizations, and companies have issued policies and recommendations to encourage the formulation of ethical guidelines and standards. International organizations such as IEEE [26], OECD [30], and the Future of Life Institute [21], as well as countries like the European Union [24], the United States [7], and the United Kingdom [5], have proposed relevant principles and policy documents. Tech companies such as Google [33], Microsoft [6], IBM [1], Baidu [22], and Tencent [28] have also taken various measures to promote AI ethics research and practice. Annex 1 lists representative international AI ethics principles. Upon analyzing the published AI ethical principles, our findings indicate a consensus among global AI ethics standards in key domains such as "maximizing human interests," "safety and reliability" "privacy," "fairness," "transparency and explainability," and "accountability." These aligning standards are depicted in Fig. 1.

As for the topic of AI ethics governance, scholars are committed to integrating theories and models from different fields to provide solutions for AI ethics governance. They research how to enable machines to engage in moral learning to make ethical decisions. AI ethics governance technologies are divided into two directions: one is to conduct ethical assessment and supervision of AI systems throughout the process, and the other is to enable the system to engage in moral learning during the algorithm execution stage through moral coding or training.

Currently, AI ethics governance research faces three major challenges: establishing a reliable ethical decision-making framework and addressing the insufficiency of embedding ethical principles and legal policies. Based on analyzing existing guidelines, policies, and practices, this work constructs a conceptual framework of AI ethics governance through collaborative efforts among law, technology, and the market. The aim is to provide references for global AI ethics governance mechanisms, promote the sustainable development of the global AI industry, facilitate a healthy and inclusive interaction among technology, society, and humans, and build a smart society that is beneficial for all.

2 The Status of Global AI Ethical Governance

2.1 AI Governance Policy

The formulation and standardization of ethical regulations and policies related to AI lag behind technological development. However, since 2016, global attention to the ethical and legal issues of AI has gradually increased, and relevant initiatives, standards, and regulations have been continuously introduced. In this process, the European Union, the United States, and China are the most typical representatives.

The EU attaches great importance to the construction of AI ethics. As early as January 2015, a working group specializing in the development of robots and AI was established. After that, the EU successively issued the "Draft Report with Recommendations to the Commission on Civil Law Rules on Robotics" and the "European Civil Law Rules in Robotics" [43]. In February 2017, the EU Parliament passed the world's first "Civil Law Rules on Robotics" [2], actively exploring civil legislation on robots and AI. In October 2020, the European Parliament passed a proposal on the regulation of AI and plans to propose an "Artificial Intelligence Act" in the first half of 2021 [25]. In addition, the Ad Hoc Committee on AI of the European Council issued a feasibility study report on the legal standards of AI, and proposed a legal framework for AI composed of European Council instruments [31].

The AI policy of the United States focuses on complying with the general trend of vigorous development of technology. The United States has passed legislation in some key areas, such as "SELF DRIVE ACT" [3] and "AV START ACT" [4] in the field of autonomous driving. In addition, California has passed a number of laws related to personal information protection and formulated a series of laws to solve the problem of discriminatory bias in the algorithm [40].

The United States has also developed AI employment-related bills to address the challenges posed by AI to employment.

China has also begun to pay attention to the ethical issues of AI, and has included related legislative projects in the five-year legislative plan. The "New Generation of Artificial Intelligence Development Plan" has set development goals for AI ethics and laws, and issued relevant guiding documents. China's National Information Security Standardization Technical Committee has also issued guidelines on the prevention of ethical security risks of AI.

In general, the EU focuses on formulating strict ethical norms and laws to constrain the development of AI, while the United States focuses on market access and security, ethical risk prevention and control mechanisms, and China prefers strict policies and regulations to regulate the development and application of AI.

2.2 AI Regulatory Practice

Under the background of the release of policies and principles, various countries have made much progress in the field of AI governance and supervision in view of the application practice of domestic AI technology. The EU has long been committed to AI governance. In 2020 and 2021, the "White Paper on Artificial Intelligence" [16] issued by the European Parliament and the Council on the development of uniform rules on AI (AI law) and the revision of certain EU legislation ', mandatory regulatory requirements for high-risk AI systems, and a clear distinction between 'prohibitive AI' and 'high-risk AI'. The German Electrical and Electronic Information Technology Commission and the German Ministry of Economic Affairs and Energy released the AI standardization roadmap in November 2020, and further proposed the "AI application evaluation pyramid". According to the AI application risk level, from top to bottom, it is set to the fifth level to the first level. Among them, the fifth level is the highest risk level, and the regulatory requirements are completely or partially prohibited. The first level with low risk has no special requirements, and the remaining AI applications belong to the scope of key supervision. According to the risk level of the level, measures such as adding real-time interface and adding pre-approval procedures are taken to strengthen supervision.

Unlike other countries, in addition to laws and regulations, Japan and Singapore rely more on industry self-discipline and empowerment of enterprises. Japan has taken a slightly different path from European and American countries in the ethical supervision of AI [29], that is, focusing on not increasing the cost of the enterprise system and not damaging the enthusiasm of technology research and development, and guiding enterprises to prevent ethical accidents through the principles and guidelines of the nature of soft law, so as to achieve the purpose of maintaining social value and promoting technological development. Japan's [29] AI ethical supervision can be divided into principle layer, rule layer, supervision layer and law enforcement layer from the institutional framework. Among them, the principle layer sets the goal of ethical supervision of AI, the rule layer clarifies the path to achieve the above goals, the supervision layer guides the enterprise to self-regulate, and the law enforcement layer pursues responsibility for violations. Japan's design of each layer of content can be said to consciously follow the idea of government setting goals, enterprise independent norms, and multi-subject participation in governance. Following the guiding principle of "AI decision-making can be explained, transparent and fair, and artificial intelligence system should be people-oriented," Singapore has issued a series of operational guidelines such as "AI governance demonstration framework" and "organization implementation and self-assessment guide" [8], which help enterprises ' AI governance practice move from principle to practice.

3 Theoretical Practice of AI Ethical Governance

AI ethics is an emerging field of ethical research dedicated to exploring ethical issues related to the development, deployment, and use of AI. In this field, scholars have proposed various conceptual frameworks and technical theories aimed at addressing AI ethics governance issues.

3.1 AI Ethical Governance Frameworks

Many scholars have attempted to integrate theories and models from different fields to provide solutions for AI ethics governance. Iyad Rahwan [34] introduced the "Society-in-the-Loop" (SITL) governance framework, which combines the "human-in-the-loop" (HITL) concept with social contract theory to balance stakeholder interests and oversee the implementation of ethical principles. This approach emphasizes human involvement in decision-making processes. Thomas Arnold and Matthias Scheutz [44] developed a testing framework within a virtual environment to evaluate the behavior of intelligent agents while ensuring minimal interference with system operation. This testing framework focuses on assessing AI behavior. Martin Abrams et al. [9] took a classical ethics approach by integrating consequentialism and non-consequentialism into organizational frameworks. Their work emphasizes ethical guidelines as an integral part of AI governance. Dorian et al. [32] proposed two frameworks to translate ethical principles into actionable strategies for addressing ethical issues in AI engineering practice. Their approach aims to bridge the gap between ethical principles and practical implementation. Reddy et al. [35] introduced a governance model tailored to the healthcare sector, regulating the introduction and implementation of AI models. This framework addresses the specific ethical challenges within healthcare AI. Ashok et al. [11] proposed an ontological framework that conceptualizes the ethical impact of AI on digital technologies and maps digital ethical principles to different digital technology prototypes. Ienca et al. [27] put forth a comprehensive global governance framework to facilitate the use of brain data in neuroscience and medicine, emphasizing the ethical aspects of data usage in these fields. These frameworks and models in AI ethics governance, setting the stage for our contribution, a conceptual framework of governance based on dynamic feedback, which offers a novel approach to address emerging challenges in AI ethics governance.

3.2   AI Ethical Supervision and Evaluation Procedures

Scholars are dedicated to designing full-process assessment and supervision procedures to ensure that AI systems comply with ethical principles. These efforts primarily focus on key issues and principles such as safety, transparency, interpretability, and fairness.

In terms of ensuring the safety and controllability of AI systems, the "big red button" is one approach that guarantees system safety by establishing an emergency stop mechanism. Riedl [37] utilized this theory but also proposed a grid-world-based model to avoid the problem of system manipulation with the button. Orseau and Armstrong [10] introduced the concept of "Interruptibility", enabling operators to interrupt the system while still allowing the system to make optimal decisions. Thomas Arnold and Matthias Scheutz [44] constructed an Ethical Core (EC) testing system based on a simulation environment, but it remains at the theoretical level.

To enhance the interpretability of AI systems, there are two main approaches [18]: model-centric explanations [38] and topic-centric explanations. The former aims to provide known information about algorithms, such as the DeepLIFT [42] and LRP [12] algorithms, as well as leveraging attention mechanisms and knowledge graphs to achieve interpretabilit [41,45] of recommendation models. The latter focuses on understanding the reasons behind the system's decision-making, using modular methods such as LIME [36], S-LIME [46], ALIME [39], and ILIME [19].

Ensuring fairness in AI systems mainly involves data sampling, reweighting [20], individual data record alteration [23], transformation of given datasets [15], and automatic compensation rewards [10] to mitigate data bias. Additionally, Google's What-If Tool and IBM's AI Fair 360 Toolkit can be used to evaluate and diagnose the fairness of models.

3.3   AI Moral Learning Program Design

With the development of machine learning algorithms, AI moral learning programs have evolved from static designated learning to dynamic update learning and feedback learning. Static designated learning represents ethical principles through logical rules, enabling the system to statically learn these principles and measure the degree to which instructions satisfy or violate ethical ethics through decision procedure [14].

Dynamic update learning allows the system to learn new ethical principles and update them. This can be achieved by training neural networks for learning new ethical scenarios, or by using Bayesian learning to update the ethical objective function for ethical decision-making [10].

Feedback learning enables the system to dynamically learn ethical principles and automatically adjust ethical levels according to the application environment.

This can be achieved through reinforcement learning to maximize ethical utility [17], or by incorporating value constraints to improve accuracy and automation in dealing with different environments and ethical dilemmas [13].

In conclusion, research on AI ethical governance is still in its developmental stage, lacking a comprehensive system study. Currently, it mainly focuses on key issues and principles, but the satisfaction of multiple ethical principles is one of the requirements for trustworthy AI. The feedback learning model increases the consideration of the changes in the application environment. Moral learning is more automated, and the ability to adjust moral decisions and behaviors with the environment is stronger.

4   The Proposed Framework

This work begins by conducting fundamental theoretical research on the definition of AI ethics. Subsequently, it summarizes the common ethical norms of AI worldwide and the main challenges and practical requirements within the governance process, which helps to improve the legal, regulatory and policy framework of AI globally. The study then constructs an AI ethical governance framework based on the theory of dynamic feedback reinforcement learning. This involves designing an ethical algorithm procedure, an ethical evaluation procedure, an ethical update procedure, and an ethical responsibility traceability procedure to guide the ethical decision-making of agents. Additionally, a dynamic feedback mechanism is introduced to establish a multi-party collaborative framework for AI ethical governance, encompassing the fields of law, technology, and the market, as shown in Fig. 2.

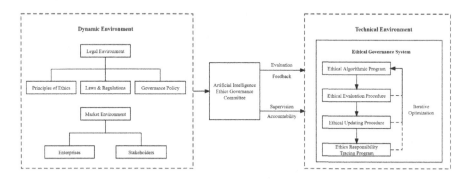

Fig. 2. AI ethical governance framework diagram

4.1 Theoretical Guidance

This work is constructed upon foundational ethical theories such as deontology, the principles of bioethics, and utilitarianism, while also incorporating the theory of reinforcement learning from applied behaviorist psychology. The framework fully considers the establishment of human control and management over the ethics of intelligent agents. It follows a process that involves human definition, the learning of ethics principles by intelligent agents, dynamic environmental feedback, and the updating of ethics principles. By establishing the theory of dynamic feedback reinforcement learning, the framework practically applies ethical principles to the sequential decision-making of intelligent agents. These principles are integrated into the agents through the design of a reward function. The ethical level is adjusted based on the evaluation feedback from the dynamic and uncertain environment. This iterative process of updating the reward function creates a model for learning ethical principles based on dynamic feedback reinforcement learning.

4.2 Construction of Legislative System

This work thoroughly examines the principles, theories and governance models of AI ethical governance across government agencies, public welfare organizations, and enterprises such as the European Union and the United States. And by analyzing the research status of AI algorithm governance, it is pointed out that there are numerous ethical challenges arising from the development of AI algorithms. This aids in forming a comprehensive and precise comprehension of the potential ethical risks linked with AI, as well as the pragmatic necessities for ethical governance during this phase of AI advancement. Additionally, it furnishes references for global AI ethics governance mechanisms and advocates for the sustainable development of the global AI industry. Furthermore, this work constructs scientifically grounded, universally applicable, and actionable AI ethical norms. It also establishes a legal framework and governance policy system as a foundation for the implementation of AI ethical governance.

4.3 Technology Governance System

The AI ethics governance system model is based on the dynamic feedback reinforcement learning model, and proposes innovation for the governance framework of AI ethics. In the model system, the agent is continuously iteratively optimized with the feedback of the dynamic environment, and finally makes an optimal strategy in this environment. It includes ethical learning algorithm procedures, ethical feedback evaluation procedures, ethical update procedures, and ethical responsibility traceability procedures.

Ethical Algorithm Program: In the reinforcement learning framework, the reward function update strategy is needed in the construction and operation of AI autonomous system. We need to embed agents in the form of reward functions according to the current state of artificial intelligence ethical principles, policies and regulations. Firstly, the AI ethical principles are quantified into specific values to measure the degree to which the system conforms to ethics, and a reasonable method is used to evaluate the ethical utility of a single AI ethical principle. After summarizing the ethical action set, the moral utility of each action is evaluated and the reward function is designed according to the quantified AI principle. The objective function is to guide the ethical decision of the agent in this program. When the agent completes the sequential decision, the objective function will call the maximum reward value in the reward function to make the most ethical decision.

Ethical Evaluation Procedure: This procedure conducts ethical evaluation of agent's decision-making. In this procedure, the agent interacts with the dynamic environment continuously. In the process of considering ethical integration, the agent is in a dynamic environment involving legal environment and market environment. The legal environment includes continuously updated and improved policies and regulations related to AI ethics. The market environment includes ethical considerations with enterprises and stakeholders throughout the process. The program stores the results of each trial and error of the agent, including decision-making actions and reward values, and provides them to the AI ethics governance committee for qualitative or quantitative evaluation feedback.

Ethical Update Procedure: In the process of learning the ethical principles of agents, according to the evaluation feedback results, this procedure constantly updates the reward function established by iterative ethical principles learning, performs optimal decision transformation in the objective function, and continuously takes the maximum reward value in the reward function to maximize the ethical utility of AI.

Ethical Responsibility Traceability Procedure: This procedure stores the objective function, reward function and feedback of the agent's decision-making. When there are relevant ethical conflicts, responsibilities and rights claims, it traces relevant responsibilities and seeks corrective measures.

4.4   AI Ethical Governance Framework

Based on an in-depth analysis of both domestic and foreign policies, domestic resources, systems, and businesses, this work presents a multi-faceted collaborative framework for ethical governance in AI that integrates legal, technological, and market perspectives.

In the realm of law, this framework endeavors to establish comprehensive guidelines and practical applications for AI ethical norms by constructing legal rules, regulations, and codes of conduct. Ethical transgressions are to be assessed, monitored, and held accountable through the oversight of the AI Ethical Governance Committee.

On the technological front, the model for the AI ethical governance system is rooted in dynamic feedback reinforcement learning theory. This approach ensures that ethical principles evolve in response to dynamic environmental feedback, fostering the development of responsible and socially acceptable AI systems and products.

Within the market domain, we aim to activate a proactive response from various social stakeholders, including individuals and organizations directly or indirectly impacted by AI. We seek to cultivate an ethical culture surrounding AI and foster collective engagement in its ethical oversight and governance.

To ensure the effective implementation of AI ethical governance, the governance framework incorporates several key elements. The AI Ethical Governance Committee assumes a central role by providing theoretical guidance for the development and deployment of AI. Furthermore, this framework establishes essential ethical governance mechanisms, including a supervisory system, an evaluation system, a feedback system, and an accountability system.

5   Conclusions

Despite the globally agreed-upon AI ethical guidelines, they are insufficient to address various ethical challenges due to the continuous changes in society and technology. Thus, we emphasize the importance of developing specific governance guidelines based on different AI application scenarios. The proposed multidimensional conceptual framework of AI ethical governance framework based on dynamic feedback reinforcement learning holds significant potential. Through feedback learning, the system can automatically adjust its ethical level in different environments, better adapting to diverse ethical requirements. This framework contributes to promoting collaborative governance among law, technology, and the market, thereby achieving sustainable development of AI.

Acknowledgement. This paper is supported by "the Fundamental Research Funds for the Central Universities", Zhongnan University of Economics and Law (202451406).

Appendix Overview of Major AI Ethical Guidelines

See Tables 1, 2, 3, 4 and 5.

Table 1. Ethical Guidelines for Representative Artificial Intelligence in International Organizations

Publishing organization or institution	Report title	Publication date	Key ethical principles
Future of Life	Asilomar AI Principles	2017.08	Safety, transparency of failures, transparency of judgments, responsibility, alignment with human values, privacy protection, respect for freedom, sharing of benefits, common prosperity, human control, non-subversion, and prohibition of AI arms race
IEEE	White Paper - Ethically Aligned Design - A Vision for Prioritizing Human Well-being with Autonomous and Intelligent Systems	2019.03	Human rights, well-being, accountability, transparency
HLEG AI	Ethics Guidelines for Trustworthy AI	2019.04	Agency and oversight of individuals, safety, privacy data management, transparency, inclusiveness, social well-being, accountability mechanisms
EU	On Artificial Intelligence-A European approach to excellence and trust	2020.02	Human-centric, ethical, sustainable development, respect for fundamental rights and values
OECD	OECD AI Principles overview	2019.05	Inclusive growth, sustainable development, and well-being; values of human-centeredness and fairness; transparency and explainability; robustness and safety reliability; and responsibility
UNESCO	Recommendation on the Ethics of Artificial Intelligence	2021.11	Proportionality and non-harmfulness, safety and security, fairness and non-discrimination, sustainability, privacy rights and data protection, human supervision and decision-making, transparency and explainability, responsibility and accountability, awareness and literacy

Table 2. Ethical Guidelines for Representative Artificial Intelligence in Government Organizations

Publishing organization or institution	Report title	Publication date	Key ethical principles
Japan	Social Principles of Human-centric AI (Draft)	2018.12	Human-centered, educational applications, privacy protection, security assurance, fair competition, fairness, accountability, transparency, innovation
USA	AI Principles: Recommendations on the Ethical Use of Artificial Intelligence by the Department of Defense	2019.1	Responsible, fair, traceable, reliable, controllable
USA	Guidance for Regulation of Artificial Intelligence Applications	2020.01	Public trust, public participation, research integrity and data quality, risk assessment and management, benefits and costs, flexibility, fairness and non-discrimination, transparency, security, cross-department coordination
UK	AI in the UK: Ready, Willing and Able?	2018.04	Serve the common interests and well-being of humanity, comprehensibility and fairness, not undermine citizens' rights and privacy, all citizens have the right to receive AI-related education, not harm, destroy, or deceive humanity
China	Governance Principles for the New Generation Artificial Intelligence–Developing Responsible Artificial Intelligence	2019.06	Harmony and friendliness, fairness and justice, inclusiveness and sharing, respect for privacy, safety and controllability, shared responsibility, open collaboration, agile governance
China	Ethical Norms for New Generation Artificial Intelligence	2021.09	Promote human well-being, foster fairness and justice, protect privacy and security, ensure controllability and trustworthiness, strengthen responsibility, enhance ethical literacy

Table 3. The representative ethical principles of artificial intelligence in colleges and universities

Publishing organization or institution	Report title	Publication date	Key ethical principles
Tsinghua University	Principles and Pivots of Artificial Intelligence Governance	2018.07	Welfare, security, sharing, peace, rule of law, cooperation
University of Montreal	The Montréal Declaration for a Responsible Development of Artificial Intelligence	2018.12	Happiness, respect for autonomy, protection of privacy and intimacy, solidarity, democratic participation, fairness, diversity, inclusion, prudence, responsibility, sustainable development
President of the Pontifical Academy for Life, President of Microsoft, IBM Executive Vice President, FAO Director-General Minister, Italian Minister of Innovation	Rome Call for AI Ethic	2020.02	Transparency, inclusiveness, responsibility, impartiality, reliability, security and privacy

Table 4. The representative ethical principles of artificial intelligence in private enterprises

Publishing organization or institution	Report title	Publication date	Key ethical principles
Microsoft	The Future Computed: Artificial Intelligence and its role in society	2018.01	Fair, inclusive, transparent, responsible, reliable, and secure, privacy and confidentiality
IBM	IBMs Principles for Trust and Transparency	2018.05	AI assists rather than replaces humans. Transparency is needed, and citizens and workers require education and training to use AI products and services
Baidu	Four principles of AI ethics	2018.05	Security and controllability promote equal access to technology and capabilities for humanity. Artificial intelligence teaches people to learn and grow, bringing more freedom and possibilities to humanity
Google	AI at Google: our principles	2018.06	Beneficial to society, avoiding or exacerbating unfair biases, ensuring security in development and testing, being responsible to humanity, establishing and embodying principles of privacy protection, supporting and encouraging high standards of technological integrity, and providing and ensuring the feasibility of the aforementioned principles

continued

Table 4. continued

Publishing organization or institution	Report title	Publication date	Key ethical principles
Tencent	The technical ethics of the intelligent era-reshaping the trust of the digital society	2019.06	Trust in technology (availability, reliability, verifiability, and controllability), individual well-being, and social sustainability
PHILIPS	Five Guiding Principles for the Responsible Use of Artificial Intelligence in Healthcare and Healthy Living	2020.01	Well-being, supervision, robustness, fairness, transparency
Jingdong Exploration Research Institute & China Institute of Information and Communications	Trusted Artificial Intelligence White Paper	2021.07	Reliable and controllable, transparent and explainable, data protection, clear responsibility, diversity and inclusiveness

Table 5. The representative ethical principles of artificial intelligence in industry association

Publishing organization or institution	Report title	Publication date	Key ethical principles
Association for Computing Machinery US Public Policy Council (USACM)	Statement on Algorithmic Transparency and Accountability	2017.05	Transparency and accountability
Amnesty International, Access Now	The Toronto Declaration: Protecting the right to equality and non-discrimination in machine learning systems	2018.05	Fairness, impartiality, transparency, reducing discrimination, equality

continued

Table 5. continued

Publishing organization or institution	Report title	Publication date	Key ethical principles
Consejo Argentino para las Relaciones Internacionales (CARI)	Towards a G20 Framework For Artificial Intelligence in the Workplace	2018	Trust, security, adaptation to needs, privacy
Beijing Academy of Artificial Intelligence (BAAI)	Beijing AI Principles	2019.05	Artificial intelligence should be beneficial and responsible
Chinese AI Alliance	Joint Pledge on Artificial Intelligence Industry Self-Discipline	2019.06	Fairness, human-centered, avoiding harm, safety and controllability, transparency and explainability
BEUC(The European consumer organisation)	Ai Rights For Consumers	2019.1	Right to Transparency, Explanation, and Objection - Right to Accountability and Control - Right to Fairness - Right to Non-discrimination - Right to Safety and Security - Right to Access to Justice - Right to Reliability and Robustness
Bosch	Bosch code of ethics for AI	2020.02	Secure and interpretable artificial intelligence products
Data Science and Ethics Group	A Framework For The Ethical Use Of Advanced Data Science Methods In The Humanitarian Sector	2020.04	Regarding responsible and ethical data collection and usage, data protection, humanitarian innovation, and humanitarian principles and standards

References

1. IBM policy. https://www.ibm.com/blogs/policy/trust-principles/. Accessed 16 Sept 2023
2. Texts adopted - civil law rules on robotics. https://www.europarl.europa.eu/doceo/document/TA-8-2017-0051_EN.html?redirect. Accessed 4 Jan 2024
3. H.R.3388 - safely ensuring lives future deployment and research in vehicle evolution act, September 2017. https://www.congress.gov/bill/115th-congress/house-bill/3388. Accessed 4 Jan 2024
4. S.1885 - AV START act, November 2017. https://www.congress.gov/bill/115th-congress/senate-bill/1885. Accessed 4 Jan 2024
5. AI in the UK: ready, willing and able? (2018). https://publications.parliament.uk/pa/ld201719/ldselect/ldai/100/10004.htm. Accessed 16 Sept 2023
6. The Future Computed: Artificial Intelligence and Its Role in Society. Independently Published, Washington (2018)
7. AI principles: Recommendations on the ethical use of artificial intelligence by the department of defense (2020). https://admin.govexec.com/media/dib_ai_principles_-_supporting_document_-_embargoed_copy_(oct_2019).pdf. Accessed 16 Sept 2023

8. Singapore launches world's first AI testing framework and toolkit to promote transparency; invites companies to pilot and contribute to international standards development, May 2022. https://www.imda.gov.sg/resources/press-releases-factsheets-and-speeches/press-releases/2022/sg-launches-worlds-first-ai-testing-framework-and-toolkit-to-promote-transparency. Accessed 4 Jan 2024

9. Abrams, M., Abrams, J., Cullen, P., Goldstein, L.: Artificial intelligence, ethics, and enhanced data stewardship. IEEE Secur. Priv. **17**(2), 17–30 (2019)

10. Armstrong, S.: Motivated value selection for artificial. In: Workshops at the Twenty-Ninth AAAI Conference on Artificial Intelligence (2015)

11. Ashok, M., Madan, R., Joha, A., Sivarajah, U.: Ethical framework for artificial intelligence and digital technologies. Int. J. Inf. Manage. **62**(102433), 102433 (2022)

12. Bach, S., Binder, A., Montavon, G., Klauschen, F., Müller, K.R., Samek, W.: On pixel-wise explanations for non-linear classifier decisions by layer-wise relevance propagation. PLoS ONE **10**(7), e0130140 (2015)

13. Balakrishnan, A., Bouneffouf, D., Mattei, N., Rossi, F.: Incorporating behavioral constraints in online AI systems. Proc. Conf. AAAI Artif. Intell. **33**(01), 3–11 (2019)

14. Briggs, G.M., Scheutz, M.: Sorry, I can't do that: developing mechanisms to appropriately reject directives in human-robot. In: AAAI Fall Symposia, pp. 32–36 (2015)

15. Calmon, F.P., Wei, D., Ramamurthy, K.N., Varshney, K.R.: Optimized data preprocessing for discrimination prevention (2017)

16. European Commission: White paper on artificial intelligence: a European approach to excellence and trust, February 2020. https://ec.europa.eu/futurium/en/system/files/ged/white_paper_ai_19_02_2020.pdf. Accessed 5 Jan 2024

17. David, A., James, M., Michael, L.L.: Reinforcement learning as a framework for ethical decision making. In: The Workshops of the Thirtieth AAAI Conference on Artificial Intelligence Providence, pp. 54–61 (2016)

18. Edwards, L., Veale, M.: Slave to the algorithm: why a right to an explanation is probably not the remedy you are looking for. Duke Law Technol. Rev. (18) (2017)

19. ElShawi, R., Sherif, Y., Al-Mallah, M., Sakr, S.: ILIME: local and global interpretable model-agnostic explainer of black-box decision. In: Welzer, T., Eder, J., Podgorelec, V., Kamišalić Latifić, A. (eds.) ADBIS 2019. LNCS, vol. 11695, pp. 53–68. Springer, Cham (2019). https://doi.org/10.1007/978-3-030-28730-6_4

20. Friedler, S.A., Scheidegger, C., Venkatasubramanian, S.: A comparative study of fairness-enhancing interventions in machine learning. In: Proceedings of the Conference on Fairness, Accountability, and Transparency, pp. 329–338 (2019)

21. Future of Life: AI principles, August 2017. https://futureoflife.org/ai-principles/. Accessed 16 Sept 2023

22. Haitao, G.: How did Chinese internet enterprises participate in internet governance-a case study based on Baidu, Alibaba and Tencent (bat). J. Commun. **28**(53–69+127) (2021)

23. Hajian, S.: Simultaneous discrimination prevention and privacy protection in data publishing and mining (2013)

24. High-Level Expert Group on Artificial Intelligence: Ethics guidelines for trustworthy AI. European Commission (2019)

25. Huang, L., Yan, H.: CICC: the EU is concerned about the impact on the development path of AI through legislative initiatives, November 2020. https://www.sohu.com/a/431693843_463913. Accessed 4 Jan 2024

26. IEEE: Ethically Aligned Design: A Vision for Prioritizing Human Well-being with Autonomous and Intelligent Systems, November 2017. Accessed 16 Sept 2023

27. Ienca, M., et al.: Towards a governance framework for brain data. Neuroethics **15**(2) (2022)
28. Tencent AI Lab: Technology ethics in the intelligent era - reshaping trust in the digital society, July 2019. https://www.tisi.org/10890. Accessed 16 Sept 2023
29. Liu, X., Xiao, H.: Ethical governance of artificial intelligence in the soft law paradigm: an analysis of the Japanese institution. Contemp. Econ. Japan **04**(28–44) (2023). https://doi.org/10.16123/j.cnki.issn.1000-355x.2023.04.003
30. OECD: AI-principles overview, May 2019. https://www.oecd.ai/ai-principles. Accessed 16 Sept 2023
31. Peets, L., Hansen, M., Choi, S.J., Drake, M.: The council of Europe publishes feasibility study on developing a legal instrument for ethical AI, January 2021. https://www.insideprivacy.com/artificial-intelligence/the-council-of-europe-publishes-feasibility-study-on-developing-a-legal-instrument-for-ethical-ai/. Accessed 4 Jan 2024
32. Peters, D., Vold, K., Robinson, D., Calvo, R.A.: Responsible AI–two frameworks for ethical design practice. IEEE Trans. Technol. Soc. **1**(1), 34–47 (2020)
33. Pichai, S.: AI at Google: our principles, June 2018. https://www.blog.google/technology/ai/ai-principles/. Accessed 16 Sept 2023
34. Rahwan, I.: Society-in-the-loop: programming the algorithmic social contract. Ethics Inf. Technol. **20**(1), 5–14 (2018)
35. Reddy, S., Allan, S., Coghlan, S., Cooper, P.: A governance model for the application of AI in health care. J. Am. Med. Inform. Assoc. **27**(3), 491–497 (2020)
36. Ribeiro, M., Singh, S., Guestrin, C.: "why should I trust you?": explaining the predictions of any classifier. In: Proceedings of the 2016 Conference of the North American Chapter of the Association for Computational Linguistics: Demonstrations. Association for Computational Linguistics, Stroudsburg, PA, USA (2016)
37. Riedl, M.: Big red button by Mark Riedl (2016)
38. Robbins, S.: AI and the path to envelopment: knowledge as a first step towards the responsible regulation and use of AI-powered machines. AI Soc. **35**(2), 391–400 (2020)
39. Shankaranarayana, S.M., Runje, D.: ALIME: autoencoder based approach for local interpretability. ArXiv, abs (1909)
40. Shen, Z.: On California consumer privacy law, July 2019. http://rmfyb.chinacourt.org/paper/html/2019-07/12/content_157608.htm?div=-1. Accessed 4 Jan 2024
41. Shimizu, R., Matsutani, M., Goto, M.: An explainable recommendation framework based on an improved knowledge graph attention network with massive volumes of side information. Knowl. Based Syst. **239**(107970), 107970 (2022)
42. Shrikumar, A., Greenside, P., Kundaje, A.: Learning important features through propagating activation differences (2017)
43. Tencent Research Institute: Ten recommendations for interpreting new trends in EU AI legislation, November 2020. https://baijiahao.baidu.com/s?id=1559578568643940&wfr=spider&for=pc. Accessed 4 Jan 2024
44. Thomas, A., Scheutz, M.: The "big red button" is too late: an alternative model for the ethical evaluation of AI systems. Ethics Inf. Technol. **20**(1), 59–69 (2018)
45. Wang, X., He, X., Cao, Y., Liu, M., Chua, T.S.: KGAT: knowledge graph attention network for recommendation. In: Proceedings of the 25th ACM SIGKDD International Conference on Knowledge Discovery & Data Mining. ACM, New York, NY, USA (2019)
46. Zhou, Z., Hooker, G., Wang, F.: S-LIME: stabilized-LIME for model explanation. In: Proceedings of the 27th ACM SIGKDD Conference on Knowledge Discovery & Data Mining. ACM, New York, NY, USA (2021)

Health Informatics

Digital Footprints of Distress: An Analysis of Mental Health Search Patterns Across Socioeconomic Spectrums in Alabama Counties

Hengyi Fu$^{(\boxtimes)}$ (iD)

School of Library and Information Studies, The University of Alabama, Tuscaloosa, USA
hfu4@ua.edu

Abstract. Mental healthcare access continues to be a significant challenge in the United States, with marked disparities across socioeconomic divides. As technology and algorithms increasingly play pivotal roles in healthcare access, understanding unique symptom manifestations in socioeconomically disadvantaged communities is crucial. In this context, we embarked on a comprehensive analysis of mental health search patterns in Alabama counties, leveraging Google search data. Distinct trends emerged between socioeconomically advantaged and disadvantaged areas. The advantaged regions predominantly showed clinically specific searches, suggesting a higher degree of mental health literacy or more considerable access to healthcare professionals. Residents in disadvantaged areas primarily utilized generalized mental health symptom terms, such as anxiety and depression, hinting at a potential awareness or resource gap. A similar pattern was evident for somatic symptoms, with the disadvantaged showing a preference towards generalized and pain-related terms. This trend could signify disparities in access to specialized care or inappropriate clinical treatments, raising concerns like potential opioid misuse. Additionally, counties with higher population density had more mental health-related searches, while predominantly African American counties showed fewer, suggesting potential cultural or linguistic barriers. Our findings emphasize the potential of refining search engines to cater to diverse user needs and the importance of tailored health campaigns for marginalized communities. However, potential ethical challenges, such as unintentional exacerbation of existing biases, must consistently be recognized. Future research will elevate this analysis to a national scope, considering the effects of significant global occurrences, such as the COVID-19 pandemic, on search behaviors.

Keywords: Mental health · Medical Informatics · Health Informatics · Search Engine · Socioeconomic Factors

1 Introduction

Mental health has become a pressing concern in the U.S. Annually, one in five adults and adolescents battle mental illnesses. Beyond the statistics, many challenges prevent individuals from seeking the assistance they need. Among these are the enduring societal stigma associated with mental health issues, burdensome financial costs, and a prevalent lack of awareness about the available mental health resources [1, 2].

I. Sserwanga et al. (Eds.): iConference 2024, LNCS 14598, pp. 125–134, 2024.
https://doi.org/10.1007/978-3-031-57867-0_9

Adding to the complexities of this landscape, the outbreak of the COVID-19 pandemic drastically intensified levels of mental distress. Amidst lockdowns, uncertainties, and the existential crisis that occurred many traditional routes to psychiatric care became less accessible, necessitating an expedited transition to virtual services [3]. The situation accelerated the adoption of technology-enabled solutions such as online supporting communities and telemedicine [4, 5].

Many mental health platforms now use algorithms to recommend resources based on user language, aiming to personalize care [6]. However, this technology often overlooks disparities in mental health experiences influenced by class, race, and gender identity. For instance, the lack of broadband access in rural, African American, and Hispanic communities in the U.S. limits the reach of these digital solutions [7]. The pandemic, with its numerous online-centric solutions, inadvertently amplified this divide, pushing the marginalized even further to the periphery in terms of health equity [8, 9].

A salient challenge in addressing these disparities is the scant knowledge surrounding the unique mental health challenges these marginalized communities face. And while socioeconomic disparities undeniably impact healthcare access, our understanding of mental health perceptions in socioeconomically disadvantaged areas remains limited. Fortunately, search engine data provides valuable insights into individual mental health understanding [4]. This study, therefore, leverages Google search data from 2017–2022 to explore the different search patterns related to mental health concerns across areas with different socioeconomic standings. The paper presents preliminary findings from a more extensive study, focusing on Alabama counties with differing socioeconomic rankings. We primarily seek to answer the question: *How do search patterns for mental health symptoms differ between counties with high and low socioeconomic standings in Alabama?*

We want to emphasize that it's crucial to interpret the results presented in this paper with precision. As it stands, our study primarily provides preliminary descriptive findings and does **not** imply **causation**. We're not suggesting that socioeconomic status is the driver or exclusive driver behind the search patterns observed or asserting its dominance over other factors. For the socioeconomic rankings, we've leaned on the established indexes provided by the County Health Rankings[1] (C.H.R) instead of devising our own. We acknowledge that C.H.R. used various socioeconomic factors to calculate their socioeconomic rankings—such as education, income, employment, social and family support, and community safety, and we do not intend to suggest that any factor has a greater influence. Additionally, our results don't rule out the potential impact of other essential determinants like race and gender.

2 Online Search for Mental Health

Search engines have become a prevalent tool for acquiring health-related information, particularly in mental health, where digital anonymity offers respite from societal judgments [10]. As reported by the Pew Research Center, a significant 72 percent of U.S. internet users sought health information online in 2012, with most starting their search

---

[1] https://www.countyhealthrankings.org/

on general search engines [11]. These platforms provide a confidential space for individuals to understand and interpret health conditions, especially those with societal stigma [12]. However, the high costs and engagement required for clinical research often lead to the underrepresentation of rural, minority, and low-income communities in U.S. mental health studies [13]. Consequently, search queries become vital in understanding mental health perspectives in these communities.

The complexity of mental health concerns is mirrored in online searches, influencing individuals' perceptions and health decisions. There's a risk of users misinterpreting symptoms based on online information, potentially causing increased anxiety or neglect of critical symptoms [14]. The algorithms and user interfaces of search engines play a significant role in shaping how individuals perceive and communicate their symptoms [15].

The nature of information obtained from search engines depends largely on query wording. For example, searches for Depression in Spanish often yield news articles focused on tragic events, which might inadvertently influence self-harm perceptions, contrasting with results from more clinical terminology [16]. This highlights the importance of query specificity in accessing relevant resources.

Despite these challenges, advancements in AI offer promising enhancements for search engines. Ethically implemented, they could provide nuanced responses and recognize critical mental health situations, potentially serving as preliminary intervention tools [17].

3   Method

3.1   Data

To analyze the variation in mental health symptom searches across diverse counties, we utilize the Google COVID-19 Search Trend symptoms dataset [18]. Developed during the pandemic, this dataset offers anonymized, aggregated Google search trends for 422 symptoms, including mental health conditions[2]. The data is organized by Counties on a weekly basis. Previous studies have demonstrated the dataset's utility in forecasting COVID-19 transmission and fatality rates [19]. For our analysis, we analyze data spanning 2017–2022 for all 67 counties in Alabama.

3.2   Socioeconomic Ranking for Counties

We utilized the County Health Rankings (C.H.R.) [20] to determine the socioeconomic ranking of each county in Alabama. The C.H.R, a project of the University of Wisconsin Population Health Institute, offers various rankings that contribute to health outcomes for every U.S. County. Each county gets a state-level rank for each item, categorized into four quartiles. The results of this project, supported by multiple surveillance methods,

---

[2] For a full description of the method Google used to create this dataset, see: https://storage.goo
gleapis.com/gcp-public-data-symptom-search/COVID-19%20Search%20Trends%20symp
toms%20dataset%20documentation%20.pdf.

have become widely used for studying county-level health, including mental health [21–23].

The strength of C.H.R.'s socioeconomic rankings lies in incorporating several social determinants influencing health outcomes. The Socioeconomic rankings within the C.H.R. comprise five elements: education, income, employment, social and family support, and community safety. Previous studies have associated income disparities and educational attainment with health outcomes [24–27]. For instance, higher educational levels correlate with improved health knowledge, fewer exposures to hazards, and greater access to health benefits through employment. Full-time employment has been found to promote better self-perceived health, while unemployment can have direct and indirect negative health implications. Notably, job loss can result in physiological changes such as increased cholesterol levels, weakened immune responses, and a rise in unhealthy behaviors [28–31].

Alabama's 67 counties are grouped into four quartiles based on their socioeconomic standings as per the C.H.R. With our research, we aimed to compare mental health search patterns between the top 34 counties and the bottom 33, analyzing differences between socioeconomically advantaged and disadvantaged areas.

3.3 Data Analysis

Symptom Selection
Our analysis started with a manual review by two domain experts, both having a minimum of two years of experience in either psychiatry or clinical psychology. From the 422 symptoms in the Google COVID-19 Search Trends symptoms dataset, they identified 69 symptoms that are cited in psychiatric manuals [32], achieving a Cohen's Kappa score of 0.832. This list comprised 37 direct mental health symptoms and an additional 32 somatic symptoms that frequently correlate with mental health conditions (see Appendix A).

Symptom Popularity Calculation
To protect user privacy, Google's COVID-19 Search Trends dataset uses aggregate normalized weights. These weights represent the frequency of searches for a symptom relative to other symptoms, rather than showing raw search numbers. To analyze this data effectively, we standardized our comparisons. We did this by dividing the weight of each symptom by the total weight of all symptoms for a specific county and bi-weekly period. This approach helps us understand the average popularity of a symptom compared to all other symptom searches over that period.

Specifically, we first scaled each symptom's normalized weight by dividing it by the highest scaled weight in the region for that time frame. We then divided this value by the sum of all scaled symptom weights for that period. This calculation gives us a clear picture of how popular each symptom is within the county on a bi-weekly basis. The use of bi-weekly periods allows us to track changes in symptom popularity over time, providing valuable insights into public health trends.

$$P(A) = \frac{a_A/m}{\sum_{i=1}^{n} \frac{a_i}{m}}$$

where:

- $P(A)$ is the percentage popularity of Symptom A;
- a_A is the scaled normalized weight of Symptom A, provided by Google dataset;
- m is the maximum scaled normalized weight among all symptoms in that county;
- n is the total number of symptoms, the summation $\sum_{i=1}^{n} \frac{a_i}{m}$ means sum up the normalized values of all the symptoms from the first one to the nth one.

We then compared the average popularity of each symptom on the list mentioned above between the top 34 counties (advantaged areas) and the bottom 33 counties (disadvantaged areas) on a bi-weekly basis. Additionally, we compared the cumulative popularity of all symptoms between these two areas. All comparisons were conducted using an independent two-tailed t-test to ascertain if any observed differences were statistically significant ($p < .05$).

4   Preliminary Results

In Alabama, an intriguing trend emerges when correlating mental health search patterns with socioeconomic status. The findings suggest that the top 34 counties, which fall into the socioeconomically advantaged bracket, comprise all the top ten counties most frequently searching for mental health symptoms. Conversely, in the bottom 33 counties, which are socioeconomically disadvantaged, eight out of the ten counties least engaged in such searches fall into this bracket. The disparity in numbers is worth noting: 15.46% ($\sigma = 1.78\%$) of searches in the advantaged areas relate to mental health, whereas the percentage drops to 13.85% ($\sigma = 1.42\%$) in the disadvantaged areas. If one were to focus just on the extremes – the top ten socioeconomically ranked versus the bottom ten counties – this gap widens to 17.25% ($\sigma = 2.53\%$) against 13.61% ($\sigma = 3.34\%$). Table 1 provides a six-year average percentage search of all symptoms whose bi-weekly average percentage significantly varies between advantaged and disadvantaged areas ($p < .05$).

Our findings show that residents in disadvantaged areas mostly search for general mental health symptoms like *Anxiety* (mean = 1.12%, $\sigma = .24\%$), *Depression* (mean = 1.34%, $\sigma = .12\%$), and *Confusion* (mean = .57%, $\sigma = .18\%$). For instance, a search query might be, "Why do I feel so lost?" or "Can't focus on anything."

Conversely, in advantaged areas, searches were more inclined towards specific clinical terms like *Psychosis* (mean = .58%, $\sigma = .11\%$), *Generalized Anxiety Disorder* (mean = .41%, $\sigma = .13\%$), *Attention Deficit Hyperactivity Disorder* (mean = .42%, $\sigma = .16\%$), *Fibromyalgia* (mean = .45%%, $\sigma = .12\%$), *Manic Disorder* (mean = .38%, $\sigma = .05\%$), or *Mood Disorder* (mean = .52%, $\sigma = .21\%$). For instance, someone might search "symptoms of Bipolar Disorder" or "therapies for O.C.D." The only exception is the *Major depressive disorder*, for which the search in disadvantaged areas is slightly higher than those in the advantaged areas (+0.05%). These terms are clinically recognized and commonly used by mental health professionals. This pattern could indicate better mental health literacy, a tendency towards self-diagnosis, or a more proactive approach towards understanding and addressing mental health issues in advantaged areas.

When it comes to somatic symptoms, a clear distinction emerges as well. Residents of disadvantaged areas search more frequently for general symptoms like *Fatigue* (mean

Table 1. Percentages of mental health symptoms of all health searching in advantaged and disadvantaged area with statistically significant differences (p < .05)

Symptom (6-year average)	Advantaged areas (top 34 counties) Mean (SD)	Disadvantaged areas (bottom 33 counties) Mean (SD)
Total	15.46% (1.78%)	13.85% (1.42%)
Alcoholism	0.36% (.14%)	0.52% (.19%)
Anxiety	0.94% (.08%)	1.12% (.24%)
Attention Deficit Hyperactivity Disorder	0.42% (.16%)	0.05% (.04%)
Avoidant personality disorder	0.31% (.07%)	0.15% (.12%)
Compulsive behavior	0.62% (.14%)	0.21% (.08%)
Confusion	0.24% (.25%)	0.57% (.18%)
Depression	1.02% (.17%)	1.34% (.12%)
Fibromyalgia	0.45% (.12%)	0.18% (.07%)
Generalized anxiety disorder	0.41% (.13%)	0.21% (.08%)
Major depressive disorder	0.22% (.08%)	0.27% (.21%)
Manic Disorder	0.38% (.05%)	0.05% (.02%)
Mood disorder	0.52% (.21%)	0.18% (.07%)
Panic attack	0.56% (.14%)	0.28% (.06%)
Psychosis	0.58% (.11%)	0.14% (.04%)
Back pain	0.81% (.12%)	0.98% (.06%)
Chronic pain	0.35% (.05%)	0.62% (.03%)
Dizziness	0.80% (0.5%)	0.25% (0.2%)
Fatigue	0.92% (.12%)	1.16% (.28%)
Headache	0.87% (.07%)	1.22% (.13%)
Pain	1.18% (.12%)	1.64% (.05%)
Vertigo	0.36% (.08%)	0.12% (.10%)
Weight gain	0.27% (.04%)	0.33% (.04%)
Weakness	0.74% (.09%)	1.02% (.06%)

= 1.16%, σ = .28%), *Weight Gain* (mean = .33%, σ = .04%), or *Weakness* (mean = 1.02%, σ = .06%). They may search like "*Why am I always so tired?*" or "*sudden weight gain reasons.*" It's alarming to note that for all pain-related symptoms, including *Back Pain* (mean = .98%, σ = .06%), *Chronic Pain* (mean = .62%, σ = .03%), *Headache* (mean = 1.22%, σ = .13%), and *Pain* (mean = 1.64%, σ = .05%) in general, the disadvantaged areas took the lead. This increased focus on pain could suggest limited access to specialized care or potential mismanagement in treatments, such as opioid overdoses. For instance, individuals might be inquiring online about "constant backache causes" or "persistent headache remedies" due to inadequate healthcare resources. On the other hand, in advantaged areas, the narrative might be different. With better access to healthcare, individuals might have more precise search queries based on a diagnosis or treatment plan provided by a healthcare professional. For instance, searches might be more like "physical therapy for chronic back pain" or "migraine relief exercises." This comparison underscores the disparity in healthcare access and literacy between socioeconomically advantaged and disadvantaged areas, mirrored in the nature and specificity of health-related search queries across these areas.

We also found that counties with predominantly African American populations registered fewer mental health searches. This might be attributed to the fact that the vocabulary constructs traditionally used to denote mental illness are majorly based on white populations [33]. As a result, the language African American individuals use to articulate mental distress might not be flagged by search algorithms as representative of mental illness [34]. This might be analogous to how grief, often termed "*weariness*" within some African American communities, isn't always identifiable through conventional search parameters.

5   Discussion, Implications, and Future Research

The findings of this study emphasize the urgency of refining search engine algorithms to better cater to the diverse needs of users. Search engines can help to close this inequity in care by referring individuals to specialized resources around mental health, even when the symptom categories being searched for are broader. For instance, if someone from an economically deprived region searches "*Why do I always feel down?*" or "*finding it hard to wake up,*" the search outcome could offer emotional support resources and insights into potential mental health issues, alongside general information on potential causes or solutions. This tailored approach could also help mitigate the tendency of search engines to inadvertently heighten users' health anxieties, particularly among those from disadvantaged backgrounds. When laypersons rely on search engines for a medical understanding of their symptoms, there's often a risk of overreacting to commonplace signs. By juxtaposing mental health aids with general health details, search engines can equip users with vocabulary and resources that better mirror their distress while tempering undue worries about non-critical symptoms. For users in advantaged areas, who often use clinical terms in their mental health searches, search engines might prioritize results aligned with formal treatment. However, it's crucial to recognize that the nature of these recommended resources can significantly shape individuals' perceptions of mental health. An overemphasis on biomedical approaches could be counterproductive, potentially neglecting other valuable forms of care. Therefore, it's important for search engine algorithms to present a diverse range of resources. This includes broader stress-related resources, helplines, online peer support, and alternative care options beyond the traditional biomedical framework.

Furthermore, the predominance of pain-related searches in socioeconomically disadvantaged areas underscores the necessity for proactive public health initiatives on pain management. There's a potential to raise awareness of alternative, non-pharmaceutical therapies for pain and combat the opioid epidemic through education on the dangers of misuse and over-reliance on opioids. This can be crucial, especially in regions where access to specialists, like physical therapists, might be limited, increasing the reliance on medication. The searches might include phrases like *"Why does my leg pain never go away?"* or *"headaches every day."* By redirecting such queries towards resources on holistic pain management techniques, ranging from physiotherapy exercises to mindfulness techniques, we can offer alternatives before one resort to painkillers.

Lastly, given the general trend in the data, it's evident that there is a pressing need for enhanced public health information campaigns, particularly those tailored for underserved communities. Such campaigns could aim to increase mental health literacy, destigmatize mental health discussions, and provide resources on serious concerns like suicide prevention. Directing efforts to communities that search less frequently for specific mental health terms but more for broad feelings or symptoms might improve general mental health awareness and potentially save lives.

However, while harnessing these insights, addressing ethical dimensions is imperative. Search engines must guard against perpetuating biases, ensuring that recommendations do not marginalize or misinform certain identities or communities. For example, if a predominantly African American community searches for terms rooted in their cultural expressions of distress, algorithms should recognize and respect these nuances without jumping to ill-informed conclusions. While search data can guide public health initiatives, policymakers must remember that such data offers a macro perspective, potentially missing the nuanced intricacies of individual experiences.

We are expanding the analysis to a national level to see if a person in urban New York searches similarly to someone in rural Alabama when feeling mentally unwell. Additionally, the COVID-19 pandemic undoubtedly impacts mental health searches. Preliminary observations suggest a notable decrease in mental health-related searches as the pandemic took hold. But this dip was sharper in socioeconomically disadvantaged areas [35]. Was it due to pressing concerns about physical health and survival, overshadowing mental health? Or was it indicative of a larger systemic neglect? By seeking answers to these questions, we aim to arm policymakers and healthcare professionals with data that truly echoes diverse communities' pulse, ensuring that mental health strategies are both inclusive and effective.

Appendix A

Alcoholism, Amnesia, Anxiety, Arthralgia, Attention deficit hyperactivity disorder, Auditory hallucination, Avoidant personality disorder, Back pain, Blurred vision, Binge eating, Bruxism, Cataplexy, Chest pain, Compulsive behavior, Compulsive hoarding, Chronic pain, Clouding of consciousness, Confusion, Dementia, Depression, Depersonalization, Dizziness, Dry eye syndrome, Dysphoria, Dyspareunia, Excessive daytime sleepiness, Eye strain, Fatigue, Fibromyalgia, Headache, Hypersomnia, Hyperventilation, Generalized anxiety disorder, Guilt, Hypochondriasis, Impulsivity, Insomnia, Itch, Lightheadedness, Major depressive disorder, Manic Disorder, Mood disorder, Mood swing, Muscle weakness, Myalgia, Nausea, Night sweats, Night terror, Pain, Palpitations, Panic attack, Paranoia, Psychosis, Photophobia, Rumination, Self-harm, Sensitivity to sound, Sleep deprivation, Shortness of breath, Suicidal ideation, Shyness, Sleep disorder, Tachycardia, Tinnitus, Tremor, Vertigo, Weakness, Weight gain, Yawn.

References

1. Centers for Disease Control and Prevention. About Mental Health (2023). https://www.cdc.gov/mentalhealth/learn/index.htm
2. National Institutes of Health. National Institute of Mental Health--Mental Health Information, Statistics (2022). https://www.nimh.nih.gov/health/statistics/mental-illness
3. Zangani, C., et al.: Impact of the COVID-19 pandemic on the global delivery of mental health services and telemental health: systematic review. JMIR Mental Health 9(8), e38600 (2022)
4. Jimenez, A.J., et al.: COVID-19 symptom-related Google searches and local COVID-19 incidence in Spain: correlational study. J. Med. Internet Res. 22(12), e23518 (2020)
5. Jong, W., Liang, O.S., Yang, C.C.: The exchange of informational support in online health communities at the onset of the COVID-19 pandemic: content analysis. JMIRX Med 2(3), e27485 (2021)
6. Haim, M., Scherr, S., Arendt, F.: How search engines may help reduce drug-related suicides. Drug Alcohol Depend. 226, 108874 (2021)
7. Atske, S., Perrin, A.: Home broadband adoption, computer ownership vary by race, ethnicity in the U.S (2021)
8. Faraj, S., Renno, W., Bhardwaj, A.: Unto the breach: what the COVID-19 pandemic exposes about digitalization. Inf. Organ. 31(1), 100337 (2021)
9. Li, F.: Disconnected in a pandemic: COVID-19 outcomes and the digital divide in the United States. Health Place 77, 102867 (2022)
10. Powell, J., Clarke, A.: Internet information-seeking in mental health: population survey. Br. J. Psychiatry 189(3), 273–277 (2006)
11. Wagner, T.H., Subak, L.L.: Talking about incontinence: the first step toward prevention and treatment. JAMA 303(21), 2184–2185 (2010)
12. De Choudhury, M., Morris, M.R., White, R.W.: Seeking and sharing health information online: comparing search engines and social media. In: Proceedings of the SIGCHI Conference on Human Factors in Computing Systems (2014)
13. López, C.M., et al.: Technology as a means to address disparities in mental health research: a guide to "tele-tailoring" your research methods. Prof. Psychol. Res. Pract. 49(1), 57 (2018)
14. White, R.W., Horvitz, E.: Cyberchondria: studies of the escalation of medical concerns in web search. ACM Trans. Inf. Syst. (TOIS) 27(4), 1–37 (2009)
15. Ayers, S.L., Kronenfeld, J.J.: Chronic illness and health-seeking information on the Internet. Health 11(3), 327–347 (2007)
16. Vargas, L., Comello, M.L.G., Porter, J.H.: The web's potential to provide depression literacy resources to latinx teens: a missed opportunity? Howard J. Commun. 32(4), 366–381 (2021)
17. Ybarra, M.L., Suman, M.: Help seeking behavior and the internet: a national survey. Int. J. Med. Inform. 75(1), 29–41 (2006)
18. Google, Google COVID-19 Search Trends Symptoms Dataset (2022)
19. Abbas, M., et al.: Associations between google search trends for symptoms and COVID-19 confirmed and death cases in the United States. Int. J. Environ. Res. Public Health 18(9), 4560 (2021)
20. The University of Wisconsin Population Health Institute, County Health Rankings & Roadmaps

21. Anderson, T.J., et al.: A cross-sectional study on health differences between rural and non-rural US counties using the county health rankings. BMC Health Serv. Res. **15**, 1–8 (2015)
22. Peyer, K., et al.: Relationships between county health rankings and child overweight and obesity prevalence: a serial cross-sectional analysis. BMC Public Health **16**, 1–10 (2016)
23. Spaulding, A., et al.: A community health case for psychiatric care: a cross-sectional study of county health rankings. Gen. Hosp. Psychiatry **57**, 1–6 (2019)
24. Kennedy, B.P., et al.: Income distribution, socioeconomic status, and self rated health in the United States: multilevel analysis. BMJ **317**(7163), 917–921 (1998)
25. Jarvandi, S., Yan, Y., Schootman, M.: Income disparity and risk of death: the importance of health behaviors and other mediating factors. PLoS ONE **7**(11), e49929 (2012)
26. Braveman, P.A., et al.: Socioeconomic status in health research: one size does not fit all. JAMA **294**(22), 2879–2888 (2005)
27. Shea, S., et al.: Independent associations of educational attainment and ethnicity with behavioral risk factors for cardiovascular disease. Am. J. Epidemiol. **134**(6), 567–582 (1991)
28. Dooley, D., Catalano, R., Hough, R.: Unemployment and alcohol disorder in 1910 and 1990: drift versus social causation. J. Occup. Organ. Psychol. **65**(4), 277–290 (1992)
29. Halford, W.K., Learner, E.: Correlates of coping with unemployment in young Australians. Aust. Psychol. **19**(3), 333–344 (1984)
30. Lee, A.J., et al.: Cigarette smoking and employment status. Soc Sci Med **33**(11), 1309–1312 (1991)
31. Ross, C.E., Mirowsky, J.: Does employment affect health? J. Health Soc. Behav. **36**, 230–243 (1995)
32. American Psychiatric Association, Diagnostic and statistical manual of mental disorders: *DSM-5*: American psychiatric association Washington, DC, vol. 5 (2013)
33. Alang, S.M.: "Black folk don't get no severe depression": meanings and expressions of depression in a predominantly black urban neighborhood in Midwestern United States. Soc Sci Med **157**, 1–8 (2016)
34. Bauer, A.G., et al.: "We are our own counselor": Resilience, risk behaviors, and mental health service utilization among young African American men. Behav. Med. **46**(3–4), 278–289 (2020)
35. Fu, H.: Decoding distress: how search engine data reveals socioeconomic disparities in mental health. In: ACM SIGIR Conference on Human Information Interaction and Retrieval Proceedings. Sheffield, United Kingdom: ACM (2024). https://doi.org/10.1145/3627508.363 8323

Exploring Media Framing of the Monkeypox Pandemic in Mainstream and Social Media: A Framing Theory Analysis

Lin Yang[(✉)] [iD]

Johns Hopkins University, Washington, DC 20009, USA
lyang94@alumni.jh.edu

Abstract. This study investigates the application of framing theory in the context of media coverage of the monkeypox outbreak, analyzing the divergent approaches adopted by mainstream and social media. Utilizing six framing models, the research methodically examined a corpus of 100 media items, comprising news articles and social media posts, collected from January to December 2022. The content was categorized under four principal themes: symptoms and transmission, prevention and treatment, public opinion and attitudes, and social strategies. The analysis elucidated a notable differentiation in framing preferences. Mainstream media predominantly utilized 'Framing of Situations' and 'Framing of Attributes,' denoting a tendency towards narrative and descriptive reporting. In contrast, social media exhibited a proclivity for 'Framing of Actions' and 'Framing of Issues,' reflective of an interactive and dynamic communicative style. A Chi-square statistical analysis yielded a significant association between the types of media and the employed framing models (Chi-square = 25.38, p < 0.0001). The computed Cramér's V value of 0.316 indicated a moderate degree of association, suggesting nuanced variances in framing strategies between mainstream and social media. This study contributes to the scholarly understanding of media framing in the milieu of a global health crisis. The findings underscore the distinct ways in which different media platforms engage audiences and shape public perceptions during health emergencies. These insights are instrumental for the formulation of effective public health communication strategies, highlighting the pivotal role of media framing in the dissemination and reception of health-related information.

Keywords: Monkeypox Outbreak · Framing Theory · Social Media · Mainstream Media · Media Analysis

1 Background

The emergence of COVID-19 significantly disrupted everyday life, bringing about unprecedented challenges worldwide. Despite the widespread administration of vaccines, which has played a crucial role in mitigating infection rates, the incidence of COVID-19 cases continues to rise. Amid these ongoing challenges, another infectious

I. Sserwanga et al. (Eds.): iConference 2024, LNCS 14598, pp. 135–149, 2024.
https://doi.org/10.1007/978-3-031-57867-0_10

disease, monkeypox, has gained prominence. Monkeypox is caused by a poxvirus and is characterized by pimple- or blister-like lesions accompanied by flu-like symptoms [1]. Transmission occurs through various routes, including direct physical contact, respiratory secretions, vertical transmission from mother to fetus, and contact with objects contaminated with fluids from the infected person's lesions [1]. With the global increase in monkeypox cases, it is imperative to gain a comprehensive understanding of this emerging pandemic.

2 Introduction

In the wake of the recent monkeypox outbreak, the manner in which information is communicated to the public has become increasingly vital. This paper sought to explore the application of framing theory within the realm of health communication, with a particular focus on the coverage of monkeypox by mainstream and social media. Framing theory, as introduced by Entman [2], posits that information creators select and emphasize specific aspects of reality, thereby influencing the perceptions and decision-making processes of the audience. This theory extends beyond the first level of agenda-setting, which dictates what the public should think about, to a second level that shapes how the public should think about these issues [3].

The choice of framing theory as the theoretical framework for this study was twofold. First, framing is a predominant technique in mass communication, where journalists and other communication practitioners leverage it to deliver knowledge and influence perceptions or behaviors through both linguistic and paralinguistic messages [4, 5]. Secondly, framing theory is instrumental in crafting effective health messages [6], an essential aspect of disseminating information during health crises such as monkeypox. This research examined six models of framing – framing of situations, framing of attributes, framing of actions, framing of issues, framing of choices, and framing of news [7] – to better comprehend how monkeypox is being portrayed in the media.

This paper delved into the distribution of framing types across various topics covered in social media and mainstream media, providing a comparative analysis of their approaches during the monkeypox outbreak. Media outlets of both types have played pivotal roles in disseminating information, alleviating anxieties, and highlighting the severity of the disease [8–10]. By examining the media coverage from six outlets across both media types, this study aimed to identify the predominant frames used to capture attention and shape public opinion about the outbreak. The analysis specifically focused on how these outlets have framed the symptoms and transmission of monkeypox, strategies for prevention and treatment, public opinion and attitudes towards the outbreak, and social strategies for public health promotion. Through this exploration, this study intended to provide a nuanced understanding of the impact of media framing on public perceptions and behaviors during health crises, and to offer insights into how public health experts and media professionals can collaborate more effectively to enhance public health outcomes.

3   Literature Review

Framing theory plays a crucial role in public relations, mass communication, and health communication. With monkeypox emerging as the latest pandemic, there is limited scientific research utilizing framing theory to study issues related to this disease. However, given the similarities in communication strategies and research between monkeypox and the COVID-19 outbreak, this study draws on previous research that used framing theory to explore COVID-19-related issues. According to a previous work Wildman [10], framing theory proposes that events can be portrayed through salient content, influencing audience perceptions based on the information presented. Hallahan [7] describes seven models of framing: framing of situations, framing of attributes, framing of risky choices, framing of actions, framing of issues, framing of responsibility, and framing of news. This study will exclude the framing of responsibility as it is less pertinent to the topic at hand.

3.1   Framing of Situations

Framing of situations involves using language and communication structure to organize or construct facts in interactions [7]. Schnell et al. [11] conducted a content analysis of 118 news articles to investigate how age was framed in the context of COVID-19. They found that the framing of situations model significantly impacts audiences' attitudes, behaviors, and emotions. Articles often portrayed elderly patients as frail, and some suggested that ignoring social distancing could lead to a grandparent's death. This use of language highlights salient facts, thus influencing public behavior to protect the elderly population.

3.2   Framing of Attributes

Attribute framing focuses on the characteristics of objects, people, or events [7]. This type of framing can be either positive or negative, affecting message receivers' perceptions. Barnes and Colagiuri [12] conducted an experiment with 1,222 UK participants, comparing positive and negative attribute-framed information about COVID-19 booster side effects. Participants exposed to positive attribute framing, such as "90 in 100 people may not be affected by side effects," showed increased attention towards unfamiliar COVID-19 boosters, whereas negative framing was effective for familiar vaccines [12]. This demonstrates how attribute framing can influence perceptions and behaviors.

3.3   Framing of Actions

Framing of actions emphasizes that achieving a desired goal is contingent upon performing specific behaviors. Dobrowolsk [13]'s group examined the role of framing theory in engaging people in COVID-19 vaccination programs. This research category falls under the framing of actions, where vaccination was portrayed as a means to decrease infection risks and enhance safety. The findings revealed that framing is instrumental in developing vaccination strategies and encouraging participation.

3.4 Framing of Issues

Framing of issues involves presenting information to emphasize one perspective over another, often leading to disputes over problem definitions [7]. Bolsen et al. [14] examined public opinions on different framed messages about COVID-19's origins. One group read about a natural origin, while another read a conspiracy theory. This framing significantly influenced beliefs about the virus's origin, demonstrating the power of issue framing on public opinion.

3.5 Framing of Risky Choices

According to Hallahan [7]'s work, framing of risky choices involves decision-making between two options under risk or uncertainty. Hameleers [15] studied how different framing methods influenced participants' choices between COVID-19 treatment programs. The study found that gain-framed conditions led to risk-averse choices, while loss-framed conditions resulted in risk-seeking behavior, highlighting the impact of framing on decision-making in uncertain situations.

3.6 Framing of News

News framing, as defined by Gamson and Modigliani [28] and Hallahan [7], involves organizing and highlighting ideas to emphasize a particular issue. Ogbodo et al. [17] analyzed word choices and frames in COVID-19 news coverage, finding that themes of human interest and fear were predominant. Similarly, Chen et al. [18] investigated news framing patterns in Chinese coverage of COVID-19 and tourism, identifying key themes like the pandemic's impact on tourism and public sentiment. Although these studies focus on COVID-19, their insights are relevant to the discussion of monkeypox due to similarities in urgency and scope.

4 Method

This study utilized content analysis to explore how mainstream and social media framed the monkeypox outbreak. Anchored in framing theory, the analysis specifically focused on identifying and interpreting the various framing techniques and topics covered in media content related to monkeypox.

4.1 Data Collection

Data was collected from mainstream media outlets and social media platforms, encompassing the period from January to December 2022. After manually reviewing more than 350 news articles and social media posts, a total of 100 pieces of content were analyzed. This included 50 news articles from prominent media outlets like CNN, The New York Times, and The Washington Post, and 50 posts from social media platforms such as Instagram, Facebook, and Twitter. The selection was guided by keywords like "monkeypox," "monkeypox symptoms," "monkeypox prevention," and "monkeypox infection," ensuring the inclusion of relevant and timely content related to the monkeypox outbreak.

4.2 Selection Criteria

Mainstream media outlets were selected for their wide audience reach and reputability in news reporting. Social media platforms were chosen for their role in shaping public opinion and the diversity of user-generated content. The goal was to achieve a balanced representation of various perspectives and formats, ranging from expert analysis to personal narratives.

The selection of mainstream media outlets, including Cable News Network (CNN), The New York Times (NYT), and The Washington Post, for this study was based on their extensive reach and esteemed reputation in the realm of news reporting. CNN is recognized for its significant impact in both digital and traditional media realms [19]. The New York Times is particularly noted for its distinguished reporting on global health issues [20]. Similarly, The Washington Post is acclaimed for its thorough and frequent coverage of health-related content [21].

For the selction of social media, platforms including Instagram, Facebook, and Twitter were chosen due to their widespread use and their significant influence in shaping public opinion [22, 23]. These platforms are renowned for their diverse user base and the variety of content they host, making them essential for comprehending public discourse on health issues [23].

Content from both mainstream and social media was selected based on representativeness and diversity. This approach captured varied perspectives and formats, text, images, and videos, shown in Table 1. The collected content included official updates from health authorities, personal experiences and opinions from individuals, and informative posts about monkeypox. Overall, the content was categorized into four key areas: symptoms and transmission [24], prevention and treatment [25], public opinion and attitudes [26], and social strategies [27]. This inclusive analysis encompassed a wide range of viewpoints, showcasing the multifaceted nature of public response and engagement with the monkeypox outbreak across different platforms.

Table 1. Samples Distributions on Different Media.

Media Types	Number	Format
Mainstream Media	33	Articles in Text with Image(s)
	17	Audio/Video Transcript
Social Media	10	Posts in Text only
	40	Posts with Video/Image

4.3 Content Coding

One coder was assigned the task of coding all content, which was divided into two distinct branches. The first branch concentrated on collecting and coding news articles published from January 1st to December 31st, 2022. The second branch focused on coding posts published on social media during the same timeframe.

Using a codebook aligned with the research objectives, four key topics were identified to capture public attention and shape opinions on the monkeypox outbreak: symptoms and transmission (S/T) [24], prevention and treatment (P/T) [25], public opinion and attitudes (PO/A) [26, 28], and social strategies (SS) [29].

The selected articles covered a range of aspects related to monkeypox, ensuring a comprehensive overview of the coverage from both mainstream and social media. The framing models analyzed included situation, attributes, actions, issues, risky choices, and news. Articles from reputable media outlets such as CNN, NYT, and The Washington Post provided expert insights, while content from social media platforms reflected public perceptions and reactions.

To offer a deeper understanding, the study includes a table that presents the different ways news articles related to the monkeypox outbreak are framed across the four categories: Symptoms and Transmission (S/T), Prevention and Treatment (P/T), Public Opinion and Attitudes (PO/A), and Social Strategies (SS). Each framing model—Situations, Attributes, Risky Choices, Actions, Issues, and News—brings a unique focus and perspective on how news content can be presented. For instance, the framing of situations highlights the societal impact of monkeypox, while the framing of attributes concentrates on the disease's symptoms and transmission methods. Table 2 presents provides practical examples of how each framing model can be applied to create news articles that inform, educate, and engage the audience on the topic of monkeypox outbreak. Table 3 shows some typical examples of Framing Theory models in mainstream media and social media.

Table 2. Feature Framing Models Grid in Monkeypox Outbreak Coverage.

Framing Model	S/T	P/T	PO/A	SS
F/S	Monkeypox outbreak and its impact on society. (Article ID 1)	Availability and effectiveness of vaccines	Public concern and fear of contracting the disease	Coordination between public health agencies and the government
F/AT	Symptoms and transmission methods of monkeypox (Article ID 2, 24)	Efficacy and side effects of various treatment options. (Article ID 2)	Perception of monkeypox as a severe and deadly disease (Article ID 24)	Prioritizing and implementing prevention measures
F/RC	Avoiding high-risk activities and exposure to infected individuals	Weighing the potential risks and benefits of vaccination and treatment options	Public opinion on the risks and benefits of vaccination and treatment (Article ID 7)	Encouraging individuals to make informed decisions about their health
F/AC	Public health officials taking measures to contain the spread of the disease (Article ID 33)	Healthcare professionals administering treatment and vaccines	Attitudes towards vaccination and treatment	Collaborating with others to promote prevention and treatment measures (Article ID 26,33)

(continued)

Table 2. (*continued*)

Framing Model	S/T	P/T	PO/A	SS
F/I	Importance of public health preparedness and response to infectious diseases	Adequacy of healthcare resources and infrastructure to handle outbreaks	Public awareness and education about infectious diseases	Addressing systemic issues in healthcare and public health systems (Article ID 52)
F/N	Covering the latest developments and updates on monkeypox outbreak (Article ID 67,81)	Highlighting success stories and breakthroughs in treatment and prevention (Article ID 67,81)	Shaping public opinion and attitudes towards monkeypox (Article ID 67)	Facilitating informed discussions and decision-making around monkeypox prevention and treatment (Article ID 81)

Table 3. Typical Examples of Framing Theory Models in Mainstream Media and Social Media.

Article ID	Outlet Name	Headline/Username	Date	Mainstream Media	Social Media
1	CNN	As Fauci …the window to control it 'probably has closed	07/17/2022	X	
2	CNN	What is monkeypox, and how can you stay safe as it spreads?	07/14/2022	X	
24	Instagram	6ixbuzztv	08/03/2022		X
26	Instagram	gbpublichealth	07/28/2022		X
33	Facebook	CDC	08/25/2022		X
52	Twitter	Monkeypox	08/13/2022		X
53	Twitter	Monkeypox	08/14/2022		X
7	CNN	WHO chief advises men who have sex with men …limit exposure to monkeypox	07/28/2022	X	
67	New York Times	The Unfiltered Faces of Monkeypox	08/11/2022	X	
81	Washington Post	Colleges warn students about monkeypox risk as fall term approaches	08/13/2022	X	

5   Reliability Test

To ensure accuracy and consistency in the coding process, this study engaged three researchers proficient in the English language. Before beginning the coding, these coders were provided with clear definitions and illustrative examples for each coding category to standardize their understanding and approach. To assess intercoder reliability, a random sample of 20 posts, comprising 20% of the total sample, was selected and assigned to the coders. The reliability of the coding process was evaluated using Krippendorff's alpha test, yielding results between 0.89 and 0.94. These values indicate a high level of agreement among the coders, underscoring the reliability and consistency of the coding across the entire dataset of news articles.

6 Result

Tables 4 and Table 5 displayed the distribution of framing models and topics covered across the 100 news articles and social media posts analyzed in this study. It was noteworthy that each article typically incorporated multiple framing models and topics, which were determined by the article's primary message or intended purpose.

Table 4. Distribution of Framing Types Across Social Media and Mainstream Media.

Framing Types	Social Media	Mainstream Media
Framing of Situations	19 (38.0%)	34 (68.0%)
Framing of Actions	27 (54.0%)	21 (42.0%)
Framing of Risky Choices	14 (28.0%)	25 (50.0%)
Framing of Issues	24 (48.0%)	6 (12.0%)
Framing of Attributes	13 (26.0%)	30 (60.0%)
Framing of News	15 (30.0%)	26 (52.0%)

1. Note: Each article/post may encompass multiple framing types, reflecting the diverse narrative construction in media.

Table 5. Distribution of Topics Covered Across Social Media and Mainstream Media.

Framing Types	Social Media	Mainstream Media
Symptoms and Transmission	33 (66.0%)	45 (90.0%)
Prevention and Treatment	21 (42.0%)	32 (64.0%)
Public Opinion and Attitudes	41 (82.0%)	11 (22.0%)
Social Strategies	17 (34.0%)	27 (54.0%)

1. Note: Each article/post may cover multiple topics, reflecting the diverse narrative construction in media.

In the analysis of the association between media type and framing types, as illustrated in Table 4, the contingency table revealed distinct preferences in narrative framing by different media. Social media predominantly used 'Framing of Actions' and 'Framing of Issues,' accounting for 54.0% and 48.0% respectively. Mainstream media displayed a more balanced distribution across various framing types, with 'Framing of Situations' (68.0%) and 'Framing of Attributes' (60.0%) being the most prevalent.

The comparative analysis of framing types between social media and mainstream media also showed that both media types had a relatively similar use of 'Framing of Risky Choices,' with mainstream media at 50.0% and social media at 28.0%, and mainstream media exhibited a higher usage of 'Framing of News' (52.0%) compared to social media (30.0%).

The output indicated that both news articles and social media posts covered the monkeypox outbreak by focusing on Symptoms and Transmission (S/T) to a greater extent, with 45 articles (90%) and 33 posts (66%) respectively. Prevention and Treatment (P/T) was the second most commonly covered topic, with 32 articles (64%) and 21 posts (42%). Public Opinion and Attitudes (PO/A) was less frequently covered in news articles with only 11 articles (22%), but it was more prevalent in social media with 41 posts (82%). Social Strategies (SS) received coverage from both news articles and social media, with 27 articles (54%) and 17 posts (34%), respectively.

Mainstream media showed a different pattern. 'Framing of Situations' was prominently used for 'Symptoms and Transmission,' indicating a more narrative or scenario-based approach to this topic. 'Framing of News,' with a balanced distribution across topics, suggested a consistent news-reporting style regardless of the topic.

In social media, the analysis revealed a diverse use of framing types across various topics. 'Framing of Actions' was frequently used for topics like 'Public Opinion and Attitudes,' suggesting an emphasis on dynamic and action-oriented content in these discussions. Conversely, 'Framing of Risky Choices' was most prevalent in 'Symptoms and Transmission,' pointing towards a focus on the implications and decisions related to health information.

Tables 6, 7 and 8 showed the distribution of framing types across topics covered in different media types, and the Chi-square test was used to examine the association between media types (social media vs. mainstream media) and framing types, revealing a significant association (Chi-square = 25.38, $p < 0.0001$, df = 5). This indicated that the choice of framing in content significantly varied between social media and mainstream media. The moderate Cramér's V value (V = 0.316) revealed that while there was a noticeable relationship, it was not extremely strong.

Similarly, the association between topics covered and media type was significant (Chi-square = 23.67, $p < 0.00003$, df = 3). This result underscored the distinct topical preferences between the two types of media. The Cramér's V statistic (V = 0.323) indicated a moderate degree of association between media type and the topics covered, suggesting that different media types tended to focus on different topics, but there was overlap in topic coverage across media types.

Table 6. Distribution of Framing Types Across Topics Covered in Mainstream Media.

Framing Model	S/T		P/T		PO/A		SS	
	n	%	n	%	n	%	n	%
F/S	31	37.8	23	28.05	6	7.32	22	26.83
F/AT	26	38.24	20	29.41	7	10.29	15	22.06
F/RC	23	41.07	18	32.14	5	8.93	10	17.86
F/AC	21	37.5	20	35.71	4	7.14	11	19.64
F/I	4	26.67	4	26.67	4	26.67	4	26.67
F/N	24	39.34	14	22.95	8	13.11	15	24.59

Table 7. Distribution of Framing Types Across Topics Covered in Social Media.

Framing Model	S/T		P/T		PO/A		SS	
	n	%	n	%	n	%	n	%
F/S	13	32.5	5	12.5	15	37.5	7	17.5
F/AT	12	36.36	8	24.24	9	27.27	4	12.12
F/RC	14	41.18	7	20.59	10	29.41	3	8.82
F/AC	19	26.76	18	25.35	23	32.39	11	15.49
F/I	14	25	10	17.86	22	39.29	10	17.86
F/N	6	23.08	2	7.69	11	42.31	7	26.92

Table 8. Chi-Square and Cramér's V Statistic for Degree of Association.

Association Tested	Chi-Square Statistic	p-value	Degrees of Freedom	Cramér's V Value	Interpretation
Framing Types and Media Type	25.38	< 0.00012***	5	0.316	Moderate association
Topics Covered and Media Type	23.67	< 0.00003***	3	0.323	Moderate association

1. *** $p < 0.001$, ** $p < 0.01$, * $p < 0.05$
2. The Chi-Square Statistic and p-values are based on the Chi-square test for independence.
3. Cramér's V values are used to measure the strength of association, with values closer to 1 indicating a stronger association.

7   Media Review Framing Analysis (Partial Content)

Article ID = 1 [30].

Title: CNN News Article "As Fauci Warns Monkeypox Needs to be Taken More Seriously, Former FDA Commissioner Says the Window to Control It 'Probably Has Closed".

Media Type: Mainstream Media.

Framing Model: Framing of Situations.

Overview: The news article aims to draw public and government attention to the prevention and handling of monkeypox by highlighting the confirmed case data using the framing of situations. The authors emphasize the severity of the situation by employing language techniques that highlight the temporal aspect of the issue.

Messages: The article cites Dr. Scott Gottlieb's warning that it may be too late to control the virus and the latest data from the CDC, which shows at least 1,814 probable or confirmed cases in the US and a total of 12,556 confirmed cases in 68 countries.

Analysis: The authors use framing of situations to emphasize the severity of the monkeypox issue and to raise awareness nationally and internationally. The language techniques used in the article, such as "too late to control" and "very likely an undercount," draw attention to the temporal element of the situation and emphasize its severity. This approach is used to encourage the public and governments to take necessary measures to prevent and manage the outbreak.

Article ID = 2 [31].

Title: What is monkeypox, and how can you stay safe as it spreads?

Media Type: Mainstream Media.

Framing Model: Attribute framing model.

Overview: This news article provided a lot of information about monkeypox in terms of the disease, symptoms, how it is spread and who has the risks of getting infected, what people should do if they get the disease, and how to prevent it. Given that monkeypox has recently emerged as a concern, the public might feel anxious because they do not know how it is spread and how to avoid it. Moreover, although the lesion typically concentrates on the arms and legs, some rash appears on the genital and perianal areas, and many people are afraid of infected STDs.

Messages: Dr. John Brooks, the CDC's chief medical officer of HIV prevention, … and other experts have been emphasizing that fact 'to remind people that people may come in for an evaluation of what they think is an STD, but we'd like the provider to think 'Could it be monkeypox as well?' if the circumstances fit the story.

Analysis: The author employed attribute framing to assuage the public's concerns by highlighting quotes from CDC and other experts. By emphasizing the credibility and expertise of these individuals, the author aimed to provide a fresh perspective for individuals worried about contracting STDs. This approach was taken because the cure rate for monkeypox is significantly higher than that of STDs. Additionally, Langmaid states that monkeypox can be transmitted through physical contact, respiratory secretions, and contaminated objects. Therefore, individuals who mistake their symptoms for STDs or HIV and seek consultation in hospitals may inadvertently increase the likelihood of monkeypox transmission. To change this potential behavior, the author framed the content in a way that encourages individuals to seek proper medical consultation for monkeypox.

8 Discussion and Conclusion

The literature review examined existing scientific research on COVID-19, adopting six models of framing theory, including the framing of situations, attributes, choices, actions, issues, and news [7]. Although this paper aimed to explore monkeypox through the lens of framing theory, the literature review predominantly focused on COVID-19 due to the emergent nature of monkeypox and limited research on the topic [32, 33]. Nevertheless, the studies on COVID-19, also a pandemic infectious disease, provided a valuable foundation for understanding monkeypox, particularly as both occurred within a two-year span [34, 35]. The literature utilizing the six framing theory models to study COVID-19 serves as a solid base for comprehending the monkeypox pandemic, thereby supporting the subsequent content analysis and media feature review.

The distribution outputs from the analysis indicated that the recent monkeypox outbreak was covered by both news articles and social media using various framing techniques to shape public perception and behavior. Both media types prioritized information on symptoms and transmission, which aligns with previous literature related to epidemics [36–38], followed by prevention and treatment. Social media more prominently discussed public opinion and attitudes than news articles, echoing findings by Boot's team on its role in shaping public discourse [39]. Additionally, both news articles and social media emphasized the importance of communicating public health measures through social strategies, as noted by Porat et al. [40] in 2020. The contingency tables showed that Framing of Situations and Actions were predominant across topics in mainstream media [41, 42], suggesting a preference for narrative and action-oriented approaches, reflective of a traditional journalistic style focused on storytelling and dynamic reporting. Social media widely utilized Framing of Actions and Issues, indicating a focus on immediate, dynamic content and contemporary issues, resonating with the interactive nature of these platforms.

The Chi-square statistic of 25.38 with a very low p-value suggests a statistically significant association between framing types and media type, indicating that the choice of framing in content varies significantly between social media and mainstream media. The low p-value (much lower than the standard alpha level of 0.05) implies that the observed differences in framing types between these two media types are unlikely to be due to chance. The moderate Cramér's V value ($V = 0.316$) indicates a moderate degree of association, suggesting that while certain framing styles are more prevalent in one media type over the other, there is still considerable overlap in the use of framing types across both social media and mainstream media.

Similarly, the Chi-square statistic of 23.67 with an extremely low p-value denotes a statistically significant association between the topics covered and the type of media. This finding implies that different media types tend to focus on different sets of topics, with certain topics being more prominent in either social media or mainstream media. The low p-value reinforces that these differences are not random variations but reflect distinct topical preferences or strategies of different media platforms. The Cramér's V value ($V = 0.323$), similar to the framing types of association, indicates a moderate degree of association, suggesting that each media type may have certain topics they cover more extensively, but there is significant overlap in topics covered by both social media and mainstream media.

Overall, social media demonstrated diverse utilization of framing types across different topics, reflecting the platform's dynamic and user-driven nature [43]. The variety in framing suggests a tailored approach to engage with a varied audience, adapting to user interests and interactions [44]. In contrast, mainstream media's contingency table indicated a more uniform distribution of framing types across topics, pointing to a potentially more standardized approach to news reporting and topic presentation, likely driven by traditional journalistic standards and audience expectations.

This study is fundamental for future research on the monkeypox pandemic, providing early-stage patterns of media portrayal and public perceptions of the disease. These observations are crucial for public health communication strategies. Understanding the nuances in media framing can aid health professionals and communicators in effectively disseminating information and engaging the public on various platforms [4, 45]. In health crises like the monkeypox outbreak, leveraging each media type's strengths can enhance public awareness and promote informed decision-making [46].

While this study provides foundational insights, it has limitations that future research could address. Expanding the scope of media platforms and topics could yield a more comprehensive analysis. Further exploration of qualitative aspects, such as audience engagement and the specific impact of framing techniques, could offer deeper insights into content effectiveness. Future research might also investigate temporal changes in media framing trends, especially considering the rapidly evolving nature of social media.

References

1. Mpox in the U.S., https://www.cdc.gov/poxvirus/mpox/symptoms/index.html. Accessed 24 Apr 2023
2. Entman, R.M.: Framing: Toward Clarification of a Fractured Paradigm. **43**(4), 51–58 (1993)
3. Lecheler, S., de Vreese, C.H.: News Framing Effects, 1st edn. Routledge, London (2018)
4. Guenther, L., et al.: Framing as a concept for health communication: a systematic review. Health Commun. **36**(7), 891–899 (2020)
5. D'angelo, P.: Framing Theory and Journalism. 1–10 (2019)
6. Bullock, O.M., Shulman, H.C.: Utilizing framing theory to design more effective health messages about tanning behavior among college women. **72**(3), 319–332 (2021)
7. Hallahan, K.: Seven Models of Framing: Implications for Public Relations. **11**(3), 205–242 (1999)
8. Bao, H., et al.: Digital Media's Role in the COVID-19 Pandemic. **8**(9), e20156 (2020)
9. Olagoke, A.A., et al.: Exposure to coronavirus news on mainstream media: the role of risk perceptions and depression. Br. J. Health Psychol. **25**(4), 865–874 (2020)
10. Widmann, T.: Fear, Hope, and COVID-19: emotional elite rhetoric and its impact on the public during the first wave of the COVID-19 pandemic. **43**(5), 827–850 (2022)
11. Schnell, F., et al.: Ageism and perceptions of vulnerability: framing of age during the Covid-19 pandemic. Innov. Aging **8**(2), 170–177 (2021)
12. Barnes, K., Colagiuri, B.: Positive attribute framing increases COVID-19 booster vaccine intention for unfamiliar vaccines. **10**(6), 962 (2022)
13. Dobrowolski, Z.: The strategy of vaccination and global pandemic: how framing may thrive on strategy during and after Covid-19. Eur. Res. Stud. J. **24**(1), 532–541 (2021)
14. Bolsen, T., et al.: Framing the Origins of COVID-19. Sci. Commun. **42**(5), 562–585 (2020). https://doi.org/10.1177/1075547020953603
15. Hameleers, M.: Prospect theory in times of a pandemic: the effects of gain versus loss framing on risky choices and emotional responses during the 2020 coronavirus outbreak - evidence from the US and the Netherlands. Mass Commun. Soc. **24**(4), 479–499 (2021)
16. Gamson, W.A.: Hiroshima, the holocaust, and the politics of exclusion. Am. Sociol. Rev. **60**(1), 1–20 (1995)

17. Ogbodo, J., et al.: Communicating health crisis: a content analysis of global media framing of COVID-19. Health Promot. Perspect. **10**(3), 257–269 (2020)
18. Chen, H., et al.: A content analysis of Chinese news coverage on COVID-19 and tourism. Curr. Issues Tourism **25**(2), 198–205 (2020)
19. Mutua, S.N., Ong'ong'a, D.O.: Online News Media Framing of COVID-19 Pandemic: Probing the Initial Phases of the Disease Outbreak in International Media. **1**(2), e02006 (2020)
20. Ali, S.M.A., Sherman-Morris, K.: Pandemic and health reporting: a content analysis of New York times coverage of COVID-19 from January 01, 2020, to August 31, 2022. Soc. Sci. Hum. Open **8**(1), 100739 (2022)
21. Barnes, M.D., et al.: Analysis of media agenda setting during and after Hurricane Katrina: implications for emergency preparedness, disaster response, and disaster policy. Am. J. Public Health **98**(4), 604–610 (2008)
22. Hussain, A., et al.: Artificial intelligence–enabled analysis of public attitudes on Facebook and twitter toward COVID-19 vaccines in the United Kingdom and the United States: observational study. J. Med. Internet Res. **23**(4), e26627 (2021). https://doi.org/10.2196/26627
23. Malik, A., et al.: Public health agencies outreach through Instagram during the COVID-19 pandemic: crisis and emergency risk communication perspective. Int. J. Disaster Risk Reduction **61**, 1–9 (2021)
24. Laws, R.L., et al.: Symptoms and transmission of SARS-CoV-2 among children - Utah and Wisconsin, March-May 2020. Pediatrics **147**(1), 1–15 (2021)
25. Huang, Y., et al.: Monkeypox: epidemiology, pathogenesis, treatment, and prevention. Signal Transduct. Target. Ther. **7**(373), 1–22 (2022)
26. Meo, S.A. et al.: Public perceptions of the emerging human monkeypox disease and vaccination in Riyadh, Saudi Arabia: a cross-sectional study. **10**(9), 1534 (2022)
27. Silva, P.C.L. et al.: COVID-ABS: an agent-based model of COVID-19 epidemic to simulate health and economic effects of social distancing interventions. Chaos, Solitons Fract. **139**, 110088 (2020)
28. Gamson, W.A., Modigliani, A.: Media discourse and public opinion on nuclear power: a constructionist approach. Am. J. Sociol. **95**(1), 1–37 (1989)
29. Girum, T., et al.: Optimal strategies for COVID-19 prevention from global evidence achieved through social distancing, stay at home, travel restriction and lockdown: a systematic review. Arch. Public Health **79**, 150 (2021)
30. As Fauci warns monkeypox needs to be taken more seriously, former FDA commissioner says the window to control it 'probably has closed'. https://www.cnn.com/2022/07/17/health/monkeypox-cases-undercounted-fauci/index.html. Accessed 11 Aug 2022
31. What is monkeypox, and how can you stay safe as it spreads? https://www.cnn.com/2022/07/14/health/monkeypox-questions-update/index.html. Accessed 11 Aug 2022
32. Deshmukh, P., et al.: Monkeypox: what do we know so far? A short narrative review of literature. J. Assoc. Phys. India **70**(7), 87–90 (2022)
33. Webb, E.M., et al.: Availability, scope, and quality of monkeypox clinical management guidelines globally: a systematic review. BMJ Glob. Health **7**(8), e009838 (2022)
34. Tusabe, F., et al.: Lessons Learned from the Ebola Virus Disease and COVID-19 Preparedness to Respond to the Human Monkeypox Virus Outbreak in Low- and Middle-Income Countries. Infect. Drug Resist. **15**, 6279–6286 (2022)
35. Kumar, N. et al.: The 2022 outbreak and the pathobiology of the monkeypox virus. **131**, 102855 (2022)
36. Lazard, A.J., Scheinfeld, E., Bernhardt, J.M., Wilcox, G.B., Suran, M.: Detecting themes of public concern: a text mining analysis of the centers for disease control and prevention's Ebola live Twitter chat. Am. J. Infect. Control **43**(10), 1109–1111 (2015). https://doi.org/10.1016/j.ajic.2015.05.025

37. Wicke, P., Bolognesi, M.M.: Framing COVID-19: how we conceptualize and discuss the pandemic on Twitter. PLoS ONE **15**(9), e0240010 (2020). https://doi.org/10.1371/journal.pone.0240010

38. Ophir, Y., et al.: The framing of COVID-19 in Italian media and its relationship with community mobility: a mixed-method approach. J. Health Commun. **26**(3), 161–173 (2021). https://doi.org/10.1080/10810730.2021.1899344

39. Boot, A.B., Dijkstra, K., Zwaan, R.A.: Correction: the processing and evaluation of news content on social media is influenced by peer-user commentary. Humanit. Soc. Sci. Commun. **8**(1), 209 (2021). https://doi.org/10.1057/s41599-021-00901-y

40. Porat, T., et al.: Public health and risk communication during COVID-19-enhancing psychological needs to promote sustainable behavior change. **8**, 1–15 (2020)

41. Framing of the Covid-19 pandemic and its organizational predictors. **50**, 91–112 (2021)

42. Nwakpu, E.S., Ezema, V.O., Ogbodo, J.N.: Nigeria media framing of coronavirus pandemic and audience response. Health Promot. Perspect. **10**(3), 192–199 (2020). https://doi.org/10.34172/hpp.2020.32

43. Bahtar, A.Z., Muda, M.: The impact of user – generated content (UGC) on product reviews towards online purchasing – a conceptual framework. Procedia Econ. Finance **37**, 337–342 (2016)

44. van Ruler, B.: Communication theory: an underrated pillar on which strategic communication rests. Int. J. Strateg. Commun. **12**(4), 367–381 (2018). https://doi.org/10.1080/1553118X.2018.1452240

45. Gao, R., et al.: The effects of health behaviours and beliefs based on message framing among patients with chronic diseases: a systematic review. BMJ Open **12**(1), e055329 (2022)

46. Mohammed, F., Al-Kumaim, N.H., Alzahrani, A.I., Fazea, Y.: The impact of social media shared health content on protective behavior against COVID-19. Int. J. Environ. Res. Public Health **20**(3), 1775 (2023). https://doi.org/10.3390/ijerph20031775

Prediction and Analysis of Multiple Causes of Mental Health Problems Based on Machine Learning

Shengli Deng[1] , Fan Wang[1](✉) , Yunna Cai[1] , Haowei Wang[1] ,
Zhenyu Wang[2] , Qianwen Qian[1] , and Weiwei Ding[1]

[1] School of Information Management, Wuhan University, Wuhan 430072, China
1161252028@qq.com
[2] School of Information Management, Nanjing University, Nanjing 210023, China

Abstract. To prevent other types of mental health problems from being misclassified as depression, as well as to remedy the problem of inadequate resources for mental health consultations. This study first analyzes the types of different causes of mental health problems, providing an important basis for better understanding the diversity and complexity of this field. Subsequently, a machine learning approach was used to predict the potential causes of different types of mental health problems. This research provides new perspectives and methods for early identification and personalized treatment of mental health problems. The experimental results show that depression accounts for only 16.9% of mental health problems. In the prediction of the causes of mental health problems, the SVM method performed best in predicting the causes of mental health problems, outperforming 5 machine learning methods and 3 deep learning methods. Through these studies, we hope to prevent other types of mental health problems from being misclassified as depression and to remedy the lack of resources for mental health counseling. This will help increase the success rate of early intervention and provide better mental health support for patients.

Keywords: Mental Health · Depression · Misclassification · Machine Learning · Early Prediction

1 Introduction

Mental health problems, as a common mental health disorder, have become a major public health issue globally. According to the World Health Organization, approximately 340 million people worldwide are affected by mental health problems, and this number continues to rise [1]. Mental health problems not only have a profound impact on the quality of life of the sufferer, but also place a huge burden on the family and society. Yet, in this context, resources for counseling are relatively inadequate, with an insufficient number of healthcare professionals [2]. In addition, it is often the case that people with other types of mental health problems are misdiagnosed with depression, which makes early identification and individualized treatment particularly important [3].

I. Sserwanga et al. (Eds.): iConference 2024, LNCS 14598, pp. 150–160, 2024.
https://doi.org/10.1007/978-3-031-57867-0_11

The aim of this paper is to explore the multifactorial causes of mental health problems and try to identify the different types of causes leading to mental health problems with the help of machine learning and deep learning techniques. By delving into the causes of mental health problems, we are expected to provide new perspectives and methods for accurate early diagnosis and personalized treatment.

The value of the study lies in the introduction of machine learning techniques into the field of analyzing the causes of mental health problems, which provides a new opportunity for the development of the fields of precision medicine and mental health. Through this study, doctors can understand the diversity and complexity of mental health problems more quickly, provide patients with more personalized treatment plans, and improve the success rate of treatment. At the same time, this study also provides useful lessons for research and practice in the field of mental health and is expected to promote early identification and intervention of mental health problems and improve patients' quality of life.

In the specific study, we will detail the methodology, experimental results, and conclusion part of the study, and the main contributions of this paper are as follows:

- Analysis of causes of mental health problems: This study systematically analyzed multiple factors that contribute to mental health problems, including depression. The importance and percentage of various causes in mental health problems were statistically analyzed, providing a database for in-depth research.
- Predicting the causes of mental health problems: This paper introduces machine learning and deep learning techniques to predict different types of causes of mental health problems, including depression. This innovative approach uses computer algorithms to analyze textual data to automate cause prediction, providing new methods and tools for mental health research.

2 Related Work

Early work in the field of research on mental health problems focused on symptom diagnosis and improvement of psychotherapeutic approaches [4]. However, with the rapid development of machine learning and deep learning techniques, more and more research is focusing on how these techniques can be used to analyze and predict the underlying causes of mental health problems for more accurate diagnosis and treatment [5].

In the literature, there are several studies focusing on the classification and prediction of depression [6]. Naseem et al. used natural language processing techniques and machine learning algorithms to successfully identify verbal features of depressed individuals [7]. However, no distinction was made between depression and other mental health problems.

On the other hand, some studies have focused on analyzing the multifactorial causes of mental health problems. Fraser et al. used statistical methods to retrospectively analyze multiple causes of mental health problems [8].

Relative to existing studies, the unique feature of this paper is the integrated use of machine learning techniques to analyze and predict the causes of mental health problems. This will help identify and intervene in mental health problems more accurately and improve patients' quality of life.

3 Experiments

3.1 Data Collection and Processing

BetterHelp is an online mental health platform focused on providing high-quality psychotherapy and counseling services. We obtained 2400 Q&A data from this online community for mental health counseling, and the format of each raw data is shown in Table 1. After data cleaning to remove advertisements and blank phrases, 1958 articles remain. Mental health experts and medical professionals were then asked to categorize the causes of mental health problems caused by the patients as shown in Table 2. Figures 1 and 2 show the exact number and percentage of different categories, respectively. We found that depression accounted for only 16.4% of mental health consultations. The percentage of people who were mentally healthy was 11.4%. The percentage of other types of psychological problems was 71.7. Therefore, there is a need to strictly differentiate between other types of mental health problems to prevent misdiagnosis of depression.

Table 1. Table captions should be placed above the tables.

Content	
User's Question Title:	Can I change my feeling of being worthless to everyone?
User's Question Content:	I'm going through some things with my feelings and myself. I barely sleep and I do nothing but think about how I'm worthless and how I shouldn't be here. I've never tried or contemplated suicide. I've always wanted to fix my issues, but I never get around to it. How can I change my feeling of being worthless to everyone?
Mental Health Expert's Response	If everyone thinks you're worthless, then maybe you need to find new people to hang out with. Seriously, the social context in which a person lives is a big influence on self-esteem. Otherwise, you can go round and round trying to understand why you're not worthless, then go back to the same crowd and be knocked down again...

3.2 Experimental Procedure

We divided the dataset into training, testing, and validation sets in the ratio of 6:2:3, and then used multiple machine learning methods to identify the causes of emerging mental health problems. As shown in Table 3. These methods are classical machine learning methods.

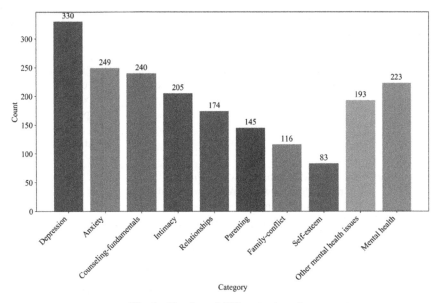

Fig. 1. Number of different categories

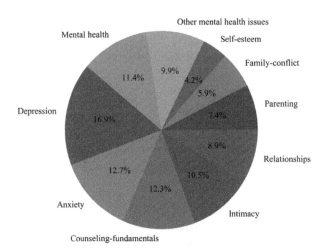

Fig. 2. Proportion of Various Mental Health Issues

Optimal Parameter Selection Experiment

SVM often performs well on text classification tasks with few samples. Therefore, we mainly chose SVM as a method for the prediction of causes of mental health problems and carried out experiments on optimal parameter selection. Since the main hyperparameters present in SVM are c-value and kernel function, we chose five groups of c-value, which are 0.01, 0.1, 1, 10, 100, 1000 and four kernel functions, which are 'linear', 'poly', 'rbf', 'sigmoid'.

Table 2. Example of Mental Health Experts Categorizing the Causes of Mental Health Issues

Category	User Problem Title	User Problem Content	Expert Response
Depression	Can I change my feeling of being worthless to everyone?	I'm going through some things with my feelings and myself....	If everyone thinks you're worthless, then maybe you need to find new people to hang out with. Seriously, the social context in which ...
Family conflict	No matter what I do, my mom will almost always find something wrong...	My mother has Alzheimer's, and she has become so nasty and mean to ...	It is challenging to see one's parents age and to cope with the new demands. Your mom means a lot to you, and that is why you get...
...	...	...	...
Mental Health	How to do personal growth and development?	I've heard that a lot of people are prone to depression ...	Ensuring mental health and personal growth is an important concern for everyone...

Table 3. Classical Machine Learning Methods

NO	Typology	Methods	Literatures
1	Machine Learning	XGBoost	[9]
2		Adaboost	[10]
3		SVM (Support Vector Machine)	[11]
4		Logistic Regression	[12]
5		Bayes	[13]
6		KNN (K-Nearest Neighbor)	[14]
7	Deep learning	FastText	[15]
8		TextCNN	[16]
9		TextRNN	[15]

The 20 sets of optimal parameter selection experiments were carried out on the validation set as shown in Fig. 3. Since the F1 value can fully represent the performance of the model, we selected the best C value of 1 and the best kernel function of 'linear' based on the F1 value in Fig. 3(d).

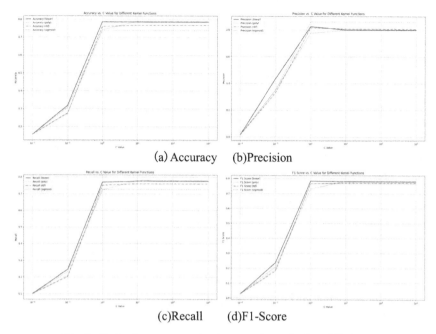

(a) Accuracy   (b)Precision

(c)Recall   (d)F1-Score

Fig. 3. Optimal parameter selection experiment in the validation set

Comparison with Machine Learning Methods
In the mental health problem cause prediction task, we evaluated different machine learning classification methods to determine their performance in identifying 10 different causes of mental health problems. Parameters were tuned to optimize in all methods. We also used Accuracy, Precision, Recall and F1 Score to get a complete picture of the performance of various methods [17]. Figure 4 shows the performance comparison results of different machine learning methods, and Fig. 5 shows the confusion matrix results of different machine learning methods.

First, SVM excels in all performance metrics and is the top ranked method with its high accuracy, precision, recall and F1 value. This could explain why SVM performs well in this task. SVM is an effective classifier especially for high-dimensional data, and textual data usually has high-dimensional features, so SVM can efficiently delineate the boundaries between different causes of mental health problems. Secondly, XGBoost also performs well, albeit slightly less well than SVM, but still excels in areas such as precision and recall. XGBoost is an integrated learning method that typically performs well in classification tasks but requires good feature engineering to realize its potential. However, Adaboost, while in the middle of the pack in terms of performance, is slightly lower than the other methods in terms of accuracy and F1 values. It can be sensitive to noisy data and therefore requires more data cleaning and preprocessing. Logistic regression performs well in terms of precision but is relatively low in terms of recall and F1 value. It is a simple linear classifier and may not be sufficient to capture complex relationships in textual data. Finally, the relatively poor performance of Bayesian methods and KNN may

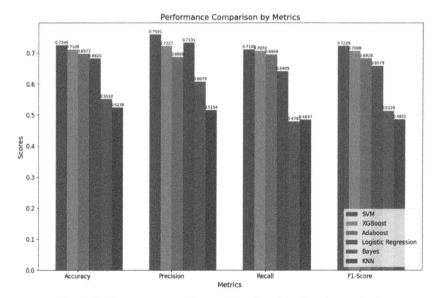

Fig. 4. Performance comparison results of machine learning methods

be due to their assumption that features are independent of each other, an assumption that is usually not true in text categorization.

In summary, SVM and XGBoost are the methods that perform well in the task of predicting the causes of mental health problems, mainly because of their ability to handle high-dimensional textual data and complex feature relationships. Logistic regression performed well in terms of precision, but more improvements are needed to increase recall and F1 values. For future work, more complex textual feature extraction methods and more training data could be considered to further improve classification performance. This will help to improve the accuracy and usefulness of mental health problem category identification.

These confusion matrices also reflect the potential for machine learning to misdiagnose. The reason is that there may be potential feature overlap between similar diseases, making it difficult for the model to accurately distinguish them. This similarity may manifest itself in the sharing of similar keywords, symptoms, or descriptions in textual data, making it difficult for the model to capture subtle differences between them during learning. From a clinical perspective, misdiagnosis may result in patients receiving inappropriate treatment. Therefore, it is recommended to use the combination of doctors and artificial intelligence for disease diagnosis.

Deep Learning Methods
The performance comparison between the deep learning method and the SVM method is shown in Fig. 6. The parameters of all these deep learning methods have been tuned to the optimum, but transfer learning has not been used. Notably.

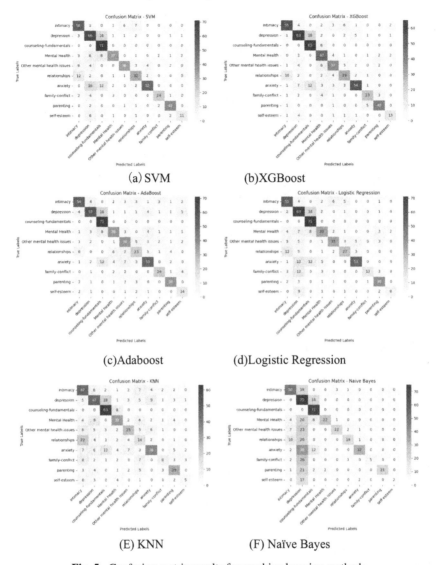

Fig. 5. Confusion matrix results for machine learning methods

Figure 6 shows that the deep learning methods are lower than the machine learning methods on all four metrics. This may be a result of the mental health data being a small sample of data.

However, psychological data often involves privacy, so it is difficult to obtain a large amount of patient data. In the future, we will try to improve the performance of deep learning methods by using transfer learning [18].

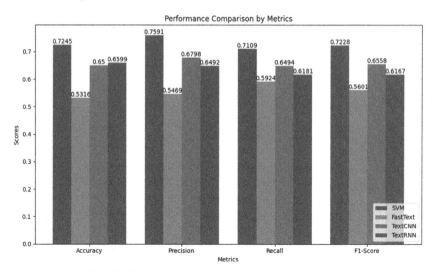

Fig. 6. Performance results for deep learning methods

4 Research Implications

4.1 Theoretical Implications

This study expands the application of machine learning in the field of mental health. By validating various machine learning classification methods, this study provides new ideas for identifying the etiology of depression. This is crucial for understanding natural language representations of emotional and mental health problems as well as highlighting potential limitations of text categorization techniques. In addition, this study highlights the scope for improvement of text categorization techniques, aiming to provide better tools and methods for accurate classification of text data in healthcare.

4.2 Practical Implications

This study offers great potential for early identification of mental health problems and personalized treatment plans. First, by identifying the underlying causes of depression, the model developed in this study can help healthcare professionals identify patients' mental health problems early. This could enable early intervention and improve the success of treatment. Second, based on the results of this study, a more personalized treatment plan can be designed. Healthcare professionals can tailor treatment strategies for each patient based on the specific cause of the condition identified, thereby improving treatment outcomes.

In addition, this study helps optimize resources. By automatically identifying patients' mental health problems and underlying etiologies, the model developed in this study can help healthcare providers better allocate resources and optimize the delivery of mental health services. This has the potential to reduce wasted resources and improve service efficiency.

Most importantly, this study provides a new approach to reducing the burden of mental health forecasting. As mental health problems continue to increase, this study has the potential to improve the early identification and treatment of these problems, ultimately improving patients' quality of life. These results are expected to advance the field of mental health and provide substantial support for policy and practice to better meet society's need for mental health care.

5 Conclusions

In this study, we first deeply analyzed the different causes of mental health problems, which provides an important reference for understanding the diversity and complexity of mental health problems and prevents misclassifying other types of mental health problems as depression. Then, through the application of machine learning and deep learning methods, the automatic identification of the etiology of different types of mental health problems was successfully realized, which provided new perspectives and solutions for research related to mental health problems. Finally, the research value and applicable fields of this study are discussed.

Despite the results of this study, there are some limitations. First, the relatively small size of the dataset in this study may limit the generalization ability of the model. In addition, the impact of the quality and completeness of the textual data on the results still needs to be further considered and improved. In addition, the causes of mental health problems are a multidimensional issue, and the features and methods used in this study may not be comprehensive enough and need to be further expanded and deepened.

Future research can improve the performance and reliability of the model in many ways, such as expanding the size of the dataset, adopting algorithms with transformer architecture, incorporating multimodal content, and so on. In addition, treatment strategies for different types of mental health problems can be explored in depth to provide more references for personalized treatment. Meanwhile, the feasibility and practicality of the model can also be further verified with actual clinical data to promote the further development of the research field of mental health problems.

References

1. Sheeran, T., Zimmerman, M.: Case identification of depression with self-report questionnaires. Psychiatry Res. **109**, 51–59 (2002)
2. Schwenzer, M., Zattarin, E., Grozinger, M., Mathiak, K.: Impaired pitch identification as a potential marker for depression. BMC Psychiatry **12** (2012)
3. Cai, J.Y., Wang, Z.J., Appel-Cresswell, S., McKeown, M.J., IEEE: feature selection to simplify BDI for efficient depression identification. In: IEEE Canadian Conference on Electrical and Computer Engineering (CCECE) (2016)
4. Narendorf, S.C., et al.: Self-identification of mental health problems among young adults experiencing homelessness. Community Ment. Health J. **59**, 844–854 (2023)
5. Chen, Y.Y., Liu, J.X., Chen, H.T., He, Y.L., Chen, H.L.: Divergence and integration of identification methods for geriatric mental health disorders in nonspecialized institutions-a qualitative study of service providers from different departments in Shanghai, China. Aging & Mental Health (2023)

6. Zhou, G.Y., Liu, X.L., Fu, S.H., Sun, Z.X.: Parallel identification and filling of depressions in raster digital elevation models. Int. J. Geogr. Inf. Sci. **31**, 1061–1078 (2017)
7. Naseem, U., Dunn, A.G., Kim, J., Khushi, M.: ACM: early identification of depression severity levels on Reddit using ordinal classification. In: 31st ACM Web Conference (WWW), pp. 2563–2572 (2022)
8. Bilz, L.: Mental Health in Schools. Padiatrie Und Padologie **58**, 8–12 (2023)
9. Chen, T.Q., Guestrin, C., Assoc Comp, M.: XGBoost: a scalable tree boosting system. In: 22nd ACM SIGKDD International Conference on Knowledge Discovery and Data Mining (KDD), pp. 785–794. Assoc. Comput. Mach. New York (2016)
10. El Rifai, H., Al Qadi, L., Elnagar, A.: Arabic text classification: the need for multi-labeling systems. Neural Comput. Appl. **34**(2), 1135–1159 (2021). https://doi.org/10.1007/s00521-021-06390-z
11. Cortes, C., Vapnik, V.: Support-vector networks. Mach. Learn. **20**, 273–297 (1995)
12. Bangyal, W.H., et al.: Detection of fake news text classification on COVID-19 using deep learning approaches. Comput. Math. Methods Med. **2021**, 1–14 (2021). https://doi.org/10.1155/2021/5514220
13. Pedregosa, F., et al.: Scikit-learn: machine learning in Python. J. Mach. Learn. Res. **12**, 2825–2830 (2011)
14. Cingillioglu, I.: Detecting AI-generated essays: the ChatGPT challenge. Int. J. Inf. Learn. Technol. **40**, 259–268 (2023)
15. Yang, X., Li, Y.J., Li, Q.K., Liu, D., Li, T.R.: Temporal-spatial three-way granular computing for dynamic text sentiment classification. Inf. Sci. **596**, 551–566 (2022)
16. Guo, B., Zhang, C.X., Liu, J.M., Ma, X.Y.: Improving text classification with weighted word embeddings via a multi-channel TextCNN model. Neurocomputing **363**, 366–374 (2019)
17. Devlin, J., Chang, M.W., Lee, K., Toutanova, K.: BERT: Pre-training of deep bidirectional transformers for language understanding. In: Conference of the North American-Chapter of the Association-for-Computational-Linguistics - Human Language Technologies (NAACL-HLT), pp. 4171–4186. Association Computational Linguistics-ACL, Stroudsburg (2019)
18. Geng, Z.C., Yan, H., Qiu, X.P., Huang, X.J.: FastHan: a BERT-based multi-task toolkit for Chinese NLP. In: Joint Conference of 59th Annual Meeting of the Association-for-Computational-Linguistics (ACL)/11th International Joint Conference on Natural Language Processing (IJCNLP)/6th Workshop on Representation Learning for NLP (RepL4NLP), pp. 99–106. Association Computational Linguistics-ACL, Stroudsburg (2021)

Automated Compliance Analysis on Clinical Notes to Improve Cancer Lifestyle Management

Yujia Hou[1]([⊠]) [iD] and Javed Mostafa[2] [iD]

[1] University of North Carolina at Chapel Hill, Chapel Hill, NC 27599, USA
yujia.hou@unc.edu
[2] University of Toronto, Toronto, ON M5S 1A1, Canada

Abstract. Maintaining a healthy lifestyle is essential for cancer patients, and certain lifestyle factors can help manage specific types of cancer. However, research has shown that lifestyle information is not effectively communicated during clinical visits, and patients may not receive appropriate guidance to manage their lifestyles during cancer treatment. This paper will develop an automatic compliance analysis method and examine the present state of lifestyle information documented in clinical notes, discover for which type of cancer patients are receiving the most appropriate lifestyle recommendations during clinical visits, and assess the extent of compliance between the lifestyle recommendations and published standard guidelines. Results indicate that the average frequency of selected lifestyle keywords appeared 4 times during each clinical visit, and only 3% of medical notes pertained to patients' lifestyle. Diet and weight-related keywords were the most frequently mentioned lifestyle factors, but the compliance was low for major types of cancer. The proposed method could have significant implications for improving cancer patients' lifestyle management by facilitating timely and accurate assessment of lifestyle recommendations from clinicians.

Keywords: Cancer · Lifestyle · Natural Language Processing · Electronic Health Record · Compliance Analysis

1 Background

1.1 Introduction

Cancer is a complex disease that requires multifaceted care. Besides cancer treatment such as surgery, chemotherapy, and radiation to cancer survivorship, lifestyle is also a crucial aspect to improve cancer management. Lifestyle factors such as diet, physical activity, sleep pattern, smoking status and alcohol consumption can have a significant impact on cancer risk and overall health outcomes. In common long-term cancers like breast, colon, prostate, and lung cancers, there is increasing evidence linking these factors to the risk of cancer development, recurrence, and mortality [1]. Therefore, it is essential for cancer patients to receive information and guidance on how to make healthy lifestyle choices, as healthy lifestyle is beneficial for them to manage cancer symptoms, reduce risk of recurrence, and improve overall quality of life [2, 3]. Notably, different types of cancer may require different lifestyle modifications to improve patient outcomes, such as dietary changes, exercise recommendations, and smoking cessation [4, 5].

I. Sserwanga et al. (Eds.): iConference 2024, LNCS 14598, pp. 161–169, 2024.
https://doi.org/10.1007/978-3-031-57867-0_12

National organizations such as the American Cancer Society (ACS) have issued guidelines on Nutrition and Physical Activity for Cancer Survivors (NPGCS) for the past few decades. Unfortunately, despite the availability of numerous lifestyle guidelines, studies have shown that such information is not always effectively communicated, and patients may not receive appropriate guidance to manage their lifestyles during cancer treatment. Most cancer patients still have low awareness and adherence to the guidelines [6]. Cancer patients often rely on professional support during and after treatment to adopt healthy lifestyle habits [7].

Medical appointments offer direct and personalized interactions between clinicians and patients, allowing a thorough discussion of lifestyle factors and recommendations. The key information is recorded in electronic health records (EHRs), the clinical notes section, which contains textual descriptions of physician-patient encounters, capturing important medical and lifestyle information. As a crucial intermediary, clinicians are supposed to be knowledgeable about the guidelines and help patients maintain good adherence during their clinical appointments. Previous research used self-reported questionnaires and group interview assessments indicating that many healthcare providers recognize the importance of lifestyle factors in cancer survivorship, and patients have shown positive attitudes towards receiving lifestyle recommendations during medical visits, however, there are still existing barriers for cancer patients to receive enough lifestyle information [8–10]. During medical encounters, the topics usually focus on diagnosis, treatment, and medications of cancer management, and patient lifestyle information is not systematically collected [11].

To better assess the importance of lifestyle factors in clinical notes, we utilized natural language processing (NLP) techniques to automatically analyze the compliance of lifestyle information in clinical notes and published lifestyle guidelines. Compliance reveals how closely the recommendations align with established guidelines. There has been previous work showing an outline and preliminary results of conducting an automatic compliance analysis on clinical notes [12]. And this study will further explore the automatic compliance analysis method and provide comparison for different cancer types. This study will provide timely feedback for clinicians and patients to discover if there is a lack of lifestyle information during clinical visits, and eventually improve lifestyle communication during clinical visits and patient adherence.

1.2 Research Questions

This paper aims to examine and present results for the following questions:

1. What is the present state of lifestyle information documented in clinical notes for cancer patients?
2. For which type of cancer are patients receiving the most accurate lifestyle management recommendations from clinicians during clinical visits?
3. What are the degrees of compliance between the lifestyle recommendations and published standard guidelines?

1.3 Related Literature

NLP has been playing a crucial role in EHR data in automating data extraction, facilitating prediction models, improving disease detection, and enhancing risk assessments.

Kasthurirathne et al. [13] evaluated the performance of common classification algorithms to detect cancer cases from free-text pathology reports using nondictionary approaches, and Napolitano et al. [15] facilitated the extraction of information relevant to cancer staging, proposing a model for semi structured reports that outperformed the model for unstructured reports alone. In Zhou et al. [16], authors applied NLP techniques to automatically extract lifestyle exposures as well and corresponding intervention strategies from clinical notes, to investigate the prevalence of lifestyle risk factor exposures among Alzheimer's disease (AD) patients. Shoenbill et al. [17] used an existing open-source NLP tool on electronic health records to automatically identify lifestyle modification documentation data and make them be ready for analysis. Feller et al. [18] examined and proved that NLP improved the predictive performance of automated HIV risk assessment by extracting terms in clinical text indicative of high-risk behavior. These applications showcase the versatility and effectiveness of NLP in transforming clinical data into valuable insights for healthcare professionals and researchers.

2 Methodology

2.1 Data and Material

MIMIC-IV-Note
MIMIC-IV-Note is a collection of deidentified free-text clinical notes for patients included in the MIMIC-IV clinical database, a standard public dataset published on Jan. 6, 2023, on PhysioNet. MIMIC-IV-Note contains deidentified discharge summaries from 145,915 patients admitted to the hospital and emergency department at the Beth Israel Deaconess Medical Center in Boston, MA, USA, between 2008 and 2019. The discharge table which contains discharge summaries for hospitalizations is used in this paper. Discharge summaries are long form narratives which describe the reason for a patient's admission to the hospital, their hospital course, and any relevant discharge instructions [19].

American Cancer Society Nutrition and Physical Activity Guideline for Cancer Survivors
The ACS published NPGCS in 2006, 2012, and 2022. The purpose of this guideline is to provide evidence-based, cancer-specific recommendations for anthropometric parameters, physical activity, diet, and alcohol intake for reducing recurrence and cancer-specific and overall mortality. The guideline is intended to serve as a resource for informing ACS programs, health policy, and the media. As the medical notes dataset covers the period between 2008–2019, reference is made to the guidelines from 2006 [4] and 2012 [5].

2.2 The Automatic Compliance Analysis Method

This section elaborates on the framework for generating an automatic compliance analysis on the designated dataset. The process involves the following steps:

Step 1: Text Preprocessing. Patients with cancer-related medical records (diagnosed with cancer or had cancer family history) were filtered as the cohort for this study. In MIMIC-IV-Note, each free-text discharge summary is a mix of clinical notes and other patient information such as medical history, lab reports, physical exam data, medication etc., and is presented as a single text string. Therefore, this step extracted full sentences from discharge summaries and removed excessive information, to obtain more accurate notes from clinicians. Moreover, even though MIMIC-IV-Note is a discharge summary dataset, patients with recurrent inpatient care had more than one record, so all records were further grouped by patient ID.

Step 2: Keyword Frequency Analysis. Designated lifestyle keywords and their frequencies were extracted and calculated. The lifestyle keyword list included diet, food, meal, eat, drink, exercise, weight, obesity, sleep, alcohol, smoking, wellness, lifestyle, which were extracted from NPGCS as they were the general aspects discussed for each cancer type. Inflection of the keywords were also considered. Lifestyle keywords were further classified as Diet (diet, food, meal, eat, drink), BMI (obesity, weight, exercise), Wellness (lifestyle, wellness, sleep) and Smoking and Alcohol (smoking, alcohol) for a detailed lifestyle information analysis.

Step 3: Information Weighting Analysis. Traditional term weighting determines the significance of each individual keyword. Since lifestyle information is more than just keywords, we improved the traditional method (counting the ratio of keywords with total words) by conducting semantic analysis, along with rules and regular expressions to detect all the content related to keywords and calculated the ratio of the number of keywords related sentences to the total sentence number as the weight. The upgraded method can better present the weighting of desired information.

Step 4: Word Dictionary. To assess the compliance of the clinical notes and NPGCS, a word dictionary was generated by listing and comparing the extracted lifestyle sentences from MIMIC-IV-Note and an NLP summarized list from NPGCS. Substring matching score was calculated for compliance analysis.

Step 5: Cancer Type Analysis. Keywords weighted frequency and the compliance score were also calculated for different cancer types to analyze if their lifestyle information in clinical notes focused most on their own criteria, and how well it matched NPGCS guidelines. For instance, smoking cessation may be more critical for lung cancer patients, while dietary habits may be more important for colon cancer patients. The selection of the top five cancer types (breast, colon, lung, prostate, bladder) was based on their frequencies in the cohort, and the key lifestyle factors for each cancer time was summarized from NPGCS.

3   Results

Among all 145,915 patients, 52,561 had cancer-related medical records (diagnosed with cancer or had cancer family history) with 124,825 visits in total. In this cohort, 48,703 of them had lifestyle information on record. The frequency of each lifestyle keyword is presented in Fig. 1.

Among all records, "Diet" and "Weight" related keywords were notably more frequently mentioned than other aspects, "Alcohol" and "Sleep" were also two relatively

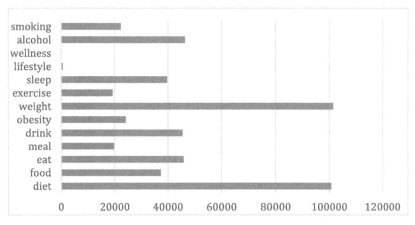

Fig. 1. Lifestyle Keywords Total Frequency

major aspects that were recorded during clinical visits. General words "Wellness" and "Lifestyle" barely appeared in the clinical notes.

The average frequency of lifestyle keywords appearing per visit is presented in Table 1. As there were recurrent visits for some patients, the average frequency of the keywords appearing in all visits for each patient is also presented. On average, each patient had lifestyle keywords involved 10.33 times for all their discharge summaries, and selected lifestyle keywords appeared 4.03 times for each clinical visit. Diet was the most frequent topic discussed which counted for over half of the time in lifestyle discussions, followed by BMI, Smoking and Alcohol, and Wellness.

Table 1. Lifestyle Keywords Average Frequency

Average Frequency	Lifestyle	Diet	BMI	Wellness	Smoking and Alcohol
per patient	10.33	5.12	2.98	0.83	1.41
per visit	4.03	2.00	1.16	0.32	0.55

Weighted frequency for lifestyle information is presented in Fig. 2. The pie chart on the left side presents the weight of the total lifestyle related information among all clinical records, and the weight for "Diet", "BMI", "Wellness", and "Smoking and Alcohol" on the right side is based on all lifestyle-related records. Results indicate that 3% of the clinical notes pertained to patients' lifestyle. "Diet" and "BMI" were accounting for 77% of the lifestyle-related discussions.

The key respective factors, the weighting of the factors (decimal representation of percentage) and the compliance ratio (0, 100), 100 represents the highest compliance) of them are listed in Table 2. For colon cancer, 89% of the lifestyle discussions were about diet, BMI, and alcohol intake, which should be taken care of the most for colon cancer. The key factors weighted frequency were about 50% for all other cancer types, which means that half of the lifestyle discussions were focusing on the most important

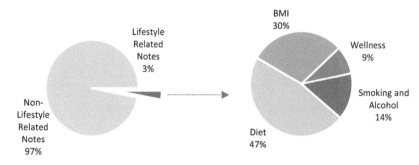

Fig. 2. Lifestyle Keywords Weighted Frequency

criteria. The compliance ratio was about 27 for all selected cancer types, indicating that the lifestyle clinical notes matched only 27% of the content in NPGCS.

Table 2. Key Lifestyle Factors Analysis by Cancer Type

Cancer Types	Breast	Colon	Lung	Prostate	Bladder
Key Lifestyle Factors	BMI, alcohol	diet, BMI, alcohol	diet, smoking	diet, BMI	BMI, smoking
Key Factors Weighted Frequency	0.47	0.89	0.47	0.54	0.48
Compliance Ratio	27.54	27.58	26.09	27.27	27.49

4   Discussion

The study presents an analysis of the frequency and compliance of lifestyle information in clinical notes for a large cohort of cancer patients. It is a positive finding that most cancer patients received lifestyle discussions during clinical visits. The results indicate that diet and weight related keywords are the most frequently mentioned lifestyle factors. This matches the finding from NPGCS that these two factors are emphasized and given the most instructions for all types of cancer. This reflects the importance of diet and BMI control in cancer lifestyle management. General words such as "wellness" and "lifestyle" were rarely mentioned in the clinical notes, which indicates that lifestyle instructions focus on more detailed aspects rather than broader concepts. More specific recommendations are beneficial for cancer patients to better understand and be coherent.

It also implies that there are no specific sections in clinical notes for lifestyle or wellness. The structure of clinical notes could be more organized on documenting lifestyle discussions.

The results also suggest that lifestyle information is not adequately discussed during clinical visits. While the average frequency of selected lifestyle keywords appeared 4 times during each clinical visit, only 3% of medical notes pertained to patients' lifestyle. Healthcare providers may need to prioritize lifestyle information more consistently to better support patients' cancer management, or the documenting method of clinical notes need to focus more on lifestyle management.

The key factors weighted frequency for different cancer types were also analyzed. Colon cancer was found to have a significant emphasis on its key factors, and the key factors were emphasized about half of the time for other cancer types. The compliance ratio shows that lifestyle clinical notes matched only 27% of the NPGCS instructions, indicating that there is a significant gap between the importance of lifestyle factors and the documentation of these factors in the clinical notes. This highlights the need for better adherence to guidelines for lifestyle management in cancer patients. Clinicians and patients should work together to ensure that lifestyle guidelines are effectively considered to better improve patients' treatment outcomes and quality of life.

5   Conclusion

Overall, this study underscores the significance of giving increased attention to lifestyle discussions during cancer clinical visits, and the need for clinicians to consistently document lifestyle information in clinical notes to better support cancer management. Compared to traditional questionnaire or interview methods, the use of an automatic compliance analysis method on clinical notes is more efficient and effective. By automating the compliance analysis, clinicians can easily identify areas where patients are not receiving appropriate lifestyle information and take steps to rectify the situation. Notably, this study makes a valuable contribution to the existing literature on the application of NLP methods for analyzing clinical notes in EHR, as it represents the first study specifically focused on cancer lifestyle management within this context.

This study has some limitations as MIMIC-IV-Note was extracted from discharge records. Newly diagnosed and under treatment cancer patients may receive more lifestyle recommendations from clinicians. Guidelines and lifestyle recommendations for patients with and without cancer family history may also vary. Furthermore, since this is a deidentified dataset, results might differ if demographic data is included. More detailed research will need to be conducted to identify specific cancer types, stages, and treatments that necessitate the highest amount of lifestyle management information for patients. This information will be used to establish a cohort for further investigation.

Based on the findings of this study, our future research will focus on improving the emphasis of lifestyle discussion in cancer clinical visits, by building deep learning models and proposing an upgraded documenting tool. Ultimately, this study will improve the quality of care for cancer patients by ensuring that clinicians are providing adequate lifestyle information, leading to more effective and personalized cancer treatment decisions and survivorship.

References

1. Vijayvergia, N., Denlinger, C.: Lifestyle factors in cancer survivorship: where we are and where we are headed. J. Personal. Med. **5**(3), 243–263 (2015). https://doi.org/10.3390/jpm 5030243
2. Demark-Wahnefried, W., Jones, L.W.: Promoting a healthy lifestyle among cancer survivors. Hematol. Oncol. Clin. North Am. **22**(2), 319–342 (2008). https://doi.org/10.1016/j.hoc.2008. 01.012
3. Hamer, J., Warner, E.: Lifestyle modifications for patients with breast cancer to improve prognosis and optimize overall health. Canadian Med. Assoc. J. **189**(7), E268–E274 (2017)
4. Doyle, C., et al. (2006)
5. Rock, C.L., et al.:Nutrition and physical activity guidelines for cancer survivors. CA: Cancer J. Clin. **62**(4), 242–274 (2012). https://doi.org/10.3322/caac.21142
6. James-Martin, G., Koczwara, B., Smith, E.L., Miller, M.D.: Information needs of cancer patients and survivors regarding diet, exercise and weight management: a qualitative study. Eur. J. Cancer Care **23**(3), 340–348 (2013). https://doi.org/10.1111/ecc.12159
7. Westhoff, E., et al.: Low awareness, adherence, and practice but positive attitudes (2019)
8. Balneaves, L.G., Truant, T.L., Van Patten, C., Kirkham, A.A., Waters, E., Campbell, K.L.: Patient and medical oncologists' perspectives on prescribed lifestyle intervention—experiences of women with breast cancer and providers. J. Clin. Med. **9**(9), 2815 (2020). https://doi.org/10.3390/jcm9092815
9. Stump, T.K., et al.: Physicians' perspectives on medication adherence and health promotion among cancer survivors. Cancer **125**(23), 4319–4328 (2019). https://doi.org/10.1002/cncr. 32410
10. Koutoukidis, D.: Lifestyle advice to cancer survivors: a qualitative study on the perspectives of Health Professionals (2017). https://doi.org/10.26226/morressier.5a05ac1fd462b80 29238a695
11. Chan, C., Cohall, A., Kaufman, D., Khan, S., Kukafka, R.: Selecting data elements to build a patient-centric electronic health record that will support adherence to therapeutic (2008)
12. Hou, Y., Mostafa, J.: IEEE/ACM CHASE 2023. In: Poster: Automatic Compliance Analysis on Clinical Notes and Lifestyle Guidelines in Cancer Survivorship, Orlando (IEEE/ACM CHASE 2023). (2023). https://doi.org/10.1145/3580252.3589422
13. Kasthurirathne, S.N., Dixon, B.E., Gichoya, J., Xu, H., Xia, Y., Mamlin, B., et al.: Toward better public health reporting using existing off the shelf approaches: the value of medical dictionaries in automated cancer detection using plaintext medical data. J. Biomed. Inform. **69**, 160–176 (2017)
14. Sheikhalishahi, S., Miotto, R., Dudley, J.T., Lavelli, A., Rinaldi, F., Osmani, V.: Natural language processing of clinical notes on chronic diseases: systematic review. JMIR Med. Inform. **7**(2), e12239 (2019). https://doi.org/10.2196/12239
15. Napolitano, G., Marshall, A., Hamilton, P., Gavin, A.T.: Machine learning classification of surgical pathology reports and chunk recognition for information extraction noise reduction. Artif. Intell. Med. **70**, 77–83 (2016)
16. Zhou, X., Wang, Y., Sohn, S., Therneau, T.M., Liu, H., Knopman, D.S.: Automatic extraction and assessment of lifestyle exposures for Alzheimer's disease using natural language processing. Int. J. Med. Informatics **130**, 103943 (2019). https://doi.org/10.1016/j.ijmedinf. 2019.08.003
17. Feller, D., Zucker, J., Yin, M.T., Gordon, P., Elhadad, N.: Using clinical notes and natural language processing for automated HIV risk assessment. J. Acquir. Immune Defic. Syndr. **77**(2), 160–166 (2018). https://doi.org/10.1097/qai.0000000000001580

18. Shoenbill, K., Song, Y., Gress, L., Johnson, H.M., Smith, M.A., Mendonça, E.A.: Natural language processing of lifestyle modification documentation. Health Informatics J. **26**(1), 388–405 (2019). https://doi.org/10.1177/1460458218824742
19. Johnson, A., Pollard, T., Horng, S., Celi, L.A., Mark, R.: MIMIC-IV-Note: deidentified free-text clinical notes (version 2.2). PhysioNet (2023). https://doi.org/10.13026/1n74-ne17

Navigating Health Information: Understanding Conflicting Adoption Mechanisms and Cognitive-Behavioral Paradoxes from the Patient's Lens

Yan Jin⬛, Di Zhao⬛, Zhuo Sun$^{(\boxtimes)}$ ⬛, Chongwu Bi, and Ruixian Yang⬛

School of Information Management, ZhengZhou University, ZhengZhou, China
sunshuo@zzu.edu.cn

Abstract. The advancement of information technology has significantly expanded the avenues and approaches through which individuals can access health-related information. However, this proliferation of information sources has also introduced challenges. Specifically, the abundance of diverse sources often generates conflicting health information, making it increasingly challenging for individuals to make informed decisions and navigate their health-related choices. While previous research has primarily focused on factors influencing adoption behavior, willingness to adopt, and the outcomes of adoption, there has been a relative neglect of the underlying processes, formation mechanisms, and the mechanics governing adoption behavior itself. To address this gap, this study takes a patient-centered approach to construct a model of Conflicting health information adoption. It seeks to comprehensively explore the adoption process and behavioral phenomena among patients, while also employing the concept of "trans-theory" to conduct a thorough analysis. The study's findings illuminate a common pattern when patients encounter conflicting health information: a misalignment between their cognitive understanding and their subsequent behavior across various facets of adoption behavior. This inconsistency arises from a complex interplay of factors, including the influence of information, individual abilities, psychological factors, and environmental conditions, all shaping the process of adopting Conflicting health information. This research, grounded in a patient-centric perspective, aims to shed light on the intricate dynamics of conflicting health information adoption. By bridging the gap between cognition and behavior, it seeks to contribute to a more informed and effective approach to health information management in a world marked by information abundance and complexity.

Keywords: Conflicting Health Information · Adoption Mechanisms · Cognitive-behavioral Paradoxes

1 Introduction

Patient-centered health information services are increasingly integrating with the Internet and social media, significantly expanding patient access to information [1]. However, this proliferation of information also heightens the likelihood of encountering Conflicting health information, which, to some extent, disrupts patients' decision-making

I. Sserwanga et al. (Eds.): iConference 2024, LNCS 14598, pp. 170–191, 2024.
https://doi.org/10.1007/978-3-031-57867-0_13

processes. Conflicting health information is typically described as information on the same healthcare topic with inconsistent content [2]. It can manifest in two forms: "inconsistent behavioral outcomes" and "inconsistent behavioral processes." Additionally, considering the strength of information conflict, it can be categorized into two types: strong conflict (beneficial-harmful) and weak conflict (beneficial-harmless).While current academic research primarily centers on strong conflicting information, addressing inconsistencies in behavioral processes like medication duration, frequency differentiation, efficacy, and side effects [3, 4], this paper will narrow its focus to weak conflicting health information, which has received less attention in existing research.

The conflicting nature of health information presents patients with significant challenges when it comes to adopting such information. Consequently, guiding patients to make rational and informed adoption decisions has become a pivotal issue in both theoretical research and practical healthcare. The existing research on information adoption has been conducted in the fields of social media [5], medical treatment [6], the travel industry [7], libraries [8], and others. However, most of these studies focus on user adoption outcomes and improve user behavior by exploring the influencing factors that lead to that outcome. Among them, the influencing factors are generally classified into three dimensions: subject [9], the object [10], and the environment [11].

Although scholars have conducted a wide range of studies on information adoption, there are still three important research gaps in studies based on the subject's perspective to explore the process of conflicting health information adoption: (1) Previous studies have mostly explored conflicting information from the perspectives of social systems and adoption programs, and there is a lack of research on conflicting health information adoption based on the patient's perspective [12, 13]. Therefore, there is a considerable need for targeted research on conflictual health information adoption around patient groups. (2) Most of the existing research focuses on the outcomes of adoption and lacks discussion of the specific adoption process of conflicting health information. Therefore, to clarify the specific aspects of the adoption process and its causes and mechanisms not only provides a new way of thinking to improve the adoption effect of patients, but also enriches the connotation of the discipline to a certain extent. (3) Although studies have examined the health information adoption behaviors of patient groups, they have not yet focused on cognitive and behavioral inconsistencies in the adoption of conflictual health information. Previous studies have discussed patients' adoption intention and behavior from a static perspective, ignoring the dynamic changes in cognition and behavior during the adoption process as well as the conflict between the two, which leads to a lack of precision in proposing measures to improve the adoption effect. Therefore, it is necessary to analyze the mechanism of dynamic changes in patients' cognition and behavior during the process of conflicting information adoption from a dynamic perspective, to understand the multidimensional reasons for the cognitive-behavioral paradox, and to provide guidance for the adoption of effective measures to improve the adoption of health information by patients.

In order to fill the research gaps mentioned above, this paper mainly adopts situational experiments, rootedness theory, questionnaire survey and other methods to design three studies [14, 15]. Firstly, based on scenario experiments and rootedness theory, we summarize the behavioral process and paradoxical phenomena of patients' adoption of conflicting health information. In this process, there are three typical phenomena of inconsistency between patients' cognition and behavior, and we have summarized the common aspects of adoption. Secondly, with the help of situational experiments and questionnaires, we confirmed that the above paradoxical phenomena are common and statistically significant. Finally, a model of conflictual health information adoption by patients is constructed based on the rootedness theory and explained by the idea of "trans-theory". At the same time, the causes and mechanisms of patients' cognitive and behavioral paradoxes are discussed. This paper not only helps to enrich the research on the granularity of the process of patients' adoption of conflicting health information, but also explores the paradox of cognitive-behavioral incongruence, which is of great theoretical value and practical significance.

Overall, this paper proposes to address the following three research questions:

(1) When patients are confronted with conflicting health information, are there common aspects of their adoption process? If so, what are they? Do patients' cognitions and behaviors show inconsistencies in the adoption process?
(2) Is the paradox of inconsistencies between patients' perceptions and behaviors universal?
(3) How do paradoxes between patients' perceptions and behaviors emerge? How are these phenomena related to various aspects of adoption?

2 Pilot Study

Research confirms that conflicting health information is not uncommon and that 13% of conflicting health information is related to health products [13, 16]. Based on this finding, we visited the First Affiliated Hospital of Zhengzhou University. The results showed that hyperglycemia is one of the important factors for current patients to consider whether to use health supplements. Therefore, conflicting health messages with the theme of "lowering/controlling sugar" were selected as experimental materials for this study. In order to exclude the influence of existing health product brands and existing perceptions on the experimental results, this paper sets "XYS health supplements are useful for reducing/controlling sugar" and "XYS health supplements are useless for reducing/controlling sugar" as a set of conflicting health information. In this case, the health supplement named XYS is a fictitious product. Furthermore, to simulate real-world information formats, we presented each viewpoint in both Science Expository Writing and Scientific Essay formats (Table 1 and Fig. 1).

In the pilot study, we utilized a questionnaire as a data collection tool to achieve two main objectives. Firstly, we sought to assess the users' ability to differentiate between information presented in different stylistic types. Secondly, we aimed to revalidate these stylistic types while also analyzing whether users could recognize the conflicting nature inherent in the messages. To validate the manipulation of genre types, we enlisted the participation of 103 patients in our study on conflicting health information genres. A five-point Likert scale format was employed for data collection. After reading the provided information, participants were instructed to rate specific questions on a scale of 1 to 5, with 1 indicating "strongly disagree" and 5 indicating "strongly agree." When participants were tasked with rating the following question, "How likely do you think

Table 1. Information on reading materials

Message number	The point of view	Genre
A	XYS health supplements are useful for reducing/controlling sugar	Science Expository Writing
B	XYS health supplements are useful for reducing/controlling sugar	Scientific Essay
C	XYS health supplements are useless for reducing/controlling sugar	Science Expository Writing
D	XYS health supplements are useless for reducing/controlling sugar	Scientific Essay

*(**Note:** Science Expository Writing uses more professional vocabulary and academic terms and is more rigorous in form; Scientific Essay is more colloquial and vivid in language and uses more rhetorical devices such as similes and metaphors.)*

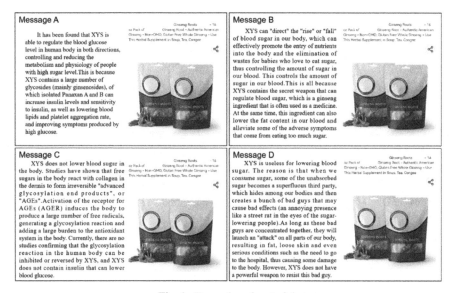

Fig. 1. Examples of materials

it is that the genre of the above material is a Science Expository Writing?" —we drew several key conclusions. Specifically, we observed a significant difference ($p < .001$) between the scores for Message A (Useful/Science Expository Writing) ($M = 4.25$, SD $= 0.860$) and Message B (Useful/Scientific Essay) ($M = 2.69$, SD $= 1.5321$). This disparity was confirmed by the analysis ($F_{(1,204)} = 82.407$). Furthermore, we designed reverse experimental materials based on Message A and Message B, resulting in Message C (Useless/Science Expository Writing) ($M = 4.28$, SD $= 0.954$) and Message D (Useless/Scientific Essay) ($M = 2.49$, SD $= 1.406$). Importantly, the scores for these two messages also exhibited significant differences (p < .001), as indicated by the analysis (F (1,204) = 155.061) (see Fig. 2).

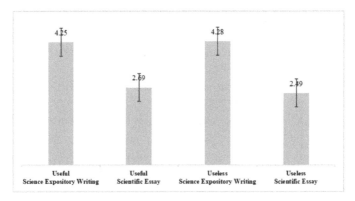

Fig. 2. Science Expository Writing scores

Next, we conducted a second verification of the genre type with the participation of 102 patients in this experiment. Participants were asked to rate the question: "How likely do you think it is that the genre of the above material is Science Expository Writing?" The results of the study yielded significant findings. Specifically, we observed a significant difference (p < .001) in the scores between Message A, labeled as "Useful/Science Expository Writing" (M = 4.25, SD = 0.906, F(1,203) = 89.750), and Message B, designated as "Useful/Scientific Essay" (M = 2.60, SD = 1.504, F(1, 203) = 89.750).Additionally, Message C, categorized as "Useless/Science Expository Writing" (M = 4.23, SD = 1.043, F(1,203) = 119.396), and Message D, identified as "Useless/Scientific Essay" (M = 2.36, SD = 1.370, F(1, 203) = 119.396), also displayed significant score differences (p < .001) (see Fig. 3).

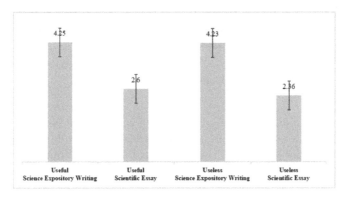

Fig. 3. Science Expository Writing scores

Lastly, we conducted an examination to determine whether the content of the information presented conflicting viewpoints. In this phase, we enlisted the participation of

102 patients in our experiment. These subjects were instructed to rate the following question: "How likely are you to think that the above message expresses a 'Useful' viewpoint?" The results of this examination unveiled noteworthy findings. Significantly, we identified a substantial difference (p < .001) in the scores between Message A, labeled as "Useful/Science Expository Writing" (M = 4.29, SD = 1.001, F (1,203) = 138.565), and Message C, categorized as "Useless/Science Expository Writing" (M = 2.33, SD = 1.352, F (1, 203) = 138.565). Furthermore, we observed a significant difference (p < 0.001) between the scores for Message B, denoted as "Useful/Scientific Essay" (M = 4.32, SD = 0.798, F (1,203) = 106.280), and Message D, characterized as "Useless/Scientific Essay" (M = 2.58, SD = 1.512, F (1, 203) = 106.280) (see Fig. 4).

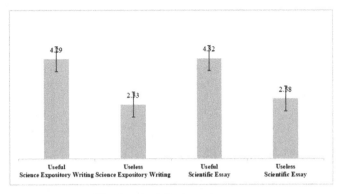

Fig. 4. "Useful" viewpoint score

3 Empirical Overview

This paper comprises three distinct research investigations. In Study 1, we conducted a meticulous examination of patients' reading behaviors, focusing on them as the target group. Subsequently, we employed a grounded theory approach to systematically organize the patients' adoption process, addressing the shortcomings identified in previous studies. Notably, during this stage, we unearthed paradoxical phenomena, revealing disparities between patients' perceptions and behaviors. Building upon the insights from Study 1, Study 2 was designed to validate the observed paradoxical phenomenon during the adoption process. The results conclusively affirmed the existence of cognitive and behavioral inconsistencies when patients confront conflicting health information. In Study 3, we synthesized the outcomes from the previous phases to construct a comprehensive model of patient adoption of conflicting health information. This model was developed based on interview results and elaborated using the concept of "trans-theory." In summary, the purpose of this paper is to provide an in-depth examination of patients' conflictual health information adoption processes and phenomena, and to provide an interpretive analysis through three studies with progressive relationships.

3.1 Study One: Patients' Conflicting Health Information Adoption Processes Experimental Methods

A random sampling method was used for the selection of the subjects, and they were screened for eligibility by prior questioning. There were two specific selection criteria [17]. First, they had the experience of seeking medical treatment for illnesses and had taken the initiative to pay attention to health information. The second is to have the ability and condition to use computer software such as Tencent Conference. There were 17 valid subjects in the experiment, as shown in Fig. 5. When the subjects completed the scenario experiment, we provided a cash reward of 50–100 RMB according to their participation level and the quality of their answers (Table 2). This experiment consisted of two distinct phases: behavioral observation and thought retrospection (see Fig. 5).

Table 2. Statistics on sample characteristics

Measurements	Categorized indicators	Number of people
Age	18–28	9
	29–45	3
	46–60	5
Evaluation of the degree of impact on life	Severe	5
	Moderate	8
	Mild	4
Academic qualifications	Master's degree or above	2
	Bachelor's degree	12
	College	2
	High school or below	1

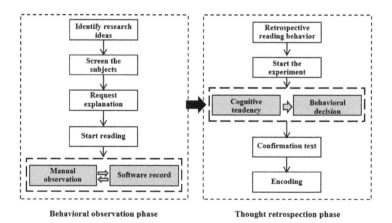

Fig. 5. Flow of Study 1

The behavioral observation stage in our study employs the scenario manipulation method. Firstly, we provided the subjects with a clear understanding of the experiment's requirements, which included:

1) Conducting the experiment online using specialized software.
2) Tracking their reading behavior using mouse movements.
3) Encouraging subjects to identify and highlight information elements they deemed important or thought had an impact on their decision-making process by circling them with the mouse.

Following these instructions, we presented the subjects with a hypothetical scenario: imagine you are experiencing symptoms like dry mouth, fatigue, or poor mental performance, which could potentially be attributed to high blood sugar levels. During this scenario, you come across several conflicting health messages. To facilitate data collection, we initially employed both manual observation and behavioral analysis software. This software enabled us to track and record the subjects' mouse reading trajectories and dwell time.

The thought retrospective phase encompassed two distinct segments. Initially, subjects were questioned about their cognitive-level inclinations and the rationale behind their adoption preferences. This segment involved specific inquiries about why they deemed the circled content as important, which material they would prefer to read, and which material they found more credible, among other aspects. Subsequently, in the second segment, subjects were prompted to delve into their behavioral inclinations. They were asked to elucidate why they were inclined toward specific actions. This line of questioning included inquiries such as: What motivates your engagement in particular behaviors? To what extent have these behaviors been influenced by the reading material? Do you foresee any changes in your current behaviors in the future?

Data Processing
Building upon the findings from the behavioral observation and thought retrospection phases, our subsequent analysis employed the grounded theory method. In the spindle coding stage, we initially identified four key adoption links: Information Attention, Information Comprehension, Information Evaluation, and Information Decision. During the selective coding stage, our focus shifted to investigating the interrelationships among these categories. This process allowed us to unveil the typical relationship structure, which is further detailed in Table 3.

Result Presentation
The coding results reveal the patient's conflicting health information adoption process, which comprises 4 distinct segments, each with 3 transformation stages (see Fig. 6).

Information Attention: This segment is characterized by two noteworthy reading behaviors. Firstly, through mouse track observations, it was observed that some subjects did not follow a linear textual or typographical order while reading. Secondly, certain information elements garnered the subjects' focused attention.

Information Comprehension: Here, we probed the subjects about parts of the material where they exhibited noticeable pauses during the reading process. Subjects uniformly

Table 3. Selective coding and typical relationship structure

Selective coding	Original statement	Fabric of relationships
Information Attention → Information Comprehension	Hospitals have suggested......attention but can't fully understand it (F7) The images look like a shopping site...... can't read foreign languages but you can search for images directly (F1)	The subject purposefully seeks out elements of information and then makes sense of the target information
Information Comprehension → Information Evaluation	Some specialized vocabulary is not well understood and needs to be queried in order to make judgments (F5) There is a lack of understanding, but it does not affect the judgment (F3)	The degree to which an individual understands information affects his or her choice of Information Evaluation for that information
Information Evaluation → Information Decision	While reading it, I also thought about whether I would buy this product if it were me (F12) After all, it's related to health, so I'm sure I'll make a decision after learning more about it (F15)	Individuals make behavioral decisions after Information Evaluation

expressed that comprehension difficulties led to these pauses, rendering the process time-consuming.

Information Evaluation: The results from the thought retrospection phase indicated that most subjects formed opinion judgments after reading the information. However, this behavioral tendency was not always demonstrated during the reading experiment itself.

Information Decision: In the retrospective stage of thinking, we explored the subjects' actual behavioral tendencies. It's important to note that Information Evaluation and Information Decision reflect the subjects' adoption tendencies at the cognitive and action levels, respectively. In the adoption process, subjects initially formulate cognitive judgments and subsequently make behavioral decisions.

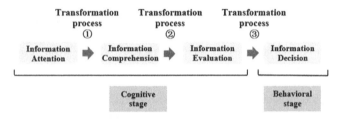

Fig. 6. Patient's Conflicting health information adoption process

Furthermore, as we transitioned between these segments, we discerned potential paradoxes within them (see Table 4).

Table 4. Paradoxical phenomena

Transformation process	Paradoxical phenomena
Information Attention → Information Comprehension	Paradox 1: Prefer to read Scientific Essay but find Science Expository Writing more credible
Information Comprehension → Information Evaluation	Paradox 2: More able to understand the content of Scientific Essay, but more agreeable to Science Expository Writing
Information Evaluation → Information Decision	Paradox 3: Inconsistency between subjects' cognitive dispositions and behavioral choices

3.2 Study Two: An Empirical Analysis of Cognitive-Behavioral Paradoxes in Patients' Adoption of Conflicting Health Information

In Study 2, we aimed to validate the three paradoxical phenomena that surfaced during the adoption process. To achieve this, we gathered data through questionnaires to assess the generalizability of these paradoxes. A total of 101 patients participated in this research on conflicting health information behavior paradoxes. We employed a five-point Likert scale, prompting participants to rate the paradoxes on a scale of 1 to 5 (1 = strongly disagree, 5 = strongly agree) after reading the informational material.

(1) **Paradox 1: An Experiment on the Relationship between Reading Preference and Level of Trust**

The validity of Paradox 1 manipulation was assessed through ANOVA. Participants were asked to rate the following questions: "Do you think Message A is more readable?" and "Do you think Message B is more readable?" Notably, there was a substantial difference in scores ($p < .001$) between Message A (Useful/Science Expository Writing) (M = 2.44, SD = 1.403, $F(1,200)$ = 94.935) and Message B (Useful/Scientific Essay) (M = 4.12, SD = 1.023, $F(1,200)$ = 94.935).Building upon Message A and Message B, we designed reverse experimental materials—Message C (Useless/Science Expository Writing) (M = 2.28, SD = 1.320, $F(1,200)$ = 94.195) and Message D (Useless/Scientific Essay) (M = 4.00, SD = 1.200, $F(1,200)$ = 94.195). It is noteworthy that both sets of materials exhibited the same significant difference in scores ($p < .001$) (see Fig. 7).

Participants were asked to rate questions regarding trust levels: "Do you think Message A is more trustworthy?" and "Do you think Message B is more credible?" Notably, a significant difference ($p < .001$) emerged in the scores between Message A (Useful/Science Expository Writing) (M = 4.22, SD = 0.844, $F(1,200)$ = 154.533) and Message B (Useful/Scientific Essay) (M = 2.43, SD = 1.178, $F(1,200)$ = 154.533). Similarly, leveraging Message A and Message B, we devised reverse experimental materials—Message C (Useless/Science Expository Writing) (M =

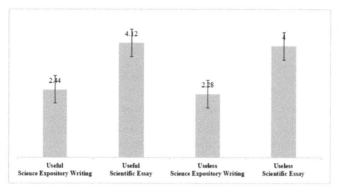

Fig. 7. Information Readability Score

4.26, SD = 0.986, F(1,200) = 102.733) and Message D (Useless/Scientific Essay) (M = 2.51, SD = 1.419, F(1,200) = 102.733). It's noteworthy that the scores for these materials also exhibited a significant difference (p < .001) (see Fig. 8).

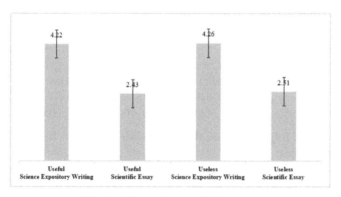

Fig. 8. Information Credibility score

In summary, concerning preference, participants showed a higher inclination to read information presented in the scientific essay. However, when it came to trust, they exhibited a greater reliance on health information conveyed in the science expository writing. Therefore, Paradox 1 remains consistent.

(2) **Paradox 2: An Experiment on the Relationship between Information Comprehension and Agreeableness**

The validity of Paradox 2 manipulation was confirmed through ANOVA. Participants were requested to assess ease of comprehension by rating the questions, "Do you think Material A is easier to understand?" and "Do you think Material B is easier to understand?" Interestingly, a significant difference (p < .001) emerged in the scores between Message A (Useful/Science Expository Writing) (M = 2.81, SD = 1.391, F(1,200) = 65.196) and Message B (Useful/Scientific Essay) (M = 4.16, SD = 0.935, F(1,200) = 65.196).Subsequently, utilizing Message A and Message B as a basis, we formulated reverse experimental materials—Message C (Useless/Science Expository Writing) (M = 2.61, SD = 1.311, F(1,200) = 79.030) and Message D (Useless/Scientific Essay) (M = 4.04, SD = 0.937, F(1,200) = 79.030). Notably, these materials also exhibited significant score differences (p < .001) (see Fig. 9).

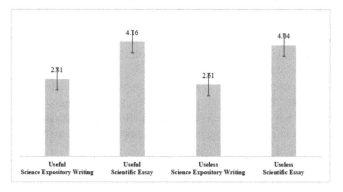

Fig. 9. Information Comprehension score

Participants were instructed to evaluate the persuasiveness of the messages by responding to the questions, "Do you think Material A is more persuasive?" and "Do you think Material B is more persuasive?" The results revealed a significant difference (p < .001) in the scores between Message A (Useful/Science Expository Writing) (M = 4.11, SD = 1.057, F(1,200) = 63.400) and Message B (Useful/Scientific Essay) (M = 2.71, SD = 1.410, F(1,200) = 63.400).Subsequently, using Message A and Message B as the foundation, we developed reverse experimental materials—Message C (Useless/Science Expository Writing) (M = 4.04, SD = 1.029, F(1,200) = 43.620) and Message D (Useless/Scientific Essay) (M = 2.97, SD = 1.261, F(1,200) = 43.620). These materials also exhibited significant score differences (p < .001) (see Fig. 10).

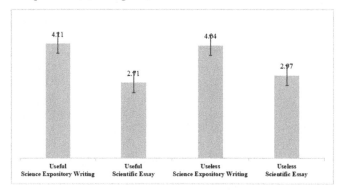

Fig. 10. Information Identity Score

In summary, participants exhibited a greater comprehension of health messages presented in the scientific essay, while perceiving health messages in the science expository writing as more persuasive. That is, they are more likely to agree with Science Expository Writing. This confirms the existence of Paradox 2.

(3) **Paradox 3: Experiments on the Relationship Between Cognitive Tendencies and Behavioral Pointing**

Subjects were asked to assess the utility of XYS supplements for sugar reduction/control and their willingness to purchase such nutraceuticals after reviewing Information A (Useful/Science Expository Writing) and Information C (Useless/Science Expository Writing). The findings revealed that 46 subjects believed that XYS supplements were effective for glucose reduction/control. However, more than half of them indicated they would not purchase this product ("Strongly Disagree": 35%; "Comparatively Disagree": 24%). Conversely, among the remaining 55 subjects who perceived XYS-type supplements as ineffective for glucose-lowering/control, 52% ("strongly agree": 27%; "somewhat agree": 25%) expressed a willingness to buy these products. These results indicate a degree of ambivalence among subjects when navigating between cognitive and behavioral dimensions, as depicted in Figs. 11 and 12.

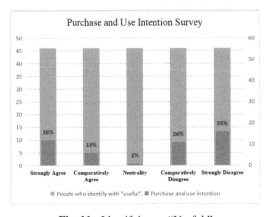

Fig. 11. Identifying as "Useful."

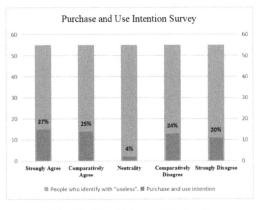

Fig. 12. Identifying as "Useless."

To rigorously validate the results, we implemented reverse experiments based on message A and message C: message B (Useful/Scientific Essay) and message D (Useless/Scientific Essay). The findings revealed that 49 subjects believed XYS-type supplements were effective for glucose reduction/control. However, more than half of them (56%) stated they would not purchase this product ("Strongly Disagree": 23%; "Comparatively Disagree": 33%). Conversely, among the remaining 52 subjects who perceived XYS-type supplements as ineffective for glucose-lowering/control, 62% ("strongly agree": 25%; "somewhat agree": 37%) expressed a willingness to buy these products. This once again underscores the presence of ambivalence in the subjects' perceptions and behaviors, as depicted in Figs. 13 and 14. Therefore, Paradox 3 holds.

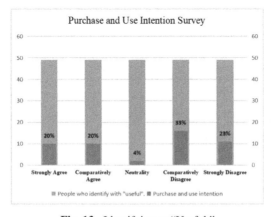

Fig. 13. Identifying as "Useful."

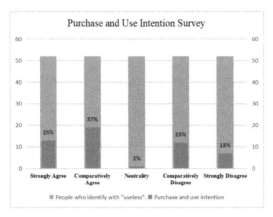

Fig. 14. Identifying as "Useless."

3.3   Study Three: An Analysis of the Causes of the Cognitive-Behavioral Paradox in the Adoption of Conflicting Health Information by Patients

The aforementioned studies have demonstrated that patients can indeed encounter cognitive and behavioral paradoxes during the adoption process. Building upon these findings, in Study 3, we formulated a model depicting patients' adoption of conflicting health information through interviews. Additionally, we introduced the concept of "transtheoretical" to conduct a comprehensive analysis of the model. Subjects for this experiment were selected based on two conditions: (1) The selection was limited to those who had experienced all three paradoxes in Study 2. (2) Subjects were individuals who were currently ill or had a history of illness (Table 5). Additionally, upon completion of the experiment, subjects were compensated with cash prizes ranging from 50 to 100 RMB.

Table 5. Statistics on sample characteristics

Measurements	Categorized indicators	Number of people
Age	18–28	10
	29–45	4
	46–60	3
Evaluation of the degree of impact on life	Severe	3
	Moderate	7
	Mild	7
Academic qualifications	Master's degree or above	5
	Bachelor's degree	10
	College	1
	High school or below	1

Data Processing
The subjects' interviews were recorded using audio recording software. Subsequently, the researcher applied the grounded theory approach to systematically sort and analyze the collected dataset. In order to maintain consistency with Study 1, subjects in this phase were identified by numbers, specifically F18 to F34. During the open coding stage, 11 initial categories were identified based on the adoption sessions, which were further condensed into 4 main categories. Moving to the selective coding stage, the study delved into the interrelationships among these categories, ultimately revealing a typical relationship structure, as illustrated in Table 6.

Result Presentation
The results of Study 3 revealed that informational, competence, psychological, and environmental factors are the primary drivers of paradox among patients. These factors sequentially influence the paradoxical phenomenon in various stages of transformation. To delve deeper into this discovery, we developed a model that elucidates patients'

Table 6. Selective coding and typical relationship structure

Selective coding	Original statement	Fabric of relationships
Information factor → Ability factor	I have heard the doctor say…… But I can't read much about it myself, so I'm not going to look at it again either (F33) Some of the content is too specialized to understand…… (F19) Thought it was just decorative pictures, didn't feel very important (F24)	Comprehension of information elements based on reading
Ability factor → Psychosocial factor	Feels pretty reasonable, but not really needed at the moment and…… Takes time to understand (F26) The doctor didn't ask for this, and I think it's better to buy the medicine in the hospital (F20) It shouldn't be a problem to buy something with a single ingredient, and the internet reviews are pretty good (F18)	The choice of Information Evaluation is supported by the individual's level of understanding and is also interfered by psychological factors
Psychosocial factor → environmental factor	Will choose to try it, I have friends who have used it and feel quite comfortable with it (F32) Still sticking with my previous opinion, there are too many ads, so I don't have a good feeling about this kind of stuff (F20)	The implementation of the act of adoption is limited by environmental factors

behaviors in adopting conflicting health information. This model is expounded upon using the concept of "trans-theory."

J.O. Prochaska introduced the concept of "trans-theory," a framework effective in elucidating the mechanisms of individual health behavior change and forecasting its progression [18]. It allows tailoring behavioral promotion strategies to individuals in different stages of behavioral change [19, 20]. This study observed that patient populations undergo various types of behavioral shifts during the adoption of conflicting health information, aligning with the fundamental tenets of Trans Theory. Consequently, we propose that this theory can serve as a valuable tool to delve into the transition from cognition to action within the patient adoption process and shed light on the reasons behind paradoxical phenomena. Throughout the adoption journey, patients' proclivity to move from cognition to behavior experiences constant fluctuations. Drawing from the "trans-theory" framework, we divide this process into four distinct phases, each corresponding to a specific facet of the adoption process (see Table 7). Building upon this foundation, we construct a comprehensive model delineating patients' adoption of conflicting health information (see Fig. 15).

Table 7. Comparison of "trans-theoretical" thinking and adoption processes.

Adoption process	Evolutionary stage	Evolutionary process	explanation	Influencing Factor
Information Attention	Precontemplation stage	Consciousness Raising	Recognizing the Realities and Perceptions of Adoption Decision Making by Receiving Conflicting Health Information	Information factor
		Dramatic Relief	Generating negative feelings that accompany the risk of Conflicting health information	
Information Comprehension	Contemplation stage	Self-Reevaluation	Individual's level of understanding of information	Ability factor
Information Evaluation	Preparation stage	Self-Liberation	Believe in your own behavioral decisions	Psychosocial factor
		Social Liberation	Preparing for adoption decisions	
Information Decision	Action stage	Helping Relationship	Seeking social support for behavioral decisions	Environmental factor
		Counter Conditioning	Finding reasons to support decision-making perspectives	
		Stimulus Control	Supporting decision perspectives by circumventing some information	

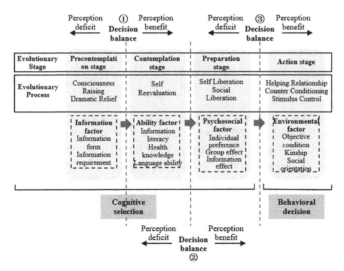

Fig. 15. Patient Conflicting health information adoption model

As depicted in Fig. 15, the adoption process can be divided into distinct stages: Precontemplation, Intention, and Preparation. These stages reflect the patient's cognitive responses to conflicting health information, while the Action stage ultimately determines the direction of the patient's behavior. The results of patient adoption are significantly influenced by balanced decision-making as they progress from mere cognition to actionable behavior [21, 22]. This often leads to the intriguing phenomenon of ambivalence. Within the framework of "trans-theoretical" thinking, the linchpin is the concept of decisional balance, serving as the foundational driver behind these transitions. Decisional balance comprises two pivotal factors: perceived benefit and perceived deficit. The former actively facilitates behavioral shifts, while the latter presents a hindrance. Therefore, we posit that user behavior undergoes transformation when the influence of perceived benefits outweighs that of perceived deficits, culminating in the emergence of paradoxes.

The paradoxical phenomena can be elucidated as follows:

Paradox 1: Initially, patients are drawn to scientific essays, forming distinct reading preferences. However, when guided by their information literacy and health knowledge, their cognitive preferences shift. At this juncture, the role of their cognitive abilities supersedes that of the information itself.

Paradox 2: While most patients tend to comprehend scientific essays due to individual cognitive limitations, their psychological inclinations lead them to favor science expository writing. In this scenario, psychological factors exert a more substantial influence than cognitive abilities.

Paradox 3: Objective conditions, familial ties, social orientation, and other external factors impose constraints on patients' psyches. Consequently, patients' behavioral decisions are influenced by environmental factors, potentially giving rise to cognitive and behavioral paradoxes.

4 Discussion and Influence

Conflicting health information environments create significant challenges for individuals striving to make informed health decisions. Therefore, this paper takes a medical field perspective to delve into the patient group's encounters with conflicting health information.

Study 1, the paper simulated a scenario where patients encounter conflicting health information and conducted interviews to explore their information adoption process. While previous research primarily focused on the holistic outcomes of adoption behaviors [23]. However, this experiment delves into the specific process of adoption. Ultimately, the paper identified four key stages in the conflictual health information adoption process: Information Attention, Information Comprehension, Information Evaluation, and Information Decision. Additionally, it revealed the presence of cognitive-behavioral paradoxes at each stage of the adoption process. Based on the above findings, Study 2 validated three cognitive-behavioral paradoxes. These were: (1) Patients preferred to read the Scientific Essay but trusted the Science Expository Writing more. (2) Patients displayed a better understanding of the Scientific Essay but favored the ideas presented in the Science Expository Writing. (3) Patients' cognitive-level choices were often inconsistent with their final behavioral decisions. A public questionnaire further confirmed that these paradoxes were widespread. Then, we invited 17 subjects who produced cognitive-behavioral paradoxes for secondary interviews with the aim of exploring the reasons why such inconsistencies arise. From the analyses, we believe that informational, ability, psychological, and environmental factors are the dominant factors in the adoption chain. Their influence increases in sequence, leading to a shift in the patient's behavior, thus creating a cognitive-behavioral paradox.

In terms of theoretical implications, first this study has contributed to the field of information adoption by delving into patients' adoption tendencies throughout various stages of the process. While previous research predominantly focused on the final decision outcome, scholars have explored factors influencing improved adoption behavior [24] but have often overlooked the specific process and transformation. Furthermore, there exists a significant gap in research concerning conflicting health information. Despite the consensus that, "information adoption is a process" [25], this process hasn't been uniformly refined. Second, this study has uncovered the paradoxical phenomenon of cognition and behavior within patient adoption, shedding light on areas where previous research has been limited. While prior studies have largely overlooked behavioral aspects of information adoption, paradoxes of cognition and behavior have been more commonly explored in fields like privacy and consumption [26, 27]. Finally, this study introduces the concept of "trans-theory" to analyze the formation mechanism of the paradoxical phenomenon in patients' adoption of conflicting health information. This paper offers an insightful perspective on the information adoption process by focusing on patients' behavioral occurrences and psychological changes.

The managerial implications of this paper are threefold. **(1) Adoption segment: health platform page setup and function optimization.** This study has identified four distinct stages in the process of patient adoption behavior: Information Attention, Information Comprehension, Information Evaluation, and Information Decision. This finding provides valuable insights for optimizing health platforms to align with users' behavioral development stages, reducing the likelihood of patients encountering conflicting health information. **(2) Paradoxical phenomena: improvement of information formats and patient self-improvement.** This study has empirically demonstrated the presence of paradoxical phenomena during the adoption process by users. To minimize such occurrences, information publishers should enhance their control over content, focusing on both content clarity and the accuracy of health information. Efforts to boost information dissemination channel credibility and user favorability should also be made. Concurrently, users should actively work on improving their skills and knowledge. **(3) Factors at play: social security systems and patient leadership mechanisms.** This paper highlights how patients' information adoption behavior is influenced by environmental factors, including objective conditions, kinship, and social orientation. To optimize the positive impact of these factors and mitigate their negative effects, we propose two strategies. Firstly, the government should offer appropriate guidance and support measures [28]. Secondly, health platforms can actively engage patients in sharing their personal experiences in adopting health information, including screening typical cases.

5 Limitations and Future Research Directions

Despite the valuable insights gained from this study, it is essential to acknowledge its limitations. Firstly, this paper focused primarily on weak conflicting health messages with inconsistent behavioral outcomes, neglecting other categories of conflicting health messages. Secondly, while examining the adoption process from a process perspective, the study did not delve deeply into the subjective characteristics of patients. Lastly, while tracing the adoption process, it did not extend its scope to cover post-decision usage. To chart a course for future research, several promising avenues emerge. Firstly, there is an opportunity to explore the applicability of the findings to different types of conflicting health information. For example, investigating whether patients opt for health products with known side effects (strong conflict). Secondly, future research could conduct in-depth investigations into individual patient characteristics. Factors such as educational background, disease duration, health status, economic well-being, and interpersonal relationships can influence the information adoption process. Analyzing and summarizing these patient group characteristics can lead to more tailored recommendations. Thirdly, guiding patients in their adoption behaviors is an ongoing and evolving process. Subsequent research should maintain the momentum, and continually refine and enhance the findings for increased reliability and practical application.

References

1. Rozenblum, R., Bates, D.W.: Patient-centered healthcare, social media and the internet: the perfect storm? BMJ Qual. Saf. **22**(3), 183–186 (2013)
2. Iles, I.A., Gillman, A.S., O'Connor, L.E., Ferrer, R.A., Klein, W.M.P.: Understanding
3. Carpenter, D.M.: Understanding the effect of conflicting information on medication adherence for vasculitis patients. Dissertations & Theses Gradworks (2010)
4. Elstad, E., Carpenter, D.M., DeVellis, R., Blalock, S.J.: Patient decision making in the face of conflicting medication information. Int. J. Qual. Stud. Health Well Being **1**, 7 (2012)

5. Khan, A.M., Soroya, S.H. Mahmood, K.: Impact of information credibility on social media information adoption behavior: a systematic literature review. Library Hi Tech (2022). https://doi.org/10.1108/LHT-03-2022-0165
6. Chen, M., Esmaeilzadeh, P.: Adoption and use of various health information exchange methods for sending inside health information in US hospitals. Int. J. Med. Informatics **177**, 105156 (2023)
7. Collado-Agudo, J., Herrero-Crespo, A., San Martín, H.: The adoption of a smart destination model by tourism companies: a ecosystem approach. J. Destin. Mark. Manag. **28**(6), 100783 (2023)
8. Akwang, N.E.: A study of librarians' perceptions and adoption of Web 2.0 technologies in academic libraries in Akwa Ibom State, Nigeria. J. Acad. Librarianship **47**(2), 102299 (2021)
9. Bao, Z., Zhu, Y.: Understanding online reviews adoption in social network communities: an extension of the information adoption model. Inf. Technol. People (2023). https://doi.org/10.1108/ITP-03-2022-0158
10. Abdulaziz, E., Smail, E., Mushfiqur, R., Deniz, Z.: Understanding mobile users' information adoption behavior: an extension of the information adoption model. J. Enterp. Inf. Manag. **35**(6), 1789–1811 (2022)
11. Albayrak, M., Ceylan, C.: Effect of eWom on purchase intention: meta-analysis. Data Technol. Appl. **55**(5), 810–840 (2021)
12. Iles, I.A., Gillman, A.S., O'Connor, L.E., Ferrer, R.A., Klein, W.M.P.: Understanding responses to different types of conflicting information about cancer prevention. Soc. Sci. Med. **311**, 115292 (2022)
13. Herrera-Perez, D., Haslam, A., Crain, T., et al.: A comprehensive review of randomized clinical trials in three medical journals reveals 396 medical reversals. eLife **8**, 45183 (2019)
14. Wu, Y., Zhang, X., Xiao, Q.: Appeal to the head and heart: the persuasive effects of medical crowdfunding charitable appeals on willingness to donate. Inf. Process. Manage. **59**(1), 102792 (2022)
15. Zhang, J., Wolfram, D., Ma, F.: The impact of big data on research methods in information science. Data Inf. Manag. **7**(2), 100038 (2023)
16. Nagler, R.H., Gollust, S.E., Yzer, M.C., Voger, R.I., Rothman, A.J.: Sustaining positive perceptions of science in the face of conflicting health information: an experimental test of messages about the process of scientific discovery. Soc. Sci. Med. **334**, 116194 (2023)
17. Paige, S.R., et al.: Communicating about online health information with patients: exploring determinants among telemental health providers. PEC Innovation **2**(10), 100176 (2023)
18. Prochaska, J.O., Redding, C.A., Evers, K.E.: The transtheoretical model and stages of change **22**(22), 97–121 (1997)
19. Mansuroğlu, S., Yasemin Kutlu, F.: The transtheoretical model based psychoeducation's effect on healthy lifestyle behaviors in schizophrenia: a randomized controlled trial. Archiv. Psychiat. Nurs. **41**, 51–56 (2022)
20. Delbosc, A., Currie, G., Jain, T., Aston, L.: The 're-norming' of working from home during COVID-19: a transtheoretical behavior change model of a major unplanned disruption. Transp. Policy **127**, 15–21 (2022)
21. Prochaska, J.: The transtheoretical model of health behavior change. Am. J. Health Promot. **12**(1), 38–48 (1997)
22. Prochaska, J.O., Redding, C.A., Evers, K.E.: The transtheoretical model and stages of change. **22**(22), 60–84 (1997)
23. Chiu, W., Oh, G.-E.(G)., Cho, H.: An integrated model of consumers' decision-making process in social commerce: a cross-cultural study of the United States and China. Asia Pacific J. Market. Logist. **35**(7), 1682–1698 (2023)
24. Liu, H., Guo, P., Yin, H.W.: Consistent comments and vivid comments in hotels' online information adoption: which matters more? Int. J. Hosp. Manag. **107**, 103329 (2022)

25. Cheung, C.M.K., Lee, M.K.O., Rabjohn, N.: The impact of electronic word-of-mouth - the adoption of online opinions in online customer communities. Internet Res. **18**(3), 229–247 (2008)

26. Gadgil, G., Prybutok, G., Prybutok, V.: Mediation of transgender impression management between transgender privacy paradox and Trans Facebook Persona: a trans perspective. Comput. Hum. Behav. **143**(6), 107700 (2023)

27. Fanning, A.L., O'Neill, D.W.: The Wellbeing-Consumption paradox: happiness, health, income and carbon emissions in growing versus non-growing economies. J. Clean. Prod. **2**(12), 810–821 (2019)

28. Zolbin, M.G., Huvila, I., Nikou, S.: Health literacy, health literacy interventions and decision-making: a systematic literature review. J. Document. **78**(7), 405–428 (2022)

Human-AI Collaboration

Does AI Fit? Applying Social Actor Dimensions to AI

Chelsea Collier[1]([✉]) [ID], Kenneth R. Fleischmann[1] [ID], Tina Lassiter[1] [ID],
Sherri R. Greenberg[2], and Raul G. Longoria[3]

[1] School of Information, The University of Texas at Austin, Austin, TX 78712, USA
cem224@my.utexas.edu
[2] Lyndon B. Johnson School of Public Affairs, The University of Texas at Austin, Austin,
TX 78712, USA
[3] The Cockrell School of Engineering, The University of Texas at Austin, Austin, TX 78712,
USA

Abstract. This paper applies one of the fundamental Social Informatics (SI) theories, the social actor approach, to Artificial Intelligence (AI). The paper builds upon the foundational scholarship of Lamb and Kling and reviews their proposed four dimensions of the social actor – Affiliations, Environments, Interactions, Identities – against the context of interviews with skilled trade workers and their perceptions of smart hand tools, which are hand tools that leverage embedded sensing, the internet of things, and edge AI. Our research reveals that the concept of social actors continues to be salient in the context of contemporary AI. We conclude that social actor theory has important implications for AI design.

Keywords: AI · Social Informatics · Skilled Trade Workers · Smart Hand Tools

1 Introduction

Artificial Intelligence (AI) inspires a re-examination of human activity, including the construction of fundamental academic theories. In this paper, we explore the social actor approach from Social Informatics (SI) and ask if AI supports previous theoretical thinking based on Information and Communications Technologies (ICTs) [1, 2]. Building on the work of Lamb and Kling [3], we ask, "does the concept of social actors still have salience in relation to contemporary AI?" We review Lamb and Kling's [3] four dimensions of the social actor: Affiliations, Environments, Interactions, and Identities.

To explore the relevance of AI to SI social actor approach, we leverage ongoing qualitative research with skilled trade workers and AI-enabled smart hand tools [4–7]. Skilled trade workers use tools and machinery in their jobs [8]. Smart hand tools contain sensing technology and intelligence capabilities that can deliver information to workers [9]. We conclude, based on insights from skilled trade workers, that the four dimensions of SI social actor approach are valid. This finding reflects that SI theories show promise in keeping up with recent advances in ICTs (e.g., AI). Beyond theoretical relevance, this work has practical implications concerning the design and application of AI by

I. Sserwanga et al. (Eds.): iConference 2024, LNCS 14598, pp. 195–203, 2024.
https://doi.org/10.1007/978-3-031-57867-0_14

social actors. The intention of this paper is to contribute to SI theory and to expand its application to the current technology landscape, which includes AI. We also lay out a longer-term approach for investigating future technologies and their relevance to SI's social actor approach.

First, in the Background section, we provide a brief overview of AI and the social actor model. In Methods, we describe our ongoing qualitative research involving 22 skilled trade workers and supervisors. In the Findings section, we showcase insights from interviews with skilled trade workers and supervisors that align with the four dimensions of a social actor. In the Discussion section, we detail how participants reinforce the social actor approach and demonstrate that skilled trade workers go beyond being simple users of technologies such as smart hand tools. Finally, in Conclusion, we assess how these findings contribute to the field and recommend additional research.

2 Background

2.1 AI

The definition of AI is a topic of scholarly debate [10]. Following Slota et al., we define AI as "oriented toward the use of large datasets, analyzed through computational methods, to engender predictions arising from that data or to attempt to replicate human intelligence" [11, p. 311].

2.2 From Users to Social Actors

Lamb and Kling [3] present a social actor model which expands the concept of the "user" related to those who interact with ICTs. Lamb and Kling [3] claim that contextual factors surrounding the user are missing and respond by introducing four dimensions of the social actor which describe the complex web of experiences that influence how social actors interact with ICTs. The four dimensions of the social actor include: Affiliations, Environments, Interactions, and Identities. (1) Affiliations describes how a social actor's professional identities and experience reflects their own interests and impacts their use of technology. (2) Environments refers to forces that impact an organization (e.g., regulation) and therefore the social actor. (3) Interactions focus on how exchanging information impacts engagement with other actors. (4) Identities reveal how an individual's personal make-up and experiences influence a technology's use and/or design. Combined, these four dimensions amount to a "metaphor that readily expands the scope and scale of the social space of people's interactions with ICTs and with other people, groups, and organizations" [3, p. 224].

3 Methods

To explore alignment between skilled trade workers and social actor theory, we interviewed 22 skilled trade workers and their supervisors, including 15 workers and seven supervisors. All 22 participants work for the City of Austin across five departments: Austin-Bergstrom International Airport, Austin Water, Fleet Mobility Services, Parks and Recreation, Watershed Protection. As part of our interview process, we inquired about the number of years of experience that both the supervisors and workers had working for the city, which varied significantly (see Table 1). We did not inquire about the total years of experience working with hand tools nor did we inquire about the age of participants.

Table 1. Participants' Employment Tenure with the City

Identifier	Years of City Employment
Supervisor 1	7.5
Supervisor 2	13.5
Supervisor 3	8
Supervisor 4	Less than one
Supervisor 5	20
Supervisor 6	28
Supervisor 7	30
Worker 1	1 year 10 months
Worker 2	9 years 6 months
Worker 3	3
Worker 4	12
Worker 5	13 years 3 months
Worker 6	More than 15
Worker 7	5
Worker 8	5
Worker 9	8
Worker 10	27
Worker 11	11
Worker 12	Almost 16
Worker 13	Almost 4
Worker 14	6
Worker 15	7

We gained access to participants through a partnership between the City of Austin and The University of Texas at Austin. We used different instruments and modalities to conduct semi-structured interviews with workers and supervisors. We interviewed supervisors for approximately 45 min via virtual conferencing tool (Zoom) to maximize convenience for the supervisors and their schedules. Following each supervisor interview, we requested their permission to interview their staff members. The participating supervisors suggested in-person, onsite interviews with workers following a staff meeting or training for a time duration of approximately 15 min per interview. We complied with the supervisors' recommendations for interviews with their staff. We slightly adjusted the interview instrument for workers to conform to the allotted time by reducing the number of questions from 25 for supervisors to 15 for workers. We also condensed the critical incident questions for workers to focus on tools use rather than departmental activities.

Participants volunteered and were uncompensated per city policy. The research protocol was approved by the authors' Institutional Review Board. The research team used thematic analysis to code interviews and develop themes [12]. The review of skilled trade workers as social actors was not one of the originally identified themes. Rather, we revisited the data to search for evidence to support or nullify our research question: does the concept of social actors still have salience in relation to contemporary AI?

The initial concept of AI-enabled smart hand tools co-designed with skilled trade workers has yielded several publications from varying data sets. A paper focusing on welding interventions, provided initial direction for the project [4]. This initial inquiry inspired additional research on virtual simulation for welding that resulted from a follow-on effort and separate dataset [5]. Next, our research on the co-design of smart hand tools with skilled workers employed at the City of Austin resulted related a paper on how smart hand tools may serve as public interest technology (PIT) [6] and serve as emancipatory technology [7]. While this paper is based on the same dataset examined in the last two cited papers, this paper reports new findings based on themes and quotes not reported in the prior papers.

4   Findings

We select insights from 22 participant responses from ongoing research with skilled trade workers who provide insights that support the design of smart hand tools. We label interviews with supervisors (S1 – 7) and with workers (W1 – 15). These findings demonstrate evidence that skilled trade workers are social actors based on alignment with the four dimensions – Affiliations, Environments, Interactions, and Identities [3]. We also provide a visualization of how Social Actor Dimensions align with participant insights (see Table 2).

4.1   Affiliations

As social actors, participants convey their work-related identities and experience and describe the relation to their technology use. One worker describes their professional experience:

> I am the operations superintendent ... I've been in this business of municipal water right at 30 years. And before that I've had various licenses, boilermaker, journeyman, landscaper, plumbing, multiple years of using hand tools (W4).

The participant goes on to describe how technology has changed over the course of their career:

So, there's been a lot of automation over the years. When I first started working in water in boilers, there was very little automation ... But I've noticed over the years that folks start to rely on automation ... You get complacent (W4).

The participant's affiliation with multiple professional identities and experiences impacts their attitude towards technology. Another participant echoes a similar observation:

I've been in the business for 44 years. I am old school ... I have personal tools that have laser guides and all this on them. I never use those. I still measure and check everything, so I don't trust them (S1).

This participants' identification as "old school" influences their attitude and proclivity towards technology use. It is important for AI-enabled tool designers to understand how expert skilled trade workers may distrust technology and instead rely on their own experience.

4.2 Environments

We consider how the safety features of hand tools have changed over time and how this impacts skilled trade workers:

The drills and all the safety stuff has changed a whole lot more compared to whenever I was 15 years old in wood shop. We got more safety stuff, but a lot of times the safety stuff is what actually gets in the way (W7).

This participant (W7) suggests how safety features impact users and the need for improved tool design:

Some of the safety issues on some of these tools, like the guards and stuff could work a little bit better ... They'll get in a bind and then it puts the operator in a bind his self. And then it gets real scary (W7).

On a similar but separate theme of safety, a participant describes how smart hand tool design could be influenced by safety regulations. The supervisor also expresses a possible approach, demonstrating how experienced skilled tradespersons can influence tool application:

So, yeah, in the system for OSHA, before you get on a pallet jack or a forklift, you have to do an inspection. So, there was a box that was on, you put in your employee number, you did the inspection, and then you came back and the inspection completed. And that could also be something that could potentially be utilized in a tool situation ... If you had basically an accident, if you bumped a pallet too hard ... That it would just shut down outta nowhere (S4).

Both the worker and supervisor participants' evaluation of safety features and suggestion for improvement is an example of how a user may influence the design of hand tools and AI-enabled applications related to safety.

4.3 Interactions

One participant describes how technical knowledge differs between generations:

> We got one guy, one Gen X guy in here and he couldn't tell you the measurements or anything. Lucky, he has somebody like me that's going to be patient with him ... Now we're on computers, he's the one that comes in ... it all falls into the question of his time (W10).

While the more experienced worker had significant advantage regarding tool use, there is an acknowledgement that the less-experienced skilled trade worker's technical acumen is valued in the workplace. This mutual respect and exchange may be an important component to consider in smart hand tool design. Another participant describes the interactions between staff and supervisors and how the bi-lateral feedback on topics such as tool use can impact job efficiency measures:

> Engagement is a big part of ensuring that the jobs we're performing can be done efficiently ... We need our frontline staff to tell us cuz there's more than one type of tool to perform a job and if we equip them with a compressor and a hose and a jackhammer and tell 'em to go and perform an application of excavation and they find that it's more effective to use the battery-operated jack hammer cuz it's not gonna take as long. And they've already done some of the work and have made that in determination that hey, it's probably easier and quicker to get the job done if we use this type of tools (S7).

The descriptions of these exchanges between skilled trade workers and supervisors have implications for how smart hand tool technology may need to accommodate a diversity of digital skill level as well as lived experience.

4.4 Identities

A participant (W13) provides insight as to how their personal style preferences impact the opportunity for technical intervention:

> So, I grew up with my dad showing me how to use tools. And so, I have a fondness for tools being very simple ... A smart tool would be phenomenal. But I know that going away from a tool that is as simple as simple can be, will take away from the tool (W13).

This worker (W13) is outlining a clear case for how their experience shapes their design perspective which is in line with the Identity dimension. A supervisor also provides insight to how their experience, namely their gender, impacts their approach to problem solving related to tool use and skilled trade work:

> Well, I mean just being realistic and knowing people, especially men. I mean, well myself ... we don't really like to look at the instruction sheet or manual that comes with the tool <laugh>. We know how to use them and it's usually trial by error that we use something and learn it that way (S3).

While S3 was providing a light-hearted comment about how skilled trade workers learn through experience, the implications for training are quite serious. These insights could indicate the need for less text-based instruction and more hand-on instruction. This could significantly impact AI-enabled smart hand tool design.

4.5 Summary of Social Actor Dimensions

Insights from participant interviews align with the four dimensions of social actor theory and reveals preliminary evidence that skilled trade workers are representative of social actors.

4.6 Data Visualization

In Table 2, we connect the four dimensions of a social actor as defined by Lamb and Kling [3] with participant insights to better visualize the data.

Table 2. Alignment of Social Actor Dimensions with Participant Insights

Social Actor Dimension	Social Actor Dimension Description	Example: Participant Insight
Affiliation	How a social actor's professional identities and experiences reflect their own interests and impact their use of technology	"I've been in the business for 44 years. I am old school…" (S1)
Environment	How forces that impact an organization (e.g., regulation) impact the social actor	"We got more safety stuff, but a lot of times the safety stuff is what actually gets in the way" (W7)
Interactions	How exchanging information impacts engagement with other actors	"Engagement is a big part of ensuring that the jobs we're performing can be done efficiently…" (S7)
Identities	How an individual's personal make-up and experiences influence a technology's use and/or design	"So, I grew up with my dad showing me how to use tools" (W13)

5 Discussion

As we contend with how AI transforms our existence, we can also review how AI impacts academic theories. SI is an appropriate community to consider AI's impact due to a focus on technology's interaction with individuals, organizations, and society [1, 2]. SI is recognized for incorporating theories from other disciplines [1, 2].

We chose the social actor approach as a backdrop to examine the applicability of AI to SI theory in the context of ongoing research with 22 skilled trade workers and supervisors related to smart hand tools. Our broader research interests include the ethical design of AI and smart hand tools provide a relevant application of this phenomenon [4–7]. Participant insights from both workers and supervisors provide preliminary but sufficient evidence that those in skilled trades are acting in concert with the four dimensions of a social actor – Affiliation, Environment, Interactions, and Identity.

One participant (W4) demonstrates Affiliation by describing the increase of automation over a 30-year career and this had made some workers "complacent." A supervisor (S4) provides evidence of AI related to Environment by describing federal safety regulations and how technology could support upholding those policies. Another participant (W10) provides evidence of Interactions by detailing how workers who are experienced in hand tool use are less proficient with technology and depend on earlier generations to support them with their digital literacy. Finally, a supervisor discusses how gender may influence training design in the context of Identities. These early insights provide sufficient fodder to inspire future inquiries on how AI and emerging technologies, such as smart hand tools, support the relevance of SI's social agent theory.

This smart hand tools research is emergent, small in scope and with sample size and location-related limitations. We recommend additional research to further test the four dimensions with skilled trade workers. We especially hope that scholars look beyond AI's immediate influencers and consider how non-traditional social actors may influence AI implementation.

We also recommend further exploration of AI relative to other SI scholarships that examine ICT. Specifically, Yang et al. [12, p. 2] ask, "How do ICTs affect the existing social order, as the tension between control, autonomy, and power shift?" It would be interesting to extend this question to consider AI's influence. We hope to contribute to the ever-evolving field of SI by exploring the longevity of foundational theories as applied to modern advanced technology, such as AI.

6 Conclusion

In this work, we take the initial steps to establish that SI's social actor theory endures beyond ICT and applies to AI through the expression of four social actor dimensions. Our conceptual framing offers an opportunity to share insights from skilled trade workers who use their skills and experience to improve AI-enabled smart hand tool design.

A contribution of social actor theory is that social agents go beyond a simplistic view of the user and instead represent their own interests and experiences [3]. Our research with skilled trade workers reinforces this theory and contributes to the continuation of the theory's application. Participants describe how their experiences and perceptions can shape the design and application of AI. This work seeks to contribute to the field of SI by expanding previous work on ICT by providing contemporary examples of how AI fits within social actor theory.

Acknowledgments. This work was supported by funding from Good Systems: Ethical AI at UT Austin; Microsoft; and The MITRE Corporation. We would like to thank all our research participants for generously sharing their time and expertise. In addition, we would especially like to recognize Mr. Charles Purma in the Office of Innovation at the City of Austin for his support and collaborative contribution.

References

1. Sawyer, S., Tyworth, M.: Social informatics: principles, theory, and practice. In: Social Informatics: An Information Society for all? In Remembrance of Rob Kling: Proceedings of the Seventh International Conference on Human Choice and Computers (HCC7), IFIP TC, vol. 9, pp. 49-62. Springer, Maribor, Slovenia (2006). https://doi.org/10.1007/978-0-387-37876-3_4

2. Kling, R., Rosenbaum, H., Sawyer, S.: Understanding and communicating social informatics: A framework for studying and teaching the human contexts of information and communication technologies, 1st edn. Information Today, Medford, NJ (2005)

3. Lamb, R., Kling R.: Reconceptualizing users as social actors in information systems research. MIS Q., 197–236 (2003)

4. Hill, K. M., et al.: Information needs of blue-collar workers: Welding challenges and the potential of smart welding tools. In: Proceedings of the Association for Information Science and Technology, Pittsburgh, PA, vol. 59(1), pp. 431–436 (2022)

5. Lassiter, T., Collier, C., Fleischmann, K.R., Greenberg, S.R.: Welding instructors' perspectives on using AI technology in welding training. In: Proceedings of the Association for Information Science and Technology, London, pp. 233–43 (2023)

6. Collier, C., Lassiter, T., Fleischmann, K.R., Greenberg, S.R., Longoria, R.G., Chinchali, S.: AI as an emancipatory technology: smart hand tools for skilled trade workers. In: Proceedings of the 57th Annual Hawai'i International Conference on System Sciences, Waikiki, HI, pp. 6490 – 6500. (2024)

7. Collier, C., Fleischmann, K.R., Lassiter, T., Greenberg, S.R., Longoria, R.G., Chinchali, S.: Co-designing socio-technical interventions with skilled trade workers. In: 2023 IEEE International Symposium on Technology and Society (ISTAS), Virtual (2023)

8. Autor, D.H., Levy, F., Murnane, R.J.: The skill content of recent technological change: an empirical exploration. Q. J. Econ. **118**(4), 1279–1333 (2003)

9. Zoran, A., Shilkrot, R., Goyal, P., Maes, P., Paradiso, J.A.: The wise chisel: The rise of the smart handheld tool. IEEE Pervasive Comput. **13**(3), 48–57 (2014)

10. Littman, M.L., et al.: Gathering strength, gathering storms: the One Hundred Year Study on Artificial Intelligence (AI100) 2021 Study Panel Report. Stanford University, Stanford, CA (2021). http://ai100.stanford.edu/2021-report, (Accessed 16 Sep 2021)

11. Slota, S.C., et al.: Locating the work of artificial intelligence ethics. J. Am. Soc. Inf. Sci. **74**(3), 311 (2023)

12. Clarke, V., Braun, V., Hayfield, N.: Thematic analysis. In: Smith, J.A. (ed.), Qualitative psychology: a practical guide to research methods, 3rd edn., pp. 222–248. Sage (2015)

13. Yang, S., Fichman, P., Zhu, X., Sanfilippo, M., Li, S., Fleischmann, K.R.: The use of ICT during COVID-19. In: Proceedings of the Association for Information Science and Technology, vol.57(1), p. e297, Virtual (2020)

Understandability: The Hidden Barrier and the Last Yard to Information Accessibility

Ian Y Song[1(✉)] and Sherry L Xie[2]

[1] Simon Fraser University Library, Burnaby, BC, Canada
isong@sfu.ca
[2] School of Information Resource Management, Remin University of China, Beijing, China

Abstract. Students with print disabilities frequently encounter the challenge of understanding alternative texts for complex, scholarly non-text contents. While a local solution exists, it is intellectually stimulating to explore this phenomenon more broadly in pertinent policies, standards, and academic literature. The process revealed that understandability appeared to be the most challenging barrier to information accessibility despite being one of the widely accepted accessibility principles. For students with print disabilities to fully participate in equal education, the challenge of understandability, the last yard to information accessibility, must be dealt with. On the basis of local practices and literature analysis, this short paper presents reflections and suggestions. It is believed that collaboration between scholarly publishers, digital librarians, and universities, in addition to technologies, assistive and otherwise, is the most optimal solution.

Keywords: Accessibility · Information Accessibility · Understandability · Academic Accommodation · Students with Print Disabilities

1 Introduction

Accessibility is one of the eight principles prescribed in the United Nations (UN) Convention on the Rights of Persons with Disabilities (Art. 3), referring to both physical accessibility and information accessibility (art. 9). This principle bears a direct impact on the Convention's goal to ensure disabled individuals to "participate fully in all aspects of life" (art. 9) [1], including their exercise of the right to education (art. 24). As a State Party to the UN Convention, Canada subscribes to the Convention's principles, and it enacted an accessibility act in 2019 to consolidate the existent protections in the Canadian Charter of Rights and Freedoms and the Canadian Human Rights Act. The aim of the Accessible Canada Act is to "ensure a barrier-free Canada" [2]. The right to education is thus expressed as barrier-free education [3, 4] or barrier-free learning [5], where a barrier is, for example, anything that hinders such right [6]. This exemplar barrier definition comes from the accessibility act of the British Columbia (BC) province, where the author's employing institution, i.e., Simon Fraser University (SFU), resides. By the Accessible British Columbia Act and its regulation [7], SFU is prescribed as an accessible organization, effective September 1, 2023. To be an accessible organization,

I. Sserwanga et al. (Eds.): iConference 2024, LNCS 14598, pp. 204–212, 2024.
https://doi.org/10.1007/978-3-031-57867-0_15

the university needs to, among other requirements, establish an accessibility committee (art. 9) and to develop an accessibility plan (art. 11) so that barriers to equal, inclusive education can be removed and prevented. While both the Accessible British Columbia Act and the Accessible British Columbia Regulation are recent (coming into effect in June 2021 and September 2023 respectively), accessibility has long been recognized as a fundamental policy area in BC and in its educational system. SFU, for example, included services for students with disabilities in its Office of Student Services prior to 1996 and in 1996, established officially the Centre for Accessible Learning (CAL), an office that is committed to educational accessibility for students with disabilities [8]. What impact will the new, legal accessibility requirements have on universities such as SFU? While a comprehensive assessment would not be possible at this time as the new requirements only started to take effect, the observation of the legal emphasis on "anything," i.e., anything that hinders accessibility, invoked a desire to look into its possible implementation. In fact, the emphasis on "anything" is the same with the Accessible Canada Act (sec. 2) [2]. This short paper explores first the relation of the "anything" requirement to the author's working experience as a digital service librarian in assisting the university's provision of accessibility to course materials for visually impaired students and then, presents some reflections and suggestions based on the SFU practice and the analysis of relevant literature.

2 Information Accessibility, Course Materials, and the Understandability Challenge

Both information and physical accessibility are addressed in the SFU Accessibility for Students with Disabilities Policy (revised 2003) [9] and the accompanying accessibility information [10], which are rather comprehensive in terms of the types of assistance provided. However, the specifics on information accessibility are much more limited than those on physical accessibility, which focuses on making general information accessible such as information on the university's website and information about the university's programs and services. Information accessibility for university students is certainly more than accessing general information and the necessity of accessing course materials goes without saying. For students with print disabilities, course materials need to be in formats other than the regular prints and only specialized efforts can make it happen. Arguably, the course materials accessibility is covered by the university policy's general provision on academic accommodations, which requires students with disabilities to individually register for accommodations [11]. In practice, the availability of course materials in alternative formats is ensured by a national-provincial-local network [12], the nodes of which include, for example, the Canadian National Institute for the Blind [13], the National Educational Association of Disabled Students [14],and the Library and Archives Canada at the national level, and the Center for Accessible Post-secondary Education Resources [15] and the British Columbia College and Institute Library Services [16] at the provincial level. Apart from making available the existent alternative textbooks and other academic materials, the network also provides customized services that create and deliver the alternatives to students upon request. Moreover, individual university libraries, such as the SFU Library, joined forces with the network to accommodate situations irregular to the standard customized services. These irregular situations include unexpected changes from either the instructors or the students, which are typically short noticed and thus difficult for the standard customized services to accommodate. When this happens to print-disabled students at SFU, the SFU Library takes over the request, creates digital counterparts of the course materials under request, add descriptive tags to the digital outcome, make sure all contents are software readable, wraps all parts in a digital package, and delivers it to the requester. This local, individual university library node reduces the service delivery time from a standard month-long period to one that can be as short as one day; as such, it has ensured a complete fulfillment of information availability to print-disabled students at the university.

Does this, however, indicate complete fulfillment of academic accommodations that the university promised to the students? Not necessarily. The on-time delivery of course materials as a digitally integrated package only completes availability, not understandability, a meaning also implied by the term accessibility. Depending on the specifics of the course materials, understandability may become a major issue with non-text contents such as images, graphs, charts, and tables, in particular when they are complicated or when they occupy central places for understanding. When this is the case, the descriptive tags, more specifically here, alternative texts for non-text contents, added by digital service librarians in accordance with informational standards and practices become insufficient as they are basic, general, and discrete. The tags are basic because they rely only on the captions supplied by the print version, they are general because they can only describe the non-text contents as a whole, and they are discrete because they are unable to bring out the relationships between and among the parts, or those between the parts and the whole. To describe the parts, the whole, and their interrelationship requires subject or domain knowledge, which is typically unavailable from digital service librarians. In other words, the added alternative texts can only be format correct but not content instructive. Thus, for understandability, listening to alternative texts for complex, significant non-text contents is not the same as eyeing them – the latter allows seamless interpretations of both the parts and the whole, and is aided by simultaneous retrieval of existing knowledge behind the eyes. Students encountering alternative text challenges had to request interpretation assistance from the Centre for Accessible Learning, which then arranged subject knowledge-equipped human interpreters for the task. Only by this step, can the university's promise for academic accommodations to students with disabilities be considered complete. This experience shows that without sufficient understandability, information accessibility must be acknowledged as incomplete and ineffective.

3   Understandability in Policies, Standards and Academic Literature

The W3C Web Accessibility Initiative (WAI) gathered a list of national and international laws and policies regarding accessibility on its site, including both web-accessibility exclusive ones and others that are more than web accessibility [17]. What the term accessibility actually means in terms of a formal, legal definition appears insignificant to the majority of these laws and policies, the focus of which is to set up sets of compliance requirements. Arguably, by going through each and every requirement, one can distill what the term specifically means in that particular context and whether or not it encompasses – when it comes to information accessibility – the two dimensions of availability and understandability. This inefficient manner of understanding the term must be recognized by the EU law makers, who, in the EU's Web Accessibility Directive (adopted in 2016), attached four principles to accessibility: perceivability, operability, understandability, and robustness [18]. While not word by word, the four principles fundamentally mean the same as the four accessibility principles offered by the W3C in its second version of Web Content Accessibility Guidelines (WCAG) [19]. Thus, the widely adapted industrial accessibility standard has eventually found its way into a major legal context and was subsequently translated into the EU standard EN 301 549 V1.1.2 Accessibility requirements suitable for public procurement of ICT products and services in Europe (2015–04). This standard, according to the Web Accessibility Directive, contains "testable success criteria" regarding the principles; however, understandability was not found to be covered by it [20]. The part that is closely related to understandability and is mostly relevant to the SFU experience is that of document success criteria (Sect. 10.2), particularly those concerning non-text content (10.2.1), which addresses, however, only the presenting and the presence of alternative texts. This observation raises questions. If the measures of having alternative texts, which is addressed by the principle of perceivability, and assistive technologies, which is addressed by the principle of robustness, is sufficient for understanding, why, then, is a separate principle for understanding needed? If understanding is indeed a different matter (as demonstrated by the SFU experience), why, then, aren't there any "success criteria" for it? And if the standard intended for enforcement [21] does not address understandability specifically and independently, how can it then be implemented?

The observation of understandability being marginalized in the accessibility legal landscape continues with academic studies on information/web content accessibility. Firstly, not all accessibility-related studies addressed understandability, e.g., the study on accessibility in higher education in Norway [22], the study on requirements for large scale web accessibility evaluation [23], and the study on the inaccessibility of websites in postsecondary education [24]. Secondly, for those that did, understandability was sometimes conceptually confusing or at other times, hardly the focus or even an independent consideration. The examples for the former include the accessibility study on the Finnish higher education institution webpages, which equated being understandable as being readable [25], and the tools for web accessibility evaluation study, which considered the understandable principle as "mainly related to cognitive accessibility" [26], seemingly to place the burden on the shoulders of the users rather than the content producer. The examples for the latter include the study on e-book accessibility [27], the accessibility automatic evaluation tools study [28], and the accessibility in digital services study [29], all of which treated understandability as a simple mention.

Some of the empirical accessibility studies seem to be able to shed light on this understandability-being-marginalized situation. From these studies, many of them originated from the library/information community, it is clear that the overall accessibility requirements implementation or the implementation of requirements that are simpler than understandability is what is at issue. For example, two studies assessing library website accessibility for visually imparted users identified usability and navigation as problematic respectively in 2016 [30] and 2019 [31], and in 2020, a study evaluating the accessibility of special education cooperative websites for individuals with disabilities observed that these organizations struggled to meet the most basic levels of accessibility compliance [32]. In 2023, the study on public library website accessibility in the US concluded that these sites overwhelmingly failed to meet the accessibility standards required by US law (i.e., Sect. 508 of the Rehabilitation Act) [33]. As a result, understandability, the apparently most challenging requirement, is typically either simplified by the existence of alternative texts or left to future studies. According to the two studies concerning alternative texts, even the presence of alternative texts is unsatisfactory. The one published in 2017 identified the "missing alternative text areas for images" as mostly common across the 219 urban public library websites being studied [34] and the one published in 2021, which focused on open textbooks, concluded that "most of the books did not meet basic accessibility requirements", i.e., they fail to have alternative text for any images or properly coding/tagging for tables [35].

4   Reflections and Suggestions

Despite occupying a place in the accessibility principles and being considered as able to aid the removal or prevention of barriers, understandability appears to be a barrier to accessibility. Its implementation is much more challenging than that of the other principles and assistive technologies are inadequate in interpreting subject or domain knowledge for academic accommodations. The current assistive technology research seems to focus still on generating alternative texts [36] for reading over despite involving the new artificial intelligence tools [37]. And this apparently is not limited to research projects. The latest topics by those big tech names such as W3C [38] and Microsoft [39] are not extending to understanding complex, scholarly non-text contents for visually disabled persons either. Can the challenge of understanding complex, scholarly non-text contents for print-disabled students be eventually dealt with by technology? Can hope be placed on the (extreme) advancement of artificial intelligence such as the Meta's segment anything model? This newly released large-scale image model claims to be able to "cut out" any object in an image when being prompted [39], presenting therefore the possibility of understanding the parts of an image. While it is unknown when the cut-outs can be automatically annotated and relationships between the cut-outs can be automatically established, it can always be anticipated, isn't it? After all, for technologists, it is technology that makes things happen for people with disabilities [41].

For non-technologists, however, more than technology is needed to prescribe confidence for solving this complicated issue. According to the European Accessibility Act, accessibility should be achieved by removing and preventing barriers in a systematic manner [See [17]]; relying on technology alone can hardly be considered as being systematic. Being systematic requires a true appreciation of the barrier, an inclusive assessment of all possible contributing forces, and a solution that is both pertinent and scalable. For the barrier of understanding complex, scholarly non-texts for print-disabled students, scholarly publishers, academic librarians, and universities should all be involved in developing the solutions. This non-technological solution should be the blueprint for the development of pertinent technologies. For example, the publisher could request from the research team/article author(s) the processes of producing the non-text contents, just as the opening up of research data in the open science movement. If the documented research processes are enough for reproducibility, they then should be adequate for understanding when listening to. On the other hand, when individual interpretations are produced, such as those arranged by the SFU Cener for Accessible Learning, the process can also be recorded and annotated. These recordings can be submitted into the university's institutional repository or to any of the nodes on the national-provincial-local network for alternative course materials. While individual at one time, the accumulation may result in a collection that can potentially benefit students and learners with print disabilities all over the world. It can also become a unique dataset for the training of algorithms that are devoted to this understandability purpose. To open up the processes of producing the non-text contents requires only awareness, willingness, and comparatively minimum set of resources. Solutions as such seem to own the rational of continuing existence with even the availability of powerful artificial intelligence tools. Humankind as a whole will have to eventually answer the question as to what should be handed over to technologies and what should be reserved for ourselves.

5 Conclusion

For learning, it is understandability that a student ultimately desires and a university fundamentally accommodate. For print-disabled individuals, understandability is the most challenging barrier to information accessibility and for print-disabled students, understandability is the last yard that needs to be paved for a complete academic accommodation. That it is a last yard as opposed to a last mile challenge is because the university libraries are typically able to pave the majority of the way for student information accessibility [42]. Regardless it all needs to be able to reach the final destination.

Without understanding, access to information is meaningless. Despite that the current information accessibility environment is limited to availability and readability, it is understandability that will make a difference for the disabled individual, students, and the world.

References

1. United Nations, Convention on the Rights of Persons with Disabilities. https://www.un.org/esa/socdev/enable/rights/convtexte.htm, (Accessed 7 Sep 2023)
2. Government of Canada, Accessible Canada Act. https://laws-lois.justice.gc.ca/eng/acts/A-0.6/FullText.html, (Accessed 21 Dec 2023)
3. Canadian Hearing Services. Barrier-Free Education. https://www.chs.ca/page/barrier-free-education, (Accessed 02 Sep 2023)
4. British Columbia Library Association, Accessibility and Vancouver Community College Library. https://bclaconnect.ca/perspectives/2015/10/31/verbeem-et-al, (Accessed 4 Sep 2023)
5. University of Toronto, The Barrierfree Learning Environment. https://barrierfree.ca/index.htm, (Accessed 03 Sep 2023)

6. British Columbia, Accessible British Columbia Act. https://www.bclaws.gov.bc.ca/civix/doc ument/id/complete/statreg/21019section2, (Accessed 02 Sep 2023)
7. British Columbia, Accessible British Columbia Act. Accessible British Columbia Regulation (B.C. Reg.105/2022). https://www.bclaws.gov.bc.ca/civix/document/id/complete/sta treg/105_2022, (Accessed 14 July 2023)
8. Centre for Accessible Learning, Simon Fraser University, About us. https://www.sfu.ca/stu dents/accessible-learning/contact-us/about-us.html, (Accessed 8 Sep 2023)
9. Simon Fraser University, Accessibility for Students with Disabilities Policies. https://www. sfu.ca/policies/gazette/general/gp26.html, (Accessed 9 Sep 2023)
10. Simon Fraser University, Accessibility Information. https://www.sfu.ca/students/iss/contact/ accessibility_information.html, (Accessed 9 Sep 2023)
11. Simon Fraser University, Accessibility for Students with Disabilities Policy. https://www.sfu. ca/policies/gazette/general/gp26.html, (Accessed 10 Sep 2023)
12. National Education Association of Disabled Students, Access to Academic Materials for Post-Secondary Students with Print Disabilities. https://www.neads.ca/en/about/projects/atam, (Accessed 13 Sep 2023)
13. CNIB Foundation, Homepage. https://www.cnib.ca/en/search/node?keys=textbook&reg ion=on, (Accessed 10 Sep 2023)
14. NEADS, Frequently Asked Questions. https://www.neads.ca/en/norc/faq/index.php?ID=11, (Accessed 11 Sep 2023)
15. CAPER-BC, Home Page, https://caperbc.ca, last accessed 2023/09/03
16. NEADS, Access to Academic Materials for Post-secondary Students with Print Disabilities. https://www.neads.ca/en/about/projects/atam/profiles_provincial.php, (Accessed 12 Sep 2023)
17. W3C, Web Accessibility Laws & Policies, Web Accessibility Initiative (WAI). https://www. w3.org/WAI/policies/, (Accessed 12 Sep 2023)
18. EUR-Lex, Directive (EU) 2016/2102 of the European Parliament and of the Council of 26 October 2016 on the Accessibility of the Websites and Mobile Applications of Public Sector Bodies. https://eur-lex.europa.eu/eli/dir/2016/2102/oj, (Accessed 9 Sep 2023)
19. W3C, Web Content Accessibility Guidelines (WCAG) 2.0. https://www.w3.org/TR/WCA G20/, (Accessed 11 Sep 2023)
20. ETSI, Accessibility Requirements Suitable for Public Procurement of ICT Products and Services in Europe. https://www.etsi.org/deliver/etsi_en/301500_301599/301549/01.01.02_60/ en_301549v010102p.pdf, (Accessed 10 Sep 2023)
21. Siteimprove, Everything you need to know about the EU Web Accessibility Directive and the European Accessibility Act, https://www.siteimprove.com/glossary/eu-web-accessibility-directive/#:~:text=The%20European%20Accessibility%20Act%20will,potential%20legal% 20and%20financial%20risks, (Accessed 11 Sep 2023)
22. Inal, Y., Torkildsby, A.B.: Web accessibility in higher education in Norway: to what extent are university websites accessible? In: Nocera, J.A., Lárusdóttir, M.K., Petrie, H., Piccinno, A., Winckler, M. (eds.) INTERACT 2023: Part I, pp. 111–122. Springer Nature Switzerland, Cham (2023). https://doi.org/10.1007/978-3-031-42280-5_7
23. Paternò, F., Pulina, F., Santoro, C., Gappa, H., Mohamad, Y.: Requirements for large scale web accessibility evaluation. In: Miesenberger, K., Manduchi, R., Covarrubias Rodriguez, M., Peňáz, P. (eds.) ICCHP 2020. LNCS, vol. 12376, pp. 275–283. Springer, Cham (2020). https://doi.org/10.1007/978-3-030-58796-3_33
24. Seale, J., Burgstahler, S., Fisseler, B.: Tackling the inaccessibility of websites in postsecondary education. In: Yesilada, Y., Harper, S. (eds.) Web Accessibility. HIS, pp. 263–279. Springer, London (2019). https://doi.org/10.1007/978-1-4471-7440-0_15

25. Laamanen, M., Ladonlahti, T., Puupponen, H., et al.: Does the law matter? An empirical study on the accessibility of Finnish higher education institutions' web pages. Universal Access Inform. Soc. (2022). https://doi.org/10.1007/s10209-022-00931-6
26. Abascal, J., Arrue, M., Valencia, X.: Tools for web accessibility evaluation. In: Yesilada, Y., Harper, S. (eds) Web Accessibility. Human–Computer Interaction Series. Springer, London (2019). https://doi.org/10.1007/978-1-4471-7440-0_26
27. Sun, Y.T., Manabat, A.K.M., Chan, M.L., Chong, I., Vu, K.-P. L., et al.: Accessibility evaluation: manual development and tool selection for evaluating accessibility of E-textbooks. Adv. Neuroergon. Cognitive Eng., 327–337 (2016). https://doi.org/10.1007/978-3-319-41691-5_28
28. Abu Doush, I., Sultan, K., Al-Betar, M.A.: Web accessibility automatic evaluation tools: to what extent can they be automated? CCF Trans. Pervasive Comput. Interact. 5, 288–320 (2023). https://doi.org/10.1007/s42486-023-00127-8
29. Kärpänen, T.: How to ensure web accessibility in digital services to improve the competitive advantage of an organization. In: Antona, M., Stephanidis, C. (eds.) Universal Access in UAHCI 2023, Part I, pp. 74–87. Springer Nature Switzerland, Cham (2023). https://doi.org/10.1007/978-3-031-35681-0_5
30. Yoon, K., Dols, R., Hulscher, L., Newberry, T.: An Exploratory study of library website accessibility for visually impaired users. Libr. Inf. Sci. Res. 38(3), 250–258 (2016)
31. Mulliken, A.: Eighteen blind library users experiences with library websites and search tools in US academic libraries: a qualitative study. College Res. Libraries (2019). https://doi.org/10.31235/osf.io/vtnr9
32. Baule, S.M.: Evaluating the accessibility of special education cooperative websites for individuals with disabilities. TechTrends 64, 50–56 (2020). https://doi-org.proxy.lib.sfu.ca/ , https://doi.org/10.1007/s11528-019-00421-2
33. Khawaja, P.: Accessibility of public library websites in the United States. Univ. Access Inform. Soc. 22(3), 1047–1057 (2023). https://doi.org/10.1007/s10209-022-00866-y
34. Liu, Y.Q., Bielefield, A., McKay, P.: Are urban public libraries websites accessible to Americans with disabilities?. Univ. Access Inform. Soc. 18(1), 191–206 (2017). https://doi.org/10.1007/s10209-017-0571-7
35. Azadbakht, E., Schultz, T., Arellano, J.: Not open for all: accessibility of open textbooks. Insights the UKSG J. 34(1), 24 (2021). https://doi.org/10.1629/uksg.557
36. Tiwary, T., Mahapatra, R.P. Enhancement in web accessibility for visually impaired people using hybrid deep belief network –bald eagle search. Multimedia Tools Appli. 82, 24347–24368 (2023). https://doi-org.proxy.lib.sfu.ca/ , https://doi.org/10.1007/s11042-023-14494-y
37. Tiwary, T., R. P. Mahapatra, R.P.: Web accessibility challenges for disabled and generation of Alt Text for images in websites using artificial intelligence. In: 2022 3rd International Conference on Issues and Challenges in Intelligent Computing Techniques (ICICT), Ghaziabad, India, pp. 1–5 (2022). https://doi.org/10.1109/ICICT55121.2022.10064545(2022)
38. W3C. Artificial Intelligence (AI) and Accessibility Research Symposium 2023. https://www.w3.org/WAI/research/ai2023/, last accessed 2023–09–13
39. Microsoft. Accessibility Tools for Vision. https://support.microsoft.com/en-us/topic/accessibility-tools-for-vision-b3c57606-e0af-46d2-97b4-fa6b5fba4fa1, (Accessed 12 Sep 2023); Cuevas, Z.: Accessibility and AI: Microsoft Details Its Plans for a More Inclusive Future. https://www.pcmag.com/news/accessibility-and-ai-microsoft-details-its-plans-for-a-more-inclusive-future, (Accessed 12 Sep 2023)
40. Segment Anything, Segment Anything Model (SAM): A New AI Model from Meta AI that Can "cut out" any Objct, in any Image, with a Single Click. https://segment-anything.com/, (Accessed 15 Sep 2023)

41. CANARIE, The Barrierfree Learning Environment. https://barrierfree.ca/overview.htm, (Accessed 10 Sep 2023)
42. Longmeier, M.M., Foster, A.K.: Accessibility and disability services for libraries: a survey of large, research-intensive institutions. Portal (Baltimore, Md.) **22**(4), 823–853 (2022). https://doi.org/10.1353/pla.2022.0044

Differences in Knowledge Adoption Among Task Types in Human-AI Collaboration Under the Chronic Disease Prevention Scenario

Quan Lu[1,2] and Xueying Peng[2(✉)]

[1] Center for Studies of Information Resources, Wuhan University, Wuhan 430072, China
[2] School of Information Management, Wuhan University, Wuhan 430072, China
pengxy1105@whu.edu.cn

Abstract. Chronic disease prevention is crucial for maintaining national health and reducing medical burden. Transmission of disease prevention knowledge to people through human-AI collaboration is an emerging disruptive and revolutionary approach. Nonetheless, little research has been aimed at the knowledge adoption in different tasks under this scenario. This study explored the differences in knowledge adoption among task types in human-AI collaboration under the chronic disease prevention scenario. Twelve participants were recruited to complete the factual, interpretive, and exploratory tasks in human-AI collaboration. The subjective efficiency and effectiveness of knowledge adoption were obtained by questionnaires. The objective efficiency, including search time, switch frequency, and number of queries, was counted by Screen Recorder, while experts scored the objective effectiveness. Furthermore, non-parametric tests were used to compare the differences. The results showed that objective efficiency varied among different task types. Participants spent more time in the interpretive task and switched more pages in the exploratory task. Then, perceived effectiveness was the worst in the interpretive task. Finally, the participants got lower scores in the factual task and higher scores in the interpretive task. Therefore, suggestions for the means of human-AI collaboration have been proposed under the chronic disease scenario, including identifying scenarios to enhance user adaptation and immersion in completing different health tasks, enhancing the transparency and explainability of AI, especially in interpretive tasks, and adding references in the process of acquiring and understanding knowledge.

Keywords: Human-AI Collaboration · Knowledge Adoption · Chronic Disease Prevention

1 Introduction

Chronic diseases including heart disease, cancer, diabetes, and arthritis have a significant impact on national health. Financial incentives, health coaching, wellness programs, and group medical appointments are four types of chronic disease prevention interventions [1]. Existing studies indicated that the average proportion of a community's jurisdictional population reached by a specific intervention varied across interventions [2]. However, implementing various interventions depends on the one-to-one promotion of community health workers (CHWs). Studies have proved studies that as the number of in-person contacts between the community health worker and the client increased, the likelihood of achieving disease prevention was greatly improved [3]. However, promoting chronic disease prevention through contact between CHWs and residents is inefficient. Robust infrastructure, education programs, and other problems [4, 5] can also interfere with chronic disease prevention. The government and society urgently need a convenient way to achieve chronic disease prevention to promote the interaction between CHWs and residents.

At present, chronic disease prevention involves multi-agent participation, such as community health workers (CHWs), community residents, hospitals, service agencies, faith-based organizations, unions, nonprofits, and government agencies [6, 7]. With the change in living habits, there are increasingly potential chronic disease patients. In addition to residents, various participants are also actively involved in preventing chronic diseases. They not only undertake chronic disease prevention work of different types, difficulties, and goals but also master a large amount of chronic disease prevention knowledge from different sources. The prevention of chronic diseases has gradually become a cause that the whole society participates in. Obviously, the previous interventions cannot effectively deal with realistic tasks of chronic disease prevention. However, the adoption of chronic disease prevention knowledge is the first and key step to achieving prevention. Knowledge can improve the operability of chronic disease prevention and subtly change the living habits of residents. The premise of chronic disease prevention is that residents adopt the knowledge published by different agents. Then, any intervention needs to be based on the adoption of chronic disease prevention knowledge. But the process of knowledge adoption hides in the daily health search task. Therefore, it is necessary to analyze knowledge adoption of chronic disease prevention involving multi-agents to facilitate the exchange of knowledge and promote in-depth and extensive prevention work.

Human-AI collaboration describes the process of developing a socio-technical system in which AI and humans can collaborate in a mutually beneficial fashion by exploiting individual strengths and coevolving through complementary improvement [8, 9]. The means of human-AI collaboration can not only support the interaction between CHWs and residents but also promote knowledge exchange among multiple agents. Therefore, the adoption of chronic disease prevention knowledge by residents can be achieved through the means of human-AI collaboration. At present, human-AI collaboration has been applied in the field of chronic disease prevention [10, 11]. Most existing studies have discussed the application and ethics of AI in chronic disease prevention from the perspective of system design and service optimization. However, little research has focused on how residents adopt knowledge in different health search tasks. Therefore, the analysis of the differences in knowledge adoption among task types in human-AI collaboration under the chronic disease prevention scenario is of great significance for promoting the prevention of chronic diseases.

2 Literature Review

2.1 Task Types

Task is a key factor that influences search behaviors and cognitions [12]. Different types of tasks have been identified and classified in the Web search environment [13–15] believed that task characteristics encompass task complexity, task differences, time orientation, goal differences, professional differences, cognitive differences, and task areas. In general, task types can be identified and classified in terms of difficulty, complexity, interacting objects, and levels [16, 17]. ①Task difficulty: [18] noted in their comprehensive task classification scheme that task difficulty can only be subjective, as assessed by task doers. Some other researchers defined task difficulty based on certain objective criteria and/or measurements. ②Task complexity: [19] indicated that complexity refers to "the number and interactions of problem variables." [20] distinguished between simple, decision, judgment, problem, and fuzzy tasks based on complexity attributes, including multiple paths, multiple desired outcomes, conflicting interdependence, and uncertainty. Task complexity can also effectively distinguish objective task difficulty. ③Interacting objects and levels: [21] provided three types of tasks based on user goal: leading search goal, current search goal, and interactive intentions. [22] provided three levels of task, including meta-task, category, and sub-categories. Meta-task can be divided into interacting with others, interacting with ideas or information, and interacting with things.

Compared to general search tasks, health information search (HIS) tasks focus more on user searches for health issues. [23] divided exploratory HIS into two phases: evidence-based and hypothesis-directed. The evidence-based phase mainly focuses on locating information regarding signs and symptoms, while the hypothesis-directed phase involves discrimination among different diseases under uncertainty. Based on this framework, [24] added another phase: decision-making search, which involves seeking information to make a treatment decision, including locating information, differentiating information, and making decisions. Another classification framework is also widely accepted and used in health information searches. [25] defined search tasks (factual, interpretive, and exploratory), which were used to design the health information-seeking experiment scenarios. Among them, the factual task is an "asking a fact" task with a closed question, such as naming, identifying, or listing. The interpretive task is a "thinking/ understanding" task to configure an answer rather than simply and concisely locate one. It is rather open-ended but more focused and goal-oriented than an exploratory task. The exploratory task is motivated by the searcher's desire to broaden their knowledge of a topic. Based on this framework, [26] explored how people with health anxiety may behave differently regarding their attentional biases when seeking health information online based on three types of tasks. This classification framework has a wider applicability than just health information search.

2.2 Human-AI Collaboration

AI with collaboration intelligence is characterized by the ability of multiple agents to exchange not only information but also knowledge and to work together and/or with humans to produce or create something in support of a shared task [27]. Only AI with a social quotient (SQ) can achieve human-AI collaboration. At present, human-AI collaboration has been applied in various fields of social life. Researchers have chosen specific AI systems to achieve human-AI collaboration based on designed experiments, including developed or existing AI systems, such as intelligent recommendation systems, robots, virtual humans, autonomous vehicles, etc. For example, [28] created a crowdsourcing campaign consisting of four human intelligence tasks (HITs) in which the participants had to indicate whether or not a set of papers belonged to the same author. [29] designed colorizing tasks and discussed the design implications for human-AI collaboration in the area of art. [30] created a fashion design task to design clothing by seamlessly mixing the real and virtual environments. [31] designed pothole inspection tasks using the drone's automatic inspection to explore the safety and efficiency of human-AI collaboration and how humans could appropriately calibrate their trust towards the AI agents.

Diagnosis is the most concerning scenario of human-AI collaboration. For example, [32] designed classification and captioning tasks to explore the clinical scenarios of human-AI-collaborative pathological diagnosis. They found that optimizing the tools for the annotation process can support a better experience of human-AI collaboration in pathological diagnosis. [33] designed a non-clinical randomized controlled trial with real-world peer supporters on TalkLife and examined how AI can collaborate with humans to facilitate peer empathy during textual, online supportive conversations. [34] developed a human-AI collaborative diagnosis tool that shares a similar examination process to that of pathologists, which can improve AI's integration into their routine examination. In addition, some studies have explored how to improve the efficiency and effectiveness of health care in the exchange of knowledge between humans and AI. For example, [35] identified implications for doctors, patients, healthcare systems, and technology design from the perspective of general practitioners in order to understand the potential roles of a future artificial intelligence (AI) documentation assistant in primary care consultations. [36] highlighted the importance of guaranteeing better cooperation within human-AI teams to enable safer and more human-sustainable care practices. However, further exploration is needed for the application and empirical testing of the means of human-AI collaboration in chronic disease prevention scenarios.

2.3 Knowledge Adoption

Knowledge is awareness and understanding about people or things in the objective world, generated by feeling, communicating, logical reasoning activities in practice and education, and maybe facts, information, or skills [37]. Adopting knowledge on chronic disease prevention means acquiring, integrating, and comparing knowledge resources before understanding, absorbing, transforming, and applying knowledge to prevent chronic diseases. This process involves many components: resource, creator, provider, inspirer, recipient, and reviewer [38]. HCWs, hospitals, service agencies, faith-based organizations, unions, nonprofits, and government agencies play one or more components in chronic disease prevention. Furthermore, the adoption of chronic disease prevention knowledge is a key step in chronic disease prevention. In general, knowledge adoption processes can be divided into a series of information-processing activities [39], such as knowledge capture, knowledge creation, knowledge storage, knowledge organization, knowledge application, and knowledge dissemination [40]. However, activities related to knowledge adoption are inseparable from search, whether the result of knowledge adoption is actively acquired or passively absorbed by users. Therefore, it is necessary and feasible to consider knowledge adoption from a search perspective.

Types of tasks influence the efficiency and effectiveness of knowledge adoption. For example, [41] found that work tasks dramatically affect users' interaction performance, particularly search efficiency and effectiveness. In her results, search efficiency and effectiveness were higher in less complex decision tasks and lower in more complex intellectual tasks. Task complexity is of great importance to search efficiency and effectiveness. [42] found that there was no significant difference among the three systems in supporting users' task completion processes for complex tasks. [43] learned that a crowdsourcing task should consist of multiple simple microtasks rather than a complicated task. On this basis, time efficiency, the number of interactions with the computer interface, and the frequency of behavior are used to measure efficiency [44–46], while perceived decision quality, accuracy, reliability, and other indicators are used to measure effectiveness [47, 48]. The performance of different indicators can reflect the characteristics of task types.

Therefore, this study attempts to address a question related to the knowledge adoption in human-AI collaboration under the chronic disease prevention scenario:

RQ: What are the differences in knowledge adoption among task types in human-AI collaboration under the chronic disease prevention scenario?

(a) What are the differences in the efficiency of the knowledge adoption among task types in human-AI collaboration under the chronic disease prevention scenario?

(b) What are the differences in the effectiveness of the knowledge adoption among task types in human-AI collaboration under the chronic disease prevention scenario?

3 Methodology

3.1 Participants and Sampling

Those who do not have Alzheimer's disease (have not been diagnosed with it) and whose family members also do not have Alzheimer's disease (have not been diagnosed with it) could participate in the experiment. Based on task types, the number of participants in the experiment should be a multiple of 3. Furthermore, we have conducted a literature review on user experiments and found that the number of participants generally ranges from 8 to 36. As a result, more than 12 participants from Wuhan University and Central China Normal University were recruited for the experiment, responding to advertisements. However, the newly obtained data did not exceed the range of three standard deviations of the existing data, and the impact on the final results was insignificant as the number of participants increased. Therefore, considering the scientific rigor of the experiment, we analyzed the data from 12 participants and presented it in this study.

All participants were required to be informed, agree to the precautions of the experiment, and sign. Participants were each paid ¥20 for their involvement in the study. Table 1. Describes information with different genders, education, and other demographic characteristics.

Table 1. Characteristics of participants ($N = 12$).

Demographic characteristics		Number	Percentage
Gender	Male	6	50%
	Female	6	50%
Age	20–22	3	25%
	23 –25	8	67%
	26 –28	1	8%
Education	Master or below	11	92%
	Doctor	1	8%
Whether you have chronic diseases	Yes	2	17%
	No	10 (3 suspected)	83%
Whether your family members have chronic diseases	Yes	5	42%
	No	7	58%

3.2 AI System

The WeChat mini program "Elderly Disability Screening and Management" was used as an AI system to achieve human-AI collaboration. The reasons are: (1) The AI system implemented social intelligence and can collaborate with users. (2) The knowledge obtained by the dual model of knowledge base and GPT. (3) What is exchanged between the AI system and users is knowledge. (4) AI systems, experts, and users all share the same goal of preventing chronic diseases. The production or creation of human-AI collaboration should be new knowledge and the understanding of knowledge, thereby further promoting the prevention of chronic diseases.

Before the experiment, all participants scanned a QR code on their mobile phones to access the AI system. They then used the AI system until they were familiar with all the functions. Finally, they checked their phone's screen-recording software and screenshots to complete the experiment (Fig. 1).

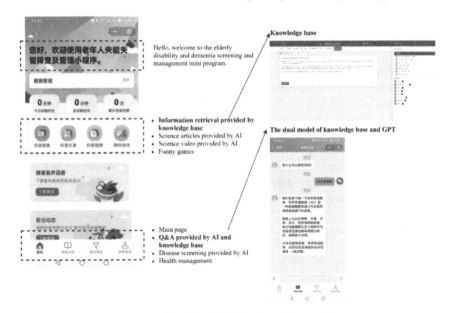

Fig. 1. AI System of Elderly Disability Screening and Management.

3.3 Procedures

The experiment was completed from April 1 to April 30, 2023. Each participant completed the experiment as follows.

① Pre-questionnaire—Participants were instructed to fill out a pre-questionnaire requesting their demographic information, whether they have chronic diseases, and whether their family members have chronic diseases. Participants were asked to fill in the pre-questionnaire at the lab.

② Search Experiment—All participants completed three types of tasks: Factual, Interpretive, and Exploratory Task in sequence [25].

Factual Task (T1): *Assuming your family is diagnosed with Alzheimer's disease by a doctor, you would like to know what Alzheimer's disease is. Please provide a definition of Alzheimer's disease through screenshots.*

Interpretive Task (T2): *Assuming that your family has recently experienced symptoms such as forgetfulness, constantly repeating the same sentence or asking a question, or decreased interest in personal interests. Please search to determine if they have Alzheimer's disease and take screenshots of the cause.*

Exploratory Task (T3): *In order to help your family prevent Alzheimer's disease, please take screenshots of 3 pieces of Alzheimer's disease prevention knowledge that you think are useful by searching.*

Active participation by the elderly and passive completion through other searchers are typical scenarios for chronic disease prevention. The completion process of the three types of tasks was recorded by screen-recording software, and participants took screenshots of the tasks. Search time, switch frequency, number of queries, and objective effectiveness could be obtained according to the results of recordings and screenshots.

③ Self-report—Participants repeated the entire process of completing the tasks based on the recorded screen file.

④ Post-questionnaire—After the participants completed the tasks, they were asked to fill in the post-questionnaire, which consisted of questions regarding subjective efficiency and effectiveness of adopting knowledge on chronic disease prevention. Participants were also requested to fill in the post-questionnaire for their experiences at the lab.

⑤ Online Follow-up Questionnaire—To track the long-term effectiveness of knowledge adoption, this study conducted an online follow-up questionnaire on the seventh day after the completion of the experiment for each participant and asked them to choose the best-matched statement. Based on [49], the four levels of the statement are as follows.

R1: Strong adoption: *After adopting Alzheimer's prevention knowledge last week, I have consciously taken action this week to help myself or my family prevent Alzheimer's disease.*

R2: Weak adoption: *After adopting Alzheimer's prevention knowledge last week, I consciously prepared to take action to help myself or my family prevent Alzheimer's disease.*

R3: Faint adoption: *Although I adopted Alzheimer's prevention knowledge last week, I'm not sure I need to use this knowledge to help myself or my family prevent Alzheimer's disease in the future.*

R4: Not adoption: *Although I adopted Alzheimer's prevention knowledge last week, I do not see the need to use this knowledge to help myself or my family prevent Alzheimer's disease.*

3.4 Measures

This study considered seven indicators and statistically tested whether there are differences between types of tasks in knowledge adoption under the chronic disease prevention scenario.

First, the search experiment provided a record of the search related to the three types of tasks.

① Search time refers to the time from the start to the end of the search. The indicator was automatically generated by screen-recording software and reviewed by investigators.

② Switch frequency refers to the number of pages that appear between the start and end of the search. The indicator was determined by investigators. Examples are shown in Fig. 2.

③ Number of queries refers to the number of queries that appear between the start and end of the search. The indicator was determined by investigators.

④ Result screenshot refers to screenshots from participants of the results of different tasks. The text in the picture was automatically extracted by the Word Processing System (WPS) and formed into a document. Two physicians from the Geriatric Health Management Department of the Chronic Disease Prevention and Control Center scored the effectiveness of the task according to the documents, ranging from 0 to 5 points. The documents were named only by numbers. After scoring by experts, this study selected the most authoritative scoring results for data analysis.

Second, post-questionnaire was used to obtain the perceived efficiency and perceived effectiveness.

⑤ Perceived efficiency refers to the user's subjective rating of the efficiency of human-AI collaboration, ranging from 1 to 5 points.

⑥ Perceived effectiveness refers to the user's subjective rating of the effectiveness of human-AI collaboration, ranging from 1 to 5 points.

Third, an online follow-up questionnaire was used to obtain the long-term effectiveness.

⑦ Long-term effectiveness refers to the tendency of users to change their chronic disease prevention habits in the long term after adopting knowledge.

The investigators analyzed quantitative data collected from the experiment and the post- and online follow-up questionnaires. Quantitative data were tallied and analyzed in SPSS 26, mainly to compare the differences in knowledge adoption under the chronic disease prevention scenario. The data collection and analysis plans are shown in Table 2.

The Mann-Whitney test is a non-parametric statistical method used to compare whether the medians of two groups of samples are equal. Its advantages include strong robustness, wide applicability, and high efficiency. Since the experimental data in this study does not meet the assumptions of normal distribution or homogeneity of variance, the sample size is small. The Mann-Whitney test was selected in this study to compare the differences.

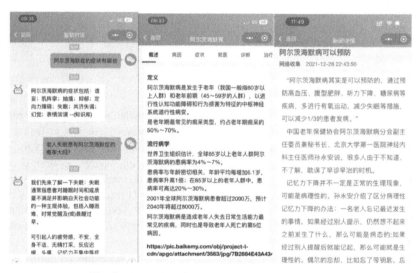

Fig. 2. Examples of pages on knowledge adoption.

Table 2. Data collection and analysis plans.

Research questions	No. of participants	Indicators	Max	Min	SD	Data collection	Data analysis
RQ (a)	12	Perceived efficiency	5	2	0.97	Post-questionnaire	non-parametric test and descriptive analysis
		Search time (s)	251	15	65.52	Search experiment	
		Switch frequency	21	1	4.58	Search experiment	
		Number of queries	3	0	0.97	Search experiment	
RQ (b)	12	Perceived effectiveness	5	2	0.86	Post-questionnaire	non-parametric test, descriptive analysis, and expert scoring
		Result effectiveness score	5	1	1.29	Search experiment	
		Long-term effectiveness	R2	R4	-	Online follow-up questionnaire	

4 Results

4.1 Efficiency of Knowledge Adoption

Table 3. Reports the perceived efficiency score in the knowledge adoption. The results show that the three types of tasks are consistent in perceived efficiency. Task 1 and Task 3 have higher scores, and Task 2 has a lower score (4.42 for Task 3, 4.25 for Task 1, and 3.67 for Task 2). It indicates that the exchange of knowledge between humans and AI systems achieves high efficiency for users. Then, the perceived efficiency in the three types of tasks is compared using a Mann-Whitney U test. The test results show no significant differences between any of the task types (P >0.05). It indicates that the three types of tasks are consistent, and users do not feel overly surprised or disappointed in either task.

Table 4. Reports the objective efficiency in the knowledge adoption, including search time, switch frequency, and the number of queries. The results show that the three task types differ in many aspects.

First, users spend much more search time to finish Task 2 and Task 3 (160.75s for Task 2, 121.67s for Task 3, and 68.92s for Task 1). It indicates that a long search is a negative signal for task difficulty. Then, the search time in the three types of tasks is compared using a Mann-Whitney U test. The test results show that the search time in Task 1 and Task 2 is significantly different (P <0.05). It indicates that differentiating chronic disease symptoms was more difficult for users to understand the definition, even if the AI system gave clear chronic disease-related knowledge of definitions and symptoms.

Second, users use many more pages to finish Task 2 and Task 3 (8.75 pages for Task 3, 7.17 pages for Task 2, and 3.83 pages for Taks 1). It indicates a strong relationship between the number of pages and the amount of knowledge. When the task requires three pieces of knowledge, the user would actively compare more knowledge on different pages. And then, the switch frequency in the three types of tasks is compared using a Mann-Whitney U test. The test results show that the switch frequency in Task 1 and Task 3 is significantly different ($P < 0.05$). It indicated that human-AI collaboration promoted increased relevance of knowledge in Task 3, allowing users to view more pages in less time.

Third, users use many more queries to finish Task 1 and Task 2 (0.92 for Task 2, 0.83 for Task 1, and 0.58 for Task 3). It indicates that human-AI collaboration can provide keywords based on the scenario, greatly reducing the number of query constructions and reconstructions. Then, the number of queries in the three types of tasks is compared using a Mann-Whitney U test. The test results show no significant differences between any of the task types ($P > 0.05$). It indicates that human-AI collaboration can facilitate users' prevention of chronic diseases by creating tags, providing prompt words, and forming knowledge associations.

To conclude, many statistics in Table 4. Show that the objective efficiency of the knowledge adoption in three types of tasks have many differences in our study. Such differences may come from the task characteristics and requirements. Our results further find that Task 1 (Factual Task) can be a benchmark for difficulty in comparing the characteristics of different tasks.

Table 3. The subjective efficiency of knowledge adoption.

Items	T1	T2	T3	$P < 0.05$ Differences
Perceived efficiency	4.25	3.67	4.42	-

Table 4. The objective efficiency of knowledge adoption.

Items	T1	T2	T3	$P < 0.05$ Differences
Search time	68.92	160.75	121.67	T1 < T2
Switch frequency	3.83	7.17	8.75	T1 < T3
Number of queries	0.83	0.92	0.58	-

4.2 Effectiveness of Knowledge Adoption

Table 5. Reports the perceived effectiveness score in the knowledge adoption. The results show that the three types of tasks are very different in perceived effectiveness. Task 1 and Task 3 have higher scores, and Task 2 has a lower score (4.42 for Task 3, 4.33 for Task 1, and 3.50 for Task 2). It indicates that human-AI collaboration achieved better effectiveness for users in Task 1 and Task 3. Then, the perceived effectiveness in the three types of tasks is compared using a Mann-Whitney U test. The test results show that the perceived effectiveness in Task 1 and Task 2, Task 2 and Task 3 is significantly different (P < 0.05). It indicated that the results of Task 2 have greater uncertainty for users because they have not clearly identified the disease corresponding to each symptom.

Table 6. Reports the effectiveness score in knowledge adoption. The results show that the three task types differ in objective effectiveness. Task 1 and Task 3 have lower scores, and Task 2 has a higher score (4.00 for Task 2, 3.67 for Task 3, and 3.25 for Task 1). It indicated that users do not have a great understanding of chronic disease prevention knowledge, and most of them passively receive knowledge provided by AI systems. Then, the effectiveness score in the three types of tasks is compared using a Mann-Whitney U test. The test results show that Task 1 and Task 2's effectiveness scores are significantly different (P < 0.05). It indicates that difficult tasks (i.e., Interpretive Task) encouraged users to actively participate in human-AI collaboration, achieving better results even if users do not feel it.

Table 7. Reports on the long-term effectiveness of knowledge adoption. The results show that short-term knowledge adoption has long-term effectiveness, regardless of the task (2 users achieved weak adoption, and nine users achieved faint adoption). It indicates that human-AI collaboration can achieve the long-term effectiveness of chronic disease prevention and, on this basis, subtly change users' living habits. However, this long-term effectiveness needs to be reinforced by other means.

Table 5. The subjective effectiveness of knowledge adoption.

Items	T1	T2	T3	P < 0.05 Differences
Perceived effectiveness	4.33	3.50	4.42	T1 > T2, T2 < T3

Table 6. The objective effectiveness of knowledge adoption.

Items	T1	T2	T3	P < 0.05 Differences
Results effectiveness score	3.25	4.00	3.67	T1 < T2

Table 7. Long-term effectiveness of knowledge adoption.

Items	R1	R2	R3	R4
Long-term effectiveness	0	2	9	1

5 Discussion

5.1 Findings

Significant contributions of this study lay in uncovering types of tasks associated with the knowledge adoption in human-AI collaboration under the chronic disease prevention scenario. Three types of tasks, Factual, Interpretive, and Exploratory tasks, were examined in relation to the efficiency and effectiveness of knowledge adoption in human-AI collaboration. Figure 3 presents a summary of the findings and implications of this study.

First, the participants' perceived effectiveness was the worst in the interpretive task, and there was no noticeable difference in perceived efficiency among the three types of tasks. The reason is that users have good adaptability to the means of human-AI collaboration, but they have an illusion of control over the AI system [50]. Users overestimate how much control they have over their health tasks and thus perceive that the functions used are equally feasible and effective in different health tasks. However, they do not trust the disease diagnosis provided by AI. Participants said, *"I think this knowledge given by AI is not credible for disease diagnosis. If I want to get an exact disease diagnosis, I will still choose to go to the hospital for a regular examination* (P9)". Many studies explained that users have been alarmed by the black-box nature of many state-of-the-art ML models and are hesitant to trust these models [51]. Therefore, how to build trusted and trustworthy AI responsibly in diagnosing diseases is the development focus of human-AI collaboration in the future.

Second, objective efficiency was closely related to task types. Obviously, the user spent more time in the interpretive task. The reason is that the user splits the symptoms and matches the disease until they get a disease that fits all the symptoms perfectly. A participant said, *"I found a disease for each symptom, but I didn't find an exact disease for all symptoms* (P7)". Then, the user switched more pages in the exploratory tasks. The reason is that users compare knowledge from multiple sources until they arrive at actionable and understandable results. Previous studies have also shown that task characteristics affect decision-making performance [52]. However, there was no significant difference in the number of queries. The reason is that the means of human-AI collaboration has provided suitable labels and prompt words, and the user does not need to enter many queries. This is quite different from the task in which the query is the main search method for a long time [53]. Therefore, it requires the functions of the AI system to be considered in human-AI collaboration according to task types.

Third, the participants got lower scores in the factual task. The reason is that the AI systems give encapsulated knowledge [54] based on databases and GPT, and users are reluctant to spend more energy on simple tasks. Most studies have set the difficulty and complexity of factual tasks as the lowest [17]. However, the participants got higher scores in the interpretive task, even if they did not think the search was good. Some studies have shown that users do not perform well in the interpretive task [24]. The reason is that users tend to continue to acquire and understand the knowledge of symptoms and disease. Accordingly, the means of human-AI collaboration certainly provides this opportunity for users, even if users do not feel it directly.

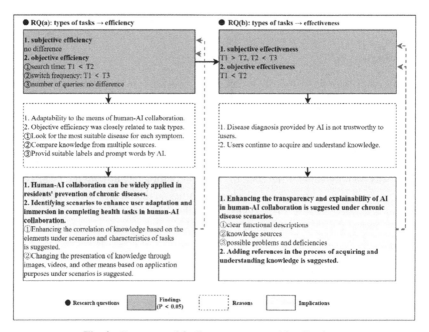

Fig. 3. Summary of findings, reasons, and implications.

5.2 Implications

Analyzing the differences in knowledge adoption among task types in human-AI collaboration was essential for understanding users' behavioral and cognitive changes in chronic disease prevention, assisting in improving knowledge services in human-AI collaboration.

First, the means of human-AI can be widely applied in residents' prevention of chronic disease, but enhancing the transparency and explainability of AI in human-AI collaboration is suggested under the chronic disease scenario. On the one hand, it should give clear functional descriptions of each component in the AI system so that users know how they work and what functions they can achieve [55]. On the other hand, the source, sample size, representativeness, and additional information of the training data used should be marked, and the possible problems and deficiencies should be explained [56]. On this basis, users can form correct and differentiated cognition of different health tasks in human-AI collaboration, thereby avoiding the illusion of control.

Second, identifying scenarios to enhance user adaptation and immersion in completing health tasks in human-AI collaboration. On the one hand, general health tasks have a high sense of urgency, relevance, and importance [57]. Therefore, enhancing the correlation of knowledge based on the elements under scenarios and characteristics of tasks is suggested. Then, AI systems can further increase the ability to empathize by analyzing the type of user emotion in a statement (text or voice) and how strong it is under scenarios. The factual task can be used as the baseline affective task. On the other hand, each country has specific cultural contexts and specific features of the health system. Changing the presentation of knowledge through images, videos, and other forms based on application purposes under scenarios is suggested [58]. Determining the knowledge presentation forms based on the age, educational background, usage habits, and purpose of users from different cultural contexts is necessary.

Third, adding references in the process of acquiring and understanding knowledge according to task types is suggested. Some users said that although they have received a lot of knowledge, they cannot judge whether it is correct because they did not know the source, especially health-related knowledge. Participants said, "*I type in my question, and the AI comes up with an answer, but I modify the keywords slightly, and the AI comes up with a similar answer. I cannot judge what knowledge to believe other than answers* (P5)". Therefore, increasing the traceability of AI feedback knowledge in human-AI collaboration helps users understand health knowledge and enhances the interaction between users and AI [59].

6   Conclusion

With the urgency of chronic disease prevention, the inefficiency of face-to-face knowledge exchange, and the requirement of multi-agent participation in prevention, it is imperative to explore the differences in knowledge adoption among task types in human-AI collaboration under the chronic disease prevention scenario. This study took the "AI System of Elderly Disability Screening and Management" as a tool for human-AI collaboration and explored the differences between knowledge adoption efficiency and effectiveness in factual, interpretive, and exploratory tasks. The results showed that the participants' perceived effectiveness was worst in the interpretive task, and there was no noticeable difference in perceived efficiency among the three types of tasks. Then, objective efficiency was closely related to task types. Finally, the participants got lower scores in the factual task and higher scores in the interpretive task. From the user-centered perspective, this study puts forward suggestions for improving the means of human-AI collaboration to promote the further application of human-AI collaboration in chronic disease prevention, help residents adopt chronic disease prevention knowledge, and thus improve the efficiency and effectiveness of chronic disease prevention.

There were some limitations that the non-parametric test method was used in this study, and the number of participants was twelve, which may cause some results to be insignificant. In the future, data sets with higher external validity should be utilized, or the number of participants should be increased to improve internal validity, thereby further increasing the credibility of the findings and implications. Future research will consider the short-term and long-term changes in the efficiency and effectiveness of knowledge adoption under the influence of multiagents such as knowledge systems of AI and experts.

Acknowledgments. This study was supported by the National Social Science Fund of China (No: 20ATQ008).

Data Statements The data in this study and the published paper (DOI: https://doi.org/10.16353/ j.cnki.1000-7490.2023.12.014.) are from the same experiment. This study supplemented the analysis of significant differences in tasks based on existing experiments.

References

1. Dona, S.W.A., Angeles, M.R., Hall, N., Watts, J.J., Peeters, A., Hensher, M.: Impacts of chronic disease prevention programs implemented by private health insurers: a systematic review. BMC Health Serv. Res. **21**(1), 1222 (2021)
2. Bunnell, R., et al.: Fifty Communities putting prevention to work: accelerating chronic disease prevention through policy, systems and environmental change. J. Community Health **37**(5), 1081–1090 (2012)
3. Chiyaka, E.T., et al.: Influence of interaction between community health workers and adults with chronic diseases on risk mitigation through care coordination. Inter. J. Care Coordin. **25**(2–3), 57–65 (2022)
4. Rodriguez, B., et al.: Community health workers during COVID-19 supporting their role in current and future public health responses. J. Ambul. Care Manage. **46**(3), 203–209 (2023)
5. Sranacharoenpong, K., Hanning, R.M.: Diabetes prevention education program for community health care workers in Thailand. J. Community Health **37**(3), 610–618 (2012)
6. Carvajal, S.C., et al.: Evidence for long-term impact of pasos adelante: using a community-wide survey to evaluate chronic disease risk modification in prior program participants. Int. J. Environ. Res. Public Health **10**(10), 4701–4717 (2013)
7. Tsai, J.H.C., Petrescu-Prahova, M.: Community interagency connections for immigrant worker health interventions, King County, Washington State, 2012–2013. prev. chronic dis. **13**, e73 (2017)
8. Loske, D., Klumpp, M.: Human-AI collaboration in route planning: an empirical efficiency-based analysis in retail logistics. Int. J. Prod. Econ. **241**, 108236 (2021)
9. Jiang, N., Liu, X.H., Liu, H.F., Lim, E.T.K., Tan, C.W., Gu, J.B.: Beyond AI-powered context-aware services: the role of human-AI collaboration. Industrial Manag. Data Syst, ahead-of-print (2022)
10. Sqalli, M.T. and Al-Thani, D.: AI-supported Health coaching model for patients with chronic diseases. In: 16th International Symposium on Wireless Communication Systems (ISWCS), pp. 452–456. IEEE, New York (2020)
11. Patel, K., et al.: A survey on artificial intelligence techniques for chronic diseases: open issues and challenges. Artif. Intell. Rev. **55**(5), 3747–3800 (2021)
12. Xie, I., Joo, S.: Factors affecting the selection of search tactics: Tasks, knowledge, process, and systems. Inf. Process. Manage. **48**(2), 254–270 (2012)
13. Li, Y.: Exploring the relationships between work and search tasks in information search. J. Am. Soc. Inform. Sci. Technol. **60**(2), 275–291 (2009)
14. Xie, I.: Dimensions of tasks: Influences on information-seeking and retrieving process. J. Documentation **65**(3), 339–366 (2009)
15. Tushman, M.L.: Technical communication in R&D laboratories: the impact of project work characteristics. Acad. Manag. J. **21**(4), 624–645 (1978)
16. Liu, J.J., Kim, C.S., Creel, C.: Exploring search task difficulty reasons in different task types and user knowledge groups. Inf. Process. Manage. **51**(3), 273–285 (2015)
17. Kim, J.: Task difficulty as a predictor and indicator of web searching interaction. In: Conference on Human Factors in Computing Systems, pp. 959–964. Assoc Computing Machinery, New York (2006)
18. Li, Y.L., Belkin, N.L.: A faceted approach to conceptualizing tasks in information seeking. Inf. Process. Manage. **44**(6), 1822–1837 (2008)
19. MacMullin, S.D., Taylor, R.S.: Problem dimensions and information traits. Inf. Soc. **3**, 91–111 (1984)
20. Campbell, D.J.: Task complexity: A review and analysis. Acad. Manag. Rev. **13**(1), 40–52 (1988)

21. Xie, I.: Planned and situated aspects in interactive ir: patterns of user interactions and information seeking strategies. Proc. ASIS Annual Meeting **34**, 101–110 (1997)

22. Algon, J.: Classifications of tasks, steps, and information-related behaviors of individuals on project teams. In: Vakkari, P., Savolainen, R., Dervin, B. (eds.) International Conference on Research in Information Needs, Seeking and Use in Different Contents, pp. 205–221. Taylor Graham, London (1997)

23. Cartright, M.A., White, R.W., Horvitz, E.: Intentions and attention in exploratory health search. In: 34th International ACM SIGIR Conference on Research and Development in Information Retrieval (SIGIR), pp. 65–74. Assoc Computing Machinery, New York (2011)

24. Chi, Y., He, D.Q., Jeng, W.: Laypeople's source selection in online health infor-mation-seeking process. J. Am. Soc. Inf. Sci. **71**(12), 1484–1499 (2020)

25. Kim, K.S., Allen, B.: Cognitive and task influences on web searching behavior. J. Am. Soc. Inform. Sci. Technol. **53**(2), 109–119 (2002)

26. Ke, Q., Du, J.T., Geng, Y.X., Xie, Y.S.: Studying health anxiety related attentional bi-as during online health information seeking: impacts of stages and task types. Inf. Process. Manage. **60**(5), 103453 (2023)

27. Cichocki, A., Kuleshov, A.P.: Future trends for human-AI collaboration: a comprehensive taxonomy of AI/AGI using multiple intelligences and learning styles. Comput. Intell. Neurosci. **2021**, 8893795 (2021)

28. Guimaraes, D., Paulino, D., Correia, A., Trigo, L., Brazdil, P., Paredes, H.: Towards a human-AI hybrid framework for inter-researcher similarity detection. In: Nurnberger, A., et al. (eds.) 2nd IEEE International Conference on Human-Machine Systems (ICHMS), pp. 123–126. IEEE, New York (2021)

29. Kim, E., Hong, J., Lee, H., Ko, M.: Colorbo: envisioned mandala coloring through human-AI collaboration. In: 27th Annual International Conference on Intelligent User Interfaces (ACM IUI), pp. 15–26. Assoc Computing Machinery, New York (2022)

30. Zhao, Z.J., Ma, X.J.: A compensation method of two-stage image generation for human-ai collaborated in-situ fashion design in augmented reality environment. In: 1st IEEE International Conference on Artificial Intelligence and Virtual Reality (AIVR), pp. 76–83. IEEE, New York (2019)

31. Okamura, K., Yamada, S.: Adaptive trust calibration for human-AI collaboration. PLoS ONE **15**(2), e0229132 (2020)

32. Zhang, H.Y., et al.: PathNarratives: Data annotation for pathological human-AI collaborative diagnosis. Front. Med. **9**, 1070072 (2023)

33. Sharma, A., Lin, I.W., Miner, A.S., Atkins, D.C., Althoff, T.: Human-AI collaboration enables more empathic conversations in text-based peer-to-peer mental health support. Nat. Mach. Intell. **5**(1), 46–57 (2023)

34. Gu, H.Y., et al.: Improving workflow integration with xpath: design and evaluation of a human-AI diagnosis system in pathology. ACM Trans. Comput.-Human Interact. **30**(2), 28 (2023)

35. Kocaballi, A.B., et al.: Envisioning an artificial intelligence documentation assistant for future primary care consultations: a co-design study with general practitioners. J. Am. Med. Inform. Assoc. **27**(11), 1695–1704 (2020)

36. Cabitza, F., Campagner, A., Sconfienza, L.M.: Studying human-AI collaboration protocols: the case of the Kasparov's law in radiological double reading. Health Inform. Sci. Syst. **9**(1), 8 (2021)

37. Wang, F., Fan, H., Liu, G.: Big data knowledge service framework based on knowledge fusion. In: Fred, A., Dietz, J., Aveiro, D., Liu, K., Bernardino, J., Filipe, J. (eds.) 8th International Joint Conference on Knowledge Discovery, Knowledge Engineering and Knowledge Management (KDIR), pp. 116–123. Scitepress, Portugal (2016)

38. Berger, A., Tymula, A.: Controlling ambiguity: The illusion of control in choice under risk and ambiguity. J. Risk Uncertain. **65**(3), 261–284 (2022)
39. Paliwoda-Pekosz, G., Dymek, D.m Grabowski, M.: Adoption of emerging information technologies through the lenses of knowledge acquisition. In: 27th Annual Americas Conference on Information Systems (AMCIS). Assoc Information Systems, Atlanta (2021)
40. Makkonen, H.: Information processing perspective on organisational innovation adoption process. Technol. Anal. Strategic Manag. **33**(6), 612–624 (2020)
41. Li, Y.L., Belkin, N.J.: An exploration of the relationships between work task and interactive information search behavior. J. Am. Soc. Inform. Sci. Technol. **61**(9), 1771–1789 (2010)
42. Li, Y.L., Yuan, X.J., Che, R.Q.: An investigation of task characteristics and users' evaluation of interaction design in different online health information systems. Inf. Process. Manage. **58**(3), 102476 (2021)
43. He, X., Zhang, H.S., Bian, J.: User-centered design of a web-based crowdsourcing-integrated semantic text annotation tool for building a mental health knowledge base. J. Biomed. Inform. **110**, 103571 (2020)
44. Gong, Y., Zhang, J.J.: Toward a human-centered hyperlipidemia management system: the interaction between internal and external information on relational data search. J. Med. Syst. **35**(2), 169–177 (2011)
45. King, K., et al.: The impact of a location-sensing electronic health record on clinician efficiency and accuracy: a pilot simulation study. Appl. Clin. Inform. **9**(4), 841–848 (2018)
46. Hilliard, R.W., Haskell, J., Gardner, R.L.: Are specific elements of electronic health record use associated with clinician burnout more than others? J. Am. Med. Inform. Assoc. **27**(9), 1401–1410 (2020)
47. Del Fiol, G., et al.: Formative evaluation of a patient-specific clinical knowledge summarization tool. Int. J. Med. Informatics **86**, 126–134 (2016)
48. Wasmann, J.W., Pragt, L., Eikelboom, R., Swanepoel, D.: Digital Approaches to automated and machine learning assessments of hearing: scoping review. J. Med. Internet Res. **24**(2), e32581 (2022)
49. Wang, N.: Knowledge adoption: a new perspective and the influence of knowledge characteristics. In: 52nd Annual Hawaii International Conference on System Sciences, pp. 5548–5557 (2019)
50. Lawson, S.: Examining the relationship between organizational culture and knowledge management. Nova Southeastern University (2003)
51. Max, W.S.: Trust in AI: interpretability is not necessary or sufficient, while black-box interaction is necessary and sufficient. In: FAccT 2022: ACM Conference on Fairness, Accountability, and Transparency. ACM, New York (2022)
52. Devine, D.J., Kozlowski, S.W.J.: Domain-specific knowledge and task characteristics in decision making. Organ. Behav. Hum. Decis. Process. **64**(3), 294–306 (1995)
53. Zhu, Y.J., Takama, Y., Kato, Y., Kori, S., Ishikawa, H., Yamaguchi, K.: Introduction of Search engine focusing on trend-related queries to market of data. In: Zhou, Z.H., et al. (eds.) 14th IEEE International Conference on Data Mining (IEEE ICDM), pp. 511–516. IEEE, New York (2014)
54. Van den Berg, H.A.: Three shapes of organizational knowledge. J. Knowl. Manag. **17**(2), 159–174 (2013)
55. Ángel, A.C., Adam, P. and Jason, I.H.: Improving Human-AI Collaboration With Descriptions of AI Behavior. In ACM Human-Computer Interaction, vol. 7. ACM, New York (2023)
56. Roberto V.Z., et al.: On assessing trustworthy AI in healthcare. machine learning as a supportive tool to recognize cardiac arrest in emergency calls. Fronti. Hum. Dynam. **3**, 673104 (2021)

57. Inthiran, A., Alhashmi, S.M., Ahmed, P.K.: A preliminary study on the usage of search assisting features when searching for a personal health task. Aslib J. Inf. Manag. **67**(2), 159–181 (2015)
58. Tusche, A., Bockler, A., Kanske, P., Trautwein, F.M., Singer, T.: Decoding the chari-table brain: empathy, perspective taking, and attention shifts differentially predict altruistic giving. J. Neurosci. **36**(17), 4719–4732 (2016)
59. Sicilia M.A.: Traceability for trustworthy AI: a review of models and tools. Big Data a Cognitive Comput. **5**(2) (2021)

Influence of AI's Uncertainty in the Dawid-Skene Aggregation for Human-AI Crowdsourcing

Takumi Tamura[1]([✉]) [iD], Hiroyoshi Ito[2] [iD], Satoshi Oyama[3] [iD],
and Atsuyuki Morishima[2] [iD]

[1] School of Informatics, University of Tsukuba, 1-2 Kasuga, Tsukuba, Ibaraki
305-8577, Japan
`tamura.takumi.ap@alumni.tsukuba.ac.jp`
[2] Faculty of Library, Information and Media Science, University of Tsukuba, 1-2
Kasuga, Tsukuba, Ibaraki 305-8577, Japan
`{ito,mori}@slis.tsukuba.ac.jp`
[3] School of Data Science, Nagoya City University, 1 Yamanobata, Mizuho-cho,
Mizuho-ku, Nagoya, Aichi 467-8501, Japan
`oyama@ds.nagoya-cu.ac.jp`

Abstract. The power and expressiveness of AIs are rapidly increasing, and now AIs have the ability to complete tasks in crowdsourcing as if they were human crowd workers. Therefore, the development of methods to effectively aggregate the results of tasks performed by AIs and humans is becoming a critical problem. In this study, we revisit the Dawid-Skene model that has been used to aggregate human votes to obtain better results in classification problems. Most of the state-of-the-art AI classifiers predict the class probabilities as their output. Considering the probabilities represent their uncertainty, utilizing them in Dawid-Skene aggregation may provide higher-quality annotations. To this end, we introduce a variation of the Dawid-Skene model to directly use the probabilities without discarding them and conduct experiments with two real-world datasets of different domains. Experimental results show that the Dawid-Skene model with probabilities improves the overall accuracy. Moreover, a detailed analysis shows that the aggregation results were improved for classification tasks with high uncertainty.

Keywords: Data Quality Control · Hybrid Intelligence · Human-AI Collaboration

1 Introduction

With the rapid development of AI technology, crowdsourcing with AI support is the focus of attention in many applications such as computer vision [3,11, 18], natural language processing [9,16], and many other fields [4]. For example, Ramírez et al. investigated the effect of an AI model's highlighting relevant parts

I. Sserwanga et al. (Eds.): iConference 2024, LNCS 14598, pp. 232–247, 2024.
https://doi.org/10.1007/978-3-031-57867-0_17

in advance on human task results in text classification tasks [16]. Despite limited human resources, the amount of data needed for annotations is increasing, and as a result, the importance of human-AI collaborative crowdsourcing is expanding.

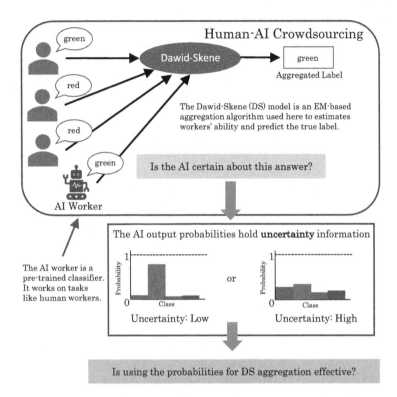

Fig. 1. We consider whether the Dawid-Skene aggregation using the AI class probabilities directly is more effective. The probability distribution provides useful information on the uncertainty of the AI worker.

There are many ways to obtain AI models, which can complete tasks, such as image classifiers and speech recognition models as well as LLMs. Many pre-trained models are widely available on online platforms including HuggingFace Hub[1]. In addition, competitive data science platforms like Kaggle[2] enable users to obtain AI models developed by crowd AI engineers.

Given this background, the idea that AIs work on microtasks like human workers is being proposed by several papers [1,6], in other words, humans and AIs will answer the tasks together. For example, Kobayashi et al. proposed a task assignment algorithm in the "Human+AI Crowd" model [8]. In the model,

---

[1] https://huggingface.co/models.
[2] https://www.kaggle.com/.

crowdsourcing microtasks are assigned to both human workers and machine learning models called "AI workers."

However, it is a critical problem how to effectively aggregate task results from human and AI workers under such human-AI collaboration crowdsourcing. As a quality control measure, microtasks are often assigned to several workers, and the results must be aggregated. In the context of human results aggregations for classification tasks such as that task for giving one from a fixed label set (e.g., positive or negative) to each tweet, *Dawid-Skene model (DS)* is known to be more effective than the simple majority vote when the abilities of human workers are not uniform [5] and is now a standard method for the result aggregation in crowdsourcing. The DS model estimates the abilities of each worker (i.e., how often he or she answers correctly for each label) in the process of aggregating labels. If we allow an AI worker to join, its behavior is usually different from humans, and we may not even know the precise ability of the worker in some cases where the models were developed by somebody else including crowd workers. Therefore, the DS model perfectly fits the situation.

The DS model takes as inputs the labels given by each worker and outputs the aggregated labels. Therefore, a simple way to apply the DS model to our context is to deal with each AI worker as a human worker and supply its final output label to the DS model. However, most state-of-the-art AI classifiers directly compute not a label but the probabilities of the class that is associated with each label and choose the label with the highest class probability. These probabilities are considered as the uncertainty or confidence of AI's prediction.

So a natural question arises (Fig. 1); if we did not discard the probability distribution, would we obtain better aggregated results? Note that this is not a trivial question. Our hypothesis is that the DS model with probabilities would improve the quality of the task results because AI's uncertainty helps estimate AI's ability. However, the interaction between the probability distribution produced by AI workers and the estimation of worker abilities makes the question non-trivial.

Research Question, Contributions and Key Findings. This paper addresses the following two research questions (Fig. 2). **(RQ1)** What is the influence of introducing the output class probabilities in the DS model? **(RQ2)** If it has a positive influence, what is the condition for the influence to appear?

To address the RQs, we first extended the DS model to deal with the probability outputs. Next, we conducted experiments based on two real-world datasets of different domains (image and text classifications). The accuracy of aggregated labels was compared between the basic and extended DS models. Then, we did a detailed analysis of when the probability outputs have effects on the result to clarify the effects of introducing the class probability into the DS model.

Our key findings are as follows. First, we found that AI's uncertainty improves the accuracy of aggregated results. Second, the improvements are observed when the AI is uncertain in its output, namely, when several classes have similar probabilities in the AI prediction. The uncertainty indicates AI's "less confidence" in the DS model and it helps estimate AI's ability accurately.

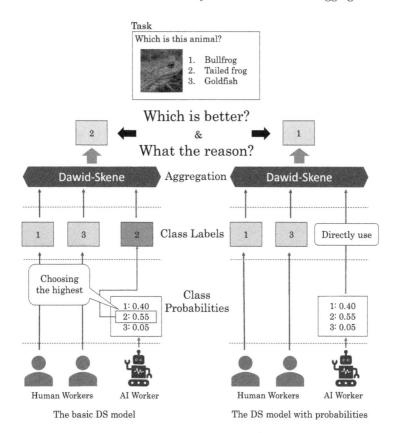

Fig. 2. We consider the following two research questions: (RQ1) Does the DS aggregation directly using probabilities perform better than the basic DS model? (RQ2) What is the reason for the effectiveness of the proposed model, if any?

Limitations. To simplify factors that affect the experimental results, we assume that we have only one AI worker in our experimental setting. In addition, we address the situation where the class probabilities are given by AI workers only. It is well known that humans have difficulty expressing their confidence in answers correctly (overconfident or underconfident [14]), which would introduce complex factors and require different attention. We chose two real-world datasets with different characteristics and our findings are based on the results of the experiments with them. Although we believe that the observation we obtained from the detailed analysis, on the condition we see a positive influence is correct, how often we see the condition will depend on datasets.

2   Related Work

2.1   Extensions of the Dawid-Skene Model

The Dawid-Skene model [5] is a well-known method to aggregate the results of human crowd workers for quality control. It predicts the true labels of tasks by estimating workers' abilities based on the EM algorithm.

Oyama et al. [14] extended the DS model with confidence scores of the task results given by human workers. Unlike our work, the work mainly focused on estimating the accuracy of the confidence score for their answer, because human workers tend to be either overconfident or underconfident. In addition, our work deals with the probability distribution output by AI workers that represents uncertain information about *every* class, not the one of the class with the highest probability.

There are other extensions of the DS model that add parameters to obtain more effective aggregations. GLAD [17] estimated worker expertise and task difficulty, and Bi et al. [2] also considered a parameter indicating the dedication of human workers. The problems they deal with are different from ours.

2.2   Human-AI Collaboration in Crowdsourcing

Many types of hybrid crowdsourcing systems have been explored from the perspective of collaboration between humans and AI systems [4].

Several different approaches have been proposed for quality control in the scenario of human and AI workers performing tasks together. For example, Kobayashi et al. [8] proposed a task assignment algorithm in the same scenario and they called this scenario the "Human+AI Crowd" model. Here, task assignment is an important step before the task result aggregation to determining who complete the tasks. Kanda et al. [7] reduced the computation cost for the task assignment by focusing on the evaluation process of AI workers in the model. Our work addresses the next step of task assignment - the aggregation of human and AI results in their human+AI crowd model, which, to the best of our knowledge, has not addressed before.

Crowdsourcing systems that combine human and AI predictions based on the DS model have also been studied. For example, HAEM [18], Lean Crowdsourcing [3], and Liao et al. [11] incorporate an AI model, which works similarly with human workers, and trains its AI model during the process of their Dawid-Skene extensions. However, in contrast to our work, they do not investigate the effect of considering the AI's probabilities in the aggregation.

3   Methods

The notations in Sect. 3 are listed in Table 1.

Table 1. Notation used in Sect. 3

Notation	Description
$\mathbb{J}$	Set of class labels
$\mathbb{I}$	Set of classification tasks
$\mathbb{K}$	Set of workers including humans and AIs
T_{ij}	The binary value whether the true class of task i is the class j ($T_{ij} = 1$ if that is true, $T_{ij} = 0$ otherwise)
E_{ij}	Expected value of T_{ij}
$n_{ij}^{(k)}$	The number of times that the worker k votes the class j on the task i
r	The number of human workers who assigned each task (redundancy)
p_j	The marginal probability of the class j
$\pi_{jl}^{(k)}$	The probability that the worker k votes the class l if the true class is j
θ_k	The parameters of the AI worker k
$P(j \mid i, \theta_k)$	The probability when the true class of task i is j output by AI worker k

3.1 Problem Definition

We consider the classification tasks that workers select only one label from fixed options about the provided task content, for example, "Which animals are in the image, a dog, cat, or rabbit?" Here, each label represents a *class* in $\mathbb{J}$. Let $\mathbb{I}$ be a set of classification tasks.

Under the scenario of this paper, both human and AI workers answer the tasks together. Let $\mathbb{K}$ be a set of workers including humans and AIs. The tasks are assigned to several workers for quality control. The number of human workers assigned to each task is defined as r "redundancy," conversely, AIs perform all tasks only once. The AI worker $k \in \mathbb{K}$ is a pre-trained machine learning model, the parameters of which are defined as θ_k. It receives the content of the task $i \in \mathbb{I}$ (e.g., images) as input and outputs probabilities $P(j \mid i, \theta_k)$ of each class $j \in \mathbb{J}$.

Our goal is to obtain high-quality classification labels by aggregating the results from human and AI workers. The noisy votes from workers are aggregated by the following models.

3.2 Dawid-Skene Model

The Dawid-Skene model [5] is a popular aggregation method based on the EM algorithm. This model predicts true labels by estimating workers' abilities and prioritizing skillful workers. Let T_{ij} be 1 if the true label of the task $i \in \mathbb{I}$ is the class $j \in \mathbb{J}$ and 0 otherwise, and let E_{ij} be the expected value of T_{ij}. The noisy labels are provided as $n_{ij}^{(k)}$ which means the number of times that the worker $k \in \mathbb{K}$ votes $j \in \mathbb{J}$ on the task $i \in \mathbb{I}$.

This method iterates the following E and M steps. In the E-step, this method predicts the label probabilities E_{ij} from the current estimates of worker parameters: p_j is the marginal probability of the class $j \in \mathbb{J}$ and $\pi_{jl}^{(k)}$ is the probability that the worker $k \in \mathbb{K}$ votes $l \in \mathbb{J}$ when ground truth is $j \in \mathbb{J}$, that is, $\pi_{jl}^{(k)}$ shows the estimated confusion matrix of the worker $k \in \mathbb{K}$. The E-step is performed as follows.

$$E_{ij} = \frac{p_j \prod_{l \in \mathbb{J}} \prod_{k \in \mathbb{K}} (\pi_{jl}^{(k)})^{n_{il}^{(k)}}}{\prod_{q \in \mathbb{J}} p_q \prod_{l \in \mathbb{J}} \prod_{k \in \mathbb{K}} (\pi_{ql}^{(k)})^{n_{il}^{(k)}}}. \tag{1}$$

In the M-step, the method estimates worker parameters from the current expected value of label probabilities.

$$p_j = \frac{\sum_{i \in \mathbb{I}} E_{ij}}{|\mathbb{I}|}, \tag{2}$$

$$\pi_{jl}^{(k)} = \frac{\sum_{i \in \mathbb{I}} E_{ij} n_{il}^{(k)}}{\sum_{m \in \mathbb{J}} \sum_{i \in \mathbb{I}} E_{ij} n_{im}^{(k)}}. \tag{3}$$

The initial value of E_{ij} is given as follows.

$$E_{ij} = \frac{\sum_{k \in \mathbb{K}} n_{ij}^{(k)}}{\sum_{l \in \mathbb{J}} \sum_{k \in \mathbb{K}} n_{il}^{(k)}}. \tag{4}$$

3.3   The Baseline and Probability-Aware Models

In experiments, we compared the two DS models with and without the probabilities output by the AI workers. The observed variable $n_{ij}^{(k)}$ needs to be extended when the worker $k \in \mathbb{K}$ is an AI. In the basic DS, the AI worker $k \in \mathbb{K}$ is to perform equivalently to human workers, and its output probabilities are transformed to the label by choosing the highest probability class.

$$n_{ij}^{(k)} = \begin{cases} 1 & \text{if } \operatorname*{argmax}_{l \in \mathbb{J}} P(l \mid i, \theta_k) \text{ is } j \;, \\ 0 & \text{otherwise} \end{cases} \tag{5}$$

Conversely, the DS with probability model uses the output probabilities directly.

$$n_{ij}^{(k)} = P(j \mid i, \theta_k). \tag{6}$$

We refer to the baseline model **DS** and the DS model with probabilities **DS-P** for short.

4   Experiment

To address the RQs, we conducted experiments on datasets, and the accuracy of the predicted labels by the DS and DS-P models was evaluated.

4.1   Datasets

Table 2 shows the properties of the two real-world datasets.

Tiny Imagenet: We used the crowdsourced image classification dataset used in Yamashita et al. [18], which extracted 5 classes from Tiny Imagenet [10] and labeled by Amazon Mechanical Turk.

Amazon Reviews: Using Crowdsourced Amazon Sentiment Dataset[3] [9], the experiment of sentiment analysis was conducted. The ground truth was based on the stars of the reviews. Notably, the tasks allowed human workers to answer "not sure." Furthermore, we used the F1 score in addition to accuracy as a measure of evaluation because the dataset was imbalanced, with a negative ratio of only 9.9%.

Table 2. The properties of the two datasets. Note that the "redundancy" means the number of human workers assigned to each task.

	Tiny Imagenet	Amazon Reviews
Task Type	Image Classfication	Text Sentiment Analysis
Class Labels	goldfish, European fire salamander, bullfrog, tailed frog, American alligator	negative, not negative
The number of tasks	2,500 (500 images per class)	1,000 (9.9% negative)
The number of human workers	188	263
Redundancy	$r = 2$	$r = 5$

Table 3. The results obtained by each dataset and aggregation method with both human and AI workers

Datasets	Tiny Imagenet	Amazon Reviews	
metrics	accuracy	accuracy	F1
AI Only	0.5424	0.946	0.727
Humans Only DS	0.7320	0.956	0.794
DS (baseline)	0.7328	0.961	0.813
DS-P (Proposed)	**0.7472**	**0.965**	**0.831**

---

[3] Available at https://github.com/Evgeneus/screening-classification-datasets/.

4.2   AI Workers

We let an AI worker participate in the experiment with each dataset. The AI workers were not calibrated for the experiment because calibrating AI workers is not always possible in the setting of human-AI crowdsourcing.

Tiny Imagenet: A toy model based on a CNN model was trained as the AI worker from a very small dataset. The dataset was composed of Tiny Imagenet images that had not been in the crowdsourced dataset above and contained 50 images for each class.

Amazon Reviews: A pre-trained BERTweet model [13] trained from the SemEval-2016 [12] tweets dataset was used as the AI worker via the pysentimiento Python library [15]. This model classified texts into 3 classes: positive, neutral, and negative. Since the tasks for this dataset require us to classify each review to "negative" or "not negative", the class probability of "not negative" was calculated as the sum of positive and neutral labels given by the model.

4.3   Result

Table 3 shows the experimental results from the DS and DS-P models with each dataset. On both of the datasets, the DS-P model performed better than the baseline DS model. As supplementary information, the evaluation of the AI worker and the DS aggregation result of only the human workers are also shown in Table 3.

Table 4. The number of the tasks and the frequency with which the predicted labels were changed between the DS and DS-P models

	Tiny Imagenet	Amazon Reviews
count	514	7
ratio	20.6%	0.7%

5   Detailed Analysis and Discussion

Table 3 shows that the DS-P model performed better than the baseline DS model with both datasets. We conducted detailed analyses of the results to determine the reasons for these results.

Ratio of Changes. Table 4 shows the number of tasks and the frequency with which the predicted labels were changed between the DS and DS-P models. The ratio was 20.6% in Tiny Imagenet and 0.7% in Amazon Reviews. This shows that the influence of AI's uncertainty depends on the attributes of task types and datasets such as difficulty or the number of classes. Thus, we mainly focus

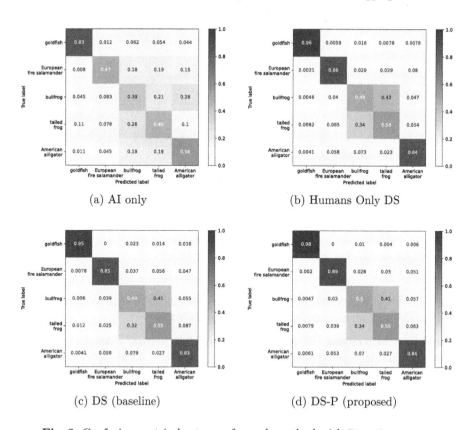

Fig. 3. Confusion matrix heatmaps for each method with `Tiny Imagenet`

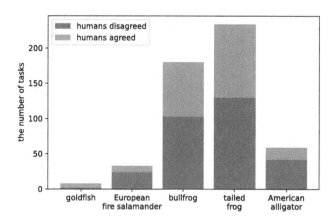

Fig. 4. The number of tasks that the predicted label changed between the DS and DS-P model in each class with `Tiny Imagenet`. The colors of the bars indicate whether the votes from two human workers are the same (the redundancy of `Tiny Imagenet` is $r = 2$).

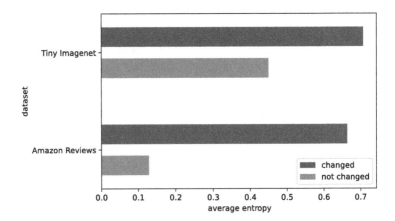

Fig. 5. The differences in average entropy when the tasks of which predicted label changed between the DS and DS-P models in each dataset

on the results of `Tiny Imagenet`, given that the number of tasks affected by the DS-P model was much greater than `Amazon Reviews`.

Confusion Matrices. Figure 3 shows confusion matrix heatmaps for each method with `Tiny Imagenet`. Comparing the DS and DS-P models, a slight increase in accuracy is shown among all classes. Moreover, these results show that e.g., distinguishing a "bullfrog" from a "tailed frog" was relatively difficult.

Distribution of Changes. Figure 4 shows that the number of tasks was changed between the DS and DS-P model in each class with `Tiny Imagenet`. This shows that the changes were much greater for the classes "bullfrog" and "tailed frog" than for other classes. It seemed that the task difficulty was related to the changes. Figure 4 also shows whether the votes from two human workers were matched. In addition to the task difficulty, the changes were greater among all when the human votes did not match than matched, but matched cases were not few.

   Given these observations, we hypothesized that the improvements occurred when the uncertainty of AI prediction about the task was high, in other words, when the AI gave an ambiguous answer to the task.

Entropy Analysis. To evaluate that hypothesis, we consider the influence of information entropy. The entropy of the task $i \in \mathbb{I}$ with the probabilities of the AI worker $k \in \mathbb{K}$ is given as follows.

$$\text{Entropy}(i, \theta_k) = -\sum_{j \in \mathbb{J}} P(j \mid i, \theta_k) \log_2 P(j \mid i, \theta_k). \tag{7}$$

The maximum entropy is shown when the distribution is uniform; therefore, if the entropy is high, the uncertainty must be high. Then, using any subsets of

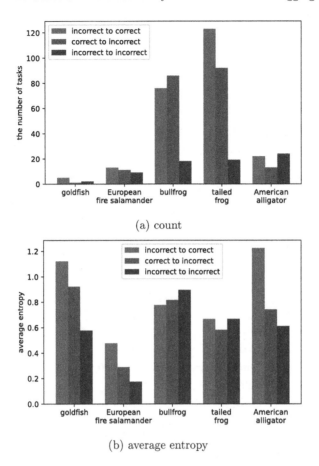

(a) count

(b) average entropy

Fig. 6. The count and average entropy of each class and changed task groups: "incorrect to correct," "correct to incorrect," and "incorrect to incorrect" with `Tiny Imagenet`

the tasks $\mathbb{S} \subseteq \mathbb{I}$, we defined "average entropy" for a part of all tasks as follows.

$$\text{AverageEntropy}(\mathbb{S}, \theta_k) = \frac{1}{|\mathbb{S}|} \sum_{i \in \mathbb{S}} \text{Entropy}(i, \theta_k). \qquad (8)$$

Figure 5 shows the differences in average entropy when the tasks of which predicted label changed between the DS and DS-P models in each dataset. These results show there were clearly notable differences in terms of entropy.

Furthermore, the changed tasks could be classified into three groups, including those changed from "incorrect to correct," from "correct to incorrect," and from "incorrect to incorrect." Fig. 6 shows the number of tasks and average entropy in each group and class with `Tiny Imagenet`. It describes the number of the "incorrect to correct" tasks was greater than of "correct to incorrect" in all classes except for "bullfrog." Moreover, average entropy exhibited the same trend that "incorrect to correct" had greater entropy than "correct to incorrect" on all classes except for "bullfrog." These results support the hypothesis: the increase in accuracy was caused when the uncertainty was high.

Given the above result, we conducted a case analysis for three distinctive cases. Case 1 and 2 were in the "incorrect to correct" group and Case 3 was in "correct to incorrect." In each case, the reason for the change was analyzed.

Case 1: This task was in Tiny Imagenet and the ground truth was "bullfrog." One human worker voted "bullfrog" and the other answered "tailed frog." The AI worker outputs the probabilities shown in Table 5. The predicted label of the DS-P model was "bullfrog" while that of the DS model was "tailed frog." In that case, the class that had the highest probability was "tailed frog." However, the difference between "tailed frog" and "bullfrog" probabilities was only 0.01. The DS-P model was able to estimate the true label using the information of the distribution, and conversely, the DS model was influenced by the highest probability and failed.

Table 5. Class probabilities predicted by the AI worker for Case 1

class	probability
goldfish	0.05
European fire salamander	0.00
bullfrog	0.45
tailed frog	0.46
American alligator	0.03

Case 2: The ground truth of that task in Amazon Reviews was "not negative." The five human workers were assigned the task and 2 of 5 voted "not negative" and 3 of 5 answered "negative." The probability distribution of the AI worker is shown in Table 6. The DS model mistook the prediction, although the DS-P model estimated the correct label. The DS model was influenced by the majority class in adding AI's predicted label "negative," which had the highest probability. In contrast, the DS-P model utilized the ambiguity of AI and predicted the label correctly.

Table 6. Class probabilities predicted by the AI worker for Case 2

class	probability
not negative	0.45
negative	0.55

Case 3: The task's true class was "tailed frog," and both human workers voted "bullfrog" incorrectly in `Tiny Imagenet`. Table 7 shows the class probabilities of the AI worker, and this describes the highest class as the correct label "tailed frog." In that case, the DS-P model predicted the label as "bullfrog" and failed to accurately classify the task. On the other hand, the DS model using the highest probability class estimated "tailed frog" correctly. It seems that the DS-P model judged the AI prediction as less confident and prioritized the human votes.

Table 7. Class probabilities predicted by the AI worker for Case 3

class	probability
goldfish	0.00
European fire salamander	0.28
bullfrog	0.02
tailed frog	0.66
American alligator	0.04

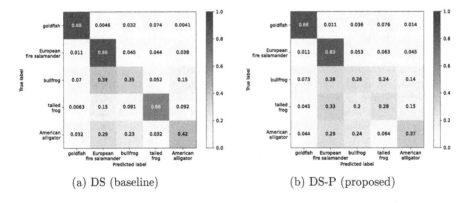

(a) DS (baseline)   (b) DS-P (proposed)

Fig. 7. AI's confusion matrix heatmaps estimated from both the models with `Tiny Imagenet`. Note that the DS models predict each worker's confusion matrix without ground truth.

Influence of AI's Uncertainty. Figure 7 shows the final estimated confusion matrix of the AI worker from the DS and DS-P models. Compared to the two estimated confusion matrices, the DS-P model predicted the AI worker as being less skillful than the DS model in some classes, as in the example given above for the label, "tailed frog." Therefore, the uncertainty in the DS-P model must have improved the accuracy of the AI's ability estimation. Overall, our results suggests that AI's uncertainty provides the information that AI had "less confidence" about the task to the DS-P model and makes the aggregation better.

6   Conclusion

In the context of human-AI collaboration, this paper revisited the Dawid-Skene model that aggregates human results of classification tasks in crowdsourcing. We explored how the probability distribution of classes in AI prediction for a classification task affects the aggregated results through experiments with two real-world datasets and revealed that it improves the quality of the aggregation results. We also conducted a detailed analysis of when they have positive effects. Future work includes more analysis of more complicated cases and extending the Dawid-Skene model to address other differences between human and AI workers such as the number of tasks they can complete.

Acknowledgements. This work was supported by JSPS KAKENHI Grant Number JP21H03552, JP22H00508, JP22K17944, JP23H03405, JST CREST Grant Number JPMJCR21D1, and JPMJCR22M2.

References

1. Amer-Yahia, S., et al.: Making AI machines work for humans in FoW. ACM SIG-MOD Rec. **49**(2), 30–35 (2020)
2. Bi, W., Wang, L., Kwok, J.T., Tu, Z.: Learning to predict from crowdsourced data. In: Proceedings of the Thirtieth Conference on Uncertainty in Artificial Intelligence (UAI), pp. 82–91 (2014)
3. Branson, S., Horn, G.V., Perona, P.: Lean crowdsourcing: combining humans and machines in an online system. In: 2017 IEEE Conference on Computer Vision and Pattern Recognition (CVPR), pp. 6109–6118 (2017)
4. Correia, A., et al.: Designing for hybrid intelligence: a taxonomy and survey of crowd-machine interaction. Appl. Sci. **13**(4), 2198 (2023)
5. Dawid, A.P., Skene, A.M.: Maximum likelihood estimation of observer error-rates using the EM algorithm. J. Roy. Stat. Soc. Ser. C (Appl. Stat.) **28**(1), 20–28 (1979)
6. He, X., et al.: AnnoLLM: Making Large Language Models to Be Better Crowdsourced Annotators. arXiv preprint arXiv:2303.16854 (2023)
7. Kanda, T., Ito, H., Morishima, A.: Efficient evaluation of AI workers for the human+AI crowd task assignment. In: Proceedings of IEEE International Conference on Big Data (BigData), pp. 3995–4001 (2022)
8. Kobayashi, M., Wakabayashi, K., Morishima, A.: Human+AI crowd task assignment considering result quality requirements. In: Proceedings of the AAAI Conference on Human Computation and Crowdsourcing (HCOMP), vol. 9, pp. 97–107 (2021)
9. Krivosheev, E., Casati, F., Baez, M., Benatallah, B.: Combining crowd and machines for multi-predicate item screening. In: Proceedings of the ACM on Human-Computer Interaction (CSCW), vol. 2, pp. 1–18 (2018)
10. Le, Y., Yang, X.: Tiny imagenet visual recognition challenge. CS 231N **7**(7) (2015)
11. Liao, Y.H., Kar, A., Fidler, S.: Towards good practices for efficiently annotating large-scale image classification datasets. In: 2021 IEEE/CVF Conference on Computer Vision and Pattern Recognition (CVPR), pp. 4348–4357 (2021)
12. Nakov, P., Ritter, A., Rosenthal, S., Sebastiani, F., Stoyanov, V.: SemEval-2016 task 4: sentiment analysis in Twitter. In: Proceedings of the 10th International Workshop on Semantic Evaluation (SemEval), pp. 1–18 (2016)

13. Nguyen, D.Q., Vu, T., Nguyen, A.T.: BERTweet: a pre-trained language model for English Tweets. In: Proceedings of the 2020 Conference on Empirical Methods in Natural Language Processing: System Demonstrations (EMNLP), pp. 9–14 (2020)
14. Oyama, S., Baba, Y., Sakurai, Y., Kashima, H.: Accurate integration of crowd-sourced labels using workers' self-reported confidence scores. In: Proceedings of the Twenty-Third International Joint Conference on Artificial Intelligence (IJCAI), pp. 2554–2560 (2013)
15. Pérez, J.M., Giudici, J.C., Luque, F.: pysentimiento: A Python Toolkit for Senti-ment Analysis and SocialNLP tasks. arXiv preprint arXiv:2106.09462 (2021)
16. Ramírez, J., Baez, M., Casati, F., Benatallah, B.: Understanding the impact of text highlighting in crowdsourcing tasks. In: Proceedings of the Seventh AAAI Conference on Human Computation and Crowdsourcing (HCOMP), vol. 7, pp. 144–152 (2019)
17. Whitehill, J., Ruvolo, P., Wu, T., Bergsma, J., Movellan, J.: Whose vote should count more: optimal integration of labels from labelers of unknown expertise. In: Proceedings of the 22nd International Conference on Neural Information Process-ing Systems (NIPS), pp. 2035–2043 (2009)
18. Yamashita, Y., Ito, H., Wakabayashi, K., Kobayashi, M., Morishima, A.: HAEM: obtaining higher-quality classification task results with AI workers. In: Proceedings of the 14th ACM Web Science Conference (WebSci), pp. 118–128 (2022)

Heuristic Intervention for Algorithmic Literacy: From the Perspective of Algorithmic Awareness and Knowledge

Jing Liu[1] 🆔, Guoye Sun[1,2], and Dan Wu[1,2(✉)] 🆔

[1] School of Information Management, Wuhan University, Wuhan 430072, China
woodan@whu.edu.cn
[2] Centre of Human-Computer Interaction and User Behavior, Wuhan University, Wuhan 430072, China

Abstract. Improving algorithmic literacy empowers people to engage with algorithm-driven products across myriad applications with material impact. However, there remains a shortage of interventions aimed at nurturing algorithmic literacy within everyday life. With algorithmic awareness and algorithmic knowledge serving as vital pillars for algorithmic literacy, we initiated a heuristic intervention. This intervention drew upon official information from platforms including Taobao, Bilibili, and Weibo, integrating stimulus questions and heuristic materials. We conducted online experiments, amassing a dataset of 622 responses. The outcomes of our data analysis substantiated the efficacy of the heuristic intervention in bolstering algorithmic awareness and advancing algorithmic knowledge. Moreover, the results indicated a positive correlation between users' algorithmic knowledge and their algorithmic awareness, suggesting that as users' algorithmic knowledge increased, so did their level of algorithmic awareness. These findings hold substantial significance for guiding future practices in the cultivation of algorithmic literacy.

Keywords: Algorithmic Literacy · Algorithmic Awareness · Algorithmic Knowledge · Heuristic Intervention

1 Introduction

Algorithms and algorithm-driven artificial intelligence (AI) technologies have been applied to all aspects of social life. In this symbiotic relationship between people and technology, algorithms have emerged as the gatekeepers of information, steadily augmenting their authority in governing the flow of information [1]. Considering the potential adverse effects posed by algorithmic utilization, including information cocoons [2], algorithmic bias [3], and the looming prospect of an algorithmic knowledge gap [4], algorithmic literacy is regarded as a series of crucial competencies for individuals to navigate the challenges posed by technological advancements in the AI era.

Despite the increasing focus on algorithmic literacy in recent years and the shift from theoretical to empirical research in this field, there remains a notable absence of discourse

I. Sserwanga et al. (Eds.): iConference 2024, LNCS 14598, pp. 248–258, 2024.
https://doi.org/10.1007/978-3-031-57867-0_18

concerning the enhancement of users' algorithmic literacy for real-world algorithmic applications in their daily lives. This gap in discussion hinders our ability to effectively address the evolving technological landscape. Only a limited number of scholars have made efforts to elevate users' algorithmic literacy through targeted intervention design [5].

The process by which people process information is understood as two systems: heuristic and systematic [6]. Heuristic refers to the use of intuition to form an understanding of things through fragmented and intuitive information, which is a way of processing information with less cognitive load. In the process of user-algorithm interaction, heuristic intervention design could use the information provided by the page as a clue to inspire users to notice and think about the process of their interaction with the algorithm. In this paper, we argue that heuristic intervention design can be an important tool for improving users' algorithmic literacy.

Furthermore, the concept of algorithmic literacy, comprising a collection of competencies with algorithmic awareness and algorithmic knowledge at its core, lacks a comprehensive exploration of their interplay and interrelation. Considering this, the present study presents two research queries:

RQ1: Can heuristic interventions be effectively designed to enhance users' algorithmic awareness and knowledge, thereby improving their algorithmic literacy?

RQ2: Can algorithmic awareness be enhanced through the supplementation of algorithmic knowledge?

The objective of this research is to use algorithmic awareness and algorithmic knowledge as focal points for devising a heuristic intervention aimed at nurturing users' algorithmic literacy. Through experimental validation, this study seeks to assess the efficacy of this intervention and uncover the connection between algorithmic knowledge and algorithmic awareness. The aim is to provide valuable insights for refining future interventions. To achieve this, this study selected three platforms, Taobao, Bilibili and Weibo, which are similar to Amazon, YouTube, and Twitter in China. Based on the above three platforms, which are frequently used by users in their daily lives, we collected 622 responses. We conducted an online experiment to analyze the alterations in algorithmic awareness and knowledge before and after exposure to heuristic information.

2 Related Works

2.1 Algorithmic Literacy

In the age of artificial intelligence, the influence of algorithms on societal culture and even its structure is increasingly pronounced. This necessitates a fresh demand for humans to comprehend, grasp, and wield algorithms effectively, giving rise to the concept of algorithmic literacy. Finn [7] calls for algorithmic literacy " that builds from a basic understanding of computational systems, their potential and their limitations, to offer us intellectual tools for interpreting the algorithms shaping and producing knowledge." Research on algorithmic literacy, which experienced a significant surge around 2020, can be classified into three overarching categories: conceptual exploration, unveiling relationships, and practical tools, depending on their research focus and subject matter. Conceptual exploration research delves into the fundamental concepts and research framework of algorithmic literacy. It centers on addressing key conceptual questions [8] like "Why is the study of algorithmic literacy important" and "What constitutes algorithmic literacy." Some scholars opt for a bottom-up method, deconstructing algorithmic literacy through an examination of users' interactions with algorithms from their perspectives [9].

Within the relationship-revealing research category, scholars have conducted investigations into the connections between algorithmic literacy and variables like algorithmic trust, algorithmic attitudes, and algorithmic behaviors. They delve into how algorithmic literacy influences human behaviors and attitudes [10, 11]. Practical tools research pertains to academic inquiries focused on the practical application of algorithmic literacy. This encompasses the creation and validation of tools for assessing algorithmic literacy [12], along with the development and examination of interventions aimed at enhancing algorithmic literacy [6, 13].

It is worth highlighting that in algorithmic literacy research, algorithmic awareness and algorithmic knowledge stand as the foundational pillars. In the formulation of the algorithmic literacy measurement scale, Dogruel [12] has categorized these into two principal components: algorithmic awareness and algorithmic knowledge.

2.2 Intervention for Algorithm-Related Topics

The increasing prevalence of AI-related technologies centered around algorithms has drawn the attention of scholars towards the significance of disseminating knowledge about algorithms, machine learning, AI, and related subjects to the public. For example, consider the intervention designed for educating laypersons in machine learning algorithms [14].

Many scholars have concentrated on cultivating fundamental knowledge of algorithms and AI-related topics within K-12 education. They have developed interventions such as family games [15, 16], summer programs [17], and smart games [18] to promote children's comprehension of categorization algorithms and AI. Nonetheless, these studies primarily target children and adolescents, aiming to establish a broad, foundational grasp of AI- related concepts and algorithmic logic. Their emphasis lies on infusing educational tools with an enjoyable learning experience.

In addition to addressing specific groups like children, teenagers, and work environments, it is imperative to craft interventions tailored for users' everyday scenarios. This approach is more effective in enhancing the algorithmic literacy of the public, as it enables them to relate the intervention content to their actual experiences, thereby reinforcing their understanding of algorithms.

3 Intervention and Experiment Design

3.1 Heuristic Intervention Design

The heuristic intervention in this study consisted of two parts: stimulus questions and heuristic reading materials. First, using stimulus questions is regarded as an efficient method to stimulate users' thought processes [19]. We initiated the creation of heuristic algorithmic recommendation reasoning questions by drawing from real account recommendation data. Users are tasked with choosing information that the system is likely to recommend and providing explanations. This exercise encourages users to engage in profound contemplation regarding the rationale behind the algorithm's recommendations (see Fig. 1).

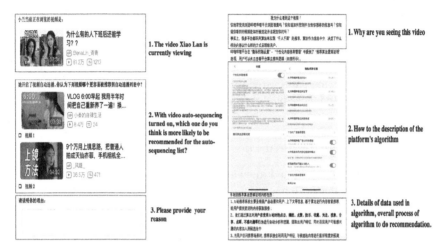

Fig. 1. Heuristic intervention (Left: Stimulus questions; Right: Heuristic reading material).

Next, users understand and assess algorithms based on their preexisting knowledge and the information (clues) provided within the interface [20]. These pieces of information and clues serve as crucial elements in inspiring users' algorithmic awareness. In this study, we gathered platform algorithm explanations from official sources. These explanations encompassed algorithmic recommendation guidelines, rules for personalized advertisement recommendations driven by algorithms, and collected user data, among other details. This information was incorporated into the survey as heuristic knowledge materials for users to read.

3.2 Experiment Design

Platforms Selection. Our approach differs from existing approaches in that it focuses on general algorithm literacy and does not focus on specific tasks and applications. To enhance the broader applicability of our study's findings, we transcend the constraints of specific platforms and focus on common scenarios where individuals engage with algorithms routinely. Consequently, our research concentrates on prevalent algorithm-driven platforms that users utilize in their everyday lives. We have selected three widely popular and extensively used platforms in China: Taobao, Bilibili, and Weibo, representing e-commerce, video-based social media, and social media, respectively.

Participants in our experiment were randomly allocated to three distinct application platforms, they all underwent the same experimental process and completed identical measurement scales.

Experiment Process. Once the user clicks on the experiment link, they will be directed to the experiment introduction and consent form. After providing informed consent, they will proceed to the main experiment section, which consists of three sessions: 1) Pre-intervention of algorithmic awareness (Questionnaire). 2) Heuristic intervention, where participants will answer three reasoning questions, skim through the heuristic reading material, and then answer three more reasoning questions. 3) Post-intervention of algorithmic awareness (Questionnaire), and basic demographic questions.

Data Quality Control. To ensure data quality, we implemented four measures: 1) Included attention-checking questions on general knowledge (e.g., the capital of China) to filter out users who answered incorrectly. 2) Excluded questionnaires were completed in less than 10 min, as the entire experiment required at least this amount of time. 3) Excluded users who used these platforms less than three times per week.

3.3 Manipulation and Measurement

Users' algorithmic awareness and knowledge before and after heuristic intervention were assessed in this study. To gauge algorithmic awareness, we adopted a framework inspired by Liu et al.'s work [21], comprising four dimensions: conceptual awareness (AC), data awareness (AD), risks awareness (AR) and functional awareness (AF). For each dimension, we formulated three questions, drawing from Shin's study [9, 10]. The cumulative result of the four dimensions contributes to the overall level of algorithmic awareness. All scales employed in this study were presented on a 7-point Likert scale, and algorithmic awareness demonstrated strong internal validity, with a Cronbach's Alpha coefficient of 0.72 for each dimension.

Table 1. Indicators and description

Indicators	Description
Pre_AC	Users' awareness of algorithms and related concepts in the pre-intervention stage
Pre_AD	Users' awareness of data usage in algorithms in the pre-intervention stage
Pre_AR	Users' awareness of the risks of algorithms in the pre-intervention stage
Pre_AF	Users' awareness of the functions of algorithms in the pre-intervention stage
Pre_knowledge	Users' performance of first 3 stimulus question, which indicates their knowledge level in the pre-intervention stage
Post_AC	Users' awareness of algorithms and related concepts in the post-intervention stage
Post_AD	Users' awareness of data usage in algorithms in the post-intervention stage
Post_AR	Users' awareness of the risks of algorithms in the post-intervention stage
Post_AF	Users' awareness of the functions of algorithms in the post-intervention stage
Post_knowledge	Users' performance of last 3 stimulus question, which indicates their knowledge level in the post-intervention stage

In addition to assessing algorithmic knowledge, we aimed to objectively measure users' algorithmic knowledge levels rather than self-report. To achieve this, we used users' performance on stimulus questions as indicators of their algorithmic knowledge, considering both their question answer scores and reasoning scores.

4 Data Analysis and Results

This online survey was conducted on Wenjuan Xing, the most widely utilized online survey platform in China. The survey was distributed between May and June 2023, resulting in a total of 872 responses. After rigorous quality control screening, 622 valid questionnaires were retained, yielding an effective response rate of approximately 71%. These valid responses were distributed as follows: 202 from the Taobao platform, 204 from the Weibo platform, and 216 from the Bilibili platform. Gender distribution was relatively even, with 308 male respondents, 309 female respondents, and 5 respondents choosing not to disclose their gender. The age of respondents ranged from 18 to 59 years, with a predominant level of education being a bachelor's degree or equivalent.

4.1 RQ1: Heuristic Interventions'Effect on Algorithmic Awareness and Knowledge

We experimentally obtain users' algorithmic awareness and algorithm knowledge in pre-intervention and post-intervention stages. Each dimension of algorithmic awareness was assessed using three questions. We initially employed factor analysis to condense the algorithmic awareness dimensions and conducted a factor analysis of total assessment (with all dimensions having a KMO value greater than 0.6 and a significant value of 0.00). To examine whether there were significant changes in user algorithmic awareness and knowledge in different stages, we utilized a one-way ANOVA test. (See Table 2). The findings indicate that following the heuristic intervention, there were notable alterations in users' algorithmic awareness (Mdiff = 0.55, P <0.05). As for details of dimensions of algorithmic awareness, the most pronounced changes observed in conceptual awareness and functional awareness. Specifically, conceptual awareness exhibited a significant increase (Mdiff = 0.61), while functional awareness experienced a significant decrease (Mdiff = 0.3). Data awareness doesn't show too much change. We attribute this shift to the fact that the intervention materials predominantly revolved around the algorithm's recommendation function, potentially causing users to perceive other functions of the algorithm less favorably after engaging in the intervention.

In Fig. 2, we present an overview of the overall changes in algorithmic awareness and knowledge before and after the heuristic intervention. Users' overall algorithmic awareness exhibited a slight increase, rising from 17.0 to 17.55 (Mdiff = 0.55), while algorithmic knowledge demonstrated a significant improvement, increasing from 2.88 to 3.70 (Mdiff = 0.82).

Table 2. Means and variability for change of algorithmic awareness and knowledge, split by pre_intervention and post_intervention.

	Algorithmic awareness	Dimensions of algorithmic awareness			
		AC	AD	AR	AF
Pre_intervention	17.0	6.64	8.09	5.76	8.03
Post_intervention	17.55	7.25	8.12	5.56	7.73
F	10.063	86.18	0.37	4.00	24.67
P	0.002**	.000***	.545	.046**	.000***

* $p < 0.1$. ** $p < 0.05$. *** $p < 0.01$.

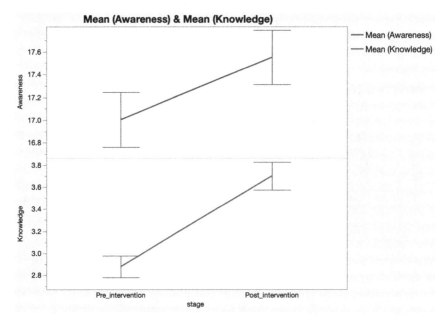

Fig. 2. Comparison of algorithmic awareness and knowledge in different stages (Error bar: 95% CI).

The analysis outcomes affirm the effectiveness of our proposed heuristic intervention. It is shown to have a modest positive impact on users' algorithmic awareness, particularly enhancing conceptual awareness and reducing risk awareness. Furthermore, the intervention led to a notable enhancement in users' performance on heuristic problems and a significant increase in their algorithmic knowledge.

4.2 RQ2: Analysis of the Influence of Algorithmic Knowledge on Algorithmic Awareness

To delve deeper into the impact of shifts in algorithmic knowledge on algorithmic awareness, we scrutinized the interplay between algorithmic knowledge and algorithmic awareness both before and after the intervention. Our analysis outcomes reveal that, overall, prior to the intervention, there was no significant correlation between algorithmic knowledge and algorithmic awareness. However, post-intervention, a substantial correlation emerged (see Fig. 3), with users' awareness of algorithms displaying an overall upward trajectory with the increase in algorithmic knowledge (P <0.0001).

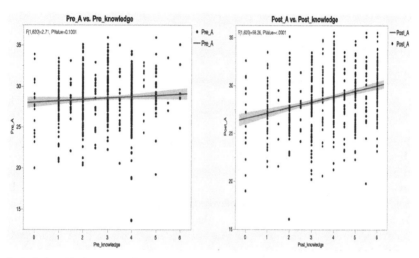

Fig. 3. Relationship between algorithmic awareness and knowledge in different stages (Left: Pre_intervention; Right: Post_intervention).

Furthermore, we conducted a detailed examination of the relationship between algorithmic knowledge and various dimensions of algorithmic awareness after the intervention. Our findings indicate that, as algorithmic knowledge increased, users' awareness of data and functionality within algorithms exhibited significant improvement (P <0.0001). In contrast, conceptual awareness and risk awareness showed no significant alterations (see Fig. 4).

This result reflects the linkage between the different competencies of the dimensions of algorithmic literacy. This means that during heuristic intervention, users learn algorithmic knowledge, and as their algorithmic knowledge increases, their algorithmic awareness tends to rise.

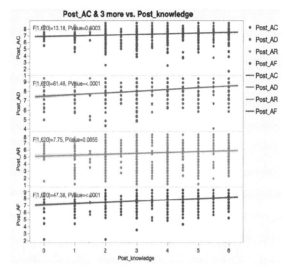

Fig. 4. Relationship between different dimensions of algorithmic awareness and knowledge in the Post_intervention stage.

5   Discussion and Conclusion

Improving algorithmic literacy empowers people to engage with algorithm-driven products across myriad applications with material impact.

Despite the growing emphasis on algorithmic literacy in recent years, there remains a limited algorithmic literacy intervention. In this research, we have developed and validated a heuristic intervention, using user experiments, aimed at enhancing users' algorithmic awareness and algorithmic knowledge to bolster their overall algorithmic literacy. The significance of this study extends beyond delivering a practical intervention for advancing algorithmic literacy; it also entails analyzing the intricate connections between various dimensions of algorithmic literacy, including algorithmic awareness and algorithmic knowledge. This empirical examination provides a valuable foundation for future efforts in cultivating algorithmic literacy.

5.1   Implications for Algorithmic Literacy Development

Enhancing Algorithmic Literacy through a User-friendly UI Design that Offers Heuristic Information. In our designed heuristic intervention, we integrate heuristic reading materials with thought-provoking stimulus questions, all sourced from readily accessible information found in a real-world platform. We present this information in a straightforward manner to users, leading to observable improvements in their awareness and knowledge. However, the fact is that these users use these platforms more often than three times a week. This means that users do not find or read relevant information when they use these platforms on their daily basis. This underscores the potential for enhancing the UI design and information structuring of these platforms. Algorithm and AI product designers and operators should strive to present algorithm-related information in a more intuitive manner through UI design. This approach can foster users' awareness and comprehension of algorithms, consequently augmenting their algorithmic literacy.

Enhancing User Algorithmic Awareness through Fundamental Algorithmic Knowledge Education. Our experiments have unveiled a link between algorithmic awareness and algorithmic knowledge, indicating that as users' algorithmic knowledge improves, their algorithmic awareness also increases. This insight offers valuable guidance for future efforts in nurturing algorithmic competency at the cognitive level. By cultivating knowledge, skills, and other externally observable competencies, we can potentially trigger meaningful transformations in users' intrinsic abilities.

5.2 Limitations and Future Research

Firstly, it is essential to acknowledge that the sample size in this study is relatively limited. Despite our dedicated efforts in collecting 622 data points, the dataset remains relatively small compared to more extensive and well-established datasets. Secondly, the heuristic intervention employed in this study is a singular short-term intervention. It represents an initial exploration into fostering algorithmic literacy and has yielded modest effects. The longer-term trajectory of changes in user awareness and assessments over an extended duration requires further investigation. As part of our future endeavors, we plan to design and implement long-term interventions and carry out follow-up assessments to gain deeper insights into this evolving landscape.

Acknowledgement. This work is sponsored by the Innovative Research Group Project of the Hubei Provincial Natural Science Foundation (No. ZRQT2023000026) and the National Natural Science Foundation of China Major Research Program Cultivation Project (No.92370112).

References

1. Bonini, T., Gandini, A.: First Week Is Editorial, Second Week Is Algorithmic': Platform Gatekeepers and the Platformization of Music Curation. Social Media+Society, Article number: 2056305119880006 (2019)
2. Sunstein, C.R.: Infotopia: How many minds produce knowledge. Oxford University Press (2016)
3. Lambrecht, A., Tucker, C.: Algorithmic bias? An empirical study of apparent gender-based discrimination in the display of STEM career Ads. Manage. Sci. **65**(7), 2947–3348 (2019)
4. Cotter, K., Reisdorf, B.: Algorithmic knowledge gaps: A new dimension of (digital) inequality. Int. J. Commun. **14**, 745–765 (2020)
5. Fouquaert, T., Mechant, P.: Making curation algorithms apparent: a case study of 'Instawareness' as a means to heighten awareness and understanding of Instagram's algorithm. Inf. Commun. Soc. **25**(12), 1769–1789 (2022)
6. Chaiken, S.: Heuristic versus systematic information-processing and the use of source versus message cues in persuasion. J. Personality Social Psychol. **39**(5), 752–766
7. Finn, E.: Algorithm of the Enlightenment. Issues Sci. Technol. **33**(3), 1–25 (2017)
8. Ridley, M., Pawlick-Potts, D.: Algorithmic literacy and the role for libraries. Inf. Technol. Libr. **40**(2), 1–15 (2021)

9. Swart, J.: Experiencing algorithms: how young people understand, feel about, and engage with algorithmic news selection on social media. Social Media+Society **7**(2), 1–11 (2021)

10. Shin, D., Rasul, A., Fotiadis, A.: Why am I seeing this? Deconstructing algorithm literacy through the lens of users. Internet Research (2021)

11. Shin, D.: How do people judge the credibility of algorithmic sources? AI & Soc. 1–16 (2021). https://doi.org/10.1007/s00146-021-01158-4

12. Dogruel, L., Masur, P., Joeckel, S.: Development and validation of an algorithm literacy scale for internet users. Commun. Methods Measures (2021)

13. Silva, D.E., Chen, C., Zhu, Y.: Facets of algorithmic literacy: information, experience, and individual factors predict attitudes toward algorithmic systems. New Media Soc. (2022)

14. Chiang, C.W., Yin, M.: Exploring the Effects of machine learning literacy interventions on laypeople's reliance on machine learning models. In: 27th International Conference on Intelligent User Interfaces. Helsinki, pp. 148–161 (2022)

15. Long, D., Teachey, A., Magerko, B.: Family Learning Talk in AI Literacy Learning Activities. In: The 2022 CHI Conference on Human Factors in Computing Systems, New Orleans, pp. 1–20 (2022)

16. Druga, S., Christoph, F.L., Ko, A.J.: Family as a third space for AI literacies: How do children and parents learn about AI together?. In: The 2022 CHI Conference on Human Factors in Computing Systems, New Orleans, pp. 1–17 (2022)

17. Lee, I., Ali, S., Zhang, H., DiPaola, D., Breazeal, C.: Developing middle school students' AI literacy. In: The 52nd ACM Technical Symposium on Computer Science Education, pp. 191–197 (2021)

18. Druga, S., Vu, S.T., Likhith, E., Qiu, T.: Inclusive AI literacy for kids around the world. In: FabLearn 2019, New York, pp. 104–111 (2019)

19. Danry, V., Pataranutaporn, P., Mao, Y., Maes, P.: Don't just tell me, ask me: AI systems that intelligently frame explanations as questions improve human logical discernment accuracy over causal AI explanations. In: The 2023 CHI Conference on Human Factors in Computing Systems, Hawai'i, pp. 1–13 (2023)

20. Shin, D.: How do users interact with algorithm recommender systems? The interaction of users, algorithms, and performance. Comput. Hum. Behav. 109, Article number: 106344 (2020)

21. Jing, L., Guoye, S., Dan, W.: A study of digital native algorithm awareness and mechanism of action. Inform. Documentation Serv. **44**(3), 80–87 (2023)

Information Retrieval

An Exploratory Study on a Physical Picture Book Representation System for Preschool Children

Pianran Wang[1(✉)], Xuan Sun[2], and Yuting Wang[1]

[1] Department of Information Management, Peking University, Beijing, China
pianranw@pku.edu.cn

[2] Department of Information Resource Management, Business School, Nankai University, Tianjin, China

Abstract. This paper describes the developing process and preliminary testing of a physical representation system aimed at supporting preschool children's picture book search. The authors first conducted named entity recognition (NER) on a corpus of 880 picture book summaries to supplement a metadata schema identified in prior research. They then designed a system using colored stripes and icons to physically represent these metadata elements on book spines. A small-scale experiment (N = 8) comparing search performance between children taught the representation system versus untaught controls was conducted. The results suggest that the representation system can be understood by children and improves recall, precision, and success rates. The findings provide initial evidence that mapping metadata to intuitive physical identifiers could enhance young children's book search experiences and engagement. Further research with larger samples is needed to evaluate the effectiveness of this approach.

Keywords: Children · Picture Book · Metadata Schema · Named Entity Recognition · User-centered Design

1 Introduction

Picture books play a crucial role in early childhood, as they not only promote children's language and literacy development but also help to cultivate children's reading interest and creativity. With the growing popularity of picture books and the increasing evidence that positive experiences with book selection can significantly enhance children's motivation to develop their literacy skills [1], it is imperative to develop effective ways to support young readers' picture book search.

Children ages 3 to 6 mainly read physical picture books, accessing them in environments like libraries and bookstores rather than websites. However, common classification systems used in these physical spaces often do not align well with how young children search for and select books. For instance, Kaplan et al. [2] point out that using the first three letters of the author's surname to organize books does not correspond with the book search and selection behavior of children. This mismatch suggests that current systems may not provide optimal support for preschoolers' book searches.

© The Author(s), under exclusive license to Springer Nature Switzerland AG 2024
I. Sserwanga et al. (Eds.): iConference 2024, LNCS 14598, pp. 261–270, 2024.
https://doi.org/10.1007/978-3-031-57867-0_19

2 Related Works

2.1 Children's Book Search Behavior and Metadata Schema

Wang et al. [3] have identified 1064 picture book description words that preschool children aged 3 to 6 use when searching for books through quasi Wizard-of-Oz and crowd-sourcing studies. These elements can be concluded into 39 metadata schema elements and further categorized into three dimensions, including entity elements (animals, humans, fantasy creatures, locations, time, etc.), story elements (main characters, supporting characters, key items, etc.), and picture book medium elements (cover, illustrations, etc.).

Some researchers have investigated school-age children's search behaviors and book selection factors, including basic bibliographical information (e.g. titles, authors), book covers, stories (fiction), subjects (nonfiction), illustrations, characters, physical characteristics, genres, understandability/difficulty, feelings, familiarity, and awards/recommendations [1, 4–6]. Correspondingly, researchers developed children-oriented book search and recommendation systems or metadata schemas, such as Druin and her colleagues' International Children's Digital Library (ICDL) [7–11], Kaplan and her colleagues' Metis system [2, 6], and Beak's child-driven metadata [1]. However, these metadata schemas are oriented toward information systems and lack connection to the management practices of physical collections.

2.2 Visual Identification for Children's Book Search

Visual identification is widely used in physical book management. Many libraries use colored bookshelves to store and identify books of different categories or target groups [12], and many libraries apply color stripes to the book spine, which represents the category of a book for preliminary arrangement. Some libraries or service providers have begun to explore the use of color to enhance the identification of book labels [13–15]. Lyttle and Walsh [13] found that children quickly embraced the new labels although they may not necessarily understand the bands, subject headings, and their surrogates.

To the best of the authors' knowledge, only the Metis system applies icon identification to physical children's books [2, 6]. Considering the low literacy and reading skills of the low- and middle-grade students, Kaplan et al. [6]. Hired a graphic designer to create hashtags for 26 categories. For example, "sports" uses the images of tennis rackets hitting a ball. These labels visually indicate what the book is about, and they are visually child-friendly [16].

Researchers discuss the positive impact of collection and organization improvement on the circulation of children's books, even yielding an increase of more than 500% [2, 15]. However, the existing research or practice on visual identification for children only focuses on the effect of improving the circulation of the library collection and lacks test and comparative research on the effect of children's book search. Therefore, whether these changes can improve the effect of children's book search and experience, is yet to be explored.

3   Problem Formulation

Preschool-aged children are in the preoperational stage of cognitive development according to Piaget's theory. In this stage, children struggle with abstract symbolic thought and logic. Therefore, traditional library classification systems that rely on abstract categories, alphanumeric codes may be difficult for preschoolers to effectively utilize during book searches. To provide developmentally appropriate support, picture book search systems for young children should incorporate concrete, physical design elements that align with preschoolers' cognitive skills. This suggests a need for research on two components: (1) developing a metadata schema oriented toward physical organization that matches children's book search behaviors, and (2) designing intuitive physical identifiers for picture books tailored to preschoolers' abilities.

Prior research has identified key metadata elements that align with preschoolers' book search behaviors [3, 17], but this work has relied on small sample sizes. Analyzing a larger corpus of picture books could help expand and refine the schema. Therefore, research is needed on:

RQ1: How can the expanded dataset contribute to the refinement of the schema?

RQ2: Can preschool children understand this physical representation system and its mapping between schema elements and visual identifiers?

RQ3: How does using the physical representation system impact preschoolers' book search performance compared to traditional organization?

4   Named Entity Recognition of Picture Bools

4.1   Method

Previous studies were conducted from the perspective of preschool children. Considering the limited number of picture books used in previous studies, with the additional purpose of extracting the metadata schema from the picture book itself, we first proposed a natural language processing study to obtain a large amount of picture book entity elements.

A trained GPT model was used to identify named entities of names, organizations, time, locations, etc. The dataset used in this study was obtained in April 2023 from the API of Dangdang, which is the largest online platform for book purchasing in China. We obtained picture book information, including title, author, publisher, and descriptive text such as "content summary" of picture books. By extracting structured information from unstructured data, we generated a dataset of annotated content summaries that can be used for further analysis.

4.2 Result

A total of 880 picture book data were collected. After the initial named entity recognition, we identified 2,553 entities. Subsequently, we conducted a frequency analysis and narrowed down the selection to 858 entities with a frequency of 2 or more.

We merged these 858 identified entities with the 1,064 descriptive words obtained in the previous study. Some of the entities overlap with the 1,064 descriptive words obtained in previous research. In this study, we did not identify any new metadata schema elements and the total remains at 39 and the dimensions remain at three. The relationship between the picture book description words from children obtained in previous studies and the NER from picture books obtained in this study, metadata schema elements, and dimensions is shown in Fig. 1.

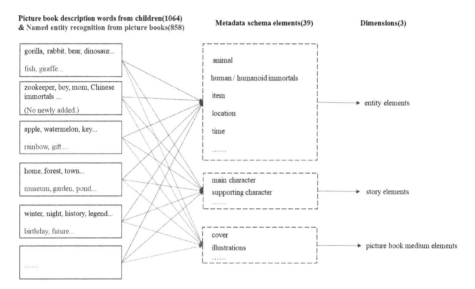

Fig. 1. The relationship between three levels of elements

It is crucial that the physical metadata schema meets the requirements and search behaviors of young children. We conducted a frequency analysis and categorized the merged dataset of picture book description words from children obtained in previous studies and the NER from picture books obtained in this study. We excluded the picture book medium elements because of the usage scenario of the representation system and formed a schema that includes entity elements and story elements. We conducted frequency analysis on the merged dataset, selected high-frequency words, and gathered feedback from children, librarians, and teachers to form the final schema.

5   Physical Picture Book Representation

A clear visual identity, such as a color stripe as a label, is effective for managing books on a shelf, while concrete images of content elements are more intuitive for young children. Therefore, we adopt both identity styles simultaneously. We select copyright-free icons to represent the high-frequency elements and color stripe label as background to represent the metadata schema.

These labels with colored stripes and icons are like call number labels in libraries and are attached to the spine of picture books. Each picture book has 4–5 label stickers according to its content. The labels and icons are shown in Table 1.

Table 1. Book labels and icons

Label Color	Label Representation	Icon	Icon representation
Yellow	Who(s) is this story about?		Cat
			Other animals not mentioned in the above ten animal icons
		20 icons more	Bear, dinosaur, human/ humanoid immortals, etc.
Purple	Is there anything special or an impressive characteristic about the main character, such as appearance and ability?		Distinctive appearance
			Superpower
		5 icons more	Occupation/profession, prince/princess, emotion, etc.
Pink	What is the relationship between the main characters of the story?		Family
			Friends
		2 icons more	Pet, enemy
Orange	Is there something that appears in the story from beginning to end or that plays a big role in the story?		Yes
		(blank)	No
Green	Where did the story take place?		House
			Kindergarten/school
		15 icons more	City/town, library, outer space, etc.
Blue	When did the story happen?		Night
			History
		7 icons more	Legend/tale, holiday, seasons, etc.

Taking the picture book *Belinda the Ballerina* (located at the far right of Fig. 2) as an example. In this story, the main character is the girl, for whom we have assigned a yellow "human" label. The girl is distinguished by her large feet, represented by a purple "distinctive appearance" label. The story unfolds in a city, represented by a green "city/town" label.

Fig. 2. Labeled picture books

6 Experiment

6.1 Method

We assessed the usability of the book label representation system, involving preschool children aged 3–6 as participants. We invited preschool children from the children's section of the library to participate in the study. These children were then divided into two groups: the experimental group, which used picture book labels, and the control group, which did not receive instructions on using picture book labels. The two groups of children were similar in terms of age, gender, and literacy levels.

Due to the limited attention span of preschool children, the test was conducted within 15 min. To expedite the process of locating picture books, we selected 30 picture books and pasted the book labels to the book spines. As the children in the control group were not instructed on how to utilize the book labels, these labels did not influence their customary book search behaviors.

According to children's search behavior, we designed three easy to difficult tasks to determine if children could understand the representation function (task 1), coordination function (tasks 2 and 3), and surrogates of the picture book labels.

- Task 1: Find one book about "friends" or "friendship."
- Task 2: Find one book about a child sleeping at night.
- Task 3: Find the book *A Piece of Cake*, which is about "Mrs. Large the elephant who wanted to lose weight; she asked her family to eat healthy food and do more work out. One day, they received a box of cakes. Mrs. Large forced the family not to eat; however, Mrs. Large kept thinking about the cake and could not sleep. Finally, Mrs. Large could not help going to the kitchen to steal the cake. However, there was only one cake left; the others were eaten by other family members. Finally, she and her family decided not to lose weight." (This task description was copied from one child's story description in our previous study.)

The procedure was conducted as follows: for children in the experimental group, the researchers initially explained the utilization of book labels, using one picture book as an example with the attached book labels. Subsequently, the researchers asked the children to select labels that represented the classic story of *Snow White* to ensure their comprehension of book label usage. This instructional session lasted approximately 5 min. Following the training session, the researchers informed the children that there would be three games involving searching for picture books based on the recently learned method. Additionally, the children were informed that the book search process would be timed, emphasizing that quicker retrieval of picture books would yield better results. During the test, the labels and their corresponding representations were placed on the table for the children's reference. For children in the control group, the researchers only explained the rules of the games. The entire search process was recorded on video.

6.2 Result

A total of 8 children with a vocabulary of less than 30 Chinese characters participated in and completed this test, with 4 in the control group and 4 in the experimental group. There are five girls and three boys. The average age is 4.125 (SD = 0.354).

Understandability. All the children who were taught the guidelines were able to use the picture book labels to find the target picture books. According to the video analysis, all the children in the experimental groups first looked at the book label sticker on the spine, which was different from the children in the control group, who looked at the cover of the picture book. This indicates that children can consciously use labels as a tool to assist in book searching.

Recall. Children often use a single picture book icon to help them discover picture books that contain the same elements. For example, in task 1, the children in the experimental group could find the first picture book containing the "pink-friend" label in a considerably short time, and thereafter, they could find the other three books with the label, which indicates that the label could assist in discovering books on the same topic. In task 2, two children caught the keyword "night"; thus, they searched for picture books with stickers of "blue-moon". In task 3, all the children extracted the keyword "elephant," and one of the children extracted all the 3 picture books with stickers of the "yellow-elephant", checked one by one, and finally found the target book.

Precision. Task 3 simulated the common situation of children searching for known picture books by informing them about the title and main content of the picture books. Four children in the experimental group first located three picture books containing "elephant". Afterward, two children found the target picture book by looking for the key item label, one child who recognized the Chinese character for "one/a" in the titles, and one child checked the three elephant picture books one by one and found the target picture book through the cake on the cover.

These strategies indicated that book labels can assist children in narrowing down the search range and using their strategies to find known picture books.

Success and Speed. The success rate of the experimental group children was higher than that of the children in the control group, who used their usual strategies to search for books. In task 1, all the children in the control group used the methods of checking the cover of the picture book and flipping through the illustrations of the picture book to search for books. However, since "friend" is an abstract relationship, it is difficult for children who have not read picture books to determine whether there is a "friend" relationship between the characters. Therefore, the success rate in the control group was significantly lower than that in the experimental group in task 1. In tasks 2 and 3, which involved more intuitive cues that could be observed on the book covers, the control group exhibited an improved success rate.

The average time spent on task 2 was 169.25 s for the experimental group and 161 s for the control group. In task 3, the average times of the experimental and control groups were 599 and 444 s, respectively. The average time for the experimental group to find the picture book was longer than the control group. By analyzing the video, we found that the reasons for the relatively long time spent by the children in the experimental group were that the children in the experimental group used the labels for the first time, and such short-term teaching could not enable them to frequently use the new labels. To assist the children in the experimental group, researchers printed the guidelines with the label table on the desk, and the children spent a lot of time looking up the labels while searching.

7 Discussion

To the best of our knowledge, our study represents the first attempt to craft a physical picture book representation system tailored explicitly for young children and assess its effectiveness in enhancing picture book search efficiency. This innovative system incorporates color stripes and icons comprehensively, aiming to augment the visual recognition of call numbers. Consequently, it holds the potential to enhance both children's picture book search experiences and the management of library collections.

For young children, this intuitive identification system streamlines the book search process considerably. It offers a child-centered perspective on representing the content of picture books while taking into account the limited literacy and reading skills of preschool-aged children. By simply scanning these labels, children can effortlessly explore books aligned with their interests. In sum, this system provides young children with an engaging and enjoyable experience of serendipitous book discovery.

The advantages of this system extend to library collection management as well. First and foremost, it employs subject indexing, which complements the traditional organizational approach often employed in the children's section of libraries. Second, the easily understandable labels can actively involve children in maintaining collection. Librarians, for instance, can instruct children to "gather picture books featuring humans as the main characters together" to maintain order in the children's section. Third, it facilitates dynamic shelving, enabling librarians to swiftly assemble books as needed. For instance, during autumn reading activities, librarians can readily locate picture books adorned with blue "fallen leaves" icons and place them together.

The primary limitation of our study is the limited sample size. Our research was conducted with a relatively small group of participants. Future research with a larger and more diverse sample is crucial to validate and refine the system further, ensuring its applicability and effectiveness in a broader range of settings.

8   Conclusions

This paper presents an exploratory study on a children-specific physical representation system for picture books. Designed to align with children's perspectives and cognitive abilities, this system simplifies their interaction with book searches. Future plans include real-world implementation, longer-term user testing in library settings, and expanding our sample size to ensure feasibility and efficiency.

Acknowledgments. This work was supported by the Chunhui Project of the Ministry of Education of China (Grant number 202200982), the National Natural Science Foundation of China (Grant number 71904091),

References

1. Beak, J.: A child-driven metadata schema: a holistic analysis of children's cognitive processes during book selection (2014)
2. Kaplan, T.B., Dolloff, A.K., Giffard, S., Still-Schiff, J.: Are Dewey's days numbered?: Libraries nationwide are ditching the old classification system. Sch. Libr. J. **58**, 24–28 (2012)
3. Wang, P., Lu, J., Wu, Y., Zhang, J.: A bundle of serendipity: a crowdsourcing program for picture book information organization oriented toward preschool children. Libr. Inf. Sci. Res. **45**, 101251 (2023). https://doi.org/10.1016/j.lisr.2023.101251
4. Milton, A., Batista, L., Allen, G., Gao, S., Ng, Y.-K.D., Pera, M.S.: "Don't judge a book by its cover": exploring book traits children favor. In: Proceedings of the 14th ACM Conference on Recommender Systems, pp. 669–674. Association for Computing Machinery, New York, NY, USA (2020). https://doi.org/10.1145/3383313.3418490

5. Hourcade, J.P., Bederson, B.B., Druin, A., Rose, A., Farber, A., Takayama, Y.: The international children's digital library: viewing digital books online. Interact. Comput. **15**, 151–167 (2003)
6. Kaplan, T.B., Giffard, S., Stillschiff, J., Dolloff, A.K.: One size does not fit all: creating a developmentally appropriate classification for your children's collections. Knowl. Quest. **42**, 30–37 (2013)
7. Druin, A., Weeks, A., Massey, S., Bederson, B.B.: Children's interests and concerns when using the international children's digital library: a four-country case study. In: ACM/IEEE-CS Joint Conference on Digital Libraries, pp. 167–176. Association for Computing Machinery, Vancouver BC, Canada (2007)
8. Druin, A.: What children can teach us: developing digital libraries for children with children. Libr. Q. **75**, 20–41 (2005)
9. Hutchinson, H., Druin, A., Bederson, B.B., Reuter, K., Rose, A., Weeks, A.C.: How do I find blue books about dogs? The errors and frustrations of young digital library users. Proc. HCII **2005**, 22–27 (2005)
10. Reuter, K.: Assessing aesthetic relevance: children's book selection in a digital library. J. Am. Soc. Inform. Sci. Technol. **58**, 1745–1763 (2007)
11. Reuter, K., Druin, A.: Bringing together children and books: an initial descriptive study of children's book searching and selection behavior in a digital library. Proc. Am. Soc. Inf. Sci. Technol. **41**, 339–348 (2004)
12. Wang, P., Xu, J., Sturm, B.W., Kang, Q., Wu, Y.: "Books, physical spaces, rules, people": a holistic analysis of young Chinese children's perceptions of public libraries. J. Librariansh. Inf. Sci. **54**, 239–250 (2022). https://doi.org/10.1177/09610006211007197
13. Lyttle, M.A., Walsh, S.D.: Color in the library – organizing materials by color, http://public librariesonline.org/2014/10/color-in-the-library/. Accessed 30 Nov 2021
14. Lyttle, M.A., Walsh, S.D.: Leaving dewey for BISAC. http://publiclibrariesonline.org/2018/11/leaving-dewey-for-bisac/. Accessed 18 Nov 2021
15. Parrott, K., Gattullo, E.: Throwing dewey overboard: Dewey lite: a model for nonfiction reorganization. Child. Libr. **11**, 3–7 (2013)
16. Kaplan, T.B., Dolloff, A., Giffard, S., Still-Schiff, J.: Labels Available!, https://sites.google.com/site/metisinnovations/home/label-images. Accessed 10 Jun 2022
17. Wang, P., Ma, Y., Xie, H., Wang, H., Lu, J., Xu, J.: There is a gorilla holding a key on the book cover: young children's known picture book search strategies. J. Am. Soc. Inf. Sci. **73**, 45–57 (2022). https://doi.org/10.1002/asi.24539

Challenges of Personal Image Retrieval and Organization: An Academic Perspective

Amit Kumar Nath[1], Forhan Bin Emdad[2(✉)], and An-I Andy Wang[1]

[1] Department of Computer Science, Florida State University, Tallahassee, USA
{anath,aawang}@fsu.edu

[2] College of Communication and Information, Florida State University, Tallahassee, USA
fe21a@fsu.edu

Abstract. With the increasing number of smartphone devices and social media platforms, many users now have large personal image collections. As these collections expand, the task of organizing and retrieving specific images becomes increasingly challenging. To quantify the scope of this emerging problem, we conducted a quantitative survey study to gain insights into users' practices concerning personal image retrieval and organization. Initially, we conducted a survey on the Florida State University campus, primarily targeting undergraduate and graduate students. The survey questionnaire delved into various aspects of how users organize and retrieve their images. Then we implemented several machine learning models (decision trees, random forest, logistic regression, and XGboost) on the collected survey data to determine the existence of problems faced by the users to retrieve their personal images. XGboost performed better than the other models with an accuracy of 73%. The model also revealed that several factors, such as the frequency of encountering difficulties in finding photos both before and after sharing, the number of photos taken by users in the previous year, the number of photos posted on social media, and the total number of photos stored on users' laptops or desktops, were among the most critical features associated with personal image retrieval challenges.

Keywords: Image retrieval · Photo Organization · Smartphone · Social media

1 Introduction

Photographs are lasting representations of our memories, and many people take photographs frequently using various devices. The emergence of smartphones, digital cameras, and tablets has enabled users to take many pictures without worrying about depleting film reels, as people used to do with old cameras. With improvements in cloud and storage technologies, users are less concerned about storage space. Most smart devices can store and upload images to cloud storage and social network-based sharing platforms as needed.

An estimated 12 trillion photos have been captured since 2012. In 2019, the worldwide count of photographs taken reached approximately 1.4 trillion (Fig. 1). However,

© The Author(s), under exclusive license to Springer Nature Switzerland AG 2024
I. Sserwanga et al. (Eds.): iConference 2024, LNCS 14598, pp. 271–282, 2024.
https://doi.org/10.1007/978-3-031-57867-0_20

the global pandemic caused a 21% reduction in the number of images taken in 2020, bringing it down to 1.1 trillion. As the effects of the pandemic subsided in 2021, the number of photos taken once again exhibited an upward trajectory, reaching 1.4 trillion. Furthermore, in 2022, the number of photos taken further increased to 1.5 trillion [1, 2].

The proliferation of social media platforms like Facebook, WhatsApp, Snapchat, and Instagram has significantly contributed to the surge in photo-taking activities. These platforms encourage users to upload and share their photos with friends and family, while also facilitating feedback and engagement from others. The daily photo-sharing statistics on these platforms are as follows: WhatsApp, 6.9 billion; Snapchat, 3.8 billion; Facebook, 2.1 billion; Instagram, 1.3 billion; and Flickr, 1 million [1].

Considering all the images owned by an individual, whether shared or not, their whole collection can be referred to as a ***personal image collection***. This collection is primarily accessible to the owner and is typically stored on local storage media, with sharing predominantly occurring through various social media platforms.

After the emergence of digital photography, several user studies were conducted emphasizing on the changes that the new technology brought about in users' photo-related activities [3–6]. These studies provided early insights into the image-related activities performed by the users. However, with the ubiquitous use of smartphones and other smart devices, user behavior has also changed significantly. Some recent studies stated that personal organization tendencies are influenced by social interactions [7, 8]. However, the existing literature on user behavior concerning personal image retrieval and organization remains notably limited and largely outdated.

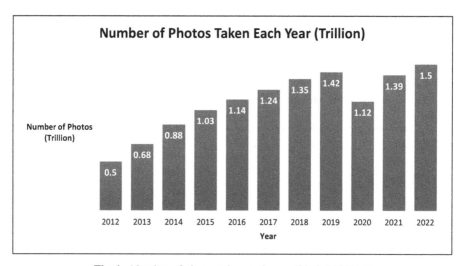

Fig. 1. Number of photos taken each year (2012–2022) [1]

As reported in a recent study [9], the failure rates among participants attempting to locate photos on their computers and smartphones were 71% and 37%, respectively. In certain scenarios, users often grapple with the challenge of recalling the precise time and location of photos they have captured. This lack of contextual information significantly complicates their ability to locate specific images or groups of images. Several factors contribute to this issue, including the sheer volume of photos, images lacking labels, and related complications.

Numerous photo-related applications and cloud-based solutions offer functionalities such as searching based on timestamps, locations, content, and facial recognition. However, many of these applications, including Curator, Imaganize, A + Gallery, and others, either require paid subscriptions or offer limited free features [20]. The default photo galleries on Android and iPhone devices offer minimal search capabilities, primarily focused on chronological ordering for time-based searches [10].

To gain deeper insights into users' activities related to photos, we conducted a survey study on the Florida State University (FSU) campus, titled "A Survey on Personal Image Retrieval and Organization", or PIRO. Exploring the challenges of personal image retrieval from the perspective of students in an academic campus setting can be invaluable, as students are generally technologically competent and well-versed in current technology trends [11]. Moreover, identifying the factors influencing issues related to personal image retrieval can contribute significantly to the mitigation of this prevalent problem.

To address the prevailing issues in the personal image retrieval process, this study has the following objectives:

1. We aim to quantify the challenges faced by users when attempting to retrieve specific images from their personal image collections. To achieve this, we will apply various machine-learning models to the survey data we have collected.
2. Subsequently, using machine-learning models, we intend to identify the major factors that play a role in personal image retrieval-related difficulties.

2   Method

Study Overview: This quantitative survey study consists of four distinct stages: data collection, data preprocessing, classification, and the identification of significant variables influencing the classification models. In the initial data collection stage, we integrated the data and transformed a few text-based columns into categorical data. Subsequently, during the data processing stage, we analyzed missing data (no missing data was found) and standardized the dataset, converting the data into a normalized range between 0 and 1. Finally, the preprocessed data was provided as input for various machine-learning models for the classification of personal image retrieval-related problems.

Data Description: The PIRO survey study was conducted on a 19-question questionnaire to examine and understand users' image organization and retrieval practices (Appendix). In the survey, we recruited participants from the FSU campus. The survey was promoted through e-mail listings and flyers. The survey flyers were also posted on the bulletin boards and bus stops all over the FSU campus. We received responses from 202 participants from FSU. The survey was conducted from September 27, 2021, to January 13, 2022 (117 days).

In this study, the sample size was determined through random sampling [12, 19], aiming for a 90% confidence level with a 5% margin of error. While the appropriate sample size would typically fall within the range of 250 to 300 participants or more than

300 participants [12], we managed to enlist a reasonably sized cohort of 202 individuals. This recruitment challenge stemmed from time constraints and the technology-oriented nature of the study, making it challenging to secure a sample size exceeding 200. Also note that most of our participants are undergraduate and graduate students, representing a younger demographic known for their technological competence [11] and penchant for capturing and sharing a substantial number of photos on various social media platforms. Consequently, this participant group offers a good distribution for our study's objectives.

Variables: The dataset included 44 variables including 'the number of computing devices used by the participants', 'device type', 'smartphone type', 'OS (Operating system) type', 'storage type', 'photo organizing app used', 'number of photos on social media', 'frequency of creating photos', 'frequency of organizing photos', 'frequency of retrieving photos', 'frequency of sharing photos', 'frequency of trouble finding photos before sharing', and 'frequency of trouble finding photos after sharing' etc. In addition, the dataset included demographic variables such as 'gender,' 'age,' and the 'major of their study.' Demographic variables have been analyzed by descriptive statistics where mean, frequency, percentage, and standard deviation have been calculated.

As this study focuses on issues related to personal image retrieval, the binary outcome variable for this classification study is "problems to find photos". In this context, a "1" signifies the presence of difficulties in retrieving desired photos (positive instances), while a "0" indicates the absence of any issues in finding photos (no difficulties encountered in photo retrieval).

Model Implementation: We implemented basic classification models such as decision tree, random forest, logistic regression, and XGBoost for the experiment [13]. A decision tree is a simple non-parametric supervised learning process, and a random forest is a combination of multiple decision trees. Logistic regression is a method for estimating the probability of a discrete result given an input variable.

Among all other simple models, XGboost is considered to be advanced and more effective. XGBoost (eXtreme Gradient Boosting) is an implementation of the gradient-boosted decision tree that has been designed for better performance and speed. To achieve an optimal XGBoost implementation, a comprehensive parameter tuning process was conducted. Learning rate, regularization parameters (lambda and alpha), and tree-based parameters such as max_depth, min_child_weight, gamma, subsample, colsample_bytree, and scale_pos_weight were tuned accordingly to find the best possible combination. In our model, we achieved the optimal combination with values such as 0.005 for reg_alpha, 0.1 for the learning rate, 4 for max_depth, 0 for gamma, 0.8 for subsample, and 1 for scale_pos_weight. Regularization parameter tuning helps to minimize complexity and improve the performance of the model. Tree-based parameters help to address imbalance class-related issues. To assess the model's performance, we used metrics including accuracy, F1 score, precision, recall, and area under the receiver operating characteristic curve (AUROC) [14].

To identify the key features of the model, we used the SHAP (SHapley Additive exPlanations) explanation technique. SHAP is used here because the interpretation approach is based on a strong theoretical foundation which is game theory, and it provides information related to the fair distribution of the feature's influence on the prediction. This approach is particularly beneficial for understanding complex machine-learning models often regarded as "black box" models [15, 16]. Moreover, SHAP interpretations provide a dual perspective by offering both global and local insights [17].

3 Results

Demographic characteristics (Table 1) show that most of the participants facing personal image retrieval-related problems are between 20 to 45 years old. In addition, male participants (67%) tend to face image retrieval-related problems more than female participants (31%). Computing-related (major course of study) student participants overwhelmingly constituted the majority of results, which can be attributed to their heightened tech-savviness.

Table 1. Analysis of demographic characteristics of the participants.

	Have Problems for Finding Photos		No Problems for Finding Photos	
Age	Number	Mean (Standard Deviation)	Number	Mean (Standard Deviation)
0–19	9	18.4 (0.73)	6	18.8 (0.41)
20–45	123	28.3 (5.24)	62	28.2 (4.41)
45–65	2	56 (8.5)	0	0
Gender	**Number**	**Percentage**	**Number**	**Percentage**
Male	92	68.7	40	58.8
Female	42	31.3	28	41.2
Major (Degree)	**Number**	**Percentage**	**Number**	**Percentage**
Computing-related	66	49.3	44	64.7
Science-related	35	26.1	10	14.7
Other	33	24.6	14	20.6

Table 2 shows the comparison of the performance of the machine-learning models. Each model's precision, recall, F1-score, accuracy, and area under curve (AUROC) are recorded in the below table.

By analyzing Table 2, we can observe that XGboost has performed best in terms of precision, accuracy, and AUROC which are considered as the main metrics of performance comparison. However, the logistic regression model scored a maximum for recall and F1-score metrics.

As the XGboost model gained the highest accuracy and AUROC, we interpreted the XGboost model with a SHAP explanation. Based on the SHAP explanation (Fig. 2), we identified the following features as the most significant ones that influence the problems related to personal image retrieval:

Table 2. Performance comparison of different machine learning models.

Model	Precision	Recall	F1-score	Accuracy	AUROC
Logistic Regression	67%	**85%**	**75%**	63%	56%
Decision Tree	60%	40%	48%	68%	62%
Random Forest	67%	40%	50%	71%	64%
XGboost	**75%**	40%	52%	**73%**	**66%**

1. The frequency of trouble finding photos before sharing
2. Number of photos the users have on their laptops/desktops
3. Number of photos taken by the users in the previous year
4. Number of photos posted by the users on social media
5. Facebook (Social media platform used for uploading photos)
6. The frequency of trouble finding photos after sharing

4 Discussions

The final question of the survey asked the participants about the reasons for their difficulty finding their photos. For the survey participants, the primary reasons for their difficulty in finding personal photos were (1) they had too many photos (47%) and (2) their photos were not labeled (44%). Other reasons were that their photos were not organized (32%), they had forgotten when and where they had taken the photos (29%), and the photos were stored on multiple devices (18%), making it difficult to track them. Thirty-three percent of the participants had no problem finding photos. So, we can conclude that about 67% of the participants did have difficulty finding their personal photos, which supports the results from the models (Table 2).

The XGboost model employed in this study demonstrated a noteworthy accuracy score of 73%, signifying its utility in identifying issues related to personal image retrieval. The model yielded a plethora of variables that exerted considerable influence on image retrieval problems. Analyzing these variables holds promise for mitigating these issues and uncovering improved solutions.

A notable portion of survey participants (33%) reported infrequent difficulties in finding photos before sharing them, while a higher percentage (40%) encountered problems when attempting to locate photos after sharing. These figures underscore that despite the widespread availability of multiple photo-sharing platforms, participants still grappled with photo retrieval challenges, possibly stemming from difficulties in recalling the specific platform used for sharing.

By conducting quartile analysis, we established that the median quantity of photos stored on participants' smartphones typically fell within the 500–600 range. Interestingly, a similar median range was observed for the number of photos stored on their laptop/desktop computers. Moreover, participants had a median of approximately 150 photos uploaded on their social media platforms, while they captured around 400 photos in the previous year (median value). Figure 3 provides a logarithmic scale-based visualization depicting the number of photos stored on smartphones, shared on social media, stored on laptops/desktops, and captured by participants over the past year.

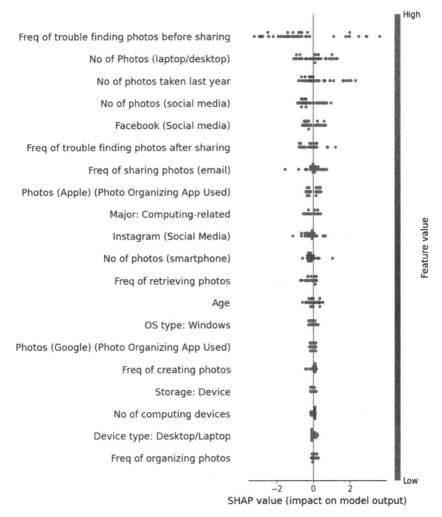

Fig. 2. Feature importance identification using SHAP values.

Other notable findings from the study include the ranking of social media platforms and image organization apps used by the participants. Note that a single user can use multiple social media platforms and several photo organization and retrieval applications, so the total percentage exceeds 100% in both cases. After analyzing the survey findings in this research, we established a ranking of platforms based on their popularity for photo sharing among the participants. According to the survey respondents, Instagram (59%) and Facebook (58%) emerged as the most popular, with Snapchat (37%) and Flickr (17%) following closely behind. Additionally, we conducted a ranking of photo organization and retrieval applications based on their popularity. Apple Photos (57%) secured the top spot, succeeded by Google Photos (48%), iCloud (21%), Samsung Gallery (15%), One Drive (13%), and the default file folders (12%).

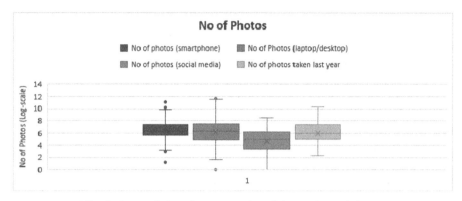

Fig. 3. Log scale-based representation of the numbers of photos.

Like many other research endeavors, this study is not without its limitations. To begin with, the study's sample size is relatively small, primarily due to the challenge of locating technology-oriented participants within an academic context. Additionally, there may be inherent bias [18] in the survey questions, as they were formulated by researchers with backgrounds in computer and information science.

To address these limitations and further enhance our understanding of the subject, future research should aim to encompass a more diverse population and utilize a larger sample size. This approach can facilitate more comprehensive investigations and offer recommendations for effectively addressing the identified issues.

5   Conclusions

The insights uncovered in this study provide valuable perspectives on users' behaviors concerning image organization and retrieval. The research substantiates the challenges faced by survey participants from FSU when attempting to locate specific photos in their personal image repositories. The analysis emphasizes the common obstacles users face when navigating extensive personal image collections to find particular photos. Moreover, the findings underscore the importance of developing effective software applications and tools to assist users in addressing these challenges. This research identifies factors that should be considered in the development of such tools. There is significant potential to enhance and streamline the processes of image organization and retrieval for users through dedicated research and development efforts.

Appendix

Survey on Personal Image Retrieval and Organization (PIRO)

User Behavior Questionnaire:

1	Email Address (provide if you want to have a chance to win a gift card)	
2	Gender	i. Male ii. Female iii. Non-binary / third gender iv. Prefer not to say
3	Age	
4	Ethnicity (check all that apply)	i. American Indian, Alaskan Native, and/or Native Hawaiian Islander ii. Asian, Asian American, and/or Pacific Islander iii. Black or African American iv. Hispanic/Latino/Latinx v. White vi. Other
5	Major	i. Computing-related major (E.g., computer science, information technology) ii. Science-related major (E.g., biology, physics) iii. Other
6	How many computing devices do you use (e.g., smartphone, tablet, laptop)?	
7	Which computing device do you use for organizing photos?	i. Smartphone ii. Laptop/Desktop iii. Tablet
8	If you have a smartphone, what type of phone do you have?	i. Android ii. iPhone iii. Other iv. Not applicable
9	Which operating system do you use on your laptop/desktop?	i. Windows ii. iOS iii. Other iv. Not applicable
10	Where do you mostly access your photos from?	i. Device ii. Cloud storage
11	Which software application do you use for organizing photos? (Select all that apply)	i. None (just use file folders) ii. Photos (Apple) iii. Photos (Google) iv. Samsung Gallery v. iCloud vi. OneDrive vii. Other:

(continued)

(*continued*)

1	Email Address (provide if you want to have a chance to win a gift card)	
12	Which software application do you use for retrieving photos? (Select all that apply)	i. None (just use file folders) ii. Photos (Apple) iii. Photos (Google) iv. Samsung Gallery v. iCloud vi. OneDrive vii. Other:
13	How many photos do you have on your smartphone?	
14	How many photos do you have on your laptop/desktop?	
15	How many photos do you have on your social media?	
16	How many photos have you taken within the past year?	
17	Which social media do you use for photo sharing? (Select all that apply)	
18	How often do you: Create photos? Organize your photos? Retrieve photos from your personal image collection? Share your photos via social media? Share photos by email? Have trouble finding photos before sharing them? Have trouble finding photos after sharing them?	Choose the most suitable answer Daily Weekly Monthly Yearly Rarely
19	Why do you have a hard time finding your photos? (Select all that apply)	i. I do not have any problems to find photos ii. My photos are not organized iii. I do not remember the time and place when the photo was taken iv. I have too many photos v. The photos are not labeled vi. The photos are stored in multiple devices vii. Other:

References

1. Enfield, S.: How many photos will be taken in 2022? https://news.mylio.com/how-many-pho
   tos-taken-in-2022/. Accessed 19 Sep 2023
2. Brogie, M.: Average number of photos taken per day around the world. https://www.repsly.
   com/blog/field-team-management/field-data-insight-average-number-of-photos-taken-per-
   day-worldwide. Accessed 19 Sep 2023
3. Frohlich, D., Kuchinsky, A., Pering, C., Don, A., Ariss, S.: Requirements for photoware.
   In: Proceedings of the 2002 ACM Conference on Computer Supported Cooperative Work,
   pp. 166–175. Association for Computing Machinery, New York, NY, USA (2002). https://
   doi.org/10.1145/587078.587102
4. Kirk, D., Sellen, A., Rother, C., Wood, K.: Understanding photowork. In: Proceedings of the
   SIGCHI Conference on Human Factors in Computing Systems, pp. 761–770. Association for
   Computing Machinery, New York, NY, USA (2006). https://doi.org/10.1145/1124772.112
   4885
5. Platt, J.C., Czerwinski, M., Field, B.A.: PhotoTOC: automatic clustering for browsing personal photographs. In: Fourth International Conference on Information, Communications and
   Signal Processing, 2003 and the Fourth Pacific Rim Conference on Multimedia. Proceedings
   of the 2003 Joint, pp. 6–10, vol.1 (2003). https://doi.org/10.1109/ICICS.2003.1292402
6. Rodden, K., Wood, K.R.: How do people manage their digital photographs? In: Proceedings
   of the SIGCHI Conference on Human Factors in Computing Systems, pp. 409–416. Association for Computing Machinery, New York, NY, USA (2003). https://doi.org/10.1145/642
   611.642682
7. Jones, W., Bruce, H., Jones, E., Vinson, J.: Providing for Paper, Place and People in Personal
   Projects. (2023)
8. Solomon, R.L.: Personal digital photograph management and the impacts of social media
   (2015)
9. Bergman, O., Gutman, D., Whittaker, S.: It's too much for us to handle—the effect of smartphone use on long-term retrieval of family photos. Pers. Ubiquit. Comput.Ubiquit. Comput.
   27, 289–298 (2023). https://doi.org/10.1007/s00779-022-01677-x
10. Nath, A.K., Wang, A.: A survey on personal image retrieval systems. http://arxiv.org/abs/
    2107.04681, (2021). https://doi.org/10.48550/arXiv.2107.04681
11. ramesh, roshini: tech teachers and tech savvy students. https://medium.com/@rroshini239/
    tech-teachers-and-tech-savvy-students-691e4b61c7bf. Accessed 19 Sep 2023
12. Cohen, L., Manion, L., Morrison, K.: Research Methods in Education. Routledge, London
    (2007)
13. Emdad, F.B., Tian, S., Nandy, E., Hanna, K., He, Z.: Towards interpretable multimodal pre-
    dictive models for early mortality prediction of hemorrhagic stroke patients. AMIA Summits
    Transl. Sci. Proc. **2023**, 128 (2023)
14. Behera, B., Kumaravelan, G., Kumar B., P.: Performance evaluation of deep learning algo-
    rithms in biomedical document classification. In: 2019 11th International Conference on
    Advanced Computing (ICoAC), pp. 220–224 (2019). https://doi.org/10.1109/ICoAC48765.
    2019.246843
15. Li, Z.: Extracting spatial effects from machine learning model using local interpretation
    method: an example of SHAP and XGBoost. Comput. Environ. Urban Syst. **96**, 101845
    (2022). https://doi.org/10.1016/j.compenvurbsys.2022.101845
16. Feng, Q., Yuan, J., Emdad, F.B., Hanna, K., Hu, X., He, Z.: Can attention be used to explain
    EHR-based mortality prediction tasks: a case study on hemorrhagic stroke (2023). http://
    arxiv.org/abs/2308.05110. https://doi.org/10.48550/arXiv.2308.05110

17. Islam, M., Shuvo, S.S., Ahmed Shohan, J., Faruque, O.: Forecasting of PV plant output using interpretable temporal fusion transformer model. In: 2023 North American Power Symposium (NAPS), pp. 01–06 (2023). https://doi.org/10.1109/NAPS58826.2023.10318698

18. Emdad, F.B., Ho, S., Ravuri, B., Hussain, S.: Towards a unified utilitarian ethics framework for healthcare artificial intelligence. In: AMCIS 2023 Proceedings (2023)

19. Israel, G.D.: Determining sample size. Institute of food and agricultural sciences (IFAS), University of Florida, PEOD-6, pp. 1–5 (2013)

20. Corpuz, J.: The best photo organizer apps in 2024. https://www.tomsguide.com/best-picks/best-photo-organizer-apps. Accessed 07 Jan 2024

Word Embedding-Based Text Complexity Analysis

Kahyun Choi[(⊠)] [ID]

Indiana University Bloomington, Bloomington, USA
choika@iu.edu

Abstract. Text complexity metrics serve crucial roles in quantifying the readability level of important documents, leading to ensuring public safety, enhancing educational outcomes, and more. Pointwise mutual information (PMI) has been widely used to measure text complexity by capturing the statistical co-occurrence patterns between word pairs, assuming their semantic significance. However, we observed that word embeddings are similar to PMI in that both are based on co-occurrence in large corpora. Yet, word embeddings are superior in terms of faster calculations and more generalizable semantic proximity measures. Given this, we propose a novel text complexity metric that leverages the power of word embeddings to measure the semantic distance between words in a document. We empirically validate our approach by analyzing the OneStopEnglish dataset, which contains news articles annotated with expert-labeled readability scores. Our experiments reveal that the proposed word embedding-based metric demonstrates a stronger correlation with ground-truth readability levels than conventional PMI-based metrics. This study serves as a cornerstone for future research aiming to incorporate context-dependent embeddings and extends applicability to various text types.

Keywords: Readability · Text complexity · Word embedding · Pointwise Mutual Information

1 Introduction

Computational analysis of text complexity has been actively explored over a century, which produced many readability metrics and algorithms [2]. Readability metrics have served a wide range of purposes; it is critical to ensure the safety of people by providing the appropriate levels of military manuals or medical documents [2,17]; students can also benefit from the right level of reading materials for a more engaging reading experience and a better learning outcome [6,12]; many writers use readability metrics from online text analytic services, such as https://readable.com, https://textinspector.com, and https://app.grammarly.com, to increase their readerships by providing more readable content.

Computational metrics for text complexity have a long history of evolution. Traditional readability metrics, for example, Flesch reading ease, Flesch-Kincaid

I. Sserwanga et al. (Eds.): iConference 2024, LNCS 14598, pp. 283–292, 2024.
https://doi.org/10.1007/978-3-031-57867-0_21

grade, Gunning Fog index, and Coleman-Liau index, were introduced decades ago [2]. Their basic principle is that short, simple, and familiar words and sentences make text easy to read, and vice versa. The final scores are based on straightforward linguistic statistics, such as the number of characters, syllables, words, familiar words, and sentences. More recently, sophisticated word-level features have been developed to quantify concreteness and lexical cohesion, and structural features of words, e.g., syntactic complexity [11]. In addition, advanced natural language processing (NLP) technology provides a new perspective to text complexity metrics by using big text corpora and data-driven machine learning techniques [5].

In this vein, Flor et al. advanced the field by introducing a text complexity metric based on pointwise mutual information (PMI), a measure rooted in the co-occurrence of words [4]. Their examples highlighted how PMI can effectively capture semantic distances between words, thereby contributing to the overall complexity of the text. For instance, in a sentence like "The dog barked and wagged its tail," the PMI score would be relatively high (PMI=5.5) due to the frequent co-occurrence of word pairs such as "dog" and "bark" or "wag" and "tail." Conversely, a sentence like 'Green ideas sleep furiously' would yield a lower PMI score (PMI=2.2), attributed to the rare co-occurrence of pairs like "green" and "idea" or "sleep" and "furiously."

Motivated by these innovations, we recognize that both word embeddings and PMI are essentially derived from co-occurrence information [7,10,13]. However, word embeddings trained on large datasets generally capture the average contextual meaning of each word, offering great generalizability in comparison tasks. On the other hand, the pairwise scores provided by PMI estimate the relationships between word pairs, which do not generalize as much as the robustly learned discriminative word-specific representations [9]. With this understanding, we propose an advanced text complexity metric based on word embedding models.

We empirically demonstrate the merit of the proposed method. To begin with, we compare PMI and the proposed word embedding-based text complexity metrics to estimate the complexity of documents. We use OneStopEnglish [16] to evaluate the estimation by comparing it to the human-labeled, thus ground-truth readability scores. The results verify that the proposed method shows a statistically more meaningful relationship with the human-labeled complexity of the text than the PMI metrics.

2   The Proposed Text Complexity Metric

Flor et al. [4] reported that a complex document tends to have words that are semantically farther from each other. The semantic distance of words is the opposite concept of word similarity, which correlates with the co-occurrence of words in a context window. To be specific, words in a less complex text, such as "The dog barked and wagged its tail," tend to co-occur in the same sentence or adjacent sentences, while the words in a more complex text, such as "Green ideas sleep furiously," rarely co-occur.

PMI can capture this concept in a statistical way by comparing the joint probability (i.e., the co-occurrence frequency) of the two words $p(x, y)$ and their *a priori* expected co-occurrence probability based on the product of their global word frequencies $p(x)p(y)$:

$$PMI(x; y) = \log \frac{p(x, y)}{p(x)p(y)}. \tag{1}$$

Hence, for example, if two words are rarely used in the corpus, i.e., both $p(x)$ and $p(y)$ are low, while they happen to co-occur frequently, i.e., $p(x, y)$ is relatively high, it means that the two words are semantically associated.

Flor et al. [4]'s proposed method is based on the average *normalized* pointwise mutual information (NPMI) scores between all pairs of words in each document. Unlike the basic PMI, NPMI values are bounded between -1 and 1: -1 indicates that the two terms never co-occur together, while 1 indicates that the two terms always co-occur in the corpus. They went one step further and used positive normalized PMI (PNPMI), which assigns 0 to any negative NPMI score, and showed that PNPMI was a promising complexity metric.

$$NPMI(x; y) = \frac{\log \frac{p(x,y)}{p(x)p(y)}}{-\log p(x, y)},$$

$$PNPMI(x; y) = \begin{cases} NPMI(x; y) & \text{if } NPMI(x; y) > 0 \\ 0 & \text{otherwise} \end{cases} \tag{2}$$

However, word embedding models such as Word2Vec have been reported to outperform more traditional count-based models such as PMI on measuring word similarity [8]. Word embedding is a multidimensional vector representation of words, derived by a shallow neural network that learns semantic relationships between words from a large corpus. Word2Vec was introduced in 2013, followed by other embedding methods, such as GloVe and FastText [1, 10, 14]. The main characteristics of these methods are that for a pair of words x and y, the encoder function f learns their D-dimensional embedding vectors $\mathbf{z}_x$ and $\mathbf{z}_y$,

$$\mathbf{z}_x \leftarrow f(x), \quad \mathbf{z}_y \leftarrow f(y), \tag{3}$$

whose distance is more likely to be high if the pair's semantic difference is high, and vice versa. While the semantic distance of two words is hard to represent as a function, the embedding vectors often preserve it in the simple Euclidean space. For example, a cosine distance could be used to quantify the semantic distance of x and y:

$$D(x; y) = 1 - \frac{\mathbf{z}_x^\top \mathbf{z}_y}{|\mathbf{z}_x||\mathbf{z}_y|}. \tag{4}$$

Training of the encoding function f utilizes various word pairs that share similar conceptual meanings. In addition, it is typical to use "negative sampling" to expose the embedding to those learned from semantically far words as well, making the learned word representation more discriminative and robust. Therefore, it is expected that a word embedding $\mathbf{z}_x$ must contain its relationship to other words. This holistic representation is helpful when the word embeddings are compared against each other because the average semantic meanings the word carries are taken into account. On the other hand, a PMI (or its variants') value records narrower meanings of the word compared only to its counterpart. For example, since the word embeddings encode the semantics of words, a new pairwise relationship can be more robustly computed by comparing their embedding vectors, even though the pair did not appear in the corpus–PMI variants, however, consider them dissimilar words.

Finally, the proposed word embedding (WE)-based text complexity metric computes pairwise cosine distance values of all possible pairs and then calculates its average:

$$WE = \frac{1}{|\mathcal{V}|} \sum_{x,y \in \mathcal{V}} D(x; y), \tag{5}$$

where $|\mathcal{V}|$ stands for the number of all words that appear in the document.

Likewise, the similarity defined in the word embedding space is conceptually similar to PMI in that word embeddings are an implicit factorization of a word-context matrix, which can be computed based on PMI [9]. However, word embedding is superior in word similarity tasks, such as automatically evaluating the coherence of topics generated by topic modeling algorithms [3]. Hence, we expect word embedding models would be equivalent to or better than PMI variants in measuring the complexity of documents.

Note that, in the rest of the paper, we treat the PMI-based complexity measures by inverting the NPMI or PNPMI values, i.e., $-NPMI(x; y)$ and $1 - PNPMI(x; y)$, as the original scores are meant to measure the similarity of the word pairs, not their distance.

3   Experimental Studies

In this section, we present a comparative analysis between the proposed word embedding-based complexity metric and existing metrics based on pointwise mutual information (PMI), using the OneStopEnglish dataset [16].

The Dataset

Corpus with Readability Level Annotation: We use the OneStopEnglish corpus to assess the proposed text complexity metric as the dataset provides human experts' annotation of complexity levels on various news articles. The OneStopEnglish corpus comprises 189 sets of texts with three reading levels for each topic. The corpus was curated by onestopenglish.com, which is a worldwide English education service with plenty of resources for English language teachers. Participating teachers there rewrote each news article from the Guardian newspaper in three different versions: Advanced (Adv), Intermediate (Int), and Elementary (Ele). Table 1 shows three different versions of the same article example. It is known that advanced texts have positive correlations with various statistical and linguistic features, such as the number of words, Flesch-Kincaid grade level (FKGL), type-token ratio (TTR), and the average number of noun phrases (NP), verb phrases (VP), and preposition phrases (PP) [16]. We select this dataset to test the effectiveness of readability metrics because its reliability levels highly correlate with all the features (see Table 2).

Table 1. Example sentences for three reading levels [16].

Level	Example Text
Advanced (Adv)	Amsterdam still looks liberal to tourists, who were recently assured by the Labour Mayor that the city's marijuana-selling coffee shops would stay open despite a new national law tackling drug tourism. But the Dutch capital may lose its reputation for tolerance over plans to dispatch nuisance neighbours to scum villages made from shipping containers.
Intermediate (Int)	To tourists, Amsterdam still seems very liberal. Recently the city's Mayor assured them that the city's marijuana-selling coffee shops would stay open despite a new national law to prevent drug tourism. But the Dutch capitals plans to send nuisance neighbours to scum villages made from shipping containers may damage its reputation for tolerance.
Elementary (Ele)	To tourists, Amsterdam still seems very liberal. Recently the city's Mayor told them that the coffee shops that sell marijuana would stay open, although there is a new national law to stop drug tourism. But the Dutch capital has a plan to send antisocial neighbours to scum villages made from shipping containers, and so maybe now people won't think it is a liberal city any more.

Table 2. Some statistics about OneStopEnglish corpus [16]

Feature	ADV	INT	ELE
avg num. words	820.49	676.59	533.17
FKGL	9.5	8.2	6.4
TTR	0.56	0.432	0.42
avg num. NP	6.08	5.52	4.92
avg num. VP	4.49	4.03	3.49
avg num. PP	2.72	2.30	1.82

Word Embedding Models: We use eight different pretrained word embedding models supported by the toolbox, Gensim[1], to compute different types of word embeddings. The pretrained models are based on three word embedding algorithms, including Word2Vec [10], GloVe [13], and FastText [7]. The models were trained on the following large-scale sources: Wikipedia, Twitter, and internet news, with varying co-occurrence statistics. Among these, `glove-twitter` and `glove-wiki-gigaword` come in multiple versions, differentiated by their vector dimensions D. A large D typically allows more representative vectors at the cost of a potential loss of linearity in the learned vector space. To investigate the

---

[1] https://github.com/RaRe-Technologies/gensim-data#models.

impact of vector size, we experimented with three different dimensions: $D = 50$, 100, and 200.

Experimental Setup

Data Pre-processing: We employ SpaCy for tokenization and part-of-speech (POS) tagging of the OneStopEnglish corpus. We consider only content words in our analysis, as we aim to measure the complexity arising from the semantic distances between words, and content words carry greater weight in determining meaning. To calculate the WE-based complexity score for each document, we aggregate and average the cosine distances of individual pairs of words. Meanwhile, we calculate PNPMI and NPMI for each document using the Palmetto API, an open-source tool that computes NPMI based on word co-occurrence in the English Wikipedia [15].

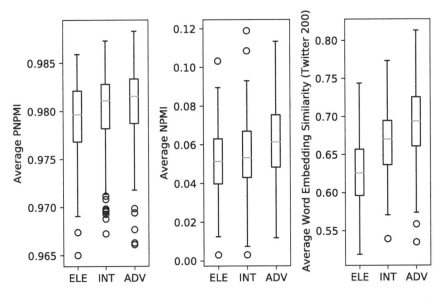

Fig. 1. Comparison of two PMI variants and one of the proposed WE similarity metrics. More widely spread boxes in the WE results indicate the proposed metric provides a stronger association with the three complexity levels (i.e., ELE, INT, and ADV).

Comparison Between the Proposed WE Complexity Metrics and PMI Variants: The experiments consist of two steps. In the first experiment, we conducted a comparison between two PMI variants, including NPMI and PNPMI, and our proposed WE complexity metric. We use the first 50 content words per document because otherwise, the number of word pairs grows intractably large for the relatively slow palmetto API. The first experiment confirmed a significant enough gap between the PMI and word embedding groups to establish the superiority of our proposed WE metric.

Comparison Among the Proposed Metrics Derived by Different WE Models: The second experiment follows to determine the best configuration among the eight pre-trained word embedding models. For this experiment, we consider all words in the documents, rather than limiting to the first 50, as computing WE vectors and their pairwise similarities is sufficiently fast.

Table 3. Comparison of Two PMI Variants and Eight Proposed WE Similarity metrics using 50 content words from each document. Each [higher reading level]-[lower reading level] entry reports the percentage of source articles where a metric returns a higher complexity score (lower similarity score) for the more advanced version of the article. avg-gap is the average of the percentages of the three pairs. Also, for each metric, the correlation coefficient score between the complexity scores and the reading levels is reported.

Models	int-ele	adv-int	adv-ele	avg-gap	Correlation Coefficient
glove-twitter-50	90%	81%	96%	89%	0.51
glove-twitter-100	92%	86%	97%	91%	0.51
glove-twitter-200	93%	86%	96%	92%	0.52
glove-wiki-gigaword-50	88%	79%	95%	87%	0.42
glove-wiki-gigaword-100	89%	81%	96%	89%	0.45
glove-wiki-gigaword-200	92%	83%	96%	90%	0.46
word2vec-google-news-300	91%	74%	93%	86%	0.42
fasttext-wiki-news-subwords-300	78%	59%	78%	72%	0.20
NPMI	56%	67%	72%	65%	0.22
PNPMI	68%	59%	68%	65%	0.17

Experimental Results

Comparison Between the Proposed WE Complexity Metrics and PMI variants: First, we compare the WE complexity metrics and NPMI and PNPMI using box plots. We report the box plot of glove-twitter-200 as the representative of the proposed method because all the WE complexity metrics except fasttext-wiki-news-subwords-300 show similar box plots. Figure 1 shows that the gaps between different reading levels are much wider in the proposed WE group than in the PMI groups. For a fair comparison to the slow NPMI and PNPMI calculation, we only use the first 50 words for the WE scores, too. These box plots show the overall superiority of the proposed WE scores. However, since a box plot aggregates all documents that belong to the same reading level, the graphs do not show how well a complexity metric distinguishes different reading-level versions derived from the same original news article.

Table 3 shows how well each metric distinguishes different reading levels of the same source article. Once again, only 50 content words from each document are used. For example, int-ele is the percentage of source articles where the intermediate version has a higher score than the elementary version, i.e., 100%

means a perfect discrimination performance. First, we observe that the average gap of those three comparisons, int-ele, adv-int, and adv-ele, summarizes that all WE-derived complexity metrics (the top 8 rows, ranging between 72 and 92%) are significantly better than the PMI variants (the bottom two rows, with an accuracy of 65%). Furthermore, the Pearson's r correlation coefficient of NPMI and PNPMI, -0.22 and -0.17, are significantly lower than those of the word embedding models, between 0.42 and 0.52 (except for the fast-text case as an outlier, 0.20).

Table 4. Comparison among the proposed metrics derived by different WE models using all words from each document instead of the first 50. Otherwise, the setup is identical to Table 3's.

Models	int-ele	adv-int	adv-ele	avg-gap	Correlation Coefficient
glove-twitter-50	98%	89%	99%	95%	0.602
glove-twitter-100	98%	92%	99%	96%	0.594
glove-twitter-200	98%	93%	99%	96%	0.597
glove-wiki-gigaword-50	98%	90%	98%	96%	0.494
glove-wiki-gigaword-100	98%	92%	99%	96%	0.534
glove-wiki-gigaword-200	98%	92%	98%	96%	0.543
word2vec-google-news-300	98%	87%	99%	95%	0.542
fasttext-wiki-news-subwords-300	90%	55%	87%	77%	0.243

Likewise, the word embedding models outperform the PMI group significantly in differentiating documents with different reading levels both per source article and regardless of source articles.

Comparison Among the Proposed Metrics Derived by Different WE models : We also compare the eight WE configurations more thoroughly. In Table 4, we repeat the same experiment done in Table 3, but on all words in the documents instead of only the first 50. Indeed, using all words led to higher scores and correlations across all pairs and pre-trained models. However, the increase in the number of words did not result in a significant change in their rankings. Overall, while fasttext-wiki-news-subwords-300 shows the lowest distinguishing power across the three pairs, the rest pre-trained models perform similarly in widening the gaps. For example, in all cases, 98% of the time, the proposed WE-based metrics succeed in distinguishing elementary-level versions from their corresponding intermediate versions, except for fasttext-wiki-news-subwords-300. When it comes to distinguishing the intermediate and advanced levels documents, glove-twitter-200 achieves the highest score, 93%. Finally, except for fasttext-wiki-news-subwords-300, with more than 98% of accuracy, all WE configurations separate the advanced and elementary versions.

We compare three different vector sizes, $D = 50, 100$, and 200, for the two WE configurations: glove-twitter and glove-wiki-gigaword, to determine the relationship between the vector size of the word embedding and the distinguishing power. Table 4 shows that there is no meaningful correlation between the two factors. Among the pre-trained word embedding models, `glove-twitter` models show higher distinguishing power in terms of Pearson's r correlation coefficient scores. Although their correlation coefficient scores are almost equivalent, `glove-twitter- 50` showed the highest score, 0.602.

4   Conclusion and Future Work

This study proposed a new text complexity metric that measures the average pairwise distance between words, relying on the assumption that more complex documents tend to have words that are semantically far from each other, as studied in Flor et al.'s work using PMI-based word similarity metrics. This study adopted the metric after modification but with greater generalizability, which was achieved by redefining the semantic distance between the two words in the word embedding space. Thanks to the representational power of word embeddings, the proposed metric showed superior performance on readability level estimation tasks, We investigated the complexity pattern of the OneStopEnglish dataset, which offers three readability levels for the same article. Our proposed method demonstrated a stronger statistical correlation with the dataset's expert-labeled readability scores than existing PMI-based approaches. In future work, we will explore other complexity metrics based on context-dependent word embeddings, and see the relationships to extended types of text.

Acknowledgments. This work was supported by RE-252382-OLS-22 from the Institute of Museum and Library Services.

References

1. Bojanowski, P., Grave, E., Joulin, A., Mikolov, T.: Enriching word vectors with subword information. Trans. Assoc. Comput. Linguist. **5**, 135–146 (2017)
2. DuBay, W.H.: The principles of readability. Impact Information (2004)
3. Fang, A., Macdonald, C., Ounis, I., Habel, P.: Using word embedding to evaluate the coherence of topics from twitter data. In: Proceedings of the 39th International ACM SIGIR Conference on Research and Development in Information Retrieval, pp. 1057–1060 (2016)
4. Flor, M., Klebanov, B.B., Sheehan, K.M.: Lexical tightness and text complexity. In: Proceedings of the Workshop on Natural Language Processing for Improving Textual Accessibility, pp. 29–38 (2013)
5. François, T., Miltsakaki, E.: Do NLP and machine learning improve traditional readability formulas? In: Proceedings of the First Workshop on Predicting and Improving Text Readability for Target Reader Populations, pp. 49–57 (2012)
6. Hiebert, E.H.: Readability and the Common Core's staircase of text complexity. TextProject Inc, Santa Cruz, CA (2012)
7. Joulin, A., Grave, E., Bojanowski, P., Douze, M., Jégou, H., Mikolov, T.: Fasttext. zip: compressing text classification models. arXiv preprint arXiv:1612.03651 (2016)

8. Levy, O., Goldberg, Y.: Neural word embedding as implicit matrix factorization. Adv. Neural. Inf. Process. Syst. **27**, 2177–2185 (2014)

9. Levy, O., Goldberg, Y., Dagan, I.: Improving distributional similarity with lessons learned from word embeddings. Trans. Assoc. Comput. Linguist. **3**, 211–225 (2015)

10. Mikolov, T., Chen, K., Corrado, G., Dean, J.: Efficient estimation of word representations in vector space. arXiv preprint arXiv:1301.3781 (2013)

11. Napolitano, D., Sheehan, K.M., Mundkowsky, R.: Online readability and text complexity analysis with textevaluator. In: Proceedings of the 2015 Conference of the North American Chapter of the Association for Computational Linguistics: Demonstrations, pp. 96–100 (2015)

12. Nelson, J., Perfetti, C., Liben, D., Liben, M.: Measures of text difficulty: testing their predictive value for grade levels and student performance. Council of Chief State School Officers, Washington, DC (2012)

13. Pennington, J., Socher, R., Manning, C.: GloVe: global vectors for word representation. In: Proceedings of the 2014 Conference on Empirical Methods in Natural Language Processing (EMNLP), Doha, Qatar, pp. 1532–1543. Association for Computational Linguistics (2014). https://doi.org/10.3115/v1/D14-1162. https://aclanthology.org/D14-1162

14. Pennington, J., Socher, R., Manning, C.D.: Glove: global vectors for word representation. In: Proceedings of the 2014 Conference on Empirical Methods in Natural Language Processing (EMNLP), pp. 1532–1543 (2014)

15. Röder, M., Both, A., Hinneburg, A.: Exploring the space of topic coherence measures. In: Proceedings of the Eighth ACM International Conference on Web Search and Data Mining, pp. 399–408 (2015)

16. Vajjala, S., Lučić, I.: Onestopenglish corpus: a new corpus for automatic readability assessment and text simplification. In: Proceedings of the Thirteenth Workshop on Innovative Use of NLP for Building Educational Applications, pp. 297–304 (2018)

17. Zheng, J., Yu, H.: Assessing the readability of medical documents: a ranking approach. JMIR Med. Inform. **6**(1), e8611 (2018)

Community Informatics

Towards a Better Understanding of Cyber Awareness Amongst Migrant Communities in Australia

Misita Anwar[1,2]([mail]) [ID], Manika Saha[1] [ID], Gillian Oliver[1] [ID], Mohamed Ibrahim[2] [ID], and Carsten Rudolphr[1] [ID]

[1] Monash University, Victoria, Australia
{Misita.anwar,Manika.Saha,Gillian.Oliver,
Carsten.Rudolph}@monash.edu
[2] Swinburne University, Victoria, Australia
mohamedibrahim@swin.edu.au

Abstract. Cyber-attack incidents are increasing while there is limited understanding of cyber safety and security awareness amongst the migrant communities in Australia. Using a mixed methodology, we design a small-scale pilot study to understand the level of cyber security awareness among three migrant communities in Australia - Indonesia, Bangladesh, and Somalia. One of our significant findings is that almost all the participants have experienced some level of cyber security and crime-related issues, while about 80% of the participants are not aware of how and where to report their incidents for legal action. Our focus-group discussion highlights participants' perceptions, experiences, and some socio-cultural and context-specific cybersecurity events, including cyberbullying and racism they face as migrants in Australia. Finally, we discussed how an enhanced understanding of culture and human context-specific factors could be helpful in designing and delivering proper awareness-raising interventions for sustainable cyber security systems for migrant communities.

Keywords: Cyber Awareness · Migrant Communities · Cyber Security · Australia

1 Introduction

The increasing frequency of cyber security risks due to the widespread use of ICT has prompted a global need for enhanced cyber awareness among citizens. A cybersecurity analysis estimates that by 2025, the worldwide cost of cybercrime will have risen from over USD 6 trillion in 2021 to USD 10.5 trillion [25]. Despite the complexity of the factors that contribute to cybercrime, human factors consistently stand out as the primary cause. A recent research report on cyber investigations of breaches implicated human error as a factor in 95% of security incidents [18]. The inadvertent and naive behaviours of computer users remain the foremost frequent cause of information security breaches [26]. Despite these alarming statistics, our understanding of the extent to which individuals differ in their awareness, knowledge, and cybersecurity behaviour, when confronted with prevalent cyber threats and hazards is still quite limited.

I. Sserwanga et al. (Eds.): iConference 2024, LNCS 14598, pp. 295–310, 2024.
https://doi.org/10.1007/978-3-031-57867-0_22

Migrant communities account for 30% of the Australian population. A sizable 30% of Australia's total population are immigrants, making up a significant part of the country's demographic landscape. Recent data on cybercrime in Australia highlights the growing vulnerability of migrant communities, highlighting the need to better understand and address the specific cybersecurity issues they face [36]. It is critical to recognize the exposure of these migrant communities to online threats, such the alarming increase in cyber racism and scamming incidents. While cyber safety and digital advice are available to these communities, a critical question arises regarding their cultural appropriateness. Cultural factors significantly influence individuals' interactions with technology, making it crucial to consider cultural appropriateness when designing effective cybersecurity awareness initiatives for these communities [1]. For example, in collectivist cultures, frequently found in many Eastern and African countries, individuals tend to define themselves in terms of their relationships and social connections to others to which they belong.

In designing awareness-raising interventions and measuring their impact, it is important to acknowledge that migrant communities have different cyber-related needs depending on their background and language. For instance, risk perception can be a widespread phenomenon, so it is critical that initiatives to raise awareness of it consider cultural differences in their design. This research aims to explore migrant communities' cyber security awareness, considering cultural background and situational context, high-lighting the limited understanding of individual differences in cyber security behaviour. We used mixed methods to understand the status of cyber awareness amongst migrants in Australia. First, we conducted three focus groups with three communities (Indonesia, Bangladesh, and Somalia) to understand their cultural contexts and perception of general cyber-related information and incidents. Based on the initial findings from these focus groups, we adapted a questionnaire from a human aspect focused cybersecurity awareness survey [27] to collect data from these three communities. Then we conducted a small-scale pilot survey to measure the current status of cyber security awareness among these three communities in Australia.

Our paper makes a significant contribution to our understanding of cyber awareness within immigrant communities by shedding light on human factors including fundamental cultural values, like trust and relationships, which influence participants' overall cyber awareness. Our study also reveals migrants' groups experiences of cyber racism and bullying and the lack of knowledge and understanding regarding cybersecurity issues and reporting. To our knowledge, this is the first empirical investigation across diverse socio-cultural backgrounds in migrant communities in Australia. The structure of this paper is organised as follows: after reviewing relevant literatures, we move on to a detailed explanation of the research methods. The results are presented first, collated into survey results, and focus group findings, followed by a discussion. Finally, in the conclusion section, we offer recommendations, including the role of public libraries in promoting cyber awareness culture, and suggestions for future work.

2   Review of Literature

The extensive development of communication technologies is increasingly adopted by individuals, organizations, and specific communities worldwide. The borderless nature and revolution of cyberspace have become an integral part of modern society. Cyberspace has shaped how individuals and organisations can access different applications, including communications, transactions, and communications, for their daily activities [29]. Despite all the benefits of cyber security, the threat of various types of cybercrime is growing steadily [37]. Some of these cybercrimes include violation of personal privacy, identity theft, harassment, malware (infection of a device, e.g., virus) and money transfer-related fraud. According to a Global State Information security survey report, the average financial loss due to security incidents is 2.5 million dollars annually [5]. People in developing countries are more prone to threats of cyber risks than in the developed world due to their limited access and knowledge of technology and context-specific challenges [14].

A study by the Global Cyber Security Capacity Centre at the University of Oxford highlighted (based on user compliance behavior towards information system security) that cyber security awareness activities are not effectively successful in changing people's behavior [1]. This study reviews behavioural psychology literature and applied psychological theories to understand the reasons behind the challenges of changing effective cyber security behaviors and awareness. Then, the research informs five potential factors that should be considered during the design of a cyber-security awareness initiative. One of the critical factors highlighted by this study is security awareness initiatives must be more than providing information to users – it needs to be targeted and diverse culture and context-specific to the different populations. To investigate how to enhance cybersecurity awareness, De Bruijn and Janssen [10] found that awareness-building messages and materials design need to be personalized, which can target strategies to develop different messages for multiple audiences, including multicultural communities.

Human aspects, including a person's demographic attributes such as age, gender, personality, and cultural contexts of cybersecurity, pose as much of a risk as technical aspects [17, 19]. According to Metalidou et al. [23] *"Many times organisations overlook the human factor, a factor that security depends upon. Technology is often falsely perceived as the immediate answer to Information Security problems. Information Security is primarily a human factors problem that remains unaddressed"* (p. 425). Recent studies highlight the scarcity and importance of understanding human-centric socio-cultural values and experiences of non-western populations to tailor educational and training initiatives to tackle the current cyber security and safety-related challenges [17, 22]. Additionally, the majority of the recent literature on cybersecurity awareness related to behavioural study has mainly focused on Western participants and their cultural influences, missing crucial aspects of culture and values of many in the non-Western context [17, 22].

One-third of the Australian population are migrants. Many come from developing countries, including South Asia, East Asia, and Africa. Studies have already acknowledged that developing countries have different contexts and characteristics and face different levels of cybersecurity challenges. For example, due to a lack of knowledge of technology, cyber security laws and regulations, African countries face tremendous cyber-related crimes and issues [3, 34]. The one-size-fits-all approach will not suit the purpose of building cybersecurity awareness due to diverse and different context-sensitive factors in developing countries compared to developed countries [8, 21]. Migrant communities are prone to online attacks with increasing cyber racism and scamming incidents. A study of small-scale migrant traders in South Africa found that most of them experienced hacking while using their mobile devices for transacting and most reported a lack of knowledge of cybersecurity and were therefore vulnerable to further threats [20]. In Austria, documented racist incidents online are increasing and they appear to be linked to a massive increase in cyber hate against refugees and migrants [31]. Cyber safety and digital advice are available to migrant communities, however they may not be developed considering migrants' cultural context, whereas studies have found that cultural factors are considered as one of the most important factors in cyber security awareness design [1]. For example, in more collectivist cultures, such as those found in many eastern countries, individuals' perception of self tends to be defined in terms of their relationships and social group which often affect trust, an important attitude to consider in cyber security.

While there has been abundant literature found where the cybersecurity-related knowledge, attitude and practices has been used to explore cybersecurity awareness and behaviors; human aspects of the information security questionnaire is a relatively new tool to measure cybersecurity-related awareness [26, 37]. Most of the studies have been focused on either individual [12, 35] or organizational levels [9, 15, 30] of awareness. To the authors' best knowledge, there has not been an attempt to understand the status, challenges, and socio-cultural perceptions of diverse migrant communities in Australia especially those coming from developing countries. Hence, this study explores current awareness status and socio-cultural aspects and experience of cybersecurity-related issues among three migrant communities in Australia.

3   Methods

The study employed survey and focus group discussion conducted among three migrant communities from developing countries, namely Indonesia, Bangladesh, and Somalia. They represent a convenience sampling where the researchers have access to the communities. The authors' Australian institution granted ethical approval for the study. A survey questionnaire was developed based on the human aspect of information security [27], distributed to 90 participants from the three migrant communities via Google Form of which 75 returned their responses (Table 1). The participants are conveniently approached by researchers' community contacts. The survey responses were analyzed using descriptive statistics to evaluate the cybersecurity knowledge level among the sample population. Our primary selection criteria for survey respondents were first-generation immigrants aged 18 and up from the three countries. Focus groups were conducted with 6–7 participants from three Australian migrant communities to understand their cultural backgrounds, situational contexts, and perceptions of cybersecurity-related issues. Focus groups were conducted via Zoom, starting with a presentation outlining the study's purpose. The discussions were audio or video recorded, transcribed, and analyzed using thematic analysis [2].

Table 1. Participants' number and gender from the three communities.

Migrant Community	FGD		Survey		Country code
	Male	Female	Male	Female	
Indonesia	2	5	14	14	IND
Bangladesh	3	3	11	11	BDS
Somalia	4	2	11	14	SOM
Total	17		75		

4 Findings

This paper aims to understand and evaluate the level of cyber security awareness within migrant communities. We also explore migrant-specific contexts of cyber security risks focusing on those originating from developing countries. The results of the survey and three focus groups are presented below to give an overview of the current state of cyber-security experiences and awareness among the three target migrant communities in Australia.

4.1 Lack of Information and Awareness

Brief Overview of Participants' Knowledge on Cyber Security Awareness. Regarding the knowledge of cyber safety from our survey, 57% of Indonesian participants strongly agree that criminals can access their devices through cyberspace, whereas less than 50% of Bengali and Somali participants believe such. More than 50% of Indonesian and Bengali participants strongly agree that their personal information can be stolen when playing online games or using apps online. Still, less than 40% of Somali participants strongly agree with this statement. Surprisingly, 24% of Somali participants are not sure whether their bank account can be compromised (through cyberspace) or not, whereas Indonesian and Bengali groups have no doubts.

Indonesian participants have more ability (54%) to handle computer and smartphone devices, whereas many Somali participants rate their knowledge (33%) as moderate (see Fig. 1). Students (90%) have more ability to use smartphone devices than the employed (78%) or unemployed (66%). About 83% of participants use banking channels to transfer money, and the rest use non-banking channels. Almost 21% of participants from all these three countries report or tell the online incident to their family or friends, 26% of total participants inform bank and credit card providers about the online incident and 9% report it to the Australian Cybercrime authority.

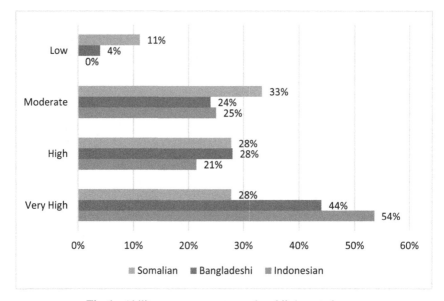

Fig. 1. Ability to use computers and mobile/smart phones.

More than 70% of Bangladeshi and Indonesian participants don't share their personal information (date of birth, location) when using social media or online games (see Fig. 2). Still, this percentage is slightly lower in the Somali community (67%). Almost 90% of participants don't share their passwords with other people, but more than 25% share their passwords with family members. About 25% are unsure whether they can identify the phishing email/message or not. About one-third (30%) of Somalian participants post content that makes them cyber victims, whereas no Indonesian and Bengali participants post such things. About 33% of Somalian participants don't know there is an antivirus program, and 38% of Somalian participants don't have any anti-virus program installed on their computers.

Among the Bangladeshi community, only 14% of Bengali participants do not use an antivirus program, while 100% of Indonesian participants use an antivirus program. More than 20% of total participants from these three countries don't use their passwords on their devices. Most of these participants from the three communities use their personal information in their passwords and the same password on their devices. Around half of the participants (50%) from these three countries write down their passwords to remember them.

Limited Access to Information and Knowledge. In terms of cyber security discussion from our focus group, it seems the three communities were aware of various issues in general but clearly did not appreciate the seriousness of the cyber security, data privacy, and protection problems. The consensus from the cybersecurity and safety aspects was an acceptance of the problem as part of living in the digital age and not a problem or a risk that can be mitigated. Even when the discussion moved into discussing solutions or ways to avoid cybersecurity problems, it was felt many in the focus group were really relaxed and less concerned about the risks. Privacy issues were discussed, and this

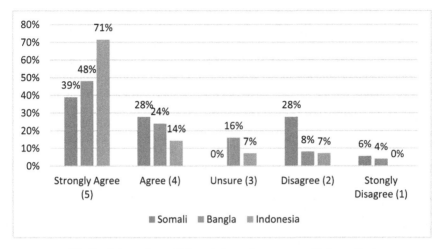

Fig. 2. Cyber privacy (I do not give out my personal information)

was the hardest issue to explain to the participants as many were not aware of privacy protection options on social media platforms or were unable to set the necessary flags or opt out. Sharing personal information with others seems to be common and was not expressed as a major concern.

More importantly, it seems many in the community do not even understand the concept of data privacy. It is important to mention for example, many Africans participants assume data collection is something the government authorised and therefore many freely give their personal data including the social media outlets.

"I have nothing to hide, so I'm not worried about data privacy. What can they do with my personal details? I am who I am and there is nothing they can do about that!" [P3, SOM]

Major issues the focus group highlighted were the limited information available to the community about the online and social media ecosystem.

"I get so many unwanted calls, I have to change my SIM card and now they are following me although I have changed my SIM cards, maybe I have to change the phone as well." [P5, SOM]

From our focus groups, we found that participants have limited access to cybersecurity and safety related information. We found there are four areas where information was missing, namely i) what to do after experiencing any cyber incidents; ii) where to go to get help; iii) how to protect themselves from cyber incidents; and iv) how to understand and respond to complex online topics. Our survey data indicated that half of the Somalian participants (57%) do not read the online policy and terms and conditions, which is much lower than among Bengali (32%) and Indonesian (29%) participants. In our focus groups, most of our participants mentioned that they do not read and understand the terms and conditions of most of the online activities. One participant said,

"They use too many technical words which are not possible to understand by the general people like us. They use too-long sentences as well!" [P1, IND).

Sometimes, they just agree without understanding anything as they need to complete their online activities which could be access to a website for information, communication, buying or sending money for their daily necessities. One participant highlighted,

"If you don't agree with their consent, you can't move to the next page, sometimes, that's why we just agree whatever they ask us to accept!" [P6, BDS].

The use of complex topics, themes and messages in cyber spaces was also noted by the participants, *"We don't have that time to read all the big messages for giving our consent for using a website"* [P7, IND]. Some of our participants think the design of complex messages are intentional by the designers. One of our participants reported that,

"Most of the consent-related messages are so hard, it's very difficult to understand. I think they do it intentionally so that people will not understand and will accept everything" [P2, SOM]

The limited knowledge and information on where to go for getting help echoed many times by the participants, *"Where can we go and listen to what we should do?"* [P5, BDS]. Another participant highlighted the need for more information dissemination among the citizens, especially among the migrants in Australia, to enhance information and awareness of cyber-security-related information and help desks. The participant noted,

"I don't know where to go if my information is stolen by others, where should I go and defend? these types of information need to disseminate more among the people" [P4, IND].

Furthermore, in most transaction related cases, people go to the bank for help but have yet to get any help from them. The participants noted the frustration of not getting help from the bank several times. One participant reported,

"Banks can't trace why this kind of thing happens from Australia, who did it, who is the authority, they can't do anything of the preventive type" [P1, SOM].

In a nutshell, our survey findings highlighted participants from three different countries' general understanding of cyber-security-related awareness. However, we noted that Somali participants appeared to be less aware of cyber-security and safety issues than our other participants. Our survey shows overall an optimistic scenario regarding migrants' knowledge, attitudes, and practices regarding cyber-security. From the focus groups, we found our participants had limited knowledge and information about cybersecurity-related incidents, privacy, help and protection guidelines and authorities' information to communicate for further assistance.

4.2 Trust and Relationships

From our survey we found that more than 50% of Indonesian participants face scamming in cyberspace, but this percentage is much lower in Somalian (43%) and Bengali (36%) communities. Related to this, more than 60% of Bengali and Indonesian participants strongly agree they perceive the risk of sharing their personal information on social sites, whereas only 43% of Somalian participants believe such. More than 75% of Indonesian and Bengali participants add unknown persons to their friend list, whereas 53% of Somalian participants do such. More than 50% of Indonesian participants strongly agree they are aware of the danger when clicking on banners, advertisements, and pop-up screens online. In contrast, the percentage is much lower than in Bengali (36%) and Somalian (29%) participants. Almost 90% of Indonesian and Bengali participants don't respond to unknown emails/SMS/messages, whereas cyber safety awareness regarding responding to unknown emails and messages is lower (52%) among Somalian participants.

However, in our focus group, we found our three groups of participants strongly believe in trust and relationships in terms of communication on any online platforms, especially in social media. It seems participants trust and consider some of the content they read online, which is a significant concern, especially medical and financial advice. Some of our participants have suffered financial losses and, in some cases, made decisions based on misleading content they have read online. Conspiracy theories about covid19 and vaccination were also significant problems highlighted. Most of our participants mentioned that for online communications and money transactions, their communities generally use phone numbers, date of birth, national ID numbers and addresses, which can easily be hacked. Lack of knowledge about using unique passwords was assumed as the main reason for online hacking and scamming. One of our Indonesian participants highlighted that,

> *"There is a link between Facebook and banking. Three pieces of information you need to know to hack a bank account include your date of birth, address, and phone number. People put everything on social media and hackers follow people. I know one of my colleague's bank accounts had been hacked using these three pieces of information. Hackers got information from FB."* [P6, IND]

All participants were aware of fake news, especially on Facebook (FB). However, migrant communities who are using social media, particularly the older generations, perceive information provided in social media as more trustworthy than other age groups. Half of the participants mentioned that their parents usually trust the information on social media instead of evaluating it. The following is an example of a participant's experience.

> *"...there are so many fake news coming now FB...our parents don't try to under-stand its fake news...they believe as it is there it's true...why someone will put fake news on fb, they don't understand...we do crosscheck the information with others but they don't know how to cross-check the news with others or from somewhere else but they actually believe everything..."* [P4, BDS].

Our participants shared several bad experiences with their parents regarding online money transfers. One of our Indonesian participants shared,

"My father got a message from the messenger that one of his friends is in big trouble and he needs money. My father was so serious and already prepared that he will send money to his friend. Then my brother tried to make him cool down and asked let's talk with your friend and find out what he needs and how he is now. Then my father called his friend and found he is completely okay and he doesn't need any money. My father did not understand why it happened and my uncle as well...they were ...." [P1, IND].

Participants emphasized experiencing various fraud issues, primarily related to money, including deceptive messages through social media, emails, and phone texts. Some encountered fraud while making online purchases, noting that certain emails and messages appeared so authentic that they were initially perceived as accurate information. A participant from Somalia shared,

"One of my friends trusted an advertisement for renting a house and she lost a large amount of money by trusting that agency!" [P6, SOM].

All of our participants confirmed that, in Australia, one of the most common fake messages they regularly receive by phone calls or messages is regarding money laundering issues. One participant shared that,

"I received a phone call a few days ago. Someone over the phone was saying, "you have a case on money laundering issues. We are now investigating the issue. We need some information. She asked for my full name with pronunciation. Then she asked my date of birth! I don't know how they got our mobile number and information. However, somehow, they get our information and make us their target." [P3, IND].

Another noteworthy instance of fraudulent activity involved impersonating government authorities such as the tax office and police. This tactic was particularly concerning to the participants, given the gravity of interacting with legitimate government entities. This was mentioned by a Bangladeshi participant:

"I often receive calls from the income tax office saying that they ask that I didn't pay my tax and the police will come to take me. This incident is most common in Australia" [P1, BDS]

One of the interesting findings from our study is that as the migrants do not know where to go for help when experiencing cyber-security-related issues, they first seek assistance from their friends and family. Most of the participants mentioned relying on friends when confronted with harassment and fraud on social media. Highlighting the strength of community bonds among migrants in Australia, they express confidence in receiving assistance from their communities in many situations. One participant from Indonesia said that,

"I first asked my friend who knows technological issues better than anyone...I talked to who knows better and after discussing with him how we can keep my Facebook account and how can I make my password stronger, I enhanced the

security of my account. I didn't know before how to do true factor authentication on Facebook. From him, I first knew how to do that..." [P2, IND].

In summary, our findings show that 'trust and relationships' is one of the most important human factors related to cyber safety among our migrant participants. This is mainly grounded in migrant communities' cultural contexts where participants easily believe and rely on each other for anything. Migrant communities rely on their friends and family to get information and solutions rather than seeking available government assistance.

4.3 Cyber Harassment and Racism

From our survey, about 11% of Indonesian participants strongly disagree that there would be any bullying and harassment in cyberspace. However, about 100% of Bengali participants agree there is bullying and harassment in cyberspace, whereas 80% of Somali participants agree. In our focus groups, many participants experienced harassment and racist remarks on social media, and a few were aware of the need to secure personal information. Harassment was the primary negative experience mentioned when using social media platforms. Many stories were shared during the focus groups, where the common issue is a lack of technical know-how and financial literacy. Five of the six female participants mentioned that they faced some sort of harassment on social media, especially on Facebook. For example,

"I got a message from the Messenger and someone wrote that, 'some of your personal pictures are with me. I was scared and then I deactivated my account. I changed my password and was detached from my FB account for a long time." [P2, BDS].

However, participants also highlighted that this kind of harassment incidents are also common in their home countries. From our focus groups, one common issue raised by most participants was the experience of racism as migrants. Our participants reported being exposed to multi-faceted forms of racial harassment on social media platforms. According to our participants, they faced three types of racism experiences: ethnicity-, religion-, skin colour and language-related racial behaviours. One participant highlighted the ethnicity-related bullying that he several times faced on social media by noting,

"I love to take and upload pictures on Facebook. One of my Aussie friends said to me you people take too many pictures and share them on social media. She said it's too funny for them. I felt very bad as she mentioned not about me but my home country! Feels like she is a racist" [P4, SOM]

The harassment and bullying of migrant communities' colour and language were also highlighted many times by our participants. The feeling of frustration of not being recognised as an Australian citizen after living and getting citizenship was also echoed many times by our migrant participants. One participant shared his frustration and anger by noting,

"I am with a photography group on Facebook. Someone one day commented on my photography and asked me which country I am from. I said I am Australian. I have citizenship here, what's wrong if I say I am Australian? Then a group of people in that photography group was bullying me about my colour, language, and photography style. They are simply just racist!" [P3, BDS]

Participants emphasized the prevalence of religious-based online bullying, particularly among Muslim communities, contributing to a negative global perception of Muslims, including in Australia. Indonesian participants, mainly from Muslim communities, shared diverse stories about their daily challenges as Muslim migrants in Australia, both online and in-person. A participant selling Islamic clothes in a Facebook marketplace group was being subjected to bullying by other vendors in the group. A lot of racist of comments were directed towards her products, including Islamic swimming garments that were said to be unsuitable to Australian culture or racist remarks like *"go back to your country!"* [P5, IND].

In summary, our participants shared other online harassment and racism experiences as migrants they face in Australia. They highlighted these experiences are more often occurring online than in their face-to-face daily lives as it is easy to comment on and difficult for them to trace or say something online. Participants also highlighted how these experiences negatively impact their self-esteem, confidence, and mental health as migrants in Australia.

5   Discussion

The preceding findings show that there is a general understanding of cyber safety and security amongst migrant participants from the three countries of origin, in particular those from Indonesia and Bangladesh. Participants from Somalia indicated as having less awareness of cyber safety issues around safeguarding personal information including passwords. This is a critical issue in terms of cyber privacy [8] as it is considered the main point of entry for individuals to be subjected to cybercrime. Different behaviours of cyber safety of people between countries of origin can also be attributed to their education background. Most Indonesian and Bangladeshi migrated to Australia through skilled visas and therefore would hold some type of qualifications. The majority of Somalians-born arrived in Australia through refugee visas [11].

Evidence of the lack of information about cyber safety incidents amongst migrant communities is also found. Not knowing what to do and where to report cyber safety incidents makes it difficult for victims to get support from relevant authorities to prevent future incidents or to take further actions. Cyber safety information is publicly available from relevant governments, for example, Federal Police (AFP) and Australian Cyber Security Centre (ACSC). However, based on our findings we would further emphasise for these resources to be tailored to ensure accessibility for people from culturally and linguistically diverse backgrounds. One such notable example can be seen from eSafety commissioner efforts in understanding the underlying issues that make certain individuals and groups are disproportionately at risk of online harm [13].

Our findings enforce what has been discussed in other studies [7, 15, 27] about the need to consider cultural and contextual factors in building cyber security awareness.

Research has found that culture can predict some security behaviour such as privacy attitude [16]. Rarely making an attempt to read and understand privacy terms and conditions when using an app is an example of privacy attitude. Language may be one barrier. Some apps and websites only translate the general content into several different languages, but keep the legal agreements in the default, official language. We also found that in some cultures, information perceived as coming from the authority is considered trustworthy and a legal document like terms and conditions is often considered as authoritative.

The findings showed that migrant communities have strong connections and trust in their relationship with family and friends. There is a tendency for participants from the three cultures to trust information presented on social media. Research shows that there are cultural differences in user perceptions of the trustworthiness of information presented in social media [6]. Their study in Spain and Lebanon suggests that having a collectivist culture, Lebanese tend to rely more on others' interactions with information including sharing and liking and subsequently influences their trust in social media as an information channel. This aligns with the collectivist characteristic of the three countries of origin for the migrant participants.

Our findings reveal that participants in Australia experienced various forms of harassment and racism online, which were consistent with similar experiences in other studies. For instance, Schultze-Krumbholz et.al [32] study on cyberbullying in a multicultural context found that ethnic/racist based cyber harassment seems prevalent especially among first generation migrant adolescents. While perceptions of cyberbullying may differ between cultures, there is an understood definition of what constitutes the experience, and it is of concern as it diminishes one's sense of wellbeing. Many countries' governments recognize that the socio-political and cultural necessity of cyber security awareness is an important factor in the wellbeing of their citizens [33].

Our study underscores vital human factors, including cultural contexts and beliefs, shaping migrant communities' views, trust, and relationships on online platforms. These, combined with a noted lack of information and knowledge, present challenges to cybersecurity. Additionally, ethnicity and religion emerge as crucial human factors influencing how migrant communities perceive and engage in online communications. A better understanding of migrant communities' voices, especially those with refugee background and with limited education, can help design community and culture-specific cyber-security awareness programmes for sustainable social inclusion. Our research also reinforces the importance of incorporating human factors into cybersecurity topics, awareness-related activities, and initiatives [7, 23, 24].

Governments and civil society organizations should collaborate closely with migrant communities to understand their concerns and provide education on accessing information and assistance for cyber-security incidents. Information institutions, like public libraries, can play a crucial role in fostering a culture of cybersecurity awareness, especially in Australia. Chang and Hawamdeh [4] stated that one of the main roles of information professionals is that users are provided with adequate information and understanding about threats to their online privacy and security In Australia, and many other countries, libraries have been at the forefront of digital literacy programs and training, often in collaboration with community partners.

6 Conclusion

Cybersecurity is a relatively new and growing field that thus needs more effort and research to improve. There is emergent work within information systems and human-centered computing that also addresses concerns regarding cultural and human factors related to technology and cyberspace in broader social contexts. In this study, we consider accommodating the experiences and perceptions of migrants to design cybersecurity-related awareness programs in Australia. We also discuss potential implications and design considerations that might have more general applicability to promote cyber security awareness among the minority and marginalized populations in a country. As there is limited formal assessment and research that has been undertaken among the migrants in Australia, our study brings the urge to do more country-wide assessments and research in the near future. We believe context-specific cyber security awareness development and design can help protect and ensure the robustness of instantaneous communications, financial transactions, and access for information to all citizens, including migrants.

This study has limitations from the small sample size and potential bias introduced by the convenience-based sampling method; thus, the findings may not be broadly applicable to other migrant communities. Nevertheless, the study is valuable for offering insights into the current state of knowledge and awareness within migrant communities. Additionally, it sheds light on certain human factors that contribute to increased risks associated with migrants' engagement in cyberspaces. This aspect, often overlooked in previous studies, adds significance to the research within the field. We recommend that future research and community engagement for designing cyber-security-related awareness programs must involve diverse migrant communities to understand their cultural contexts. These cultural contexts must include migrant communities' social, political, economic, and cultural aspects of understanding and practicing cyber-security-related issues. Finally, the findings from our study could be used to further investigations for bringing a set of cultural and other human factors and their impact on cyber security.

References

1. Bada, M., Sasse, A.M., Nurse, J.R.: Cyber security awareness campaigns: why do they fail to change behaviour? (2019). arXiv preprint arXiv:1901.02672
2. Braun, V., Clarke, V.: Thematic Analysis. American Psychological Association, Washington (2012)
3. Calandro, E., Berglund, N.: Unpacking cyber-capacity building in shaping cyberspace governance: the SADC case (2019). https://researchictafrica.net/wp/wp-content/uploads/2020/07/GIGAnet-presentation-v02.pdf
4. Chang, H.C., Hawamdeh, S. (eds.). Cybersecurity for Information Professionals: Concepts and Applications (2020)
5. Coopers, P.: Turnaround and transformation in cybersecurity: key findings from the global state of information security survey 2016 (2015)
6. Dabbous, A., Barakat, K.A., Navarro, B.Q.: Fake news detection and social media trust: a cross-cultural perspective. Behav. Inf. Technol. 41(14), 2953–2972 (2022). https://doi.org/10.1080/0144929X.2021.1963475
7. Dawson, J., Thomson, R.: The future cybersecurity workforce: going beyond technical skills for successful cyber performance. Front. Psychol. 9, 284332 (2018)

8. Da Veiga, A., Loock, M., Renaud, K.: Cyber4Dev-Q: calibrating cyber awareness in the developing country context. Electron. J. Inf. Syst. Dev. Countries **88**, e12198 (2021)
9. Dharmawansa, A.D., Madhuwanthi, R.A.M.: Evaluating the information security awareness (ISA) of employees in the banking sector: a case study. In: proceedings 13th International Research Conference, General Sir John Kotelawala Defence University, Ratmalana, Sri Lanka, pp. 147–154, 15 October 2020).
10. De Bruijn, H., Janssen, M.: Building cybersecurity awareness: the need for evidence-based framing strategies. Gov. Inf. Q. **34**(1), 1–7 (2017)
11. Department of home affairs, Somalia born community information summary (2016). https://www.homeaffairs.gov.au/mca/files/2016-cis-somalia.pdf
12. Egelman, S., Harbach, M., Peer, E.: Behavior ever follows intention? A validation of the Security Behavior Intentions Scale (SeBIS). In: Proceedings of the SIGCHI Conference on Human Factors in Computing Systems (CHI 2016), pp. 5257–5261. ACM (2016). https://blues.cs.berkeley.edu/wp-content/uploads/2016/02/article1.pdf
13. eSafety Commissioner, Protecting Voices At Risk (2020). https://www.esafety.gov.au/sites/default/files/2020-08/Protecting%20voices%20at%20risk%20online_0.pdf
14. Grobler, M., Dlamini, Z., Ngobeni, S., Labuschagne, A.: Towards a cyber security aware rural community. In: Proceedings of the 2011 Information Security for South Africa (ISSA) Conference, Hayatt Regency Hotel, Rosebank, Johannesburg, South Africa (2011). http://hdl.handle.net/10204/5183
15. Hadlington, L., Binder, J., Stanulewicz, N.: Fear of missing out predicts employee information security awareness above personality traits, age, and gender. Cyberpsychol. Behav. Soc. Netw. **23**(7), 459–464 (2020). https://doi.org/10.1089/cyber.2019.0703
16. Halevi, T., Memon, N., Lewis, J., Kumaraguru, P., Arora, S., Dagar, N., Chen, J.: Cultural and psychological factors in cyber-security. In: Proceedings of the 18th International Conference on Information Integration and Web-based Applications and Services, pp. 318–324 (2016)
17. Henshel, D., Sample, C., Cains, M., Hoffman, B.: Integrating cultural factors into human factors framework and ontology for cyber attackers. In: Nicholson, D. (eds.) Advances in Human Factors in Cybersecurity. Advances in Intelligent Systems and Computing, vol. 501, pp. 123–137. Springer, Cham (2016). https://doi.org/10.1007/978-3-319-41932-9_11
18. IBM global technology services. IBM Security Services 2014 Cyber Security Intelligence Index: Analysis of cyber-attack and incident data from IBM's worldwide security operations, Research Report, IBM (2014). https://i.crn.com/sites/default/files/ckfinderimages/userfiles/images/crn/custom/IBMSecurityServices2014.PDF
19. Jeong, J. Mihelcic, J., Oliver, G., Rudolph, C.: Towards an improved understanding of human factors in cybersecurity. In: IEEE 5th International Conference on Collaboration and Internet Computing (CIC), Los Angeles, CA, USA, pp. 338–345 (2019). https://doi.org/10.1109/CIC48465.2019.00047
20. Kariuki, P., Ofusori, L.O., Subramaniam, P.R.: Cybersecurity threats and vulnerabilities experienced by small-scale African migrant traders in Southern Africa. Secur. J. 1–30 (2023). https://doi.org/10.1057/s41284-023-00378-1
21. Lewis, M.: Game or shame - how to teach employees to be cybersecurity aware. MOBILECORP, 22 September 2020. https://www.mobilecorp.com.au/blog/game-or-shame-how-to-teach-employees-to-be-cybersecurity-aware
22. Nisbett, R.: The geography of thought: how Asians and westerners think differently... and why. Simon and Schuster (2004)
23. Metalidou, E., Marinagi, C., Trivellas, P., Eberhagen, N., Skourlas, C., Giannakopoulos, G.: The human factor of information security: unintentional damage perspective,". Procedia Soc. Behav. Sci. **147**, 424–428 (2014)
24. Moon, T.: Organizational cultural intelligence: dynamic capability perspective. Group Org. Manag. **35**(4), 456–493 (2010)

25. Morgan, S.: Cybercrime to cost the world $10.5 trillion annually by 2025, Special Report: cyber warfare in the c-suite, Cybercrime magazine (2020). https://cybersecurityventures.com/cybercrime-damages-6-trillion-by-2021/

26. Parsons, K., McCormac, A., Butavicius, M., Pattinson, M., Jerram, C.: Determining employee awareness using the human aspects of information security questionnaire (HAIS-Q). Comput. Secur. **42**, 165–176 (2014)

27. Parsons, K., Calic, D., Pattinson, M., Butavicius, M., McCormac, A., Zwaans, T.: The human aspects of information security questionnaire (HAIS-Q): two further validation studies. Comput. Secur. **66**, 40–51 (2017). https://doi.org/10.1016/j.cose.2017.01.004

28. Reid, R., Van Niekerk, J.: From information security to cyber security cultures. In: IEEE Information Security for South Africa, pp. 1–7 (2014)

29. Reid, R., Van Niekerk, J.: Decoding audience interpretations of awareness campaign messages. Inf. Comput. Secur. **24**(2), 177–193 (2016). https://doi.org/10.1108/ICS-01-2016-0003

30. Saridewi, V.S., Sari, R.F.: Feature selection in the human aspect of information security questionnaires using multi cluster feature selection. Int. J. Adv. Sci. Technol. **29**(7 Special Issue), 3484–3493 (2020)

31. Schäfer, C., Schadauer, A.: Online fake news, hateful posts against refugees, and a surge in xenophobia and hate crimes in Austria. In: Refugee News, Refugee Politics, pp. 109–116. Routledge (2018)

32. Schultze-Krumbholz, A., Pfetsch, J.S., Lietz, K.: Cyberbullying in a multicultural context—forms, strain, and coping related to ethnicity-based cybervictimization. Front. Commun. **7**, 846794 (2022). https://doi.org/10.3389/fcomm.2022.846794

33. Siponen, M.: Five dimensions of information security awareness. ACM SIGCAS Comput. Soc. **31**(2), 24–29 (2001)

34. Van der Spuy, A.: Collaborative cybersecurity: the mauritius case. (Policy Brief No. 1; Africa Digital Policy). Research ICT Africa (2018). https://researchictafrica.net/wp/wp-content/uploads/2018/11/Policy-Brief-ADPP-N-1-Collaborative-Cybersecurity-Mauritius-Case.pdf

35. Velki, T., Šoli, K.: Development and validation of a new measurement instrument: the behavioral-cognitive internet security questionnaire (BCISQ). Int. J. Electr. Comput. Eng. Syst. **10**, 19–24 (2019). https://doi.org/10.32985/ijeces.10.1.3

36. Voce, I., Morgan, A.: Cybercrime in Australia 2023. AIC reports Statistical Report 43. Australian Institute of Criminology (2023)

37. Zwilling, M., Klien, G., Lesjak, D., Wiechetek, L., Cetin, F., Basim, H.N.: Cyber security awareness, knowledge, and behavior: a comparative study. J. Comput. Inf. Syst. **2**(5), 99–110 (2016) (2020). https://doi.org/10.1080/08874417.2020.1712269

Towards a Critical Data Quality Analysis of Open Arrest Record Datasets

Karen M. Wickett[(✉)] [iD] and Jarrett Newman

School of Information Sciences, University of Illinois at Urbana-Champaign, Illinois, USA
{wickett2,jn23}@illinois.edu

Abstract. This short paper presents early results from a data quality analysis of an open arrest record dataset from the Los Angeles Police Department. We use data quality metrics from a framework for the evaluation of open government data. We present our results, along with critiques and discussion of the metrics, and describe an ongoing project to analyze the data quality of police arrest datasets and connect data quality to critical accounts of information systems.

Keywords: Data Quality · Open Government Data · Critical Information Studies

1 Introduction

The data used and produced by police departments reflect interactions between communities and criminal justice systems. In recent years, political pressure on police departments [1] and an interest in open government data [2] have led to greater publishing and sharing of police data. The City of Los Angeles Police Department (LAPD) publishes 23 datasets on the city's open data portal [3], including datasets on crime, arrests, traffic stops and calls for service. Interactions with police and police information systems are significant personally and socially and have widely ranging consequences for individuals [5] and communities [6]. The analysis presented in this paper is part of an on-going project to understand how systematic oppressive forces such as racial bias play out in police information systems. The research questions of the project focus on how data representation choices shape the public perception of police and crime in a community, and how well the datasets serve community members.

Given the intertwining of nature of public perception, open government data, and police operations, one of our project goals is to develop and refine methods of analysis for police information systems that enable us to trace power relationships and better understand how data collection and processing contribute to structural inequalities. Therefore, we use a critical data modeling approach that bridges social critique and the technical realities of information systems.

Critical data modeling uses tools and techniques from systems analysis to build technical close readings of information systems and data objects [7]. Data quality analyses characterize the "fit" of some "collection of data" for the purposes of a user for a task in a particular context [8]. Our project is exploring data quality frameworks as critical

I. Sserwanga et al. (Eds.): iConference 2024, LNCS 14598, pp. 311–318, 2024.
https://doi.org/10.1007/978-3-031-57867-0_23

data modeling tools and we take the position from the W3C Data on Web Best Practices Working Group that "that there is no objective, ideal definition" of data quality [9]. In this paper we present preliminary results from a data quality analysis of LAPD's "Arrest Data from 2020 to Present" dataset as it appears on the open data portal [4]. We use metrics from [10], which provides a data quality framework designed for open government data and demonstrates its use on municipal data.

It is important to note that in the context of critical data modeling, data quality metrics should not be presented as absolute or objective. They should function as starting points for technically informed close readings of an object or system. Additionally, data quality analysis requires consideration of stakeholders [9]. Our work deliberately foregrounds technically naïve users and laypersons, and we are particularly interested in foregrounding the people represented in an arrest record dataset (i.e., arrested individuals) as stakeholders in the dataset.

2   Data Quality Analysis

2.1   Methods and Dataset

The dataset "Arrest Data from 2020 to Present" (the Arrest Record Dataset) is published with an open license on the City of Los Angeles open data portal [4]. We downloaded a version of the dataset that was updated August 30, 2023. The data quality results shown here were determined using this version of the dataset. We used OpenRefine [11] to create filtered and faceted views of the dataset as described below.

The data quality framework [10] organizes data quality into seven characteristics: traceability, currentness, expiration, completeness, compliance, understandability, and accuracy. Figure 1 shows a summary of the data quality metrics and definitions.

Table 3
Metric definitions and description.

Characteristic	Metric	Level	Description
Traceability	Track of creation	Dataset	Indicates the presence or absence of metadata associated with the process of creation of a dataset.
	Track of updates	Dataset	Indicates the existence or absence of metadata associated with the updates done to a dataset.
Currentness	Percentage of current rows	Cell	Indicates the percentage of rows of a dataset that have current values. It means that they don't have any value that refers to a previous or a following period of time.
	Delay in publication	Dataset	Indicates the ratio between the delay in the publication (number of days passed between the moment in which the information is available and the publication of the dataset) and the period of time referred by the dataset (week, month, year).
Expiration	Delay after expiration	Dataset	Indicates the ratio between the delay in the publication of a dataset after the expiration of its previous version and the period of time referred by the dataset (week, month, year).
Completeness	Percentage of complete cells	Cell	Indicates the percentage of complete cells in a dataset. It means the cells that are not empty and have a meaningful value assigned (i.e. a value coherent with the domain of the column).
	Percentage of complete rows	Cell	Indicates the percentage of complete rows in a dataset. It means the rows that don't have any incomplete cell.
Compliance	Percentage of standardized columns	Cell	Indicates the percentage of standardized columns in a dataset. It just considers the columns that represent some kind of information that has standards associated with it (i.e. geographic information).
	eGMS Compliance	Dataset	Indicates the degree to which a dataset follows the e-GMS standard (as far as the basic elements are concerned, it essentially boils down to a specification of which Dublin Core metadata should be supplied)
Understandability	Five star Open Data	Dataset	Indicates the level of the 5 star Open Data model in which the dataset is and the advantage offered by this reason.
	Percentage of columns with metadata	Cell	Indicates the percentage of columns in a dataset that has associated descriptive metadata. This metadata is important because it allows to easily understanding the information of the data and the way it is represented.
	Percentage of columns in comprehensible format	Cell	Indicates the percentage of columns in a dataset that is represented in a format that can be easily understood by the users and it is also machine-readable.
Accuracy	Percentage of accurate cells	Cell	Indicates the percentage cells in a dataset that has correct values according to the domain and the type of information of the dataset.
	Accuracy in aggregation	Cell	Indicates the ratio between the error in aggregation and the scale of data representation. This metric only applies for the datasets that have aggregation columns or when there are two or more datasets referring to the same information but in a different granularity level.

Fig. 1. Data quality metric definitions and descriptions from Vetrò, et al. [10].

2.2 Preliminary Data Quality Analysis

We present our data quality observations of the dataset according to the characteristics specified in [10], with commentary on our observations of the Arrest Record Dataset and the data quality framework.

Traceability

The traceability metrics "Track of creation" and "Track of updates" assess the metadata connected to a dataset that gives information about the creation and updating of that data. The Arrest Record Dataset has metadata on the creation of the dataset in the form of the dataset description, which states "This dataset reflects arrest incidents in the City of Los Angeles from 2020 to present. This data is transcribed from original arrest reports that are typed on paper and therefore there may be some inaccuracies within the data." The dataset metadata, shown in Fig. 2, also includes "date created" information. However, the metadata is not at a level of detail sufficient for interpreting the data, especially for building interpretation that trace power relationships or dependencies in the data. For example, from examination of the dataset, "Charge" clearly uses alphanumeric code systems not indicated in the metadata. Furthermore, transcription processes between the internal police databases and the data published on the portal are totally opaque.

Updates are described on the portal with dates indicating "Updated" (which is shown in large bold text), "Data last updated" and "Metadata last updated." While this information is present, no detailed versioning information is provided. Users cannot see the frequency of updates, only the date of the most recent update to the data or metadata. Users also cannot see any details about updates, for example how many rows were added, whether data cells changed, or what metadata was updated.

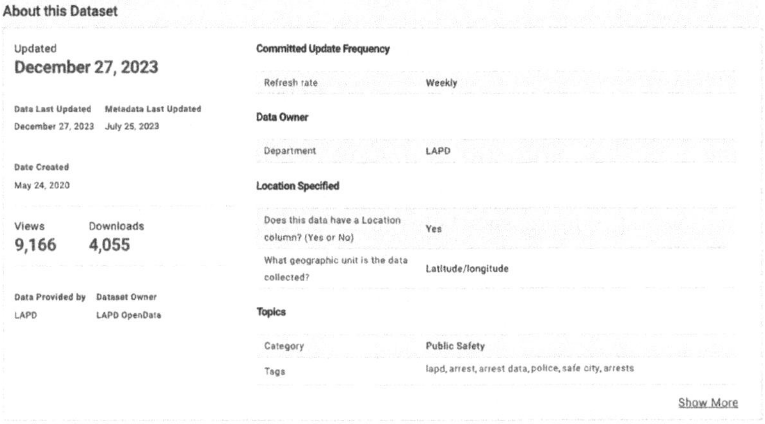

Fig. 2. Screenshot of summary metadata, taken January 2024

Currentness

For currentness, "percentage of current rows" is calculated on the difference between rows that are current and those that are not current. From what we can observe and measure from the dataset as published, according to this metric, all rows in the dataset are current. We determined "publication delay" by filtering the dataset on "Arrest Date" to find the most recent arrests in the data and comparing that date to the publication date of the dataset version. The August 30, 2023, version of the dataset has rows with arrest dates of August 26, 2023, a four-day publication delay. During the period of mid-August to early September 2023, the dataset was updated on August 22, August 30, and September 13. Therefore, for this period, the delay in publication is significantly lower than the frequency of updates, which represents an extremely low publication delay.

Expiration

The Arrest Record Dataset has the form of observational data—it records information about an event that happened at some point in the past—which is not a genre of data that is fluid over time. While it is possible that rows in the dataset may be updated over time, versioning information is not available. Detecting changes to rows will require longitudinal study that collects dataset versions over time. Since this dataset records previous events, there is no expiration of the data, and we did not assess "Delay after expiration."

Completeness

The completeness metrics "Percentage of complete cells" and "Percentage of complete rows" characterize the degree to which a dataset is filled out according to its data model. For completeness in terms of cells, we calculated the number of cells in the dataset by multiplying the number of rows (238,473 rows) by the number of columns (25 columns) to reach the number of cells (5,961,825 cells). Using OpenRefine to find blanks, we determined that there were 398,840 blank cells, meaning 93.32% of the cells were complete.

For completeness in terms of rows, we used OpenRefine to filter the dataset by "Blank values per column" and found 11 columns that had at least one blank cell, as shown in Fig. 3. This showed that 161,379 rows had at least one column with missing data. Therefore, 77,094 rows, or 32.33% of rows, were complete. Certain columns seem to play a significant role in the discrepancy between cell completeness and row completeness. For example, "Cross Street" is blank for 122,502 rows, or 51.37% of rows in the dataset. However, for 14 columns, every row has data. Therefore, we can see that completeness varies strongly across columns in this dataset, which is an area for further study.

Compliance

The metrics "Percentage of standardized columns," "eGMS Compliance," and "Five-star Open Data" assess the degree to which a dataset uses and meets the requirements of standards for the recording and publishing of data. The use and impact of standards is a focal point for critical data studies, so we aimed for a complete assessment of standardization across the dataset. We refined this metric by dividing standardized columns into two types: those that use or refer to external codes or data formats, and those that appear to use an internal standard. The use of internal standards was determined by reading the

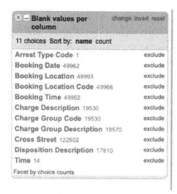

Fig. 3. Blank values per column in the August 30, 2023, dataset version

dataset metadata and counting unique data values for each column in OpenRefine. Our analysis showed that 20 columns (68%) use some degree of standardization. 6 Columns used external codes or data formats: Arrest Date, Charge, LAT, LON, Location, and Booking Date. 11 columns used internal codes or categories: Report ID, Report Type, Area ID, Area Name, Reporting District, Sex Code, Descent Code, Charge Group Code, Charge Group Description, Arrest Type Code, Charge Description, Disposition Description, Booking Location, and Booking Location Code. 5 columns showed no evidence of using standards: Time, Age, Address, Cross Street, and Booking Time.

The metric "eGMS compliance" reflects the presence of metadata about the source, creation date, category, title, description, identifier, publisher, coverage, and language of a dataset [12]. The Arrest Record Dataset metadata, shown above in Fig. 2, includes source, date of creation, category, title, description, and publisher. The dataset metadata does not include explicit elements for identifier, coverage, or language. Although coverage is not explicitly stated in structured metadata, the temporal and geographic coverage of the dataset is conveyed in the dataset description text which states "This dataset reflects arrest incidents in the City of Los Angeles from 2020 to present."

The metric "Five-star Open Data" is derived from the linked data design recommendations published by the W3C [13] and assesses availability of a dataset in terms of openness, reusability and entity linking. The Arrest Record Dataset is available on the web with an open license and is available for download in a non-proprietary format. Since the dataset does not use RDF or URIs, or link to other sources, we assess that the dataset is at Level 3 of the Five-star Open Data model.

Understandability

The metrics "Percentage of columns with metadata" and "Percentage of columns in comprehensible format" reflect a concern with the reusability of open government data. In order for data to be reused in different contexts and for different purposes, that data must be documented with metadata and in comprehensible format. The Arrest Record Dataset has metadata available for all 25 columns (100%) of the dataset. While the metadata is present, there are issues with the usefulness and accuracy of this metadata. For example, "Report ID" is described as "ID for the arrest" with no further information about the sources of the data values that appear in the dataset. Examination of the dataset shows a pattern of 7-digit values for Report ID that correlate with the Report Type "BOOKING" and 9-digit values for Report ID that correlate with the Report Type "RFC" (meaning "released from custody"). This pattern strongly suggests that there are distinct information sources or processes for the Report ID, but there is no detail given in the metadata.

Our data quality analysis is grounded in the assumption that lay persons, including community members who may be represented in the dataset should be acknowledged as stakeholders. Therefore, our definition of "columns in comprehensible format" requires that data should be comprehensible to a layperson. In other words, data should be meaningful when read directly from the dataset (with access to metadata), and without further access to external references (such as penal codes) or processing. By this definition, we determined that 16 columns (64%) were in a comprehensible format: Report Type, Arrest Date, Time, Area Name, Age, Sex Code, Descent Code, Charge Group Description, Arrest Type Code, Charge Description, Disposition Description, Address, Cross Street, Booking Date, Booking Time, and Booking Location. 9 columns were not in a comprehensible format: Report ID, Area ID, Reporting District, Charge Group Code, Charge, LAT, LON, Location, and Booking Location Code. The comprehensibility and usability of this information is another area for continuing work.

Accuracy

The data quality metric "Percentage of accurate cells" assesses individual data cells, and "Accuracy in aggregation" reflects the accuracy of columns that aggregate data from other sources that use "a different granularity level." Since we are only considering the Arrest Record Dataset in the context of the City of Los Angeles open data portal, and it does not aggregate information in any columns, we only discuss "Percentage of accurate cells" here.

For a large dataset like the Arrest Record Dataset, accuracy is challenging to assess in an intuitive sense—the degree to which a dataset reflects external reality without error. The authors of [10] reflect on this challenge and their use of the data quality model refined accuracy to "Percentage of syntactically accurate cells," shifting focus to datatype conformance. An analysis of syntactic accuracy of a previous version of the Arrest Record Dataset [7] showed that while syntactic accuracy is high, especially for temporal and geographic columns, those columns also consistently show semantically inaccurate data that reflects the use of default values for missing data.

The accuracy issues described in [7] persist in the August 30, 2023, version of the dataset. For example, every row in the dataset has a value for Arrest Date that includes date and time information, and every cell in this column has time information (12:00:00 AM) that conflicts with information in the Time column. While the dataset publishers may have intended to only include time information in Time and use Arrest Date for date information, this inaccurate information sets a threshold for "Percentage of accurate cells." One entire column out of 25 (4% of cells) is inaccurate, therefore no more than 96% of the cells in the dataset can be accurate. The fact that Arrest Date combines seemingly accurate date information with obviously inaccurate time information also demonstrates the complexity of determining accuracy, even at the cell level. Similarly, 4,623 rows in the dataset use the geo-located point (0,0) for location, which appears across 3 columns (LAT, LON, and Location), resulting in another 13,869 cells we know are inaccurate. This brings the possible accurate cell count down to 95.77%. While the (0,0) point is noted as a convention for missing data in the metadata, a direct reading of dataset frames it as an inaccuracy. Those rows can be easily filtered during visualization, but that will raise questions about the kinds of biases that would then be introduced.

3   Conclusions and Continuing Work

We have presented results from an ongoing project to develop critical readings of police information systems. As we are continuing our analysis of the LAPD open data products and the City of Los Angeles open data portal, we are interrogating the processing of these data. The data portal does not provide information about the processes through which data is published or the people or positions in the LAPD that interact with this data. Additionally, we are examining the relationships between city departments and corporations such as Tyler Technologies, the company who owns the data platform that the portal is built on [14].

We plan to conduct longitudinal analysis of dataset versions to detect changes in rows over time. In examining Location values in this data quality analysis, we found that (0,0) appeared as a location in 4,640 rows in a version of the dataset downloaded in September 2022, while it appeared in 4,623 rows in the August 30, 2023, version of the dataset. This decrease indicates that individual rows are updated during dataset updates. To fully analyze such cases, we are downloading newly updated versions and using OpenRefine and other tools to find and analyze changes to rows within the dataset.

Columns in the dataset vary strongly in terms of completeness. As we continue our project, we will examine the dataset to investigate patterns of incompleteness across the columns. "Blank Values by Column" shows shared or similar numbers of rows with missing data that we will characterize systematically to understand dependencies in the data. For example, the columns Booking Date and Booking Time are blank in 49,962 rows, while Booking Location is blank in 49,993 rows and Booking Location Code is blank in 49,966. We would expect an exceptionally large number of rows without booking information, as not all arrests lead to a person being booked into a detention facility. In fact, 49,962 rows in the dataset have the Report Type "RFC", which means "released from custody." So certain blank values do not indicate lower quality data. However, from examination of these numbers it would seem that some RFC reports include Booking Locations, which may indicate a semantic inaccuracy or other quality issue in the dataset.

As we continue this work, we will extend our analysis to arrest datasets from other municipalities. We are identifying candidate datasets through the Police Data Accessibility Project [15] and we will conduct comparative analyses of data quality. We aim to develop methods that provide rich interrogation of police data that foregrounds community members and arrested individuals as stakeholders. We are working toward critical readings of police information systems and data products that connect technical aspects of system design to the impact of policing on communities and human lives.

References

1. Brayne, S.: Predict and Surveil Data, Discretion, and the Future of Policing. Oxford University Press, New York (2020)
2. Currie, M.: Participation in the city: A typology of open government data use. In: Proceedings of iConference 2013 (2013). http://hdl.handle.net/2142/42062
3. Los Angeles Open Data. https://data.lacity.org/. Accessed 15 Sep 2023
4. Arrest Data from 2020 to Present. https://data.lacity.org/Public-Safety/Arrest-Data-from-2020-to-Present/amvf-fr72. Accessed 15 Sep 2023
5. Currie, M., Paris, B. S., Pasquetto, I., Pierre, J.: The conundrum of police officer-involved homicides: counter-data in Los Angeles county. Big Data Soc. **3**(2) (2016). https://doi.org/10.1177/2053951716663566
6. Jefferson, B.: Digitize and punish: Racial criminalization in the digital age. University of Minnesota Press, Minneapolis (2020)
7. Wickett, K.M.: Critical data modeling and the basic representation model. J. Assoc. Inf. Sci. Technol. 1–11 (2023). https://doi.org/10.1002/asi.24745
8. Tepandi, J., et al.: The data quality framework for the estonian public sector and its evaluation. In: Hameurlain, A., Küng, J., Wagner, R., Sakr, S., Razzak, I., Riyad, A. (eds.) Transactions on Large-Scale Data- and Knowledge-Centered Systems XXXV, LNCS, vol. 10680, pp. 1–26. Springer, Berlin (2017). https://doi.org/10.1007/978-3-662-56121-8_1
9. Data on the Web Best Practices: Data Quality Vocabulary. W3C Working Group Note 15 December 2016. https://www.w3.org/TR/vocab-dqv/
10. Vetrò, F., Canova, L., Torchiano, M., Minotas, C.O., Iemma, R., Morando, F.: Open data quality measurement framework: definition and application to open government data. Gov. Inf. Q. **33**, 325–337 (2016)
11. OpenRefine. https://openrefine.org/. Accessed 15 Sep 2023
12. e-Government Metadata Standard, Version 3.1 29 August 2006. https://cdn.nationalarchives.gov.uk/documents/information-management/egms-metadata-standard.pdf. Accessed 15 Sep 2023
13. Star Linked Data. https://www.w3.org/2011/gld/wiki/5_Star_Linked_Data. Accessed 15 Sep 2023
14. Tyler Technologies. https://www.tylertech.com/. Accessed 15 Sep 2023
15. Police Data Accessibility Project. https://pdap.io/index.html. Accessed 15 Sep 2023

Reading Habits and Inter-generational Influence of Women with Child-Raising Obligations in Rural Areas

Yi Xiao[ID] and Shijuan Li[(✉)][ID]

Peking University, Beijing 100871, People's Republic of China
{xyxyi,shijuan.li}@pku.edu.cn

Abstract. The national reading campaign in China is a strategically important initiative aiming at promoting citizens' reading literacy. It has been recognized that the need to specifically target at rural areas, which shows lower reading levels compared to the national average. Family involvement is one of the crucial elements in driving reading promotion efforts. This study utilizes data from the Individual Confirmation database and the Child Proxy database of China Family Panel Studies (CFPS), and combines theories from sociology and pedagogy field related to family education and inter-generational transmission. This study employs descriptive statistics and structural equation modeling to examine the current state of women reading status in rural areas, as well as incorporates various factors such as educational perceptions, educational participation, offspring personality, and offspring educational performance to validate models of inter-generational influence on reading habits. The findings indicate that women in rural areas with child-raising responsibilities exhibit lower overall reading rates and volumes compared to the general population, although their reading behavior surpasses the regional average in the country. Notably, the study reveals that the reading behavior of these women significantly influences their offspring's reading behavior and academic achievements through four dimensions: parenting perceptions, educational participation, family relationships and family expectations.

Keywords: Rural women · Reading · Inter-generational Influence

1 Introduction

Reading constitutes a fundamental activity facilitating the acquisition of knowledge and information, a practice rooted in the emergence of written language. In this scholarly exposition, the term reading is defined as follows: a social behavior, a pragmatic process, and a psychological endeavor aimed at extracting meaning from written language and symbolic representations [20].

This study is funded by CNSSF (No. 23BTQ018).

The findings of the National Reading Survey (NRS) conducted in China over the past six years reveal a marginal increase in overall reading engagement and pace among rural denizens. Nevertheless, these metrics still significantly lag behind their urban counterparts. Within the rural demographic, special attention should be directed towards women, who encounter additional impediments in accessing reading resources. Gender inequality disproportionately affects women, and their traditional familial roles position them as pivotal figures in the educational development of their offspring. Consequently, an examination of the intergenerational impact of reading habits among rural women on the educational attainment of their progeny becomes imperative in comprehending the role of reading in individual growth within the familial sphere. This inquiry also affords us an opportunity to elucidate the mechanisms involved in the inter-generational transfer of cultural capital [17, 24, 30].

2   Literature Review and Research Design

2.1   Literature Review

In preceding research endeavors, investigations into the reading habits of women in rural areas have exhibited a somewhat fragmented and non-systematic character. Scholars have predominantly employed qualitative case studies and interviews as their data collection and analysis methods. The primary focal points of these studies encompass reading advocacy initiatives targeting rural women, the intrinsic value and significance of reading in rural women's lives, and the correlation between individual traits and reading engagement [5, 22, 23, 28]. Additionally, narratives featuring rural women as central characters have garnered considerable attention from researchers, albeit without delving into the actual reading habits of rural women concerning such literature. Nevertheless, the investigation of such narratives reflects the cultural capital-driven empowerment of women [1, 21, 33]. Scholars in China have expressed considerable concern regarding the constraints faced by rural women in their reading pursuits, highlighting factors such as cultural literacy, reading attitudes, technological infrastructure, and societal perceptions [29, 35].

At the rural level, efforts to promote reading have witnessed notable advancements, both in theory and practice. The theoretical dimension primarily involves the assimilation of theories from adjacent disciplines, encompassing welfare pluralism theory, activity theory, and bioecology theory [10, 19, 27]. Furthermore, authors have devised a rural reading promotion model that deconstructs the reading behaviors and their determinants among rural residents, especially children [2]. This model serves as the foundation for summarizing strategies to advance reading in rural areas. On the practical front, the promotion of reading largely centers on children, with services emphasizing the provisioning of resources, infrastructural enhancements, and other fundamental amenities. The approach strategically integrates online and offline services, harnessing contemporary technologies to facilitate accessibility and enhance engagement through video content and digital reading materials [6, 31].

2.2 Research Methods and Materials

This study aims to address the following research question: (1) What is the current status of basic reading levels of women's groups in rural areas? The focus is on the role of literacy promotion in overcoming the bottleneck of grassroots outreach and improving resource utilisation. (2) Focusing on family-related factors and using the educational concepts and behaviors of the mother's generation as a mediator, this study explores the ultimate impact of the mother's reading behaviors on the offspring with the concept of *inter-generational transmission* within the purview of sociology [3,9], and analyzes the role of reading in class mobility. Building upon existing research that examines the transference of parental reading habits to their offspring's reading proclivities [17,25,30], this study places particular emphasis on the impact of reading on children's educational achievements and personal development to build the theoretical framework. The research design is visually represented in Fig. 1.

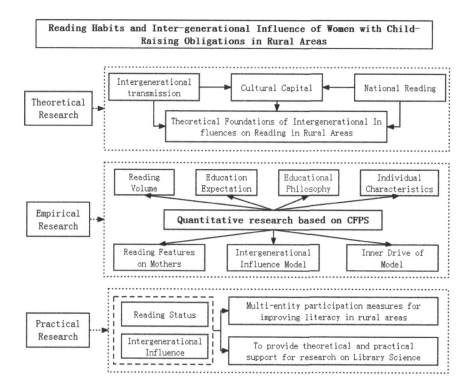

Fig. 1. Research Design

Sample selection for this study was predicated on rural household registration and offspring age, leveraging data from the 2020 China Family Panel Studies (CFPS). Descriptive statistics were employed to scrutinize the core reading characteristics of young and middle-aged rural women, comparing them to the broader population. Additionally, this analysis sought to identify the principal factors impeding the cultivation of reading habits among rural women, as delineated in extant literature. To empirically test the theoretical hypotheses concerning the inter-generational influence of reading among rural women [4,7,8,11,13–16,18,26,32,34], structural equation modeling (SEM) was employed. Ultimately, a listwise approach was utilized to retain 1791 valid samples devoid of missing data. In this research endeavor, we employed the Mplus statistical software to conduct a comprehensive analysis of our meticulously curated dataset. Our analysis incorporated the Maximum Likelihood with Robust Standard Errors (MLM) estimation technique for models involving continuous variables, while the Weighted Least Squares Mean and Variance-Adjusted (WLSMV) method was applied to models featuring categorical variables. Figure 2 delineates the underlying theoretical model.

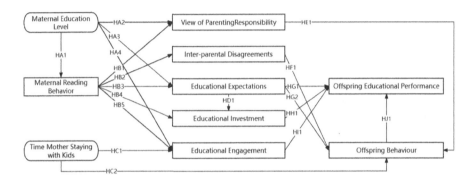

Fig. 2. Hypothesis of Inter-generational Influence Model of Women with Child-Raising Obligations in Rural Areas

3   Findings

The mothers' generation has a low reading rate and a low level of engagement (Reading Rate = 29.7%, Reading Volume = 1.56), while the overall reading rate of the sample was 35% and they read an average of 2.49 books. However, their reading behavior surpasses the average level in rural areas (Reading Rate = 25.3%, Reading Volume = 1.45). Concerning the offspring generation, family education expectations primarily revolve around aspirations for upward social mobility, although overall, there remains a preference for maintaining a stable life environment. For instance, 70.9% of the mothers expect their children to obtain an undergraduate education, while only 13.4% expect them to pursue postgraduate education and beyond. And the most sought-after professions include teachers (20.8%) and healthcare professionals (17.7%). This constraint hinders families from advancing to higher levels of expectation. Moreover, families allocate less investment towards their offspring (Investment Rate = 12%), prioritizing the attainment of favorable outcomes within the natural environment.

With the structural equation modeling, Table 1 presents the outcomes of our efforts to fit structural and measurement models for two distinct aspects of the maternal generation's reading behavior: reading habits and reading volume. The results pertaining to the fit indices fall within the desired ranges, affirming the adequacy of the models under consideration. Consequently, we deem these models to be statistically acceptable for our research purposes. On the other hand, Table 2 and Fig. 3 provide a comprehensive presentation of the fully standardized solutions stemming from our two structural models. These standardized solutions furnish a clearer understanding of the relationships and pathways elucidated within the structural framework of our study.

Based on the standardized solutions, maternal education level has a positive impact on maternal reading behaviour, educational expectations, and educational engagement. However, it has a negative impact on perceptions of parenting responsibility. Maternal reading behaviour has a significant impact on inter-parental disagreements and positively affects maternal educational investment and educational participation. Additionally, the time that a mother spends with her child has a positive impact on her educational participation but a negative impact on the child's behaviour. The way mothers perceive their parenting responsibilities and educational expectations has a positive impact on their children's behaviour, while inter-parental disagreements have a negative effect. Educational expectations, investment, participation, and offspring behaviour all significantly influence offspring educational performance [12].

Table 1. The Fit of the Measurement Model and the Two Structural Models in SEM

Model	X^2	df	X^2/df	RMSEA	SRMR	CFI	TLI
Measurement Model	45.026	19	2.370	0.028	0.017	0.993	0.989
Model 1	279.778	103	2.716	0.031	–	0.944	0.927
Model 2	264.492	103	2.568	0.030	0.030	0.959	0.946

4 Discussions

4.1 Interpretation of the Model Results

First of all, the reading behavior of the mother's generation is affected by the level of education, but the level of education does not affect the quantity of reading by the mother's generation, so while paying attention to the quality of education in rural areas and the improvement of women's education level, it is also necessary to closely promote reading promotional activities to enhance

Table 2. The Result of the Two Structural Models

Path	Estimate(M1)	Estimate(M2)	S.E.(M1)	S.E.(M2)	Sig(M1)	Sig(M2)
HA1	0.403	−0.035	0.027	0.055	0.000***	0.519
HA2	−0.115	−0.130	0.031	0.028	0.000***	0.000***
HA3	0.095	0.095	0.028	0.024	0.001***	0.000***
HA4	0.139	0.132	0.031	0.017	0.000***	0.000***
HB1	−0.064	−0.018	0.039	0.035	0.103	0.611
HB2	0.094	−0.024	0.030	0.010	0.002**	0.022*
HB3	0.065	−0.013	0.036	0.022	0.071	0.555
HB4	0.135	0.019	0.025	0.014	0.000***	0.169
HB5	−0.007	0.043	0.030	0.012	0.004**	0.560
HC1	0.309	0.275	0.036	0.015	0.000***	0.000***
HC2	−0.126	−0.128	0.027	0.024	0.000***	0.000***
HD1	0.055	0.076	0.018	0.026	0.002**	0.004**
HE1	0.233	0.239	0.028	0.031	0.000***	0.000***
HF1	−0.132	−0.132	0.024	0.027	0.000***	0.000***
HG1(Chinese)	0.241	0.240	0.018	0.025	0.000***	0.000***
HG1(Math)	−0.149	−0.148	0.020	0.023	0.000***	0.000***
HG2	0.108	0.094	0.025	0.029	0.000***	0.001***
HH1(Chinese)	0.028	0.033	0.026	0.015	0.288	0.026*
HH1(Math)	−0.043	−0.053	0.023	0.022	0.062	0.017*
HI1(Chinese)	0.126	0.101	0.024	0.021	0.000***	0.000***
HI1(Math)	−0.120	−0.103	0.024	0.022	0.000***	0.000***
HJ1(Chinese)	0.239	0.207	0.023	0.026	0.000***	0.000***
HJ1(Math)	−0.317	−0.288	0.024	0.024	0.000***	0.000***

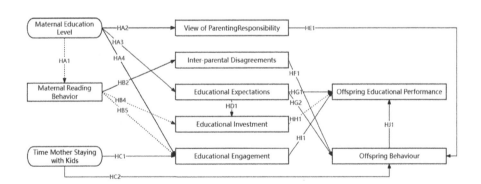

Fig. 3. Standardized Solutions of Inter-generational Influence Model of Women with Child-Raising Obligations in Rural Areas(The solid lines indicate significance in both models, while the dashed lines indicate significance in only one of the models.)

the interest in reading and the quantity of reading by rural women. This is especially urgent under the impact of the popularity of short videos in rural areas. In addition, the reading behavior of the mother's generation affects the mother's investment in her offspring and their participation in education, which in turn affects their academic performance. However, this mechanism of influence does not show significant differences in the level of reading volume, that is, the increase in reading volume does not have a significant impact on the educational investment and direct educational behavior of rural women in their adolescent offspring. Therefore, in the process of promoting reading in the above-mentioned areas, in addition to reading quantity as a measurement indicator, attention should also be paid to the type and quality of reading materials. At the level of family relations, women's reading behavior in rural China reduces the frequency of disagreements between husband and wife, and has a positive impact on improving understanding between husband and wife and fostering a good family atmosphere. In China, offspring's language achievement is clearly affected by maternal educational investment, educational expectation, educational participation and offspring's personality, but only in language subjects, there is a significant positive effect, i.e., the more the mother invests in the offspring's education and the higher the expectation, the easier it is for the offspring to achieve satisfactory results in language subjects. In the subject of mathematics, the above factors, on the contrary, have a negative effect. This may be due to the nature of the subject and the limited teaching resources available in rural areas.

4.2 Recommendations on Rural Women Reading

Based on the current status of reading levels of women's groups in rural areas and the inter-generational influence model, we have proposed the following recommendations:

Collaborative Efforts for Resource Enrichment: We advocate for collaborative efforts involving multiple stakeholders to furnish a comprehensive array of reading resources, services, and activities. This collaboration should aim to enhance the utilization rates of available resources.

Segmentation of Readership: To cater to the varied reading preferences and habits of rural women, it is advisable to segment them into distinct groups. This approach facilitates the promotion of niche reading materials and activities, aligning with the specific interests and inclinations of different segments of the readership population.

Active Women as Reading Role Models: Cultivating local reading promoters who understand the unique ecological context of the region can promote a culture of reading and have a lasting impact on motivating others to embrace reading.

Inter-generational Reading Initiatives: By encouraging parents and children to read together, we can enhance awareness about the benefits of shared reading experiences and strengthen family bonds through this joint endeavor.

Alignment with Educational Goals: Exploring the reading needs of mothers in alignment with the educational objectives of their children is essential. This approach involves tapping into the urgency and motivation stemming from the educational requirements of their offspring. By connecting reading activities to the educational aspirations of the younger generation, we can ignite an intrinsic drive among rural women to read. Ultimately, this inter-generational influence through reading can substantially improve the overall quality of education.

5   Conclusions

This study combines previous research with data from the CFPS survey to examine the current reading status of rural women raising young children, and includes variables such as their personal characteristics, educational philosophy and participation in education to explore the inter-generational influence of their reading behaviour on their offspring's behaviour. The Standardized Solutions of the two structural models show that the reading behavior of women in rural areas has a significant impact on their educational perceptions, expectations, proactiveness, initiative and family relationships. These factors exert an influence on the behavior and academic achievement of their offspring.

Owing to the constraints imposed by the relatively restricted set of variables present within the dataset, it is presently unfeasible to integrate alterations in reading mediums into the model elucidated within this paper. The nuanced dynamics underpinning digital and print-based reading, along with their respective inter-generational ramifications, will be subject to more exhaustive exploration in forthcoming research endeavors. Our future investigations will center on assessing the repercussions of the pervasive adoption of various media, notably digital platforms, on the reading practices of women residing in rural settings. Furthermore, these inquiries will delve into the intricate interactions underpinning the inter-generational transmission of cultural capital.

References

1. Ardizzoni, S.: The paradigm of Hakka women in history. Asian Stud. 9(1), 31–64 (2021)
2. Bingsi, F.: Reading promotion and library science: analysis on basic theory. J. Librar. Sci. China 40, 4–13 (2014)
3. Blau, P.M., Duncan, O.D.: The American occupational structure (1967)
4. Blissett, J., Meyer, C., Haycraft, E.: Maternal and paternal controlling feeding practices with male and female children. Appetite 47(2), 212–219 (2006). https://doi.org/10.1016/j.appet.2006.04.002
5. Buyukbay, E.O., Uzunoz, M., et al.: The behaviour of personal development of rural women in relation to their physical appearance: a case study from the province of Tokat, Turkey. J. Food Agric. Environ. 8(2), 1000–1004 (2010)
6. Chaohai, L., Xiaoliang, Y., Zhuo, L., Ying, L.: The present dilemma and optimization of the supply of book resources for primary and secondary schools in rural areas. Modern Educ. Manage. 5, 58–63 (2017)
7. Craig, L.: How employed mothers in Australia find time for both market work and childcare. J. Family Econ. Issues 28(1), 69–87 (2007). https://doi.org/10.1007/s10834-006-9047-2

8. Crosnoe, R., Kalil, A.: Educational progress and parenting among Mexican immigrant mothers of young children. J. Marriage Fam. **72**(4), 976–990 (2010). https://doi.org/10.1111/j.1741-3737.2010.00743.x

9. DiMaggio, P.: Cultural capital and school success: the impact of status culture participation on the grades of us high school students. Am. Sociol. Rev. **47**, 189–201 (1982)

10. Dong, D., Changxiu, Z., Wenjuan, Z., Shu, X., Liang, L.: The construction of the whole element system of rural children's reading promotion-based on the perspective of activity theory. Libr. Inf. Serv. **2**, 1–7 (2017)

11. Ferrer, E., McArdle, J.J., Shaywitz, B.A., Holahan, J.M., Marchione, K., Shaywitz, S.E.: Longitudinal models of developmental dynamics between reading and cognition from childhood to adolescence. Dev. Psychol. **43**(6), 1460–1473 (2007). https://doi.org/10.1037/0012-1649.43.6.1460

12. Grunig, L., Toth, E.L., Hon, L.C.: Women in Public Relations: How Gender Influences Practice. Women in Public Relations: How Gender Influences Practice, pp. 1–424 (2013). https://doi.org/10.4324/9781315045573

13. Hall, S.: Encoding and decoding in the television discourse. CCCS Stencilled Occasional Papers, vol. SP 7. Gray, A., et al. (eds.) University of Birmingham, Birmingham, vol. 2, pp. pp. 386-398, September 1973 (2007). http://epapers.bham.ac.uk/2962/

14. Jacob, A.M.: The Human Capital Earnings Function, pp. 83–96. NBER Chapters, National Bureau of Economic Research, Inc. (1974). https://ideas.repec.org/h/nbr/nberch/1767.html

15. Jeynes, W.H.: The relationship between parental involvement and urban secondary school student academic achievement. Urban Educ. **42**, 110–82 (2007)

16. Keith, T.Z.: Parent Involvement and Achievement in High School, pp. 125–141. Elsevier Science/JAI Press, US (1991)

17. Khanolainen, D., Salminen, J., Eklund, K., Lerkkanen, M.K., Torppa, M.: Intergenerational transmission of dyslexia: how do different identification methods of parental difficulties influence the conclusions regarding children's risk for dyslexia? Read. Res. Q. **58**(2), 220–239 (2023). https://doi.org/10.1002/rrq.482, https://ila.onlinelibrary.wiley.com/doi/abs/10.1002/rrq.482

18. Lange, R.: How college affects students: a third decade of research (review). J. General Educ. **55**, 160 – 163 (2006). https://api.semanticscholar.org/CorpusID:144226658

19. Lei, X., Shaohui, L.: Practical mechanism and strategy selection for social organizations participating in rural reading promotion: taking "three plus two books" as an example. Librar. Work Study **41**(4), 64 (2022)

20. Terminology Validation Committee on Library Science, I.S., Bibliography: Nouns on Library Science, Intelligence Science and Bibliography 2019. Beijing China Science Publishing & Media Ltd (2019)

21. Ligaga, D.: Rethinking motherhood through afro feminism: reading Jennifer Makumbi's the first woman. J. Afr. Cult. Stud. **35**(2), 141–151 (2023)

22. Lindell, L.R.: "So long as I can read": farm women's reading experiences in depression-era south Dakota. Agric. Hist. **83**(4), 503–527 (2009)

23. Ness, T.M., Hellzen, O., Enmarker, I.: "embracing the present and fearing the future": the meaning of being an oldest old woman in a rural area. Int. J. Qual. Stud. Health Well Being **9**(1), 25217 (2014)

24. Notten, N., Kraaykamp, G., Konig, R.P.: Family media matters: unraveling the intergenerational transmission of reading and television tastes. Sociol. Perspect. **55**(4), 683–706 (2012). https://doi.org/10.1525/sop.2012.55.4.683

25. Notten, N., Kraaykamp, G., Konig, R.P.: Family media matters: unraveling the intergenerational transmission of reading and television tastes. Sociol. Perspect. **55**(4), 683–706 (2012)
26. Patrick, K., et al.: Demographic predictors of consistency and change in heterosexuals' attitudes toward homosexual behavior over a two-year period. J. Sex Res. **50**(6), 611–619 (2013). https://doi.org/10.1080/00224499.2012.657263
27. Ponitz, C.C., Rimm-Kaufman, S.E., Grimm, K.J., Curby, T.W.: Kindergarten classroom quality, behavioral engagement, and reading achievement. Sch. Psychol. Rev. **38**(1), 102–120 (2009)
28. Puckett, A.: "Let the girls do the spelling and DAN will do the shooting": literacy, the division of labor, and identity in a rural Appalachian community. Anthropol. Quart. **65**, 137–147 (1992)
29. Qian, D.: Research on farmhouse library service based on the reading states of left-behind women, taking Chongqing municipality as an example. Librar. Work Study **1**(7), 91 (2020)
30. Raudenska, P., Basna, K.: Individual's cultural capital: intergenerational transmission, partner effect, or individual merit? Poetics **89**, 101575 (2021). https://doi.org/10.1016/j.poetic.2021.101575
31. Shilian, T., Junhua, X.: Research on reading promotion for "left-behind children" in rural areas based on field investigation. Libr. Dev. **8**, 54–61 (2017)
32. Sriganesh, R., Ponniah, R.J.: Impact of reading on the biological foundations of language, cognition, and emotion. Rupkatha J. Interdiscip. Stud. Human. **12**(6), 1–12 (2020). https://doi.org/10.21659/rupkatha.v12n6.09b
33. Tunc, T.E.: From "golden girl" to "yellow peril": reading the transgressive body in Ruthanne Lum McCunn's thousand pieces of gold. Asian J. Women's Stud. **14**(2), 59–79 (2008)
34. Yakubu, I., Salisu, W.J.: Determinants of adolescent pregnancy in sub-Saharan Africa: a systematic review. Reprod. Health **15**, 15 (2018). https://doi.org/10.1186/s12978-018-0460-4
35. Yongfeng, L., Haijing, H.: Survey analysis and strategy study on reading status of rural remaining women. Librar. Theory Pract. **3**, 23–25 (2016)

Characterizing State Governments' Administrative Capacity for Broadband

Caroline Stratton[1] [ID] and Hanim Astuti[1,2]([✉]) [ID]

[1] Florida State University, Tallahassee, FL 32304, USA
hastuti@fsu.edu
[2] Institut Teknologi Sepuluh Nopember, Sukolilo, 60111 Surabaya, Indonesia

Abstract. This study investigates how the state governments of the United States may differ in their organizational and operational administrative capacity to manage broadband availability and expansion. State governments are currently preparing for an influx of funding for broadband from the Infrastructure Investment and Jobs Act (IIJA) passed in 2021, which will be devolved from the federal government to the state level. As such, we seek to characterize how the states may differ in their preparedness to manage funds and achieve desired impacts. We construct a dataset using publicly available information about state governments to investigate similarities and differences, as well as consider how and why variation in administrative capacity may or may not be consequential in the future. This exploratory work sets up future study about the influence that pre-IIJA administrative capacity for broadband may have on IIJA policy implementation and its overall effectiveness.

Keywords: Broadband · Planning · Broadband policy

1 Background

The US federal government and state governments have long demonstrated an interest in ensuring the availability of broadband internet service. The Covid-19 pandemic intensified this interest, as it became clear that individuals without access to broadband would be at a disadvantage for participating in essential daily activities, such as working, attending school, and accessing healthcare. The passage of the Infrastructure Investment and Jobs Act (IIJA) in 2021 demonstrated the federal government's strong commitment to ubiquitous availability of high-quality internet service in the form of $65 billion in funding for broadband, including $2.75 billion to promote digital equity.

The funding to expand broadband infrastructure and pursue digital equity is to be distributed to the states, based on their fulfillment of certain prerequisites, such as the establishment of plans indicating how they will distribute funds to other entities to expand broadband availability and adoption. This model of distributing funding and delegating decision-making, or devolution, is intended to allow the states to address their unique challenges rather than prescribe a single course of action to them. Broadband funding in the IIJA has successfully incentivized the governments of US states (and territories) to work on issues of broadband availability and adoption, with all 50 states and six territories having applied for funding [1].

Prior to the establishment of new broadband funding programs in the IIJA, state governments had demonstrated variable interest in and capacity to expand broadband availability and adoption. Some states had established offices charged with tasks such as developing strategic plans, convening stakeholders, and grantmaking, while other states had little officially designated capacity. Though all states are now acting to obtain funding for broadband, their pre-IIJA activity suggests that they were not uniformly prepared to do so. In this study, we examine state governments' pre-IIJA approaches to broadband access and adoption to allow future investigation of their post-IIJA approaches, which are in development at present. Furthermore, this research initiates an exploration into the factors contributing to the diverse levels of broadband development across various US states.

Devolving implementation of the IIJA draws our attention to differences in the administrative capacity of states, those resources (human, financial, and others) necessary to "effectively implement policy plans and programs" [2]. The National Telecommunication and Information Agency's (NTIA) guidance to states [3] about how to begin preparing for broadband funding distribution advises governments to develop organizational administrative capacity, in the form of an office or authority, and to undertake activities to build operational administrative capacity, such as compiling, collecting, and mapping data about broadband availability and adoption, which adopts some characteristics stated in the new institutional theory [4].

Presumably, governments with longstanding organizational-operational administrative capacity for broadband should be better prepared for the process of applying for, distributing federal broadband funding, and achieving goals of expanding availability and adoption. This is not necessarily to say that governments without a long history of work on broadband cannot develop administrative capacity quickly (either internally or through contracting third parties) nor that once capacity has been established that it remains at the same strength over time. Future work may test the effects of administrative capacity on outcomes of IIJA, following the notion that the current broadband policy environment has effectively created a natural experiment [5]. In this exploratory work, we pose a research question to characterize the initial conditions for the experiment: *In what ways does the organizational-operational administrative capacity for broadband differ among the states?*

2   Method

2.1   Data Collection

We constructed a dataset to investigate administrative capacity regarding broadband and states past activities to expand access and adoption. Drawing on information previously compiled by Pew Charitable Trusts in 2021 [6], we identified for each state if it had a broadband office, the agency that the broadband office was located within (parent agency), its most recent broadband plan (predating IIJA-required planning), its oldest broadband plan, and state broadband mapping. To ensure the validity of the data, we also searched the current and archived versions of this data from state government websites and obtained plan documents. Our first attempts to identify when broadband offices were established led to ambiguity about differences in office establishment through legislation, funding, and staffing, or renaming and relocating to different parent agencies, so we use publication of a state's oldest broadband plan as an indicator of how long a government has demonstrated operational administrative capacity.

We sought additional evidence of operational capacity for the activities of mapping broadband availability and grantmaking, both of which are germane to obtaining and distributing IIJA funding [3, 7]. Based on broadband plan documents and state government websites, we recorded what sources of data a state's broadband mapping efforts drew on (e.g., solely on Federal Communications Commission (FCC) data or demonstrating state-level data collection efforts). We also sought the presence or absence of grantmaking activity using state funds (i.e., funds not originating from a federal source, such as the American Rescue Plan or ARPA) from state government websites and federal government sites, such as NTIA.

2.2 Data Analysis

For each state's pre-IIJA broadband plan (where available), we conducted an iterative content analysis [8], in which we began with a small set of items of interest and allowed the analysis process to surface additional similarities and differences in plans. At a fundamental level, we observed notable differences in the specificity of plans. Some plans contained discrete action items with designated owners, timelines, and strategies for monitoring and evaluation of those action items, while others offered more general recommendations or ideas about what could be done. From this observation, we coded plans for the presence of actions, which we define as distinct tasks indicating who would execute them and when, or recommendations, which we define as distinct tasks that are actionable but lack a designated owner, timeframe, follow-up strategy, or otherwise do not indicate that government had committed to acting. Our coding also noted plans featuring a lack of actions and/or recommendations.

We identified if plans contained actions or recommendations regarding three kinds of activities to expand broadband availability and adoption that are relevant to obtaining IIJA funding: expanding broadband infrastructure, supporting affordability of broadband service, and supporting digital literacy and inclusion programs.

Both authors completed this coding for actions, recommendations, and the three types of activities independently. However, to ensure the coding consistency, some coding guides were determined at first and the results were documented in an excel sheet. Both authors met to identify disagreements, state their reasoning, and reiterated the analysis across all 50 states to come to a mutually agreeable determination. Next, we report on patterns in our constructed dataset that speak to the administrative capacity for broadband across states.

3   Findings

3.1   Organizational Administrative Capacity – Office Location, Age

As of September 2023, nearly all states (46 of 50) have an office designated to manage broadband. Table 1 presents an overview of the responsibilities of parent agencies that broadband offices are situated within. Departments of Commerce and/or Economic Development are the most common arrangement for office location, followed by Departments of Community Affairs and IT. Five states established broadband offices as a unique public agency or authority. Four states do not have any specifically designated broadband office but integrate their broadband programs into an existing agency's agenda, such as Montana's ConnectMT program in its Department of Administration.

Table 1. Broadband offices and parent agencies

Category	Type of Parent Agency	Number of States
States with a Specifically Designated Broadband Office	Commerce and/or Economic Development	22
	Community Affairs	3
	IT	6
	Public Utilities	5
	Independent Agency	5
	Administration	3
	Transportation	1
	Executive	1
States with No Specifically Designated Broadband Office	–	4

Additional variation in organizational administrative capacity emerged in our efforts to identify which states were first movers in establishing broadband administrative capacity and which states had more recently done so. Due to ambiguity in using the date of designated office establishment as a datapoint, we opt instead to consider the year in which broadband offices first published a publicly available plan for broadband.

Figure 1 presents publication years of states' earliest broadband plans. We note that Minnesota appears to have published the first state-level broadband plan in 2008, two years before the FCC released the 2010 National Broadband Plan [9]. While a number of states followed suit in the five years after the 2010 NBP, the greatest quantity of states' first broadband plans was published between 2015 and 2020.

3.2   Priorities for Administrative Capacity in Pre-IIJA Broadband Plans

There are 35 states that published a broadband plan prior to the requirement introduced to obtain IIJA funding. Table 2 indicates the publication years of the pre-IIJA broadband plans included in our content analysis.

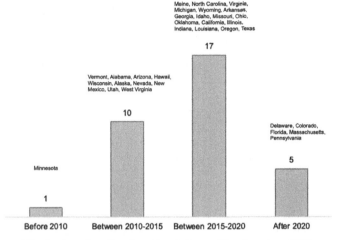

Fig. 1. States' earliest broadband plan publications (pre-IIJA).

Table 2. States according to the year of broadband plan's publication

Plan year of publication	# of States	States
2017	1	North Carolina
2018	2	Arizona, Wyoming
2019	9	Alaska, Georgia, Maine, Missouri, North Dakota, Ohio, Oklahoma, South Dakota, West Virginia
2020	8	California, Hawaii, Illinois, Indiana, Louisiana, New Mexico, Oregon, Utah
2021	7	Alabama, Delaware, Michigan, Nevada, Vermont, Virginia, Wisconsin
2022	8	Arkansas, Colorado, Florida, Massachusetts, Minnesota, Pennsylvania, Texas

A portion of plans (13 of 35) credited consultants for partial or complete authorship, six of which named firms that work on a national or international scale (e.g., McKinsey, Connected Nation, CTC). The use of third-party expertise and labor has implications for measuring capacity, as it suggests both the operational administrative capacity to contract and manage consultants and a need to supplement internal resources.

Table 3 presents our findings from content analysis of plans. Our coding of actions and recommendations identified that about three quarters of them (27 of 35) had discernible actions or recommendations. Among these plans, nearly all (26 of 27) presented actions or recommendations to expand broadband infrastructure. A smaller quantity of plans included actions or recommendations to support affordability of broadband service (14 of 35) and digital literacy and inclusion programs (13 of 35).

Table 3. Plan content with respect to IIJA priorities

Plan contains	Number of plans	Includes action or recommendation for:		
		Infrastructure expansion	Affordability	Digital literacy/inclusion
Actions	15	14	9	8
Recommendations	12	12	5	5
No discernible actions or recommendations	8	–	–	–
Total	35	26	14	13

While a portion of states' plans were not written at a level of specificity for the reader to identify discrete tasks that would be performed, our findings from analyzing pre-IIJA broadband plans do demonstrate some state governments' plans to act were already aligned with IIJA priorities. We might posit that state broadband offices with a history of action on IIJA priorities will be better positioned to obtain funding and achieve desired outcomes. Nine states' plans (those of Alabama, California, Colorado, Hawaii, Louisiana, Michigan, North Carolina, Pennsylvania, and Texas) showed alignment with the three priorities that we coded for (Table 4).

Table 4. Plan content according to broadband parent office responsibilities.

Type of parent agency	# of plans with action or recommendations	Plan includes action or recommendations for:		
		Infrastructure expansion	Affordability	Digital literacy/inclusion
Commerce and/or Economic Development	12	12 (46%)	5 (19%)	6 (23%)
IT	5	5 (19%)	4 (15%)	3 (12%)
Community Affairs	2	2 (8%)	1 (4%)	–
Public Utilities	1	1 (4%)	1 (4%)	–
Administration	2	2 (8%)	2 (8%)	2 (8%)
Independent Agency	4	3 (12%)	1 (4%)	1 (4%)
Total	26	25	14	12

The greatest quantity of pre-IIJA plans already demonstrating alignment with IIJA priorities around infrastructure, expansion, affordability, and digital literacy/inclusion are those produced within Departments of Commerce and/or Economic development, which may simply reflect that the greatest quantity of broadband offices follows this kind of arrangement.

3.3 Operational Administrative Capacity: Mapping and Grantmaking

Of the 50 states, 42 of them have a publicly available state broadband map as of September 2023. Table 5 records the types of data sources that states employ in broadband maps. Our analysis of plans flagged that plan text often referred to the flaws present in FCC broadband availability data collected through Form 477 (cf. [10]). Some offices with knowledge of these flaws and capacity to collect new or correct existing FCC data report taking action, such as requesting cooperation of internet service providers (ISPs) and asking the public to report availability. Our review of states' current broadband maps showed nearly equal portions relying on FCC data only, FCC data supplemented with data from ISPs, and FCC data supplemented with data from ISPs and additional sources.

Table 5. Data sources used in state broadband maps.

Data Sources	Number of States
FCC only	12
FCC and ISPs	15
FCC, ISPs, and additional sources	15

That state governments successfully establish and manage funding competitions will be paramount for the overall effectiveness of the IIJA. Past grantmaking activity is relevant to states' upcoming activities. Our review yielded evidence that 41 states had experience doing so by providing grants to expand broadband infrastructure between 2018 and 2023. The funding sources for these grants included Covid-19 era federal grant programs, such as ARPA. Prior to the infusion of federal funding for broadband during the pandemic, 39 states had previously allocated funding from state-level sources through competitive grant programs. In other words, the majority of states have recently had some level of operational administrative capacity in place.

4   Discussion and Conclusion

This study aimed to identify differences in administrative capacity among states that might be influential for their efforts to expand broadband availability and adoption. In general, we found that most states have demonstrated organizational administrative capacity through the establishment of offices responsible for broadband-related tasks and that although there is no specific guidance from NTIA about where broadband offices should be situated, the most common arrangement is within a Department of Commerce and/or Economic Development. While our analysis of broadband plans does not necessarily note major differences in capacity or priorities in relation to the type of parent agency, their situation in agencies that may have distinct strengths and resources in areas such as economic development, IT, and public utilities, for example, may be influential for their implementation of funding programs and the impacts they produce.

If states generally demonstrated uniformity around organizational administrative capacity, the iterative content analysis process surfaced more notable distinctions in their broadband plans with respect to their actionability and how binding they seemed to be. As noted in the methods, plans like those from California, Colorado, and Michigan detailed tasks, timelines, and performance indicators, signaling their high actionability. Although implementation was not assessed, such plans suggest clear guidance and a commitment of resources. Plans with recommendations or no discernable actions or recommendations offered some ideas about why they might not be as binding, for example, being authored by external consultants or developed for a future scenario in which a broadband office would be adequately staffed to carry out the plan. In general, simply having a broadband plan is only part of the story when it comes to administrative capacity; how actionable and binding a plan is would also seem significant. In terms of states' efforts to obtain IIJA funding, previous publication of a less actionable or binding plan might become irrelevant in the future, as all state governments have now demonstrated increased interest in broadband and must meet specific requirements with their plans to obtain funding [11].

For the nine state broadband plans demonstrating relatively stronger alignment with IIJA planning requirements and priorities, we do not necessarily note any patterns in their history of administrative capacity for broadband, their type of parent agency, or other apparent characteristics. Five of these plans come from some of the most populous US states (California, North Carolina, Michigan, Pennsylvania, and Texas), which we might take as an indicator of greater government resources; however, measures of resources, such as per capita state expenditures do not necessarily support such a claim [12]. And while two of these states are among the national first movers in broadband planning (Alabama and Hawaii, both published their first broadband plans in 2012), others such as Colorado, Louisiana, Pennsylvania, and Texas are not. The use of consultants in planning for Alabama and Colorado further suggests that characterizing administrative capacity is complex: it may be complemented, supplemented, or otherwise enhanced by third parties. Additionally, it is not necessarily constant or increasing over time.

We note relative uniformity across states regarding operational administrative capacity and grantmaking. Most states have engaged with broadband grants from both federal and state sources, even prior to the availability of pandemic-era funding. As expanding broadband infrastructure effectively depends on accurate maps of where service is available, most states have also sought to develop more comprehensive broadband maps than were previously available relying only on FCC data. Our reading of plan texts indicated broad awareness about obtaining high-quality data about broadband availability and strategies to do so that involve ISP cooperation.

To conclude, the new infusion of funding for broadband availability and adoption has prompted action from state governments to marshal resources to manage devolution. It highlights the roles of organizational capacities in the new institutional theory [4]. The extent to which prior administrative capacity will be influential in the outcomes of funding competitions and real-world impacts is yet to be measured. The case of broadband and the natural experiment that is soon to occur will yield important insight into questions about the effectiveness of devolution and the relative advantage, if any, that administrative capacity presents to the successful utilization of funding. This study enables future work to explore these questions during and after IIJA implementation.

References

1. NTIA 2022a. https://ntia.gov/press-release/2022/biden-harris-administration-awards-more-74-million-florida-internet-all-planning
2. El-Taliawi, O.G., Van Der Wal, Z.: Developing administrative capacity: an agenda for research and practice. Policy Des. Pract. **2**(3), 243–257 (2019)
3. NTIA 2022b. https://broadbandusa.ntia.doc.gov/sites/default/files/2022-02/State%20Prepara tion%20for%20BIL%20Broadband%20Grant%20Programs.pdf
4. Barman, E., MacIndoe, H.: Institutional pressures and organizational capacity: the case of outcome measurement. Sociol. Forum **27**(2), 70–93 (2012)
5. Bauer, J.M.: Federal-local realignments of broadband policy and digital equity in the United States. In: 2023 Urban Affairs Association Conference, Nashville (2023). https://quello.msu.edu/wp-content/uploads/2023/04/Bauer-Paper-Urban-Affairs-Ass ociation-Conference-2023-DRAFT-20230423-1.pdf
6. Pew Charitable Trusts. https://www.pewtrusts.org/en/research-and-analysis/articles/2021/06/28/which-states-have-dedicated-broadband-offices-task-forces-agencies-or-funds. Accessed 16 Sept 2023
7. Rinehart, W.: A program evaluation of state-based grant programs. In: TPRC49: The 49th Research Conference on Communication, Information and Internet Policy (2021). https://pap ers.ssrn.com/sol3/papers.cfm?abstract_id=3900228
8. Krippendorff, K.: Content Analysis: An Introduction to Its Methodology. Sage Publications, Thousand Oaks (2018)
9. FCC. https://transition.fcc.gov/national-broadband-plan/national-broadband-plan.pdf. Accessed 13 Mar 2010
10. Grubesic, T.H.: The US national broadband map: data limitations and implications. Telecommun. Policy **36**(2), 113–126 (2012)
11. NTIA 2022c. https://broadbandusa.ntia.doc.gov/sites/default/files/2022-09/BEAD-Digital_E quity_Alignment_Guide.pdf
12. Urban Institute (n.d.). https://www.urban.org/policy-centers/cross-center-initiatives/state-and-local-finance-initiative/state-and-local-backgrounders/state-and-local-expenditures

Assisting International Migrants with Everyday Information Seeking: From the Providers' Lens

Yongle Zhang$^{(\boxtimes)}$ and Ge Gao

University of Maryland, College Park, USA
{yongle,gegao}@umd.edu

Abstract. International migrants face difficulties obtaining information to improve quality of life and well-being in their host country. Prior research indicates that international migrants often seek information from their co-national contacts. The downside of this practice is a small-world clustering, hindering the information seekers' social adaptation. In our research, we investigated the ongoing practices and future opportunities to connect international migrants with those beyond their co-national contacts. Our work focuses on information providers' perspectives, which complements previous studies that pay exclusive attention to the information seekers. We conducted in-depth interviews with 21 participants who had assisted fulfilling the information needs of migrants to the United States. Some participants were migrants from different home countries than the information seekers, whereas the rest were U.S. nationals. Our data reveals how participants dealt with language barriers, overcame knowledge disparities, and calibrated their commitment as information providers. Based on our findings, we discuss directions for future information and communication technology design that can facilitate international migrants' daily information seeking, and accounts for information providers' needs and concerns.

Keywords: Information provider · International migrant · Adaptation · Language barrier · Knowledge gap · Commitment

1 Introduction

International migrants or people temporarily living outside their country of birth and citizenship require information for daily tasks in a new society, such as seeking healthcare and transportation services, understanding local laws, and finding jobs or housing. Access to adequate information helps migrants overcome everyday challenges [9,56] and alleviate their acculturative stress [62].

That said, obtaining the necessary information can be challenging for migrants in their host country. In particular, many people lack basic knowledge about where to begin an information search [15,70]. Language barriers also pose an issue for people whose native language differs from the host country's majority [40,57]. Official resources for international migrants often prioritize academic or professional development [37,39], which fail to cover other aspects of a person's everyday information needs.

Previous scholars have recognized migrants' social contacts as their critical information sources in everyday information seeking [24,40,44]. Social contacts who share the same country of origin (i.e., co-nationals), as well as similar cultural and migration experiences, often play a pivotal role [3,32,33,42,44,60]. These co-nationals, while usually motivated to assist, can sometimes limit migrants' exposure to diverse perspectives due to their small-size and homogeneous network in the host country [29,49,63].

Two additional groups of contacts exist in an international migrant's network: fellow migrants from different home countries and domestic residents who have grown up and consistently lived in the migrant's host country. These groups offer the potential to introduce diverse information resources [18,64], yet migrants often do not fully utilize them [45]. While several initiatives have been developed to bridge the gap [25,52], their sustainability remains a challenge. Many of these projects heavily emphasize the viewpoints of information seekers, potentially overlooking the challenges faced by the information providers [53].

Our work incorporates this missing perspective by conducting in-depth interviews with 21 information providers, including 11 fellow migrants to and 10 domestic residents of the United States. Our study offers two key contributions: 1) theoretical contributions in our examination of the information providers' practice of assisting international migrants with daily information seeking, a group largely overlooked by prior research, and 2) practical contributions in our highlighting of barriers and design recommendations shared by participants. We compared our work with previous research and discussed how our work contributes to information studies and human-computer interaction for improving international migrants' quality of life. In particular, we explored answers to the following research questions (RQ):

RQ1: What challenges, if any, do information providers face in their current practice of assisting international migrants' daily information seeking?

RQ2: How can future information and communication technologies (ICTs) be designed to help information providers overcome those challenges?

2   Related Work

We review existing literature within two facets of international migrants' daily information seeking: the challenges they face and the potential information sources they utilize.

2.1   Daily Information Seeking for International Migrants

Information seeking is essential for international migrants as they navigate various aspects of life in a new environment [15,32,44,55]. In our study, international migrants are defined as individuals temporarily living outside their country of birth or citizenship [10], such as international students and migrant workers. They often encounter challenges in everyday life [9,10], such as, finding suitable housing [40,42], managing finances [72], and accessing healthcare services [44]. These obstacles impede migrants from effectively navigating their new environment [40,42,55,59,61,72], highlighting the importance of better comprehension of local information and enhancement of international migrants' information-seeking practices.

Existing research indicates that international migrants often lack awareness of local information resources in the host country. For example, Mehra and Bilal interviewed Asian international students in the United States [42] and found that locating essential daily information was both cognitively taxing and time-consuming for participants. Similarly, the diary studies conducted by Yoon and Chung suggested that migrant participants frequently did not know where to source information needed for their lives abroad [72]. Unfamiliarity with local resources and differences in ICT between migrants' home and host countries contribute to these navigational barriers [58,67].

Another challenge faced by many migrants is gathering and understanding information in a host country where their native language is not predominantly spoken [4]. For instance, Rózsa et al. observed how Hungarian students performed online information seeking in English [48] and found that participants often crafted vague or incomplete English queries, yielding low-quality search results. Such language barriers have been frequently reported by participants in studies examining newcomer adaptation [19,29,33]. While providing resources in multiple languages can be a solution, existing infrastructures in host countries typically cater to the language(s) spoken by the majority, leaving smaller linguistic groups underserved [5,16,23,46].

International migrants often underutilize resources offered by professionals and officials [28,37,38,40,42,72]. For instance, public libraries with trained staff ready to help international visitors are frequently underused [54]. Some researchers attribute this underutilization of institutional resources to the limited range of services offered. In other words, the information available at public libraries mainly pertains to an international migrant's academic performance or specific domain achievements [37,71], which does not encompass the full array of everyday information needs in society [29,39,50]. Considering the above complexities, it is important to examine ways that support international migrants' information-seeking practices.

2.2 Social Contacts as Information Providers

Information studies scholars have examined how people interact with information sources. For example, in Wilson's framework [65,66], choice of information sources are influenced by variables such as the characteristics of the sources (e.g., accessibility, reliability, and relevance). Johnson's model examines the characteristics and utility of information channels selected and used by seekers [31]. It discusses how antecedent factors (e.g., an individual's demographics and needs) shape the uses of sources. In the context of everyday life information seeking (ELIS), Savolainen emphasizes individuals' tendencies to utilize informal sources, particularly outside of academic or professional settings [51]. Researchers have applied the concept of ELIS to investigate migrants' information sources and found that their social networks are a primary information source offering valuable information across their settlement process [29,44,54]. These social contacts fall into three categories: co-national migrants, fellow migrants, and domestic residents [6].

Co-nationals as Information Providers. Co-nationals or international migrants from the same country of origin serve as vital information providers for their peers. Their shared linguistic, cultural, and experiential backgrounds make co-nationals invaluable sources of both emotional and informational support [33,41]. Ample evidence highlights the importance of co-nationals in helping migrants navigate their daily lives [44,45]. For example, a study by Mao [40] involving Chinese migrants in Canada indicated a preference for co-nationals when seeking everyday information and services. Newly arrived migrants often experience high stress and anxiety, making them inclined to seek comfort in the familiar environment provided by their co-national community [27].

Empirical studies have shown that international migrants' networks often contain a high proportion of co-nationals [1,6,68,69]. Despite benefits, previous research has cautioned against over-dependence on co-nationals as information sources [36,60]. The size of an international migrant's network in the host country can be relatively small. Such composition of international migrants' networks may not change easily as migrants' social interactions do not necessarily become more intertwined with locals over time [21,73]. Repeated information exchange within this small network may trap migrants in an echo chamber [14,29,63], which negatively impacts their adaptation process in the long run [12,13].

Potential Information Providers Beyond a Migrant's Co-nationals. Besides co-nationals, a migrant's social contacts include domestic residents and fellow migrants from other countries. These groups are recognized for their potential to introduce new perspectives and resources to a migrant's information world [22,56]. For example, Alho interviewed international migrants with experience of seeking employment in the host country [2]. Participants acknowledged that expanding their social network beyond co-nationals could allow them to better comprehend local job market and personnel selection process. Surveys conducted by Forbush et al. suggested that international students with more diverse networks reported better social adaptation than those with fewer domestic connections [18].

Several research projects have leveraged ICT to connect newcomers with these prospective information providers and utilize them for daily information seeking. For instance, Hirsch and Liu designed Speakeasy, an integrated web and telephone-based service connecting newcomers with knowledgeable local volunteers in the Boston area [25]. These providers register their contact details and language skills, allowing the system to match them with information seekers who require assistance. Similarly, Brown and colleagues designed Rivtran, a system that enables the asynchronous exchange of audio and text messages about everyday information seeking between immigrants and mentors assigned by the local community center [8].

While the above systems provide the technical framework for international migrants to connect with local contacts [8,20,25,43], field testing data indicate that finding available and qualified volunteers to satisfy the migrants' information needs is often difficult [52]. Many initiatives are small scale and short term, presenting sustainability concerns.

Furthermore, a common theme across previous projects is the predominant focus on the perspectives of information seekers, sidelining challenges that providers might encounter [53]. In successful information-seeking practices, both information seekers and providers play crucial roles in ensuring effective communication and knowledge exchange [11,34,47]. The information seeking and communication model proposed by Robson and Robinson, in particular, considers the information provider as one major component in information seeking [47], drawing attention to their "needs, wants, and goals." For greater efficacy and longevity of relevant practice, it is vital to address these gaps and craft systems that accommodate needs of multiple stakeholders.

3   Methods

We conducted in-depth interviews with 21 participants in the United States (hereinafter referred to as the host country). Among them, 11 were international migrants (7 females, 4 males; average age = 26, S.E. = 1.69) with an average duration of 6.70 years of residency in the host country. The other 10 were domestic residents (5 females, 4 males, 1 non-binary; average age = 35, S.E. = 6.87).

3.1   Recruitment

All migrant and domestic participants in our sample were individuals with experience providing information to international migrants who need help. The recruitment took place through social media posts and physical flyers spread among our local community. The final research sample comprised 21 information providers, varying in host country status, language background, and other demographic features.

3.2   Data Collection

We conducted semi-structured interviews with participants. Each interview lasted for about one hour. Migrant participants reflected on their life experience in the host country, detailed cases of assisting with other migrants' information seeking, and any support they had or wished to receive. For participants who were domestic residents, we asked about their interactions with international migrants and their successes or failures in assisting them with daily information seeking. All interviews occurred face-to-face or via Zoom, based on the participant's preference. We reimbursed each participant with a 15 dollar gift card as a token of appreciation for their time.

4   Analysis

We performed thematic analysis with the textual data transcribed from audio recordings [7]. This analysis occurred iteratively as new data was obtained. We stopped data collection and its analysis when clear and stable themes were identified. At the beginning, the leading author of this paper read through all interview transcripts at hand and developed an initial set of codes to cover ideas discussed by participants. In later steps, the entire research team examined this initial set of codes together, iterating between reviewing the existing interview data, obtaining new data, and revising the codes. By the end, we generated a codebook including 192 codes and 1370 quotations. It centered on themes that describe an information provider's ways to establish connections with international migrants, information that they can offer to the migrants, challenges that prevent them from issuing support, and reflections regarding possible strategies to overcome the challenges.

5   Findings

Overall, our data analysis revealed three types of challenges encountered by our migrant and domestic participants when offering informational support to others (RQ1). It also uncovered several directions of technology design to enhance the information exchange between these people and the international migrants they hope to help (RQ2).

5.1   Challenges Encountered by Information Providers

Language Barriers and Relevant Social Concerns. Participants reported language barriers as their fundamental issue when providing informational support to international migrants. For example, P1 shared his challenges of articulating his thoughts in front of other international migrants:

> "For a long time, I struggled to grasp the needs of other internationals. Many of us have accents. I didn't know what they were talking about, and they couldn't understand me either. We even tried typing texts during a face-to-face conversation to assist our communication in English." [P1, fellow migrant]

Additionally, many of our domestic participants reported that language barriers not only hindered the effective information exchange between migrants and themselves, it also resulted in negative social consequences for the migrants, such as the worry about being devalued by native speakers and a sense of insecurity. P15 shared their experiences and observations on this topic, which echoes similar points made by other migrant participants (e.g., P3):

"Many international newcomers cannot speak or write English very well. My view is like, everybody has constraints, and we are not the most intelligent people out there. It's common if you and I do not understand each other even among native speakers. However, I can tell they are hesitant to let me know that they can't master the language. It is mostly because they lack confidence. They feel embarrassed." [P15, domestic resident]

"There are multiple levels of worries when I think of migrants seeking information from local people around. Of course, one of the worries is that people may not be able to articulate thoughts clearly. But there are also social concerns beyond that, like the worry that local people may view second-language speakers as outsiders and think they are not capable of doing stuff." [P3, fellow migrant]

Domestic participants felt ill-equipped to alleviate such social concerns of international migrants. They expressed that they "couldn't offer effective assistance if migrants remained hesitant to reach out." Notably, migrants in our sample never mentioned these social consequences when they spoke of interactions with other international migrants, even though language barriers also existed in exchanges among migrants with different native languages.

Dynamic Information Landscapes and Knowledge Disparities. When participants reflected on the qualifications necessary for individuals to effectively assist others with their daily information seeking, they converged on one particular point: holding sufficient knowledge about the local systems, infrastructure, and services. Participants noted that while both fellow migrants and domestic residents can act as information providers, each group brings distinct benefits and confronts unique challenges when aiding migrant information seekers.

Migrant participants shared that to develop sufficient local knowledge, individuals usually need to stay long enough in the host country. Many gained knowledge through their daily experiences or word of mouth in their social circle. Migrants in our sample felt that international migrants usually experienced common struggles while navigating local resources and services. These shared problems enabled these participants to offer a unique local knowledge that is helpful to other migrants:

"For all the internationals who study or work overseas, we might not be facing the exact same problem, but we face the same set of stressors. For example, most of us have trouble understanding the local healthcare system or buying a car. If one of us has learned something, this person can share the information with anybody who is not familiar with the system." [P3, fellow migrant]

Also, multiple migrant participants noted that they often provided informational support regarding knowledge specifically tied to their migration status, such as nuances related to visa regulations, the process of renewing a work permit, or the experience of transitioning from student to employment status in the host country. This distinct information, largely unfamiliar to domestic residents, can be helpful for international migrants navigating similar paths. For example:

"We tend to know more about the rules and laws that apply to their visa for a temporary stay in this country. One example is optional practical training (OPT) required for us to work after graduation. It is specific to international students. Domestic people do not really understand that information or they may not care much, to be honest." [P11, fellow migrant]

Meanwhile, migrant participants mentioned their difficulties of keeping up with the changing information landscape. While some of these participants reflected on their experience of acting as providers for other migrants, they reported that staying up to date with the latest resources, services, and practices could be challenging. This is particularly true for migration-related information needs. Participants acknowledged the importance of such information but also recognized its intermittent nature: some migration-related information needs are critical, but once the issue is resolved, it generally does not require attention again for several years. Thus, it can be challenging for a person to keep up with all the recent updates. As explained by one participant:

"The policies are changing fast. I knew another international student in the program. He asked me about travel regulations with our visa. I suggested scheduling an in-person appointment with his advisor to update his travel signature. However, it turned out my suggestion was not helpful. He sent couple of emails and found out it can be done online now. Many practices were updated during the pandemic, and obviously, neither me nor my friend could not keep track of all this information." [P10, fellow migrant]

Compared with migrants, one distinct benefit of domestic residents is that the latter have rich experiential knowledge about local systems and essential services in the host country. As described by our participants, this knowledge can help the former stay aware of resources that they would not be able to discover otherwise:

"Domestic people know all the choices that can help. They also understand the pros and cons of each choice. However, migrants usually do not have much background knowledge [about the host country's local situation], and it can be hard for them to choose among different information sources. So, domestic people can definitely help others to decide which one is more helpful." [P4, fellow migrant]

"A lot of the information and support would be more local, wouldn't it? Banking, employment opportunities, grocery stores... Local people know where they are and how to access them. That's where a local helper would be most beneficial. A newcomer can certainly learn the bus route and timetable by searching things online. But a local person will be able to tell them like, 'this bus always runs 10 min late' or 'there's 2 different bus lines.' This detailed information can be visible only to the locals and it is very helpful." [P21, domestic resident]

Meanwhile, domestic participants in our sample shared that it was sometimes difficult to comprehend the challenges of migrants. They made a note that there was often "a gap between what local people think the migrants know and what the migrants actually know." Domestic participants often carried over their assumptions of international migrant groups when offering help. For instance, P14 and P16 worked as volunteers who assisted migrants in their local communities. They emphasized the importance of removing themselves from certain assumptions before communicating with migrants and learning their needs:

"Many local people assume that, because migrants passed the TOEFL exam or something like that, they must be ready to go. You can just throw them into the world. That assumption is not true. You can't assume people have resources internally based on one standardized test. Also, local people often assume that migrants can use the local infrastructure that's in place, which is not necessarily true either." [P16, domestic resident]

"It would be helpful if I knew what systems this migrant has in their home country and how they work. When a migrant comes to me for help, I often start with asking them questions like, 'how would you seek a medical appointment in your home country?' After they share, I will realize how their systems differ from ours. Knowing that difference will help me explain things clearly." [P14, domestic resident]

Paradox Between "Feeling Motivated" and "Hesitating to Commit." Participants acknowledged that fostering and maintaining the motivation of information providers to offer assistance is crucial, as the sustainability of these networks relies upon individuals' willingness to help. In particular, our analysis uncovered that the two groups of information providers had distinct motivations but faced similar challenges related to commitment.

Many migrants hold information that may benefit the daily practices of one another, regardless of their national background. This commonality served as the foundation for our migrant participants to build emotional alignment with other information seekers who are also international migrants. Their motivation to help is rooted in shared experiences and the desire to alleviate similar hardships for others. As elaborated by one migrant participant:

"I often grapple with my own issues, whether it is about housing or finding out the restrictions for a job search. I have been in these situations and want to ease the journey for others. I know how important my help can be to those in the same boat." [P1, fellow migrant]

In contrast, our domestic participants identified the sense of personal fulfillment as their primary motivation to assist migrant information seekers in their new journey. They described the rewards of witnessing firsthand the impact of their support, as migrants became more confident and independent in their new environment.

Furthermore, migrant participants in our sample all reported that much of their assistance with other migrants' information seeking happened during their initial year of settlement. They recalled that acting as a helper for others often burdened their own life that was already filled with acculturation stress. As a result, they found themselves lacking the bandwidth to commit to more responsibilities. As P10 noted:

> "For a lot of internationals, we have to try very hard to focus on academic performance, meet the requirements at work, and deal with homesickness. There is a lot to handle while we still struggle with listening and understanding everyone in English. We just do not have enough time to take care of anything else." [P10, fellow migrant]

Similarly, domestic participants expressed hesitation to engage in volunteer programs, especially those that require longer-term support and one-on-one mentorship for migrants. Participants shared that the commitment to continuous assistance can be substantial, requiring considerable time and energy. They voiced concerns about their capacity to sustain such intensive involvement in the face of their personal and professional obligations. Instead, participants desired some ways to contribute in a more flexible manner, as shared by P17 and P15:

> "I spent half a year volunteering in a program matched with two mentees from China and Mexico. It was a rewarding experience, but sometimes overwhelming. My job [in the company] involves a lot of fieldwork, and can get pretty busy, leaving little room for my commitment [to supporting others]. I would need more flexible ways to get involved, just trying to support others while still maintaining balance in our personal lives." [P17, domestic resident]

> "My wife saw the value and impact of what we do [as volunteers]. But she's concerned about over-committing as she isn't retired yet. Often, she would gather flyers in our neighborhoods to pass on me for distribution in my [volunteer] group. I mean, considering people like her, there's a vast potential support network out there; people would need to explore ways to tap into it without imposing overwhelming obligations." [P15, domestic resident]

5.2 ICT Design for the Information Exchange Between Information Providers and Seekers

Making Deliberate Use of Language Technologies. Participants reflected on the pros and cons of leveraging AI-powered language technologies, such as machine translation, for communication between information providers and seekers of different language backgrounds. Several domestic participants in our sample considered machine translation a promising technology to bridge language barriers. They believed that these tools have the potential to offer international migrants more independence, as they would "give migrants a sense of control on their second language."

In contrast, the migrant participants were more aware of this technology's limitations due to their prior experiences. For them, it is essential that ICT platforms not only incorporate a machine translation module but also indicate the risk of counting on sometimes-imperfect translation output:

> "Google Translate could generate translation outcomes that do not follow people's natural way of talking. It could be weird to use their words or phrases when we provide information to people. It could let others form the wrong impression about you. For example, you may sound condescending when helping others because Google translates your message in a way that includes uncommon words and complex sentence structures." [P7, fellow migrant]

> "People can talk through the emotional aspect of their needs. However, machines may have a really difficult time understanding the emotion conveyed in a message and the severity of it. If I was using machines to translate information I offered, they [seekers] should pay more attention to the factual aspect of the request. Emotions should be handled by human translators." [P8, fellow migrant]

Identifying Shared Knowledge for Effective Information Exchange.
Domestic participants reflected on their practices that aimed to contextualize the information seeker's needs. They reported using shared vocabularies and knowledge as a starting point to fully comprehend the information needs of migrant seekers. Several participants shared examples from they experience serving as volunteers at the city library to assist migrants with information seeking. When seekers' information needs were ambiguous, volunteers tried to find words and concepts that were likely to be understood by both parties. Volunteers started with simple openers such as "Do you have a library card?" or "What do you need today"? to initiate the conversation with the information seeker. P14 explained the rationale behind these actions:

> "When they [migrant seekers] come in the library and say hi, the first question I will ask is, do you have a library card? What do you need today? Because that's the starting point to know their needs. If I have problems understanding their requests, I will catch the keywords and try to figure out the shared vocabulary and knowledge between us. When I catch the keyword resume, I will ask if they need to make a cover letter and such. I just ask questions using more common words so that people can easily answer with yes or no. Then I put these pieces together to figure out what people really need." [P14, domestic resident]

Asking "Do you have a library card?" is a tactical approach in this context. The library card symbolizes a shared understanding between the information provider and seeker. This question, as well as other yes/no ones, is part of the information provider's strategy to narrow down the seeker's needs and guide the interaction toward a productive outcome.

We communicated the above strategies to migrant participants in our sample to gather their feedback. They considered the practice helpful, but soon realized it would be inefficient and time-consuming for complex queries as "some of the requests might be too broad to be addressed by yes/no questions." More importantly, continuous probing with questions might frustrate some migrant participants and make them "feel like being talked down to." Our participants envisioned tools that would enable an efficient discovery of common ground between information seekers and providers. For example, participant P17 shared:

"A cheat sheet outlining similarities and differences between systems in a migrant's home country and here could be a great help. For example, while online banking is globally similar, paper-based banking like check deposits here confuses many migrants. A guide that provides a side-by-side comparison of systems, tailored to a person's nationality, could highlight the contrasts between two countries. This, in turn, would allow us to provide specifically adapted guidance based on their contexts." [P17, domestic resident]

Enabling the Communication of Know-How. In the long term, migrants may benefit more from learning how to navigate the host country's information system themselves than by relying on the help of others. To this end, several participants shared their thoughts regarding future ICT tools that could equip migrants with the skills and knowledge to become independent, rather than just offering timely assistance. Such insights revolved around generating user-tailored tutorials as the core feature of the design.

"If a migrant comes to me for help, I am always happy to give them the information they need. However, it is more important to scaffold them for the future. For example, I can screen capture what I do, and then share it with the person in a file. Because that way they can watch what it is and then be like, 'oh that was easy'. It is not really easy until you have seen the whole process being done. In the future, maybe the system can automatically generate a video for the person to follow. They will get the right information by following the video." [P13, domestic resident]

6   Discussion

By incorporating the perspectives of information providers, we identify the barriers encountered by fellow migrants and domestic residents in providing effective assistance to migrants. These barriers include, but not limited to, the imbalance in language proficiency between migrant information seekers and their information providers. Our findings build upon those reported in other studies [32,40] and add new insights to prior research that indicates the importance to understand the characteristics and utility of diverse information sources.

Specifically, existing models within library and information science studies focus primarily on the information seeker and the information being requested [17,30,65], offering a simplified view of the information provider. The analysis of our data revealed distinct challenges faced by information providers who are fellow migrants and domestic residents, respectively. Fellow migrants, for example, often struggled to stay updated with the ever-evolving migration policies and regulations, while domestics sometimes found it hard to contextualize migrants' inquiries.

Previous work has developed various messaging platforms facilitating the information exchange on diverse daily topics between resettling migrants and other individuals living in the host country [8,35,52]. Most projects demonstrate the potential of domestic residents to assist migrants using their local knowledge. However, they overlooked the impact of not understanding the migrant's home country systems on effective communication. Some research in this area emphasized the need to bridge the knowledge gap between international migrants and their information providers, but it paid exclusive attention to assisting migrants in learning about local knowledge. Our results hint at the opportunity for information providers to grasp more about migrants' backgrounds which, consequently, may lessen the stress experienced by the migrants [62]. We suggest future ICTs incorporate features that share relevant contextual information about migrants with domestic providers.

Furthermore, information providers in our research reflected on their practices and concerns toward balancing their own lives with helping international migrants. They expressed the desire to assist with migrants' information seeking in a more flexible manner, such as through task-based commitments (e.g., resolving single information searches) rather than longer-term engagements (e.g., paired mentorship). We suspect that taking a task-based approach can alleviate common issues reported by existing programs serving the migrant information seeker's needs. For example, Schwarz et al. reported their research with an information exchange program that paired immigrants with local volunteers in Austria and the United Kingdom [52]. Due to the burden of providing long-term service, multiple Arabic-speaking volunteers ceased participating after the first few weeks. Their withdrawal let to a reduced willingness among Arabic migrants to engage with and trust the service. We propose that a future system connecting migrant information seekers and potential providers should integrate alternative mechanisms to ensure sustainability. To this end, adopting the model of an online freelance marketplace (e.g., TaskRabbit) can benefit the management of workload distribution and ensure a steady and diverse pool of participants serving the information provider's role over time [26].

7 Limitations

Our research has several limitations. Despite efforts for diverse recruitment, our sample may not exhaust the full range of potential information providers beyond a migrant's co-nationals. We primarily leveraged online platforms for data collection, possibly excluding those with limited digital literacy. Migrant participants in our final sample all have lived in the host country for less than 10 years. Compared with other individuals qualified for our definition of fellow migrants, these participants may share unique commonalities in assisting another migrant's daily information seeking. Also, all participants in our research were asked to reflect on their experiences assisting with the information needs of international migrants in any self-selected areas. While this choice enabled us to identify representative challenges and practices in information seeking and providing across areas, it limited our ability delve deep into a specific domain (e.g., information seeking for job search). The transferability of our findings should be considered with these constraints in mind.

8 Conclusion

Through in-depth interviews with 21 information providers, including fellow migrants from different home countries and domestic residents, we identified challenges that hinder people from offering information support to international migrants. These challenges consider how information providers deal with language barriers, overcome knowledge disparities, and calibrate their effort commitment when assisting with a migrant's informational needs. Our work sheds light on design directions for future ICTs that facilitate international migrants' daily information seeking by accounting for information providers' needs and concerns.

Acknowledgement. This work receives support from the Research Improvement Grants provided by the University of Maryland's INFO College. We thank the anonymous reviewers for their valuable comments on earlier versions of our paper.

References

1. Alberts, H.C., Hazen, H.D.: "there are always two voices..." International students intentions to stay in the United States or return to their home countries. Int. Migr. **43**(3), 131–154 (2005)
2. Alho, R.: 'you need to know someone who knows someone': international students' job-search experiences. Nordic J. Work. Life Stud. **10**, 3–22 (2020)
3. Alzougool, B., Chang, S., Gomes, C., Berry, M.: Finding their way around: international students' use of information sources. J. Adv. Manage. Sci. **1**(1), 43–49 (2013)
4. Berendt, B., Kralisch, A.: A user-centric approach to identifying best deployment strategies for language tools: the impact of content and access language on web user behaviour and attitudes. Inf. Retr. **12**, 380–399 (2009)

5. Blasi, D.E., Mishra, V., García, A.M., Dexter, J.P.: Linguistic fairness in the us: the case of multilingual public health information about COVID-19. medRxiv pp. 2021–09 (2021)
6. Bochner, S., McLeod, B.M., Lin, A.: Friendship patterns of overseas students: a functional model 1. Int. J. Psychol. **12**(4), 277–294 (1977)
7. Braun, V., Clarke, V.: Using thematic analysis in psychology. Qual. Res. Psychol. **3**(2), 77–101 (2006)
8. Brown, D., Grinter, R.E.: Designing for transient use: a human-in-the-loop translation platform for refugees. In: Proceedings of the 2016 CHI Conference on Human Factors in Computing Systems, pp. 321–330 (2016)
9. Caidi, N., Allard, D., Dechief, D.: Information practices of immigrants to Canada: a review of the literature. Unpublished report to Citizenship and Immigration Canada (2008)
10. Caidi, N., Allard, D., Quirke, L.: Information practices of immigrants. Ann. Rev. Inf. Sci. Technol. **44**(1), 491–531 (2010)
11. Case, D.O.: A model of the information seeking and decision making of online coin buyers. Inf. Res. **15**(4), 15–4 (2010)
12. Chang, S., Gomes, C.: Digital journeys: a perspective on understanding the digital experiences of international students. J. Int. Stud. **7**(2), 347–466 (2017)
13. Chang, S., McKay, D., Caidi, N., Mendoza, A., Gomes, C., Ekmekcioglu, C.: From way across the sea: information overload and international students during the COVID-19 pandemic. Proc. Assoc. Inf. Sci. Technol. **57**(1), e289 (2020)
14. Chatman, E.A.: Life in a small world: applicability of gratification theory to information-seeking behavior. J. Am. Soc. Inf. Sci. **42**(6), 438–449 (1991)
15. Chung, E., Yoon, J.: An exploratory analysis of international students' information needs and uses/exploration et analyse des besoins et des utilisations d'information des étudiants internationaux. Can. J. Inf. Libr. Sci. **39**(1), 36–59 (2015)
16. Cobo, C.: Exploration of open educational resources in non-English speaking communities. Int. Rev. Res. Open Distrib. Learn. **14**(2), 106–128 (2013)
17. Ellis, D.: A behavioural approach to information retrieval system design. J. Doc. **45**(3), 171–212 (1989)
18. Forbush, E., Foucault-Welles, B.: Social media use and adaptation among Chinese students beginning to study in the united states. Int. J. Intercult. Relat. **50**, 1–12 (2016)
19. Gao, G., Zheng, J., Choe, E.K., Yamashita, N.: Taking a language detour: how international migrants speaking a minority language seek COVID-related information in their host countries. Proc. ACM Human-Comput. Interac. **6**(CSCW2), 1–32 (2022)
20. Gatteschi, V., Lamberti, F., Demartini, C.: Lo-match: a semantic platform for matching migrants' competences with Labour market's needs. In: Proceedings of the 2012 IEEE Global Engineering Education Conference (EDUCON), pp. 1–5. IEEE (2012)
21. Gomes, C., Berry, M., Alzougool, B., Chang, S.: Home away from home: international students and their identity-based social networks in Australia. J. Int. Stud. **4**(1), 2–15 (2014)
22. Hamid, S., Bukhari, S.: Information seeking behaviour and international students: the role of social media in addressing challenges while abroad, pp. 590–596. Istanbul, Turkey, August 2015. http://www.icoci.cms.net.my/proceedings/2015/TOC.html

23. Han, M., Pong, H.: Mental health help-seeking behaviors among Asian American community college students: the effect of stigma, cultural barriers, and acculturation. J. Coll. Stud. Dev. **56**(1), 1–14 (2015)
24. Hendrickson, B., Rosen, D., Aune, R.K.: An analysis of friendship networks, social connectedness, homesickness, and satisfaction levels of international students. Int. J. Intercult. Relat. **35**(3), 281–295 (2011)
25. Hirsch, T., Liu, J.: Speakeasy: overcoming barriers and promoting community development in an immigrant neighborhood. In: Proceedings of the 5th Conference on Designing Interactive Systems: Processes, Practices, Methods, and Techniques, pp. 345–348 (2004)
26. Hoque, F.: How The Rising Gig Economy is Reshaping Businesses, September 2015. https://www.fastcompany.com/3051315/the-gig-economy-is-going-global-heres-why-and-what-it-means
27. Hurh, W.M., Kim, K.C.: Religious participation of Korean immigrants in the United States. J. Sci. Study Relig. **29**, 19–34 (1990)
28. Jackson, P.A.: Incoming international students and the library: a survey. Ref. Serv. Rev. **33**(2), 197–209 (2005)
29. Jeong, W.: Unbreakable ethnic bonds: information-seeking behavior of Korean graduate students in the united states. Librar. Inf. Sci. Res. **26**(3), 384–400 (2004)
30. Johnson, J.D.: Cancer-related Information Seeking. Hampton Press, Creskill, NJ (1997)
31. Johnson, J.D., Case, D.O.: Health Information Seeking, vol. 52. Peter Lang, New York (2012)
32. Komito, L., Bates, J.: Migrants' information practices and use of social media in Ireland: networks and community, pp. 289-295. iConference 2011, Association for Computing Machinery, New York, NY, USA (2011). https://doi.org/10.1145/1940761.1940801
33. Kudo, K., Simkin, K.A.: Intercultural friendship formation: the case of Japanese students at an Australian university. J. Intercult. Stud. **24**(2), 91–114 (2003)
34. Kuhlthau, C.C.: Inside the search process: information seeking from the user's perspective. J. Am. Soc. Inf. Sci. **42**(5), 361–371 (1991)
35. Kukulska-Hulme, A., Gaved, M., Paletta, L., Scanlon, E., Jones, A., Brasher, A.: Mobile incidental learning to support the inclusion of recent immigrants. Ubiquit. Learn. Int. J. **7**(2), 9–21 (2015)
36. Lee, E.J., Lee, L., Jang, J.: Internet for the internationals: effects of internet use motivations on international students' college adjustment. Cyberpsychol. Behav. Soc. Netw. **14**(7–8), 433–437 (2011)
37. Liao, Y., Finn, M., Lu, J.: Information-seeking behavior of international graduate students vs. American graduate students: a user study at Virginia tech 2005. College. Res. Librar. **68**(1), 5–25 (2007)
38. Liu, G., Winn, D.: Chinese graduate students and the Canadian academic library: a user study at the University of Windsor. J. Acad. Librariansh. **35**(6), 565–573 (2009)
39. Liu, M., Redfern, B.: Information-seeking behavior of multicultural students: a case study at San Jose State University. College Res. Librar. **58**(4), 348–354 (1997)
40. Mao, Y.: Investigating Chinese migrants' information-seeking patterns in Canada: media selection and language preference. Glob. Media J. **8**(2), 113 (2015)
41. Maundeni, T.: The role of social networks in the adjustment of African students to British society: students' perceptions. Race Ethn. Educ. **4**(3), 253–276 (2001)

42. Mehra, B., Papajohn, D.: "glocal" patterns of communication-information convergences in internet use: cross-cultural behavior of international teaching assistants in a culturally alien information environment. Int. Inf. Librar. Rev. **39**(1), 12–30 (2007)

43. Ngan, H.Y., Lifanova, A., Jarke, J., Broer, J.: Refugees welcome: supporting informal language learning and integration with a gamified mobile application. In: Verbert, K., Sharples, M., Klobučar, T. (eds.) EC-TEL 2016. LNCS, vol. 9891, pp. 521–524. Springer, Cham (2016). https://doi.org/10.1007/978-3-319-45153-4_54

44. Oh, C.Y., Butler, B.S.: Newcomers from the other side of the globe: international students' local information seeking during adjustment. Proc. Assoc. Inf. Sci. Technol. **53**(1), 1–6 (2016)

45. Oh, C.Y., Butler, B.S., Lee, M.: Information behavior of international students settling in an unfamiliar geo-spatial environment. Proc. Am. Soc. Inf. Sci. Technol. **51**(1), 1–11 (2014)

46. Pavlenko, A.: "I'm very not about the law part": nonnative speakers of English and the Miranda warnings. TESOL Q. **42**(1), 1–30 (2008)

47. Robson, A., Robinson, L.: Building on models of information behaviour: linking information seeking and communication. J. Doc. **69**(2), 169–193 (2013)

48. Rózsa, G., Komlodi, A., Chu, P.: Online searching in English as a foreign language. In: Proceedings of the 24th International Conference on World Wide Web, pp. 875–880 (2015)

49. Rui, J.R., Wang, H.: Social network sites and international students' cross-cultural adaptation. Comput. Hum. Behav. **49**, 400–411 (2015)

50. Sakurai, T., McCall-Wolf, F., Kashima, E.S.: Building intercultural links: the impact of a multicultural intervention programme on social ties of international students in Australia. Int. J. Intercult. Relat. **34**(2), 176–185 (2010)

51. Savolainen, R.: Everyday life information seeking: approaching information seeking in the context of "way of life.". Librar. Inf. Sci. Res. **17**(3), 259–294 (1995)

52. Schwarz, S., Salazar, E.P., Bobeth, J., Bersia, N., Tscheligi, M.: Help radar: ubiquitous assistance for newly arrived immigrants. In: Proceedings of the 14th International Conference on Mobile and Ubiquitous Multimedia, pp. 183–194 (2015)

53. Seguin, J.P., Varghese, D., Anwar, M., Bartindale, T., Olivier, P.: Co-designing digital platforms for volunteer-led migrant community welfare support. In: Designing Interactive Systems Conference, pp. 247–262 (2022)

54. Sin, S.C.J.: Demographic differences in international students' information source uses and everyday information seeking challenges. J. Acad. Librariansh. **41**(4), 466–474 (2015)

55. Sin, S.C.J., Kim, K.S., Yang, J., Park, J.A., Laugheed, Z.T.: International students' acculturation information seeking: personality, information needs and uses. Proc. Am. Soc. Inf. Sci. Technol. **48**(1), 1–4 (2011)

56. Smith, R.A., Khawaja, N.G.: A review of the acculturation experiences of international students. Int. J. Intercult. Relat. **35**(6), 699–713 (2011)

57. Suh, M., Hsieh, G.: The "had mores": exploring Korean immigrants' information behavior and ICT usage when settling in the United States. J. Am. Soc. Inf. Sci. **70**(1), 38–48 (2019)

58. Tang, C., Gui, X., Chen, Y., Magueramane, M.: New to a country: barriers for international students to access health services and opportunities for design. In: Proceedings of the 12th EAI International Conference on Pervasive Computing Technologies for Healthcare, pp. 45–54 (2018)

59. Thomas, F.: Transnational health and treatment networks: meaning, value and place in health seeking amongst Southern African migrants in London. Health Place **16**(3), 606–612 (2010)
60. Tsai, C.H., Gui, X., Kou, Y., Carroll, J.M.: With help from afar: cross-local communication in an online COVID-19 pandemic community. Proc. ACM Human-Comput. Interact. **5**(CSCW2), 1–24 (2021)
61. Wang, L., Kwak, M.J.: Immigration, barriers to healthcare and transnational ties: a case study of South Korean immigrants in Toronto, Canada. Soc. Sci. Med. **133**, 340–348 (2015)
62. Ward, C., Bochner, S., Furnham, A.: The Psychology of Culture Shock (2001). https://doi.org/10.4324/9781003070696
63. Ward, C., Searle, W.: The impact of value discrepancies and cultural identity on psychological and sociocultural adjustment of sojourners. Int. J. Intercult. Relat. **15**(2), 209–224 (1991)
64. Williams, C.T., Johnson, L.R.: Why can't we be friends?: Multicultural attitudes and friendships with international students. Int. J. Intercult. Relat. **35**(1), 41–48 (2011)
65. Wilson, T.D.: On user studies and information needs. J. Doc. **37**(1), 3–15 (1981)
66. Wilson, T.D.: Information needs and uses: fifty years of progress. Fifty Years Inf. Progr. J. Doc. Rev. **28**(1), 15–51 (1994)
67. Wyche, S.P., Grinter, R.E.: "this is how we do it in my country" a study of computer-mediated family communication among Kenyan migrants in the united states. In: Proceedings of the ACM 2012 conference on Computer Supported Cooperative Work, pp. 87–96 (2012)
68. Yan, K., Berliner, D.C.: Chinese international students' personal and sociocultural stressors in the united states. J. Coll. Stud. Dev. **54**(1), 62–84 (2013)
69. Ye, J.: Traditional and online support networks in the cross-cultural adaptation of Chinese international students in the United States. J. Comput. Mediat. Commun. **11**(3), 863–876 (2006)
70. Yeh, C.J., Inose, M.: International students' reported English fluency, social support satisfaction, and social connectedness as predictors of acculturative stress. Couns. Psychol. Q. **16**(1), 15–28 (2003)
71. Yi, Z.: International student perceptions of information needs and use. J. Acad. Librariansh. **33**(6), 666–673 (2007)
72. Yoon, J., Chung, E.: International students' information needs and seeking behaviours throughout the settlement stages. Libri **67**(2), 119–128 (2017)
73. Yuan, C.W., Setlock, L.D., Cosley, D., Fussell, S.R.: Understanding informal communication in multilingual contexts. In: Proceedings of the 2013 Conference on Computer Supported Cooperative Work, pp. 909–922 (2013)

Recordkeeping Practices of Grassroots Community Organizations: Exploring the Potential Application of Push-Pull-Mooring Theory

Md Khalid Hossain[✉] ⓘ, Viviane Frings-Hessami ⓘ, and Gillian Christina Oliver ⓘ

Monash University, Victoria 3800, Australia

{md.khalid.hossain,viviane.hessami,Gillian.Oliver}@monash.edu

Abstract. Across the world, grassroots community organizations contribute to local socioeconomic development and community empowerment. Most of these grassroots community organizations initially start as informal groups autonomously formed by like-minded members of the community or shaped due to the influence of external agencies like large non-government organizations in the development sector. Different factors, notably the vision of leaders, desire for sustaining long-term operations, and financial gains, often influence these entities to embrace the formal shape of an organization. Owing to this transition from informality to formality, grassroots community organizations also have to change their approach to recordkeeping practices from reactive to proactive ones. Although the recordkeeping literature has a strong focus on organizational practices, the literature hardly looked at the specific case of grassroots community organizations. The literature did not investigate the influencing factors that reshape the recordkeeping practices of grassroots community organizations. In this regard, the push-pull-mooring theory adopted initially by scholars in migration studies has the potential to be applied to grassroots community organizations' recordkeeping practices to explain the influencing factors. Considering this, we aim to explore the potential application of the push-pull-mooring theory in the context of the transitional recordkeeping practices of grassroots community organizations.

Keywords: Grassroots Community Organization · Recordkeeping Practices · Push Factors · Pull Factors · Mooring Factors

1 Recordkeeping Practices of Organizations

From an organizational perspective, preserving 'complete, reliable, and accurate evidence of decisions and transactions' influenced the evolution of the concept of recordkeeping [11: 137]. They argued that requirements related to legal and statutory regulations push the organizations to have a recordkeeping system that facilitates the creation and capture of records. These records become an integral part of the business process of an organization considering the nature of business. Organizations also need to show

I. Sserwanga et al. (Eds.): iConference 2024, LNCS 14598, pp. 356–364, 2024.
https://doi.org/10.1007/978-3-031-57867-0_27

evidence of transactions, both financial and non-financial, over a time to indicate their transparent and accountable business processes. Records act as evidence for organizations and organizations adopt numerous recordkeeping practices [11]. While the records management literature used the terms 'recordkeeping' and 'record keeping', Upward et al. [35] clarified that along with creating and capturing records, recordkeeping also entails the process of organizing and pluralizing records. They further highlighted that when the term 'record keeping' is used in an organizational setting, it refers to the way of keeping records as physical artefacts. Here, we are using the term 'recordkeeping' as we are more interested in focusing on the holistic idea of managing records over time.

This holistic idea was advanced in the records continuum model by Upward [34] and widely cited in the academic literature on recordkeeping [7, 18, 32]. From an organizational perspective, the four continua highlighted in the model were identity, Transactionality, evidentiality, and recordkeeping containers. In the model, identity is related to the authorities or entities within the organization that make and keep records while making decisions on other actors to be involved in the process and facilitating their empowerment from socio-cultural perspectives. Secondly, Transactionality in the model refers to records as products of different organizational activities that are generated from the organization's transactions or dealings. Next, evidentiality is included in the model since records are key verified evidence of organizational memory indicating organizational process over the years. Finally, recordkeeping containers are the objects where records are deposited like files where organizational documents are deposited [35]. Overall, organizations' recordkeeping allows them to administer and operate effectively. Touray [33] argued that it is the 'basis for accountability, transparency, protection of rights and entitlements, anti-corruption strategies, poverty reduction and effective management of resources.

Recordkeeping literature has been predominantly developed from the perspective of formal organizations (like academic, government, business, non-government etc.) and less from individual, community, or professional group perspectives. For example, Shankar [27] studied recordkeeping in the setting of an academic research laboratory by using an ethnographic methodology. She found that in that setting, scientists kept handwritten and typed records to tell the story of physical actions that happened in the laboratory and the mental processes behind those actions in the forms of dated narratives, graphs, charts, drawings, etc. She argued that judicial, cultural, institutional, and professional factors influence recordkeeping [27]. In relation to government organizations, Klareld [12] studied recordkeeping in a Swedish public agency that had adopted an outsourcing policy. She found that due to a particular focus on outsourcing, related recordkeeping practices need to be customized and guided by a legal framework. The study indicates that despite having generic practices for recordkeeping for usual functions, organizational recordkeeping may have to be readjusted for some distinct functions.

Sundberg and Wallin [29] studied recordkeeping in business organizations by exploring five banks and one insurance company from the Swedish financial sector. They found that the ability to access customer records from any part of the organization, irrespective of subsidiary office or headquarters, influences the electronic recordkeeping of business organizations operating as multinational organizations. In the context of Ghana, Mintah et al. [20] studied recordkeeping in small and medium-sized enterprises (SMEs) and found that business records management training and policies are positively associated with business records management. For Ghanaian SMEs, business records management was found to positively influence the business growth.

Overall, we observed that the recordkeeping literature is strongly focused on formal organizations for both conceptual and empirical works but offers a solid foundation to expand the recordkeeping research in semi-formal and informal settings. In this regard, Courtney [6] studied recordkeeping in a choir, a musical organization, which she described as being 'freestanding' and 'amateur' to indicate its informal nature as an organization. She highlighted that this type of organizations is rarely studied in record-keeping research while arguing the importance of studying such organizations due to their distinct volunteer-based nature of organizational activities as opposed to salaried staff-based business organizations. Since volunteers are almost all at the same level in this type of informal organization, identity as referred to in the records continuum model remains blurry as all volunteers can make decisions on recordkeeping. Most of the grass-roots community organizations have a similar nature of volunteer-based operations at the beginning and those organizations are empirically understudied in recordkeeping research. In this regard, in the context of Aboriginal community archives in Australia, Thorpe [31] mentioned the role of community organizations as a source of records, hinting that some recordkeeping practices exist in community organizations despite having not been studied adequately.

Consequently, considering their importance in the society and their potential to turn into larger organizations from informal groups (by increasing geographic coverage and scope of works), the purpose of this paper is to scope out a relevant theoretical framework that can systematically highlight the influencing factors behind recordkeeping of grassroots community organizations. After setting the background of the paper and highlighting recordkeeping literature, the paper presents literature on grassroots community organizations and our insights on their recordkeeping. The proposed theoretical framework is discussed next, and the paper subsequently concludes by indicating its academic and practical implications.

2   Grassroots Community Organizations

Across the world, community organizations at the grassroots level have been forming over many years, having different forms, and serving different purposes. Initiating initially as informal groups, grassroots community organizations take the forms of social or political pressure groups, locally organized action groups or self-help groups [25]. Grassroots community organizations are sometimes formed to serve the purpose of a group serving the interests of a particular labor or professional group. Often the formation of these organizations is related to serving the purpose of advocating for a particular issue or several issues like transparent and accountable delivery of government services. These organizations are also formed as informal groups to take social, economic, or environmental action beneficial for their communities like stopping gender-based violence, delivering community health programs, or greening the village [25, 38]. Due to their important roles, the transition of grassroots community organizations from informal groups to formal organizations is an interest of community development professionals including the government and non-government organizations [4, 5, 8].

Since the intent of many grassroots community organizations is initially to achieve social justice, these organizations need to be collectively empowered to take power. In this regard, these organizations need to have task-oriented groups involving the active members as well as general members to enable community participants to access and use valuable information, build their skills, learn ways to express opinions and take actions, and make decisions. Through this process, members of the task-oriented groups and other general members of grassroots community organizations experience their collective power and develop a sense of ownership for their organization [28]. While volunteers acting as leaders or members of task-oriented groups are the main strength of grassroots community organizations, the major challenges these organizations face during the organizational journey are related to ensuring continuous and sustained participation of members, attracting new members, and keeping the organizational leaders engaged [25].

As drop-out of members and leaders is a reality for grassroots community organizations, retaining collective organizational memory and evidence of organizational processes is significant for these organizations to transition from an unstructured informal group to a structured formal organization where recordkeeping plays a vital role [1–3]. In most of the cases of formalization, grassroots community organizations take the shape of 'cooperative organizations' or 'cooperatives' and adhere to related government regulations [10]. Government policies also encourage such formalization process since it helps to ensure the transparency and accountability of those organizations, assists in regulating their operations and facilitates in advancing the government's development agenda through them [13, 19, 24]. Consequently, recordkeeping becomes an integral part of the operation of grassroots community organizations when they take more formal shapes in the long run. External exposure to regulations and engagements exerted at that point may push the community organizations to adopt different measures including actions on their recordkeeping [36]. At the same time, being a formal organization, grassroots community organizations also feel an internal urge to improve their organizational processes, including recordkeeping [30]. Since these organizations have been empirically understudied in recordkeeping research as mentioned previously, scoping out a relevant theoretical framework to systematically highlight external and internal influencing factors behind their recordkeeping practices is important for future empirical recordkeeping research.

3   Push-Pull-Mooring Theory as the Theoretical Framework

Although the recordkeeping literature mentioned numerous factors that influence recordkeeping practices in organizations, the literature did not categorize those factors as push, pull and mooring factors. Since recordkeeping studies on grassroots community organizations are scarce as highlighted in the following section, discussions on their recordkeeping practices highlighting apparent push, pull and mooring factors influencing those practices are non-existent. However, we argue that for grassroots community organizations (along with other informal, semi-formal and transitional organizations), identification and categorization of the influencing factors are important for focusing on those specifically for improving recordkeeping. In this regard, as the first step, we aim to propose a theoretical framework that can apprehend push, pull and mooring factors based on the evolution of grassroots community organizations' recordkeeping practices with a forward-looking approach.

Consequently, we propose that the push-pull-mooring theory adopted initially by Lee [14] and subsequently expanded by Moon [21] in migration studies be customized in academic studies on recordkeeping of grassroots community organizations. In his original argument, Lee [14] indicated that physical migration from a physical place of origin to another physical place of destination is the interaction between the push effects at the origin and the pull effects at the destination. Push effects are generally regarded as negative external factors present at the place of origin that push people to leave their place of origin. Such factors could be insecurity, climate change impacts and natural disasters, lack of economic opportunities etc. In general, people do not wish to migrate to another place where similar negative factors exist that pushed them out of their origin. They rather choose destinations for migration where there are positive factors that create the pull effects attracting people to migrate to that destination. Opposite to the push factors, the pull factors could understandably be improved security situation, better climate, available economic opportunities, etc. [14].

While expanding the work of the push-pull model proposed by Lee [14], Moon [21] emphasized considering other aspects of human motivation related to the field of social psychology by progressing from the behavioral and cognitive approaches. While the push-pull model is largely focused on the push effects and pull effects of origin and destination that are largely external and beyond someone's control, Moon [21] attempted to look internally by suggesting the combination of theories of human motivation with the understanding of cultural influences. He argued that such a holistic consideration will not only emphasize the personal realm of migration but also the institutional framework of politico-economic structure and socio-cultural values that influence people to make their migration decisions [21]. Consequently, Moon [21] expanded the Push-Pull model of Lee [14] by incorporating the concept of mooring and proposed the Push-Pull-Mooring (PPM) theory to explain migration intention of people from one place to another.

The PPM theory has been customized and adopted by other academic disciplines since it was proposed. For example, Nimako and Ntim [23] applied the PPM theory in business and management studies to explain consumer switching behavior from one product to another [23]. In education studies, Zhu et al. [41] applied the PPM theory to explain the university teachers' switching intention from a traditional classroom to a smart classroom. Hati et al. [9] used the theory in the context of religious studies to explain people's migration to Islamic banks from traditional banks. On the other hand, Zeng et al. [40] found the scope to adopt the PPM theory in policy studies by explaining public servants' switching from the traditional paper-based work pattern to land information system (LIS) applications in China. Since recordkeeping studies did not attempt to use the PPM theory unlike some other diverse disciplines, based on our review of the recordkeeping practices of grassroots community organizations and the nature of these organizations, we argue that there is a strong potential to apply the PPM theory in recordkeeping studies.

4 Recordkeeping of Grassroots Community Organizations

Adopting different recordkeeping practices does not happen autonomously in formal organizations. Corporate governance as well as regulatory pressures influence those practices a great deal [11]. For grassroots community organizations, autonomous adoption of recordkeeping practices may not even exist when these organizations start as an informal group. Since there are not adequate studies on grassroots community organizations' recordkeeping, we argue that grassroots community organizations gradually strengthen their recordkeeping due to different push factors based on gradual transition from informality to formality. The major push factor in this regard is government regulations [26]. Grassroots community organizations formalize themselves under government regulations to get formal recognition and to operate legally. Those regulations push them to create, capture, organize and pluralize their records so that grassroots community organizations can demonstrate their eligibility to become a formal organization and subsequently operate transparently and accountably. Besides, after formalization, separate government regulations on recordkeeping (different from the regulations to be a formal organization like a cooperative) for formal organizations further push grassroots community organizations to adopt additional recordkeeping standards. We also argue that community members as well as the broader society push formalized grassroots community organizations to adopt recordkeeping practices to demonstrate transparency and accountability since they are increasingly involved with those organizations in financial and non-financial transactions [37].

From the cases of grassroots community organizations' development across the world, we observe that many of those organizations grew and became stronger due to internal desires of organizational members and leaders for socio-economic and socio-ecological change by becoming a formal organization rather than due to any external pressure or push [6, 22]. When such internal desire exists within these organizations, members and leaders pull together different innovative and sustaining activities and practices [17]. We argue that in this type of scenario, recordkeeping of the grassroots community organizations will also experience the influence of pull factors generated within the organizations to excel in creating, capturing, organizing, and pluralizing their records to demonstrate their activities publicly and establish themselves as accountable organizations so that other stakeholders feel enthusiastic to collaborate with them. Similar to the external factors, the internal factors may also facilitate or prevent grassroots community organizations' decision to migrate from one recordkeeping practice to another.

Since every organization has its own preferences, ideologies, values, and motivations, often driven by their members and leaders, those factors, termed as mooring factors [15], could also facilitate or prevent grassroots community organizations' decision to migrate from one recordkeeping practice to another. Besides, organizations also operate through navigating different social and cultural values in their surroundings. Those are also considered as mooring factors Yu et al. [39] and can facilitate or prevent grassroots community organizations' decision to migrate from one recordkeeping practice to another.

5 Conclusion

The primary focus for pursuing a future research agenda using the Push-Pull-Mooring theory in recordkeeping studies highlighted in this paper is grassroots community organizations given their significance in society and the lack of specific focus in the recordkeeping literature on these organizations. We argue that the use of PPM theory after exploring recordkeeping practices of grassroots community organizations through empirical research will be helpful to categorize influencing factors as push, pull and mooring factors as the potential of its use discussed in the paper is largely conceptual based on studies of grassroots community organizations. This will benefit the government organizations and NGOs that are promoting and contributing to the organizational development of grassroots community organizations.

References

1. Arcand, J.L., Wagner, N.: Does community-driven development improve inclusiveness in peasant organizations?–Evidence from Senegal. World Dev. **78**, 105–124 (2016)
2. Barraud-Didier, V., Henninger, M.C., El Akremi, A.: The relationship between members' trust and participation in governance of cooperatives: the role of organizational commitment. Int. Food Agribus. Manage. Rev. **15**(1), 1–24 (2012)
3. Battley, B.: Authenticity in places of belonging: community collective memory as a complex, adaptive recordkeeping system. Arch. Manuscr. **48**(1), 59–79 (2020)
4. Choudry, A., Shragge, E.: Disciplining dissent: NGOs and community organizations. Globalizations **8**(4), 503–517 (2011)
5. Clarke, G.: Non-governmental organizations (NGOs) and politics in the developing world. Polit. Stud. **46**(1), 36–52 (1998)
6. Courtney, A.: Recordkeeping in freestanding amateur organisations: a case study of a choir. Arch. Rec. **43**(3), 267–284 (2022)
7. Frings-Hessami, V., Sarker, A., Oliver, G., Anwar, M.: Documentation in a community informatics project: the creation and sharing of information by women in Bangladesh. J. Doc. **76**(2), 552–570 (2020)
8. Glaser, M.A., Soskin, M.D., Smith, M.: Local government-supported community development: community priorities and issues of autonomy. Urban Affairs Rev. **31**(6), 778–798 (1996)
9. Hati, S.R.H., Gayatri, G., Indraswari, K.D.: Migration (Hijra) to Islamic bank based on push–pull–mooring theory: a services marketing mix perspective. J. Islam. Mark. **12**(8), 1637–1662 (2021)
10. Hussain, M.S.: The role of cooperative organizations in rural community development in Nigeria: Prospects and challenges. Acad. Res. Int. **5**(3), 189 (2014)
11. Ismail, A., Jamaludin, A.: Towards establishing a framework for managing trusted records in the electronic environment. Rec. Manag. J. **19**(2), 135–146 (2009)
12. Klareld, A.S.: Recordkeeping in an outsourcing public agency. Rec. Manag. J. **28**(1), 99–114 (2018)
13. Kumar, V., Wankhede, K.G., Gena, H.C.: Role of cooperatives in improving livelihood of farmers on sustainable basis. Am. J. Educ. Res. **3**(10), 1258–1266 (2015)
14. Lee, E.S.: A theory of migration. Demography **3**(1), 47–57 (1966)
15. Lisana, L.: Factors affecting university students switching intention to mobile learning: a push-pull-mooring theory perspective. Educ. Inf. Technol. **28**(5), 5341–5361 (2023)

16. Lucas, E.: Social development strategies of a non-governmental grassroots women's organisation in Nigeria. Int. J. Soc. Welf. **10**(3), 185–193 (2001)
17. Martiskainen, M.: The role of community leadership in the development of grassroots innovations. Environ. Innov. Soc. Trans. **22**, 78–89 (2017)
18. McKemmish, S.: Placing records continuum theory and practice. Arch. Sci. **1**, 333–359 (2001)
19. Medina, M.: Scavenger cooperatives in Asia and Latin America. Resour. Conserv. Recycl. **31**(1), 51–69 (2000)
20. Mintah, C., Gabir, M., Aloo, F., Ofori, E.K.: Do business records management affect business growth? PLoS ONE **17**(3), e0264135 (2022)
21. Moon, B.: Paradigms in migration research: exploring 'moorings' as a schema. Prog. Hum. Geogr. **19**(4), 504–524 (1995)
22. Newman, L., Waldron, L., Dale, A., Carriere, K.: Sustainable urban community development from the grassroots: challenges and opportunities in a pedestrian street initiative. Local Environ. **13**(2), 129–139 (2008)
23. Nimako, S.G., Ntim, B.A.: Construct specification and misspecification within the application of push-pull-mooring theory of switching behaviour. J. Bus. Manage. Sci. **1**(5), 83–95 (2013)
24. Ortmann, G.F., King, R.P.: Agricultural cooperatives I: history, theory and problems. Agrekon **46**(1), 40–68 (2007)
25. Perkins, D.D., Brown, B.B., Taylor, R.B.: The ecology of empowerment: predicting participation in community organizations. J. Soc. Issues **52**(1), 85–110 (1996)
26. Riswanto, E., Riswadi, R.: Judicial review of the law on community organisations in Indonesia. In: Proceedings of the First Multidiscipline International Conference, MIC 2021, Jakarta, Indonesia, 30 October 2021, January 2022
27. Shankar, K.: Recordkeeping in the production of scientific knowledge: an ethnographic study. Arch. Sci. **4**, 367–382 (2004)
28. Staples, L.: Community organizing for social justice: grassroots groups for power. Soc. Work Groups **35**(3), 287–296 (2012)
29. Sundberg, H.Å.K.A.N., Wallin, P.: Recordkeeping and information architecture-a study of the Swedish financial sector. Int. J. Publ. Inf. Syst. **3**(1), 31–45 (2007)
30. Thomas, B., Hangula, M.M.: Reviewing theory, practices, and dynamics of agricultural cooperatives: understanding cooperatives development in Namibia. J. Dev. Agric. Econ. **3**(16), 695–702 (2011)
31. Thorpe, K.: Aboriginal community archives. In: Gilliland, A.J., McKemmish, S., Lau, A.J. (eds.) Research in the Archival Multiverse, pp. 900–934. Monash University Publishing, Clayton (2016)
32. Tintswalo, S., Mazenda, A., Masiya, T., Shava, E.: Management of records at Statistics South Africa: challenges and prospects. Inf. Dev. **38**(2), 286–298 (2022)
33. Touray, R.: A review of records management in organisations. Open Access Libr. J. **8**(12), 1–23 (2021)
34. Upward, F.: Modelling the continuum as paradigm shift in recordkeeping and archiving processes, and beyond - a personal reflection. Rec. Manag. J. **10**(3), 115–139 (2000)
35. Upward, F., Reed, B., Oliver, G., Evans, J.: Recordkeeping informatics: re-figuring a discipline in crisis with a single minded approach. Rec. Manag. J. **23**(1), 37–50 (2013)
36. Wickman, D.: Recordkeeping legislation and its impacts: the PARBICA Recordkeeping for Good Governance Toolkit. Arch. Manuscripts **36**(1), 32–45 (2008)
37. Yates, D., Gebreiter, F., Lowe, A.: The internal accountability dynamic of UK service clubs: towards (more) intelligent accountability? In: Accounting Forum, vol. 43, no. 1, pp. 161–192. Routledge, January 2019
38. Yesudian, C.A.K.: Community organisation as an approach to community health. J. Manag. Med. **4**(1), 43–48 (1989)

39. Yu, S.W., Liu, J.Y., Lin, C.L., Su, Y.S.: Applying the push-pull mooring to explore consumers' shift from physical to online purchases of face masks. Mathematics **10**(24), 4761 (2022)
40. Zeng, Z., Li, S., Lian, J.W., Li, J., Chen, T., Li, Y.: Switching behavior in the adoption of a land information system in China: a perspective of the push–pull–mooring framework. Land Use Policy **109**, 105629 (2021)
41. Zhu, Z., Peng, Z., Yang, K.: Utilizing the push–pull–mooring framework to explore university teachers' intention to switch from traditional classrooms to smart classrooms in China. Educ.+ Train. **65**(3), 470–491 (2023)

Psychosocial Portraits of Participation in a Virtual World: A Comparative Analysis of Roles and Motives Across Three Different Professional Development Subreddits

Subhasree Sengupta[1]([✉]) [iD], Jasmina Tacheva[2] [iD], and Nathan McNeese[1] [iD]

[1] Clemson University, Clemson, SC 29634, USA
{subhass,mcneese}@clemson.edu
[2] Syracuse University, Syracuse, NY 13210, USA
ztacheva@syr.edu

Abstract. Work and learning are essential facets of our existence, yet women continue to face multiple restrictions that hinder and impede their professional outcomes. These restrictions are especially pronounced in the technical domains of Information technology and Computer science. This paper explores the power of informal online communities to act as a collective shield of care and support in resisting and disrupting gender-based barriers. By comparing three professional development forums on Reddit, we explore the emergent social roles and how these engender community extending support, solidarity, and collective enrichment. Through a novel exploration of psychosocial linguistic markers, we identify four roles and outline key signatures delineating differing motives, intent, and commitment to the community. Expanding prior research that distinguishes between communal and agentic dispositions of actors in online communities, we postulate how these emergent roles characterize a spectrum of communal vs. agentic behaviors that set the contour of conversation and type of care practices supported by the forums. Depending on these forums' underlying relational affinity traits, these roles can focus on knowledge sharing, depicting a weaker communal link, or a more collective close-knit bond that furthers support, empowerment, and resilience-building initiatives. Novel insights also offer inferences about automated actors' position within communities and influence on community norms and values. Cumulatively, these insights can have crucial implications for online discussion forums' design and policy-related issues, especially towards empowering and emboldening professional development initiatives for minoritized groups such as women.

Keywords: Care and Resilience Building · Role formation in Online communities · Women and Technical Workplace

© The Author(s), under exclusive license to Springer Nature Switzerland AG 2024
I. Sserwanga et al. (Eds.): iConference 2024, LNCS 14598, pp. 365–381, 2024.
https://doi.org/10.1007/978-3-031-57867-0_28

1   Introduction

Work, learning, and establishing one's professional footprint can be integral to our day-to-day lives. Work and the type of career one pursues can be essential to carve and extend one's social identity [7]. However, access to opportunities and the ability to sustain one's professional footprint may be contingent upon one's social standing and be dictated by informal sociocultural logics of hierarchy and prejudice, which may inhibit exploration and fulfillment of professional goals [19],?. Historically, women have faced multiple sociocultural limitations that have impeded their professional aspirations and explorations [25]. Recent scholarship has particularly pointed to glaring concerns of exclusion and ostracism manifesting in the everyday organizational practices of technical domains. This has led scholars to coin the notion of 'systems of exclusion' [15]. Such 'systems of exclusion' can be found in the context of hiring practices, roles, and workplace cultures [56]. Such structurally embedded exclusionary forces may cause strife, turmoil, and crisis in the everyday context, thus calling for finding channels and avenues for everyday resilience building [48].

Social media platforms in recent times have emerged as tools to build collectives of resilience that offer a haven for those facing multiple intersecting social hindrances and stigma [31]. Aligned with this vision of empowerment, studies have indicated how social media can act as a powerful venue for social justice and aid in forming alliances, providing a space for advocacy, solidarity, and amplifying collective voices [47]. Given that online discussion forums are maintained and nurtured by content created by those who engage in them, it becomes critical to understand the different types of users and the latent roles through which people participate and contribute to such forums [6]. Such roles can have a vital impact in stimulating conversational habits that effectively lay the ground for how support and resilience-building initiatives are nurtured and sustained [1]. Yet roles may develop based on the relational affinity a community supports and nurtures. Prior explorations have indicated how specific forums may have a more communal flavor, yet some may have a more agentic or individualistic pattern of association [14]. While several studies have inspected role formation in online social networks through varied metrics [29], how such roles develop, and nurture practices that extend empowerment and care through online forums remain under-explored. Thus, the critical aim of this analysis is mainly to focus on role formation to understand better how online forums can scaffold and nurture women in their professional trajectories.

While content and network measures have predominantly been used to investigate role formation [61], these insights do not provide an understanding of the deeper motives, outlooks, and perspectives that drive how people act and behave. Thus, in this investigation, the goal is to uncover and find glimpses of how the psychosocial (cognitive, social, and behavioral characteristics) intertwine with how people express and perform in an online community, manifesting as and through the roles that the community performs [42]. Armed with this social premise, the goal of this work is to perform a comparative investigation of the type of roles based on the psychosocial markers that emerge in three different online professional forums to explicate how these virtual avenues may provide support, care, and resilience-building activities for women as they carve out their professional footprints.

Reddit has emerged as a popular forum that supports various causes, including providing a safe space for disclosure and extended social support [13]. Given that Reddit has emerged as a powerful avenue for communal exchange and deliberation on a wide cross-section of topics [3], the study focuses on the following three subreddits: r/cscareerquestions (r/csc) (created in 2011, with a total of 832,000 members) - a general forum focused on technical careers, and r/girlsgonewired (r/ggw) (created in 2012, with 22,300 users) and r/careerwomen (r/cw) (created in 2013, with 4,479 users) - two women-centric career forums [3]. We selected these online communities to examine community dynamics, support provisions, and resilience-building tactics on one hand and to explore how women-centric forums may offer unique ways to resist and subvert gender-related tensions in professional development, especially in technical fields, on the other. By investigating roles driven by psychological participation markers, we can gauge the engagement trends that sustain and maintain the collaborative efforts and associated care practices that define the collective identity of each platform of interest.

The key questions that drive this investigation are thus:

1. *What central roles emerge in these spaces as discerned from the different groups of psychological markers?*
2. *How do these roles vary and differ across the examined forums?*

The central contributions of this study are:

1. Presenting a novel typology of roles using psychosocial markers of communication.
2. Presenting a comparative viewpoint on roles to situate how care, support-seeking, and resilience-building tactics seep into role characteristics, especially for women-centric forums, and how these role signatures may differ from a general forum. Such insights can have design and policy implications for online channels.
3. Theoretically, connecting roles to the underlying relational pattern of integration within communities motivates the apparent separation between the role functions across the forums of interest.

2 Related Work

2.1 Struggles of Gendered Expression in the Workplace: Subversion, Resilience and Care

Several feminist and social constructivist frameworks have alluded to how gender is often a product of sociocultural practice, manifesting as a condition and implicitly defining the disposition or the individual's day-to-day routines, beliefs, and demeanor [5]. Even in the workplace, studies have shown that implicit norms and standards, often with a masculine undertone, are established, and women are expected to conform to them [52]. Such systemic subjugation can undermine an individual's self-esteem and self-identity, especially in technical fields [26]. These may manifest in the type of roles, tensions in the relational dynamic established between co-workers, markers of performance, and expectations of behavior and demeanor [38]. Several interlocking mechanisms of oppression may restrict and impair how women and other minoritized voices navigate and adapt to the technical workplace. For example, empirical research has shown that biased recruitment systems may disproportionately reject female candidates due to an oversampling of data from male employees, which skews the performance of such systems [28]. Studies also highlight how women face barriers to participation and expression in online discussion forums, especially those oriented toward technical issues (such as software programming) [33]. All such investigations indicate the need for finding spaces of inclusion, solidarity, and peer-parity that can help minoritized voices, especially women, to find support and resilience, especially to configure their professional footprints [50]. Drawing on feminist HCI frameworks, studies have indicated how communities develop that focus on advocacy, solidarity, and empowerment by creating niche spaces for those voices that in the larger social fabric may feel silenced and ostracized [20]. Such relational acts of nurturing coalition engender care with a deep-rooted sense of embeddedness and fellow feeling [34]. To ensure such spaces' survival, participating members' roles become crucial in advancing the community's goals and visions. Yet, understanding the roles and communities that empower women in the context of the technical workplace remains under-explored, further motivating this investigation.

2.2 Roles and Nurturing Collective Agency in Online Communities

A parallel stream of scholarship highlights the use of social media as a source of support for a diverse spectrum of issues. Specifically, constructivist frameworks have sought to understand how an emergent structure arises amidst unregimented engagement patterns. This creates a schema of participation and action driven by norms and values and [43]. In this view, roles are fundamental to maintaining community, as they characterize specific norms, values, and routines that define the myriad functions community members serve and, at the same time, in their way, expand knowledge and the overall expertise of the community [29]. Roles in online forums can be explicit (like moderators) or implicit (like discussion-focused or answered-focused) [10]. Implicit roles are the focus of this narrative since they are pivotal to managing information exchange and maintaining the conversational palette of the community. Role formation has received attention from social media scholars, particularly in defining roles as functions and identifying roles through behavioral signatures (captured through text and network identifiers) [46]. Thus, roles capture a type of competency that community members assume to characterize their orientation and purpose within the group [22].

2.3   A Brief Background on Psycholinguistic Markers of Communication

As motivated in prior sections, psychosocial attributes capture how the collective or the "social" influences an individual's habits, actions, and beliefs [36]. Given that social media forums thrive on text and conversational exchange, identifying such psychosocial markers through the discourse of online forums can be very helpful in understanding the varied motives and rationales that drive community and individual participation in these forums [35]. These can relay intent and latent expectations and even serve as a basis to identify the underlying moral perspectives guiding participation and group formation in virtual formats [45]. Aligned with the goals of this investigation, prior work has indicated how psycholinguistic markers can help to understand forms of care and the emotional exchange that manifests latently [44]. Parallel scholarship has also identified how such linguistic trends manifest in gendered communication patterns and are essential to understanding group formation and collaborative intent [59]. In exploring varied expression and narrative styles found in virtual forums, studies have also leveraged psycholinguistic markers to identify emotional valence and other linguistic attributes of conversations, such as language acquisition skills [39,57]. Given the importance of psycholinguistic markers in identifying and characterizing an individual's group affiliation and associated engagement, it becomes important to understand how roles align with such psycholinguistic communication markers. This can help better capture how group norms and values are etched on the psyche of individual community members, shedding light on their intent and motivational aspects associated with the conversational palette perceived.

3   Methods

3.1   Computational Psycholinguistic Analysis

To conduct the psycholinguistic analysis as outlined, we used LIWC (Linguistic Inquiry and Word Count tool), which detects words associated with multiple psychosocial categories such as emotion and affect, social, cognitive, and biological processes, and personal concerns related to work, money, and family, among others [54]. The newest version (LIWC-22) contains more than 120 psychosocial linguistic dimensions [8]. LIWC reads a given text, compares each word in the text to the list of dictionary words, and calculates the percentage of total words that match each dictionary category. In LIWC-22, four top-level LIWC categories combine multiple sub-dimensions - "Analytic," "Clout," "Authentic," and "Tone" language. Analytic has been associated with formal and logical thinking, with markers of professional success [37]. Clout is a marker of social status, confidence, and leadership. Authentic captures an honest and open style of conversation, where there is less self-regulation and speech filtering. The tone is an aggregate measure of positive and negative emotions (also categories of the LIWC dictionary), where a higher number signifies a more positive tone and vice versa. This tool captures several facets of human life, including social status, hierarchy, relationships, group processes, and individual differences [54]. Given its widespread popularity and use for various psychosocial measurements, we selected this tool as the basis for uncovering latent roles [8].

3.2 Data Preparation and Analysis Approach

The dataset was compiled using a mixture of existing databases of Reddit data (PSAW) and Python API wrappers (PRAW) for each of the examined subreddits. Data was collected for the period between January 2018 to June 2022. Given that the forums have different churn rates in terms of the total number of threads and total number of responses associated with each thread, the total number of threads collected from these forums in this time frame greatly differs. This has also been observed by other studies that have conducted comparative analyses across Reddit forums [53]. Following best practices in the study of Reddit, conversational threads that were removed, deleted, or did not have author attributes were excluded from the analysis [53]. This was also done to ensure that those conversations that best captured the values and goals of the collectives were retained for further inspection [17].

Since role formation requires actor-level intervention, a process similar to the procedure used by [29] was followed to transform the dataset with actor-level aggregations. First, for each community, the actors in the top quartile were shortlisted and grouped together into one dataset. This process yielded a set of 14,687 actors. Next, using the LIWC outputs associated with the conversational vectors for each actor, k-means clustering using the elbow method for determining the optimal number of clusters was used [12]. Recommended parameter selection and preprocessing steps specified in extant literature were followed for the k-means approach [63]. Figure 1 depicts the iterations of the k-means method using the elbow method. Based on the different values of k, the model with k = 4 was selected for further investigation to define the final schema of roles subsequently outlined.

4   Results

The clustering approach yielded four distinct psychosocial portraits that further delineate the nature of roles that emerge in these spaces. These include (1) Communal champions, (2) Communal pivots, (3) Self-directed agents (4) Resource managers. Investigation of these four psychosocial profiles reveals a spectrum of communal vs. agentic attributes, with communal champions ranking the highest in communal linguistic markers, followed by communal pivots. The two categories of self-directed agents and resource managers rank higher on the agentic spectrum. This observation extends the binary differentiation between agentic and communal relational perspectives postulated by [14] to a more continual spectrum. Such insights are akin to observations made by [49], highlighting how

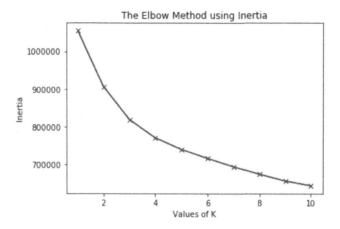

Fig. 1. Kmeans result by varying the number of clusters

three engagement models emerge. While one category captures a more communal essence, another is more agentic, and a middle category blends the two perspectives.

Further discussions and descriptions of these profiles are explained below:

1) **Communal Champions**: As the category name suggests, these actors drive the cause for collective affinity development in the forums. In terms of the linguistic markers (using the Centroid scores for each of the underlying LIWC categories), we find that this category is characterized by greater use of function words (such as we, assent, pronouns, affiliation) that are indicative of solid group bonding and cohesion [54]. Further, it is also described by a more significant social outlook, with a strong indication of prosocial behavior. According to [8], the category of prosocial captures the essence of helping and nurturing others, indicating that this category of actors is committed to others and uplifting the community. Akin to prior work by [27], this category is also associated with affect, positive emotion, and social markers. All these indicate that this category of actors depicts a strong affiliation with the collective (also captured through the strong presence of the affiliation construct), is highly embedded, and fosters a sense of collective collegiality with others in the group, which has also been captured for women embedded in groups [30].

To complement the inferences drawn from the LIWC analysis, we also explored content traces across all three forums to gain deeper insights into the activity traces that characterize this category of actors. Overall, champions exhibit deep wisdom about the community and strive to enhance the development of collective spirit. Based on Fig. 2, there is a high prevalence of this category in the women-centric forums, so on investigating further, it is evident that forum participants embodying this role in such spaces (especially in r/ggw) are focused on championing the goals of inclusivity and collective upliftment by empowering, advocating and calling for collective action. For example, an actor in this category stated - *"I am going to participate in a meetup for women and non-binary folks in computing soon, I would encourage others to consider participating as well"*. Champions also help nurture discussions on the issues of ethics and inclusivity in the technical workplace while ensuring that the conversations adhere to the community's norms and encourage multiple standpoints and opinions [40]. In doing so, these actors commit to the community and maintain community values of transparency and equivocality [60].

Champions in r/cw engaged in conversations to provide strategies and tips for navigating organizational challenges, imparting their experiential wisdom by engaging in acts of teaching and nurturing [16]. For example, in a post addressing concerns about reacting to criticism, a champion stated, *"I would suggest thanking him for this feedback also saying that you are happy to discuss through the feedback. It shows that you have an open-door policy and are open to conversation"*. For r/csc, it is interesting to observe that automated agents (such as Auto-moderators) emerged as category champions. This shows that these agents are critical in absorbing communal wisdom and becoming embedded in the community. The Automoderator's role in controlling traffic could be likened to a more profound sense of the community's norms. Thus, by such actions, it also becomes a highly communal entity. In summary, champions are, in a way, leaders of their spaces. They are vital in motivating, guiding, and sparking thought, action, and vision, adding innovation and enrichment to these forums [51].

2) **Communal Pivots**: These actors in the linguistic frontier share quite a few aligning attributes with the category of communal champions. Second to champions, in terms of LIWC attributes, pivots also engage in conversations that characterize group and community as well as gendered expressions, as supported by [30]. However, this group's most pronounced and distinguishable features are cognitive processes that capture a keen sense of thinking, prominently manifesting through the linguistic attribute of insight. This depicts more profound intuition, wisdom, and understanding [8]. Also, second to the category of self-directed agents (described next), linguistic markers such as pronouns like 'I' and expressions of achievement characterize these contributions to a large extent. Thus, given these linguistic descriptors, it is evident that an individualistic flavor of discussion manifests in this forum. Hence, in the communal-agentic spectrum, these actors are more agentic than champions but less so than the other two categories and capture a middle ground of psychosocial motives manifesting in these spaces. These actors thus play a substantial role in balancing the communal and agentic aspects that set the pattern of contributions associated with these spaces and, therefore, are termed as pivots. The strong cognitive dimension could indicate acts that require more cognitive effort, such as thinking and knowledge sharing in a group, akin to a collaborative learning setting, as observed in prior investigations by [11]. Additional conversational analysis is presented to further elaborate on these observations.

Akin to collaborative learning settings [11], pivots participate in collective sharing and engage in collective efforts to enrich and empower one another by boosting professional development outcomes for those engaged in these spaces.

Based on Fig. 2, we can see that while a large percentage of actors from r/ggw & r/cw fall under this category, one can also observe a strong presence of this category in r/csc. Looking at activity traces first from r/ggw & r/cw; we see that the actors in this category aim to foster communal affinity by proactively encouraging engagement and knowledge-centric collaborative pursuits. For example, a pivot posted - *"I am studying algorithms, and it is a topic I feel many might be presently studying, struggling with. It would be great to have someone to study this with. Although I am not sure how much I can contribute! If anyone wants to join, my DMs are open."*. Collaborative learning can also involve encouraging and validating each other to express a form of togetherness and value contributions from different team members [11]. Such encouragement was also evident in conversations pivots engaged in, an example being- *"I completely missed that aspect of the exercise, you are so correct about this clarification, I wish you luck and hope we can both get our results soon"*. Such posts also depict how pivots create a sense of parity and synergy and attempt to encourage, reinforce, and motivate each other, capturing how cognitive acts and care together create the contour of learning practices crafted in these channels [4].

Regarding the cognitive dimension that characterizes this category, the linguistic attribute of certitude can be captured in how people expressed certain certainty while attempting to mask a certain degree of uncertainty [8]. For example, a post in r/csc stated, *"I have tried the best I could; beyond that, I'll just wait for the results."* Associated with such messages were also posts that captured a deep sense of reflection, insight, and inner wisdom, manifesting in spiritual or moral wisdom [50]. These were often captured in how these actors attempted to heal from failure while encouraging community members to become more resilient [58]. An example post from r/ggw capturing such sentiment stated, *"I have resolved to keep going on with my life, no matter what the outcome, it would be rather painful otherwise, we learn, and we move forward."* In conclusion, pivots are communal and agentic; fusing these characteristics adds to collective knowledge and expands the pool of expertise. Further, these pivots also act as pillars for support and advice and thus form the backbone of communal enterprise across the three forums.

3) **Self-directed Agents**: These actors lean more towards the agentic side of the communal-agentic spectrum. Thus, agentic attributes are more prominent when investigating the associated LIWC metrics for this category. Self-directed agents have a high indicator of cognitive processes (higher than pivots), especially captured through the certitude attribute. Further, a strong presence of agentic indicators, such as 'I,' was also observed. Interestingly, this category has a high manifestation of the linguistic marker of discrepancy. The attribute of discrepancy indicates a disparity between two states of existence [8]. It captures the essence of conflict or some form of dissimilarity. While social markers such as emotion and feeling are also salient, these are less prevalent than champions and pivots.

Interestingly, self-directed agents were highly present in r/csc compared to the other two forums. On investigating the trends, it is evident that self-directed agents use anecdotal references from their experiences to share or inspire others in the community. Such posts usually attempted to provide more insights into how the organizational context, especially the technical workplace, functioned and thus were often prefaced with "I would" or "From my experience," - which is why these seem so salient in the agentic dimensions of LIWC. For example, discussing ways to counter procrastination, he stated, *"Procrastination affects me too; I have found diving and setting priorities to my work very useful. The key for me is to set routines. But everyone finds a different route; this is what I do and find works for me"*. Such posts reveal an intent to help; however, they also signal a sense of precaution in advising interlocutors to ensure that personal preferences are made evident, thereby reflecting a sense of self-regulation and speech monitoring [18]. This kind of self-regulation can potentially explain the higher values along the cognitive dimension [41].

Interestingly, one of the actors in this role category is a moderator on r/ggw. While this might seem counter-intuitive, on investigating the activity trace further, we find that this could be because when explaining the reason why a post was removed, this actor often shoulders the responsibility of enforcing community-centric norms and tends to word such messages from an individualistic standpoint, for example: *"I feel posting such content is against a rule for this forum. I shall discuss further with admins and take necessary action."* Further, beyond being a custodian, this actor also engages in self-reflective conversations, saying, *"I always feel I am the only one, yet on further reflection, I have realized that there might be others who might be struggling just as I am."* Such comments further reinforce the cognitive aspect and reflect how individuals try to reason their position within a larger collective. Thus, in a sense, such phrasing may seem detached from the collective, yet latent in them is a core commitment to helping others while ensuring that the individual aspect of one's rationale is highlighted and signified. Hence, while these actors driven by linguistic markers may align more with the agentic orientation, their contributions capture the community's spirit and attempt to infuse perspectives and thoughts to boost collective enrichment and empowerment.

4) **Resource Managers**: Regarding LIWC attributes, these actors present an interesting mixture of psychosocial markers. The most distinguishing attributes that define the boundaries of this category include the markers of perception, work, leisure, and money [8]. It is also interesting to note a high agentic presence in this category. Second to self-directed agents, several function words that indicate an agentic disposition were observed [14]. Out of all the four categories, this one ranked the lowest in capturing any effects of community (group cohesiveness, emotion, feeling, social orientation). All these indicate an evident objectified existence and focus on the self. Further explanation of these themes and their association with this category will be unpacked using activity traces from the forums.

Across all three forums (r/csc, r/cw & r/ggw), these actors engage in conversations about sharing references and links. For example, one actor in r/cw posted, *"There are two components of success, networking, and knowledge. In this article series, I discuss tips and tricks for developing yourself and finding the right people to connect with. To read more, check out this link. ".* Such posts also help justify the presence of the perception linguistic attribute; as evident in this quoted text, a strong intuition and experiential wisdom come forth [23]. Such perceptive remarks reveal an intent for not only sharing one's materials and promoting one's work (which is a very agentic aspect) but also understanding the community's goals and aligning such messages accordingly. Such endeavors may induce cognitive effort, which is further captured in the dimensions of perception. While the communal intent is more subtle and subdued, sharing such resources can also indicate a desire to help the community grow and stimulate knowledge growth within these spaces [24].

What is interesting to note is that there were a few automated agents spanning the different forums. They participated by sharing links or providing corrected links previously incorrectly offered by others. Thus, they help to curate and retain information while only engaging by giving references. Notable in this regard is an automated agent (not Auto moderator) that only participates in the r/csc community by creating threads and urging others to post topic-specific discussions. Further, this is a common trend of participation in r/csc. While such sharing helps enhance the informational potential of these forums, it also highlights a weaker group association, as surmised by other investigations [49]. These forms of sharing depict an on-demand learning and sharing outlook, which is more impersonal and captures a weaker association with the group [9].

5 Discussion

Through the different roles that emerge, we essentially gauge how community members propel the identity and collective spirit of the community, imbuing each forum with a unique sense of purpose, vision, and values. Figure 2 clearly distinguishes between the emerging roles. The women-centric forums have a more significant presence of champions and pivots (i.e., the more communal roles). In contrast, the general forum has a higher concentration of resource managers and self-directed agents, exhibiting a more agentic and individualistic character. It is interesting to find a more significant presence of pivots in the general forum; it shows the community's commitment to nurturing peer-led resource-sharing initiatives, again highlighting the community's thrust towards knowledge and task-specific visions. This contrast in relational association indicates different levels of bonding. It highlights how the women-centric forums are focused on advocacy, empowerment, encouragement, and support to enable and embolden one another, as if a form of sisterhood, collective solidarity, is established and drives the community [32].

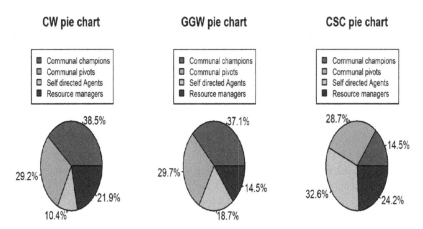

Fig. 2. Distribution of psychosocial portraits across the three forums

This comparative arc sheds light on how communities establish a distinct form of care (whether focused on solidarity and support or a more detached knowledge-sharing perspective) through different roles that set the schema of participation and engagement. This is also visible in how certain actors assume contrasting roles depending on the community. For example, some actors who are more engaged as champions in r/ggw take the role of pivots in r/csc. This could also allude to how identity and associated expressions are not encouraged in the general forum (r/csc); in fact, conversations highlight how often identity and gendered expressions are redirected to other forums, resulting in a form of implicit silencing of specific issues and causes which might result in the type of role migration observed [62]. Such insights can have several design and policy implications regarding how care and care-centric information exchange mechanisms are nurtured and sustained online [2]. For example, reward mechanisms and algorithmic content presentation systems can consider the type of care acts that community members perform [55]. Such design visions can empower and direct the right kind of content, support, and peers, enhancing and enriching the experiences of those who engage in and through these forums [13].

Another critical insight involves the role of automated agents. In the case of r/csc, for instance, the auto moderator and other automated actors assume prominent positions within the community. The impact of these actors in the communal-agentic spectrum yields exciting insights into how automated agents develop a social standing within communities. Yet, they also impact and define certain community norms and characteristics [21]. Yet, we also see a noticeable distinction between the different forums. For example, in r/csc, auto moderator emerges as a champion, yet in r/ggw, we see human moderators acting as advocates and taking up the role of champions. While in r/ggw, we see auto moderators present and regulate content, human moderators control and express an awareness and attentiveness towards the potential pitfalls of such automated agents (such as blocking traffic to specific posts). This example illustrates how human-AI partnerships may also differ and be defined by the type of relational pattern of engagement such communities scaffold. In summary, such insights can significantly impact how automated agents are infused and the nature of *complementarity* established with humans. Based on the insights from r/csc, we see that having automated agents individually leading and managing content may benefit managing large volumes of posts. Yet, its limited experiential wisdom may inadvertently harm human participation and engagement, impairing the extent of access and equitable participation such channels offer [21]. Such inferences can have policy insights and influence regulatory guidelines on how such automated actors are infused into the relational fabric of online discussion spaces.

6 Conclusion and Future Work

Through a comparative role analysis, we outline and delineate key role characteristics and habits that define the conversational routines that shape the forums inspected. Consistent with previous research, we find that a sense of community influences the types of roles that emerge and the unique characteristics that define these roles. Contrary to the binary division between agentic and communal attributes suggested by previous studies [14]. However, our analysis yields a spectrum of roles that range from being more communal to being more agentic. Interestingly, the women-centric forums show a greater presence of roles with a collaborative mindset, empowering and emboldening one another. In contrast, the general form is characterized by more agentic individualistic tastes with a sharp focus on knowledge and task performance. Such insights can motivate further inspection into the differing types of communal identities that emerge and the types of multidimensional support and care initiatives these support, which ultimately can have enriching implications for advocating the position of historically minoritized voices such as women, especially those working in the technical workforce.

Future work can further delve into more robustly classifying the roles, with additional inferences drawn from network and content-related attributions. Temporal trends of how such roles emerge, transition, and evolve can be another extra layer of investigation. Finally, complementary qualitative insights can provide further details regarding the perception and embeddedness of these roles, drawing on the lived experiences of those participating in these online forums. This can give a more nuanced view of the motives of participation and a deeper insight into the background details of the community members, which cannot be fully understood based on the secondary data used for the present study. Such qualitative insights can also help to overcome the potential pitfalls of the quantitative approach propelling LIWC. This can help to provide more robust inferences on top of the estimates and conclusions drawn from the LIWC insights, enriching the overall understanding of how community members perceive and absorb the norms and values of these forums.

References

1. Ahmed, S., Jaidka, K., Cho, J.: Tweeting India's Nirbhaya protest: a study of emotional dynamics in an online social movement. In: Technology, Media and Social Movements, pp. 65–83. Routledge (2020)
2. Andalibi, N., Haimson, O.L., Choudhury, M.D., Forte, A.: Social support, reciprocity, and anonymity in responses to sexual abuse disclosures on social media. ACM Trans. Comput. Hum. Interact. (TOCHI) **25**(5), 1–35 (2018)
3. Anderson, K.E.: Ask me anything: what is reddit? Libr. Hi Tech News **32**(5), 8–11 (2015)
4. Ares, N.: Appropriating roles and relations of power in collaborative learning. Int. J. Qual. Stud. Educ. **21**(2), 99–121 (2008)
5. Arnot, M.: Male hegemony, social class and women's education. J. Educ. **164**, 64–89 (1982)
6. Baxter, J.A., Haycock, J.: Roles and student identities in online large course forums: Implications for practice. Int. Rev. Res. Open Distrib. Learning **15**(1) (2014)
7. Blustein, D.L., Noumair, D.A.: Self and identity in career development: implications for theory and practice. J. Couns. Dev. **74**(5), 433–441 (1996)
8. Boyd, R., Ashokkumar, A., Seraj, S., Pennebaker, J.: The Development and Psychometric Properties of LIWC-22. University of Texas at Austin, Austin (2022)
9. Budhathoki, N.R., Haythornthwaite, C.: Motivation for open collaboration: crowd and community models and the case of OpenStreetMap. Am. Behav. Sci. **57**(5), 548–575 (2013)
10. Buntain, C., Golbeck, J.: Identifying social roles in reddit using network structure. In: Proceedings of the 23rd International Conference on World Wide Web, pp. 615–620 (2014)
11. Curşeu, P.L., Chappin, M.M., Jansen, R.J.: Gender diversity and motivation in collaborative learning groups: the mediating role of group discussion quality. Soc. Psychol. Educ. **21**, 289–302 (2018)
12. Davidson, B.I., Jones, S.L., Joinson, A.N., Hinds, J.: The evolution of online ideological communities. PLoS ONE **14**(5), e0216932 (2019)
13. De Choudhury, M., De, S.: Mental health discourse on reddit: self-disclosure, social support, and anonymity. In: Eighth International AAAI Conference on Weblogs and Social Media (2014)
14. Decter-Frain, A., Frimer, J.A.: Impressive words: linguistic predictors of public approval of the us congress. Front. Psychol. **7**, 240 (2016)
15. D'ignazio, C., Klein, L.F.: Data Feminism. MIT Press, Cambridge (2020)
16. Dillard, C.B.: To address suffering that the majority can't see: lessons from black women's leadership in the workplace. New Directions Adult Continuing Educ. **2016**(152), 29–38 (2016)
17. Dosono, B., Semaan, B.: Decolonizing tactics as collective resilience: identity work of AAPI communities on reddit. Proc. ACM Hum.-Comput. Interact. **4**(CSCW1), 1–20 (2020)
18. Dunn, K.E., Rakes, G.C., Rakes, T.A.: Influence of academic self-regulation, critical thinking, and age on online graduate students' academic help-seeking. Distance Educ. **35**(1), 75–89 (2014)
19. Ellemers, N., De Gilder, D., Haslam, S.A.: Motivating individuals and groups at work: a social identity perspective on leadership and group performance. Acad. Manag. Rev. **29**(3), 459–478 (2004)

20. Fiesler, C., Morrison, S., Bruckman, A.S.: An archive of their own: a case study of feminist HCI and values in design. In: Proceedings of the 2016 CHI Conference on Human Factors in Computing Systems, pp. 2574–2585 (2016)
21. Gillespie, T.: The relevance of algorithms. Media Technol. Essays Commun. Material. Soc. **167**(2014), 167 (2014)
22. Golder, S.A., Donath, J.: Social roles in electronic communities. Internet Res. **5**(1), 19–22 (2004)
23. Gunawardena, C., Frechette, C., Layne, L.: Culturally Inclusive Instructional Design: A Framework and Guide to Building Online Wisdom Communities. Routledge, Milton (2018)
24. Hall, H., Graham, D.: Creation and recreation: motivating collaboration to generate knowledge capital in online communities. Int. J. Inf. Manage. **24**(3), 235–246 (2004)
25. Hatmaker, D.M.: Engineering identity: gender and professional identity negotiation among women engineers. Gend. Work. Organ. **20**(4), 382–396 (2013)
26. Herman, C.: Rebooting and rerouting: women's articulations of frayed careers in science, engineering and technology professions. Gend. Work. Organ. **22**(4), 324–338 (2015)
27. Iosub, D., Laniado, D., Castillo, C., Fuster Morell, M., Kaltenbrunner, A.: Emotions under discussion: gender, status and communication in online collaboration. PLoS ONE **9**(8), e104880 (2014)
28. Kodiyan, A.A.: An overview of ethical issues in using AI systems in hiring with a case study of Amazon's AI-based hiring tool. Researchgate Preprint, pp. 1–19 (2019)
29. Kou, Y., Gray, C.M., Toombs, A.L., Adams, R.S.: Understanding social roles in an online community of volatile practice: a study of user experience practitioners on reddit. ACM Trans. Soc. Comput. **1**(4), 1–22 (2018)
30. Li, L., Zhou, J., Zhuang, J., Zhang, Q.: Gender-specific emotional characteristics of crisis communication on social media: case studies of two public health crises. Inf. Process. Manag. **60**(3), 103299 (2023)
31. Lucero, L.: Safe spaces in online places: social media and LGBTQ youth. Multicult. Educ. Rev. **9**(2), 117–128 (2017)
32. McAdam, M., Harrison, R.T., Leitch, C.M.: Stories from the field: women's networking as gender capital in entrepreneurial ecosystems. Small Bus. Econ. **53**, 459–474 (2019)
33. Morgan, S.: How are programming questions from women received on stack overflow? A case study of peer parity. In: Proceedings Companion of the 2017 ACM SIGPLAN International Conference on Systems, Programming, Languages, and Applications: Software for Humanity, pp. 39–41 (2017)
34. Mowle, A.: Safe spaces on social media platforms: selective censorship and content moderation in Reddit's r/TwoXchromosomes. In: Wiesslitz, C. (ed.) Women's Activism Online and the Global Struggle for Social Change, pp. 221–238. Springer, Cham (2023). https://doi.org/10.1007/978-3-031-31621-0
35. Neubaum, G., Rösner, L., Rosenthal-von der Pütten, A.M., Krämer, N.C.: Psychosocial functions of social media usage in a disaster situation: a multi-methodological approach. Comput. Hum. Behav. **34**, 28–38 (2014)
36. Newman, B.M., Newman, P.R.: Development Through Life: A Psychosocial Approach. Cengage Learning, Belmont (2017)
37. Pennebaker, J.W., Chung, C.K., Frazee, J., Lavergne, G.M., Beaver, D.I.: When small words foretell academic success: the case of college admissions essays. PLoS ONE **9**(12), e115844 (2014)

38. Peterson, H.: Gendered work ideals in Swedish it firms: valued and not valued workers. Gend. Work. Organ. **14**(4), 333–348 (2007)
39. Pikhart, M., Botezat, O.: The impact of the use of social media on second language acquisition. Procedia Comput. Sci. **192**, 1621–1628 (2021)
40. Preece, J., Maloney-Krichmar, D., Abras, C.: History of online communities. Encycl. Commun. **3**(1023–1027), 86 (2003)
41. Robinson, L.: Investigating critical thinking disposition, self-efficacy, self-regulation, and self-identity amongst online students. Coll. Stud. J. **55**(3), 325–337 (2021)
42. Rodgers, S., Chen, Q.: Internet community group participation: psychosocial benefits for women with breast cancer. J. Comput.-Mediated Commun. **10**(4), JCMC1047 (2005)
43. Rosenbaum, H., Shachaf, P.: A structuration approach to online communities of practice: the case of Q&A communities. J. Am. Soc. Inform. Sci. Technol. **61**(9), 1933–1944 (2010)
44. Ryan, E.B., Giles, H., Bartolucci, G., Henwood, K.: Psycholinguistic and social psychological components of communication by and with the elderly. Lang. Commun. **6**(1–2), 1–24 (1986)
45. Saha, K., Torous, J., Caine, E.D., De Choudhury, M.: Psychosocial effects of the COVID-19 pandemic: large-scale quasi-experimental study on social media. J. Med. Internet Res. **22**(11), e22600 (2020)
46. Saxena, A., Reddy, H.: Users roles identification on online crowdsourced q&a platforms and encyclopedias: a survey. J. Comput. Soc. Sci. **5**, 1–33 (2021)
47. Schejter, A.M., Tirosh, N.: "seek the meek, seek the just": social media and social justice. Telecomm. Policy **39**(9), 796–803 (2015)
48. Semaan, B.: 'Routine infrastructuring' as 'building everyday resilience with technology' when disruption becomes ordinary. Proc. ACM Hum.-Comput. Interact. **3**(CSCW), 1–24 (2019)
49. Sengupta, S.: A tale of two virtual communities: a comparative analysis of culture and discourse in two online programming communities (2021)
50. Sengupta, S., Semaan, B.: 'A guiding light in a virtual haven': a preliminary analysis of conversations around navigating and repairing self-worth in an online professional community for women. In: Companion Publication of the 2021 Conference on Computer Supported Cooperative Work and Social Computing, pp. 158–162 (2021)
51. Seraj, M.: We create, we connect, we respect, therefore we are: intellectual, social, and cultural value in online communities. J. Interact. Mark. **26**(4), 209–222 (2012)
52. Simpson, A., Bouhafa, Y.: Youths' and adults' identity in stem: a systematic literature review. J. STEM Educ. Res. **3**, 167–194 (2020)
53. Staudt Willet, K.B., Carpenter, J.P.: Teachers on reddit? Exploring contributions and interactions in four teaching-related subreddits. J. Res. Technol. Educ. **52**(2), 216–233 (2020)
54. Tausczik, Y.R., Pennebaker, J.W.: The psychological meaning of words: Liwc and computerized text analysis methods. J. Lang. Soc. Psychol. **29**(1), 24–54 (2010)
55. Taylor, S.H., Bazarova, N.N.: Always available, always attached: a relational perspective on the effects of mobile phones and social media on subjective well-being. J. Comput.-Mediat. Commun. **26**(4), 187–206 (2021)
56. Tokbaeva, D., Achtenhagen, L.: Career resilience of female professionals in the male-dominated it industry in Sweden: toward a process perspective. Gend. Work. Organ. **30**(1), 223–262 (2023)

57. Trifan, A., Antunes, R., Matos, S., Oliveira, J.L.: Understanding depression from psycholinguistic patterns in social media texts. In: European Conference on Information Retrieval, pp. 402–409. Springer (2020)

58. Vaast, E., Levina, N.: Speaking as one, but not speaking up: dealing with new moral taint in an occupational online community. Inf. Organ. **25**(2), 73–98 (2015)

59. Vogel, E.A., Pechmann, C.: Application of automated text analysis to examine emotions expressed in online support groups for quitting smoking. J. Assoc. Consum. Res. **6**(3), 315–323 (2021)

60. Weld, G., Zhang, A.X., Althoff, T.: Making online communities 'better': a taxonomy of community values on reddit. arXiv preprint arXiv:2109.05152 (2021)

61. Welser, H.T., Gleave, E., Fisher, D., Smith, M.: Visualizing the signatures of social roles in online discussion groups. J. Soc. Struct. **8**(2), 1–32 (2007)

62. Workman, H.: Formation of safe spaces in gendered online communities Reddit and "the front page of the internet". Ph.D. thesis, Texas Christian University (2014)

63. Wu, J., Xiong, H., Chen, J.: Adapting the right measures for k-means clustering. In: Proceedings of the 15th ACM SIGKDD International Conference on Knowledge Discovery and Data Mining, pp. 877–886 (2009)

The Legacy of Slavery and COVID-19 Mortality in Southern U.S. States

Mary Dalrymple and Vanessa Frias-Martinez[(✉)] [iD]

University of Maryland, College Park, UMD, College Park, USA
{mdalrymp,vfrias}@umd.edu

Abstract. Public health experts have observed higher risks of COVID-19 infection, hospitalization, and death for some racial groups compared with others. Studies into racially disparate COVID-19 outcomes have concentrated on the medical and public health reasons for disparities, while other work has looked generally at historic slavery's continuing effect on health. None has looked specifically at the link between COVID-19 outcomes and historical slavery. This study looks at the disparity between Black Non-Hispanic and White Non-Hispanic deaths by asking whether the American legacy of slavery contributes to racial disparity. Specifically, we interpret the regression coefficients in linear regressions that explore the relationship between slavery and COVID-19 mortality for Black and White Non-Hispanic Americans, while controlling for other demographic characteristics. This study finds statistically significant evidence that slavery, outlawed more than 150 years ago, nevertheless influences disease today by contributing to higher mortality among Black Americans and lower mortality among White Americans in selected counties of U.S. Southern states.

Keywords: COVID-19 Mortality · U.S. History of Slavery

1 Introduction

According to the World Health Organization, COVID-19 killed more than 6.4 million people globally by mid-August 2022, including more than 1 million Americans [1]. Adjusting for age, the U.S. Centers for Disease Control and Prevention (CDC) has calculated that Black Non-Hispanic people die from COVID-19 infection at 1.7 times the rates of White Non-Hispanic people [2].

Occurring simultaneously with Black Lives Matters protests around the United States, awareness of disparate COVID-19 hospitalization and death for Black Americans ignited debates about racial disparity in health and healthcare. Public health authorities continue to search for medical causes underlying racial disparities in the U.S. population in areas that range from higher rates of underlying health risks [3] to unequal access to medical care [4].

In the United States, questions of racial disparity for Black Americans remain intertwined with the country's legacy of slavery. Researchers have sought and found evidence that the legacy of slavery continues to contribute to health disparities for Black Americans in cardiovascular [5] and cardio-cerebral health [6]. This paper contributes to the

© The Author(s), under exclusive license to Springer Nature Switzerland AG 2024
I. Sserwanga et al. (Eds.): iConference 2024, LNCS 14598, pp. 382–392, 2024.
https://doi.org/10.1007/978-3-031-57867-0_29

discussion of how the past shapes the present by extending foundational work on health, history, and slavery into the COVID-19 pandemic. Specifically, we explore the question of whether an ongoing legacy of slavery contributes to higher COVID-19 mortality for Black Americans. The main contribution of this paper is to show that when the White and Black populations of selected counties in the U.S. South are considered separately, historically higher rates of slavery are shown to be a statistically significant factor that contributes both to higher rates of Black COVID-19 mortality and lower rates of White COVID-19 mortality.

2 Related Work

2.1 COVID-19 Mortality

General work on the risk factors for COVID-19 mortality have identified a number of conditions that contribute to risk of death, regardless of race or ethnicity. A meta-analysis of 42 studies done in 13 locations identified old age, male sex, obesity, diabetes, current smoking, acute kidney injury, chronic obstructive pulmonary disease, hypertension, cardiovascular disease, cancer, and increased D-dimer as risk factors for COVID-19 mortality [7].

In an ongoing synthesis for clinical professionals, the CDC summarizes the available evidence in scientific and medical literature for risk factors that predict a severe outcome from COVID-19 infection, defined as hospitalization, admission to a hospital intensive care unit, intubation or mechanical ventilation, or death [8]. The most recent synthesis, reflecting literature available as of January 1, 2022, found age to be the strongest risk factor, along with higher risk of severe outcomes for people with conditions that include chronic disease of a major body system (kidney, lung, liver, heart, cerebrovascular), asthma, cancer, diabetes, dementia, obesity, current and former smoking, and selected mental health disorders, immune conditions, infections, and disabilities. The analysis also noted the observed disparity in severe COVID-19 outcomes for some racial and ethnic minority groups.

More illustrative of Black Americans living in the U.S. South, a study done during the early months of the COVID-19 pandemic in rural Georgia found that age 65 and over, hypertension, morbid obesity, and use of immunosuppression therapies predicted COVID-19 mortality. Female sex was found to predict decreased mortality. The patient population studied was 87% Black [9]. These foundational works identified two demographic attributes related to severe COVID-19 outcomes, age, and sex, that we used as variables in our analysis.

2.2 Disparate COVID-19 Outcomes

As evidence of COVID-19's heavier toll on Black Americans started to accumulate, researchers looked at disparity more systematically, comparing smaller geographic areas. Early in the U.S. pandemic, and in light of limited but growing evidence of racial disparity, Scannell et al. [10] conducted a national, county-level analysis. They found that after adjusting for possible confounders (including county-level variables for female sex, age 65-and-up, uninsured, mean household size, and other factors related to environment, access to healthcare, and COVID-19 interventions) that counties with a higher proportion of Black residents had a larger number of cases and deaths.

Li et al. [11] looked at all 3,142 U.S. counties to identify characteristics associated with higher cumulative and weekly COVID-19 cases and deaths. They found that rural counties, counties with more minorities and more racial segregation, and counties with more people who did not graduate high school who also had medical comorbidities were associated with higher cumulative COVID-19 case and death rates. A separate county-level analysis [12] found counties with more Black or Native American residents had more deaths.

A better knowledge of COVID-19 outcomes at the county level for minority populations suffers from lack of data. Formal (and lagging) CDC counts of death by county and race suppress information for counties that experienced fewer than 100 deaths, thereby providing data for little more than one-third of 1,462 southern counties [13]. Analysts have stepped into the void to try to understand county-level racial trends.

Focusing narrowly on the most highly populated counties in Texas, Xu et al. [14] found a strong correlation between COVID-19 outcomes and a higher proportion of Black and Hispanic residents but no correlation with local pollution.

Two data analyses [11, 12] described the narrowing and widening disparities between Blacks and Whites over time during various phases of COVID-19 variants, noting that Black and White populations experienced similar rates of mortality at some points, wider disparities at other points, but a disparity persisting. These works established evidence of racial differences in COVID-19 mortality among U.S. counties, where racial demographics and history vary widely. This inspired us to investigate more deeply and explore whether part of the racial discrepancies could be explained by the residual effects of a county's historic experience of slavery.

2.3 Geographic Legacy of Slavery and Health

Looking into the question of how and why health disparities develop, Phelan and Link [17] show evidence that disparities in health occur in circumstances where medical science has developed treatments that successfully control or mitigate disease or death. They looked at outcomes for two diseases (brain and ovarian cancer) for which medical science can do little to ameliorate the course of disease and found no disparity in outcomes by race or socioeconomic status over time. However, for diseases that treatment can control or mitigate, they found evidence that populations "richer in resources," which include knowledge, money, power, prestige, and social connection, saw reduced mortality as knowledge spread. As a result, racial disparities emerged.

Looking not specifically at health but at the continuing effects of historic slavery by place, Curtis and O'Connell [18] showed that racial discrimination acts differently in different places. Using poverty rate as a proxy for discrimination in varied social institutions, they found that in counties that had lower than 30% slave populations in the 1860 census (so-called low-slavery states), the patterns of poverty supported the "racial threat" theory, which posits that a more powerful group discriminates against a less powerful group to preserve dominance, and that discrimination stabilizes when the economic threat to the more powerful seems to be neutralized. The theory surfaced in the low-slavery-state counties as a log relationship between percentage Black population and poverty. In counties that had 30% or more slave population in 1860, the relationship between percent Black population and poverty showed a linear relationship, supporting the "exploitation thesis," which holds that the benefits economically exploiting the Blacks population increases for the White population as the concentration of Black population grows. This work showed that the attributes of racial discrimination do not simply reflect the "percentage Black" population and that the process of discrimination acts differently in historically low-slave and high-slave counties.

Historic slavery has been investigated in connection with certain health conditions. In a study of stroke mortality [6], researchers investigated the 2- to 4-times higher risk of stroke among Blacks living in the Southern U.S. compared with non-Hispanic Whites and found higher rates of stroke and stroke mortality in counties with a history of slavery. In counties with slavery in 1860, they found for every 1% increase in historic slave density, there was a 0.82% increase in Black stroke mortality per 100,000 people.

Similarly, Kramer et al. [5] investigated whether the legacy of slavery explained some of the slower improvement in heart disease mortality in the U.S. South, especially among Blacks, from 1968 to 2014. This study looked at differences between Deep South states, which had a higher concentration of slavery, and Upper South states and found Black populations in the Deep South experienced a 17% slower decline in heart disease mortality, slower than blacks in the Upper South and Whites.

Looking at racial disparity from a different perspective, Reece [19] studied the advantages garnered by Whites in areas with a legacy of slavery and showed a relationship between the proportion of slavery by county and lasting effects on Whites to be higher median income, lower rates of uninsured, lower poverty rates, higher homeownership rates, and lower food stamp usage.

Extending the research around White advantage into health, Gabriel et al. [20] investigated the relationship between a county's slave past and its present-day White opioid mortality and found a significant negative association between the slave population in 1860 and White opioid deaths during the 2009–2018 span of the opioid epidemic. Our work builds on these investigations into the modern-day effects of historical slavery in U.S. Southern counties with a focus specifically on COVID-19 deaths.

3 Methodology

To evaluate whether the legacy of slavery contributed to differing COVID-19 mortality rates in different populations living in U.S. Southern states, we propose two multiple regression models to carry out coefficient analysis.

The first – Model 1 – looks at the relationship between a county's percent slavery in the 1860 census (independent variable, *pctSlavery*) and the Non-Hispanic Black COVID-19 mortality in the county (dependent variable). Model 1 controls for race-specific demographics – age greater than 65 (*pctBlack > 65*) and male sex (*pctBlackMale*) – that have been shown in other literature to be risk factors for increased COVID-19 mortality.

(**Model 1**) $Non - HispanicBlackMortality$

$= \alpha * pctSlavery + \beta * \text{pct}BlackMale + \theta * (\text{pct}Black > 65) + \varepsilon$

The second – Model 2 – looks at the relationship between a county's percent slavery in the 1860 census (independent variable, *pctSlavery*) and the Non-Hispanic White COVID-19 mortality in the county (dependent variable). Like Model 1, Model 2 controls for two known demographic risk factors for COVID-19 mortality, race-specific age over 65 (*pctWhite > 65*) and male sex (*pctWhiteMale*).

(**Model 2**) $Non - HispanicWhiteMortality$

$= \alpha * pctSlavery + \beta * \text{pct}WhiteMale + \theta * (\text{pct}White > 65) + \varepsilon$

Using two models allows us to explore historic slavery's contribution to modern COVID-19 mortality from two perspectives, Black and White. Each model can potentially show whether, even when controlling for two of the most significant risks, the historic legacy of slavery remains a contributing factor for COVID-19 mortality.

4   Datasets

To evaluate Models 1 and 2, we need data at the county level for COVID-19 mortality; the demographics of age, sex, and race; and the historic proportions of slavery. We employed three data sets, described in more detail here.

First, we obtained COVID-19 mortality stratified by race (Black Non-Hispanic and White Non-Hispanic) from the CDC's National Center for Health Statistics' Provisional COVID-19 Deaths by County, and Race and Hispanic Origin [9].

Second, we obtained race-specific age and gender data for use in controlling for COVID-19 mortality risk from the U.S. Census Bureau's 2020 American Community Survey 5-year data [21].

Third, we derived the percentage slave population in U.S. Southern states from 1860 Census figures provided by the IPUMS National Historical Geographic Information System [22]. The 1860 U.S. Census was the last before the abolishment of slavery.

To establish a modern reference for historic slavery in U.S. Southern counties, the percentage enslaved population recorded in the 1860 U.S. Census was mapped from 1860 county boundaries to modern county boundaries and the percentage of enslaved population was adjusted using the R areal interpolation package areal [23]. Figure 1 shows the 1860 distribution of slavery in U.S. Southern counties within their 1860 geographic borders. Figure 2 shows the interpolated distribution of slavery within modern county borders. States include: TX, LA, AR, MO, AL, GA, FL, TN, SC, NC, KY and VA.

Fig. 1. Percent enslaved population in 1860, historic county boundaries

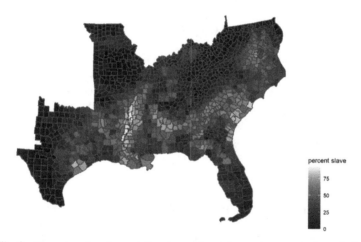

Fig. 2. Percent enslaved population interpolated for modern county boundaries.

Counties in the U.S. South (excluding regions of Texas without county subdivisions in 1860) were then intersected with counties in the CDC's dataset of COVID-19 mortality by county and race. As noted previously, the CDC releases race-stratified COVID-19 mortality data only in counties with 100 more deaths. The resulting intersection produced a dataset containing 505 counties in the U.S. South for which historical enslavement and modern COVID-19 deaths by race could be known. Figure 3 displays the interpolated distribution of slavery for the U.S. Southern counties with available COVID-19 mortality data.

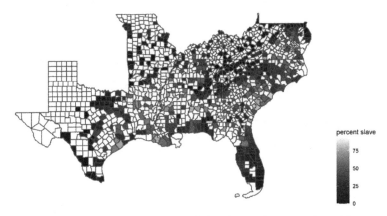

Fig. 3. Percent of interpolated enslaved population for modern counties with race-stratified COVID-19 mortality data.

5   Experimental Evaluation

5.1   Model 1 – Black COVID-19 Mortality

Model 1 found a significant positive relationship between Black COVID-19 mortality and historic rates of slavery when controlling for race-specific age and sex ($F_{3,500} = 1452$, $p = \ < 2.2e{-}16$). A 1% increase in historic slavery rates was associated with a 0.08% increase in Black COVID-19 mortality ($p = 6.33e{-}08$) when controlling for sex and older age in the Black population. As suggested by studies of COVID-19 risk factors, male sex and age over 65 years also show a statistically significant positive relationship with COVID-19 mortality in the Black population. Table 1 and Fig. 4 show Model 1 results.

Table 1. Model 1 – Black COVID-19 Mortality Coefficients

	Estimate	Std Error	t-value	Pr($>$|t|)	
	−0.0069427	0.0042313	−1.641	0.1015	
pctSlavery	0.0008526	0.0001559	5.492	6.33e−08	***
pctBlackMale	0.0172812	0.0009434	18.317	<2e−16	***
pctBlack > 65	0.0074606	0.0031544	2.365	0.0184	*

Multiple R-squared: 0.897
Adjusted R-squared: 0.896
Significance Codes: *** 0; * 0.01

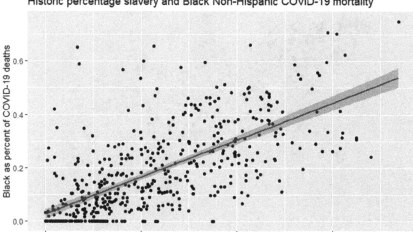

Fig. 4. Historic percentage enslavement by county vs percent COVID-19 deaths attributed to Black Non-Hispanic residents.

5.2 Model 2 – White COVID-19 Mortality

Model 2 found a significant negative correlation between White COVID-19 mortality and historic rates of slavery when controlling for race-specific age and sex ($F = 1344_{3,500}$, $p = \ < 2.2\text{e}{-}16$). A 1% increase in historic slavery rates was associated with a 0.04% reduction in White COVID-19 mortality ($p = 0.00544$) when controlling for gender and age in the White population. Like Model 1, Model 2 also shows the already established relationship between COVID-19 mortality and both male sex and older age in the White population. Table 2 and Fig. 5 show Model 2 results.

Table 2. Model 2 – White COVID-19 Mortality Coefficients

	Estimate	**Std Error**	**t-value**	**Pr(> |t|)**	
	0.1040316	0.0139347	7.466	3.71e−13	***
pctSlavery	−0.0004513	0.0001616	−2.792	0.00544	**
pctWhiteMale	0.0187196	0.0004657	40.200	<2e−16	***
pctWhite > 65	0.0017722	0.0007373	2.403	0.01660	*

Multiple R-squared: 0.889
Adjusted R-squared: 0.889
Significance Codes: *** 0; ** 0.001; * 0.01

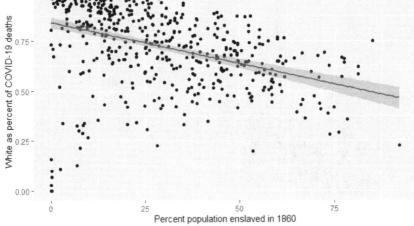

Fig. 5. Historic percentage enslavement by county vs percent COVID-19 deaths attributed to White Non-Hispanic residents.

6 Discussion

The proposed models find the relationship of historic enslavement to be positive with Black COVID-19 mortality and negative with White COVID-19 mortality in selected counties of the U.S. South. The relationships suggest the continued legacy of historic slavery acts against Non-Hispanic Black survival and slightly benefits Non-Hispanic White survival in the COVID-19 pandemic. It also suggests that variations in geography and history may underlie some of the currently observed racial disparities in health, as shown by work prior to COVID-19 [5, 6, 19].

Unable to control for underlying health conditions by race and by county, however, this study does not separate the lasting legacy of slavery from underlying medical risk factors. This limitation points to the need for race-stratified data that describe chronic disease and other underlying health conditions by racial population, at the county level.

U.S. health authorities have begun to show an interest in producing race-stratified data to help hospitals and other health providers see and ameliorate differences in health outcomes by race [25]. Such data measuring both underlying health conditions by racial groups and geography can help public health experts design interventions that effectively target medical and historical reasons for racial disparities in health outcomes.

7 Limitations

This study could not control for underlying health conditions due to a lack of race-stratified data for disease by county. (The nation's largest behavioral health survey [24], which models the rates of many health conditions shown to contribute to COVID-19 mortality, makes data available at the state level.) This omission prevents the model from teasing apart the contribution of slavery from other health conditions that may exist at higher or lower prevalence among Black or White populations by county. Also, only counties with COVID-19 deaths over 100 were used.

8 Conclusion

This study finds a significant relationship between historic rates of enslavement and both higher Black COVID-19 mortality and lower White COVID-19 mortality in selected counties of the U.S. South. Unable to control for underlying health conditions by race and by county, however, this study could not separate the effects of slavery from underlying medical risk factors. Future work will look into the use of large-scale behavioral datasets to model present COVID-19 health behaviors with respect to historic enslavement [26–28].

References

1. World Health Organization Coronavirus (COVID-19) Dashboard. https://covid19.who.int/. Accessed 13 Aug 2022
2. Centers for Disease Control and Prevention Risk for COVID-19 Infection, Hospitalization, and Death By Race/Ethnicity. https://www.cdc.gov/coronavirus/2019-ncov/covid-data/invest igations-discovery/hospitalization-death-by-race-ethnicity.html. Accessed 13 Aug 2022
3. Secretary's Advisory Committee on National Health Promotion and Disease Prevention Objectives for 2030 Report #2: Recommendations for Developing Objectives, Setting Priorities, Identifying Data Needs, and Involving Stakeholders for Healthy People 2030. https://www.healthypeople.gov/sites/default/files/Advisory_Committee_Obj ectives_for_HP2030_Report.pdf. Accessed 13 Aug 2022
4. Institute of Medicine Committee on the Consequences of Uninsurance: Care Without Coverage: Too Little, Too Late. National Academy Press, Washington, D.C. (2002)
5. Kramer, M.R., Black, N.C., Matthews, S.A., James, S.A: The legacy of slavery and contemporary declines in heart disease mortality in the U.S. South. SSM Popul. Health **3**, 609–617 (2017)
6. Esenwa, C., Tshiswaka, D.I., Gebregziabher, M., Ovbiagele, B.: Historical slavery and modern-day stroke mortality in the United States stroke belt. Stroke **49**, 465–469 (2018)
7. Dessie, Z.G., Zewotir, T.: Mortality-related risk factors of COVID-19: a systemic review and meta-analysis of 42 studies and 423,117 patients. BMC Infect. Dis. **21**, 855 (2021)
8. Centers for Disease Control and Prevention Underlying Medical Conditions Associated with Higher Risk for Severe COVID-19: Information for Healthcare Professionals. https://www.cdc.gov/coronavirus/2019-ncov/hcp/clinical-care/underlyingconditions.html. Accessed 13 Aug 2022
9. Shah, P., et al.: Demographics, comorbidities and outcomes in hospitalized COVID-19 patients in rural southwest Georgia. Ann. Med. **52**(7), 354–360 (2020)
10. Scannell, C.A., Oronce, C.I.A., Tsugawa, Y.: Association between county-level racial and ethnic characteristics and COVID-19 cases and deaths in the USA. J. Gen. Intern. Med. **35**, 3126–3128 (2020)
11. Li, D., et al.: Identifying US county-level characteristics associated with high COVID-19 burden. BMC Publ. Health **21**, 1007 (2021)

12. Samuel, L.J., Gaskin, D.J., Trujillo, A.J., Szanton, S.L., Samuel, A., Slade, E.: Race, ethnicity, poverty and the social determinants of the coronavirus divide: U.S. county-level disparities and risk factors. BMC Publ. Health **21**, 1250 (2021)
13. National Center for Health Statistics Provisional COVID-19 Deaths by County, and Race and Hispanic Origin. https://data.cdc.gov/d/k8wy-p9cg. Accessed 8 May 2022
14. Xu, A., et al.: Race and ethnic minority, local pollution, and COVID-19 deaths in Texas. Sci. Rep. **12**, 1002 (2022)
15. Jones, B.: The changing political geography of COVID-19 over the last two years. Pew Research Center. https://www.pewresearch.org/politics/2022/03/03/the-changing-political-geography-of-covid-19-over-the-last-two-years/. Accessed 13 Aug 2022
16. Hill, L., Artiga, S.: COVID-19 cases and deaths by race/ethnicity: current data and changes over time. Kaiser Family Foundation. https://www.kff.org/coronavirus-covid-19/issue-brief/covid-19-cases-and-deaths-by-race-ethnicity-current-data-and-changes-over-time/. Accessed 13 Aug 2022
17. Phelan, J.C., Link, B.G.: Controlling disease and creating disparities: a fundamental cause perspective. J. Gerontol. B Psychol. Sci. Soc. Sci. **60**(2), 27–33 (2005)
18. Curtis, K.J., O'Connell, H.A.: Historical racial contexts and contemporary spatial differences in racial inequality. Spat. Demogr. **5**, 73–97 (2017)
19. Reece, R.L.: Whitewashing slavery: legacy of slavery and white social outcomes. Soc. Probl. **67**(2), 304–323 (2020)
20. Gabriel, R., Esposito, M., Ward, G., Lee, H., Hicken, M.T., Cunningham, D.: White health benefits of histories of enslavement: the case of opioid deaths. Ann. Am. Acad. Pol. Soc. Sci. **694**(1), 142–156 (2021)
21. U.S. Census Bureau 2016–2020 American Community Survey 5-Year Data. https://www.census.gov/data/developers/data-sets/acs-5year.html. Accessed 1 May 2022
22. Manson, S., Schroeder, J. Van Riper, D., Kugler, T., Ruggles, S.: IPUMS National Historical Geographic Information System: Version 16.0. IPUMS, Minneapolis (2021)
23. Prener, C., Revord, C.: Areal: an R package for areal weighted interpolation. J. Open Source Softw. **4**(37), 1221 (2019)
24. Centers for Disease Control and Prevention Behavioral Risk Factor Surveillance System. https://www.cdc.gov/brfss/. Accessed 13 May 2022
25. Department of Health and human Services Centers for Medicare and Medicaid Services: Medicare Program; Hospital Inpatient Prospective Payment Systems for Acute Care Hospitals and the Long-Term Care Hospital Prospective Payment System and Proposed Policy Changes and Fiscal Year 2023 Rates (CMS-1771-P). Federal Register **87**(90), 28108–28746 (2022)
26. Ghurye, J., Krings, G., Frias-Martinez, V.: A framework to model human behavior at large scale during natural disasters. In: IEEE International Conference on Mobile Data Management (MDM), vol. 1, pp. 18–27. IEEE (2016)
27. Frias-Martinez, V., Virseda, V.: Cell phone analytics: scaling human behavior studies into the millions. Inf. Technol. Int. Dev. **9**(2), 35 (2013)
28. Isaacman, S., Frias-Martinez, V., Frias-Martinez, E.: Modeling human migration patterns during drought conditions in La Guajira, Colombia. In: Proceedings of the 1st ACM SIGCAS Conference on Computing and Sustainable Societies, pp. 1–9, June 2018

Scholarly, Communication and Open Access

A WOS-Based Investigation of Authors for English Predatory Journals

Qian Tan◉, Xiaoqun Yuan(✉)◉, and Zixing Li◉

School of Information Management, Wuhan University, Wuhan 430072, China
Yuan20030308@whu.edu.cn

Abstract. This study focuses on the author' profile publishing articles in English predatory journals. To this end, we utilize bibliometrics and statistical analysis methods to investigates the statistical patterns and characteristics of authors publishing their articles in English predatory journals from the perspective of time distribution, spatial breadth, citation distribution, and topic distribution. Our study may help to gain a comprehensive understanding of this group's overall situation and characteristics, uncover specific characteristics and publication patterns among authors and identify commonalities among authors of predatory journals worldwide.

Keywords: Author profile · Predatory Journals · Author academic influence

1 Introduction

Predatory journals, also known as deceptive or write-only publications, pose a significant threat to the trustworthiness and legitimacy of mainstream scientific research [1]. These journals cater to the demand among scholars to have their research published, but they often do not adhere to standard peer-review procedures. This lack of proper review affects subsequent studies and the accuracy of information disseminated to the public. The rage of predatory journals can be attributed to the pressure faced by academics to publish in order to secure academic promotions, tenure, and job opportunities. These factors, which are based on publication numbers, author order, and journal impact, create a strong incentive for scholars to submit their work to these journals [2]. This pressure is particularly intense in developing countries like India and South Africa, where scientists face tremendous pressure to have their research cited. As universities and research institutes require scholars to publish journals with high rankings, there is a growing concern about identifying and avoiding predatory and low-quality journals.

The original version of the chapter has been revised. The title has been corrected and the pagination has been updated. A correction to this chapter can be found at
https://doi.org/10.1007/978-3-031-57867-0_32

© The Author(s), under exclusive license to Springer Nature Switzerland AG 2024, corrected publication 2024
I. Sserwanga et al. (Eds.): iConference 2024, LNCS 14598, pp. 395–408, 2024.
https://doi.org/10.1007/978-3-031-57867-0_30

Although research on predatory journals has focused on their origins [3, 4], characteristics [5–7], impact [8], and measures to control them [9, 10], there has been a neglect in examining the authors who publish in these journals. However, the author of the paper plays a crucial role in determining the quality of a journal. To address this gap in research, our study aims to conduct group research on authors who publish English predatory journals. To the end, we take China as an example and investigate the statistical patterns and characteristics of authors who published articles in English predatory journals, which may help people to gain a comprehensive understanding of this group's overall situation and characteristics. This research can also help uncover specific characteristics and publication patterns among authors and identify commonalities among authors of predatory journals worldwide. To achieve this, our study will utilize bibliometrics and statistical analysis methods to analyze predatory journals listed on the Bell Independent Journal Blacklist at a macro level. We will focus on author profiles from four perspectives: time distribution, spatial breadth, citation distribution, and topic distribution. This analysis will provide valuable insights into the behavior and the characteristics of authors who published in predatory journals, contributing to efforts to combat this problem and promote trustworthy scientific research.

2 Data and Research Design

The framework of our research is shown as Fig. 1, which is the following steps to ensure accurate and meaningful results. The first step is to refer to the list of "Potentially Predatory Academic Open Access Journals" compiled by Beall on his blog. This list serves as a reference point for identifying the predatory journals that need to be investigated. Once the list is obtained, the next step is to conduct a thorough search for each of the predatory journals mentioned. To ensure a comprehensive analysis, the search is performed using the Web of Science core collection, a reputable and reliable database. To narrow down the focus and concentrate on papers published by Chinese authors, the search criteria include selecting "PEOPLES R CHINA" as the country/region and filtering the document types to include only papers, conference proceedings papers, and review papers. A total of 46 predatory journals are identified and subsequently searched within the Web of Science core collection. This comprehensive search yields a substantial dataset consisting of 27,695 documents. The time range for these publications spans from 1982 to 2023, providing a comprehensive overview of the research output from these predatory journals over several decades. Once the dataset is obtained, it is essential to clean and preprocess the data to ensure its quality and reliability. This involves removing any duplicate or irrelevant entries, standardizing the format, and addressing any missing or erroneous information. This cleaning process ensures that the subsequent analysis is based on accurate and reliable data. After cleaning the dataset, the next step is to extract and visualize the important data. This involves identifying key variables and metrics that are relevant to the research objectives. By visualizing the data through charts, graphs, and other visual representations, patterns and trends can be identified and explored. This visual exploration allows for a deeper understanding of the dataset and facilitates the identification of any significant findings or insights.

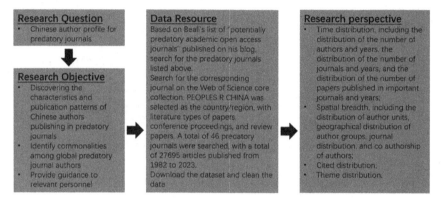

Fig. 1. The framework of our research

3 Result

3.1 The Temporal Evolution of the Author

The red line in Fig. 2 dominates the changes of the number of papers published by Chinese authors in predatory journals from 1982 to 2023. It clearly shows that the number of papers published by Chinese authors in predatory journals was relatively small in the 1980s and early 1990s. However, there was a rapid increase in the number of papers after 2005, with a significant surge observed after 2012. The number of papers reached a peak of 6,214 in 2017 but dropped sharply to 1,070 in 2018. It is worth noting that there are only 219 data points available for 2023, which may be due to the dataset ending in that year or incomplete data collection. The period from 2012 to 2018 accounted for 77.7% of the total number of papers, indicating a substantial growth in predatory journal publications during this time. The emergence of "predatory journals" can be attributed to the rise of the Open Access (OA) model in the 1980s and 1990s. The term "predatory journals" was first coined by Bell in 2012, drawing attention from researchers and leading to increased scrutiny and disapproval of such journals.

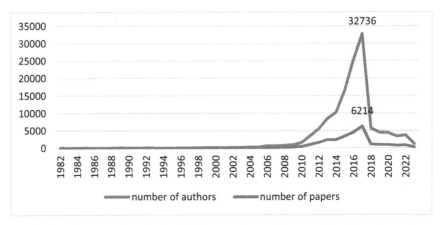

Fig. 2. The temporal evolution of Chinese authors and papers of predatory journal.

The blue line in Fig. 2 shows the number of authors publishing in these predatory journals each year. Obviously, it reveals a similar trend. The number of authors was relatively small in the 1980s and early 1990s but began to increase rapidly in 2005. A significant increase in the number of authors was observed in 2011 and 2012, followed by a rapid rise from 2015 to 2017. However, after 2018, the number of authors showed an overall downward trend. These findings align with the trends observed in the number of papers published each year. It can be inferred that changes in the number of papers are deeply influenced by changes in the number of authors, with the number of authors playing a decisive role. As the number of authors publishing in predatory journals increased, so did the number of articles in these journals. Conversely, as authors became more skeptical and stopped choosing predatory journals to publish their papers, the number of papers in such journals declined. Although there has been a recent downward trend in the number of papers and authors, it does not indicate an extinction of predatory journals. However, it does suggest a decline in their prevalence. The logical connection between the number of authors and the number of papers supports this conclusion. Overall, the analysis demonstrates a clear relationship between the number of authors, the number of papers, and the changing attitudes towards predatory journals.

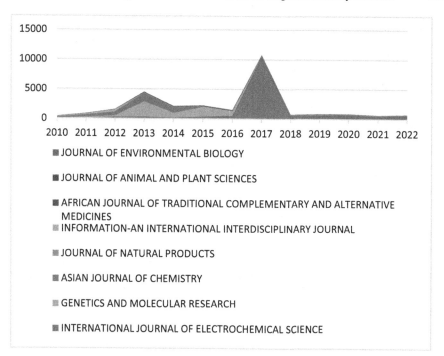

Fig. 3. The temporal evolution of publications by Chinese authors for different predatory journal.

Detailly, we investigate the number of papers published each year in journals, which predominantly feature Chinese authors as shown in Fig. 3. Figure 3 shows that it is evident that there was a significant surge in publications from 2012 to 2018, followed by a rapid decline. Overall, there is a clear trend of initial growth followed by a subsequent decrease. Among the journals examined, ONCOTARGET stands out as the journal with the highest number of articles published. Starting from 2011, the number of articles published in this journal experienced a rapid increase, peaking at 10,016 articles in 2017. This suggests a preference among Chinese authors to publish in this particular predatory journal in recent years. On the other hand, the INTERNATIONAL JOURNAL OF ELECTROCHEMICAL SCIENCE has shown a consistent upward trend in the number of articles published. This journal has steadily gained popularity among Chinese authors, with a significant number of articles being published in recent years. However, it is worth noting that certain journals, such as ASIAN JOURNAL OF CHEMISTRY, GENETICS

Table 1. The distribution of Chinese authors publishing articles in predatory journals.

Region	number of papers	Region	number of papers
Jiangsu	6633	Fujian	1235
Shanghai	6162	Jilin	1134
Guangdong	5470	Hebei	1063
Shandong	4661	Guangxi	1043
Zhejiang	3760	Jiangxi	898
Sichuan	2907	Hong Kong	737
Hubei	2670	Shanxi	657
Liaoning	2492	Gansu	625
Henan	2412	Xinjiang	560
Shaanxi	2402	Inner Mongolia	458
Beijing	2271	Hainan	426
Hunan	2022	Guizhou	425
Tianjin	1921	Ningxia	136
Anhui	1917	Qinghai	110

AND MOLECULAR RESEARCH, and ONCOTARGET, have been excluded from the Science Citation Index (SCI) since around 2015. Additionally, in 2020, the Chinese Academy of Sciences included the international journal of electrochemical science, ONCOTARGET, and others in its international journal warning list. These actions suggest a recognition of potential issues with the credibility and quality of these journals. Obviously, the analysis of publication trends in journals featuring Chinese authors reveals a pattern of initial growth followed by a subsequent decline. While ONCOTARGET has seen a surge in popularity among Chinese authors, the INTERNATIONAL JOURNAL OF ELECTROCHEMICAL SCIENCE has steadily gained favor. However, the exclusion of certain journals from SCI and their inclusion in warning lists by the Chinese Academy of Sciences indicate concerns regarding their reliability and reputation.

3.2 The Distribution of Chinese Author of Predatory Journal

It is evident that institutions that have a preference for publishing in predatory journals tend to produce a larger volume of papers. This trend can be attributed to the intense competitive pressure faced by teachers and students in these institutions, who are compelled to publish more scientific research papers and results. Furthermore, it is worth noting that the majority of the universities with the highest number of published articles are comprehensive and medical universities, indicating a predominant focus on medical research. This suggests that the main research direction of these institutions is primarily in the field of medicine.

In conclusion, in terms of publication volume, the top ten institutions collectively contribute a significant portion of the total papers published, indicating a higher propensity for publishing in predatory journals among these institutions. The prevalence of comprehensive and medical universities among the top publishers suggests a strong emphasis on medical research in these institutions.

Table 1 illustrates the distribution of Chinese authors publishing articles in predatory journals. The data reveals that Jiangsu Province has the highest number of papers, reaching 6,633, followed by Shanghai Municipality and Guangdong Province with 6,162 and 5,470 papers, respectively. Furthermore, Shandong Province, Zhejiang Province and Sichuan Province also issued more papers, with 4,661, 3,760 and 2,907 papers, respectively. The number of papers issued in Jiangsu, Zhejiang and Shanghai accounted for 26.5% of the total number of papers issued in China. And Taiwan Province has the least number of papers with only 2 articles. Additionally, Hong Kong Special Administrative Region and Macao Special Administrative Region also have a higher number of papers, with 737 and 105 papers, respectively. Geographically, the eastern region exhibits a higher number of papers compared to the western region. This discrepancy may be attributed to the more developed economy in the east, which provides greater funding for publishing papers and covering high publication fees in predatory journals.

By comparing the number of universities across different provinces with the afore-mentioned data, it becomes apparent that provinces with a larger number of universities tend to publish more articles in predatory journals. This correlation suggests that the higher number of papers in the eastern region may be due to the presence of more universities, a larger population of young and inexperienced researchers, and greater scientific research pressure. In summary, the distribution of Chinese authors publishing articles in predatory journals is uneven across different regions. The eastern region, char-acterized by a more developed economy and a higher number of universities, exhibits a greater number of papers. This may be attributed to the availability of funds and the pressure faced by young researchers. Conversely, the western region demonstrates a relatively smaller number of papers, potentially due to limited resources and research opportunities.

From Table 2, it clearly shows that among these 46 predatory journals, ONCO-TARGET stands out with the largest number of publications, totaling 10,180 papers. Other notable journals with over 100 articles include INTERNATIONAL JOURNAL OF ELECTROCHEMICAL SCIENCE, GENETICS AND MOLECULAR RESEARCH, ASIAN JOURNAL OF CHEMISTRY, JOURNAL OF NATURAL PROD-UCTS, INFORMATION-AN INTERNATIONAL INTERDISCIPLINARY JOURNAL, AFRICAN JOURNAL OF TRADITIONAL COMPLEMENTARY AND ALTERNA-TIVE MEDICINES, JOURNAL NAL OF ANIMAL AND PLANT SCIENCES, and JOURNAL OF ENVIRONMENTAL BIOLOGY. These journals have published 5800, 3982, 3813, 2187, 636, 266, 202, and 152 articles, respectively. Collectively, these 9 journals account for 98.3% of the total number of articles published by the 46 journals mentioned. It is worth noting that these journals serve as the primary platform for Chinese authors to publish in predatory journals. Notably, the important authors tend to publish their work in the aforementioned journals with the highest number of publications. It is worth mentioning that out of the total number of authors, 2,079 have published more than 10 articles, accounting for 2.4% of the total. Conversely, a significant majority of authors, 58,562 to be precise, have only published one article, making up approximately 66.8% of the total number of authors. On average, authors have published 2.1 articles.

Table 2. The distribution of articles by Chinese authors in different journals.

Journal	number of papers
ONCOTARGET	10180
INTERNATIONAL JOURNAL OF ELECTROCHEMICAL SCIENCE	5800
GENETICS AND MOLECULAR RESEARCH	3982
ASIAN JOURNAL OF CHEMISTRY	3813
JOURNAL OF NATURAL PRODUCTS	2187
INFORMATION-AN INTERNATIONAL INTERDISCIPLINARY JOURNAL	636
AFRICAN JOURNAL OF TRADITIONAL, COMPLEMENTARY AND ALTERNATIVE MEDICINES	266
JOURNAL OF ANIMAL AND PLANT SCIENCES	202
JOURNAL OF ENVIRONMENTAL BIOLOGY	152
JOURNAL OF PHYSICAL THERAPY SCIENCE	69
INDO AMERICAN JOURNAL OF PHARMACEUTICAL SCIENCES	57
INTERNATIONAL PROCEEDINGS OF CHEMICAL, BIOLOGICAL AND ENVIRONMENTAL ENGINEERING	55
INTERNATIONAL JOURNAL OF COMPUTER SCIENCE AND NETWORK SECURITY	43
MATHEMATICAL AND COMPUTATIONAL APPLICATIONS	42
BIOINTERFACE RESEARCH IN APPLIED CHEMISTRY	37
ROMANIAN BIOTECHNOLOGICAL LETTERS	30
BIOINFORMATION	19
BIOSCIENCE BIOTECHNOLOGY RESEARCH COMMUNICATIONS	14
JOURNAL OF ADVANCED VETERINARY AND ANIMAL RESEARCH	14

Overall, these findings highlight the dominance of ONCOTARGET and a few other journals in terms of publication numbers, as well as the prevalence of certain authors who contribute significantly to the output of these predatory journals.

Based on the analysis of the author co-authorship, we can find that authors with a higher number of publications tend to collaborate more frequently with other authors. Furthermore, it is observed that authors who prefer publishing in predatory journals tend to have a higher publication count. Notably, there were 460 papers published by a single author, which accounts for only 1.7% of the total number of papers. This indicates that the majority of papers are co-authored, with only a few being authored by a single individual. Obviously, the analysis of the author co-authorship provides valuable insights into the centrality of authors, their publication counts, and their collaboration patterns. The findings highlight the importance of collaboration in academic publishing and shed light on the prevalence of co-authored papers in comparison to those authored by a single individual.

3.3 The Analysis of the Article Topic and Citation

According to the research fields classified by WOS, as shown in Fig. 4, oncology and cell biology emerge as the most popular fields, with a staggering 10,180 papers published by Chinese authors. Following closely behind are biomedicine, molecular biology, and genetics, each boasting 3,982 papers. Chemistry and plant sciences have also made significant contributions with 3,850 and 2,187 papers, respectively. However, it is disheartening to note that integrative and complementary medicine lags far behind with a mere 266 papers, significantly lower than other fields. Similarly, the number of papers in Rehabilitation, Computer Science, and Biotechnology and Applied Microbiology remains relatively low. Furthermore, the data reveals that certain fields such as orthopedics, plant sciences, medical laboratory technology, and sports science exhibit a lower average number of publications. This could be attributed to several factors such as limited funding, fewer researchers, or a lack of emphasis on publishing within these disciplines.

Moreover, the analysis highlights that the majorities of published papers are concentrated in the field of natural sciences, while the fields of humanities and social sciences have comparatively fewer publications. This discrepancy may be attributed to the larger number of individuals engaged in natural science research compared to humanities and social sciences. Additionally, the production and publication of papers in the humanities and social sciences tend to be more challenging due to their weaker "scientific nature" and the inherent complexities associated with these disciplines. In conclusion, the research fields classified by WOS indicate a clear dominance of oncology and cell biology, followed closely by biomedicine and molecular biology and genetics. However, it is crucial to acknowledge the lower number of publications in certain fields and the

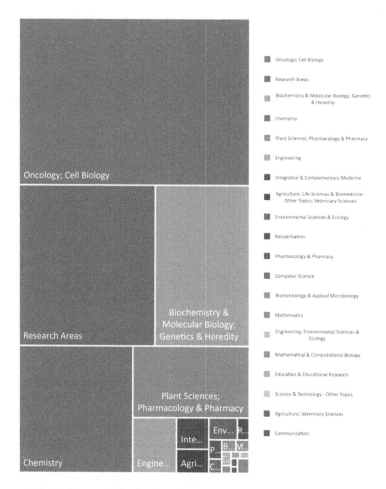

Fig. 4. The topic distribution of articles published by Chinese authors.

relatively fewer papers in the humanities and social sciences. This analysis underscores the need for further exploration and support in these areas to foster a more balanced and comprehensive research landscape.

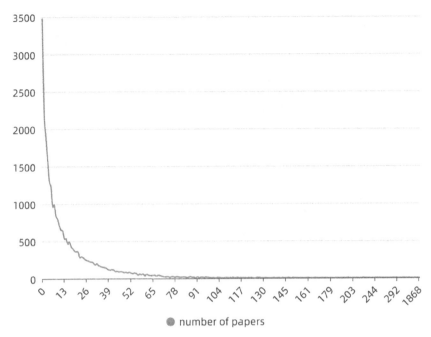

number of papers

Fig. 5. The distribution of article citation.

When evaluating the academic impact and value of a paper, the commonly used metric is the "number of citations." By analyzing the relationship between the number of citations and the number of papers, as shown in Fig. 5, we can find out that most papers receive fewer citations, while only a few papers receive a significant number of citations. Specifically, approximately 57.7% of papers receive between 0–10 citations, while only 1.2% of papers receive more than 100 citations. These statistics indicate that a large number of papers fail to garner attention and citations from the academic community, suggesting a prevalence of low-quality papers that occupy valuable publishing resources. Furthermore, the fact that one paper received 1868 citations highlights the scarcity of papers with genuine academic value in predatory journals. Additionally, as the number of citations increases, the number of papers gradually decreases, further emphasizing the scarcity of highly cited papers. On average, each article receives approximately 15.86 citations. However, there are 18,801 articles that fall below this average, accounting for 67.9% of the total. These findings collectively suggest that authors who publish in predatory journals produce works of low overall quality, lacking scientific research rigor and academic value.

4 Conclusions and Future Work

The inclusion of 46 journals with Chinese authors in the Bell Independent Journal Blacklist from the Web of Science (WOS) provides valuable insights into the publishing situation of Chinese authors in predatory journals. Conducting a study on the profile of Chinese authors in predatory journals is of great significance for the academic community and the industry. In this study, bibliometric analysis and data statistical analysis methods were employed to analyze the publication status and author characteristics of 27,695 papers published in these 46 predatory journals, aiming to create a comprehensive portrait of Chinese authors in predatory journals.

The findings of this research reveal several important observations. Firstly, it is evident that many Chinese authors had a preference for publishing in predatory journals as early as ten to five years ago. However, due to discussions in policy and academic circles, the choice of predatory journals by Chinese authors has significantly decreased in recent years. Although it has remained at a low but stable level, there is no indication of a complete extinction trend. Secondly, the number of papers published in predatory journals is significantly higher in the eastern region of China compared to the western region. Specifically, Jiangsu, Zhejiang, and Shanghai account for a quarter of the total number of publications. This can be attributed to the higher number of universities in these regions, which leads to greater scientific research pressure and availability of funding, resulting in more articles being published in predatory journals. Thirdly, Chinese authors tend to prefer publishing in predatory journals within Asia. The overall quality of literature produced by these authors is generally low, with most articles receiving very few citations. However, there are a few articles of high quality and academic value among them. Fourthly, the analysis reveals that while some authors publish as solo authors, most papers are co-authored by multiple individuals. The topics covered by Chinese authors predominantly focus on natural sciences, particularly the medical field, with relatively fewer studies in humanities and social sciences. This trend is expected to persist for a considerable period. Lastly, the published papers are primarily concentrated in the field of natural sciences, with a limited number in humanities and social sciences. This indicates a need for greater emphasis on research and publication in these fields among Chinese authors.

However, the Bell Independent Journal Blacklist stopped being updated in 2017, and these predatory journals may be outdated and not representative of the current population of predatory journals. The predatory journals included in the WOS are mostly in the fields of biology and medicine and may be unrepresentative. In the future, we will continue this research by analyzing the author group portrait of the most recent predatory journals and exploring how these publications fall into the predatory journal category and what motivates authors to choose these journals.

In conclusion, the study provides valuable insights into the publishing behavior of Chinese authors in predatory journals. The findings highlight the decreasing trend in the choice of predatory journals by Chinese authors, the regional disparities in publication numbers, the preference for publishing within Asia, and the focus on natural sciences. This research contributes to a better understanding of the publishing landscape and can guide future efforts to promote ethical publishing practices among Chinese authors.

References

1. Chen, L.X., Su, S.W., Liao, C.H., et al.: An open automation system for predatory journal detection. Sci. Rep. **13**, 2976 (2023)
2. Frandsen, T.F.: Authors publishing repeatedly in predatory journals: an analysis of Scopus articles. Learn. Publ. **35**, 598–604 (2022)
3. Beall, J.: Predatory publishers are corrupting open access. Nat **489**(7415), 179 (2012)
4. Sharma, H., Verma, S.: Predatory journals: the rise of worthless biomedical science. J. Postgrad. Med. **64**(4), 226 (2018)
5. Ezinwa, N., Williams, O.O.: Penetration of Nigerian predatory biomedical open access journals 2007–2012: a bibiliometric study. Learn. Publ. **28**, 23–34 (2015)
6. Beall, J.: Predatory publishers threaten to erode scholarly communication. Sci Edit **36**, 18–19 (2013)
7. Shen, C., Björk, B.C.: 'Predatory' open access: a longitudinal study of article volumes and market characteristics. BMC Med. **13**, 230 (2015)
8. Beall, J.: Predatory journals threaten the quality of published medical research. J. Orthop. Sports Phys. Ther. **47**, 3–5 (2017)
9. Philips, O.A., Niran, A.: Growth of predatory open access journals: implication for quality assurance in library and information science research. Libr. Hi Tech News **1**, 17–22 (2017)
10. Al-Khatib, A.: Protecting authors from predatory journals and publishers. Publ. Res. Q. **32**(4), 281–285 (2016). https://doi.org/10.1007/s12109-016-9474-3

A Content-Based Novelty Measure for Scholarly Publications: A Proof of Concept

Haining Wang[(✉)] [ORCID]

Department of Information and Library Science, Indiana University Bloomington, Bloomington, USA
hw56@indiana.edu

Abstract. Novelty, akin to gene mutation in evolution, opens possibilities for scholarly advancement. Although peer review remains the gold standard for evaluating novelty in scholarly communication and resource allocation, the vast volume of submissions necessitates an automated measure of scholarly novelty. Adopting a perspective that views novelty as the atypical combination of existing knowledge, we introduce an information-theoretic measure of novelty in scholarly publications. This measure quantifies the degree of 'surprise' perceived by a language model that represents the word distribution of scholarly discourse. The proposed measure is accompanied by face and construct validity evidence; the former demonstrates correspondence to scientific common sense, and the latter is endorsed through alignment with novelty evaluations from a select panel of domain experts. Additionally, characterized by its interpretability, fine granularity, and accessibility, this measure addresses gaps prevalent in existing methods. We believe this measure holds great potential to benefit editors, stakeholders, and policymakers, and it provides a reliable lens for examining the relationship between novelty and academic dynamics such as creativity, interdisciplinarity, and scientific advances.

Keywords: Novelty · Measure · Language Model · Information Theory · Open Science

1 Introduction

From alchemy to AlphaFold, the progress of academic endeavor is undeniable. Much as gene mutation drives evolution, novelty often seen as the recombination of existing knowledge elements allows for scientific breakthroughs from known terrain. It also serves as a key criterion for academic institutions and funding agencies, with submissions frequently required to showcase novel findings and insights. Of the 1.8 million papers published on PubMed in 2022, more than 8% included the word 'novel' in their titles or abstracts [18].

This research was supported in part by Lilly Endowment, Inc., through its support for the Indiana University Pervasive Technology Institute.

I. Sserwanga et al. (Eds.): iConference 2024, LNCS 14598, pp. 409–420, 2024.
https://doi.org/10.1007/978-3-031-57867-0_31

While recognizing novelty is crucial for pushing research boundaries, its presence and extent are often subjectively assessed by domain experts. Given the huge volume of scientific outputs and applications, an automatic measure of scholarly novelty can be beneficial for reviewers, editors, stakeholders, and policymakers. The pursuit of such a measure, in alignment with human judgment, emerges as both a technical and philosophical imperative.

In this study, we conceptualize novelty as 'atypical combinations of knowledge' within the framework of information theory, and adopt the information-theoretic measure *surprisal* to evaluate the novelty present in scholarly publications based on their *content* in the context of current scholarly landscapes. Specifically, we treat each word in the main content of a manuscript as a unit of knowledge. The atypicality of a sequence of these units, i.e., a manuscript, can be calculated based on the sequence's deviation from a distribution that approximates word distribution in scholarly discourse. This enables the identification and measurement of novelty in a bottom-up manner, from the word level onward. Furthermore, the measure's numeric values are interpretable due to its information-theoretic nature, a characteristic not possessed by other existing novelty measures. The measure, code, and data are accessible under a permissive license, available at github.com/Wang-Haining/noveval.

2   Literature Review

Historical inquiries have shed light on the defining characteristic of novelty in scholarly publications as the *recombination of existing knowledge in atypical ways* [2]? ?. We use the terms 'originality' and 'novelty' interchangeably in the context of scholarly communication [9]. However, creativity often entails both usefulness ? and impact [6,21], whereas novelty does not necessarily lead to scientific advances [8,24].

2.1   Novelty Measures Based on Reference, Keyword, Title, and Abstract

Operationalizing knowledge components at the levels of journals [12,34,36,37] and documents [5,16,32], the atypicality is obtained by contrasting observed combinations against local or global co-occurrences found in past literature. Apart from hesitation regarding citations made for non-intellectual [7,19] or casual reasons [4,17,30], the main critique is that the granularity of the knowledge unit is coarse and ignores the content of individual manuscripts. With co-occurrence networks, knowledge units are also operationalized using keywords, where rarely paired keywords [31] and controlled vocabulary [3] are used as heuristics to gauge novelty. Semantically divergent titles [10] and abstracts [29] are also considered as indicators of novelty.

2.2   Novelty Measures Based on Content

Interestingly, the content of a manuscript is rarely examined. A straightforward way to explore the full text of a manuscript is to cast novelty evaluation as a regression task [11,38] using discriminative models, perhaps enhanced with reviews from experts [11] and social media [13]. However, discriminative models assume that the word distribution in the papers being examined has an independent and identically distributed (IID) relationship with respect to the training data. Therefore, it is theoretically untenable for such models to be applied to papers that do not conform to the IID assumption, as this violates the definition of novelty, which entails unconventional distributions of words. Using the concept of terminology life stages and distance in the semantic space of contextual embeddings, Luo et al. [15] examine rare combinations of terms in the question and method sections of a paper, while possibly overlooking other sections where novelty may also be present.

2.3   Considerations for Designing a Novelty Measure

We distill the essential attributes of an effective novelty measure by drawing upon the identified limitations of current measures and incorporating the best practices established within relevant fields. The acronym 'CORE' captures the attributes we consider indispensable: a *content*-based novelty measure that is *open, reproducible,* and *explainable.*

First, common sense holds that novelty resides in a manuscript's content. Seeking novelty from the content closely mirrors what a human reviewer would do and clearly delineates between the measuring of novelty and interdisciplinarity [6]. Second, as trust stems from explainability, a numerical value for a measure cannot be relied upon unless it can be adequately interpreted. Explainability is also closely related to the third consideration, context, which is used for contrasting atypical from commonplace content, thereby distinguishing novelty from known scholarly landscapes. The evaluation of a word's novelty varies with context; for example, a discussion of graph theory may be perceived differently in a philosophy journal compared to an applied physics setting [1,14,27]. Fourth, simply stretching network theories or examining semantic distance does not provide sufficient granularity when investigating whether a snippet of a paper is novel or less so. A smaller, relevant knowledge unit can enable a more thorough examination for novelty. Lastly, most novelty measures have heavily relied on proprietary, paywalled citation databases. While these databases are useful, the reality is that the vested interests of dataset publishers, such as subscriptions, promotions, and language services, present challenges to the principles of accessibility and transparency in academic research. An ideal solution would involve releasing measures under permissive licenses, accompanied by all the essential materials required for replication, while avoiding alignment with commercial interests.

3   An Information-Theoretical Understanding of Novelty in Scholarly Publications

Let us further ground the defining characteristic of novelty, 'atypical recombination of existing knowledge units,' in the language of probability and information theory.

First, because a scholarly manuscript includes a sequence of words as its primary content, we consider the unit of knowledge to be words, composed of letters, punctuation marks, numerals, and special characters. Second, because the narrative is naturally sequential, 'recombination' means a sequence of words. Third, 'atypical' essentially means that the likelihood of observing a particular event is low. Put together, scholarly novelty in an article implies that *the joint probability of observing the sequence of words is low* in the universe of scholarly discourse.

In information theory, a low probability indicates a deviation from the expected distribution of a random variable. In this context, the random variable represents the occurrence of each word within the realm of scholarly discourse, denoted P. By measuring a word's probability relative to P, we assess its deviation from the expected norm in scholarly discourse.

This deviation is quantified as Shannon information [28], or surprisal [33] for short. The surprisal of a word x_i from a set of possible words X, given its probability under the distribution P, is computed as its base-2 logarithm:

$$I(x_i) = -\log P(x_i), \quad x_i \in X \tag{1}$$

This formula highlights the inverse relationship between probability and surprisal: as the probability of a token decreases, its surprisal increases, indicating a higher level of novelty or unexpectedness in the random variable representing scholarly discourse.

The cumulative surprisal of a sequence of words $x_1, x_2, \ldots, x_n$ in a manuscript, given their joint probability under the distribution P, is computed as follows:

$$I(x_1, x_2, \ldots, x_n) = -\log \prod_{i=1}^{n} P(x_i) = -\sum_{i=1}^{n} \log P(x_i) \tag{2}$$

In essence, words that are highly probable in P result in lower cumulative or average surprisal values, indicating their commonality in scholarly discourse. This scenario mirrors an academic manuscript discussing well-established data or theories. Such a paper's surprisal value is minimal, as it largely reaffirms what the academic community already knows, offering little to no new information. Conversely, a paper that introduces a novel concept or method significantly deviating from established norms carries a high surprisal value. This indicates a substantial divergence from standard scientific expectations and, consequently, a high degree of novelty in the research.

4 Approximating Scholarly Discourse with a Language Model

4.1 Language Modeling

The novelty of an academic manuscript is gauged by its divergence from the distribution of scholarly discourse P. However, since P is not directly observable, we use a surrogate distribution, Q, to approximate typical scholarly discourse. Specifically, we operationalize distribution Q using a causal language model, where the probability of the presence of a word is conditioned on the preceding words and is estimated from English Wikipedia.

We adopted the Generative Pretrained Transformer (GPT-2) architecture [26], employing its smallest model variant with approximately 124 million parameters, and trained it from scratch.[1] GPT-2 was selected for its widespread use and the superior ability to model complex language patterns.

For ease of understanding, we narrate using 'words' as the unit of knowledge. In practice, language models typically use 'tokens,' which correspond to shorter words or sub-words, to effectively capture semantic relationships and address out-of-vocabulary issues. For example, the word 'bioinformatics' can be tokenized into 'bio,' 'inform,' and 'atics,' allowing the model to process both familiar and novel terms by breaking them down into recognizable components. Token-level granularity renders models sensitive to subtle signals of novelty. In total, there are 50,304 tokens, the combinations of which constitute academic discourse.

During training, the parameters of the GPT-2 are updated so as to maximize the probability of observing the next token based on its preceding tokens. If the language model is well-trained, it can serve as a good proxy for scholarly discourse. For example, given the history 'The theory of relativity was proposed by __,' we would expect the language model to predict the next token as 'Albert' instead of tokens such as 'Ludwig' or 'that.' The probability of observing a sequence from the manuscript of interest is a joint probability of the tokens in the sequence:

$$Q(w_{1:n}) = Q(x_1)Q(x_2)Q(x_3)...Q(x_n)$$
$$= Q(x_1)Q(x_2|x_1)Q(x_3|x_{1:2})...Q(x_n|x_{1:n-1})$$
$$= \prod_{i=1}^{n} Q(x_i|x_{1:i-1}) \tag{3}$$

Note that, in theory, each token's probability is conditioned on *all* its preceding tokens (or history). The joint probability can then be readily plugged into Eq. 2 for cumulative surprisal calculation.

---

[1] Our implementation adhered to the original version, featuring a maximum input length of 1,024 tokens, 12 transformer layers, 12 self-attention heads per layer, and a model dimensionality of 768. We refrained from applying any dropout or bias terms.

4.2 Modeling Scholarly Discourse

The English Wikipedia corpus was created by cleaning a publicly available dump of all Wikipedia articles as of March 2022 [39]. The training set contained approximately 6.5 million documents and 4.6 billion tokens.[2]

Wikipedia articles represent one genre of scholarly discourse that offers a wide range of facts, common sense, and established theory in diverse research fields [22,23]. They share the explanatory nature of typical academic manuscripts. Additionally, Wikipedia articles are written by many authors spanning a long period, which may help to account for stylistic and temporal variations in language. Generally, Wikipedia articles are better suited to our goals than corpora that consist only of academic abstracts or full texts parsed from PDF files. The former fail to provide a more accurate representation of the structure of full-length articles; the latter often contain OCR artifacts and require further consideration of disciplinary balance, which trades off generality and specificity.

4.3 Notes on Surprisal Calculation

The accurate estimation of a surprisal score for a token requires a sufficiently long text, as the probability of the token is conditioned on all its preceding tokens (Eq. 3). In practice, however, constructing a language model to account for an extremely long context window is computationally expensive, so we adopt a fixed window of 1,024 tokens, faithfully mirroring the original GPT-2 architecture. To achieve reliable estimations, each token's calculation was conditioned on a history of at least 256 or 512 preceding tokens.[3]

5 Assessing Face Validity Using Illustrative Examples

Having established the theory of measuring novelty using surprisal derived from a proxy distribution of scholarly discourse, our next step is to assess its face validity. To this end, we will start with two token-level examples for illustration in the realm of quantum physics and move to examining surprisal's capacity to distinguish novelty from two groups of sentences paraphrased from the examples.

---

[2] We used four A100 GPUs (40 GB memory each), set a batch size of 16 per GPU, and accumulated 5 gradients before updating the model's parameters. This results in a total of approximately 0.33 million tokens per update. We fixed a total training course of 141,000 steps, resulting in a total of approximately 46 billion tokens processed (ten times the size of the Wikipedia corpus). AdamW optimization was used with $\beta_1 = 0.9$ and $\beta_2 = 0.95$. The optimizer had a weight decay rate of 0.1, and the learning rate was reduced from a maximum of 6e–4 to a minimum of 6e–5 over the training course, with a warm-up period of 2,000 steps. The training of the GPT-2 took approximately 43 h.

[3] An 'end of document' symbol (`<|endoftext|>`) is prepended to the start of each document for these calculations.

5.1   A Token-Level Examination

Consider the following sentence:[4]

> Quantum physics started with Max Planck's 'act of desperation', in which he assumed that energy is quantized in order to explain the intensity profile of the black-body radiation... [ca. 500 tokens omitted] Building upon this research background, we propose a method that uses photonic crystals at
>
> --

An intuitive continuation might be 'low temperature,' as current methods typically focus on low-temperature observation. This is due to quantum states being sensitive to temperature changes, which poses difficulties in maintaining entangled states. In contrast, observing quantum entanglement at 'room temperature' indicates significant novelty, presenting a formidable challenge to the current capabilities of our technology and equipment. Although there is only one token difference (i.e., 'room' and 'low' as shown in Fig. 1), we expect the surprisal associated with 'room' to be higher than that for 'low.'

We calculated the surprisal for the two tokens sharing the same history using the GPT-2 model trained on Wikipedia data (i.e., Q). The token 'low' scores a surprisal of 2.58 bits, corresponding to a probability of 0.17 (i.e., $2^{-2.58}$), and is ranked first among all 50,304 tokens in the vocabulary. The token 'room' has a much higher surprisal score of 4.42 bits, corresponding to a lower probability of 0.05 (i.e., $2^{-4.42}$), and is ranked sixth. This corroborates common sense in quantum entanglement research: performing experiments at low temperatures is commonplace, carrying little novelty, hence higher probability and lower surprisal.

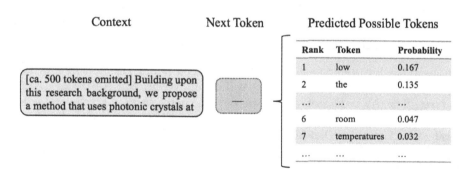

Fig. 1. Illustrative examples showing the probability rankings of potential subsequent tokens given a common preceding context. Based on the same history, the GPT-2 model, trained exclusively on English Wikipedia, predicts the next token as 'room' with a probability of 0.05 and 'low' with a probability of 0.17, indicating that room-temperature observation of quantum states is more novel.

---

[4] The context text is adopted from Vedral (2014) [35].

5.2   A Sentence-Level Examination

We further tested the face validity at the sentence level using two groups of sentences sharing the same history: each of the two sentences mentioned before was paraphrased twenty times using ChatGPT. The average surprisal score was calculated for each paraphrase in the two groups. Our null hypothesis posited that there would be no significant difference in surprisal scores between the groups, with the expectation that the paraphrases of 'room-temperature' sentences would not yield higher scores.

A one-tailed Welch's t-test yielded a t-statistic of 2.9 and a p-value of 0.003, with the degrees of freedom approximately 36.5. This finding indicates a significantly higher average surprisal score for room-temperature paraphrases than for low-temperature ones, thereby reconfirming the effectiveness of surprisal as a measure of novelty.

6   Assessing Construct Validity Using Known Groups

Beyond face validation at the token and sentence levels with synthetic examples, we extend our investigation to ascertain the applicability of surprisal at the section level for measuring novelty in a real-world dataset, using the known-groups technique. This technique is instrumental in testing construct validity, as it involves comparing two distinct groups expected to differ in the construct being measured [25]. In our case, the validity check may operate on two groups of scientific papers, one of which is perceived as more novel than the other by a group of domain experts. Creating a dataset consisting of two comparable groups of papers presents significant challenges due to the multifaceted nature of novelty in academic research [9].

6.1   Authorship Verification Anthology Dataset

To make the investigation feasible, we focused on novelty in methodology and findings sections and developed the Authorship Verification Anthology (AVA) dataset. The AVA dataset comprises working notes from a seven-year series of the Authorship Verification task, part of the Conference and Labs of the Evaluation Forum in Digital Text Forensics and Stylometry [20]. The shared task annually challenges global teams using shared datasets and requires teams to publish their working notes, detailing their experiments, models, setups, and data processing. This consistent framework across years ensures a controlled environment for comparing novelty in methodologies and findings sections.

We collected all 83 working notes in PDF format and converted them to plain text. Three domain experts independently evaluated each paper using binary scoring to determine the novelty of each working note. The criteria for novelty focused on methodological innovations in feature engineering, algorithms, and model architecture, as well as novelty from the findings, with a knowledge cutoff in mid-2022. A conservative threshold was set: papers selected as novel were those

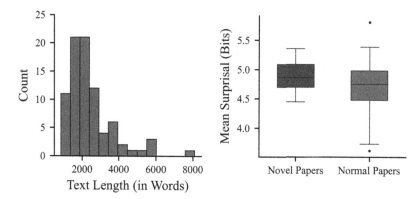

Fig. 2. The left panel presents the distribution of text lengths in the AVA dataset, measured in words. The right panel shows box plots of the average surprisal scores for two groups of papers, one of which is unanimously deemed more novel according to assessments by domain experts.

unanimously agreed upon by all raters. The statistics of length distribution and the average surprisal of each manuscript in both groups are shown in Fig. 2.

Each paper's novelty is calculated based on the concatenation of abstract and body text using the model Q. We computed the average surprisal of 1,024 tokens, each conditioned on at least 256 preceding tokens, because the papers are typically short (see Fig. 2). Finally, 25 of 80 papers were assigned to the novel group, while the remaining ones formed the normal group.[5]

6.2 A Section-Level Examination

We conducted a one-tailed Welch's t-test on two sets of academic manuscripts categorized as 'novel' and 'normal,' comparing their average surprisal values derived from a GPT-2 model exposed only to English Wikipedia. We found a t-statistic of 2.6 and a p-value of 0.005, with approximately 66.3 degrees of freedom, indicating a statistically significant difference in average surprisal value. The novel papers exhibited higher average surprisal than those in the normal group, suggesting greater novelty in their content.

We manually examined the 'false alarms'—the eight papers with average surprisal values above 5.0 that were nevertheless deemed less novel by our domain experts—to identify potential causes for these anomalies. Two of these papers contain excessive use of in-line mathematical formulas and notations. One other paper contains nonstandard syntax and informal usage, e.g., directly addressing the audience as 'you.' Three papers, authored by the same research team and reporting a series of incremental improvements on the same method, appear to have their surprisal scores influenced by the consistency in the narrative style of this particular group. The remaining two papers, with average surprisal scores just above the 5.0 threshold, are considered marginal cases.

---

[5] Three papers were too short for calculation in our setup.

7   Conclusion

In this proof-of-concept study, we reported a content-based measure for assessing novelty in scholarly publications, accompanied by a Shannonian explanation beginning at the word level. The measure is reproducible and openly accessible, supported by face and construct validity evidence. Next, we aim to conduct more rigorous validity tests using datasets involving peers from various global regions [2,11] and in multiple languages. We will also explore the trade-offs between generality and disciplinary specificity, along with the caveats associated with the use of this measure.

References

1. Acar, S., Burnett, C., Cabra, J.F.: Ingredients of creativity: originality and more. Creat. Res. J. **29**(2), 133–144 (2017). https://doi.org/10.1080/10400419.2017. 1302776
2. Bornmann, L., Tekles, A., Zhang, H.H., Fred, Y.Y.: Do we measure novelty when we analyze unusual combinations of cited references? A validation study of bibliometric novelty indicators based on F1000Prime data. J. Informet. **13**(4), 100979 (2019). https://doi.org/10.1016/j.joi.2019.100979
3. Boudreau, K.J., Guinan, E.C., Lakhani, K.R., Riedl, C.: Looking across and looking beyond the knowledge frontier: intellectual distance, novelty, and resource allocation in science. Manage. Sci. **62**(10), 2765–2783 (2016). https://doi.org/10.1287/ mnsc.2015.2285
4. Callaert, J., Pellens, M., Van Looy, B.: Sources of inspiration? Making sense of scientific references in patents. Scientometrics **98**, 1617–1629 (2014). https://doi. org/10.1007/s11192-013-1073-x
5. Dahlin, K.B., Behrens, D.M.: When is an invention really radical?: defining and measuring technological radicalness. Res. Policy **34**(5), 717–737 (2005). https:// doi.org/10.1016/j.respol.2005.03.009
6. Fontana, M., Iori, M., Montobbio, F., Sinatra, R.: New and atypical combinations: an assessment of novelty and interdisciplinarity. Res. Policy **49**(7), 104063 (2020). https://doi.org/10.1016/j.respol.2020.104063
7. Gilbert, G.N.: Referencing as persuasion. Soc. Stud. Sci. **7**(1), 113–122 (1977). https://doi.org/10.1177/03063127770070011
8. Godart, F., Seong, S., Phillips, D.J.: The sociology of creativity: elements, structures, and audiences. Ann. Rev. Sociol. **46**, 489–510 (2020). https://doi.org/10. 1146/annurev-soc-121919-054833
9. Guetzkow, J., Lamont, M., Mallard, G.: What is originality in the humanities and the social sciences? Am. Sociol. Rev. **69**(2), 190–212 (2004). https://doi.org/10. 1177/0003122404069002
10. Jeon, D., Lee, J., Ahn, J.M., Lee, C.: Measuring the novelty of scientific publications: a fastText and local outlier factor approach. J. Informet. **17**(4), 101450 (2023). https://doi.org/10.1016/j.joi.2023.101450
11. Kang, D., et al.: A dataset of peer reviews (PeerRead): collection, insights and NLP applications. In: Walker, M., Ji, H., Stent, A. (eds.) Proceedings of the 2018 Conference of the North American Chapter of the Association for Computational Linguistics: Human Language Technologies, New Orleans, Louisiana, Volume 1 (Long Papers), pp. 1647–1661. Association for Computational Linguistics, June 2018. https://doi.org/10.18653/v1/N18-1149

12. Lee, Y.N., Walsh, J.P., Wang, J.: Creativity in scientific teams: unpacking novelty and impact. Res. Policy **44**(3), 684–697 (2015). https://doi.org/10.1016/j.respol. 2014.10.007
13. Li, X., Wen, Y., Jiang, J., Daim, T., Huang, L.: Identifying potential breakthrough research: a machine learning method using scientific papers and Twitter data. Technol. Forecast. Soc. Change **184**, 122042 (2022). https://doi.org/j.techfore.2022. 122042
14. Long, H.: More than appropriateness and novelty: judges' criteria of assessing creative products in science tasks. Think. Ski. Creat. **13**, 183–194 (2014). https:// doi.org/10.1016/j.tsc.2014.05.002
15. Luo, Z., Lu, W., He, J., Wang, Y.: Combination of research questions and methods: a new measurement of scientific novelty. J. Inform. **16**(2), 101282 (2022). https:// doi.org/j.joi.2022.101282
16. Matsumoto, K., Shibayama, S., Kang, B., Igami, M.: Introducing a novelty indicator for scientific research: validating the knowledge-based combinatorial approach. Scientometrics **126**(8), 6891–6915 (2021). https://doi.org/10.1007/s11192-021-04049-z
17. Nagaoka, S., Yamauchi, I.: The use of science for inventions and its identification: patent level evidence matched with survey. Technical report, Research Institute of Economy, Trade and Industry (RIETI) (2015). https://www.rieti.go.jp/en/ publications/summary/15080017.html. Accessed 5 Apr 2023
18. National Institutes of Health: FY 2022 by the numbers: Extramural grant investments in research (2022). https://nexus.od.nih.gov/all/2022/12/13/fy-2022-by-the-numbers-extramural-grant-investments-in-research/. Accessed 28 Mar 2023
19. Nisonger, T.E.: A review and analysis of library availability studies. Libr. Resour. Tech. Serv. **51**(1), 30–49 (2011). https://doi.org/10.5860/lrts.51n1.30
20. PAN: Shared tasks (2024). http://pan.webis.de/shared-tasks.html. Accessed 10 Dec 2023
21. Park, M., Leahey, E., Funk, R.J.: Papers and patents are becoming less disruptive over time. Nature **613**(7942), 138–144 (2023). https://doi.org/10.1038/s41586-022-05543-x
22. Patton, J.D.: The role of problem pioneers in creative innovation. Commun. Res. J. **14**(1), 111–126 (2002). https://doi.org/10.1207/S15326934CRJ1401_9
23. Petroni, F., et al.: Improving Wikipedia verifiability with AI. Nat. Mach. Intell. **5**(10), 1142–1148 (2023). https://doi.org/10.1038/s42256-023-00726-1
24. Poincaré, H.: Mathematical creation. Monist **20**(3), 321–335 (1910)
25. Portney, L.G., Watkins, M.P.: Foundations of Clinical Research: Applications to Practice. Appleton & Lange, Norwalk, Conn (1993)
26. Radford, A., Sutskever, I., et al.: Language models are unsupervised multitask learners. OpenAI Blog **1**(8), 9 (2019)
27. Runco, M.A., Charles, R.E.: Judgments of originality and appropriateness as predictors of creativity. Personality Individ. Differ. **15**(5), 537–546 (1993). https:// doi.org/10.1016/0191-8869(93)90337-3
28. Shannon, C.E.: A mathematical theory of communication. Bell Syst. Tech. J. **27**, 379–423 (1948). https://doi.org/10.1002/j.1538-7305.1948.tb01338.x
29. Shibayama, S., Yin, D., Matsumoto, K.: Measuring novelty in science with word embedding. PLoS ONE **16**(7), e0254034 (2021). https://doi.org/10.1371/journal. pone.0254034
30. Smith, L.C.: Citation analysis. Libr. Trends **30**(1), 83–106 (1981)

31. Tahamtan, I., Bornmann, L.: Creativity in science and the link to cited references: is the creative potential of papers reflected in their cited references? J. Informet. **12**(3), 906–930 (2018). https://doi.org/10.1016/j.joi.2018.07.005

32. Trapido, D.: How novelty in knowledge earns recognition: the role of consistent identities. Res. Policy **44**(8), 1488–1500 (2015). https://doi.org/10.1016/j.respol.2015.05.007

33. Tribus, M.: Thermostatics and Thermodynamics: An Introduction to Energy, Information and States of Matter, with Engineering Applications. D. Van Nostrand Company, Inc., Princeton (1961)

34. Uzzi, B., Mukherjee, S., Stringer, M., Jones, B.: Atypical combinations and scientific impact. Science **342**(6157), 468–472 (2013). https://doi.org/10.1126/science.1240474

35. Vedral, V.: Quantum entanglement. Nat. Phys. **10**, 256–258 (2014).https://doi.org/10.1038/nphys2904

36. Veugelers, R., Wang, J.: Scientific novelty and technological impact. Res. Policy **48**(6), 1362–1372 (2019). https://doi.org/10.1016/j.respol.2019.01.019

37. Wang, J., Veugelers, R., Stephan, P.: Bias against novelty in science: a cautionary tale for users of bibliometric indicators. Res. Policy **46**(8), 1416–1436 (2017). https://doi.org/10.1016/j.respol.2017.06.006

38. Wang, Z., Zhang, H., Chen, J., Chen, H.: Measuring the novelty of scientific literature through contribution sentence analysis using deep learning and cloud model (2023). https://doi.org/10.2139/ssrn.4360535. Available at SSRN 4360535

39. Wikimedia Foundation: Wikimedia downloads (2023). https://dumps.wikimedia.org/backup-index.html. Accessed 1 Feb 2023

Correction to: A WOS-Based Investigation of Authors for English Predatory Journals

Qian Tan, Xiaoqun Yuan, and Zixing Li

Correction to:
Chapter 30 in: I. Sserwanga et al. (Eds.): *Wisdom, Well-Being, Win-Win*, **LNCS 14598,**
https://doi.org/10.1007/978-3-031-57867-0_30

In the original version of this paper, the title was not correct. This also affected parts of the text. These have been corrected and the pagination has been updated accordingly.

The updated version of this chapter can be found at
https://doi.org/10.1007/978-3-031-57867-0_30

Author Index

I. Sserwanga et al. (Eds.): iConference 2024, LNCS 14598, pp. 421–424, 2024.
https://doi.org/10.1007/978-3-031-57867-0

Printed in the United States
by Baker & Taylor Publisher Services